D1664122

FORMAL DESCRIPTION OF PROGRAMMING CONCEPTS - III

IFIP TC 2 / WG 2.2. Working Conference on
Formal Description of Programming Concepts - III
Ebberup, Denmark, 25-28 August, 1986

Organized by
IFIP Technical Committee 2 Programming
International Federation for Information Processing (IFIP)

Program Committee
K. R. Apt *(Chairman),* J. W. de Bakker, A. Blikle, C. Böhm
J. B. Dennis, R. Milner, E. J. Neuhold, M. Nivat, A. Pnueli
J. W. Thatcher, M. Wirsing

NORTH-HOLLAND
AMSTERDAM · NEW YORK · OXFORD · TOKYO

FORMAL DESCRIPTION OF PROGRAMMING CONCEPTS - III

Proceedings of the IFIP TC 2/WG 2.2 Working Conference on
Formal Description of Programming Concepts
Ebberup, Denmark, 25-28 August, 1986

edited by

Martin WIRSING
Fakultät für Mathematik und Informatik
Universität Passau, FRG

IS 3159
AUSGESONDERT AM:
06. JULI 2010
BIBLIOTHEK

1987

NORTH-HOLLAND
AMSTERDAM · NEW YORK · OXFORD · TOKYO

© IFIP, 1987

All rights reserved. No part of this publication may be reproduced, stored in a retrieval system, or transmitted, in any form or by any means, electronic, mechanical, photocopying, recording or otherwise, without the prior permission of the copyright owner.

ISBN: 0 444 70253 9

Published by:
ELSEVIER SCIENCE PUBLISHERS B.V.
P.O. Box 1991
1000 BZ Amsterdam
The Netherlands

Sole distributors for the U.S.A. and Canada:
ELSEVIER SCIENCE PUBLISHING COMPANY, INC.
52 Vanderbilt Avenue
New York, N.Y. 10017
U.S.A.

AUSGESONDERT

PRINTED IN THE NETHERLANDS

Preface

The aim of the Working Conferences organized by IFIP is to bring together leading scientists in a given area of computer science. Participation is by invitation only which allows for competent and extensive discussions. In total only 35 papers were submitted but it still allowed us to select 17 interesting contributions. Their presentation led to lively and interesting discussions as hopefully this volume gives evidence for.

The Program Committee consisted of K.R. Apt (chairperson), J.W. de Bakker, A. Blikle, C. Böhm, J. Dennis, R. Milner, E. Neuhold, M. Nivat, A. Pnueli, J. Thatcher and M. Wirsing. The selection of the papers took place in Paris on April 18 this year by the Selection Committee which consisted of J.W. de Bakker, A. Blikle, J. Dennis, E. Neuhold, M. Nivat and myself.

I would like to thank the members of the Program Committee and the referees for their help in selecting the papers. Also, I appreciated very much the cooperation with Martin Wirsing, the editor of these Proceedings and Dines Bjørner, the local arrangements chairperson and his team . We never met to discuss the matters but it turned out to be unnecessary - good will and cooperative spirit completely sufficed.

At various stages of the preparation of this conference I was assisted by Nancy Perry, Arlette Dupont and Danusia Czamarska to whom I express my sincere thanks.

During the conference an award for the best presentation was presented. It was offered to E.-R. Olderog who was elected by a general vote. Let me express the hope that this public distinction of Ernst-Rüdiger's lecturing qualities will encourage others to present their lectures in an equally thoughtful and inspiring way.

Krzysztof R. Apt

Paris, October 17, 1986

Editor´s Preface

The *Formal Description of Programming Concepts* is the subject of a series of conferences which are organized by the IFIP Working Group 2.2 under the auspices of the Technical Committee 2 (Programming) of IFIP. The fourth conference (being the third under this title) has been held at Ebberup, Denmark, August 25 - August 28, 1986.

This present volume contains the 17 papers which were selected by the program committee. As for the previous working conferences the questions and answers following each presentation of a paper are reported in an ad verbatum style in order to preserve hopefully the liveliness and outspokenness of the discussions. Following a warning of the editor of the previous volume, D. Bjørner, I decided to do the editing of the discussions without exposing the transcription to the questioners and answerers.

As the editor of the proceedings I would like to thank all those who contributed to the scientific program of the conference: the authors of papers for their interest in this conference, the program committee chairman K. Apt and the other members of the program committee for their excellent selection of the papers as well as all the referees who assisted the program committee in the evaluation of the submitted papers.

I am particularly indebted to D. Bjørner and his team (P. Christensen, M.R. Hansen, B.S. Hansen, U. Jørring, H.H. Løvengreen, M. Nielsen, A. Rasmussen) who did a marvellous job in organizing this conference, recording the discussions and editing the preliminary volume. The transcription of the discussions was done by H. Gründl, G. Killing and myself; word processing by H. Gründl, G. Killing, M. Pockes and T. Ramke. I gratefully acknowledge their kind and patient help.

Finally, I would like to gratefully acknowledge the DDC and the University of Passau for secretarial services and the North-Holland Publ. Co. editors (in particular Mrs. J. Mitchell and Mrs. St. Smit) for their patience in awaiting the delayed manuscript and for their cooperation in the publication of this volume.

Passau, February 1987 Martin Wirsing

Acknowledgement

Every paper was carefully reviewed by (at least) three referees. Their assistence is gratefully acknowledged.

M. Baaz
R. Barbuti
J. Bergstra
F.S. de Boer
L. Bougé
A. de Bruin
Tam-Anh Chu
M. Coppo
G. Costa
P.L. Curien
W. Damm
M. Dezani-Ciancaglini
M.C. Ferbus
R. Gerth
A. Geser
M. Grabowski
J. Gruska
M. Hennessy
R. Hennicker
H. Hussmann
J.N. Kok
P.L. Kanellakis
S. Kaplan
H.-J. Kreowski
F. Kröger
R. Kubiak
A. Martelli
E. Mayr
J.-J. Ch. Meyer
B. Möller
U. Montanari
F. Nickl
R. de Nicola
F. Oles
M. Ornaghi
P. Padawitz
D. Park
J. Parrow
M. Paul
T. Pinegger
J. Rheinhold
W.P. de Roever
S. Ronchi della Rocca
A.W. Roscoe
M.W. Shields
S. Sokolowski
C. Stirling
T. Streicher
A. Tarlecki
J. Tiuryn
F.W. Vandrager
M. Venturini-Zilli
E.G. Wagner
E. Waldin

Table of Contents

SESSION 1

Logic of Programs

Chairman: E. J. Neuhold

G. Mirkowska and A. Salwicki
Axiomatic definability of programming language semantics

F.S. de Boer
A proof rule for process - creation

Formal Description of Programming Concepts - III
M. Wirsing (Editor)
Elsevier Science Publishers B.V. (North-Holland)

© IFIP, 1987

AXIOMATIC DEFINABILITY OF PROGRAMMING LANGUAGE SEMANTICS

G.Mirkowska, A.Salwicki

University of Warsaw
Department of Mathematics and Informatics
PKiN room 850
00-901 Warsaw POLAND

The paper reveals a new application of the axiomatic systems of algorithmic logics. It is well understood that algorithmic logic can be used in analysis of semantic properties of programs. Here we show that moreover, it implicitly defines the execution method for programs. Since other components of the programming language e.g. primitive and composed data structures can be axiomatized by algorithmic theories, we conclude that the whole semantics of programming languages can be axiomatically defined.

1. INTRODUCTION

We are showing that the semantics of program connectives like **while...do...od**, **if...then...else...fi**, **begin...end** is completely defined by a set of axioms and inference rules of algorithmic logic [AL]. A similar result has been announced in [AS]. Here we present another and more detailed approach explaining that the standard method of computation, or in other words, the standard execution method is implicitly defined by axioms of algorithmic logic. As it frequently happens, we are avoiding an explicit definition of the objects and propose a set of axioms. Should certain objects satisfy the axioms we shall call them a model. It is of importance to show that a model exists and that any two models are "similar" e.g. isomorphic ones. Here we shall prove that this well known method can be applied to the goal of defining the semantics of a programming language. We propose to use the axiomatic system of AL as a criterion which accepts certain implementations and rejects others. Namely, we shall accept any interpretation (implementation) of program connectives provided that it satisfies all requirements expressed by axioms of AL. By the results of this paper it turns out that the interpretation is equivalent to the standard, commonly accepted execution method.

If the interpretation does not meet a requirement specified in an axiom we shall reject it.

In order to define a programming language one has to define two principal parts, 1° the programming constructs, and 2° the data types. It was argued elsewhere that data types, whether primitive or composed are axiomatizable by means of algorithmic theories, cf. [S1, SA]. This paper presents arguments that programming constructs are completely definable by axioms of AL. This leads to a conclusion that a union of axioms of algorithmic logic with axioms of specific data types axiomatizes a programming language's semantics. The authors believe that this approach allows to conceive the problem of axiomatic definition in a new light. We prove that not only the valid semantical properties of programs are provable from axioms but also that among many possible interpretations of the language the axioms distinguish a narrow class of standard implementations which can differ among themselves only up to irrelevant details of implementation. Every implementation accepted by axiomatization defines the same input-output relation between data and results of programs. Let us remark that in fact algorithmic formulas establish deeper similarities between various implementations. Consider the following formulas

$(\textbf{if } \gamma \textbf{ then } M \textbf{ fi})^i \neg \gamma \qquad\qquad (\textbf{if } \gamma \textbf{ then } M \textbf{ fi})^{i-1} \gamma$

they express the properties: after i-1 iterations of M the condition γ holds and after i-th iteration of M the condition γ is falsified. This clearly relates to the iterative program **while** γ **do** M **od** and allows to estimate the complexity of the program. Should these properties be proved from certain assumptions concerning data one can assure that they hold in all implementations satisfying the assumptions. Therefore, not only the input-output relations of a program considered in two implementations are equal, but more than this, the lengths of computations are equal.

The goal of defining programming language semantics has been approached by many authors. Two trends dominate 1° denotational semantics, an approach inspired by D.Scott [SD], and 2° axiomatic approach, initiated by papers of R.Floyd [Fl] and C.A.R.Hoare [Ho]. Here we present an approach which combines the virtues of both approaches mentioned above. Like in denotational semantics theory we prove that the meaning of a program is a mathematical object defined by axioms. Like in other axiomatic approaches we are able to use the axioms and inference rules as tools in the analysis of the behaviour of programs. We would like to remark on a few papers that claim to solve the problem of semantics definition on an axiomatic way. In a paper by Hoare and Wirth [HW] an axiomatic definition of Pascal programming language is promised. A closer look reveals that the paper brings certain requirements but it is far from beeing a complete axiomatic definition of Pascal. Let us remark that primitive data type integer can not be axiomatized by the formulas given in the paper. Similarly, one can ask whether the inference rule for **while**-program connective is its complete characterization. There is a paper by Greif and Meyer [GM] in which we find an interesting result stating that for every two nonequivalent programs K, M there is a pair of pre- and post- conditions α, β such that the partial correctness assertions $\{Ktrue \Rightarrow (\alpha \Rightarrow K\beta)\}$ and $\{Mtrue \Rightarrow (\alpha \Rightarrow M\beta)\}$ are non-equivalent. In other words any two non-equivalent programs can be distinguished by a partial correctness assertion. This does not mean that the semantics of programming constructs is defined, conversely, the standard meaning of program connectives is assumed. It is worth to mention a section in a book by D.Harel [Ha] which is devoted to the problem which semantics of non-deterministic programs corresponds to the axioms of the weakest precondition given by Dijkstra [Di]. We find that both authors leave the problem unsolved. We hope that the method proposed here can be adapted in order to define axiomatically the semantics of non-deterministic programs, cf.[Mi].

2. ALGORITHMIC LOGIC

Let L_1 denote a language of the classical predicate calculus, cf. [RS].

DEFINITION 1

Let π denote the least set *(of programs)* such that

(i) all expressions of the form $x:=\tau$ or $q:=\gamma$, where x is an individual and q is a propositional variable, τ is a term and γ is an open (quantifier free) formula in L , belong to π,

(ii) **if** K and M are in π and γ is an open formula then **begin** K;M **end**, **if** γ **then** K **else** M **fi**, **while** γ **do** K **od** (i.e.

the *composition* , *branching* and *iteration* constructs respectively) are in π.

□

DEFINITION 2

The set $F(\pi)$ of all *algorithmic formulas* contains all classical formulas of the language L, all expressions of the form $(M\alpha)$, where $M\in\pi$ and $\alpha\in F$ and is closed with respect to the logical connectives: $\wedge$, $\vee$, $\neg$, $\Rightarrow$.

□

Let us denote by V(w) the set of all variables that occur in w.

DEFINITION 3

By *algorithmic logic wrt to* π we shall understand an axiomatic system $AL(\pi)$ which consists of all schemes of axioms known from *classical propositional calculus* , all schemes of axioms and inference rules of *classical predicate calculus* and moreover it contains the following schemes of algorithmic formulas and rules of inference:

Algorithmic axioms

AX1 $K(\alpha \wedge \beta) \equiv (K\alpha \wedge K\beta)$ AX2 $K(\alpha \vee \beta) \equiv (K\alpha \vee K\beta)$

AX3 $K(\alpha \Rightarrow \beta) \Rightarrow (K\alpha \Rightarrow K\beta)$ AX4 $K(\neg\alpha) \Rightarrow \neg(K\alpha)$

AX5 **begin** K; M **end** $\alpha \equiv K(M\alpha)$ AX6 $(x{:=}\omega)\gamma \equiv \gamma(x/\omega)$

AX7 **if** γ **then** K **else** M **fi** $\alpha \equiv (\gamma \wedge K\alpha) \vee (\neg\gamma \wedge M\alpha)$

AX8 **while** γ **do** K **od** $\alpha \equiv$
$(\neg\gamma \wedge \alpha) \vee (\gamma \wedge K($**while** γ **do** K **od**$(\neg\gamma \wedge \alpha)))$

AX9 $\neg K(\alpha \wedge \neg\alpha)$

Rules of inference

R1 $$\frac{\alpha ,\ (\alpha \Rightarrow \beta)}{\beta}$$ R2 $$\frac{(\alpha \Rightarrow \beta)}{(K\alpha \Rightarrow K\beta)}$$

R3 $$\frac{\{(\textbf{if}\ \gamma\ \textbf{then}\ K\ \textbf{fi})^{i}\ (\neg\gamma \wedge \alpha) \Rightarrow \beta\}_{i\in N}}{(\textbf{while}\ \gamma\ \textbf{do}\ K\ \textbf{od}\ \alpha \Rightarrow \beta)}$$

In all the above formulas (and in what follows) α, β denote arbitrary formulas from the set $F(\pi)$, γ is an open classical formula, K ,M are programs from the set π , $x{:=}\omega$ is an assignment instruction and $\gamma(x/\omega)$ denotes the formula obtained from γ by the simultaneous replacement of all occurrences of x by the expression ω.

□

3. AXIOMS DEFINE SEMANTICS

A semantics for an algorithmic language L consists of three elements:

(i) an interpretation of functors and predicates,
(ii) a satisfiability relation,
(iii) an execution method for programs.

Generally the execution method is defined with the help of the notion of computation. The definition of computation is by no means a unique one. There are many different possible definitions. Most authors assume common, standard execution method based on the standard notion of computation.

DEFINITION 1

By an *execution method* we shall mean a function which to every program of the algorithmic language L assigns a binary relation in the set of all valuations in a given data structure. □

DEFINITION 2

We shall say that the execution method I for programs is *proper for algorithmic logic* AL iff the satisfiability relation which is based on I allows the soundness of AL axiomatization to be proved. □

DEFINITION 3

By a *semantic structure* for L we shall mean the triple $\langle A, I, \models \rangle$ where A is a data structure for L, I is an execution method and $\models$ is a satisfiability relation. □

DEFINITION 4

Let $\langle A, I, \models \rangle$ be a semantic structure. We shall say that I is *the standard execution method* if the following conditions hold

$I(x:=w) = \{(v,v'): v'(x)=w_A(v) \text{ and } v(z)=v'(z) \text{ for } z \neq x\}$,

$I(\textbf{begin } K; M \textbf{ end}) = I(K) \circ I(M)$ (the composition of relations)

$I(\textbf{if } \gamma \textbf{ then } K \textbf{ else } M \textbf{ fi}) = id(\gamma) \circ I(K) \cup id(\neg\gamma) \circ I(M)$

$I(\textbf{while } \gamma \textbf{ do } M \textbf{ od}) = \bigcup_{i \in N} I(\textbf{if } \gamma \textbf{ then } M \textbf{ fi})^i \circ id(\neg\gamma)$

where $K, M \in \pi$, γ is an open formula and $id(\gamma)$ denotes the set $\{(v,v): A,v \models \gamma\}$. □

Obviously the standard execution method is proper for AL [AL]. This is stated in the adequacy theorem on algorithmic logic which says that all axioms of AL are tautologies and all inference rules of AL are sound. There is a premise in the theorem which is seldom explicitly stated, namely we consider the semantics based on the standard execution method. The question naturally arises as to whether there are other different execution methods proper for AL. The program execution method is strictly connected to the problem of implementation. Can we treat our axiomatic system as a criterion for the correctness of an implementation? The main conclusion of the paper is that all conceivable proper execution methods of programs are similar in the sense that they induce the same input-output relations. The theorem presented here is in a sense converse to the adequacy theorem, it states that if a given notion of computation enjoys the property that the semantics based on it satisfies all axioms of AL (more exactly, they are to be tautologies with respect to the given semantics) then the computation can not differ from the standard notion of computation very much. The completeness theorem can be then interpreted in a way which shows that the standard notion of computation is the only one natural execution method for programs.

In the sequel we shall restrict our considerations to the class of semantic structures $\langle A, I, \models \rangle$ such that

(1) the data structure A is normalized, i.e. for arbitrary valuations v_1, v_2 in A if for every formula α $A,v_1 \models \alpha$ iff $A,v_2 \models \alpha$ implies that $v_1 = v_2$ (different valuations can be distinguished by means of a formula in the language L) and

the satisfiability relation $\models$ is such that

(2) $A,v \models (\alpha \vee \beta)$ iff $A,v \models \alpha$ or $A,v \models \beta$

$A,v \models (\alpha \wedge \beta)$ iff $A,v \models \alpha$ and $A,v \models \beta$

$A,v \models \neg\alpha$ iff non $A,v \models \alpha$

(3) $A,v \models M\alpha$ iff $(\exists v')$ $(v,v') \in I(M)$ and $A,v \models \alpha$

for arbitrary formulas α, β, program M and arbitrary valuation v. Our restrictions (2) are inessential, we introduced them for the sake of simplicity and in order to concentrate on the most important issues. One can prove namely, that if satisfiability relation is such that all axioms of classical propositional calculus are satisfied then it enjoys the properties (2).

Let $< A, I, \models >$ be a fixed semantic structure of the above defined class.

LEMMA 1

For every program M, if the semantic structure $\mathbf{A} = < A, I, \models >$ is a model for AX1 then I(M) is a partial function. □

For the proof see Appendix 1

LEMMA 2

Let K, M be arbitrary programs and $\mathbf{A} = < A, I, \models >$ be a semantic structure such that axioms AX1, AX5 hold, then

I(**begin** K; M **end**) $\equiv$ I(K) $\circ$ I(M) . □

LEMMA 3

Let K and M be arbitrary programs, γ an arbitrary open formula and $\mathbf{A}=<A,I,\models>$ the semantic structure which is a model of AX1 and AX7 then

I(**if** γ **then** K **else** M **fi**) $=$ (id(γ)$\circ$I(K)) $\cup$ (id($\neg\gamma$)$\circ$I(M)). □

LEMMA 4

If γ is an open formula and $\mathbf{A} = < A, I, \models >$ is a model of AX1, AX5, AX7, AX8 then

$$\bigcup_{i \in N} I(\mathbf{if}\ \gamma\ \mathbf{then}\ M\ \mathbf{fi})^{i} \circ id(\neg\gamma) \subset I(\ \mathbf{while}\ \gamma\ \mathbf{do}\ M\ \mathbf{od})$$

For the proof see Appendix 1. □

Let us assume that the algorithmic language L contains the binary predicate $=$. Moreover, let us assume that the semantic structure $< A, I, \models >$ is such that $=$ is interpreted as identity relation in A and for every element a of the data structure A there exists a term τ_a of L such that $a = \tau_{aA}(v)$ for every valuation v in A. We shall call such semantic structure *Herbrand structure*.

LEMMA 5

Let **A** = < A, I, ⊨ > be a Herbrand structure such that **A** is a model for AX1, AX5, AX7, AX8 and assume the rule R4 is sound then for arbitrary program M, every open formula γ

$$I(\textbf{while } \gamma \textbf{ do } M \textbf{ od}) = \bigcup_{i \in N} I(\textbf{if } \gamma \textbf{ then } M \textbf{ fi})^{i} \circ id(\neg\gamma)$$

For the proof see Appendix 1. □

LEMMA 6

If A is a Herbrand structure and **A** = < A, I, ⊨ > is a model for AX6 then for every assignment instructions of the form x := ω and for every open formula γ,

$$I(x{:=}\omega) = \{(v,v'){:}\ \ v'(z)=v(z) \ \text{ for } \ z=x \ \text{ and } \ v'(x)=\omega_A(v)\ \}.$$ □

As a straightforward consequence of the above lemmas we obtain the main result of this paper. We assume that the semantic structures considered below are Herbrand structures.

THEOREM

Algorithmic logic determines the unique execution method for programs. More strictly, if a given semantic structure **A**=< A, I, ⊨ > enjoys the property that all axioms of AL(π) are valid and all inference rules are sound in the structure **A** then I is the standard execution method, i.e. it satisfies the following equalities:

$$I(\textbf{begin } K;\ M \textbf{ end}) = I(K) \circ I(M),$$

$$I(\textbf{if } \gamma \textbf{ then } K \textbf{ else } M \textbf{ fi}) = id(\gamma) \circ I(K) \cup id(\neg\gamma) \circ I(M)$$

$$I(\textbf{while } \gamma \textbf{ do } M \textbf{ od}) = \bigcup_{i \in N} I(\textbf{if } \gamma \textbf{ then } M \textbf{ fi})^{i} \circ id(\neg\gamma)$$

$$I(x{:=}\omega) = \{(v,v'){:}\ v'(z)=v(z) \text{ for non } z=x \text{ and } v'(x)=\omega_A(v)\ \}$$

for arbitrary programs K, M, for every open formula γ and for arbitrary assignment instruction (x := ω). □

APPENDIX 1 PROOFS

PROOF OF LEMMA 1

Let (v,v')∈I(M) and (v,v")∈I(M) and v"=v'. From the assumption that the semantic structure is normalized it follows that there exists a formula α such that $\mathbf{A},v'' \models \alpha$ and $\mathbf{A},v' \models \neg\alpha$. Hence $\mathbf{A},v \models M\alpha$ and $\mathbf{A},v \models M\neg\alpha$. However, non $\mathbf{A},v \models M(\alpha\wedge\beta)$, contrary to AX1. □

PROOF OF LEMMA 4

Suppose $(v_1, v_2) \in \bigcup_{i\in N} I(\textbf{if } \gamma \textbf{ then } M \textbf{ fi})^i \circ id(\neg\gamma)$.

Hence there exists a natural number m such that $\mathbf{A},v_2 \models \neg\gamma$ and $(v_1,v_2) \in I(\textbf{if } \gamma \textbf{ then } M \textbf{ fi})^m$. Let us assume that for some formula α, $\mathbf{A},v_2 \models \alpha$. Thus $\mathbf{A},v_1 \models (\textbf{if } \gamma \textbf{ then } M \textbf{ fi})^m(\neg\gamma \wedge \alpha)$. As a consequence of axiom AX8 we find that for every valuation v if $\mathbf{A},v \models (\textbf{if } \gamma \textbf{ then } M \textbf{ fi})^m(\neg\gamma \wedge \alpha)$ then $\mathbf{A},v \models \textbf{while } \gamma \textbf{ do } M \textbf{ od } \alpha$. Hence $\mathbf{A},v_1 \models \textbf{while } \gamma \textbf{ do } M \textbf{ od } \alpha$ and there exists a valuation v' such that

$$(v_1,v') \in I(\textbf{while } \gamma \textbf{ do } M \textbf{ od}) \text{ and } \mathbf{A},v' \models \alpha.$$

Thus $v' = v_2$ by the assumption that the semantic structure is normalized . Therefore $(v_1,v_2) \in I(\textbf{while } \gamma \textbf{ do } M \textbf{ od})$. □

PROOF OF LEMMA 5

Suppose $(v_1,v_2) \in I(\textbf{while } \gamma \textbf{ do } M \textbf{ od})$ and $\mathbf{A},v_2 \models \alpha_1$. Let us assume that β is a formula which describes the valuation v_1 with respect to the set $V(\gamma,M,\alpha_1)$, i.e.

$\beta \equiv (x_1=\tau_{v1(x1)} \wedge \dots \wedge x_n=\tau_{v1(xn)} \wedge q_1\equiv c_1 \wedge \dots \wedge q_m\equiv c_m)$,

where $x_1,\dots,x_n$ are all individual variables and $q_1,\dots,q_m$ are all propositional variables that occurr in $\textbf{while } \gamma \textbf{ do } M \textbf{ od } \alpha_1$ and $c_j = v_1(q_j)$. Hence $\mathbf{A},v_1 \models \textbf{while } \gamma \textbf{ do } M \textbf{ od } \alpha_1$ and $\mathbf{A},v_1 \models \beta$, i.e. non $\mathbf{A} \models (\textbf{while } \gamma \textbf{ do } M \textbf{ od } \alpha_1 \Rightarrow \neg\beta)$. By the rule R4 there exists a natural number m such that

non $\mathbf{A} \models ((\textbf{if } \gamma \textbf{ then } M \textbf{ fi})^m(\neg\gamma \wedge \alpha_1) \Rightarrow \neg\beta)$.

As a consequence there exists a valuation v' such that

$$\mathbf{A},v' \models (\textbf{if } \gamma \textbf{ then } M \textbf{ fi})^m(\neg\gamma \wedge \alpha_1) \text{ and } \mathbf{A},v' \models \beta.$$

By the last property and assumption on β we have

(1) $\mathbf{A},v_1 \models (\textbf{if } \gamma \textbf{ then } M \textbf{ fi})^m(\neg\gamma \wedge \alpha_1)$

Asssume that m is the minimal natural number with such property. By the above fact there exists a valuation v_2' such that

$$(v_1,v_2')\in I(\textbf{if } \gamma \textbf{ then } M \textbf{ fi})^m \text{ and } \mathbf{A},v_2' \models (\neg\gamma \wedge \alpha_1).$$

Let us consider an arbitrary formula α_2 and let $\mathbf{A},v_2 \models \alpha_2$. We shall prove that $\mathbf{A},v_2' \models (\neg\gamma \wedge \alpha_2)$. Following considerations presented above we have

$$\mathbf{A},v_1 \models (\textbf{if } \gamma \textbf{ then } M \textbf{ fi})^j(\neg\gamma \wedge \alpha_2)$$

for some natural number j. Suppose $j < m$. By axiom AX7

$$\mathbf{A},v_1 \models (\mathbf{if}\ \gamma\ \mathbf{then}\ M\ \mathbf{fi})^m(\neg\gamma\wedge\alpha_1) \equiv (\mathbf{if}\ \gamma\ \mathbf{then}\ M\ \mathbf{fi})^j(\neg\gamma\wedge\alpha_1)$$

and by (1)

$$\mathbf{A},v_1 \models (\mathbf{if}\ \gamma\ \mathbf{then}\ M\ \mathbf{fi})^j(\neg\gamma \wedge \alpha_1)$$

contrary to the assumption that m is the smallest number with such property. Thus $j \geq m$ and therefore

$\mathbf{A},v_1 \models (\mathbf{if}\ \gamma\ \mathbf{then}\ M\ \mathbf{fi})^m(\neg\gamma \wedge \alpha_2)$.

Hence by axiom AX1, $\mathbf{A},v_2' \models (\neg\gamma \wedge \alpha_2)$. Thus there exists a natural number m and a valuation v_2' such that for an arbitrary for-formula α, $\mathbf{A},v_2 \models \alpha$ implies $(v_1,v_2')\in I(\mathbf{if}\ \gamma\ \mathbf{then}\ M\ \mathbf{fi})^m$ and $\mathbf{A},v_2' \models (\alpha \wedge \neg\gamma)$. Hence $v_2' = v_2$ and consequently

$$(v_1,v_2) \in I(\mathbf{if}\ \gamma\ \mathbf{then}\ M\ \mathbf{fi})^m \circ id(\neg\gamma).$$

□

APPENDIX 2 BLOCKS

Let us denote by π_1 the class of programs such that $\pi\subset\pi_1$ and

-if $\mathbf{x}$ is a sequence of variables and $M\in\pi_1$ then the expression of the form **block var x; begin** M **end** is an element of π_1,

-if γ is an open formula and $K,M \in \pi_1$ then **begin** K; M **end**, **if** γ **then** K **else** M **fi**, **while** γ **do** K **od** are elements of π_1.

Let $F(\pi_1)$ denote the corresponding set of algorithmic formulas and $AL(\pi_1)$ the corresponding algorithmic logic .

The system $AL(\pi_1)$ contains all schemes of axioms and rules of the system $AL(\pi)$ (considered in the extended language) and the following scheme of axiom.

AXblock $\mathbf{x}=\boldsymbol{\tau} \Rightarrow (\mathbf{block\ var}\ \mathbf{x};\ \mathbf{begin}\ M\ \mathbf{end}\ \alpha \equiv M((\mathbf{x}:=\boldsymbol{\tau})\alpha))$

where $M\in\pi_1$, $\mathbf{x}$, $\boldsymbol{\tau}$ are sequences of variables and terms of the same length such that $V(\boldsymbol{\tau})\cap V(\mathbf{x} \cup M)=\emptyset$ and if $\mathbf{x}=x_1,\ldots,x_n$ and $\boldsymbol{\tau}=\tau_1,\ldots,\tau_n$ then $\mathbf{x}=\boldsymbol{\tau}$ is an abbreviated form of

begin $x_1:=\tau_1;\ldots;x_n:=\tau_n$ **end**.

LEMMA 1

For arbitrary semantic structure $\mathbf{A}=\langle A,I,\models\rangle$, if $\mathbf{A} \models$ Axblock then

$$I(\mathbf{block\ var}\ \mathbf{x};\mathbf{begin}\ M\ \mathbf{end}) = R,$$

where $R=\{(v,v'):(\exists v'')\ (v,v'')\in I(M)$ and $v'(y)=v''(y)$ for $y\in V(M)-\mathbf{x}$ and $v'(y)=v(y)$ for non $y\in V(M)-\mathbf{x}$ $\}$.

PROOF

Let $(v,v')\in I($**block var x**; **begin** M **end**$)$ and let α be an arbitrary formula such that $\mathbf{A},v' \models \alpha$. Suppose that for some sequence of terms $\boldsymbol{\tau}$, $\mathbf{A},v \models \mathbf{x}=\boldsymbol{\tau}$. By properties of interpretation $\mathbf{A},v \models$ **block var x**; **begin** M **end** α and by AXblock, $\mathbf{A},v \models M(\mathbf{x}:=\boldsymbol{\tau})\alpha$. Hence there exists a valuation v'' such that $(v,v'')\in I(M)$ and $\mathbf{A},v'' \models (\mathbf{x}:=\boldsymbol{\tau})\alpha$. Let us consider the valuation v_1 such that $v_1(z)=v(z)$ for $z\in\mathbf{x}$ and $v_1(z)=v''(z)$ for non $z\in\mathbf{x}$. We have then $\mathbf{A},v_1 \models \alpha$. As the above considerations can be repeated for arbitrary formula α, we can infer $\mathbf{A},v_1 \models \alpha$ iff $\mathbf{A},v' \models \alpha$. By the assumption that the structure $\mathbf{A}$ is normalized $v_1=v'$ and therefore $(v,v')\in R$.

Conversely, suppose $(v,v')\in R$ and $\mathbf{A},v' \models \alpha$. Then there exists a valuation v'' as defined in the formulation of the lemma. Let $v(\mathbf{x})=\boldsymbol{\tau}_A(v)$ for some terms τ such that $V(\tau)\cap(V(M)\cup V(\mathbf{x}))$. Hence $(v'',v')\in I(\mathbf{x}:=\boldsymbol{\tau})$ and therefore $\mathbf{A},v \models M(\mathbf{x}:=\boldsymbol{\tau})\alpha$. By axiom AXblock $\mathbf{A},v \models$ **block var x** ; **begin** M **end** α and there exists a valuation v_1 such that $\mathbf{A},v_1 \models \alpha$ and $(v,v_1)\in I($**block var x**; **begin** M **end**$)$ Since α is an arbitrary formula and the structure $\mathbf{A}$ is normalized then $v'=v_1$ and therefore $(v,v')\in I($**block var x**; **begin** M **end**$)$. □

APPENDIX 3 PROCEDURES

Let us consider an extension of the algorithmic language L by the set of variables called procedure identifiers. We assume that each procedure identifier has a defined signature which is a pair of natural numbers. We shall define below the class of programs π_2 with blocks and procedures. We shall assume that each procedure instructions will be preceded by a corresponding procedure declaration.

DEFINITION 1

By a *procedure declaration* we shall understand every expression of the following form

procedure p(in **x**; out **y**); M **endproc**;

where **x** ,**y** are finite sequences of variables of length n,m respectively, p is a procedure identifier of the signature (n,m) and $M\in\pi_2$. We shall call the program M *the body of the procedure* p.

□

DEFINITION 2

By the *procedure instruction* we shall understand every expression of the form **call** p(**a**;**b**), where p is a procedure identifier of signature (n,m) and **a** is a sequence of terms, **b** is a sequence of variables. The lengths of sequences **a**,**b** are n,m respectively.

□

Let us denote by π_2' the least set of programs which contains all assignment instructions, all procedure instructions and is closed with respect to the usual constructs like composition, branching and iteration and the following formation rule - if D is a sequence of procedure declarations and $M \in \pi_2'$ then the expression **block var** z ;D **begin** M **end** is an element of π_2'.

DEFINITION 3

We shall say that a program $M \in \pi_2'$ is formally correct iff for each occurrence of a procedure instruction **call** p(**a**;**b**) in M there is a block instruction K in M which embeds **call** p(**a**;**b**) and which contains a declaration D of the procedure p. If K is the least block instruction in M with the above property then we shall call D a procedure declaration corresponding to this occurrence of p(**a**;**b**). By π_2 we shall denote a subset of π_2' containing the correct programs only.

□

Let us consider the following procedure declaration

(1) **procedure** p(in **x**;out **y**); Body(p) **endproc**;

Let **a**,**b** be sequences of terms and variables respectively. The lengths of **a** and **b** are equal to these of **x** and **y**.

By Mod(**a**,**b**,p) we shall understand the following program

block var u;**var w**;**begin u**:=**a**; Body(p); **b**:=**w end**

where $(V(\mathbf{u}) \cup V(\mathbf{w})) \cap (V(\mathbf{a}) \cup V(\mathbf{b})) = \emptyset$.

Let M be a program which contains a procedure instruction **call** p(**a**;**b**) and the corresponding declaration of this procedure instruction in M is the declaration (1), then Mod(M) is a program obtained from M by the replacement of the considered occurrence of **call** p(**a**;**b**) by Mod(**a**;**b**;p).

Let Der(M) be the set of programs which contains Mod(M) and such that if K∈Der(M) then Mod(K)∈Der(M).

For every K∈Der(M) by $K_\emptyset$ we shall denote program obtained from K by the simultaneous replacement of all procedure instructions by program $\emptyset$:=**while** true **do** x::=x **od** and by removing all procedure declarations.

DEFINITION 4

Let us denote by $F(\pi_2)$ the set of algoritmic formulas corresponding to the class of programs π_2, and by $AL(\pi_2)$ the corresponding algorithmic logic. The system $AL(\pi_2)$ contains all schemes of axioms and rules of the system $AL(\pi_1)$(cf.Appendix 2) and the following axiom scheme AXproc and the inference rule R4

AXproc $\qquad M\alpha \equiv Mod(M)\alpha$

R4 $$\frac{\{(K_{\emptyset}\alpha \Rightarrow \beta)\} \quad K \in Der(M)}{(M\alpha \Rightarrow \beta)}$$

where $M\in\pi_2$, $\alpha,\beta\in F(\pi_2)$. □

LEMMA 1

Let $\langle A,I,\models\rangle$ be an arbitrary semantic structure which is a model of $AL(\pi_2)$. Then for arbitrary program $K\in Der(M)$ and arbitrary $M\in\pi_2$ we have $I(K_{\emptyset}) \subset I(K)$.

PROOF

The lengthy strict proof is ommited. Let us argue informally that we never come to the execution of the instruction $\emptyset$ while executing $K_{\emptyset}$ with success. Thus replacing $\emptyset$ by any relation we come to a richer set. □

LEMMA 2

If the semantic structure **A**$:=\langle A,I,\models\rangle$ is a model for AXproc then $I(M)=I(K)$ for arbitrary $K\in Der(M)$.

PROOF

It is easy to see that by the assumption $I(M) = I(Mod(M))$ From this the result follows by the induction on the number of modifications done in M. □

As a consequence of the above and lemma 1 we have the following result.

LEMMA 3

If $\mathbf{A}=\langle A,I,\models\rangle$ is a model for $AL(\pi_2)$ without the rule R4 then for arbitrary program $M\in\pi_2$, $\bigcup\{I(K_\emptyset): K\in Der(M)\} \subset I(M)$.

□

LEMMA 4

If A is a Herbrand structure and $\mathbf{A}=\langle A,I,\models\rangle$ is a model for $AL(\pi_2)$ then $I(M) = \bigcup\{I(K_\emptyset) : K\in Der(M)\}$

PROOF.

Suppose $(v_1,v_2)\in I(M)$ and let α_1 be a formula such that $\mathbf{A},v_2 \models \alpha_1$. Let us assume that β is a formula which describes the valuation v_1 with respect to all variables occurring in M. Thus $\mathbf{A},v_1 \models (M\alpha_1)$ and $\mathbf{A},v_1 \models \beta$, i.e. non $\mathbf{A} \models (M\alpha_1 \Rightarrow \neg\beta)$. As a consequence of the rule R4, there exists $K\in Der(M)$ such that non $\mathbf{A} \models (K_\emptyset\ \alpha_1 \Rightarrow \neg\beta)$ and moreover there exists a valuation v' such that $\mathbf{A}, v' \models K_\emptyset\ \alpha_1$ and $\mathbf{A}, v' \models \beta$. Thus v', v_1 are identical on the set of variables $V(M)$ and therefore $\mathbf{A},v_1 \models K_\emptyset\ \alpha_1$. By the definition of interpretation of algorithmic formulas, there exists a valuation v_2' such that

(2) $(v_1,v_2')\in I(K_\emptyset)$ and $\mathbf{A},v_2' \models \alpha_1$.

We shall argue now that for every other formula α taken as α_1 we shall come to the valuation v_2' and $\mathbf{A},v_2' \models \alpha$.

Assuming that $\mathbf{A},v_2 \models \alpha$ we have non $\mathbf{A},v_1 \models (M\alpha \Rightarrow \neg\beta)$. Hence following above considerations we have $\mathbf{A},v_1 \models K'_\emptyset\alpha$ for some $K'\in Der(M)$. Thus there is a valuation v'' such that

(3) $(v_1,v'')\in I(K'_\emptyset)$ and $\mathbf{A},v'' \models \alpha$

It means, by Lemma 1 that $(v_1,v'')\in I(K')$ and therefore, by Lemma 2, $(v_1,v'')\in I(K)$. As the interpretation I associates to every program a partial function and $(v_1,v_2')\in I(K)$, then $v''=v_2'$. Hence by (3) $\mathbf{A},v_2' \models \alpha$.

The data structure is normalized hence $v_2=v_2'$ and by (2) $(v_1,v_2)\in I(K_\emptyset)$, therefore $(v_1,v_2)\in\bigcup\{I(K_\emptyset) : K\in Der(M)\}$ □

FINAL REMARKS

We have proposed a method of defining semantics of programming constructs. We hope that it can be used in the process of validation of compilers. Namely, one can present a compiler together with a proof that the axioms and rules of a programming language in question, are satisfied by the submitted implementation of the language. Similarly, the authors of implementation can submit the proofs of statements that their implementation of primitive and composed data types as well as other parts of running system (e.g. the storage management system) is correct. On the other hand the users of programming languages specified in this axiomatic way can profit from it in many ways.

We would like to point out that the method sketched here seems feasible. We have in hands all necessary components of axiomatic specification. The goal of full axiomatic description of a programming language requires however a serious effort. We remark that modern constructions like prefixing (inheritance rule) requires separate studies. We hope that the concepts of concurrent computations will be also defined axiomatically in some future.

REFERENCES

[AL] Mirkowska,G.,Salwicki,A., Algorithmic logic (Polish Scientific Publ., Warsaw, D.Reidel Dordrecht 1986)

[AS] Salwicki, A., Axioms of algorithmic logic univocally determines semantics of programs, in Proc.MFCS'80 (P.Dembinski ed.) LNCS 88, Springer Verlag,Berlin (1980) 552-561

[DI] Dijkstra, E.W., Discipline of Programming (Prentice Hall Englewood Cliffs 1978)

[Fl] Floyd,R.W., Assigning Meanings to Programs, in: Schwartz,J.T.(ed.) Proc.Symp.Appl. Math. AMS19, Mathematical aspects of Computer Science (AMS AnnArbor 1967) 19-32

[GM] Greif,I.,Meyer,A. Specifying programming language semantics in Proc. ACM Symp.POPL (1980), 180-189

[Ha] Harel,D., First Order Dynamic Logic, (Springer Verlag, Berlin 1978, LNCS 68)

[Ho] Hoare,C,A.R., An Axiomatic Basis for Computer Programming, CACM 12 (1969) 576-583

[HW] Hoare,C.A.R.,Wirth,N. An axiomatic definition of the Programming PASCAL, Acta Informatica 2 (1973) 335-355

[Mi] Mirkowska,G., Algorithmic Logic with non-deterministic Programs, Fundamenta Informaticae 3 (1980) 45-64

[RS] Rasiowa,H., Sikorski,R., Mathematics of Metamathematics (Polish Scientific Publ., Warsaw 1963)

[SA] Salwicki, A., On algorithmic theory of stacks, Fundamenta Informaticae 3, (1980) 311-332.

[S1] Salwicki, A., Algorithmic Theories of Data Structures in: Nielsen,M., Meineche-Schmidt,E., Proc. ICALP'82 Aarhus (Springer Verlag, Berlin 1982) 458-472

[SD] Scott,D., Domains for Denotational Semantics, ibid.

Acknowledgement: Thanks go to Krzysztof Apt for pointing out a number of errors in the preliminary version of the paper.

QUESTIONS AND ANSWERS

Apt: I have two questions about your use of local variables: first, how do you treat blocks and second, how do you treat parameters and procedures? From the competing logic, Hoare's logic, I know that there are two problems in this particular subject: one is that if the variables are not initialized in the block then one runs into troubles. The way you defined the axiom for blocks here does not take into account the possibility that the local variables could be uninitialized.

Mirkowska: Variables can be uninitialized since there is always an initial state of memory.

Apt: But on the level of logic there is no initial value.

Mirkowska: The meaning of a program is a state transformation which is defined relative to any given initial value. If you would like to check the following formula AXblock:

$$x = \tau \Rightarrow (\text{block var } x;\ \text{begin } M \text{ end } \alpha \ \equiv\ M((x := \tau)\alpha))$$

The meaning of M is a given state transformation relative to the initial values of the local variables. α is evaluated after the execution of M and the actualization $x := \tau$ of the global variables.

Apt: I have to think about this. But the other question is about the use of parameters in the program Mod(**a**; **b**; p) [cf. Appendix 3 of the paper].

Mirkowska: I know that this is neither exactly call by value nor call by name, but this is simpler. So I have presented this simpler version.

Apt: [For the semantics of procedures] we are using a similar device as years ago Jaco De Bakker to model parameter mechanisms in PASCAL. Our conclusion is that one has to distinguish between possible occurrences of a variable ´x´ in ´**a**´ and the local variable ´x´. As a result you first have to perform a renaming to avoid name clashes between the global variable which could be passed as a parameter in ´**a**´ and the local variable ´x´.

Mirkowska: Yes, I agree.

Pnueli: You mention one competitor's logic, Hoare's logic. I would like to consider dynamic logic. In some sense algorithmic logic is simpler than dynamic logic because you assume deterministic programs. The main question is: are you going to expect difficulties, if you try to generalize this to nondeterminism before going to parallelism, just nondeterminism on it´s own?

Mirkowska: First, in dynamic logic you cannot express the same as I expressed here. You cannot define exactly one semantics [up to isomorphism] by dynamic logic formulas. This is the first point. Second, I think that for nondeterminism it is much more difficult, especially as there are some other problems connected with logic which simply do not allow to define one semantics exactly. The result, which I have mentioned here, was that algorithmic logic is rich enough to define just one [isomorphism] class of understanding of programming constructs. For nondeterminism I think that it will be much more difficult and I don´t know what the solution could be.

Kröger: Your emphasis in your results is on algorithmic logic. But I think, the crucial point of showing the results is to use ω - rules.

Mirkowska: Yes, this is a crucial point.

Kröger: Don´t you think that you could for example use Hoare´s logic with ω – rules to get the same results?

Mirkowska: I think, yes. If you have ω - rules for dynamic logic, this is obviously the same.

Kröger: The point is not to use algorithmic logic but to use this special kind of axioms.

Mirkowska: Algorithmic logic contains a special kind of axioms. It is a set of axioms and rules.

Kröger: OK

Möller: Could you replace your ω - rules also by usual fixpoint induction as defined by Scott?

Mirkowska: I think yes, but it is much more difficult.

Möller: It is much more effective also.

Mirkowska: Effective? I think, it is just the same. It depends on the style of proving.

de Nicola: One can prove that the ω - induction rule implies Scott - induction, but not vice versa. So, in some sense you use a stronger mechanism with your ω - rule.

de Roever: Just a minor question: it is still not exactly clear to me what is supposed to be new. I try to find out what your contribution exactly is. What is for example the difference between the problem you solved and the problem solved by Greif and Meyer [cf. the reference in the paper] for a similar language? Could you explain the difference?

Mirkowska: The difference is just mentioned in the main theorem, I think. This theorem holds under the assumption of ′normalization′. Without this assumption I cannot prove this result which says that just one semantics is defined by the axioms and rules of algorithmic logic.

de Roever: What does ′normalized′ mean again?

Mirkowska: ′Normalized′ means that two valuations, if they are different, can be distinguished by one formula. It means, there exists a formula which holds with respect to one valuation but not with respect to the other.

de Roever: It reminds me of the assumption Brookes made in recent work, related with full abstraction [S.D. Brookes: A fully abstract semantics and a proof system for an ALGOL-like language with sharing. In: A. Melton (ed.): Mathematical foundations of programming semantics. Lecture Notes in Computer Science 239, Berlin: Springer 1985, 59 -100].

Tennent: Surely ′normalization′ is a strong assumption. For example, if you have integers, aren′t you claiming that you don′t have nonstandard models?

Mirkowska: I′m not excluding nonstandard models.

de Roever: I could give two valuations to the natural numbers: one by giving nonstandard values and the other one by giving standard values. How do you distinguish them? The definitions you have just given: you can distinguish valuations which are different. So one evaluates the natural numbers in the nonstandard part and the other evaluates them in the standard part. How do you distinguish them then?

Mirkowska: For the standard notion of natural numbers, I have an axiom which just describes the natural numbers. It is:

(x:=0 ; while x≠y do x:=x+1 od) true,

$x+1=y+1 \Rightarrow x=y$, $\neg x=0$

This defines the standard natural numbers.

de Roever: So, you are speaking about standard interpretation?

Mirkowska: Yes, obviously! And I can distinguish it from other interpretations by this formula.

Bednarczyk: The problem arises whether you can distinguish two valuations which comprise only the nonstandard values. There is no program to check whether the nonstandard values are different or not.

de Roever: The conclusion is that you are using only standard models and that you are axiomatizing standard models because your language is strong enough to do so.

Tennent: I have a comment on the question of normalization. That seems to be a form of relativization, where you are trying to establish in a sense categoricity of the algorithmic part and you are sort of assuming it with the nonalgorithmic part. I think, this is a strong assumption from the logical point of view, but I think, in the context what we are doing it is a reasonable assumption. But I am less happy with your general claims that you have combined the virtues of axiomatic and denotational semantics, because it seems to me, you combined the disadvantages. Because you have ω - rules, that´s not usable as a practical tool for program verification. And at the same time you don´t have something that has the intuitive character of denotational semantics with compositionality and so on, because it is all mixed in together. Here are the axioms and inference rules and you can´t look at these and say: this is the meaning of this construct. You have to look at several axioms and inference rules to figure out what the meaning is. Would you like to comment on my interpretation?

Mirkowska: I agree that the ω - rule is not convenient for proving properties of programs. But from this ω - rule I can prove other rules which are of use for programmers. The ω - rule is only for the theoretical part of algorithmic logic in order to have completeness.

Formal Description of Programming Concepts - III
M. Wirsing (Editor)
Elsevier Science Publishers B.V. (North-Holland)

© IFIP, 1987

A PROOF RULE FOR PROCESS-CREATION

Frank S. de Boer

Centre for Mathematics and Computer Science
P.O. Box 4709, 1009 AB Amsterdam, The Netherlands

ABSTRACT

A Hoare-style proof-system for partial correctness is defined for a language which embodies the kind of parallelism which stems from process-creation. We make use of the following proof theoretic concepts: Cooperation test, Global invariant, Bracketed section and Auxiliary variables. These concepts have previously been applied to CSP ([4], [12]), DP ([7]) and to a subset of ADA containing the ADA-rendezvous ([6]). We shall study the proof theory of a language with a generalisation of the synchronous message-passing mechanism of CSP. The syntactic construct of process creation and its semantic definition is taken from the language POOL ([1]). One of the main characteristics of proof-theoretical interest of this language is that the communication partner referred to by an output statement (or input statement) is not syntactically identifiable, in contrast with the previously mentioned languages. Basically our proof system is built upon the way the semantic mechanism of process identification is brought to the syntactic level. We have proven the proof system to be sound and relative complete.

1. Introduction.

In this paper we show how the concepts of Cooperation test, Bracketed section, Global invariant and Auxiliary variables can be used to formulate a proof rule for Process-creation. The application of these concepts to CSP we assume known ([4]).
We shall study the proof-theory of a language with process-creation as it occurs in POOL ([1]), an acronym for Parallel Object-Oriented Language. Processes making up the concurrent systems formulated in this language can interact only by synchronous message passing. We shall call this language just **P**. The rest of this introduction will be used to give some idea of the proof theoretical difficulties involved in Process-creation.
In CSP concurrent systems are defined as follows:

$$<P_1 \leftarrow S_1, \ldots, P_n \leftarrow S_n : P_1 \| \cdots \| P_n>,$$

where $S_1, \ldots, S_n$ are sequential programs containing IO-statements (input-output statements). Execution of an input-statement $P_j?x$ by process P_i is synchronised with the the execution of an output-statement $P_i!t$ by process P_j and results in assigning the value of expression t to variable x. Execution of $P_1 \| \cdots \| P_n$ consists of an interleaving of executions of $S_1, \ldots, S_n$. Given specifications $\{\phi_i\}S_i\{\psi_i\}$, $1 \leq i \leq n$, we can specify the input-output behaviour of the total system as follows: as precondition we take the conjunction of the preconditions ϕ_i , as postcondition the conjunction of ψ_i.

The research was partially sponsored by Esprit project 415: Parallel Architectures and Languages for AIP.

In languages which embody Process-creation things are a bit more complicated: we can not view a concurrent system formulated in such a language as consisting of a fixed number of certain processes. To be more specific consider the following program in **P:**

$U \equiv < C_1 \leftarrow S_1, C_2 \leftarrow S_2, C_3 \leftarrow S_3 >$

where

$S_1 \equiv$ if *true* $\rightarrow x := new(C_2) \mid true \rightarrow x := new(C_3)$ *fi*

$S_2 \equiv R,$

$S_3 \equiv R'$,

R, R' being ordinary sequential programs.

Evaluation of an expression *new(C)* consists of creating a new process and results in a reference to that process. This new process is going to execute the program associated with the identifier C. So after an assignment $x := new(C)$ x refers to the newly activated C-process. Execution of the above system starts with a process, the socalled root-process, which executes S_1. This process ends with having activated a C_2-process or a C_3-process.
So given postconditions ψ, ψ' of R resp. R' after execution of U $\psi \vee \psi'$ will hold and not $\psi \wedge \psi'$. It will be clear that neither as precondition of U can be taken the conjunction of the preconditions for R resp. R'. The problem is how to define a postcondition resp. precondition for such a concurrent system in general.
Another difficulty consists in the following: during execution of concurrent systems formulated in languages which embody Process-creation there can be active several processes executing the same program, but the sets of memory locations each process associates with the set of variables occurring in that program are disjoint. Consider the following **P** -program:

$U \equiv < C_1 \leftarrow S_1, C_2 \leftarrow S_2 >,$

where

$S_1 \equiv x := new(C_2); x!0; x := new(C_2); x!1,$

$S_2 \equiv ?y.$

The statements $x!0$, $x!1$ and $?y$ are IO-statements and can be viewed as generalisations of CSP IO-statements. In this example execution of the output statement $x!0$ resp. $x!1$ is synchronised with the corresponding input statement $?y$ and results in assigning the value 0 resp. 1 to the variable y of the process referred to by x. Thus after the execution of the above system the value of the variable y of the first activation of S_2 is 0 and that of the second 1. To be able to prove this we shall define a mechanism of process identification in such a way that its expression at the syntactic level makes a definition of a proof-system possible.
Let $U \equiv < C_1 \leftarrow S_1, \ldots, C_n \leftarrow S_n >$ be a program of **P**. At the semantic level processes will be identified by pairs of natural numbers $<k,m>$, $1 \leqslant k \leqslant n$, such that process $<k,m>$ will be the mth activation of program S_k. Semantically $C_1, \ldots, C_n$ will be treated as counters, each one counting the number of activations of the corresponding program. Given this semantic description we can formulate a creation axiom as follows: $\{p[C_k+1 / C_k, <k, C_k+1> / x]\} x := new(C_k)\ \{p\}$ (where $[\cdots]$ denotes substitution). Note that we assume $C_1, \ldots, C_n$ to be variables of the assertion language (the language used to describe states) and that this assertion language contains terms which denote pairs of natural numbers.
We shall treat a variable occurring in, say, S_i, semantically as a function with domain the set of natural numbers and with range the set of integers, booleans etc.. The second component of a process name we use as pointer to its workspace, that is, the process identified by $<k,m>$ will operate on $f(m)$, f the function denoted by x, x a variable of S_k.
Proof-theoretically this interpretation of program variables lends itself to the treatment of these variables as one-dimensional arrays ([9]). So we can refer to the value of the variable

y w.r.t. the first activation of S_2 (of the example) by the term $y[1]$. To prove that, w.r.t. the first activation of S_2, the value of y is 0, we must prove that $\{true\}?y[1]\{y[1]=0\}$ holds. But it will be clear that it is unsatisfactory and, in case of an infinity of activations of some program, impossible, to have to construct a correctness proof for every activation of some program. We must be able to construct a canonical proof for each program. This is made possible by abstracting from the specific value of the second component of a process name, the pointer to the workspace of the process denoted by that name. We introduce a new variable *i*, not occurring as a program variable, and axioms and proof rules to construct proofs for parameterized correctness- assertions like $\{p_k\}S_k^{(i)}\{q_k\}$, $1 \leqslant k \leqslant n$. $S_k^{(i)}$ denotes $S_k[x_1[i]/x_1, \ldots, x_m[i]/x_m]$, where $\{x_1, \ldots, x_m\}$ is the set of variables occurring in S_k. Thus the execution of $S_k^{(i)}$ in a particular state consists of the execution of S_k by the process $<k,m>$, m the value of the variable i in that state. So for the example just given we would have to prove that $\{true\}?y[i]\{i=1 \rightarrow y[i]=0 \wedge i=2 \rightarrow y[i]=1\}$.
In the following two sections we will fill in the technical details of this framework.
In section four we show how the proof-theoretic concepts: cooperation test, global invariant, bracketed section and auxiliary variables fit in this framework and present a proof-system for partial correctness assertions for **P** -programs.
The sections five and six discuss the soundness and completeness of the proof system.
In the appendix we discuss an example of a correctness proof.

2. The language P

Given the following sets of syntactic objects:
$Cname = \{C, \cdots\}$, the set of class names,
$Pvar = \bigcup_{C \in Cname} Pvar^C = \{x, \cdots\}$, the set of program-variables,
such that for any two distinct class names the associated sets of program variables are disjoint,
$Icon = \{n : n \in \mathbf{N}\}$, the set of integer-constants,
$Lab = \{l, \cdots\}$, the set of labels,
the syntax of the language P is given by the following grammar:

$$S ::= l{:}x:=e \mid l{:}x?y \mid l{:}?y \mid l{:}x!t \mid l{:}!t \mid S_1 \; ; \; S_2 \mid l{:}\mathop{\Box}_{i=1}^{n} b_i \rightarrow S_i \mid l{:}*\mathop{\Box}_{i=1}^{n} b_i \rightarrow S_i .$$

$$e ::= t \mid self \mid new(C)$$

$$t ::= \underline{n} \mid x \mid t_1+t_2 \mid t_1 \times t_2 \mid \cdots$$

$$b ::= t_1=t_2 \mid t_1<t_2 \mid \cdots \mid \neg b \mid b_1 \wedge b_2 \mid \cdots$$

$$u ::= <C_1 \leftarrow S_1, \ldots, C_n \leftarrow S_n>$$

where, for $1 \leqslant k \leqslant n$, C_k is a class name and $\mathrm{var}(S_k) \subseteq Pvar^{C_k}$.

A syntactic construct u is called a unit. We introduced a set of labels to be able to distinguish between different occurrences of a particular subprogram of a unit. Therefore we demand that all the labels occurring in a unit are different. We shall make use of this labelling in the proofs of the soundness and completeness theorems. Execution of a unit $u \equiv <C_1 \leftarrow S_1, \ldots, C_n \leftarrow S_n>$ consists of the execution of S_1. Evaluation of an expression $new(C)$ results in a reference to a new process which associates new memory locations to the variables occurring in the program corresponding with C and which starts executing that program. Evaluation of the expression *self* by a process results in a reference to that process. The communication mechanisms are generalisations of the way processes in CSP communicate. Execution of $x\,!t$ by a process P is synchronised with the execution of $?y$ or $z\,?y$ by a process P' if x refers to P' and, in case $z\,?y$ is being executed, z refers to P. In the same way execution of $x\,?y$ by a certain process is synchronised with the execution of $!t$ or $z\,!t$ by another process. So two processes can communicate when at least one refers to the other. Note that we do not allow statements like $x\,!new(C)$. "$\overset{n}{\underset{i=1}{\Box}} b_i \rightarrow S_i$" and "$*\overset{n}{\underset{i=1}{\Box}} b_i \rightarrow S_i$" we use as notations for the generalised IF resp. DO statement.

3. Semantics

We shall define an interleaving operational semantics for **P**, making use of the way it is done for POOL ([2]). For general information about this technique for semantic description we refer to [10]. To facilitate the description of the semantics of **P** we extend **P** to the language **P′** by adding to the previously given grammar the following rules:

$S ::= \underline{l}:\alpha!t \mid \underline{l}:\alpha?y \mid \underline{nil}.$

$t ::= d.$

Where: $\alpha \in Pname = \{\alpha : \alpha \in \mathbf{N}\times\mathbf{N}\}$. *Pname* is the set of code names for processes. During execution of a unit each process is given a unique name, by which other processes can refer to it.

And: $d \in \mathbf{D} = \mathbf{N} \cup \mathbf{N}\times\mathbf{N}$, **D** denotes the domain of all possible values.

N denotes the set of natural numbers.

Next we define the class of states. A state consists of three components: the first component assigns values to the program variables; the second assigns values to the set of logical variables, denoted by lvar, these variables do not occur in programs, and are used to express assertions about states; the third component assigns (positive) integer values to the class names occurring in u. Semantically we will treat these class names as global counters, each counting the number of active instances of that particular class.

The value ω, in the definition below, stands for undefined.

DEFINITION 3.1

We define **states**, elements of which are denoted by σ,... , as follows:

$\sigma \in$ **states** $\Leftrightarrow$

a. $\sigma = (\sigma_0, \sigma_1, \sigma_2)$

b. $\sigma_0 \in Pvar \times \mathbf{N}^+ \rightarrow \mathrm{D} \cup \{\omega\}$

c. $\sigma_1 \in \mathrm{lvar} \rightarrow \mathbf{N}$

d. $\sigma_2 \in Cname \rightarrow \mathbf{N}$

e. when $x \in Pvar^C$, $C \in Cname$, then for $k > \sigma_2(C)$, $\sigma_0(<x,k>) = \omega$.

where

$\mathrm{D} = \mathbf{N} \cup \mathbf{N}\times\mathbf{N}$.

D is the domain of all possible values, elements of which are denoted by d,....

3.$\mathbf{N}^+$ denotes the set of natural numbers greater than zero.

In the sequel we shall not distinguish the different components of a state, that is we shall just write $\sigma(C)$, $\sigma(<x,n>)$, $\sigma(i)$, C a class name , x a program variable, i a logical variable. Subscription of states will be used to be able to introduce new states when needed.

Before defining an operational semantics for **P** we define the assertion language L used to describe $\sigma \in$ **states**.

DEFINITION 3.2

The syntax of the class of terms of L is described as follows (these terms we denote by $f, f_1, \cdots$):

$term ::= Dt \mid At$
$Dt ::= It \mid Pt$
$It ::= n,\ n \in \mathbf{N} \mid It_1 + It_2 \mid \ \cdots \ \mid (Pt)_1 \mid (Pt)_2 \mid At[It] \mid C \mid i,\ i \in \text{lvar}$
$Pt ::= <It_1, It_2> \mid At[It] \mid nil$
$At ::= x,\ x \in Pvar \mid (At;[It]:Dt).$

We distinguish two kinds of terms: *Dt,* the Data terms, and *At,* the Array terms. We view every variable occurring in a unit as an one-dimensional array with lowerbound 1, so the basic array terms are program variables. The array term $(At;[It]:Dt)$ ([9], chapter 5.) denotes the array resulting from assigning the value of the data term *Dt* to the nth element of the array denoted by *At*, *n* the value of the integer term *It*. There are two kinds of data terms: *It,* the integer terms, *Pt,* the process terms. Process terms denote pairs of natural numbers. The integer term $(Pt)_1$ resp. $(Pt)_2$ denotes the first resp. the second component of the pair of numbers denoted by *Pt*. W.r.t. the assertion language we treat class names as variables.

DEFINITION 3.3

Next we define for a term $f \in L$, $\sigma \in$ **states**, $V(f)(\sigma)$, the value of term f in state σ. We treat the following cases:

1. $V(x) = g(x),\ x \in Pvar,$

where $g \in Pvar \rightarrow (\mathbf{N}^+ \rightarrow \mathbf{D})$, such that $g(x)(n) = \sigma(<x,n>)$.

2. $V(At[It])(\sigma) = V(At)(\sigma)(V(It)(\sigma))$ if $V(It)(\sigma) \in \mathbf{N}^+$
$= \omega$ otherwise

3. $V((At;[It]:Dt))(\sigma) = V(At)(\sigma)$ if $V(It)(\sigma) \notin \mathbf{N}^+$
$= V(At)(\sigma)\{V(Dt)(\sigma) \,/\, V(It)(\sigma)\}$ otherwise.

In clause 3 of the definition just given we used $g\{\cdots / \cdots\}$, g a function, as the variant notation.

First-order formulae are defined in the usual way, but for quantification which is permitted only over logical variables. The truth-definition differs slightly from the usual one w.r.t, for example, the following case:
$\models (It_1 \leq It_2)(\sigma)$ if and only if $V(It_1)(\sigma)$, $V(It_2)(\sigma) \in \mathbf{N}$ and $V(It_1)(\sigma) \leq V(It_2)(\sigma)$.

We are now able to give a deduction system for transitions like $<X,\sigma,u> \underset{k}{\overset{h}{\rightarrow}} <X',\sigma',u>$.

$<X,\sigma,u>$ and $<X',\sigma',u>$ are called configurations. X, X' are sets of pairs $<\alpha,S>$, $\alpha\in\mathbf{N}\times\mathbf{N}$, S the piece of program still to be executed by the process denoted by α. The variable k ranges over the set of natural numbers, it denotes the number of "steps" the derivation of the configuration to the right of the arrow from the one to the left takes. The variable h ranges over the set of histories, a history being a sequence of pairs $<\alpha,\beta>$, and triples $<d,\alpha,\beta>$, α, $\beta\in\mathbf{N}\times\mathbf{N}$, the intended meaning of the first being "α creates β" and that of the second being " the value d is sent by α to β". The last component of a configuration is a unit. The information encoded by h and k is used in the proofs of the soundness and the relative completeness of the proof system. Basic to the following definition of a deduction system for transitions is the coding of processes by pairs $<m,k>$, where m, k are natural numbers, such that the process coded by $<m,k>$ will be the kth activated instance of class C_m and operates on $x[k]$, where $x\in var(S_m)$, the variable x treated as a one-dimensional array. In the following definition when we write $X\cup\{\cdots\}$ this implies $\{\cdots\}\cap X=\varnothing$.

DEFINITION 3.4

axioms:

[1] $<X\cup\{<\alpha,new(C_k)>\},\sigma,u> \xrightarrow[1]{<\alpha,\beta>} <X\cup\{<\alpha,\underline{\beta}>,<\beta,S_k>\},\sigma', u>$
where $\beta=<k,\sigma(C_k)+1>$ and
$\sigma'=\sigma\{nil\,/\,<y_1,\beta_2>\,,\ldots,nil\,/\,<y_n,\beta_2>,\beta_2{}^*\,/\,C_k\}$,
$\{y_1,\ldots,y_n\}=var(S_k)$.

[2] $<X\cup\{<\alpha,self>\},\sigma,u> \xrightarrow[1]{\epsilon} <X\cup\{<\alpha,\underline{\alpha}>\},\sigma,u>$

[3] $<X\cup\{<\alpha,l:y:=\underline{d}>\},\sigma,u> \xrightarrow[1]{\epsilon} <X\cup\{<\alpha,\underline{nil}>\},\sigma',u>$
where $\sigma'=\sigma\{d\,/\,<y,\alpha_2>\}$.

[4] $<X\cup\{<\alpha,t>\},\sigma,u> \xrightarrow[1]{\epsilon} <X\cup\{<\alpha,\underline{d}>\},\ \sigma,u>$
$d=V(t[x_1[\underline{k}]\,/\,x_1,\ldots,x_m[\underline{k}]\,/\,x_m])(\sigma)$, $k=\alpha_2,\{x_1,\ldots,x_m\}=FV(t)$ **
$t\not\equiv\underline{d}$, $d\in\mathbf{D}^-$

[5] $<X\cup\{<\alpha,\underline{nil};S>\},\sigma,u> \xrightarrow[1]{\epsilon} <X\cup\{<\alpha,S>\},\sigma,u>$

[6] $X\cup\{<\alpha,l:\underline{\beta}?y>,<\beta,l':\underline{\alpha}!\underline{d}>\},\sigma,u> \xrightarrow[1]{<d,\beta,\alpha>} <X\cup\{<\alpha,\underline{nil}>,<\beta,\underline{nil}>\},\sigma', u>$
where $\sigma'=\sigma\{d\,/\,<y,\alpha_2>\}$.

[7] $<X\cup\{<\alpha,l:\underline{\beta}?y>,<\beta,l':!\underline{d}>\},\sigma, u> \xrightarrow[1]{<d,\beta,\alpha>} <X\cup\{<\alpha,\underline{nil}>,<\beta,\underline{nil}>\},\sigma', u>$
where $\sigma'=\sigma\{d\,/\,<y,\alpha_2>\}$.

[8] $<X\cup\{<\alpha,l:?y>,<\beta,l':\underline{\alpha}!\underline{d}>\},\sigma, u> \xrightarrow[1]{<d,\beta,\alpha>} <X\cup\{<\alpha,\underline{nil}>,<\beta,\underline{nil}>\},\sigma', u>$
where $\sigma'=\sigma\{d\,/\,<y,\alpha_2>\}$.

[9] $<X\cup\{<\alpha,l:\mathop{\Box}\limits_{k=1}^{n} b_k\rightarrow S_k>\},\ \sigma,u> \xrightarrow[1]{\epsilon} <X\cup\{<\alpha,S_r>\},\sigma,u>$
if $\models b_r[x_1[\underline{v}]\,/\,x_1,\ldots,x_m[\underline{v}]\,/\,x_m](\sigma)$,

---

*:for $\beta\in\mathbf{N}\times\mathbf{N}$ β_1,β_2 denotes the first resp. the second component of β.

**:for *e*, an expression, and *p*, a formula, *FV(e)* and *FV(p)* denote the set of free variables of e resp. p.

where $\{x_1, \ldots, x_m\} = FV(b_r)$, and $v = \alpha_2$.

[10] $<X \cup \{<\alpha, l:* \overset{n}{\underset{k=1}{\Box}} b_k \rightarrow S_k\},\ \sigma, u> \overset{\epsilon}{\underset{1}{\rightarrow}} <X \cup \{<\alpha, S_r; l:* \overset{n}{\underset{k=1}{\Box}} b_k \rightarrow S_k>\}, \sigma, u>$

if $\models b_r[x_1[\underline{v}]/x_1, \ldots, x_m[\underline{v}]/x_m](\sigma)$, where $\{x_1, \ldots, x_m\} = FV(b_r)$ and $v = \alpha_2$.

[11] $X \cup <\{<\alpha, l:* \overset{n}{\underset{k=1}{\Box}} b_k \rightarrow S_k>\}, \sigma, u> \overset{\epsilon}{\underset{1}{\rightarrow}} X \cup \{<\alpha, \underline{nil}>\}, \sigma, u>$

if $\models \bigwedge_{k=1}^{n} \neg b_k[x_1[\underline{v}]/x_1, \ldots, x_m[\underline{v}]/x_m](\sigma)$

where $\{x_1, \ldots, x_m\} = \bigcup_{k=1}^{n} FV(b_k)$, $v = \alpha_2$.

[12] $<X, \sigma, u> \overset{\epsilon}{\underset{0}{\rightarrow}} <X, \sigma, u>$

rules

[1]

$$\frac{<X \cup \{<\alpha, e>\}, \sigma, u> \overset{h}{\underset{1}{\rightarrow}} <X' \cup \{<\alpha, \underline{d}>\}, \sigma', u>}{<X \cup \{<\alpha, l:y := e>\}, \sigma, u> \overset{h}{\underset{1}{\rightarrow}} <X' \cup \{<\alpha, l:y := \underline{d}>\}, \sigma', u>}$$

[2]

$$\frac{<X \cup \{<\alpha, x>\}, \sigma, u> \overset{h}{\underset{1}{\rightarrow}} <X \cup \{<\alpha, \underline{\beta}>, \sigma', u>}{\begin{array}{l} i) <X \cup \{<\alpha, l:x!t>\}, \sigma, u> \overset{h}{\underset{1}{\rightarrow}} <X \cup \{<\alpha, l:\underline{\beta}!t>\}, \sigma', u> \\ ii) <X \cup \{<\alpha, l:x?y>\}, \sigma, u> \overset{h}{\underset{1}{\rightarrow}} <X \cup \{<\alpha, l:\underline{\beta}?y>\}, \sigma', u> \end{array}}$$

[3]

$$\frac{<X \cup \{<\alpha, t>\}, \sigma, u> \overset{h}{\underset{1}{\rightarrow}} <X \cup \{<\alpha, \underline{d}>\}, \sigma', u>}{\begin{array}{l} i) <X \cup \{<\alpha, l:\underline{\beta}!t>\}, \sigma, u> \overset{h}{\underset{1}{\rightarrow}} <X \cup \{<\alpha, l:\underline{\beta}!\underline{d}>\}, \sigma', u> \\ ii) <X \cup \{<\alpha, l:!t>\}, \sigma, u> \overset{h}{\underset{1}{\rightarrow}} <X \cup \{<\alpha, l:!\underline{d}>\}, \sigma', u> \end{array}}$$

[4]

$$\frac{<X \cup \{<\alpha, S_1>\}, \sigma, u> \overset{h}{\underset{1}{\rightarrow}} <X' \cup \{<\alpha, S_2>\}, \sigma', u>}{<X \cup \{<\alpha, S_1; S>\}, \sigma, u> \overset{h}{\underset{1}{\rightarrow}} <X' \cup \{<\alpha, S_2; S>\}, \sigma', u>}$$

[5]

$$\frac{<X, \sigma, u> \overset{h_1}{\underset{k_1}{\rightarrow}} <Y, \sigma', u>,\ <Y, \sigma', u> \overset{h_2}{\underset{k_2}{\rightarrow}} <Z, \bar{\sigma}, u>}{<X, \sigma, u> \overset{h_1 \circ h_2}{\underset{k_1 + k_2}{\rightarrow}} <Z, \bar{\sigma}, u>}$$

Now we are able to state the meaning of a unit u.

DEFINITION 3.5

Let $u \equiv <C_1 \leftarrow S_1, \ldots, C_n \leftarrow S_n>$ then:

$<\sigma,\sigma'> \in M(u) \Leftrightarrow$

$\exists X_0, X_1, h, k:$

a. $X_0 = \{<<1,1>, S_1>\}$
b. $\sigma(C_1)=1, \sigma(C_j)=0, 1<j \leq n,$
c. $<X_0,\sigma,u> \overset{h}{\underset{k}{\rightarrow}} <X_1,\sigma',u>$
d. $\forall <\alpha,S> \in X_1 \ S = \underline{nil}$
$<X_0,\sigma,u>$ we call an initial configuration.

Having defined the meaning of a unit $u \equiv <C_1 \leftarrow S_1, \ldots, C_n \leftarrow S_n>$ we want to define the meaning of R, $R;R'$, $R \| R'$, where R, R' are subprograms of, say, S_k resp. S_m, $1 \leq m,k \leq n$. But given a σ, $\sigma \in$ **states**, there can be active several instances of classes C_k, C_m (in case $\sigma(C_m), \sigma(C_k) > 0$) all of which are candidates to execute R resp. R'. One way to specify the particular instance one wants to consider can be described as follows:
We will define, for example, $M(R^{(i)})$, R a subprogram of S_k, i a logical variable, such that $<\sigma,\sigma'> \in M(R^{(i)})$ if execution of R by the process $<k,\sigma(i)>$ results in σ'.

DEFINITION 3.6

Let $u \equiv <C_1 \leftarrow S_1, \ldots, C_n \leftarrow S_n>$, R a subprogram of $S_k, 1 \leq k \leq n$,
$i \in$ lvar,

$<\sigma,\sigma'> \in M(R^{(i)}) \Leftrightarrow$

a. $\exists <X_l,\sigma_l,u>_{l=0,\ldots,m}$ such that for every $0 \leq l < m$:

$<X_l,\sigma_l,u> \overset{h_l}{\underset{1}{\rightarrow}} <X_{l+1},\sigma_{l+1},u>$ for some history h_l
and $\sigma_0 = \sigma$, $\sigma_m = \sigma'$.

b. $X_0 = \{<<k,\sigma(i)>, R>\}$
c. $0 < \sigma(i) \leq \sigma(C_k)$
d. $\forall 0 \leq l \leq m \ \forall <\beta,S> \in X_l \ (\beta \neq <k,\sigma(i)> \rightarrow <\beta,S> \in X_{l+1})$
e. $<<k,\sigma(i)>, \underline{nil}> \in X_m$

Clause a of the above definition states the existence of a sequence of configurations, a so called computation, such that every element, but the first, of this sequence is derivable from the previous one in one step. Clause b expresses that we want to consider the behaviour of the process $<k,\sigma(i)>$ executing the subprogram R. The number of active instances of class C_k in a state σ is given by $\sigma(C_k)$, so clause c must be included. Clause d states that every step of the computation, mentioned in clause a, is done by the process $<k,\sigma(i)>$. Clause e states that the process $<k,\sigma(i)>$ has finished executing R.

DEFINITION 3.7

Let $u \equiv <C_1 \leftarrow S_1, \ldots, C_n \leftarrow S_n>$,

R, R' subprograms of S_k, resp. S_m, $1 \leqslant k,m \leqslant n$,
i, $j \in$ lvar,

$<\sigma,\sigma'> \in M(R^{(i)};R'^{(j)})$ if and only if
there is a $\bar{\sigma}$: $<\sigma,\bar{\sigma}> \in M(R^{(i)})$, $<\bar{\sigma},\sigma'> \in M(R'^{(j)})$

DEFINITION 3.8

Let $u \equiv <C_1 \leftarrow S_1, \ldots, C_n \leftarrow S_n>$,
R, R' subprograms of S_k, S_m, $1 \leqslant k,m \leqslant n$, i, $j \in$ lvar,

$<\sigma,\sigma'> \in M(R^{(i)} \| R'^{(j)})$ if and only if

a. $\exists <X_l,\sigma_l,u>_{l=0,\ldots,p}$ such that for every $0 \leqslant l < p$:

$<X_l,\sigma_l,u> \overset{h_l}{\underset{1}{\rightarrow}} <X_{l+1},\sigma_{l+1},u>$ for some history h_l
and $\sigma_0 = \sigma, \sigma_p = \sigma'$

b. $X_0 = \{<<k,\sigma(i)>,R>,<<m,\sigma(j)>,R'>\}$

c. $k = m \rightarrow \sigma(i) \neq \sigma(j)$, $0 < \sigma(i) \leqslant \sigma(C_k)$, $0 < \sigma(j) \leqslant \sigma(C_m)$

d. $\forall 0 \leqslant l < p \forall <\beta,S> \in X_l$ $(\beta \neq <k,\sigma(i)> \wedge \beta \neq <m,\sigma(j)> \rightarrow <\beta,S> \in X_{l+1})$

e. $<<k,\sigma(i)>,\underline{nil}>,<<m,\sigma(j)>,\underline{nil}> \in X_p$

Having defined $M(u)$, $u \equiv <C_1 \leftarrow S_1,..,C_n \leftarrow S_n>$, and $M(R^{(i)})$, $M(R_1^{(i)};R_2^{(j)})$, $M(R_1^{(i)} \| R_2^{(j)})$, where i, $j \in$ lvar, R, R_1, R_2 subprograms of one of the programs S_k, $1 \leqslant k \leqslant n$, we can define the partial-correctness assertions: $\{p\}u\{q\}, \{p\}R^{(i)}\{q\} \cdots$, the truth-definition of the first as usual and that of the second, for example, is given w.r.t $M(R^{(i)})$.

4. The Proof System

The following axioms and proof rules are modifications of the axioms and proof-rules of the Hoare-style proof-system for sequential programs ([3]). These modifications are introduced because we treat the program variables as one-dimensional arrays. These axioms and proof rules enable one to reason about the correctness of the components of a concurrent system, given assumptions about those parts which depend on the behaviour of the environment.

Let $u \equiv <C_1 \leftarrow S_1, \ldots, C_n \leftarrow S_n>$, $i \in$ lvar.

A1. $(u:\{p[(x;[i]:t^{(i)})/x]\}\ (l:x:=t)^{(i)}\{p\})$,
where $t^{(i)} \equiv t[x_1[i]/x_1, \ldots, x_m[i]/x_m]$, $\{x_1, \ldots, x_m\} = FV(t)$

A2. $(u:\{p[(x;[i]:<\underline{k},i>)/x]\}\ (l:x:=self)^{(i)}\ \{p\})$,
where "$x:=self$" occurs in S_k.

R1.

$$\frac{(u:\{p \wedge b_k^{(i)}\}\ R_k^{(i)}\ \{q\}), 1 \leqslant k \leqslant m}{(u:\{p\}\ (\overset{m}{\underset{k=1}{\Box}} b_k \rightarrow R_k)^{(i)}\ \{q\})}$$

where $b_k^{(i)} \equiv b_k[x_1[i]/x_1, \ldots, x_{n_k}[i]/x_{n_k}]$, $\{x_1, \ldots, x_{n_k}\} = FV(b_k)$.

R2.

$$\frac{(u:\{p \wedge b_k^{(i)}\}\ R_k^{(i)} \{p\}), 1 \leq k \leq m}{(u:\{p\}(*\mathop{\Box}_{k=1}^{m} b_k \rightarrow R_k)^{(i)}\ \{p \wedge \bigwedge_{k=1}^{m} \neg b_k^{(i)}\}).}$$

R3.

$$\frac{(u:\{p\}\ R_1^{(i)}\ \{r\}), (u:\{r\}\ R_2^{(i)}\ \{q\})}{(u:\{p\}\ (R_1;R_2)^{(i)} \{q\})}$$

R4.

$$\frac{p \wedge i \leq C_k \rightarrow p_1\ ,\ (u:\{p_1\} R^{(i)}\ \{q_1\}), q_1 \wedge i \leq C_k \rightarrow q}{(u:\{p\}\ R^{(i)}\ \{q\}),\ R \text{ occurs in } S_k}$$

W.r.t. axiom 2 we translated the expression *self* by the term $<k,i>$ because the value of the variable i denotes in the context $(l:x:=self)^{(i)}$ the second component of the name of a process executing $l:x:=self$. Without the modification of the parameterized rule of consequence our proof-system would be incomplete: consider the following valid correctness-assertion, $(u:\{i>C_k\}(l:x:=1)^{(i)}\{x[i]=0\})$. It is valid because $\models i>C_k(\sigma)$ means that there is no process $<k, \sigma(i)>$ active in state σ. This assertion is deducible from the system consisting of the axioms A1, A2 the rules R1 , . . . , R3 and the unmodified parameterized rule of consequence if and only if $i>C_k \rightarrow (x;[i]:1)[i]=0$ is valid, which is not the case.

In the following definitions we show how the proof theoretic concepts: Bracketed Section, Global Invariant, Cooperation Test and Auxiliary Variables, can be applied to the language **P**.

DEFINITION 4.1

A BS (Bracketed Section) is of the form $<S>$ where:
$S \equiv R_1;R';R_2$, R' an IO (a communication statement) or a new-statement and in R_1 , R_2 there are no occurrences of IO or new- statements and if $R' \equiv l:x:=new(C)$ then $x \notin change(R_2)$,where $x \in change(R)$ if and only if x occurs at the l.h.s. of an assignment or the r.h.s. of a "?" of an input-statement.

DEFINITION 4.2

The bracketed sections $<R_1>,<R_2>$ match if:
$R_1 \equiv R_3;R;R_4$, $R_2 \equiv R_5;R';R_6$.
1. $R \equiv l:x?z$, $R' \equiv l:y!t$ or $R' \equiv l:!t$
2. $R \equiv l:?z$, $R' \equiv l:y!t$.

Note that bracketed sections are syntactic constructs. Let $u \equiv <C_1 \leftarrow S_1, \ldots, C_n \leftarrow S_n>$, such that each IO and new-statement occurring in u appears in a bracketed section. To be able to deduce correctness-assertions $\{p\}S_k^{(i)}\{q\}$, $1 \leq k \leq n$, for some logical variable i, we introduce sets of assumptions A_k, $1 \leq k \leq n$, an assumption being a correctness-assertion about a bracketed section. We say that two assumptions about bracketed sections containing IO statements match if the corresponding IO statements do. Having established the deducibility of $\{p_k\}S_k^{(i)}\{q_k\}$, $1 \leq k \leq n$, using the sets of assumptions A_k (notation: $A_k \vdash \{p_k\}S_k^{(i)}\{q_k\}$) we have to show that these assumptions cooperate. The formal definition of this cooperation test is given below, the notion of global invariant, a first-order formula, occurring in this definition is introduced to restrict the cooperation test to the semantically matching assumptions. By semantically matching assumptions we mean a pair of assumptions containing IO-statements execution of which can be synchronised.

DEFINITION 4.3

let $u \equiv <C_1 \leftarrow S_1, \ldots, C_n \leftarrow S_n>$, u bracketed. Given are the proofs $A_k \vdash \{p_k\}S_k^{(i)}\{q_k\}$, $1 \leq k \leq n$, i some logical variable. These proofs cooperate w.r.t the global invariant I if for some logical variable j distinct from i:

a. $FV(\mathrm{I}) \cap \{i,j\} = \varnothing$,
and there are no free occurrences in I of variables which can be changed outside a bracketed section.

b. let $\{pre(R_1)\}<R_1>\{post(R_1)\} \in A_k$,
$\{pre(R_2)\}<R_2>\{post(R_2)\} \in A_m$, be two matching assumptions then :
$\vdash (u:\{\mathrm{I} \wedge pre(R_1) \wedge (pre(R_2)[j/i])\} R_1^{(i)} \| R_2^{(j)} \{\mathrm{I} \wedge post(R_1) \wedge (post(R_2)[j/i])\})$

c. let $\{pre(R)\}<R>\{post(R)\} \in A_m$, $R \equiv <R_1; x := new(C_k); R_2>$ then:
$\vdash \{\mathrm{I} \wedge pre(R)\} R^{(i)} \{\mathrm{I} \wedge post(R)\}$
and $\mathrm{I} \wedge post(R) \wedge \bigwedge_{y \in var(S_k)} y[(x[i])_2] = \underline{nil} \rightarrow p_k[(x[i])_2 / i]$.

d. For every $\{p\}R\{q\} \in A_k$, $1 \leq k \leq n$, $FV(p,q,p_k,q_k) \cap (var(S_l) \cup \{C_1, \ldots, C_n\}) = \varnothing$, $1 \leq k \neq l \leq n$,
$j \notin FV(p,q)$, and every $x \in FV(p,q,p_k,q_k) \cap var(S_k)$ occurs only subscripted by a free occurrence of i in p,q,p_k,q_k.

Comment:

We do not allow i, j occurring free in the global invariant because this formula is introduced to express some global information. Clause d guarantees freedom from interference. We do not allow j occurring in the formulae mentioned in clause d because we have chosen the variable i to enable one to relate the values of some program variables of, say S_k, to a particular instance of class C_k. The clauses b and c together establish the invariance of the formula I over the bracketed sections. Clause a implies invariance of I over the remaining parts. Clause c states among others that for every statement $x := new(C_k)$ we have to establish that the precondition p_k is satisfied by the newly activated instance of class C_k. Because $x \notin change(R_2)$ we can access that instance.

Given the above definition we can now formulate a proof rule for process-creation.

R5.

$$\frac{\textit{there exist proofs } A_k \vdash (u:\{p_k\}S_k^{(i)}\{q_k\}),\ 1 \leq k \leq n, \textit{ which cooperate w.r.t the global invariant } I}{\{I \wedge p_1[\underline{1}/i]\} u \{I \wedge \bigwedge_{k=1}^{n} \forall \underline{1} \leq i \leq C_k\ q_k\}}$$

To derive the correctness assertions mentioned in the clauses b and c of the cooperation test we introduce the following axioms and rules:

Let i, j be distinct logical variables.

A3. $R \equiv \cdots ?x, R' \equiv \cdots !t$:
$(u:\{p[(x;[i]:t^{(j)})/x]\}R^{(i)} \| R'^{(j)}\{p\})$
where if $\vec{y} = FV(t) \cap var(u)$ then $t^{(j)} = t[y[\vec{j}]/\vec{y}]$.

A4. $(u:\{p[C_k+1/C_k, t_1/y_1, \ldots, t_m/y_m, (x;[i]:<\underline{k}, C_k+1>)/x]\}(l:x:=new(C_k))^{(i)}\{p\})$
where $\{y_1, \ldots, y_m\} = var(S_k)$, and $t_r = (y_r;[C_k+1]:\underline{nil})$, $1 \leqslant r \leqslant m$.

R6. Let $R \equiv l:x?y$ occur in S_k and $R' \equiv l':z!t$ in S_m.

a. $k \neq m$: $$\frac{(u:\{p \wedge x[i]=<m,j> \wedge z[j]=<k,i> \wedge i \leqslant C_k \wedge j \leqslant C_m\}R^{(i)} \| R'^{(j)}\{q\})}{(u:\{p\}R^{(i)} \| R'^{(j)}\{q\})}$$

b. $k = m$: $$\frac{(u:\{p \wedge x[i]=<m,j> \wedge z[j]=<k,i> \wedge i \neq j \wedge i \leqslant C_k \wedge j \leqslant C_m\}R^{(i)} \| R'^{(j)}\{q\})}{(u:\{p\}R^{(i)} \| R'^{(j)}\{q\})}$$

R7. Let $R \equiv l:?y$ occur in S_k and $R' \equiv l':x!t in S_m$.

a. $k \neq m$: $$\frac{(u:\{p \wedge x[j]=<k,i> \wedge i \leqslant C_k \wedge j \leqslant C_m\}R^{(i)} \| R'^{(j)}\{q\})}{(u:\{p\}R^{(i)} \| R'^{(j)}\{q\})}$$

b. $k = m$: $$\frac{(u:\{p \wedge x[j]=<k,i> \wedge i \neq j \wedge i \leqslant C_k \wedge j \leqslant C_m\}R^{(i)} \| R'^{(j)}\{q\})}{(u:\{p\}R^{(i)} \| R'^{(j)}\{q\})}$$

R8. $R \equiv l:x?y$, $R' \equiv l':!t$ analogously.

R9.

$$\frac{(u:\{p\}R_1^{(i)};R_3^{(j)}\{p_1\}),\ (u:\{p_1\}R^{(i)} \| R'^{(j)}\{q_1\}),\ (u:\{q_1\}R_2^{(i)};R_4^{(j)}\{q\})}{(u:\{p\}<R_1;R;R_2>^{(i)} \| <R_3;R';R_4>^{(j)}\{q\})}$$

R10.

$$\frac{(u:\{p\}R_1^{(i)}\{q_1\}),\ (u:\{q_1\}R_2^{(j)}\{q\}),}{(u:\{p\}R_1^{(i)};R_2^{(j)}\{q\})}$$

Axioms 3 and 4 model communication resp. creation by (implicit) assignment. The rules 7, 8, 9 state that to prove some correctness assertion about a communication we can use some additional information: the relation, which must hold for the communication to take place, between the values of the variables used as references to the communication partners and the values of the logical variables i and j. We conclude the exposition of the proof-system with the following rules:

R11.

$$\frac{\{p \wedge C_1 = 1 \wedge \bigwedge_{k=2}^{n} C_k = 0\} u \{q\}}{\{p\} u \{q\}}$$

R12.

$$\frac{p \rightarrow p_1 \quad \{p_1\} u \{q_1\} \quad q_1 \rightarrow q}{\{p\} u \{q\}}$$

R13.

$$\frac{\{p\} u' \{q\}}{\{p\} u \{q\}}$$

Provided $FV(q) \cap AUX = \varnothing$, where u results from u' by deleting all assignments to $x \in AUX$, AUX a set of (auxiliary) variables appearing only in assignments of the form $x := t$ such that for every occurrence of an assignment $x := t$ in u' if $FV(t) \cap AUX \neq \varnothing$ then $x \in AUX$.

R14.

$$\frac{\{p\} u \{q\}}{\{p[f/x]\} u \{q\}}$$

where f is an array term, x a program variable, and x does not occur in u, and $x \notin FV(q)$.

5. Soundness

In this section we shall sketch a proof of the soundness of the proof-system for **P**. We consider only the case of rule 5, the process-rule, soundness of the other rules and axioms being a routine matter. We will make use of the following definitions and lemma:

DEFINITION 5.1

Let u be a bracketed unit. R, a subprogram of u, we call normal iff $R \equiv \underline{nil}$ or every bracketed section of u occurs inside or outside of R.

DEFINITION 5.2

let $u \equiv \langle C_1 \leftarrow S_1, \ldots, C_n \leftarrow S_n \rangle$. R a (labelled) subprogram of one of the S_k, $1 \leqslant k \leqslant n$. We define $after(R, S_k)$ as follows:

[1] If $R \equiv S_k$ then $after(R, S_k) \equiv nil$.

[2] If $S_k \equiv \square_{k=1}^{m} b_m \rightarrow R_m$ and R occurs in R_p then $after(R, S_k) \equiv after(R, R_p)$.

[3] If $S_k \equiv * \square_{k=1}^{m} b_k \rightarrow R_k$ and R occurs in R_p then $after(R, S_k) \equiv after(R, R_p); S_k$.

[4] If $S_k \equiv R_1; R_2$ then $after(R, S_k) \equiv after(R, R_1); R_2$ if R occurs in R_1 else $after(R, S_k) \equiv after(R, R_1)$.

Next we define $before(R, S_k)$ such that $before(R, S_k) \equiv R; R'$ where $after(R, S_k) \equiv nil; R'$. The intuition behind these concepts should be clear.

LEMMA 5.1

let $u \equiv < C_1 \leftarrow S_1, \ldots, C_n \leftarrow S_n >$, u bracketed, A_k, $1 \leqslant k \leqslant n$, sets of assumptions, then:

$A_k \vdash \{p_k\} S_k^{(i)} \{q_k\}$, i some logical variable, iff there exists for every normal subprogram R assertions $pre(R)$, $post(R)$ such that: (Let R be a subprogram of S_k, $1 \leqslant k \leqslant n$)

[0] $\{pre(R)\} R \{post(R)\} \in A_k$, R a bracketed section,

[1] $p_k \wedge i \leqslant C_k \rightarrow pre(S_k)$, $post(S_k) \wedge i \leqslant C_k \rightarrow q_k$.

[2] $pre(R) \wedge i \leqslant C_k \rightarrow post(R)[(x;[i]:t^{(i)}) / x]$, $R \equiv x := t$, $t \not\equiv self$.

[3] $pre(R) \wedge i \leqslant C_k \rightarrow post(R)[(x;[i]:<\underline{k},i> / x]$, $R \equiv x := self$.

[4] $pre(R) \wedge i \leqslant C_k \rightarrow pre(R_1)$, $post(R_1) \wedge i \leqslant C_k \rightarrow pre(R_2)$, $post(R_2) \wedge i \leqslant C_k \rightarrow post(R)$, $R \equiv R_1 ; R_2$.

[5] $pre(R) \wedge b_l^{(i)} \wedge i \leqslant C_k \rightarrow pre(R_l)$, $post(R_l) \wedge i \leqslant C_k \rightarrow post(R)$, $l = 1, \ldots, m$, $R \equiv \underset{k=1}{\overset{m}{\Box}} b_k \rightarrow R_k$.

[6] $pre(R) \wedge b_l^{(i)} \wedge i \leqslant C_k \rightarrow pre(R_l)$, $post(R_l) \wedge i \leqslant C_k \rightarrow pre(R)$, $l = 1, \ldots, m$, $pre(R) \bigwedge_{l=1}^{m} \neg b_l^{(i)} \wedge i \leqslant C_k \rightarrow post(R)$, $R \equiv^* \underset{k=1}{\overset{m}{\Box}} b_k \rightarrow R_k$.

PROOF: routine.

Given $A_k \vdash \{p_k\} S_k^{(i)} \{q_k\}$ we define $VC(\{p_k\} S_k^{(i)} \{q_k\})$ to be the set of assertions corresponding with the clauses 1, . . . ,6 of the above mentioned lemma.
Given $u \equiv C_1 \leftarrow S_1, \ldots, C_n \leftarrow S_n >$ and for $1 \leqslant k \leqslant n$ proofs $A_k \vdash \{p_k\} S_k^{(i)} \{q_k\}$, for some logical variable i, a first-order formula I, $CP(A_1, \ldots, A_n, I)$ denotes the set of (correctness-) assertions corresponding with the clauses b and c of the cooperation-test.
These (correctness-) assertions are formulated w.r.t to some logical variable j distinct from i, such that $i, j \notin FV(I)$ and j does not occur in the pre (post)-condition of any assumption.
Now we can phrase the soundness of the process-rule as follows: if all assertions of $VC(\{p_k\} S_k^{(i)} \{q_k\})$, $1 \leqslant k \leqslant n$ and $CP(A_1, \ldots, A_n, I)$ are true and for every bracketed section R of, say, $S_k, 1 \leqslant k \leqslant n$, $\{pre(R)\} R \{post(R)\} \in A_k$ (and I and the assertions $pre(R)$, $post(R)$, p_k, q_k, R a bracketed section of S_k, $1 \leqslant k \leqslant n$, satisfy the additional restrictions mentioned in the cooperation test) then $\{p[\underline{1} / i] \wedge I\} u \{\bigwedge_{k=1}^{m} \forall 1 \leqslant i \leqslant C_k q_k \wedge I\}$ is true.
It is easy to see that this formulation of the soundness of the process-rule is implied by the following lemma:

LEMMA 5.2

Let $u \equiv < C_1 \leftarrow S_1, \ldots, C_n \leftarrow S_n >$, u bracketed. Assume there exists for every normal subprogram R of S_k, $1 \leqslant k \leqslant n$ assertions $pre(R)$, $post(R)$ and sets A_k, $1 \leqslant k \leqslant n$ of correctness assertions of bracketed sections occurring in u such that all assertions of $VC(\{p_k\} S_k^{(i)} \{q_k\})$, $1 \leqslant k \leqslant n$, $CP(A_1, \ldots, A_n, I)$ are true (i some logical variable) and for every bracketed section R of, say, S_k, $1 \leqslant k \leqslant n$, $\{pre(R)\} R \{post(R)\} \in A_k$ (and I and the assertions $pre(R)$, $post(R)$, p_k, q_k, R a bracketed section of S_k, $1 \leqslant k \leqslant n$ satisfy the restrictions mentioned in the cooperation test). Let $c : < X_l, \sigma_l, u >_{l=1, \ldots, m}$ such that for $1 \leqslant l < m$ $< X_l, \sigma_l, u > \overset{h_l}{\underset{1}{\rightarrow}} < X_{l+1}, \sigma_{l+1}, u >$ and for every $< \alpha, S > \in X_m$: $S \equiv before(R, S_{\alpha_1})$ or $S \equiv after(R, S_{\alpha_1})$, R a bracketed section, or $S \equiv nil$.
Further: $\models p_1[1 / i] \wedge I(\sigma_1)$
Then:

$\models I(\sigma_m)$ and

$\forall < \alpha, S > \in X_m$:
If $S \equiv before(R, S_{\alpha_1})$ then $\models pre(R)(\sigma')$,
if $S \equiv after(R, S_{\alpha_1})$ and for some $1 \leqslant k \leqslant m$, $< \alpha, before(R, S_{\alpha_1}) > \in X_k$ such that for every $k < l \leqslant m$ $< \alpha, before(R', S_{\alpha_1} > \in X_l$ implies that R' is a subprogram of R, then $\models post(R)(\sigma')$,
if $S \equiv nil$ then $\models q_{\alpha_1}(\sigma')$.
Where $\sigma' = \sigma_m\{\alpha_2 / i\}$

PROOF:
Induction to $|h|$, the length of the history of the computation c.
$|h| = 0$:
We note that in this case $\models I(\sigma_m)$ because $\models I(\sigma_1)$ and for $x \in FV(I) \cup \{C_1, \ldots, C_n\}$ $\sigma_1(x) = \sigma_m(x)$.
The proof of this case proceeds further by induction to the length of the computation c. We omit this part due to lack of space, it essentially generalises the soundness theorem of the Hoare-logic of sequential programs.

REMARK:
In the sequel we will write $< X, \sigma >$ instead of $< X, \sigma, u >$ when it is clear from the context which unit u is meant.
End of remark.

$|h| > 0$:
1. $h = h_1 \circ < \alpha, \beta >$:
It is not difficult, but tedious, to prove that we can assume that
$c = < X_1, \sigma_1 >, \ldots, < X_{k_1}, \sigma_{k_1} >, \ldots, < X_{k_2}, \sigma_{k_2} >, \ldots, < X_{k_3}, \sigma_{k_3} >, \ldots, < X_m, \sigma_m >$,
where:
1.$< \alpha, before(R_1; x := new(C_{\beta_1}); R_2, \quad S_{\alpha_1}) > \in X_{k_1}$, $< \alpha, after(R_1; x := new(C_{\beta_1}); R_2, S_{\alpha_1}) > \in X_{k_2}$,
2.from configuration $< X_{k_1}, \sigma_{k_1} >$ to $< X_m, \sigma_m >$ only the processes α, β are active.
3.from $< X_{k_1}, \sigma_{k_1} >$ to $< X_{k_3}, \sigma_{k_3} >$ only the process α is active, the result of this activity being the activation of β.
4.from $< X_{k_3}, \sigma_{k_3} >$ to $< X_m, \sigma_m >$ only β is performing.

Let $< \gamma, before(R, S_{\gamma_1}) > \in X_{k_1}$, R a bracketed section, ind.hyp.:
$\models pre(R)(\sigma_{k_1}\{\gamma_2 / i\})$, in case $\gamma \neq \alpha$, β: $\sigma_{k_1}(< x, \gamma_2 >) = \sigma_m(< x, \gamma_2 >)$, $x \in var(S_{\gamma_1})$, so $\models pre(R)(\sigma_m\{\gamma_2 / i\})$
(remember that all the free program-variables of $pre(R)$ are subscripted by a free occurrence of i and that $C_1, \ldots, C_n$ do not occur in $pre(R)$).
The same reasoning applies to the case that $< \gamma, after(R, S_{\gamma_1}) > \in X_{k_1}$, (R, a bracketed section, satisfying the additional demands of the lemma), or $< \gamma, \underline{nil} > \in X_{k_1}$.
In particular:$\models I \wedge pre(S)(\sigma_{k_1}\{ \alpha_2 / i\})$, $S \equiv R_1; x : new(C_{\beta_1}); R_2$.
We may assume that $\models \{I \wedge pre(S)\} S^{(i)} \{I \wedge post(S)\}$.
We know that $< \sigma_{k_1}\{\alpha_2 / i\}, \sigma_{k_2}\{\alpha_2 / i\} > \in M(S^{(i)})$.
So $\models I \wedge post(S)(\sigma_{k_2}\{\alpha_2 / i\})$. Following the same pattern of reasoning used in the case of $|h| = 0$ we conclude that $\models pre(R)(\sigma_{k_3}\{\alpha_2 / i\})$, $\models post(R)(\sigma_{k_3}\{\alpha_2 / i\})$, resp. $\models q_{\alpha_1}(\sigma_{k_3}\{\alpha_2 / i\})$ in case $< \alpha, before(R, S_{\alpha_1}) >$, $< \alpha, after(R, S_{\alpha_1}) >$ resp. $< \alpha, \underline{nil} > \in X_m$.
Because the free program-variables of I are not changed by the computation $< X_{k_2}, \sigma_{k_2} >, \ldots, < X_m, \sigma_m >$ we conclude that $\models I(\sigma_m)$.

Finally because $\models \bigwedge_{y \in var(S_{\beta_1})} y[(x[i])_2] = \underline{nil}(\sigma_{k_2}\{\alpha_2/i\})$ we know that $\models p_{\beta_1}[(x[i])_2/i](\sigma_{k_2}\{\alpha_2/i\})$ in other words $\models p_{\beta_1}(\sigma_{k_2}\{\beta_2/i\})$.
Thus: $\models p_{\beta_1}(\sigma_{k_3}\{\beta_2/i\})$. Again reasoning as in the case $|h|=0$ gives us the desired result.

2. $h=h_1 \circ \langle d,\alpha,\beta\rangle$:
It is not difficult but tedious to prove that:
$c=\langle X_1,\sigma_1\rangle, \ldots, \langle X_k,\sigma_k\rangle, \ldots, \langle X_l,\sigma_l\rangle, \ldots, \langle X_{l'},\sigma_{l'}\rangle, \ldots, \langle X_m,\sigma_m\rangle$,
where,
1.$\langle \alpha, before(R,S_{\alpha_1})\rangle$, $\langle \beta, before(R',S_{\beta_1})\rangle \in X_k$,
(α, β are to enter the bracketed sections R resp. R' execution of which consists of the transfer of the value d from α to β)
2. from $\langle X_k,\sigma_k\rangle$ to $\langle X_m,\sigma_m\rangle$ only α and β are performing steps.
3. $\langle \alpha, after(R,S_{\alpha_1})\rangle$, $\langle \beta, after(R',S_{\beta_1})\rangle \in X_l$.
4. From $\langle X_l,\sigma_l\rangle$ to $\langle X_{l'},\sigma_{l'}\rangle$ only the process α is executing.
5. From $\langle X_{l'},\sigma_{l'}\rangle$ only β is performing.
For $\gamma \neq \alpha$, β we reason as in the previous case.
Ind.hyp.: $\models I(\sigma_k)$, $\models pre(R)(\sigma_k\{\alpha_2/i\}$, $\models pre(R')(\sigma_k\{\beta_2/i\}$.
So for some logical variable j distinct from i, such that $i,j \notin FV(I)$, $j \notin FV(pre(R),pre(R'))$, $\models I \wedge pre(R) \wedge pre(R')[j/i]\ (\sigma_k\{\alpha_2/i,\beta_2/j\})$.
Furthermore: $\langle \sigma_k\{\alpha_2/i,\beta_2/j\}, \sigma_l\{\alpha_2/i,\beta_2/j\}\rangle \in M(R^{(i)} \| R'^{(j)})$.
Thus: $\models I \wedge post(R) \wedge post(R')[j/i]\ (\sigma_l\{\alpha_2/i,\beta_2/j\})$.
From which we conclude: $\models I(\sigma_l)$, $\models post(R)(\sigma_l\{\alpha_2/i\})$, $\models post(R')(\sigma_l\{\beta_2/i\})$.
Because for $x \in FV(I) \cup \{C_1, \ldots, C_n\}$ $\sigma_l(x)=\sigma_m(x)$ we deduce that $\models I(\sigma_m)$.
Reasoning as in the case $|h|=0$ gives us the desired result, (making use of the fact that the assertions we must show to hold in the last state of the computation, w.r.t. some particular process, are invariant over the actions of all the other processes).

6. Completeness

Let $\models\{p\}u\{q\}$, u a unit. We will show that this correctness assertion is deducible. Say $u \equiv \langle C_1 \leftarrow S_1, \ldots, C_n \leftarrow S_n\rangle$. We introduce the auxiliary variables $h_1, \ldots, h_n$. Each variable h_k will record for each activation of C_k the sequence of communications, activations it has executed. For each variable $x \in var(S_1)$ we introduce a corresponding fresh program variable $z_x \in Pvar^{C_1}$ (not occurring in p, q, u). These variables are used to freeze the initial values of the variables of $var(S_1)$.
Let $\vec{v}=FV(q)/(var(u) \cup \{C_1, \ldots, C_n\})$. Let $F=\{h_1, \ldots, h_n\} \cup \{z_x : x \in var(S_1)\} \cup \vec{v}$.
$F'=F/\{h_1, \ldots, h_n\}$.
we extend u to u' as follows:
Substitute
$x?y$ in S_k by $\langle x?y; h_k := h_k \circ \langle y,x,self\rangle\rangle$,
$x!e$ in S_k by $\langle x!e; h_k := h_k \circ \langle e,self,x\rangle\rangle$,
$!e$ in S_k by $\langle !e; h_k := h_k \circ \langle e,self,U\rangle\rangle$,
$?x$ in S_k by $\langle ?x; h_k := h_k \circ \langle x,U,self\rangle\rangle$,
$x := new(C)$ in S_k by $\langle x := new(C); h_k := h_k \circ \langle self,x\rangle\rangle$.
We define $nil \circ \langle d,\alpha,\beta\rangle = \langle d,\alpha,\beta\rangle$. We will use the value *nil* as the empty string. The symbol U stands for "unknown".

Let $u' \equiv <C_1 \leftarrow S'_1, \ldots, C_n \leftarrow S'_n>$.

DEFINITION 6.1

We define $[h]_\gamma$, $\gamma \in \mathbf{N} \times \mathbf{N}$, h a sequence of communication, activation records as follows:

$length(h)=0$: $[h]_\gamma = nil$ (the empty string)

$length(h)=n+1$:

$h = h' \circ <d, \alpha, \beta>$:

$[h]_\gamma = [h']_\gamma \circ <d, \alpha, \beta>$ if $\gamma = \alpha$ *or* β,

$= [h']_\gamma$ *otherwise*

$h = h' \circ <\alpha, \beta>$:

$[h]_\gamma = [h']_\gamma \circ <\alpha, \beta>$ if $\gamma = \alpha$,

$= [h']_\gamma$ *otherwise.*

DEFINITION 6.2

Let $x, y \in (\mathbf{D} \cup \{U\})^3$ or x, $y \in (\mathbf{D} \cup \{U\})^2$:
$x =_U y$ *iff* $|x| = |y|$ and $\forall 1 \leqslant i \leqslant |x| (x_i = y_i \neq U \vee x_i = U \vee y_i = U)$

DEFINITION 6.3

Let h, h' be sequences of communication, activation records:
$h =_U h'$ *iff* $length(h) = length(h')$ and $\forall 1 \leqslant i \leqslant length(h)$ $(h_i =_U h'_i)$.

Using the expressiveness of the underlying domain of values we will construct proof-outlines for the components of the unit u' and a global invariant.
Let $p' \equiv p \wedge h_1[1] = nil \wedge \bigwedge_{x \in var(S_1)} x = z_x$.

DEFINITION 6.4

$\models I(\sigma)$ iff $\exists Y, h, k, \bar{\sigma}, \sigma'$:

[a] $<X, \bar{\sigma}> \underset{k}{\overset{h}{\rightarrow}} <Y, \sigma'>$, $<X, \bar{\sigma}>$ an initial configuration.

[b] $\models p'(\bar{\sigma})$

[c] $\sigma(x) = \sigma'(x)$, $x \in F$

[d] $\sigma(C_k) = \sigma'(C_k)$, $1 \leqslant k \leqslant n$

[e] $\forall 1 \leqslant i \leqslant C_k (\sigma'(h_k)(i) =_U [h]_{<k,i>})$, $k = 1, \ldots, n$.

Stated very roughly this formula I collects all those states in which all the activated processes occur outside a bracketed section.

LEMMA 6.1

The above mentioned clauses $a, \ldots, e$ are expressible in the assertion language such that the resulting formula I contains as free only the variables of the set F.

PROOF :

Apply some recursion theory in combination with the technique of coding syntactic objects (see [6] pp 444-465).

DEFINITION 6.5

Let R be a normal (see definition 5.1) subprogram of, say, S'_k, i some logical variable,

$\models pre(R)^{(i)}(\sigma)$ iff $\exists Y, h, k, \bar{\sigma}, \sigma'$:

[a] $<X,\bar{\sigma}> \underset{k}{\overset{h}{\rightarrow}} <Y,\sigma'>$, $<X,\bar{\sigma}>$ an initial configuration.

[b] $\models p'(\bar{\sigma})$

[c] $\exists <\alpha,S> \in Y\ (\alpha = <k,\sigma(i)> \wedge S \equiv before(R,S_k))$.

[d] $\sigma(x)(\sigma(i)) = \sigma'(x)(\sigma(i))$, $x \in var(S_k)$.

[e] $\sigma(x) = \sigma'(x)$, $x \in F'$.

This formula $pre(R)^{(i)}$ collects all those states σ where the process $<k,\sigma(i)>$ is going to execute R.

LEMMA 6.2

The previously mentioned clauses $a, \ldots, e$ are expressible in the assertion language such that the free variables of the resulting formula $pre(R)$ are contained in $var(S'_k) \cup \{i\} \cup F'$ and all the program variables of $var(S'_k)$ occur only subscripted by a free occurence of the logical variable i.

PROOF:

See proof of lemma 6.1

DEFINITION 6.6

Let R be a normal subprogram of S'_m, i some logical variable,

$\models post(R)^{(i)}(\sigma)$ iff there exists k, $h_1,\ldots,h_{k-1}$, $X_1, \ldots, X_k$, $\sigma_1, \ldots, \sigma_k$ such that:

[a] $<X_1,\sigma_1>$ is an initial configuration,

[b] $<X_l,\sigma_l> \underset{1}{\overset{h_l}{\rightarrow}} <X_{l+1},\sigma_{l+1}>$, $1 \leqslant l < k$,

[c] there exists a $1 \leqslant l \leqslant k$ with $<<m,\sigma(i)>,before(R,S_m)> \in X_l$ such that:
for every $l \leqslant l' \leqslant k$ $<<m,\sigma(i)>,before(R',S_m)> \in X_{l'}$ implies that R' is a subprogram of R,

[d] $<<m,\sigma(i)>,after(R,S_m)> \in X_k$,

[e] $\sigma(x)(\sigma(i)) = \sigma_k(x)(\sigma(i))$, $x \in var(S_m)$,

[f] $\models p'(\sigma_1)$.

[g] $\sigma(x) = \sigma_k(x)$, $x \in F'$.

This formula $post(R)^{(i)}$ collects all those states σ in which the process $<m,\sigma(i)>$ has just finished executing R.

LEMMA 6.3

The clauses $a, \ldots, g$ of the previous definition are expressible in the assertion language such that the free variables of the resulting formula $post(R)$ are contained in $var(S'_m) \cup \{i\} \cup F'$ and all the program variables of $var(S'_m)$ occur only subscripted by a free occurence of i.

PROOF:

See proof of lemma 6.1.

We consider a routine matter to check that w.r.t a particular component of u' the assertions, $pre(R)^{(i)}$, $post(R)^{(i)}$, i some fresh logical variable, R a normal subprogram of that componenent, constitute a valid proof-outline (use lemma 5.1). What remains to be shown is that these proof-outlines cooperate. This is done by first establishing the truth of the following correctness assertions:
$\models\{pre(R_1)^{(i)} \wedge pre(R_2)^{(i)}[j/i] \wedge I\}\ R_1^{(i)} \| R_2^{(j)}\ \{post(R_1)^{(i)} \wedge post(R_2)^{(i)}[j/i] \wedge I\}$, R_1, R_2 being matching bracketed sections, j a fresh logical variable, and $\{I \wedge pre(R)^{(i)}\} R^{(i)} \{I \wedge post(R)^{(i)}\}$, R a bracketed section containing a new-statement. After that we show that arbitrary true correctness assertions like the ones mentioned are deducible. To establish the truth of these correctness assertions we need the following definition and lemma, the so called "merging lemma".

DEFINITION 6.7

Let A be finite set of pairs of natural numbers (= processes). Let for $\alpha \in A$ R_α be a subprogram of S'_{α_l} or be equal to $\underline{nil}$.
Then we call the set $\{R_\alpha: \alpha \in A\}$ $(\overline{\sigma}, A)-reachable$
iff
$\exists Y, h, k, \sigma, \sigma'$:

[a] $<X,\overline{\sigma}> \underset{h}{\overset{k}{\rightarrow}} <Y,\sigma'>$, $<X,\overline{\sigma}>$ an initial configuration.

[b] $\models p'(\overline{\sigma})$

[c] $\forall \alpha \in A\ \exists <\alpha, S> \in Y$ such that: if $R_\alpha \equiv \underline{nil}$ then $S \equiv \underline{nil}$ else $S \equiv before(R_\alpha, S_{\alpha_1})$ and $\sigma(x)(\alpha_2) = \sigma'(x)(\alpha_2)$, $x \in var(S_{\alpha_1})$.

[d] $\sigma(x) = \sigma'(x)$, $x \in F'$

[e] If furthermore $\sigma(x) = \sigma'(x)$, $x \in \{h_1, \ldots, h_n, C_1, \ldots, C_n\}$ and $\sigma'(h_k)(i) = {}_U[h]_{<k,i>}$, $1 \leq k \leq n$, $1 \leq i \leq \sigma'(C_k)$
we speak of $(I, \sigma, A)-reachability$ of $\{R_\alpha: \alpha \in A\}$.

Note that $\models pre(R)^{(i)}(\sigma)$ implies that R is $(\sigma, <k, \sigma(i)>)-reachable$ (R occurring in S_k). The following lemma states the conditions under which we can fuse different computations of u' into one computation.

LEMMA 6.4 (merging-lemma):

Let A be a finite set of processes such that for every $\alpha \in A$ R_α is a normal subprogram and $(\sigma, \alpha)-reachable$. Let furthermore $\models I(\sigma)$.
then:
$\{R_\alpha: \alpha \in A\}$ $(I, \sigma, A)-reachable$

PROOF:

Due to lack of space we have omitted this proof. For a detailed exposition of the proof see the full paper. The pattern of the proof is similar to the corresponding theorem for CSP ([5]).

Given this lemma we can prove the following lemma:

LEMMA 6.5

Let R_1, R_2 be two matching bracketed sections, occurring in, say, S'_l resp. S'_m, i, j some logical variables such that $i, j \notin FV(I)$.
Then:
$\models\{pre(R_1)^{(i)} \wedge pre(R_2)^{(i)}[j/i] \wedge I\}\ R_1^{(i)} \| R_2^{(j)}\ \{post(R_1)^{(i)} \wedge post(R_2)^{(i)}[j/i] \wedge I\}$.

PROOF:

Let $\models pre(R_1)^{(i)} \wedge pre(R_2)^{(i)}[j/i] \wedge I)(\sigma)$ From the definition of the formulas $pre(R_1)^{(i)}$, $pre(R_2)^{(i)}$ and the merging-lemma it follows that (note that $pre(R)^{(i)}[j/i] \Leftrightarrow pre(R)^{(j)}$):
$\exists X, Y, \bar{\sigma}, \sigma', h, k$ such that

a. $<X,\bar{\sigma}> \underset{k}{\overset{h}{\rightarrow}} <Y,\sigma'>$ $<X,\bar{\sigma}>$ an initial configuration.

b. $\models p(\bar{\sigma})$

c. $\sigma'(x)=\sigma(x),\ x \in FV(I) \cup \{C_1, \ldots, C_n\}$.

d. $\sigma'(x)(\sigma(i))=\sigma(x)(\sigma(i)),\ x \in var(S_l)$

e. $\sigma'(x)(\sigma(j))=\sigma(x)(\sigma(j)),\ x \in var(S_m)$

f. $\sigma'(x)=\sigma(x),\ x \in F'$

g. $<<l,\sigma(i)>, before(R_1,S_l)>,\ <<m,\sigma(j)>, before(R_2,S_m)> \in Y$

h. $\sigma'(h_k)(i)={}_U[h]_{<k,i>},\ 1 \leqslant k \leqslant n,\ 1 \leqslant i \leqslant \sigma'(C_k)$.

Let $<\sigma,\sigma_0> \in M(R^{(i)} \| R^{(j)})$.
We remark that:$\sigma_0(C_j)=\sigma(C_j)=\sigma'(C_j),\ j=1,\ldots,n$.
We define for $1 \leqslant p \leqslant n$, $1 \leqslant q \leqslant \sigma_0(C_p)$:

$$\sigma_1(x)(q)=\sigma_0(x)(q),\ x \in \{h_1, \ldots, h_n\},$$

$$\sigma_1(C_j)=\sigma_0(C_j), j=1,\ldots,n,$$

$$\sigma_1(x)(q)=\sigma_0(x)(q), x \in var(S_p),\ (p=l \wedge q=\sigma(i)) \vee (p=m \wedge q=\sigma(j)).$$

$$\sigma_1(x)(q)=\sigma'(x)(q), \text{for the remaining cases.}$$

It follows that:
$<X,\bar{\sigma}> \underset{k}{\overset{h}{\rightarrow}} <Y,\sigma'> \underset{k'}{\overset{h'}{\rightarrow}} <Y',\sigma_1>$
where
$Y'=Y/\{<<l,\sigma(i)>, before(R_1,S_l)>,\ <<m,\sigma(j)>, before(R_2,S_m)>\} \cup Z$,
($Z=\{<<l,\sigma(i)>, after(R_1,S_l)>,\ <<m,\sigma(j)>, after(R_2,S_m)>\}$).
We conclude: $\models (post(R_1)^{(i)} \wedge post(R_2)^{(i)}[j/i] \wedge I)\ (\sigma_1\{\sigma(i)/i, \sigma(j)/j\})$ ($i,j \notin FV(I)$).
So:$\models (post(R_1)^{(i)} \wedge post(R_2)^{(i)}[j/i] \wedge I)(\sigma_0)$. Which finishes the proof.

We shall now prove that arbritrary true correctness assertions about I/O bracketed sections are deducible.

LEMMA 6.6

Let R_1, R_2 be two matching bracketed sections, occurring in S'_k resp. S'_m. Then $\models\{p\}R_1^{(i)} \| R_2^{(j)}\{q\}$ implies $\vdash\{p\}R_1^{(i)} \| R_2^{(j)}\{q\}$.

PROOF:

Let: $\models p_1(\sigma) \Leftrightarrow \exists \sigma'(\models p(\sigma') \wedge <\sigma',\sigma> \in M(S_1^{(i)};\ S_3^{(j)}))$, and

$\models p_2(\sigma) \Leftrightarrow \forall\sigma'(<\sigma,\sigma'> \in M(S_2^{(i)};S_4^{(j)}) \rightarrow \models q(\sigma'))$,
where $R_1 \equiv S_1;C;S_2,\ R_2 \equiv S_3;A;S_4$.
It follows that: $\models\{p\}S_1^{(i)};S_3^{(j)}\{p_1\}$ and $\models\{p_2\}S_2^{(i)};S_4^{(j)}\{q\}$.
From the completeness of the Hoare logic for sequential programs (which carries over to its parameterized version) it follows that: $\vdash\{p\}S_1^{(i)};S_3^{(j)}\{p_1\}$ and $\vdash\{p_2\}S_2^{(i)};S_4^{(j)}\{q\}$.
Further: $\models\{p_1\}C^{(i)}\|A^{(j)}\{p_2\}$.
Let: $C \equiv x?y,\ A \equiv z!e$, the other cases are treated similar. It is easily shown that:
$\models p_1 \wedge x[i] = <m,j> \wedge z[j] = <k,i> \rightarrow p_2[(y;[i]:e^{(j)})/y]$
Thus: $\vdash\{p_1\}C^{(i)}\|A^{(j)}\{p_2\}$. Finally apply the formation rule (R9).

The only thing left to do is to prove the following lemma:

LEMMA 6.7

Let $<R> \equiv <x:=new(C_k);h_m:=h_m \circ <self,x>>$ in S_m.
Then $\vdash\{I \wedge pre(R)^{(i)}\}\ R^{(i)}\{I \wedge post(R)^{(i)}\}$ and
$\models I \wedge post(R)^{(i)} \wedge \bigwedge_{y \in var(S_k)} y[(x[i])_2] = \underline{nil} \rightarrow pre(S_k)^{(i)}[(x[i])_2/i]$.
Where $i \in$ lvar, $i \notin FV(I)$.

PROOF:

We omit this proof, which is rather straightforward due to the fact that we modelled a new-statement by a multiple assignment. The truth of the implication follows immediately from the definition of $post(R)^{(i)}$, and $pre(S_k)^{(i)}$.

This finishes the cooperation test.

We may apply now rule 7: $\vdash\{I \wedge pre(S'_1)^{(i)}[1/i]\}u'\ \{I \wedge \bigwedge_{k=1}^{n}(\forall 1 \leq i \leq C_k post(S'_k)^{(i)})\}$.

It is easy to see that: $\models p' \wedge C_1 = 1 \wedge \bigwedge_{k=2}^{n} C_k = 0 \rightarrow I \wedge pre(S'_1)^{(i)}[1/i]$ (use axiom 12 of the transition system).

We next prove that:

$\models I \wedge \bigwedge_{k=1}^{n}(\forall 1 \leq i \leq C_k post(S'_k)^{(i)}) \rightarrow q$.

Let $\models I \wedge \bigwedge_{k=1}^{n}(\forall 1 \leq i \leq C_k post(S'_k)^{(i)})(\sigma)$.

Define: $A = \{<k,l>: 1 \leq k \leq n,\ 1 \leq l \leq \sigma(C_k)\}$.

Apply the merging-lemma for $R_\alpha \equiv \underline{nil},\ \alpha \in A$.

So for some $X,\ Y,\ h,\ k,\ \bar{\sigma},\ \sigma'$: $<X,\bar{\sigma}> \underset{h}{\overset{k}{\rightarrow}} <Y,\sigma'>$, $\alpha \in A$ implies $<\alpha,\underline{nil}> \in Y$ and $\sigma(x)(\alpha_2) = \sigma'(x)(\alpha_2)$, $x \in var(S'_{\alpha_1})$, furthermore: $\sigma'(C_k) = \sigma(C_k)$, $k = 1,\ldots,n$, and $\sigma'(x) = \sigma(x)$, $x \in F'$.

So $\forall <\alpha,R> \in Y\ R \equiv nil$.

Thus from $\models\{p\}u'\{q\}$ (which follows from $\models\{p\}u\{q\}$) and $\models p(\bar{\sigma})$ ($<X,\bar{\sigma}>$ being an initial configuration) we conclude that $\models q(\sigma')$.

But σ' agrees with σ w.r.t. the free variables of q. Thus: $\models q(\sigma)$. Applying rule 12 gives $\{p'\}u'\{q\}$. Application of rule 13: $\{p'\}u\{q\}$. Application of rule 14: $\{p\}u\{q\}$ (substituting for z_x, $x \in var(S_1)$, x and for h_1 $(h_1;[1]:nil)$).

7. Conclusion.

We have shown in this paper how we can apply the concepts of cooperation test, global invariant, bracketed section and auxiliary variables to the proof-theory of a language containing process creation.
In the full paper we show how to handle within this framework total correctness and safety properties.
We have proven the proof system to be sound and (relative) complete.
Further research to the proof theory of process creation will be dedicated to the problem of how to construct a more compositional proof system for process creation.

acknowledgement

The idea of the language the proof-theory of which we studied in this paper has been inspired by the language POOL designed by Pierre America. We wish to thank Pierre America, Jaco de Bakker, Joost Kok, John-Jules Meyer, Jan Rutten and Erik de Vink for their part in the discussion of this proof-system.

references

[1] P.America, Definition Of The Programming Language POOL-T, ESPRIT project 415, Doc Nr. 0091, Philips Research Laboratories, Eindhoven, the Netherlands, June 1985.

[2] P.America, J.W. de Bakker, J.N. Kok, J.J.M.M. Rutten, Operational Semantics Of A Parallel Object-Oriented Language, 13th ACM Symposium on Principles of Programming Languages, St. Petersburg, Florida, January 13-15, 1986.

[3] K.R.Apt, Ten Years Of Hoare's Logic:A Survey - part 1, TOPLAS **3** (4) (1981) 431 -484 .

[4] K.R.Apt, N.Francez, W.P. de Roever, A Proof-system For CSP, TOPLAS **2** (3) (1980) 359 -385.

[5] K.R.Apt, Formal Justification Of A Proof-system For CSP, J.ASSOC. COMPUT. MACH., 30 **1** (1983) 197 -216.

[6] J.W. de Bakker: Mathematical Theory of Program Correctness. Prentice-Hall International, 1980.

[7] R. Gerth, A Proof System For Concurrent Ada Programs in: Science of Computer Programming 4 (1984) 159-204, North-Holland.

[8] R.Gerth, W.P.de Roever, M.Roncken, Procedures And Concurrency: A Study In Proof, in:Lecture Notes In Computer Science; International Symposium On Programming, nr.137, Turin, April, 1982.

[9] D.Gries, The Science Of Programming, Springer-Verlag, New York Heidelberg Berlin, 1981.

[10] G.D. Plotkin, A Structural Approach To Operational Semantics, Report **DAIMI** FN-19, Comp.Sci.dept., Aarhus Univ. 1981.

[11] G.D.Plotkin, An Operational Semantics For CSP, in:Formal Description Of Programming Concepts **2** (D.Bjorner ed.), North Holland, Amsterdam (1983) 199-223

[12] J. Zwiers, W.P. de Roever, P. van Emde Boas: Compositionality and concurrent nerworks: soundness and completeness of a proof system.
Proceedings of the 12th International Colloquium on Automata, Languages and Programming (ICALP), Nafplion, Greece, July 15-19, 1985, Springer-Verlag, Lecture Notes in Computer Science, Vol. 194, pp. 509-519.

8. appendix

An example: a parallel prime generator.
This program is a translation, modification of a program written in the language POOL by L. Augusteijn.
The original program generates all prime numbers and is thus a non-terminating program. We have modified the original program to make it terminating, that is we introduced a variable m such that the program generates all prime numbers not greater than m. Let $u \equiv < C_1 \leftarrow S_1, C_2 \leftarrow S_2 >$ where

```
S1:
c:=new(C2)
; n:=2
; do n≤m → c!n ; n:=n+1 od
; c!0
```

```
S2:
?p ;
if p≠0 →     next:=new(C2)
            ; do q≠0 →        ?q
                              ; if p MOD q≠0∨q=0 →     next!q
                                otherwise →            skip
                                fi
              od
   p=0 →     skip
fi
```

We want to prove the following partial correctness assertion:
$\{m[1] \geq 2\} u \{\forall 1 \leq i < C_2 \; p[i] = \text{' } i^{th} \text{ prime number'} \wedge C_2 - 1 = |\{p : prime(p) \wedge p \leq m[1]\}|\}$.
(for X a set $|X|$ denotes the cardinality of X.)
We extend u to a annotated and bracketed unit u' as follows:

```
S'1:
{φ0}
<c:=new(C2)
;bool:=false
;n:=2>
{φ1}
;do n≤m →      {φ2}
               <c!n;n:=n+1>
               {φ1}
 od
{φ3}
; <c!0>
{φ4}
```

Where,

1. $\phi_0 \equiv bool[i]=nil \wedge m[i] \geqslant 2$,
2. $\phi_1 \equiv c[i]=<2,1> \wedge n[i] \leqslant m[i]+1 \wedge bool[i] \neq nil$,
3. $\phi_2 \equiv n[i] \leqslant m[i] \wedge c[i]=<2,1> \wedge bool[i] \neq nil$,
4. $\phi_3 \equiv n[i]=m[i]+1 \wedge c[i]=<2,1> \wedge bool[i] \neq nil$,
5. $\phi_4 \equiv n[i]=m[i]+1 \wedge bool[i] \neq nil$.

```
S'2:
{ψ0}
<?p> ;
{ψ1}
if p≠0 →     {ψ2}
             <next:=new(C2)
             ;last:=false>
             {ψ3}
             ; do q≠0 →          {ψ3}
                                 <?q;r:=true>
                                 {ψ4}
                                 ; if p mod q≠0∨q=0→     {ψ5}
                                                         <next!q;r:=false>
                                                         {ψ3}
                                   otherwise →           {ψ3}skip{ψ3}
                                 fi
                                 {ψ3}
               od
             {ψ6}
   p=0 →     {ψ6}skip{ψ6}
fi
{ψ6}
```

Where,

1. $\psi_0 \equiv last[i]=r[i]=nil$,
2. $\psi_1 \equiv last[i]=r[i]=nil \wedge (p[i]=0 \vee p[i]=i^{th}$ *prime number*$)$
3. $\psi_2 \equiv last[i]=r[i]=nil \wedge p[i]=i^{th}$ *prime number*
4. $\psi_3 \equiv r[i]=true \rightarrow \neg(prime(q[i]) \vee q[i]=0) \wedge next[i]=<2,i+1> \wedge last[i]=false$,
5. $\psi_4 \equiv next[i]=<2,i+1> \wedge r[i]=true \wedge last[i]=false$,
6. $\psi_5 \equiv (p[i] \nmid q[i] \vee q[i]=0) \wedge next[i]=<2,i+1> \wedge last[i]=false \wedge r[i]=true$,
7. $\psi_6 \equiv r[i] \neq true \wedge last[i]=nil \rightarrow p[i]=0$.

We define for X a finite set of prime numbers $NP(X)$ the least prime number greater than all the numbers of X. Note that $NP(\varnothing)=2$.
Let $n \lhd NP(X)$ iff $n \leqslant NP(X)$ and $\forall x \in X\ n>x$.
Next we define our global invariant I.

1. $\forall 1 \leqslant i \leqslant C_2 (p[i]=i^{th}$ *prime number* $\vee (i=C_2 \wedge (p[i]=nil \vee p[i]=0)))$,
2. $\forall 1 \leqslant i \leqslant C_2 (r[i]=true \wedge q[i] \neq 0 \rightarrow \forall 1 \leqslant j < i\, p[j] \nmid q[i])$,
3. $\forall 1 \leqslant i \leqslant C_2 (r[i]=true \wedge q[i] \neq 0 \rightarrow q[i] \lhd NP(\{p[k]:1 \leqslant k \leqslant C_2 \wedge prime(p[k])\} \cup \{q[k]:i<k \leqslant C_2 \wedge r[k]=true \wedge prime(q[k])\})$,
4. $bool[1] \neq nil \rightarrow n[1] \lhd NP(\{p[i]:1 \leqslant i \leqslant C_2 \wedge prime(p[i])\} \cup \{q[i]:1 \leqslant i \leqslant C_2 \wedge r[i]=true$

$\wedge prime(q[i])\}),$

5. $bool[1]=nil \rightarrow C_2=0,$
6. $C_1=1,$
7. $\forall 1 \leqslant i \leqslant C_2(last[i]=nil \Leftrightarrow i=C_2).$

I is the conjunction of the formulas 1, . . . ,7.
Next we have to prove that these proof outlines cooperate. We have selected the following two cases, the others are left to the reader to verify.
We prove that:
$\{I \wedge \phi_0\}(c:=new(C_2);bool:=false;n:=2)^{(i)}\{I \wedge \phi_1\}.$

PROOF:

a. $I \wedge \phi_0 \wedge 0<i \leqslant C_1 \rightarrow C_1=1 \wedge C_2=0 \wedge i=1 \wedge m[i] \geqslant 2,$

b. $C_1=1 \wedge C_2=0 \wedge i=1 \wedge m[i] \geqslant 2 \rightarrow$
$C_1=1 \wedge C_2+1=1 \wedge i=1 \wedge m[i] \geqslant 2 \wedge (c;[i]:<2,C_2+1>)[i]=<2,C_2+1> \wedge$
$\bigwedge_{x \in var(S'_2)} (x;[C_2+1];nil)[C_2+1]=nil$

c. $\{I \wedge \phi_0 \wedge 0<i \leqslant C_2\}$
$(c:=new(C_2))^{(i)}$
$\{C_1=1 \wedge C_2=1 \wedge i=1 \wedge m[i] \geqslant 2 \wedge c[i]=<2,1> \wedge \bigwedge_{x \in var(S'_2)} x[1]=nil\}(\equiv \chi)$ (application of A4 and R4),

d. $\chi \rightarrow \chi \wedge (n;[i]:2)[i]=2 \wedge (bool;[i];false)[i]=false$

e. $\{\chi\}(bool:=false;n:=2)^{(i)}\{\chi \wedge bool[i]=false \wedge n[i]=2\}$
(application of A1 and R3),

f. $\{I \wedge \phi_0 \wedge 0<i \leqslant C_2\}(c:new(C_2);bool:=false;n:=2)^{(i)}\{\chi \wedge bool[i]=false \wedge n[i]=2\}$
(application of R3),

g. $\chi \wedge bool[i]=false \wedge n[i]=2 \rightarrow I \wedge \phi_1$

h. $\{I \wedge \phi_0\}(c:=new(C_2);bool:=false;n:=2)^{(i)}\{I \wedge \phi_1\}$
(application of R4).

Next we prove that:
$\{I \wedge \psi_5 \wedge \psi_3[j/i]\}\ (next!q;r:=false)^{(i)} \| (?q;r:=true)^{(j)}\ \{I \wedge \psi_3 \wedge \psi_4[j/i]\}.$

PROOF:
Let $\psi_i \equiv last[i]=false$ and $\psi_j \equiv next[j]=<2,j+1> \wedge last[j]=false.$

a. $I \wedge \psi_5 \wedge \psi_3[j/i] \wedge 0<i \leqslant C_2 \wedge 0<j \leqslant C_2 \wedge next[i]=<2,j> \rightarrow$
$I[(q;[j]:q[i])/q,((r;[i]:false);[j]:true)/r] \wedge \psi_i \wedge \psi_j)$

b. $\{I \wedge \psi_5 \wedge \psi_3[j/i]\}\ (next!q)^{(i)} \| (?q)^{(j)}\ \{I[((r;[i]:false);[j]:true)/r)] \wedge \psi_i \wedge \psi_j\}$
(application of A3 and R7)

c. $\{I[((r;[i]:false);[j]:true)/r] \wedge \psi_i \wedge \psi_j\}\ (r:=false)^{(i)}\ \{I[(r;[j]:true)/r] \wedge \psi_3 \wedge \psi_j\}$
(application of A1),

d. $\{I[(r;[j]:true)/r] \wedge \psi_3 \wedge \psi_j\}\ (r:=true)^{(j)}\ \{I \wedge \psi_3 \wedge \psi_4[j/i]\}.$

e. One application of R9 finishes the proof.

Remark:the truth of the implication mentioned in clause a. follows from the following observation; if $r[i+1]=true$ then $q[i+1]$ is not a prime number so
$NP(\{p[k]:1 \leqslant k \leqslant C_2 \wedge p[k] \neq nil\} \cup \{q[k]:i<k \leqslant C_2 \wedge r[k]=true \wedge prime(q[k])\})$

equals $NP(\{\cdots\} \cup \{q[k]: i+1<k \leqslant C_2 \wedge r[k]=true \wedge prime(q[k])\})$.
End of remark.

Applying rule 5. yields:
$\{I \wedge \phi_0[1/i]\} u' \{I \wedge \forall 1 \leqslant i \leqslant C_1 \phi_4 \wedge \forall 1 \leqslant i \leqslant C_2 \psi_6\}$.
Now the following implications can be shown to hold:
1. $C_1 = 1 \wedge C_2 = 0 \wedge \phi_0[1/i] \rightarrow I \wedge \phi_0[1/i]$
2. $I \wedge \forall 1 \leqslant i \leqslant C_1 \phi_4 \wedge \forall 1 \leqslant i \leqslant C_2 \psi_6 \rightarrow$
$\forall 1 \leqslant i < C_2 p[i] = i^{th}$ *prime number* $\wedge C_2 - 1 = |\{p : prime(p) \wedge p \leqslant m[1]\}|$.

Applying the rules 11, 12, 13 and 14 in that order gives us the desired result.

QUESTIONS AND ANSWERS

Lauer: There was a paper by Stephen Brookes at the Carneghie-Mellon Conference on Semantics of Concurrency in which he had a formalization of the semantics of CSP, allowing him to avoid having to deal with interference. Are you aware of that paper? And if you are: is there something inherent of what you are doing here that requires you to reintroduce interference?

de Boer: I am not aware of this paper. Interference freedom is just a very simple notion in this proof system. It just says that for giving a proof outline of one component of a program, the occurrences of variables of the proof outline are restricted. You don´t want the proof outline to speak about other components.

Lauer: Stephen Brookes doesn´t need that concept at all. Maybe I´ll show you the paper [S.D. Brookes: On the axiomatic treatment of concurrency. In: S.D. Brookes, A.W. Roscoe, G. Winskel (eds.): Seminar on Concurrency. Lecture Notes in Computer Science 197, Berlin: Springer 1984, 1-34].

Pnueli: Just a question about the design of your assertion language. You choose to count activations. That might give a sort of a bias. If you have two programs that differ only in the permutation of two activations, it would not appear intuitive that the semantics associated with this distinguishes between those cases. An alternative would be to have a set of processes corresponding to each class. Did you consider that alternative? Could you comment on it?

de Boer: That alternative is not considered, and I don´t know in which case it will solve problems. It is sure that this numbering of processes is not really abstract. We are looking for a way to device a more abstract proof system which doesn´t number the processes. But first I wanted to show that proof techniques that follow CSP can be applied.

Mirkowska: Can you say in which sense your axioms define the meaning of the constructs?

de Boer: It is more stated informally because in this talk I did not want to speak about the semantics. In the conventional way I defined an operational semantics and a proof system. With respect to that particular operational semantics, I have proved the system sound and complete. The proof system does not fix uniquely the semantics.

Mirkowska: In which sense is your system complete?

de Boer: In the usual sense, more strictly for arithmetical domains.

Mirkowska: It is not strong completeness?

de Boer: Yes, with respect to certain expressive domains.

Bjørner: Do you have a denotational semantics? And if so, what were the problems in establishing this?

de Boer: First, this is not really my field. I am supposed to work on the proof theory. At the CWI Jaco de Bakker andd Pierre America are working on the denotational semantics and their problems are not my problems in the first.

de Roever: The question is too well conceived. (laughter)

de Boer: Sure, it is interesting to compare the proof system with the denotational semantics, or to ask what restrictions are necessary to the denotational model to be useful for the proof system. But that´s not considered at this stage.

de Roever: You make your assertion language rather not abstract, anti-abstract. But this is not completely the case because if you have a class of reserved variables (the counters) then these occur over and over in your assertions, too. Whatever assertions you express about your program units, these counters will always be fixed. So, once you do this trick consistently in your language there is nothing wrong with respect to the basic meaning of the program units which has been given with respect to these counters. But one principal source of lack of abstractness is that the order in which your, let´s say, incarnation counters are increased, is a linear order, for example, it´s ´3´, ´4´, ´5´, ´6´. But if these processes are created concurrently you cannot say ´3´, ´4´ or ´4´,´3´.
Now my question is: is this in fact the only source of lack of abstractness? Can you think of other sources of lack of abstractness?

de Boer: Now you could say, that is investigated by Pierre America.

de Roever: No, it isn´t. Given your particular assertion language which is completely different from that of Pierre America, given your particular semantics, there is nothing wrong with counters or, let´s say, with subscripting.

de Boer: In the case of maximal parallelism this assertion language will not work. One has to do some other coding trick. Perhaps one could use the trick that is used by Jan Willem [Klop], Pierre [America] and Jaco [de Bakker]. They have defined an operational semantics for maximal parallelism and they have also solved the problem of coding the processes, when they can be created strictly in parallel. But I have not investigated yet how to device proof systems in that case. So I don´t know how it will work out.

Felleisen: There is a very similar problem in denotational semantics when allocating locations for variables that declare the entity for a block. If you declare x,y you get two locations and they are distinct. So if you declare y,x you get different locations although you are in the same block. The denotational semantics has one solution that just came out by Steven Brookes [S.D. Brookes: A fully abstract semantics and a proof system for an ALGOL-like language with sharing. In: A. Melton (ed.): Mathematical foundations of programming semantics. Lecture Notes in Computer Science 239, Berlin: Springer 1985, 59-100]. He works with equivalence classes that really work out well in the denotational semantics.There could be a similar way to solve the same problem.

de Boer: I don´t know, because here you have the problem of a program variable denoting different memory locations. It comes up also in the cooperation test. And there I have to show that one proof outline cooperates with itself. So I have one assumption and another assumption, say, to speak about the same variables and then you could say, I just do some renaming of these variables. But then you get the problem how this will relate to some global invariant.

Tennent: There is an earlier solution to that problem of the denotational semantics due to Frank Oles and John Reynolds, the ´possible world semantics´ [cf. e.g. F.J. Oles: Type algebras, functor categories and block structure. In: M. Nivat, J. Reynolds (eds.): Algebraic methods in semantics. Cambridge: Cambridge University Press 1985, 543-574]. This technique may also be applicable in this context.

de Roever: Brookes solved this primarily for the semantics, then he went in a separate paper to the proof theory.

SESSION 2

Concurrency I

Chairman: J. W. de Bakker

J.C.M. Baeten, J.A. Bergstra and J.W. Klop

Conditional axioms and α/β - calculus in process algebra

J.A. Bergstra, J.W. Klop and E. - R. Olderog

Failures without chaos : a new process semantics for fair abstraction

P. Degano, R. de Nicola and U. Montanari

Observational equivalences for concurrency models

Formal Description of Programming Concepts - III
M. Wirsing (Editor)
Elsevier Science Publishers B.V. (North-Holland)
IFIP, 1987

Conditional axioms and α/β-calculus in process algebra

J.C.M. Baeten,
University of Amsterdam

J.A. Bergstra,
University of Amsterdam,
State University of Utrecht

J.W. Klop,
Centre for Mathematics and Computer Science, Amsterdam

We define the alphabet of finite and infinite terms in ACP_τ, the algebra of communicating processes with silent steps, and also give approximations of it. Using the alphabet, we formulate some conditional axioms. The usefulness of the axioms is demonstrated in examples.

1985 Mathematics Subject Classification: 68Q55, 68Q45, 68Q10, 68N15.
1982 CR Categories: F.1.2, F.3.2, F.3.1, D.3.1.
Key words & Phrases: concurrency, process algebra, alphabet, conditional axiom.
Note: This work was sponsored in part by ESPRIT contract nr. 432, Meteor. This paper is a revised version of reference [1].

1. Introduction.

During the last decade, various process models, or models for concurrency, have been proposed; we mention Milner's synchronisation trees in CCS (see [13]), the metrical process spaces of De Bakker and Zucker [4], the models based on preorders between processes of Hennessy and Plotkin [11] and the failure semantics of Brookes, Hoare and Roscoe [9] and Hoare [12]. (For more complete references we must refer to Bergstra and Klop [6].) Starting with Milner, there has been a growing interest in an *algebraic* treatment of concurrency. Here is our point of departure: rather than fixing a particular process model, we start with axioms describing a class of models. There are two reasons for this axiomatic methodology. One is that when so many different (but often related) process models arise as the last years have witnessed, it is becoming profitable to attempt an organisation into an axiomatic framework. The second reason is that, being interested in actual specification of processes and verification of process behaviour, we adhere to the principle that one must be able to perform such specifications and verifications exclusively in algebraical terms - rather than in one particular process model. Thus we hope to get, eventually, at a greater manageability of specifications and verifications: ideally, we want pure algebraic formula manipulations, rather than having to resort to particular process representations, such as transition diagrams, Petri nets, or failure sets. This, for the obvious reason that such particular representations are much harder to represent mechanically than equations in an algebraic format, where we can hope to profit from the experience obtained in the culture of abstract data type specifications.

A consequence is that we wish to adhere as much as possible to *equations.* However, as this purely equational medium would not be sufficiently expressive (viz. to prove equations between expressions denoting infinite processes), we will also admit, as is usual in an algebraic/axiomatic style, *proof rules,* or as we will also call them, **conditional axioms**. A typical example of such a proof rule is the Recursive Specification Principle below, stating that if processes p,q satisfy the same (guarded) equation, one may infer the equation p = q.

Not surprisingly, it turns out that in computations with infinite processes one often needs information about the **alphabet** $\alpha(p)$ of a process p. E.g. if p is the process uniquely defined (specified) by the recursion equation $x = a\cdot x$ (where 'a' is an atomic action), we have $\alpha(p) = \{a\}$. An example of the use of alphabet information is given by:

$$\alpha(x) \cap I = \emptyset \;\Rightarrow\; \tau_I(x) = x \qquad \text{(CA4)}$$

in words: if no action from I occurs in process x, then hiding (abstracting from) actions of I in x has no effect. A more interesting axiom is conditional axiom CA2, which allows one to commute abstraction and parallel composition (in appropriate circumstances); it is vital for the verification of systems with three or more components put in parallel.

In order to attach a precise meaning to conditional axioms of the above form we need some insight in the notion of the alphabet $\alpha(p)$ of process p. We assume that p has been specified by means of a recursive specification with guarded recursion. Then one can effectively find sets $\alpha_1(p)$, $\alpha_2(p)$, $\alpha_3(p)$, ..., and $\beta_1(p)$, $\beta_2(p)$, $\beta_3(p)$, ..., such that

$$\alpha_1(p) \subseteq \alpha_2(p) \subseteq \alpha_3(p) \subseteq \ldots\ldots \subseteq \alpha(p)$$

$$\beta_1(p) \supseteq \beta_2(p) \supseteq \beta_3(p) \supseteq \ldots\ldots \supseteq \alpha(p)$$

(see 3.2, 4.5). In general $\bigcup_{n\geq 1} \alpha_n(p) = \alpha(p)$ but $\bigcap_{n\geq 1} \beta_n(p) = \alpha(p)$ need not hold (this is connected with the fact that on the basis of a given recursive specification of p the alphabet $\alpha(p)$ cannot in general be effectively computed, see 3.5). In practical cases, either one finds n,m such that $\alpha_m(p) = \beta_n(p)$ $(=\alpha(p))$, or $\beta_n(p)$ is sufficiently small to verify the condition of a conditional axiom. We call this small theory about alphabets the α/β-calculus. Though very simple, this α/β-calculus seems to be an indispensable tool in system verification based on process algebra (as we will call an algebraic framework such as the one presented below).

In the last sections we describe three examples of simple system verifications which extensively demonstrate the use of the conditional axioms CA1-7.

System verifications of a related nature, but performed in a model, can be found in Sifakis [15] and Olderog [14].

The consistency of CA1-7 on top of ACP_τ + KFAR + RSP is a nontrivial issue. We refer to [3] for such a consistency proof. In this paper, we just check each of the laws in detail for all finite processes. Here RSP is the Recursive Specification Principle, already mentioned above (see 2.9), and KFAR is Koomen's Fair Abstraction Rule, explained in 3.4. There, we find a rather unexpected connection between KFAR and determination of alphabets.

2. Algebra of communicating processes with silent steps.

2.1 The axiomatic framework in which we present this document is ACP_τ, the algebra of communicating processes with silent steps, as described in Bergstra & Klop [7]. In this section, we give a brief review of ACP_τ.

Process algebra starts from a finite collection A of given objects, called atomic actions, atoms or steps. These actions are taken to be indivisible, usually have no duration and form the basic building blocks of our systems. The first two compositional operators we consider are $\cdot$, denoting sequential composition, and + for alternative composition. If x and y are two processes, then $x \cdot y$ is the process that starts the execution of y after the completion of x, and x+y is the process that chooses either x or y and executes the chosen process. Each time a choice is made, we choose from a set of alternatives. We do not specify whether the choice is made by the process itself, or by the environment. Axioms A1-5 in table 1 below give the laws that + and $\cdot$ obey. We leave out $\cdot$ and brackets as in regular algebra, so xy + z means $(x \cdot y) + z$.

On intuitive grounds x(y + z) and xy + xz present different mechanisms (the moment of choice is different), and therefore, an axiom x(y + z) = xy + xz is not included.

We have a special constant δ denoting deadlock, the acknowledgement of a process that it cannot do anything anymore, the absence of an alternative. Axioms A6,7 give the laws for δ.

Next, we have the parallel composition operator $\|$, called merge. The merge of processes x and y will interleave the actions of x and y, except for the communication actions. In $x \| y$, we can either do a step from x, or a step from y, or x and y both synchronously perform an action, which together make up a new action, the communication action. This trichotomy is expressed in axiom CM1. Here, we use two auxiliary operators $\mathbin{\|\!\!\_}$ (left-merge) and $|$ (communication merge). Thus, $x \mathbin{\|\!\!\_} y$ is $x \| y$, but

with the restriction that the first step comes from x, and $x \mid y$ is $x \| y$ with a communication step as the first step. Axioms CM2-9 give the laws for $\lfloor\!\lfloor$ and $\mid$. On atomic actions, we assume the communication function given, obeying laws C1-3. Finally, we have on the left-hand side of table 1 the laws for the encapsulation operator ∂_H. Here H is a set of atoms, and ∂_H blocks actions from H, renames them into δ. The operator ∂_H can be used to encapsulate a process, i.e. to block communications with the environment.
The right-hand side of table 1 is devoted to laws for Milner's silent step τ (see [13]). Laws T1-3 are Milner's τ-laws, and TM1,2 and TC1-4 describe the interaction of τ and merge. Finally, τ_I is the abstraction operator, that renames atoms from I into τ.
In table 1 we have $a,b,c \in A_\delta$ (i.e. $A \cup \{\delta\}$), x,y,z are arbitrary processes, and $H,I \subseteq A$.

$x + y = y + x$	A1	$x\tau = x$	T1
$x + (y + z) = (x + y) + z$	A2	$\tau x + x = \tau x$	T2
$x + x = x$	A3	$a(\tau x + y) = a(\tau x + y) + ax$	T3
$(x + y)z = xz + yz$	A4		
$(xy)z = x(yz)$	A5		
$x + \delta = x$	A6		
$\delta x = \delta$	A7		
$a \mid b = b \mid a$	C1		
$(a \mid b) \mid c = a \mid (b \mid c)$	C2		
$\delta \mid a = \delta$	C3		
$x \| y = x \lfloor\!\lfloor y + y \lfloor\!\lfloor x + x \mid y$	CM1		
$a \lfloor\!\lfloor x = ax$	CM2	$\tau \lfloor\!\lfloor x = \tau x$	TM1
$ax \lfloor\!\lfloor y = a(x \| y)$	CM3	$\tau x \lfloor\!\lfloor y = \tau(x \| y)$	TM2
$(x + y) \lfloor\!\lfloor z = x \lfloor\!\lfloor z + y \lfloor\!\lfloor z$	CM4	$\tau \mid x = \delta$	TC1
$ax \mid b = (a \mid b)x$	CM5	$x \mid \tau = \delta$	TC2
$a \mid bx = (a \mid b)x$	CM6	$\tau x \mid y = x \mid y$	TC3
$ax \mid by = (a \mid b)(x \| y)$	CM7	$x \mid \tau y = x \mid y$	TC4
$(x + y) \mid z = x \mid z + y \mid z$	CM8		
$x \mid (y + z) = x \mid y + x \mid z$	CM9	$\partial_H(\tau) = \tau$	DT
		$\tau_I(\tau) = \tau$	TI1
$\partial_H(a) = a$ if $a \notin H$	D1	$\tau_I(a) = a$ if $a \notin I$	TI2
$\partial_H(a) = \delta$ if $a \in H$	D2	$\tau_I(a) = \tau$ if $a \in I$	TI3
$\partial_H(x + y) = \partial_H(x) + \partial_H(y)$	D3	$\tau_I(x + y) = \tau_I(x) + \tau_I(y)$	TI4
$\partial_H(xy) = \partial_H(x) \cdot \partial_H(y)$	D4	$\tau_I(xy) = \tau_I(x) \cdot \tau_I(y)$	TI5

Table 1. ACP$_\tau$.

2.2 Definition: The set of **basic terms**, BT, is inductively defined as follows:

i. $\tau, \delta \in$ BT
ii. if $t \in$ BT, then $\tau t \in$ BT
iii. if $t \in$ BT and $a \in A$, then $at \in$ BT
iv. if $t, s \in$ BT, then $t+s \in$ BT.

2.3 Elimination theorem: (Bergstra & Klop [7]) Let t be a closed term over ACP_τ. Then there is a basic term s such that $ACP_\tau \vdash t=s$.

2.4 Theorem 2.3 allows us to use induction in proofs. The set of closed terms modulo derivability (the initial algebra) forms a model for ACP_τ. However, most processes encountered in practice cannot be represented by a closed term, but will be specified recursively. Therefore, most models of process algebra also contain infinite processes, that can be recursively specified. First, we develop some terminology.

2.5 Definitions: i) Let t be a term over ACP_τ, and x a variable in t. Suppose that the abstraction operator τ_I does not occur in t. Then we say that an occurrence of x in t is **guarded** if t has a subterm of the form $a \cdot s$, with $a \in A_\delta$ (so $a \neq \tau$!) and this x occurs in s. (I.e. each variable is *preceded* by an atom.)
ii) A **recursive specification** over ACP_τ is a set of equations $\{x = t_x : x \in X\}$, with X a set of variables, and t_x a term over ACP_τ and variables X (for each $x \in X$). No other variables may occur in t_x.
iii) A recursive specification $\{x = t_x : x \in X\}$ is **guarded** if no t_x contains an abstraction operator τ_I, and each occurrence of a variable in each t_x is guarded.

2.6 Notes: i) The constant τ cannot be a guard, since the presence of a τ does not lead to unique solutions: to give an example, the equation $x = \tau x$ has each process starting with a τ as a solution.
ii) A definition of guardedness involving τ_I is very complicated, and therefore, we do not give such a definition here. The definition above suffices for our purposes.

2.7 Definition: On ACP_τ, we can define a **projection operator** π_n, that cuts off a process after n atomic steps are executed, by the axioms in table 2 ($n \geq 1$, $a \in A_\delta$, x,y are arbitrary processes).

$\pi_n(a) = a$	$\pi_n(\tau) = \tau$
$\pi_1(ax) = a$	$\pi_n(\tau x) = \tau \cdot \pi_n(x)$
$\pi_{n+1}(ax) = a \cdot \pi_n(x)$	
$\pi_n(x + y) = \pi_n(x) + \pi_n(y)$	

Table 2. Projection.

Remarks: Because of the τ-laws, we must have that executing a τ does not increase depth. A process p is **finite** if it is equal to a closed term; otherwise p is **infinite**. Note that if p is finite, there is an n such that $\pi_n(p) = p$.

2.8 Theorem: If the set of processes P forms a solution for a guarded recursive specification E, then $\pi_n(p)$ is equal to some closed ACP_τ-term for each $p \in P$ and $n \geq 1$, and this term does not depend on the particular solution P.

Proof: Let E^n be the **n-th expansion** of E, i.e. the recursive specification obtained by substituting terms t_x for variables x occurring in the right-hand sides of its equations, repeating this procedure n times. Since E is guarded, we see that in the n-th expansion of E, each variable is n times guarded. Since the set P is a solution of E, and E^n is obtained by substitution, P is also a solution of E^n. Now we calculate $\pi_n(p)$ using the equation for p in E^n, with the axioms in table 3 above. We see that $\pi_n(p)$ does not depend on which processes we substituted in the right-hand side of this equation: since each variable was n times guarded, the calculation stops before the variable is reached. It is easy to finish the proof.

2.9 Theorem 2.8 leads us to formulate the following two principles, which together imply that each guarded recursive specification has a unique solution (determined by its finite projections).

The **Recursive Definition Principle (RDP)** is the assumption that each guarded recursive specification has at least one solution, and the **Recursive Specification Principle (RSP)** is the assumption that each guarded recursive specification has at most one solution. In this paper, we assume RDP and RSP (for more about these principles, see [3]).

To give an example, if p is a solution of the guarded recursive specification $\{x = a \cdot x\}$, we find $\pi_n(p) = a^n$ for all $n \geq 1$, so we can put $p = a^\omega$. For more information, see [3].

Abusing language, we also use the variables in a guarded recursive specification for the process that is its unique solution.

2.10 In Baeten, Bergstra & Klop [3], a model is presented for ACP_τ, consisting of rooted, directed multigraphs, with edges labeled by elements of $A \cup \{\delta, \tau\}$, modulo a congruence relation called rooted $\tau\delta$-bisimulation (comparable to Milner's observational congruence, see [13]). In this model all axioms presented in this paper hold, and also principles RDP and RSP hold.

Moreover, each element in this model can either be specified by a guarded recursive specification, or can be found from such a process by abstraction (by an application of the operator τ_I).

2.11 The axioms of **Standard Concurrency** (displayed in table 3, on the following page) will also be used in the sequel. A proof that they hold for all closed terms can be found in Bergstra & Klop [7].

$(x \lfloor\!\lfloor y) \lfloor\!\lfloor z = x \lfloor\!\lfloor (y \| z)$
$(x \mid ay) \lfloor\!\lfloor z = x \mid (ay \lfloor\!\lfloor z)$
$x \mid y = y \mid x$
$x \| y = y \| x$
$x \mid (y \mid z) = (x \mid y) \mid z$
$x \| (y \| z) = (x \| y) \| z$

Table 3. Standard concurrency.

3. Alphabets.

3.1 Definition: The **alphabet** of a process is the set of atomic actions that it can perform, so is a subset of A. In order to define the alphabet function α on closed terms, we have the axioms in table 4 ($a \in A$, x,y are arbitrary processes).

$\alpha(\delta) = \emptyset$	AB1
$\alpha(\tau) = \emptyset$	AB2
$\alpha(ax) = \{a\} \cup \alpha(x)$	AB3
$\alpha(\tau x) = \alpha(x)$	AB4
$\alpha(x + y) = \alpha(x) \cup \alpha(y)$	AB5

Table 4. Alphabet.

Note that $\alpha(\delta) = \alpha(\tau) = \emptyset$ is necessary by axioms A6 and T1.

3.2 Now we want to define α on infinite processes.
We define the alphabet for solutions of guarded recursive specifications (which are in general infinite processes) by adding the following axiom to table 4:

$$\alpha(x) = \bigcup_{n \geq 1} \alpha(\pi_n(x)) \qquad \text{AB6.}$$

By theorem 2.8, each $\pi_n(x)$ is a closed term, if x is the solution of a guarded recursive specification, so $a(\pi_n(x))$ can be determined with the axioms in table 4. It is not hard to see that equation AB6 holds for all closed terms (using structural induction), so this axiom does not contradict axioms AB1-5. Further note, that since the partial unions $\alpha(\pi_1(x)) \cup ... \cup \alpha(\pi_n(x))$ form an increasing sequence (as $n \to \infty$), and the set of alphabets is finite (since A is finite), the sequence will be eventually constant, and the limit will always exist.

3.3 We still have not defined the alphabet for all processes that we want to consider. To give an example, if x is given by the guarded recursive specification {x = ax} (we say x = a^{ω}), put y = $\tau_{\{a\}}(x)$, and then the process y cannot be given by a guarded recursive specification (y is the process τ^{ω}). To define the alphabet of such processes, found by abstraction from certain actions in a process given by a guarded recursive specification, we add one more axiom to table 4:

$$\alpha(\tau_I(x)) = \alpha(x) - I \qquad \text{AB7.}$$

Again, it is clear that this axiom holds for all closed terms.

3.4 Example: Let x be given by {x = ax}, and define y = $\tau_{\{a\}}(x)$, z = y·b (with b≠a). What is the alphabet of z? Well, we know $\alpha(x) = \{a\}$ (for $\pi_n(x) = a^n$ for each n≥1), so $\alpha(y) = \alpha(x) - \{a\} = \emptyset$. Then, $\alpha(z) = \alpha(y \cdot b) = \alpha(\tau_{\{a\}}(x) \cdot b) = \alpha(\tau_{\{a\}}(x) \cdot \tau_{\{a\}}(b)) = \alpha(\tau_{\{a\}}(x \cdot b)) = \alpha(x \cdot b) - \{a\} = \emptyset$, for $\pi_n(xb) = a^n$ for each n≥1.
We can motivate this result in a different way, if we use Koomen's Fair Abstraction Rule (KFAR, see [3], and Vaandrager [16]):

$$x = i \cdot x + y,\ i \in I \Rightarrow \tau_I(x) = \tau \cdot \tau_I(y) \qquad \text{KFAR.}$$

KFAR expresses the fact that, due to some fairness mechanism, i (usually some *internal* action) resists being performed infinitely many times consecutively. Here, we have $x = a \cdot x = a \cdot x + \delta$, so by KFAR $y = \tau_{\{a\}}(x) = \tau\delta$. Then $z = yb = \tau\delta b = \tau\delta$, and we see again that $\alpha(y) = \alpha(z) = \emptyset$.

3.5 Theorem: it is in general *undecidable,* to which set α(x) is equal.
Proof: Let K be a recursively enumerable, but not recursive subset of ℕ (the set of natural numbers). In Bergstra & Klop [5] a recursive specification, parametrised by n ∈ ℕ, over finitely many variables $x_1,\ldots,x_k$ is given (k depends on K), such that we have the following:

$$x_1(n) = b^{\omega} \text{ if } n \notin K$$
$$x_1(n) = b^m \cdot \text{stop if } n \in K \text{ (for some } m \in \mathbb{N})$$

(here b, stop are atomic actions). Thus we have $\alpha(x_1(n)) = \{b\}$ if n ∉ K and $\alpha(x_1(n)) = \{b,\text{stop}\}$ if n ∈ K. Since K is not recursive, determining whether n ∈ K, for a given n, is undecidable, so determining $\alpha(x_1)$ is undecidable.

4. α/β-calculus and conditional axioms.

4.1 Axiom AB6 in 3.2 gives a sequence of subsets of α(x), which will converge to α(x). However, as we remarked, finding α(x) itself can sometimes be very difficult. Luckily, in applications it is often sufficient to have a superset of α(x), which is not too big. With such a superset, we can even determine α(x) in many cases. For this reason, we define β(x) in 4.4. First we need theorem 4.2. A piece of notation: if $B,C \subseteq A \cup \{\delta,\tau\}$, we define $B|C = \{b|c : b \in B, c \in C\} - \{\delta\}$ (we leave out δ, so that B|C is an alphabet).

4.2 <u>Theorem:</u> The following hold for all closed ACP_τ-terms t,s:

i. $\alpha(t{\cdot}s) \subseteq \alpha(t) \cup \alpha(s)$

ii. $\alpha(t\|s) = \alpha(t) \cup \alpha(s) \cup \alpha(t)\,|\,\alpha(s)$

iii. $\alpha(t \lfloor\!\lfloor s) \subseteq \alpha(t\|s)$

iv. $\alpha(t\,|\,s) \subseteq \alpha(t\|s)$

v. $\alpha(\partial_H(t)) \subseteq \alpha(t) - H$

<u>Proof:</u> By theorem 2.3, we only have to prove these statements for all basic terms.

i. We use induction on the structure of t, as defined in 2.2.

<u>Case 1:</u> if $t = \tau$, $\alpha(ts) = \alpha(\tau s) = \alpha(s) = \alpha(\tau) \cup \alpha(s)$; if $t = \delta$, $\alpha(ts) = \alpha(\delta s) = \alpha(\delta) = \varnothing \subseteq \alpha(\delta) \cup \alpha(s)$.

<u>Case 2:</u> if $t = \tau t'$, then $\alpha(ts) = \alpha(\tau t's) = \alpha(t's) \subseteq \alpha(t') \cup \alpha(s)$ (by induction hypothesis) $= \alpha(\tau t') \cup \alpha(s)$.

<u>Case 3:</u> if $t = at'$ ($a \in A$), then $\alpha(ts) = \alpha(at's) = \{a\} \cup \alpha(t's) \subseteq \{a\} \cup \alpha(t') \cup \alpha(s)$ (by induction hypothesis) $= \alpha(at') \cup \alpha(s)$.

<u>Case 4:</u> if $t = t' + t''$, then $\alpha(ts) = \alpha((t' + t'')s) = \alpha(t's + t''s) = \alpha(t's) \cup \alpha(t''s) \subseteq \alpha(t') \cup \alpha(s) \cup \alpha(t'') \cup \alpha(s)$ (by induction hypothesis) $= \alpha(t' + t'') \cup \alpha(s)$.

ii. This is more complicated. We do simultaneous induction on t and s, and write

$$t = \sum_{1\le i\le I} a_i t_i + \sum_{1\le j\le J} \tau t'_j + (\tau) + \delta,$$

$$s = \sum_{1\le k\le K} b_k s_k + \sum_{1\le n\le N} \tau s'_n + (\tau) + \delta$$

with $I,J,K,N \ge 0$, $a_i, b_k \in A$, and the single τ may or may not occur. By induction hypothesis we can assume that ii holds for all terms

$$t\|s_k,\ t\|s'_n,\ t_i\|s,\ t_i\|s_k,\ t_i\|s'_n,\ t'_j\|s,\ t'_j\|s_k,\ t'_j\|s'_n.$$

To expand $t\|s$, we use the rules of table 1.

$$\begin{aligned} t\|s &= \delta + \sum a_i(t_i\|s) + \sum \tau(t'_j\|s) + (\tau s) + \\ &+ \sum b_k(t\|s_k) + \sum \tau(t\|s'_n) + (\tau t) + \sum (a_i\,|\,b_k)(t_i\|s_k) \\ &+ \sum a_i t_i\,|\,\tau s'_n + \sum \tau t'_j\,|\,b_k s_k + \sum \tau t'_j\,|\,\tau s'_n. \end{aligned}$$

Now the three summands on the last line can be skipped, since they are summands of other terms (for instance, each $a_i t_i\,|\,\tau s'_n = a_i t_i\,|\,s'_n$ is a summand of $\tau(t\|s'_n)$, see Bergstra & Klop [7], 3.6). Next we use definition 3.1, and obtain:

$$\begin{aligned} \alpha(t\|s) = &\bigcup_{i\in I} \{a_i\}\cup\alpha(t_i\|s) \cup \bigcup_{j\in J} \alpha(t'_j\|s) \cup (\alpha(s)) \cup \bigcup_{k\in K} \{b_k\}\cup\alpha(t\|s_k) \cup \\ &\bigcup_{n\in N} \alpha(t\|s'_n) \cup (\alpha(t)) \cup \bigcup_{i,k \text{ with } a_i|b_k\ne\delta} \{a_i\,|\,b_k\}\cup\alpha(t_i\|s_k). \end{aligned}$$

Now we apply the induction hypothesis, and obtain

$$\begin{aligned} \alpha(t\|s) = &\bigcup_{i\in I} \{a_i\}\cup\alpha(t_i)\cup\alpha(s)\cup\alpha(t_i)\,|\,\alpha(s) \cup \bigcup_{j\in J} \alpha(t'_j)\cup\alpha(s)\cup\alpha(t'_j)\,|\,\alpha(s) \cup \\ &\bigcup_{k\in K} \{b_k\}\cup\alpha(t)\cup\alpha(s_k)\cup\alpha(t)\,|\,\alpha(s_k) \cup \bigcup_{n\in N} \alpha(t)\cup\alpha(s'_n)\cup\alpha(t)\,|\,\alpha(s'_n) \end{aligned}$$

$$\bigcup_{i,k \text{ with } a_i | b_k \neq \delta} \{a_i | b_k\} \cup \alpha(t_i) \cup \alpha(s_k) \cup \alpha(t_i) | \alpha(s_k) =$$

$$= \bigcup_{i\in I} \{a_i\} \cup \alpha(t_i) \cup \bigcup_{j\in J} \alpha(t'_j) \cup \alpha(t) \cup \bigcup_{k\in K} \{b_k\} \cup \alpha(s_k) \cup \bigcup_{n\in N} \alpha(s'_n) \cup \alpha(s) \cup$$

$$\bigcup_{i\in I} \alpha(t_i) | \alpha(s) \cup \bigcup_{j\in J} \alpha(t'_j) | \alpha(s) \cup \bigcup_{k\in K} \alpha(t) | \alpha(s_k) \cup \bigcup_{n\in N} \alpha(t) | \alpha(s'_n) \cup$$

$$\bigcup_{i,k \text{ with } a_i | b_k \neq \delta} \{a_i | b_k\} \cup \alpha(t_i) | \alpha(s_k).$$

Now it is not hard to see, that the union of the first part of the first line is $\alpha(t)$, of the second part $\alpha(s)$, and the union of the last two lines is $\alpha(t) | \alpha(s)$. This finishes the proof of statement ii.

iii, iv: these follow immediately from axioms CM1 and AB5.

v: We use induction on the structure of t, as given in 2.2.

Case 1: if $t=\delta$, $\alpha(\partial_H(t)) = \alpha(\partial_H(\delta)) = \alpha(\delta) = \alpha(\delta) - H$, if $t=\tau$, $\alpha(\partial_H(t)) = \alpha(\partial_H(\tau)) = \alpha(\tau) = \alpha(\tau) - H$.

Case 2: if $t=\tau t'$, $\alpha(\partial_H(t)) = \alpha(\partial_H(\tau t')) = \alpha(\partial_H(t')) \subseteq \alpha(t') - H$ (by induction hypothesis) $= \alpha(\tau t') - H$.

Case 3: if $t=at'$, and $a \in H$, we have $\alpha(\partial_H(t)) = \alpha(\partial_H(at')) = \alpha(\delta \cdot \partial_H(t')) = \alpha(\delta) = \emptyset \subseteq \alpha(at') - H$; if $a \notin H$, $\alpha(\partial_H(t)) = \alpha(\partial_H(at')) = \alpha(a \cdot \partial_H(t')) = \{a\} \cup \alpha(\partial_H(t')) \subseteq \{a\} \cup (\alpha(t') - H)$ (by induction hypothesis) $= (\{a\} \cup \alpha(t')) - H = \alpha(at') - H$.

This finishes the proof of theorem 4.2.

Remark: In the sequel we will assume that theorem 4.2 holds for *all* processes x,y. We refer to [3] for a proof that it is consistent to do so.

4.3 Definition: suppose $t(x_1,....,x_n)$ is an ACP_τ-term with variables $x_1,....,x_n$. We define a set-term corresponding to t, involving the alphabets of these variables. We do that by applying the rules in 3.1, 3.3 and 4.2 to $\alpha(t)$, working from the outside in. We go on until we only have unknowns $\alpha(x_j)$ left, so α is not applied to any composite term. We obtain $\alpha(t) \subseteq t^*(\alpha(x_1),.......,\alpha(x_n))$, where t^* is a term over the signature with as sort the powerset of A, as functions set union $\cup$, set difference -H (a unary operator for each H appearing as a subscript in a ∂_H or τ_H), and communication $|$ (as defined in 4.1), and as constants {a} for each $a \in A$, and $\emptyset$.

Example: if $t \equiv a \cdot x_4(x_1 \| x_2 + \partial_H(x_3))$, then $t^* \equiv \{a\} \cup \alpha(x_4) \cup \alpha(x_1) \cup \alpha(x_2) \cup \alpha(x_1) | \alpha(x_2) \cup (\alpha(x_3)-H)$.

4.4 Definition: Let $\{x = t_x : x \in X\}$ be a guarded recursive specification, and let $x \in X$. Suppose t_x contains variables $x_1,....,x_n$. Then define $\beta(x)$ to be least fixed point of the equation

$$\beta(x) = t_x^*(\beta(x_1),.......,\beta(x_n)).$$

Note that this least fixed point will always exist, since terms t^* over (Pow(A), $\cup$, -H, $|$, {a}) are *monotonic* (i.e. a relation $X \subseteq Y$ is preserved under the operations). Thus, $\beta(x)$

is the limit of successive approximations $t_x^*(\varnothing,....,\varnothing)$, $t_x^*(t_{x1}^*(\varnothing,...,\varnothing),.......,t_{xn}^*(\varnothing,...,\varnothing))$, etc..

4.5 Theorem: Let $E = \{x = t_x : x \in X\}$ be a guarded recursive specification and let $x \in X$. Then $\alpha(x) \subseteq \beta(x)$.

Proof: Let E^n be the n-th expansion of E, as defined in 2.8. Let $\beta_n(x)$ be the $\beta(x)$ belonging to the equation for x in E^n.

We claim that then $\beta(x) \supseteq \beta_n(x)$, for each $x \in X$. Let $t^n{}_x$ be the right-hand side of the equation for x in E^n. To prove the claim, first take n=2. Suppose $t^2{}_x$ has variables $x_1,...,x_k$. Then $t^2{}_x^*(\beta(x_1), ..., \beta(x_k)) = t_x^*(t_{x1}^*(\beta(x_{1,1}), ...), ..., t_{xk}^*(\beta(x_{k,1}), ...)) =$

$$= t_x^*(\beta(x_1), ..., \beta(x_k)) = \beta(x) \text{ (for certain variables } x_{i,j}).$$

Therefore, $\beta(x)$ is a fixed point of equation $x = t^2{}_x^*(x_1, ..., x_k)$. Since $\beta_2(x)$ is the *least* fixed point of this equation, we must have $\beta(x) \supseteq \beta_2(x)$. The general case follows by iteration. This proves the claim.

By theorem 2.8, $\pi_n(x)$ is equal to some closed term, which is independent of the processes substituted for the variables in t_x. Therefore

$$\alpha(\pi_n(x)) = \alpha(\pi_n(t^n{}_x)) = \alpha(\pi_n(t^n{}_x(x_1,...,x_k))) = \alpha(\pi_n(t^n{}_x(\delta,...,\delta))) \subseteq$$
$$\subseteq \alpha(t^n{}_x(\delta,...,\delta)) \subseteq t^n{}_x^*(\varnothing,...,\varnothing) \subseteq \beta_n(x) \subseteq \beta(x),$$

and with axiom AB6 it follows that $\alpha(x) \subseteq \beta(x)$.

4.6 Notes: i) It can be shown that the fixed point $\beta(x)$ can be reached from $\varnothing$ in finitely many iterations, if we assume that the specification is finite and assume the Handshaking Axiom $a \mid b \mid c = \delta$ (the Handshaking Axiom says that only two-way communications can occur; assuming it holds ensures that all possible communication actions are generated the first time).

ii) We cannot have in general that $\bigcap_{n\geq 1} \beta_n(x) = \alpha(x)$, because that would make the determination of $\alpha(x)$ decidable, contradicting 3.5.

4.7 Example: A bag B^{ij} with input port i and output port j ($i \neq j$) is given by the guarded recursive specification

$$B^{ij} = \sum_{d \in D} ri(d)\cdot(sj(d) \| B^{ij}) \qquad \text{(see Bergstra \& Klop [5]).}$$

Here D is a finite set of data, ri(d) means **receive** d along i, and sj(d) means **send** d along j. We find $\alpha(\pi_2(B^{ij})) = \alpha(\sum_{d \in D} ri(d)[sj(d) + \sum_{e \in D} ri(e)]) = \{ri(d),sj(d) : d \in D\}$, and on the other hand $\alpha(B) = \{ri(d),sj(d) : d \in D\} \cup \alpha(B) \cup \{sj(d) : d \in D\} \mid \alpha(B)$ using 4.2, so $\beta(B) = \{ri(d),sj(d) : d \in D\}$. Since $\alpha(\pi_2(B)) \subseteq \alpha(B) \subseteq \beta(B)$, we must have $\alpha(B) = \{ri(d),sj(d) : d \in D\}$. In this way we can calculate the alphabets of many interesting specifications. In the proofs of the following theorems, extensive use is made of this so-called α/β-calculus.

4.8 In the following table 4, we present 7 conditional axioms:

$\alpha(x) \mid (\alpha(y) \cap H) \subseteq H$	$\Rightarrow$	$\partial_H(x \| y) = \partial_H(x \| \partial_H(y))$	CA1
$\alpha(x) \mid (\alpha(y) \cap I) = \emptyset$	$\Rightarrow$	$\tau_I(x \| y) = \tau_I(x \| \tau_I(y))$	CA2
$\alpha(x) \cap H = \emptyset$	$\Rightarrow$	$\partial_H(x) = x$	CA3
$\alpha(x) \cap I = \emptyset$	$\Rightarrow$	$\tau_I(x) = x$	CA4
$H = J \cup K$	$\Rightarrow$	$\partial_H(x) = \partial_J \circ \partial_K(x)$	CA5
$I = J \cup K$	$\Rightarrow$	$\tau_I(x) = \tau_J \circ \tau_K(x)$	CA6
$H \cap I = \emptyset$	$\Rightarrow$	$\tau_I \circ \partial_H(x) = \partial_H \circ \tau_I(x)$	CA7

Table 4. Conditional axioms.

4.9 Theorem: Axioms CA1-7 hold for all closed ACP_τ-terms.

Proof: By theorem 2.3, we only have to prove these statements for all basic terms t,s.

CA1: We do simultaneous induction on t and s, as in the proof of 4.2, and write

$$t = \sum_{1 \leq i \leq I} a_i t_i + \sum_{1 \leq j \leq J} \tau t'_j + (\tau) + \delta,$$

$$s = \sum_{1 \leq k \leq K} b_k s_k + \sum_{1 \leq m \leq M} h_m s''_m + \sum_{1 \leq n \leq N} \tau s'_n + (\tau) + \delta$$

with $I,J,K,M,N \geq 0$, $a_i \in A$, $b_k \in A\text{-}H$, $h_m \in H$, and the single τ may or may not occur. Now $a_i \in \alpha(t)$ and $h_m \in \alpha(y) \cap H$, so by assumption $a_i \mid h_m \in H$ for each $i \leq I$, $m \leq M$. Now

$$\partial_H(t \| s) = (\tau) + \delta + \sum \partial_H(a_i) \cdot \partial_H(t_i \| s) + \sum \tau \cdot \partial_H(t'_j \| s) +$$
$$+ \sum b_k \cdot \partial_H(t \| s_k) + \sum \tau \cdot \partial_H(t \| s'_n) + \sum \partial_H(a_i \mid b_k) \cdot \partial_H(t_i \| s_k) +$$
$$+ \sum \partial_H(a_i t_i \mid \tau s'_n) + \sum \partial_H(\tau t'_j \mid b_k s_k) + \sum \partial_H(\tau t'_n \mid \tau s'_n).$$

As in the proof of 4.2, we see that we can omit the last three summands. Now we apply the induction hypothesis, which is possible since $\alpha(t_i)$, $\alpha(t'_j) \subseteq \alpha(t)$ and $\alpha(s_k)$, $\alpha(s'_n) \subseteq \alpha(s)$. We obtain

$$\partial_H(t \| s) = (\tau) + \delta + \sum \partial_H(a_i) \cdot \partial_H(t_i \| \partial_H(s)) + \sum \tau \cdot \partial_H(t'_j \| \partial_H(s)) +$$
$$+ \sum b_k \cdot \partial_H(t \| \partial_H(s_k)) + \sum \tau \cdot \partial_H(t \| \partial_H(s'_n)) + \sum \partial_H(a_i \mid b_k) \cdot \partial_H(t_i \| \partial_H(s_k)).$$

We use the same argument to add the terms

$$\sum \partial_H(a_i t_i \mid \tau \cdot \partial_H(s'_n)) + \sum \partial_H(\tau t'_j \mid b_k \cdot \partial_H(s_k)) + \sum \partial_H(\tau t'_j \mid \tau \cdot \partial_H(s'_n)).$$

Then we see that the sum of the last two expressions is $\partial_H(t \| \partial_H(s))$, and the proof is finished.

CA2: the proof that CA2 holds for all closed terms is entirely similar to the proof of CA1. Note that now we have to have $a_i \mid h_m = \delta$ (if $a_i \in \alpha(t)$, $h_m \in \alpha(s) \cap I$), so that $\tau_I(a_i t_i \mid h_m s''_m) = \tau_I((a_i \mid h_m)(t_i \| s''_m)) = \delta$, and all these terms drop out.

CA3: this is by induction on the structure of t. We have four cases:

Case 1: $t = \delta$ or τ. Immediate.

Case 2: if $t = \tau t'$, we have by assumption $\emptyset = \alpha(t) \cap H = \alpha(t') \cap H$, so $\partial_H(t) = \partial_H(\tau t') = \tau \cdot \partial_H(t') = \tau t' = t$.

Case 3: if $t = at'$ ($a \in A$), we have by assumption $\emptyset = \alpha(t) \cap H = (\{a\} \cup \alpha(t')) \cap H$, so $a \notin H$

and $\alpha(t') \cap H = \emptyset$, whence $\partial_H(at') = \partial_H(a)\partial_H(t') = at' = t$.

Case 4: if $t = t' + t''$, we have by assumption $\emptyset = \alpha(t) \cap H = (\alpha(t') \cup \alpha(t'')) \cap H$, so $\alpha(t') \cap H = \emptyset$ and $\alpha(t'') \cap H = \emptyset$. Then $\partial_H(t) = \partial_H(t' + t'') = \partial_H(t') + \partial_H(t'') = t' + t'' = t$.

CA4: entirely similar to the proof of CA3.

CA5: by induction on the structure of t. We have four cases:

Case 1: $t = \delta$ or τ. Immediate.

Case 2: if $t=\tau t'$, $\partial_H(t) = \partial_H(\tau t') = \tau\cdot\partial_H(t') = \partial_J\circ\partial_K(\tau)\cdot\partial_J\circ\partial_K(t')$ (induction hypothesis) = $\partial_J\circ\partial_K(\tau t') = \partial_J\circ\partial_K(t)$.

Case 3: if $t=at'$ and $a \notin H$, then also $a \notin J$ and $a \notin K$. Thus $\partial_H(t) = \partial_H(at') = a\cdot\partial_H(t') = \partial_J\circ\partial_K(a)\cdot\partial_J\circ\partial_K(t')$ (induction hypothesis) = $\partial_J\circ\partial_K(at') = \partial_J\circ\partial_K(t)$; if $a \in H$, we have two cases:

Case 3.1: $a \in K$. Then $\partial_H(t) = \partial_H(at') = \delta = \partial_J(\delta) = \partial_J\circ\partial_K(at') = \partial_J\circ\partial_K(t)$.

Case 3.2: Otherwise. Then $a \in J\text{-}K$, so $\partial_H(t) = \partial_H(at') = \delta = \partial_J(a\cdot\partial_K(t')) =$
$= \partial_J(\partial_K(a)\cdot\partial_K(t')) = \partial_J\circ\partial_K(at') = \partial_J\circ\partial_K(t)$.

Case 4: if $t=t' + t''$, $\partial_H(t) = \partial_H(t' + t'') = \partial_H(t') + \partial_H(t'') = \partial_J\circ\partial_K(t') + \partial_J\circ\partial_K(t'')$ (induction hypothesis) = $\partial_J(\partial_K(t') + \partial_K(t'')) = \partial_J\circ\partial_K(t' + t'') = \partial_J\circ\partial_K(t)$.

CA6: similar to CA5.

CA7: by induction on the structure of t. We have four cases:

Case 1: $t = \delta$ or τ. Immediate.

Case 2: if $t=\tau t'$, $\tau_I\circ\partial_H(t) = \tau_I\circ\partial_H(\tau t') = \tau\cdot\tau_I\circ\partial_H(t') = \tau\cdot\partial_H\circ\tau_I(t')$ (induction hypothesis) = $\partial_H\circ\tau_I(\tau t') = \partial_H\circ\tau_I(t)$.

Case 3: if $t=at'$ ($a \in A$), we consider three subcases:

Case 3.1: $a \notin I$, $a \notin H$. Then $\tau_I\circ\partial_H(t) = \tau_I\circ\partial_H(at') = a\cdot\tau_I\circ\partial_H(t') = a\cdot\partial_H\circ\tau_I(t')$ (induction hypothesis) = $\partial_H\circ\tau_I(at') = \partial_H\circ\tau_I(t)$.

Case 3.2: $a \notin I$, $a \in H$. Then $\tau_I\circ\partial_H(t) = \tau_I\circ\partial_H(at') = \tau_I(\delta) = \delta = \partial_H(a\cdot\tau_I(t')) =$
$= \partial_H(\tau_I(a)\cdot\tau_I(t')) = \partial_H\circ\tau_I(at') = \partial_H\circ\tau_I(t)$.

Case 3.3: $a \in I$, $a \notin H$. Then $\tau_I\circ\partial_H(t) = \tau_I\circ\partial_H(at') = \tau_I(a\cdot\partial_H(t')) = \tau\cdot\tau_I\circ\partial_H(t')) =$
$= \tau\cdot\partial_H\circ\tau_I(t')$ (induction hypothesis) = $\partial_H(\tau\cdot\tau_I(t')) = \partial_H(\tau_I(a)\cdot\tau_I(t')) = \partial_H\circ\tau_I(at') =$
$= \partial_H\circ\tau_I(t)$.

Case 4: if $t=t' + t''$, $\tau_I\circ\partial_H(t) = \tau_I\circ\partial_H(t' + t'') = \tau_I\circ\partial_H(t') + \tau_I\circ\partial_H(t'') = \partial_H\circ\tau_I(t') + \partial_H\circ\tau_I(t'')$ (induction hypothesis) = $\partial_H(\tau_I(t') + \tau_I(t'')) = \partial_H\circ\tau_I(t' + t'') = \partial_H\circ\tau_I(t)$.

4.10 Remark: Conditional axioms CA5-7 are special cases of more general properties of renaming operators, of which ∂_H and τ_I are two examples.
For more information about renaming operators, see Vaandrager [16].

5. Examples

5.1 Suppose we have two bags, linked together as in fig. 1.

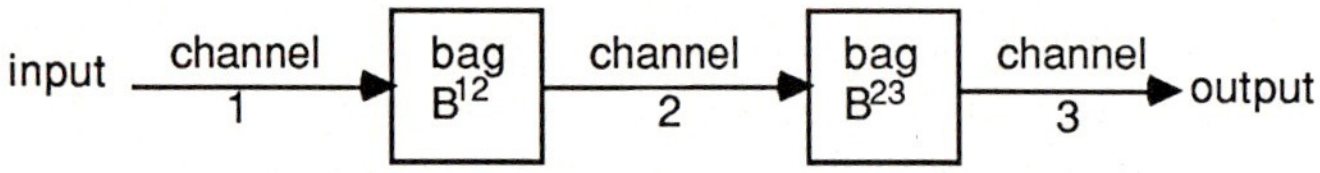

Fig. 1

We want to prove that the external behaviour of this system again is a bag. Therefore, we want to 'hide' the internal channel 2.

Let D be a finite set of data, and let the atomic actions ri(d), sj(d) be as in example 4.7. We define $c2(d) = r2(d) \mid s2(d)$, the **communication** of a $d \in D$ along channel 2. All other communications yield δ. Further, we define:

Encapsulation: $H = \{r2(d), s2(d) : d \in D\}$ (all unsuccessful communications).

Abstraction: $I = \{c2(d) : d \in D\}$ (all internal actions).

5.2 <u>Theorem:</u> $B^{13} = \tau_I \circ \partial_H(B^{12} \| B^{23})$.

<u>Proof:</u> $\partial_H(B^{12} \| B^{23}) = \sum_{d \in D} r1(d) \cdot \partial_H(s2(d) \| B^{12} \| B^{23})$ (using standard concurrency, see 2.11) =

$= \sum_{d \in D} r1(d) \cdot \partial_H \circ \partial_{\{s2(d)\}}(B^{12} \| (s2(d) \| B^{23}))$ (by CA5) =

$= \sum_{d \in D} r1(d) \cdot \partial_H \circ \partial_{\{s2(d)\}}(B^{12} \| \partial_{\{s2(d)\}}(s2(d) \| B^{23}))$ (by CA1, see note 1 below) =

$= \sum_{d \in D} r1(d) \cdot \partial_H(B^{12} \| (c2(d) \cdot s3(d) \| B^{23}))$ (CA5, and see note 2 below) =

$= \sum_{d \in D} r1(d) \cdot \partial_H(c2(d) \cdot s3(d) \| (B^{12} \| B^{23}))$ (standard concurrency) =

$= \sum_{d \in D} r1(d) \cdot \partial_H(c2(d) \cdot s3(d) \| \partial_H(B^{12} \| B^{23}))$ (by CA1, see note 3 below) =

$= \sum_{d \in D} r1(d) \cdot (c2(d) \cdot s3(d) \| \partial_H(B^{12} \| B^{23}))$ (by CA3, see note 4 below).

Using this result, we get that $\tau_I \circ \partial_H(B^{12} \| B^{23}) =$

$= \sum_{d \in D} r1(d) \cdot \tau_I(c2(d) \cdot s3(d) \| \partial_H(B^{12} \| B^{23})) =$

$= \sum_{d \in D} r1(d) \cdot \tau_I(\tau_I(c2(d) \cdot s3(d)) \| \tau_I \circ \partial_H(B^{12} \| B^{23}))$ (CA3 twice, use note 3) =

$= \sum_{d \in D} r1(d) \cdot \tau_I(\tau \cdot s3(d) \| \tau_I \circ \partial_H(B^{12} \| B^{23})) =$

$= \sum_{d \in D} r1(d) \cdot (\tau \cdot s3(d) \| \tau_I \circ \partial_H(B^{12} \| B^{23}))$ (by CA4, see note 5 below) =

$= \sum_{d \in D} r1(d) \cdot (s3(d) \| \tau_I \circ \partial_H(B^{12} \| B^{23}))$ (see note 6 below).

Therefore, the process $\tau_I \circ \partial_H(B^{12} \| B^{23})$ satisfies the defining equation of B^{13}. By the Recursive Specification Principle (see 2.9), we obtain $B^{13} = \tau_I \circ \partial_H(B^{12} \| B^{23})$.

<u>Note 1:</u> $\alpha(B^{12}) \mid (\alpha(s2(d) \| B^{23}) \cap \{s2(d)\} \subseteq \{r1(e), s2(e) : e \in D\} \mid \{s2(d)\} = \emptyset$ (each $d \in D$).

<u>Note 2:</u> Let $d \in D$. Then on the one hand

$$c2(d)s3(d) \| B^{23} = c2(d) \cdot (s3(d) \| B^{23}) + \sum_{e \in D} r2(e) \cdot (s3(e) \| c2(d)s3(d) \| B^{23}),$$

and on the other hand

$$\partial_{\{s2(d)\}}(s2(d) \| B^{23}) = c2(d) \cdot \partial_{\{s2(d)\}}(s3(d) \| B^{23}) + \sum_{e \in D} r2(e) \cdot \partial_{\{s2(d)\}}(s3(e) \| s2(d) \| B^{23}) =$$

$$= c2(d)(s3(d) \| B^{23}) + \sum_{e \in D} r2(e) \cdot \partial_{\{s2(d)\}}(s3(e) \| s2(d) \| B^{23})$$ (by CA3, see note 7 below) =

$$= c2(d)(s3(d) \| B^{23}) + \sum_{e \in D} r2(e) \cdot \partial_{\{s2(d)\}}(s3(e) \| \partial_{\{s2(d)\}}(s2(d) \| B^{23}))$$ (by CA1, argue as in note 1) =

$$= c2(d)(s3(d) \| B^{23}) + \sum_{e \in D} r2(e) \cdot (s3(e) \| \partial_{\{s2(d)\}}(s2(d) \| B^{23}))$$ (by CA3, see note 8 below) =

Thus we see that both process $c2(d)s3(d) \| B^{23}$ and process $\partial_{\{s2(d)\}}(s2(d) \| B^{23})$ satisfy the guarded equation

$$x = c2(d) \cdot (s3(d) \| B^{23}) + \sum_{e \in D} r2(e) \cdot (s3(e) \| x).$$

Therefore, by the Recursive Specification Principle,

$$c2(d)s3(d) \| B^{23} = \partial_{\{s2(d)\}}(s2(d) \| B^{23}).$$

<u>Note 3:</u> $\{c2(d), s3(d) : d \in D\} \mid A = \emptyset$, since r3(d) does not occur.

<u>Note 4:</u> $\alpha(c2(d)s3(d) \| \partial_H(B^{12} \| B^{23})) \cap H \subseteq$
$\subseteq [\{c2(d), s3(d)\} \cup (A\text{-}H) \cup \{c2(d), s3(d)\} \mid (A\text{-}H)] \cap H = (A\text{-}H) \cap H = \emptyset$, for each $d \in D$.

<u>Note 5:</u> $\alpha(\tau_I \circ \partial_H(B^{12} \| B^{23}) \| \tau s3(d)) \cap I \subseteq [(A\text{-}I) \cup \{s3(d)\} \cup (A\text{-}I) \mid \{s3(d)\}] \cap I = [A\text{-}I] \cap I =$
$= \emptyset$, for each $d \in D$.

<u>Note 6:</u> $r1(d)(\tau s3(d) \| x) = r1(d)\tau s3(d) \lfloor\!\lfloor x = r1(d)s3(d) \lfloor\!\lfloor x = r1(d)(s3(d) \| x)$.

<u>Note 7:</u> $\alpha(s3(d) \| B^{23})) \cap \{s2(d)\} = [\{s3(d)\} \cup \{r2(e), s3(e) : e \in D\} \cup$
$\cup \{s3(d)\} \mid \{r2(e), s3(e) : e \in D\}] \cap \{s2(d)\} \subseteq [A\text{-}\{s2(d)\}] \cap \{s2(d)\} = \emptyset$, for each $d \in D$.

<u>Note 8:</u> $\alpha(s3(e) \| \partial_{\{s2(d)\}}(s2(d) \| B^{23})) \cap \{s2(d)\} \subseteq (\{s3(e)\} \cup (A\text{-}\{s2(d)\}) \cup \{s3(e)\} \mid A) \cap$
$\cap \{s2(d)\} \subseteq (A\text{-}\{s2(d)\}) \cap \{s2(d)\} = \emptyset$, for each $d,e \in D$.

This finishes the proof of theorem 5.2.

5.3 We can easily generalise the theorem above to the situation where we have more than 2 bags connected in a row. To illustrate, we will consider the case of 3 bags. We define ri(d), si(d), ci(d) as before (see 4.7, 5.1), and further:

Encapsulation: $Hn = \{sn(d), rn(d) : d \in D\}$ $(n=2,3)$; $H = H2 \cup H3$;

Abstraction: $In = \{cn(d) : d \in D\}$ $(n=2,3)$; $I = I2 \cup I3$.

5.4 <u>Theorem:</u> $B^{14} = \tau_I \circ \partial_H(B^{12} \| B^{23} \| B^{34})$.

<u>Proof:</u> By 5.2, we have $B^{24} = \tau_{I3} \circ \partial_{H3}(B^{23} \| B^{34})$ and $B^{14} = \tau_{I2} \circ \partial_{H2}(B^{12} \| B^{24})$.

Therefore $\tau_I \circ \partial_H(B^{12} \| B^{23} \| B^{34}) =$

$$= \tau_{I2} \circ \tau_{I3} \circ \partial_{H2} \circ \partial_{H3}(B^{12} \| B^{23} \| B^{34})$$ (CA5, CA6) =

$= \tau_{I2} \circ \partial_{H2} \circ \tau_{I3} \circ \partial_{H3}(B^{12} \| B^{23} \| B^{34})$ (CA7) =
$= \tau_{I2} \circ \partial_{H2} \circ \tau_{I3} \circ \partial_{H3}(B^{12} \| \partial_{H3}(B^{23} \| B^{34}))$ (CA1, see note 1 below) =
$= \tau_{I2} \circ \partial_{H2} \circ \tau_{I3}(B^{12} \| \partial_{H3}(B^{23} \| B^{34}))$ (CA3, see note 2 below) =
$= \tau_{I2} \circ \partial_{H2} \circ \tau_{I3}(B^{12} \| \tau_{I3} \circ \partial_{H3}(B^{23} \| B^{34}))$ (CA2, see note 3 below) =
$= \tau_{I2} \circ \partial_{H2} \circ \tau_{I3}(B^{12} \| B^{24})$ (by theorem 5.2) =
$= \tau_{I2} \circ \partial_{H2}(B^{12} \| B^{24})$ (CA4) =
$= B^{14}$ (by theorem 5.2).

To finish the proof, we only need to check some alphabets:
Note 1: $\alpha(B^{12}) \mid (\alpha(B^{23} \| B^{34}) \cap H3) \subseteq \{r1(d), s2(d) : d \in D\} \mid H3 = \emptyset$.
Note 2: $\alpha(B^{12} \| \partial_{H3}(B^{23} \| B^{34})) \cap H3) \subseteq [(A\text{-}H3) \cup (A\text{-}H3) \cup (A\text{-}H3) \mid (A\text{-}H3)] \cap H3 = \emptyset$.
Note 3: $\alpha(B^{12}) \mid \alpha(\partial_{H3}(B^{23} \| B^{34})) \cap I3) \subseteq A \mid I3 = \emptyset$.

5.5 Our final example is somewhat more involved. It considers a bag with test for empty. Such a bag (with input port 1 and output port 2) can be defined by the following guarded recursive specification (notations as before):

$$B\emptyset = \sum_{d \in D} (r1(d)B_d + s2(\emptyset)) \cdot B\emptyset$$

$$B_d = s2(d) + \sum_{e \in D} r1(e)(B_e \| B_d)$$

To see that this indeed defines a bag with test for empty, consider the following lemma.

5.6 Lemma: $\partial_{\{s2(\emptyset)\}}(B\emptyset) = B^{12}$ (notation from 4.7)
Proof: We prove the lemma with the Recursive Specification Principle, here applied to an *infinite* recursive specification. We will show that for all multisets G of elements of D we have

$$B^{12} \| (\underset{e \in G}{\|} s2(e)) = (\underset{e \in G}{\|} B_e) \cdot \partial_{\{s2(\emptyset)\}}(B\emptyset) \qquad (*)$$

(for G=∅, we define $B^{12} \| (\underset{e \in \emptyset}{\|} s2(e)) = B^{12}$ and $(\underset{e \in \emptyset}{\|} B_e) \cdot \partial_{\{s2(\emptyset)\}}(B\emptyset) = \partial_{\{s2(\emptyset)\}}(B\emptyset)$),

by showing that both sides satisfy the same recursive specification.
We see that the lemma follows immediately from (*). To show (*), we consider two cases:
Case 1: G=∅. Then $\partial_{\{s2(\emptyset)\}}(B\emptyset) = \sum_{d \in D} (r1(d) \cdot \partial_{\{s2(\emptyset)\}}(B_d) + \delta) \cdot \partial_{\{s2(\emptyset)\}}(B\emptyset) =$

$= \sum_{d \in D} r1(d) \cdot B_d \cdot \partial_{\{s2(\emptyset)\}}(B\emptyset)$ (by CA3, see note below),

and on the other hand $B^{12} = \sum_{d \in D} r1(d)(B^{12} \| s2(d))$ by definition.

Note: $\alpha(B_d) = \{s2(d)\} \cup \{r1(e) : e \in D\} \cup \bigcup\{\alpha(B_e \| B_d : e \in D\} = \{s2(d)\} \cup \{r1(e) : e \in D\} \cup \cup \bigcup\{\alpha(B_e : e \in D\} \cup \alpha(B_d) = \cup \bigcup\{\alpha(B_e \mid B_d : e \in D\}$. Since $\beta(B_d)$ is the least fixed point of this equation, it follows easily that $\beta(B_d) = \{s2(e), r1(e) : e \in D\}$. Thus $\beta(B_d) \cap \{s2(\emptyset)\} = \emptyset$, whence $\alpha(B_d) \cap \{s2(\emptyset)\} = \emptyset$.

Case 2: $G \neq \emptyset$. In this case, we need the **Expansion Theorem** of Bergstra & Tucker [8]: let processes $x_1,...,x_n$ be given and assume the Handshaking Axiom (see 4.6). Then we can prove:

$$x_1 \| x_2 \| ... \| x_n = \sum_{1 \le i \le n} x_i ⌊⌊ (\mathop{\|}_{\substack{1 \le k \le n \\ k \neq i}} x_k) + \sum_{1 \le i < j \le n} (x_i | x_j) ⌊⌊ (\mathop{\|}_{\substack{1 \le k \le n \\ k \neq i,j}} x_k).$$

The Expansion Theorem (ET) says that if we have a merge of a number of processes, then we can start with an action of one of the processes, or with a communication between two of them. Using the Expansion Theorem here, we get:

$$B^{12} \| (\mathop{\|}_{e \in G} s2(e)) = \sum_{d \in G} s2(d)(B^{12} \| (\mathop{\|}_{e \in G-\{d\}} s2(e))) + \sum_{d \in D} r1(d)(B^{12} \| (\mathop{\|}_{e \in G \cup \{d\}} s2(e))), \text{ and}$$

$$(\mathop{\|}_{e \in G} B_e) \cdot \partial_{\{s2(\emptyset)\}}(B\emptyset) = \sum_{d \in G} s2(d)(\mathop{\|}_{e \in G-\{d\}} B_e) \cdot \partial_{\{s2(\emptyset)\}}(B\emptyset) +$$

$$+ \sum_{d \in D} r1(d)(\mathop{\|}_{e \in G \cup \{d\}} B_e) \cdot \partial_{\{s2(\emptyset)\}}(B\emptyset).$$

5.7 Now suppose we want to link this bag with empty test to a regular bag. Between the two, we interpose a one-place buffer, that 'forgets' the empty test, i.e. a process defined by the following guarded recursive equation:

$$T\emptyset = \sum_{d \in D} (r2(d)s3(d) + r2(\emptyset)) \cdot T\emptyset.$$

Thus we have the situation of fig. 2.

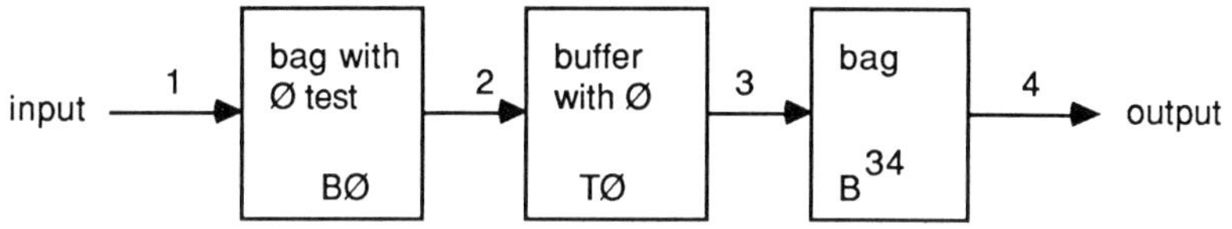

Fig. 2.

5.8 We define H2, H3, I2, I3 as in 5.3, and define in addition:

Encapsulation: $H\emptyset = \{r2(\emptyset), s2(\emptyset)\}$, $H = H2 \cup H3 \cup H\emptyset$;

Abstraction: $I = I2 \cup I3 \cup \{c2(\emptyset)\}$.

We want to prove the following theorem:

$$\tau_I \circ \partial_H(B\emptyset \| T\emptyset \| B^{34}) = \tau B^{14}.$$

Before we can prove this theorem, we need to prove a number of lemmas. First, define a (regular) one-place buffer T by:

$$T = \sum_{d \in D} r2(d)s3(d) \cdot T.$$

5.9 <u>Lemma:</u> $\partial_{\{r2(\varnothing)\}}(T\varnothing) = T$.

<u>Proof:</u> $\partial_{\{r2(\varnothing)\}}(T\varnothing) = \sum_{d\in D} (r2(d)s3(d) + \delta)\cdot\partial_{\{r2(\varnothing)\}}(T\varnothing) = \sum_{d\in D} r2(d)s3(d)\cdot\partial_{\{r2(\varnothing)\}}(T\varnothing)$.

Now use the Recursive Specification Principle.

5.10 <u>Lemma:</u> Define $P = \partial_{H2\cup H\varnothing}(B\varnothing \| T\varnothing)$. Then there is a process Q such that

$$P = c2(\varnothing)\cdot P + Q\cdot P \text{ and } c2(\varnothing) \notin \alpha(Q).$$

<u>Proof:</u> We will give an infinite guarded recursive specification for Q. This specification has variables P(G) and P(G,d), for each multiset G of elements of D, and each $d\in D$. The intuitive meaning of these processes is that P(G) describes the bag with contents G, while the buffer is empty, and P(G,d) describes the bag with contents G, the buffer filled with d. We have the following equations:

<u>Case 1:</u> $G=\varnothing$.

$$Q = \sum_{d\in D} r1(d)\cdot P(\{d\})$$

$$P(\varnothing) = P$$

$$P(\varnothing,d) = s3(d) + \sum_{e\in D} r1(e)\cdot P(\{e\},d)$$

<u>Case 2:</u> $G\neq\varnothing$.

$$P(G) = \sum_{d\in G} c2(d)\cdot P(G-\{d\},d) + \sum_{d\in D} r1(d)\cdot P(G\cup\{d\})$$

$$P(G,d) = s3(d)\cdot P(G) + \sum_{e\in D} r1(e)\cdot P(G\cup\{e\},d)$$

Then we have $P = \partial_{H2\cup H\varnothing}(B\varnothing \| T\varnothing) =$

$= c2(\varnothing)\cdot\partial_{H2\cup H\varnothing}(B\varnothing \| T\varnothing) + \sum_{d\in D} r1(d)\cdot\partial_{H2\cup H\varnothing}(B_d\cdot B\varnothing \| T\varnothing) =$

$= c2(\varnothing)\cdot P + \sum_{d\in D} r1(d)\cdot P(\{d\})\cdot P = c2(\varnothing)\cdot P + Q\cdot P,$

which follows from the following two equations:

(1) $$\partial_{H2\cup H\varnothing}((\|_{e\in G} B_e)B\varnothing \| T\varnothing) = P(G)\cdot P$$

(2) $$\partial_{H2\cup H\varnothing}((\|_{e\in G} B_e)B\varnothing \| s3(d)T\varnothing) = P(G,d)\cdot P$$

We prove these equations by showing that both sides satisfy the same guarded recursive specification.

<u>Case 1:</u> $G=\varnothing$. Equation (1) is shown above. To show (2):

$\partial_{H2\cup H\varnothing}(B\varnothing \| s3(d)T\varnothing) = s3(d)\cdot\partial_{H2\cup H\varnothing}(B\varnothing \| T\varnothing) + \sum_{e\in D} \partial_{H2\cup H\varnothing}(B_e\cdot B\varnothing \| s3(d)T\varnothing)$,

and $P(\varnothing,d)\cdot P = (s3(d) + \sum_{e\in D} r1(e)\cdot P(\{e\},d))\cdot P = s3(d)\cdot P + \sum_{e\in D} r1(e)\cdot P(\{e\},d)\cdot P$.

<u>Case 2:</u> $G\neq\varnothing$. For equation (1), see the following:

$\partial_{H2\cup H\varnothing}((\|_{e\in G} B_e)B\varnothing \| T\varnothing) = \sum_{e\in G} c2(d)\cdot\partial_{H2\cup H\varnothing}((\|_{e\in G-\{d\}} B_e)B\varnothing \| s3(d)T\varnothing) +$

$+ \sum_{d\in D} r1(d)\cdot\partial_{H2\cup H\emptyset}((\ \|_{e\in G\cup\{d\}} B_e)B\emptyset\|s3(d)T\emptyset)$ (by Expansion Theorem), and

$P(G)\cdot P = \sum_{d\in G} c2(d)P(G\text{-}\{d\},d)\cdot P + \sum_{d\in D} r1(d)P(G\cup\{d\})\cdot P.$

For equation (2), consider the following statements:

$\partial_{H2\cup H\emptyset}((\ \|_{e\in G} B_e)B\emptyset\|s3(d)T\emptyset) = s3(d)\cdot\partial_{H2\cup H\emptyset}((\ \|_{e\in G} B_e)B\emptyset\|T\emptyset) +$

$+ \sum_{f\in D} r1(f)\cdot\partial_{H2\cup H\emptyset}((\ \|_{e\in G\cup\{f\}} B_e)B\emptyset\|s3(d)T\emptyset)$ (by Expansion Theorem), and

$P(G,d)\cdot P = s3(d)P(G)\cdot P + \sum_{f\in D} r1(f)P(G\cup\{f\},d)\cdot P.$

This finishes the proof of the first half of the lemma. To prove the second half, it is not much trouble to show that for all multisets G and all $d\in D$,

$$\beta(P(G)) = \{r1(d), c2(d), s3(d) : d\in D\} \quad (G\neq\emptyset), \text{ and}$$

$$\beta(P(G,d)) = \{r1(d), c2(d), s3(d) : d\in D\}.$$

Thus, $\beta(Q) = \{r1(d), c2(d), s3(d) : d\in D\}$, whence $c2(\emptyset) \notin \beta(Q)$ and $c2(\emptyset) \notin \alpha(Q)$.

5.11 Note: If we can use *priorities* on atomic actions (see Baeten, Bergstra & Klop [2]), then Q can be defined by a finite recursive specification, as follows. If all actions s3(d) (for $d\in D$) have priority over all c2(e) (for $e\in D$), and θ implements this priority (i.e. $\theta(s3(d)x + c2(e)y) = s3(d)\theta(x)$), we can define

$$C_d = c2(d)T_d + \sum_{e\in D} r1(e)(C_e\|C_d) \quad (\text{for } d\in D)$$

$$T_d = s3(d) + \sum_{e\in D} r1(e)(T_d\|C_e) \quad (\text{for } d\in D)$$

$$Q = \sum_{d\in D} r1(d)\cdot\theta(C_d).$$

5.12 Lemma: $\tau_{\{c2(\emptyset)\}}(P) = \tau\cdot\partial_{\{c2(\emptyset)\}}(P)$.

Proof: By 5.10, we have $P = c2(\emptyset)P + QP$. Applying KFAR (see 3.4) to this equation, we get

$$\tau_{\{c2(\emptyset)\}}(P) = \tau\cdot\tau_{\{c2(\emptyset)\}}(QP) = \tau\cdot\tau_{\{c2(\emptyset)\}}(Q)\cdot\tau_{\{c2(\emptyset)\}}(P) =$$
$$= \tau\cdot Q\cdot\tau_{\{c2(\emptyset)\}}(P)$$

by CA4, since $c2(\emptyset) \notin \alpha(Q)$. On the other hand

$$\tau\cdot\partial_{\{c2(\emptyset)\}}(P) = \tau\cdot\partial_{\{c2(\emptyset)\}}(c2(\emptyset)P + QP) = \tau(\delta + \partial_{\{c2(\emptyset)\}}(QP)) =$$
$$= \tau\cdot\partial_{\{c2(\emptyset)\}}(Q)\cdot\partial_{\{c2(\emptyset)\}}(P) = \tau\cdot Q\cdot\partial_{\{c2(\emptyset)\}}(P) \text{ by CA3,}$$

so by the Recursive Specification Principle $\tau_{\{c2(\emptyset)\}}(P) = \tau\cdot\partial_{\{c2(\emptyset)\}}(P)$.

5.13 Lemma: $\tau_{I2\cup\{c2(\emptyset)\}}\circ\partial_{H2\cup H\emptyset}(B\emptyset\|T\emptyset) = \tau\cdot\tau_{I2}\circ\partial_{H2}(B^{12}\|T)$.

Proof: $\tau_{I2\cup\{c2(\emptyset)\}}\circ\partial_{H2\cup H\emptyset}(B\emptyset\|T\emptyset) =$

$= \tau_{I2}\circ\tau_{\{c2(\emptyset)\}}\circ\partial_{H2\cup H\emptyset}(B\emptyset\|T\emptyset)$ (by CA6) =

$= \tau_{I2}(\tau\cdot\partial_{\{c2(\emptyset)\}}\circ\partial_{H2\cup H\emptyset}(B\emptyset\|T\emptyset)$ (by 5.12) =

$= \tau\cdot\tau_{I2}\circ\partial_{H2}\circ\partial_{\{c2(\emptyset)\}\cup H\emptyset}(B\emptyset \| T\emptyset)$ (by CA5) =

$= \tau\cdot\tau_{I2}\circ\partial_{H2}\circ\partial_{\{c2(\emptyset)\}\cup H\emptyset}(\partial_{\{c2(\emptyset)\}\cup H\emptyset}(B\emptyset) \| \partial_{\{c2(\emptyset)\}\cup H\emptyset}(T\emptyset))$

(by CA1, see note 1 below) =

$= \tau\cdot\tau_{I2}\circ\partial_{H2}\circ\partial_{\{c2(\emptyset)\}\cup H\emptyset}(\partial_{\{c2(\emptyset),\ r2(\emptyset)\}}\circ\partial_{\{s2(\emptyset)\}}(B\emptyset) \| \partial_{\{c2(\emptyset),\ s2(\emptyset)\}}\circ\partial_{\{r2(\emptyset)\}}(T\emptyset))$

(by CA5) =

$= \tau\cdot\tau_{I2}\circ\partial_{H2}\circ\partial_{\{c2(\emptyset)\}\cup H\emptyset}(\partial_{\{c2(\emptyset),\ r2(\emptyset)\}}(B^{12}) \| \partial_{\{c2(\emptyset),\ s2(\emptyset)\}}(T))$

(by 5.6 and 5.9) =

$= \tau\cdot\tau_{I2}\circ\partial_{H2}\circ\partial_{\{c2(\emptyset)\}\cup H\emptyset}(B^{12} \| T)$ (by CA3, see note 2 below) =

$= \tau\cdot\tau_{I2}\circ\partial_{H2}(B^{12} \| T)$ (by CA3, see note 3 below).

Note 1: This is because $\{c2(\emptyset)\}\cup H\emptyset$ is closed under communication.

Note 2: $\alpha(B^{12}) = \{r1(d), s2(d) : d\in D\}$ by 4.7, and $\alpha(T) = \{r2(d), s3(d) : d\in D\}$ is easily proved.

Note 3: $\alpha(B^{12} \| T) = \alpha(B^{12}) \cup \alpha(T) \cup \alpha(B^{12}) | \alpha(T) = \{r1(d), s2(d), c2(d), r2(d), s3(d) : d\in D\}$.

5.14 Lemma: $\tau_{I3}\circ\partial_{H3}(T \| B^{34}) = B^{24}$.

Proof: $\tau_{I3}\circ\partial_{H3}(T \| B^{34}) = \tau_{I3}(\sum_{d\in D} r2(d)\cdot\partial_{H3}(s3(d)T \| B^{34}) =$

$= \sum_{d\in D} r2(d)\cdot\tau_{I3}(c3(d)\cdot\partial_{H3}(T \| B^{34} \| s4(d)) =$

$= \sum_{d\in D} r2(d)\cdot\tau\cdot\tau_{I3}\circ\partial_{H3}(\partial_{H3}(T \| B^{34}) \| s4(d))$ (by CA1, note that $A | \{s4(d)\} = \emptyset$) =

$= \sum_{d\in D} r2(d)\cdot\tau_{I3}(\partial_{H3}(T \| B^{34}) \| s4(d))$ (by CA3) =

$= \sum_{d\in D} r2(d)\cdot\tau_{I3}(\tau_{I3}\circ\partial_{H3}(T \| B^{34}) \| s4(d))$ (by CA2) =

$= \sum_{d\in D} r2(d)\cdot(\tau_{I3}\circ\partial_{H3}(T \| B^{34}) \| s4(d))$ (by CA4).

Therefore, $\tau_{I3}\circ\partial_{H3}(T \| B^{34})$ satisfies the defining equation of B^{24}, so by the Recursive Specification Principle $\tau_{I3}\circ\partial_{H3}(T \| B^{34}) = B^{24}$.

5.15 Lemma: (Van Glabbeek [10]) $ACP_\tau \vdash \tau x \| y = \tau(x \| y)$.

Proof: $\tau x \| y = \tau x \lfloor\!\lfloor y + y \lfloor\!\lfloor \tau x + \tau x | y = \tau(x \| y) + y \lfloor\!\lfloor \tau x + \tau x | y$. Therefore $\tau x \| y = \tau x \| y + \tau(x \| y)$. On the other hand $\tau(x \| y) = \tau x \lfloor\!\lfloor y = \tau\tau x \lfloor\!\lfloor y = \tau(\tau x \| y) = \tau(\tau x \| y) + \tau x \| y$. Therefore $\tau(x \| y) = \tau(x \| y) + \tau x \| y$.

5.16 Now we can finally prove the theorem refered to in 5.8.

Theorem: $\tau_I\circ\partial_H(B\emptyset \| T\emptyset \| B^{34}) = \tau B^{14}$.

Proof: $\tau_I\circ\partial_H(B\emptyset \| T\emptyset \| B^{34}) =$

$= \tau_{I3}\circ\tau_{I2\cup\{c2(\emptyset)\}}\circ\partial_{H3}\circ\partial_{H2\cup H\emptyset}(B\emptyset \| T\emptyset \| B^{34})$ (by CA5 and CA6) =

$= \tau_{I3}\circ\partial_{H3}\circ\tau_{I2\cup\{c2(\emptyset)\}}\circ\partial_{H2\cup H\emptyset}(B\emptyset \| T\emptyset \| B^{34})$ (by CA7) =

$= \tau_{I3} \circ \partial_{H3} \circ \tau_{I2 \cup \{c2(\emptyset)\}} \circ \partial_{H2 \cup H\emptyset}(\partial_{H2 \cup H\emptyset}(B\emptyset \| T\emptyset) \| B^{34})$

(by CA1, see note 1 below) =

$= \tau_{I3} \circ \partial_{H3} \circ \tau_{I2 \cup \{c2(\emptyset)\}}(\partial_{H2 \cup H\emptyset}(B\emptyset \| T\emptyset) \| B^{34})$ (by CA3, see note 1 below) =

$= \tau_{I3} \circ \partial_{H3} \circ \tau_{I2 \cup \{c2(\emptyset)\}}(\tau_{I2 \cup \{c2(\emptyset)\}} \circ \partial_{H2 \cup H\emptyset}(B\emptyset \| T\emptyset) \| B^{34})$

(by CA2, see note 1 below) =

$= \tau_{I3} \circ \partial_{H3}(\tau_{I2 \cup \{c2(\emptyset)\}} \circ \partial_{H2 \cup H\emptyset}(B\emptyset \| T\emptyset) \| B^{34})$ (by CA4, see note 1 below) =

$= \tau_{I3} \circ \partial_{H3}(\tau \cdot \tau_{I2} \circ \partial_{H2}(B^{12} \| T) \| B^{34})$ (by 5.13) =

$= \tau \cdot \tau_{I3} \circ \partial_{H3}(\tau_{I2} \circ \partial_{H2}(B^{12} \| T) \| B^{34})$ (by 5.15) =

$= \tau \cdot \tau_{I3} \circ \partial_{H3} \circ \tau_{I2} \circ \partial_{H2}(\tau_{I2} \circ \partial_{H2}(B^{12} \| T) \| B^{34})$ (by CA3, CA4, see note 2 below) =

$= \tau \cdot \tau_{I3} \circ \partial_{H3} \circ \tau_{I2} \circ \partial_{H2}(B^{12} \| T \| B^{34})$ (by CA1, CA2, see note 3 below) =

$= \tau \cdot \tau_{I2} \circ \partial_{H2} \circ \tau_{I3} \circ \partial_{H3}(B^{12} \| T \| B^{34})$ (by CA7) =

$= \tau \cdot \tau_{I2} \circ \partial_{H2} \circ \tau_{I3} \circ \partial_{H3}(B^{12} \| \tau_{I3} \circ \partial_{H3}(T \| B^{34}))$ (by CA1, CA2, see note 4 below) =

$= \tau \cdot \tau_{I2} \circ \partial_{H2}(B^{12} \| \tau_{I3} \circ \partial_{H3}(T \| B^{34}))$ (by CA3, CA4, see note 4 below) =

$= \tau \cdot \tau_{I2} \circ \partial_{H2}(B^{12} \| B^{24})$ (by 5.14) =

$= \tau \cdot B^{14}$ (by 5.2).

Note 1: By 4.7, $\alpha(B^{34}) = \{r3(d), s4(d) : d \in D\}$. Thus $\alpha(B^{34}) \mid (A - \{s3(d) : d \in D\}) = \emptyset$, and also $((A - (H2 \cup H\emptyset)) \cup \alpha(B^{34})) \cap (H2 \cup H\emptyset) = \emptyset$, and $((A - (I2 \cup \{c2(\emptyset)\})) \cup \alpha(B^{34})) \cap (I2 \cup \{c2(\emptyset)\}) = \emptyset$.

Note 2: Likewise, we show $((A - H2) \cup \alpha(B^{34})) \cap H2 = \emptyset$ and $((A - I2) \cup \alpha(B^{34})) \cap I2 = \emptyset$.

Note 3: $\alpha(B^{12} \| T) \mid \alpha(B^{34}) =$

$= (\{r1(d), s2(d) : d \in D\} \cup \{r2(d), s3(d) : d \in D\} \cup \{c2(d) : d \in D\}) \mid \{r3(d), s4(d) : d \in D\} =$

$= \{c3(d) : d \in D\}$. The result is $\emptyset$ if we intersect $\alpha(B^{12} \| T)$ with I2 or H2.

Note 4: $\alpha(B^{12}) \mid \alpha(T \| B^{34}) = \{r1(d), s2(d) : d \in D\} \mid \{r2(d), s3(d), c3(d), r3(d), s4(d) : d \in D\}$ $= \{c2(d) : d \in D\}$. The result is $\emptyset$ if we intersect $\alpha(T \| B^{34})$ with I3 or H3.

References.

[1] J.C.M.Baeten, J.A.Bergstra & J.W.Klop, *Conditional axioms and α/β-calculus in process algebra,* report CS-R8502, Centre for Mathematics and Computer Science, Amsterdam 1985.

[2] J.C.M.Baeten, J.A.Bergstra & J.W.Klop, *Syntax and defining equations for an interrupt mechanism in process algebra,* Fund. Inf. IX (2), pp. 127-168, 1986.

[3] J.C.M.Baeten, J.A.Bergstra & J.W.Klop, *On the consistency of Koomen's Fair Abstraction Rule,* report CS-R8511, Centre for Mathematics and Computer Science, Amsterdam 1985, to appear in Theor. Comp. Sci.

[4] J.W. de Bakker & J.I. Zucker, *Processes and the denotational semantics of concurrency,* Information & Control 54 (1/2), pp. 70-120, 1982.

[5] J.A.Bergstra & J.W.Klop, *The algebra of recursively defined processes and the algebra of regular processes,* Proc. 11th ICALP, Antwerpen (ed. J.Paredaens), Springer LNCS 172, pp. 82-95, 1984.

[6] J.A.Bergstra & J.W.Klop, *Process algebra for synchronous communication,* Information & Control 60 (1/3), pp. 109-137, 1984.
[7] J.A.Bergstra & J.W.Klop, *Algebra of communicating processes with abstraction,* Theor. Comp. Sci. 37, pp. 77-121, 1985.
[8] J.A.Bergstra & J.V.Tucker, *Top-down design and the algebra of communicating processes,* Sci. of Comp. Progr. 5 (2), pp. 171-199, 1984.
[9] S.Brookes, C.Hoare & W.Roscoe, *A theory of communicating sequential processes,* JACM 31 (3), pp. 560-599, 1984.
[10] R.J. van Glabbeek, personal communication, 1986.
[11] M.Hennessy & G.Plotkin, *A term model for CCS,* Proc. 9th MFCS, Poland (1980), Springer LNCS 88.
[12] C.A.R.Hoare, *Communicating Sequential Processes,* Prentice Hall 1985.
[13] R.Milner, *A calculus of communicating systems,* Springer LNCS 92, 1980.
[14] E.-R.Olderog, *Specification oriented programming,* to appear.
[15] J.Sifakis, *Property preserving homomorphisms of transition systems,* Proc. Logics of Programs (1983), Springer LNCS 164, 1984.
[16] F.W.Vaandrager, *Verification of two communication protocols by means of process algebra,* report CS-R8608, Centre for Mathematics and Computer Science, Amsterdam 1986.

QUESTIONS AND ANSWERS

Olderog: How do you get axioms for your system without having a particular model?

Baeten: We analyse the axioms by comparing different models such as the initial algebra and the process graph model.

Best: You also need another trick: the 'recursive specification principle'!

Baeten: This principle means that every guarded recursive specification has a unique solution. This is an assumption in our approach and non-trivial to prove, for particular algebras. But since I am not talking about one model, I am just assuming it and have only to show that it is consistent. If you deal with models, of course, you have to prove it.

Jouannaud: Did you try to automate these proofs, and in particular the system verifications?

Baeten: No, I believe the proof we have presented is not automatizable. I cannot say these proofs can be automatized, this may be possible in the future, I don't know. Maybe then there will be some large system verifications where automatized proofs could be useful. But we are not at a point that we can say we can do such things.

de Nicola: Are there any problems with the conditional axioms of the α/β - calculus for alphabets, since you say the alphabet is undecidable?

Baeten: No, you can work with approximations.

de Nicola: Do you know a method of deciding which subcalculi of your calculus can be completely and effectively axiomatized?

Baeten: I don't know. This is still in the future. We are all looking at such small examples, but it becomes important, if we get large systems. We do not have enough experience to really say something about that.

de Nicola: If one starts by writing axioms instead of starting from an operational model, one should start with axioms which can be put on the machine. I see two ways of using the axioms: either to justify the operational model or to start with some axioms which make definitely sense and then to put them on the machine and to see what their consequences are.

Baeten: I think, the use of the axioms is to be able to prove algebraically whether two processes are equal in order to understand the meaning of processes.

de Nicola: I agree.

Hehner: You wanted to have an effective approximation to the alphabet based on projections. The *n*th projection was defined informally and I am wondering, if that can be made effective. Can you at least give me the intuition for the effective calculation of the *n*th projection?

Baeten: You start from the given guarded recursive specification. And this means that every variable is preceeded by an atom.

Hehner: Yes, o.k., in the case of guarded definitions I can understand that. The projection does not apply then when it is not guarded?

Baeten: Well, every process can be given in three ways: either as a closed term or as a solution of a guarded recursive specification or as an abstraction from such a process. Only the third case is probably nontrivial with respect to projections.

Formal Description of Programming Concepts - III
M. Wirsing (Editor)
Elsevier Science Publishers B.V. (North-Holland)

© IFIP, 1987

FAILURES WITHOUT CHAOS: A NEW PROCESS SEMANTICS FOR FAIR ABSTRACTION

J.A. Bergstra *
Computer Science Department, University of Amsterdam ,
Kruislaan 409, 1098 SJ Amsterdam;
Department of Philosophy, State University of Utrecht,
Heidelberglaan 2, 3584 CS Utrecht, The Netherlands.

J.W. Klop *
Centre for Mathematics and Computer Science,
P.O. Box 4079, 1009 AB Amsterdam, The Netherlands.

E.-R. Olderog
Institut für Informatik und Praktische Mathematik,
Christian-Albrechts-Universität Kiel,
2300 Kiel 1, Federal Republic of Germany.

We propose a new process semantics that combines the advantages of fair abstraction from internal process activity with the simplicity of failure semantics. The new semantics is obtained by changing the way the original failure semantics of Brookes, Hoare and Roscoe or the equivalent acceptance semantics of de Nicola and Hennessy deal with infinite internal process activity, known as divergence. We work in an algebraic setting and develop the new semantics stepwise, thereby systematically comparing previous proposals.

(*): Authors partially supported by ESPRIT project 432, Meteor.

1. Introduction.

The concept of abstraction is most important for mastering the complexity of process verification. The reason is that abstraction allows larger processes to be constructed and verified hierarchically as systems of smaller ones. For example, imagine a system SYS consisting of three components connected as in Figure 1(a). Typically, the task of verification is then to prove that such a system behaves like a much simpler process SPEC serving as system specification.

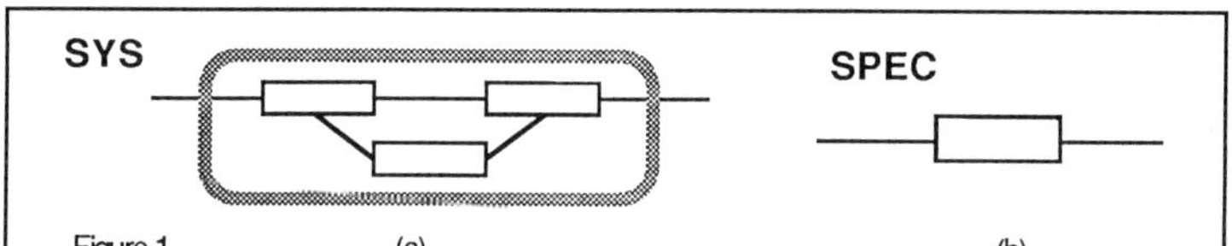

Figure 1

This proof is possible only by "abstracting" from the internal structure of the system as shown within the confined area in Figure 1(a) and comparing the specification with the remaining external behaviour of the system outside the confined area.

Combining ideas of Milner [Mi 1] and Hoare [Ho], abstraction can be modelled by distinguishing two kinds of actions in a process, viz. *external* or *observable* actions, and *internal* or *hidden* actions, and by introducing an explicit hiding operator that transforms observable actions into internal ones.

One of the difficult issues linked with abstraction is how to deal with divergence, i.e. with the capability of a process to execute an infinite sequence of internal actions. That is what our paper is about. We work in an algebraic setting where the intended semantics of processes is described by algebraic laws or axioms, and where process models prove the consistency of these axiomatisations (cf. [BK 1-4]).

We are specifically interested in the notion of fair abstraction as exemplified in Koomen's Fair Abstraction Rule (KFAR) [Ko, BBK 2]. This rule has proved particularly useful in algebraic protocol verification because it can deal with unreliable, but fair transmission media. For example, in [BK 3] and [Va] Alternating Bit and Sliding Window Protocols were verified using Koomen's Fair Abstraction Rule. Formally, KFAR allows to condense a divergence into a single internal action. KFAR is justified in Milner and Park's bisimulation semantics [Mi 1,3, Pa]. This is a very discriminating semantics where (divergence free) processes can be identified only if their global branching structure coincides [BBK 2].

Starting from the idea that only linear histories or traces of communications with a process can be observed, bisimulation semantics is too discriminating, and the linear failure semantics of [BHR] or the equivalent ("must"-version of) acceptance semantics in [dNH, He] seems appropriate (cf.[Pn]). This brings us to the main question of our paper:

Can the advantages of fair abstraction be combined with the simplicity of a trace consistent, linear process semantics?

At first sight, the answer seems to be "no". Firstly, the original failure semantics of [BHR] equates divergence with the "catastrophic" process CHAOS that makes any distinction of the subsequent process behaviour impossible. Moreover, in [BKO] it was proved that failure semantics is inconsistent with the rule KFAR in the sense that it forces us to identify finite processes which are distinguished in failure semantics.

Nevertheless, in this paper we shall present a new failure semantics without CHAOS which admits a restricted rule $KFAR^-$ for the fair abstraction of so-called unstable divergence. It is interesting to note that $KFAR^-$ turns out to be sufficient for the protocol verifications in [BK 3, Va]. We demonstrate the usefulness of $KFAR^-$ by treating a small, idealised protocol due to [Par]. The proposed semantics differs also from all versions of acceptance semantics discussed in [dNH, He].

In fact, we shall present a systematic analysis of axiom systems and semantic models centering around the notions of abstraction and divergence. Both the exposition and the elegance of the various axiomatisations are greatly enhanced by introducing a process Δ (pronounced "delay") modelling divergence. Δ is inspired by Milner's delay operator in SCCS [Mi 3]. With the symbols

δ and τ denoting deadlock and internal action, the main theories about divergence can be characterised by simple equations about Δ:

- as starting point a (new) bisimulation semantics with explicit divergence Δ,

- bisimulation semantics of [Mi 1, Pa] with fair abstraction: $\Delta = \tau$,

- a (new) failure semantics with explicit divergence Δ,

- failure semantics of [BHR, BR] with catastrophic divergence which is equivalent to the "must"-version of acceptance semantics in [dNH, He]: $\Delta\delta = \Delta$,

- finally, the main new failure semantics with fair abstraction of unstable divergence: $\Delta\tau = \tau$.

The details are explained in the rest of this paper.

2. Bisimulation Semantics with Explicit Divergence: BS_Δ

2.1. Algebraic setting.

The signature of processes contains a set A of *atomic processes* a,b,c,... modelling observable atomic actions, and the following *characteristic processes*:

δ - modelling *deadlock*,
ε - empty process modelling *termination*,
τ - modelling an *internal* or *hidden* action.

As process operations we admit, for $I \subseteq A$:

$+$ - binary infix operation modelling *nondeterminism*,
$.$ - binary infix operation modelling *sequential composition*,
τ_I - unary infix operation modeling *abstraction* from or *hiding* of all actions in I.

The above notation is chosen for its conciseness. Deadlock δ corresponds to NIL in CCS [Mi 1] and STOP in TCSP [BHR, Ho]. Termination ε and sequential composition x.y are not present in CCS but in TCSP where they are denoted by SKIP and x;y, respectively. Often we simply write xy instead of x.y. The symbols τ and $+$ are taken from CCS. For finite sums we use the convenient abbreviation Σ, e.g.

$$\Sigma_{k \in \{1,...,n\}} x_k = x_1 + ... + x_n.$$

(This notation is justified because + is commutative and associative: see the axioms in Table 1.)

The hiding operator $\tau_I(x)$ is from TCSP where it is written as x\I. The notation $\tau_I(x)$ is chosen to remind us that in x all actions a ∈ I are renamed into τ (see Table 1 again). In CCS hiding is always coupled with parallel composition, a solution which would obscure our present analysis. In fact, we do not consider parallel composition || here because the problems with abstraction and divergence arise already without this operation. However, we see no difficulties in adding the || of [BK 1] to the results in our paper.

Observably infinite processes are introduced by recursive definitions. We consider possibly infinite, guarded systems

$$E(\mathbf{x}) = \{x_k = T_k(\mathbf{x}) \mid k \in K\}$$

of recursive equations where **x** is a finite or infinite set $\mathbf{x} = \{x_k \mid k \in K\}$ of variables with index set K and where each right hand side term $T_k(\mathbf{x})$ is constructed from variables of **x**, constants of A ∪ {δ, ε, τ} and the operations + and . but not τ_I. *Guarded* means that for every k ∈ K there is some expansion $S_k(\mathbf{x})$ of x_k by E(**x**) such that each occurrence of x_k in $S_k(\mathbf{x})$ is preceded by some observable action a ∈ A. Thus a hidden action τ is not sufficient for guardedness. For example, the system $\{x_1 = x_2, x_2 = a.x_1\}$ is guarded, but $\{x_1 = \tau.x_1\}$ is not.

We require that such systems have solutions (Recursive Definition Principle RDP) which are moreover unique (Recursive Specification Principle RSP). These principles together with the basic axioms about ε, δ, τ and +, ., τ_I are given in Table 1 (next page).

Axioms A1-5 describe the general properties of . and +. Axioms A6 and A7 deal with deadlock δ: by A7 there is no subsequent behaviour possible after δ, and by A6 deadlock is discarded in the presence of another nondeterministic alternative. A6 is typical for global nondeterminism (cf. [BMOZ]). Axiom A8 characterises ε as the purely terminating process. Abstraction is described in two groups of axioms: TI1-4 describes the hiding operator τ_I as a simple renaming operator that renames every action a ∈ I into τ; how to deal with τ is then described by Milner's τ-laws T1-3 [Mi 1].

To illustrate the use of these axioms we derive the following consequence.

PROPOSITION 1. *For any* z *the term* $x = \tau(z + y)$ *solves the (unguarded) equation* $x = \tau x + y$.

PROOF. $x =_{[\text{def. } x]} \tau(z + y) =_{[T2]} \tau(z + y) + z + y =_{[A3]} \tau(z + y) + z + y + y =_{[T2]}$

$$\tau(z + y) + y =_{[T1]} \tau\tau(z + y) + y =_{[\text{def. } x]} \tau x + y. \qquad \square$$

Proposition 1 implies that in any trace consistent model (see section 2.4) of the axioms in Table 1 the equation $x = \tau x + y$ has infinitely many solutions. This explains why we restrict ourselves to guarded systems of equations when specifying processes via RDP and RSP.

Table 1

General Properties:

	$x + y = y + x$	A1
	$(x + y) + z = x + (y + z)$	A2
	$x + x = x$	A3
	$(x + y)z = xz + yz$	A4
	$(xy)z = x(yz)$	A5
	$\delta + x = x$	A6
	$\delta x = \delta$	A7
	$\varepsilon x = x\varepsilon = x$	A8
Abstraction:		
	$\tau_I(a) = \tau$ where $a \in I$	TI1
	$\tau_I(\gamma) = \gamma$ where $\gamma \notin I$	TI2
	$\tau_I(x + y) = \tau_I(x) + \tau_I(y)$	TI3
	$\tau_I(x.y) = \tau_I(x).\tau_I(y)$	TI4
	$\alpha\tau = \alpha$	T1
	$\tau x + x = \tau x$	T2
	$\alpha(\tau x + y) = \alpha(\tau x + y) + \alpha x$	T3
Recursion:		
	$\exists \mathbf{x}: E(\mathbf{x})$	RDP
	$\dfrac{E(\mathbf{x}) = E(\mathbf{y})}{\mathbf{x} = \mathbf{y}}$	RSP

In the above axioms, a ranges over A, α over $A \cup \{\tau\}$, γ over $A \cup \{\delta, \varepsilon, \tau\}$ and $E(\mathbf{x})$ stands for a guarded system of equations.

2.2. Abstraction and Divergence.

The main concern of our paper is how to apply the abstraction operator τ_I to recursively defined, infinite processes. Consider the equation

$$x = i.x + y \qquad (*)$$

with $i \in I$. In fact, take $I = \{i\}$. Applying $\tau_{\{i\}}$ to x with the help of TI1-4 just gives

$$\tau_{\{i\}}(x) = \tau.\ \tau_{\{i\}}(x) + \tau_{\{i\}}(y),$$

an unguarded recursive equation which by Proposition 1 has infinitely many solutions. But looking at the unique process x satisfying (*) the behaviour of $\tau_{\{i\}}(x)$ should be clear intuitively: $\tau_{\{i\}}(x)$ either takes (after finitely many i-steps) the y-branch to behave like $\tau_{\{i\}}(y)$ or it pursues an infinite sequence of hidden i-steps, i.e. it diverges.

Thus abstraction (or hiding) and divergence are intimately linked with each other. To express this fact, we use an idea of Milner [Mi 3] and introduce a new characteristic process:

Δ - pronounced "delay" modelling divergence.

The application of τ_I to recursive processes can now be explained by the following Delay Rule DE, which is parameterised with $n \geq 1$:

$$\frac{\forall k \in \mathbb{Z}_n: \quad x_k = i_k.x_{k+1} + y_k, \quad i_k \in I}{\tau_I(x_0) = \Delta.\tau_I(\Sigma_{k \in \mathbb{Z}_n}\ y_k)} \qquad \mathrm{DE}_n$$

Here $\mathbb{Z}_n = \{0,...,n\text{-}1\}$ and addition in the subscripts works modulo n. For n = 1 the rule applies to (*), yielding

$$\tau_{\{i\}}(x) = \Delta.\tau_{\{i\}}(y).$$

Putting $y = \varepsilon$ we obtain $\Delta = \tau_{\{i\}}(x)$ which by the previous axioms yields:

COROLLARY 1. (i) $\Delta = \Delta + \varepsilon$, (ii) $\Delta = \tau\Delta$, (iii) $\Delta = \tau\Delta + \varepsilon$.

PROOF. First we derive (iii):

$$\Delta = \tau_{\{i\}}(x) =_{[\text{def. } x]} \tau_{\{i\}}(ix + \varepsilon) =_{[TI1\text{-}4]} \tau.\ \tau_{\{i\}}(x) + \varepsilon = \tau\Delta + \varepsilon.$$

Now (i) and (ii) follow immediately:

$$\Delta = \tau\Delta + \varepsilon =_{[A3]} \tau\Delta + \varepsilon + \varepsilon = \Delta + \varepsilon,$$
$$\Delta = \tau\Delta + \varepsilon =_{[A3]} \tau\Delta + \tau\Delta + \varepsilon = \tau\Delta + \Delta =_{[T2]} = \tau\Delta.$$

□

Equation (i) says Δ may terminate, (ii) says Δ can perform arbitrarily many hidden τ-steps, and (iii) combines both properties. We add one further axiom about Δ saying that Δ has no observable actions:

$$\tau_I(\Delta) = \Delta \qquad \text{TI5}$$

The resulting axiom system, i.e. Table 1 + DE_n + TI5, we call BS_Δ.

2.3. A model for BS_Δ.

Axiomatic systems must be *logically consistent*, i.e. possess a model satisfying their axioms. Well-known are tree models for processes [Mi 1, He]. Here we build a model by dividing out a suitable equivalence on the domain of process graphs which represent the state-transition diagrams of nondeterministic automata.

A *process graph* is a rooted, directed multigraph. In this paper a process graph will always be finitely branching. Its nodes (states) are marked "open" (final states) or "closed" (other states) and its edges (transitions) are labelled by elements of $A \cup \{\tau\}$. Process graphs may contain cycles but not at their roots.

Let $\mathfrak{G}$ be the set of all finitely branching process graphs, with $g,h \in \mathfrak{G}$. Atomic and characteristic processes are represented as follows:

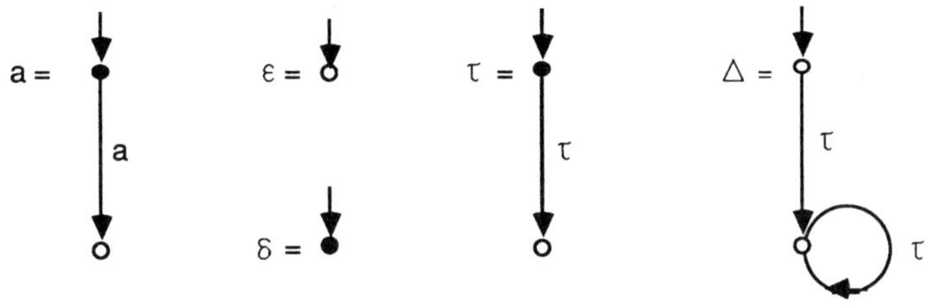

Figure 2 (a) (b) (c) (d)

The sum g + h is obtained by identifying the roots of g and h where "open" wins, the product g.h by appending h at all "open" nodes of g, the abstraction $\tau_I(g)$ by changing all labels $a \in I$ in g to τ.

As equivalence on $\mathfrak{G}$ we take a version of Milner's original observational equivalence [Mi 1] or better Park's bisimilarity [Pa, Mi 3] which keeps track of all divergences, called here *Δ-bisimilarity* $\leftrightarrow_\Delta$.

First we have to distinguish between different types of nodes in process graphs. A node is a *divergence node* if it is the starting point of an infinite path with all edges labelled by τ. A node is called *exit node* if it is the starting point of a finite path with all edges labelled by τ and ending in an open node (modelling a final state). As usual we write for nodes s,t of a process graph g and a trace $\sigma \in A^*$:

$$s \Longrightarrow^{\sigma}_{g} t$$

if there exists a finite path from s to t in g labelled by a sequence $\lambda_1,...,\lambda_n \in (A \cup \{\tau\})^*$ such that σ results from $\lambda_1,...,\lambda_n$ by skipping all τ's.

For example, consider the following process graph with nodes r, s, t, u:

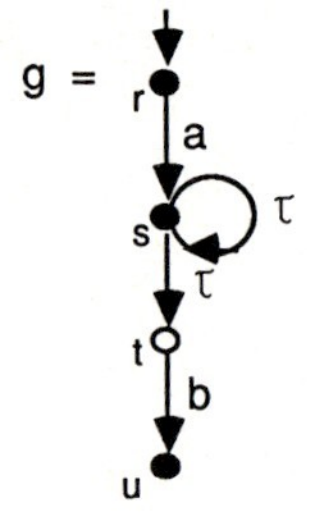

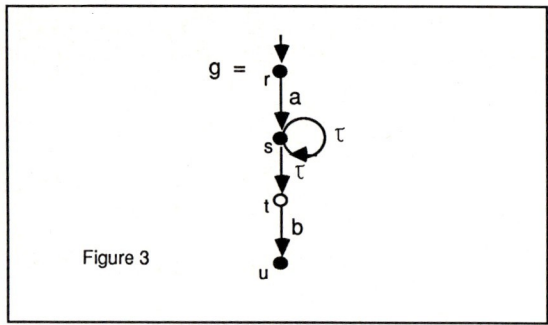

Figure 3

Then s and t are exit nodes, but not r and u. Moreover, g contains exactly one divergence node, viz. s. Finally, we have

$$r \Longrightarrow^{a}{}_{g}\, s,\ \ r \Longrightarrow^{a}{}_{g}\, t,\ \ r \Longrightarrow^{ab}{}_{g}\, u.$$

A *weak bisimulation* [Pa, Mi 3] between process graphs g and h is a relation R between the nodes of g and h satisfying the following conditions:

(B1) The roots of g and h are related.

(B2) Whenever sRt and $s \Longrightarrow^{\sigma}{}_{g}\, s'$ then, for some node t' in h, s'Rt' and $t \Longrightarrow^{\sigma}{}_{h}\, t'$.

(B3) Conversely, whenever sRt and $t \Longrightarrow^{\sigma}{}_{h}\, t'$ then, for some node s' in g, s'Rt' and $s \Longrightarrow^{\sigma}{}_{g}\, s'$.

Now, two process graphs g and h are *Δ-bisimilar*, abbreviated $g \leftrightarrow_{\Delta} h$, if there exists a weak bisimulation R additionally satisfying the following conditions:

(B4) A root may only be related to a root.

(B5) An exit node may only be related to an exit node.

(B6) A divergence node may only be related to a divergence node.

Also Milner considers a version of bisimilarity which takes divergence into account ([Mi 2]). However, his version differs from ours. For example in Milner's context the equation $\Delta(ab + a\Delta) = \Delta ab$ holds, but not with our definition of bisimilarity. Condition B5 is not needed in Milner's framework of CCS ([Mi 1]) because the notion of successful termination is not considered there. However, recall that Milner's definitions of observational equivalence do not yield a congruence w.r.t. the nondeterminism operator +. By adding condition B4, we avoid this problem.

We state without proof (see [BBK 2] for a similar proof):

THEOREM 1. (i) $\Leftrightarrow_\Delta$ *is a congruence w.r.t. the operations in* $\mathbb{G}$.
(ii) $\mathbb{G}/\Leftrightarrow_\Delta \models BS_\Delta$, *i.e. modulo Δ-bisimilarity the process graphs satisfy all axioms of* BS_Δ.

Notation: $\mathcal{A}(BS_\Delta) = \mathbb{G}/\Leftrightarrow_\Delta$. It is well-known that bisimilarity preserves the branching structure of process graphs.

2.4. Trace Consistency.

Exhibiting a model for a process axiomatisation rules out logical contradictions, but it does not guarantee that the axiomatisation captures the operational intuitions about processes. The simplest such intuition is that of a trace. We therefore require that a process axiomatisation T is *trace consistent*, i.e. whenever

$$T \vdash x = y$$

holds for two finite and closed process terms x and y involving only $A \cup \{\varepsilon, \delta, \tau\}$ and + and . then their set of complete traces must agree:

$$\underline{trace}(x) = \underline{trace}(y).$$

A *complete trace* is a trace ending with a symbol √ or δ indicating successful termination ($\sigma\surd$, $\sigma \in A^*$) or deadlock ($\sigma\delta$, $\sigma \in A^*$). Formally, the set $\underline{trace}(x)$ is defined as follows. First, *normalise* the finite, closed term x by applying the "rewrite rules" of Table 2. (In fact, we work with finite closed terms x modulo A1, A2, A5 of Table 1.)

Table 2

$(x + y)z$	$\rightarrow$	$xz + yz$
$\delta + x$	$\rightarrow$	x
δx	$\rightarrow$	δ
εx	$\rightarrow$	x
$x\varepsilon$	$\rightarrow$	x
$\alpha\tau$	$\rightarrow$	α

Above α ranges over $A \cup \{\tau\}$

For normalised x, $\underline{trace}(x)$ is defined inductively as shown in Table 3.

Table 3

$\underline{trace}(\delta) = \{\delta\}$

$\underline{trace}(\varepsilon) = \{\surd\}$

$\underline{trace}(\tau) = \{\surd\}$

$\underline{trace}(a) = \{a\surd\}$

$\underline{trace}(y + z) = \underline{trace}(y) \cup \underline{trace}(z)$

$\underline{trace}(a.y) = a.\underline{trace}(y)$

$\underline{trace}(\tau.y) = \underline{trace}(y)$

Above a ranges over A

All our models will be such that they imply trace consistency. Thus:

PROPOSITION 2. BS_Δ *is trace consistent.*

3. Bisimulation Semantics with Fair Abstraction: BS.

3.1. Fair Abstraction.

The Delay Rule DE_n allows us to apply abstraction to infinite recursive processes, but the result always contains Δ signalling divergence. This is disturbing because often one can assume *fairness* in the sense that a process will never stay forever in a cycle of hidden τ-steps but will eventually exit it. Can we axiomatise this assumption? Yes, simply by adding the axiom

$$\Delta = \tau$$

to the system BS_Δ. We will examine the resulting system BS. The Delay Rule DE_n now specialises to Koomen's Fair Abstraction Rule $KFAR_n$

$$\frac{\forall k \in \mathbb{Z}_n: \quad x_k = i_k.x_{k+1} + y_k, \quad i_k \in I}{\tau_I(x_0) = \tau.\tau_I(\Sigma_{k \in \mathbb{Z}_n}\ y_k)} \qquad KFAR_n$$

of [BBK 2]. KFAR formalises an observation by Milner about his calculus CCS [Mi 1] and was first used by C.J. Koomen of Philips Research, Eindhoven, in a formula manipulation system for CCS (see also [Ko]). *Fair abstraction* means that $\tau_I(x_0)$ will eventually exit the hidden i_0-i_1-...-i_{n-1} cycle.

A model for BS is obtained from the process graphs $\mathbb{G}$ by dividing out a slight variation $\leftrightarrows$ of the original bisimilarity relation of [Pa, Mi 3]: $\mathcal{A}(BS) = \mathbb{G}/\leftrightarrows$ (see [BBK 2]). In fact, $\leftrightarrows$ is defined as $\underline{\leftrightarrow}_\Delta$, but without condition B6. Thus BS is essentially the semantics of [Mi 1,3, Pa].

3.2. Protocol Verification in BS.

The rule KFAR has proved a crucial tool in a number of algebraic protocol verifications including Alternating Bit [BK 3] and Sliding Window Protocols [Va]. This is because KFAR can capture well the idea of a faulty, but fair transmission medium. We will demonstrate this by treating a small example.

Intuitively, a protocol is a set of rules describing how two processes, a sender and a receiver, communicate with each other over a transmission medium [Ta]. The task of protocol verification is to show that sender and receiver achieve a reliable communication despite a possibly unreliable medium that may lose or corrupt the messages sent [vB, Ha]. Formally, a protocol can be described as a system constructed hierarchically from the sender process, the receiver process, and a process modelling the medium [BK 2, Par]. The rules of communication are then incorporated in these processes.

We consider now an idealised protocol P essentially due to [Par]. Its components, the sender S, the medium M and the receiver R, are connected via directed communication channels named send, in, error, out, ack and rec:

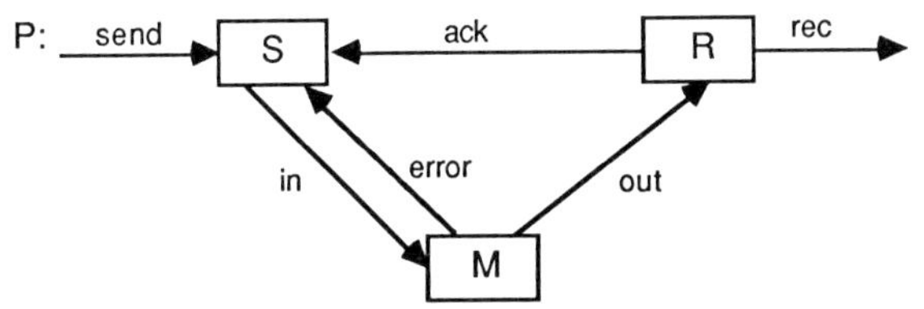

Figure 4

Their behaviour is described by the following recursive equations:

$$\begin{aligned} S &= send?.S_0 \\ S_0 &= in!.(ack?.S + error?.S_0) \\ M &= in?.(out!.M + error!.M) \\ R &= out?.rec!.ack!.R \end{aligned}$$

For illustration, we exhibit in Figure 5 (next page) the process graphs denoted by S, M and R.

Using the CSP notation [Ho], input of a message along a communication channel ch $\in$ {send,...,rec} is denoted by the action ch? and output by ch!. Intuitively, the sender S inputs a message from channel send and forwards it to the medium along channel in. If S gets an acknowledgement ack (from the receiver), it can input the next message from send. If, however, S gets the indication error representing loss or corruption of the message (inside the medium), S retransmits the present message before inputting a new one from channel send. The intuition about M and R can be explained in a similar way.

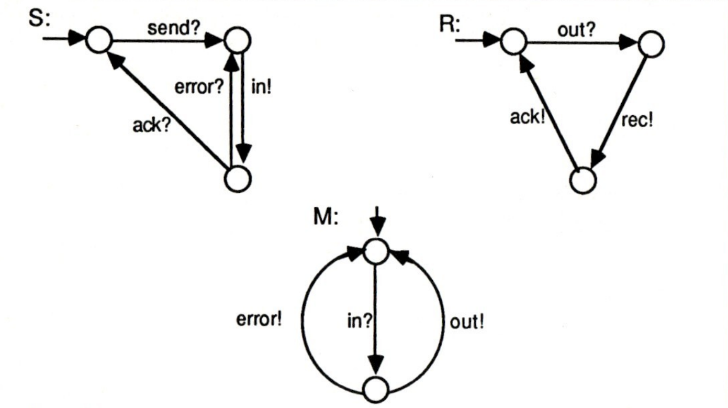

Figure 5

The protocol P explains how the components S, M, R work together. As in [BK 3] P can be described using parallel composition || and encapsulation ∂_H:

$$P = \partial_H (S \,||\, M \,||\, R).$$

We omit these details here and record only the result of this construction:

$$P \;= \text{send?}.P_0$$
$$P_0 = \underline{\text{in}}.P_1$$
$$P_1 = \underline{\text{error}}.P_0 + \underline{\text{out}}.\text{rec!}.\underline{\text{ack}}.P$$

denoting the process graph in Figure 6.

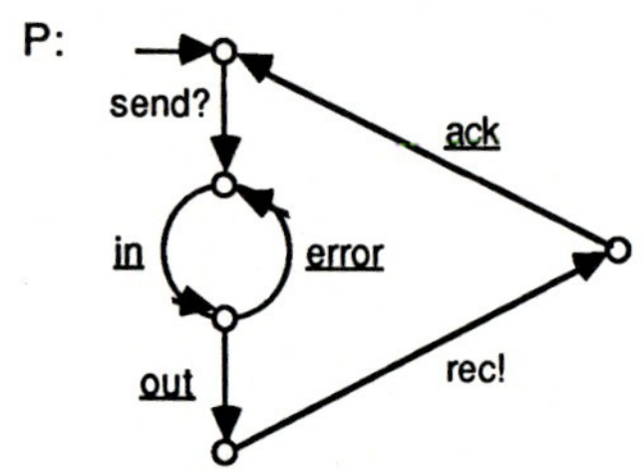

Figure 6

Here the action $\underline{\text{in}}$ denotes the result of a handshake communication between in? and in! performed through parallel composition || (see [BK 1,3]). Analogously for $\underline{\text{error}}$, $\underline{\text{out}}$ and $\underline{\text{ack}}$.

These communications should be treated as internal actions of the protocol, not observable from the outside. Therefore the remaining task of protocol verification is now to show that the system

$$\mathrm{SYS} = \tau_I(\mathrm{P}),$$

obtained from P by hiding all communications in $I = \{\underline{\text{in}}, \underline{\text{error}}, \underline{\text{out}}, \underline{\text{ack}}\}$, behaves like a reliable transmission line specified by

$$\mathrm{SPEC} = \mathrm{send?.rec!.SPEC},$$

i.e. to derive the equation

$$\mathrm{SYS} = \mathrm{SPEC}.$$

Intuitively, this verification depends on the fairness assumption that the medium M and hence the protocol P will eventually leave its cycle of errors and correctly output the current message to the receiver R. Algebraically, this assumption is treated by Koomen's Fair Abstraction Rule KFAR. Its application to P_0 yields

$$\tau_I(\mathrm{P}_0) = \tau.\tau_I(\underline{\text{out}}.\mathrm{rec!}.\underline{\text{ack}}.\mathrm{P}).$$

By the axioms TI1-4 and T1 of BS, we continue

$$\begin{aligned} \tau_I(\mathrm{P}) &= \mathrm{send?}.\ \tau_I(\mathrm{P}_0) \\ &= \mathrm{send?}.\tau.\tau.\mathrm{rec!}.\tau.\tau_I(\mathrm{P}) \\ &= \mathrm{send?.rec!}.\ \tau_I(\mathrm{P}). \end{aligned}$$

Now the Recursive Specification Principle RSP yields

$$\mathrm{SYS} = \tau_I(\mathrm{P}) = \mathrm{SPEC}$$

as desired.

4. Failure Semantics with Explicit Divergence: FS_Δ.

4.1. The Question.

As we have seen, Koomen's Fair Abstraction Rule KFAR is an attractive means for the algebraic verification of processes that involve some notion of fairness. KFAR is justified in bisimulation semantics BS, a very discriminating semantics which preserves the full branching structure of processes. Often this seems too detailed so that we would like to "simplify" the results obtained in BS.

To illustrate this point we consider an example from [BBK 1] describing a small part of an operating system, viz. the interaction of a printer with a file handler that might crash when attempting to send its data to the printer. Let action "c" denote the occurrence of a crash and action "d_k" the succesful output of the k-th data item by the printer, $k \geq 0$. Then the final observable effect of the interaction printer-file is given by the process x_0 defined as follows:

(B) $$x_k = \tau.y_k + \tau.c$$
$$y_k = d_k.x_{k+1} + \tau.d_k.y_{k+1} + \tau.d_k.c$$

where $k \geq 0$. The process graph of x_0 is shown in Figure 7.

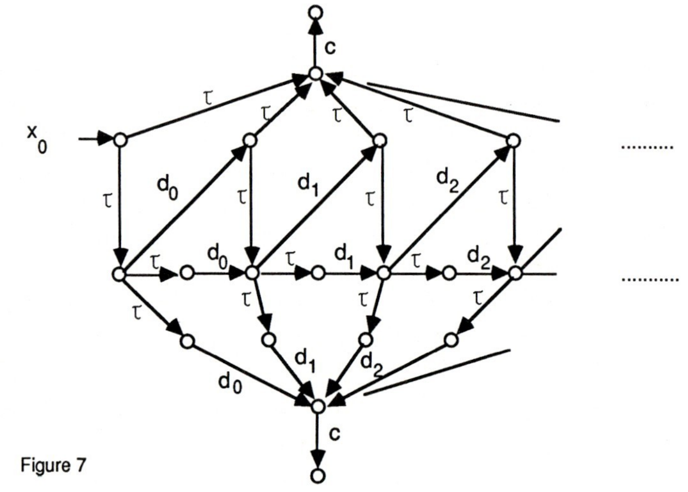

Figure 7

In the axiom system BS the equations for x_0 cannot be simplified any further. This fact is proved by showing that in the model $\mathcal{A}$(BS) none of the nodes in the process graph of x_0 can be collapsed or deleted.

However, looking at communication traces the behaviour of x_0 can be summarised very easily: x_0 outputs the data items $d_0, d_1, d_2, \ldots$ in a row, but at any moment a crash "c" can occur after which no further action happens. In general, such a linear, i.e. trace-like description of processes is often adequate (cf. [Pn]). This observation brings us to the main question of our paper:

> *Can the advantages of fair abstraction be combined with the simplicity of a trace consistent, linear process semantics?*

4.2. Towards a Solution.

We begin with the description of a linear semantics, first with explicit divergence Δ. The simplest way of introducing such a semantics would be to add the linearity axiom

$$x(y + z) = xy + xz \qquad \text{L}$$

to BS_Δ. Unfortunately, we have:

PROPOSITION 3. BS_Δ + L *is trace inconsistent.*

PROOF. Clearly, the equation $a(b + \delta) = ab + a\delta$ is an instance of L. Nevertheless $\underline{trace}(a(b + \delta)) = \underline{trace}(ab) = \{ab\surd\} \neq \{ ab\surd, a\delta\} = \underline{trace}(ab + a\delta)$. □

To achieve trace consistency, we take the more discriminating failure semantics of [BHR]. As shown in [Br, dNH, He, OH, BKO], this semantics enjoys a number of remarkable properties. For example, in [BKO] it is shown that for finite processes without τ failure semantics yields the largest trace consistent congruence. Thus failure semantics identifies as much as possible without producing any trace inconsistency. Moreover, in [dNH, He] it is shown that for (divergence free) processes failure semantics coincides with a so-called acceptance semantics obtained through a very natural idea of testing processes.

Here we axiomatise failure semantics in the presence of τ and Δ. Starting from BS_Δ we add the following axioms with α,β ranging over $A \cup \{\delta,\tau\}$:

$$\alpha(\beta x + u) + \alpha(\beta y + v) = \alpha(\beta x + \beta y + u) + \alpha(\beta x + \beta y + v) \qquad \text{R1}$$

$$\tau x + y = \tau x + \tau(x + y) \qquad \text{T4}$$

$$\frac{\forall k \in \mathbb{N}: \quad x_k = i_k.x_{k+1} + y_k, \quad i_k \in I}{\tau_I(x_0) = \Delta.\tau_I(\Sigma_{k\in\mathbb{N}}\ y_k)} \qquad \text{DE}_\infty$$

The resulting axiom system we call FS_Δ.

Axioms R1 and T4 are derivable from the axioms for failure and acceptance semantics in [Br] and [dNH]. For finite processes R1 completely characterises the readiness semantics of [OH]. This is shown in [BKO] where a complete axiomatisation of that semantics is given. We therefore call R1 the *readiness axiom.* T4 augments Milner's τ-laws T1-3 of bisimulation semantics; it is explicitly listed as a derived axiom in [dNH]. For finite processes T4 and R1 completely characterise the failure semantics. This is proved in [Br, BKO], but also in [dNH] for the equivalent acceptance semantics.

New is our way of dealing with divergence in connection with failure semantics. It is axiomatised in the "infinitary" Delay Rule DE_∞ which extends the"periodical" version DE_n in BS_Δ. To obtain a finite sum in the conclusion, we apply DE_∞ only in case of finitely many different y_k.

We examine the impact of the new axioms in FS_Δ. The readiness axiom R1 is a restricted form of the linearity axiom L; indeed, for $\alpha,\beta \in A \cup \{\delta,\tau\}$ we obtain:

PROPOSITION 4. $FS_\Delta \vdash \alpha(\beta x + \beta y) = \alpha\beta x + \alpha\beta y$.

PROOF. Put $u = v = \delta$ in R1 and use axioms A3 and A6. □

Clearly, this equation is wrong under bisimulation semantics BS_Δ. We demonstrate the effect of Proposition 4 by applying it to the final result of the printer-file example from above. In FS_Δ the equations (B) for x_0 can be simplified drastically, viz. to

(F) $$x_k = \tau.d_k.x_{k+1} + \tau.c$$

where $k \geq 0$. Note that (F) results from (B) by dropping in each equation for y_k the summand

$$+ \tau.d_k.y_{k+1} + \tau.d_k.c \ .$$

The simplicity of (F) is best illustrated by looking at the new process graph for x_0 shown in Figure 8.

Figure 8

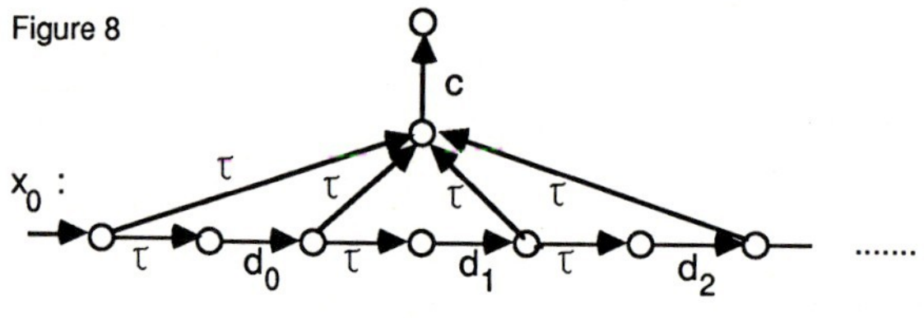

To derive (F) formally from (B), it suffices to show for $k \geq 0$:

$$FS_\Delta \vdash \tau.y_k = \tau.d_k.x_{k+1}.$$

PROOF. $\tau.y_k =$ [def.y_k]
$\tau.(d_k.x_{k+1} + \tau.d_k.y_{k+1} + \tau.d_k.c) =$ [def. x_{k+1}]
$\tau.(d_k(\tau.y_{k+1}+ \tau c) + \tau.d_k.y_{k+1} + \tau.d_k.c) =$ [T1]
$\tau.(d_k(\tau.y_{k+1}+ \tau c) + \tau.d_k.\tau.y_{k+1} + \tau.d_k.\tau c) =$ [twice Prop.4]
$\tau.(d_k(\tau.y_{k+1}+ \tau c) + \tau.d_k(\tau.y_{k+1} + \tau c)) =$ [T2]
$\tau.\ \tau.d_k(\tau.y_{k+1} + \tau c) =$ [T1]
$\tau.d_k(\tau.y_{k+1} + \tau c) =$ [def. x_{k+1}]
$\tau.\ d_k.x_{k+1}$ □

An immediate consequence of the Delay Rule DE_∞ is the finitary rule DE(2):

$$\frac{x_0 = i_0.x_1 + y_0, \quad x_1 = i_1.x_1 + y_1, \quad i_0,i_1 \in I}{\tau_I(x_0) = \Delta.\tau_I(y_0 + y_1)} \qquad DE(2)$$

(Note that DE(2) does not follow from from the "periodical" versions DE_n, $n \geq 1$, of BS_Δ.)

PROOF. To apply DE_∞, replace the second premise of DE(2) by the infinite system of equations

$$x_k = i_k.x_{k+1} + y_1$$

where $k \geq 1$. □

With DE(2) we derive the following fact about Δ:

PROPOSITION 5. (i) $FS_\Delta \vdash \Delta = \Delta\delta + \varepsilon$, (ii) $FS_\Delta \vdash \Delta(x + y) = \Delta x + \Delta y$.

PROOF. For (i) consider the system of equations

$$x_0 = ix_1 + \varepsilon$$
$$x_1 = ix_1 + \delta$$

Then

Δ	=	[A6,8]
$\Delta(\varepsilon + \delta)$	=	[TI1-4]
$\Delta\tau_{\{i\}}(\varepsilon + \delta)$	=	[DE(2)]
$\tau_{(i)}(x_0)$	–	[def.x_0]
$\tau_{\{i\}}(ix_1 + \varepsilon)$	=	[TI1-4]
$\tau.\tau_{\{i\}}(x_1) + \varepsilon$	=	[DE_1]
$\tau\Delta\delta + \varepsilon$	=	[Cor.1]
$\Delta\delta + \varepsilon$.		

Now (ii) follows immediately:

$$\Delta(x + y) = \Delta\delta + x + y = \qquad [A3]$$
$$\Delta\delta + x + \Delta\delta + y = \Delta x + \Delta y.$$

□

The failure specific linearity (ii) of Δ is remarkable in view of the rejected linearity axiom L.

4.3. A Model for FS_Δ.

We obtain a model for the axiom system FS_Δ by taking the process graphs $\mathfrak{G}$ modulo a suitable modification of the failure equivalence ≡ in [Br], called here Δ-failure equivalence $\equiv_\Delta$.

Its definition is based on the mapping F_Δ assigning to each process graph $g \in \mathfrak{G}$ a set

$$\mathfrak{F}_\Delta[g] \subseteq A^* \times \wp(A \cup \{\surd\}) \cup \{\tau\} \cup A^*.\{\surd\} \cup A^*.\{\Delta\}.$$

The elements of this set record the following information:

- failure pairs (σ, X) with $\sigma \in A^*$ and $X \subseteq A \cup \{\surd\}$ record the deadlock possibilities, i.e. the moves that can be refused after σ [BHR, OH];
- the element τ indicates an initial τ-edge in g;
- elements $\sigma\surd$ record complete traces leading to an exit node and elements $\sigma\Delta$ traces leading to a divergence node or a 'subdivergence' node.

Formally, we define for a node s in a process graph g the set

$$init(s) = \{a \mid a \in A \text{ and } \exists t: s \Longrightarrow^a{}_g t\} \cup \{\surd \mid s \text{ is an exit node}\}.$$

Thus init(s) records the initial moves from s and the possibility of termination. Further on, a node is called *stable node* if it is not the starting point of an edge labelled by τ; otherwise it is called *unstable node*. For use only in this section, a node s is called a *subdivergence node* if it can be reached from the root by a trace σρ such that there is a divergence node t reachable by σ from the root. So in particular divergence nodes are subdivergence nodes. It is not required that the subdivergence node s is actually reachable from the divergence node t; however, after inserting a suitable 'τ-jump' (to be defined shortly) s is indeed below t in the graph.

Given a process graph $g \in \mathfrak{G}$ with root r we define $\mathfrak{F}_\Delta[g]$ as the least set satisfying the following conditions:

(F1)	$(\sigma, X) \in \mathfrak{F}_\Delta[g]$		if $r \Longrightarrow^\sigma{}_g s$ for some stable node s and the set $X \subseteq A \cup \{\surd\}$ is disjoint from init(s),
(F2)	τ	$\in \mathfrak{F}_\Delta[g]$	if r is an unstable node,
(F3)	$\sigma\surd$	$\in \mathfrak{F}_\Delta[g]$	if $r \Longrightarrow^\sigma{}_g s$ for some exit node s,
(F4)	$\sigma\Delta$	$\in \mathfrak{F}_\Delta[g]$	if $r \Longrightarrow^\sigma{}_g s$ for some subdivergence node s.

Now, Δ-failure equivalence $\equiv_\Delta$ on $\mathfrak{G}$ is defined by

$$g \equiv_\Delta h \text{ iff } \mathfrak{F}_\Delta[g] = \mathfrak{F}_\Delta[h].$$

Except for its reference to stable nodes, condition F1 is as in [Br]. Conditions F2-4 are not needed in [Br] because only finite processes without termination ε and without Milner's nondeterminism operator + are studied there. In particular, condition F2 ensures, similarly to condition B4 of Δ-bisimilarity in Section 2.3, that Δ-failure equivalence is a congruence even for +. Note that a divergence node does not contribute any failure pair (σ,X) due to the stability requirement in F1. Especially remarkable is clause F4: if there 'subdivergence' is replaced by 'divergence', the resulting equivalence is not a congruence. (This observation is due to R. van Glabbeek.)

We can now state:

THEOREM 2. (i) $\equiv_\Delta$ *is a congruence on* $\mathfrak{G}$. (ii) $\mathfrak{G}/\equiv_\Delta \models FS_\Delta$, *i.e. modulo Δ-failure equivalence the process graphs satisfy all the axioms of* FS_Δ.

Note. The proof is routine, tedious and omitted. We remark that - unlike Theorem 1 - this theorem crucially depends on the restriction that $\mathfrak{G}$ contains only finitely branching graphs.□

Notation: $\mathcal{A}(FS_\Delta) = \mathfrak{G}/\equiv_\Delta$. We remark that the way in which the model $\mathcal{A}(FS_\Delta)$ treats divergence differs from the full failure model [BHR, BR] (see Section 5) and from the acceptance models developed in [dNH, He]. In contrast to these models $\mathcal{A}(FS_\Delta)$ continues to record failure pairs (σ,X) even after a divergence is encountered. It is this model property which enables us to add in Section 6 fair abstraction on top of FS_Δ.

In Proposition 5 we noticed the linearity of Δ in FS_Δ. We can now "explain" this property using a simple process graph transformation that is valid in the model $\mathcal{A}(FS_\Delta)$. This transformation we call the *τ-jump*; it is shown in Figure 9.

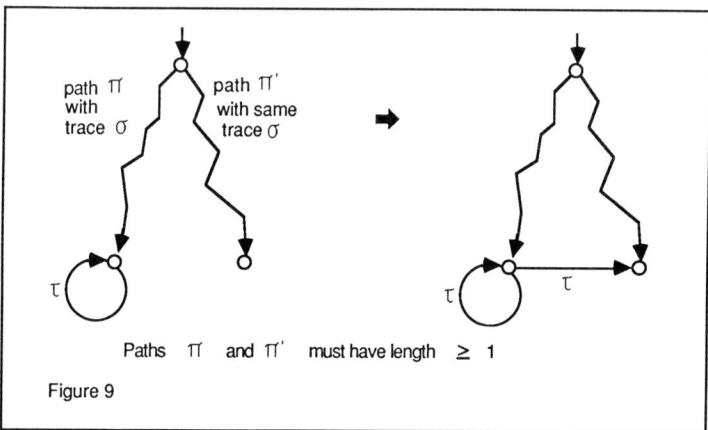

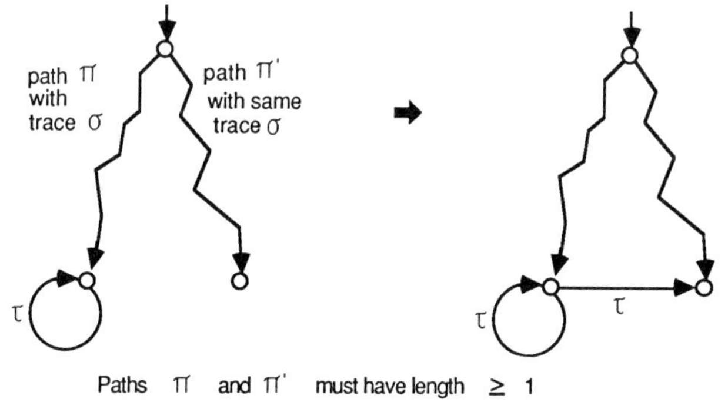

Figure 9

With the τ-jump (and Δ-bisimilarity $\leftrightarrow_\Delta$) we derive in Figure 10 the linearity of Δ pictorially.

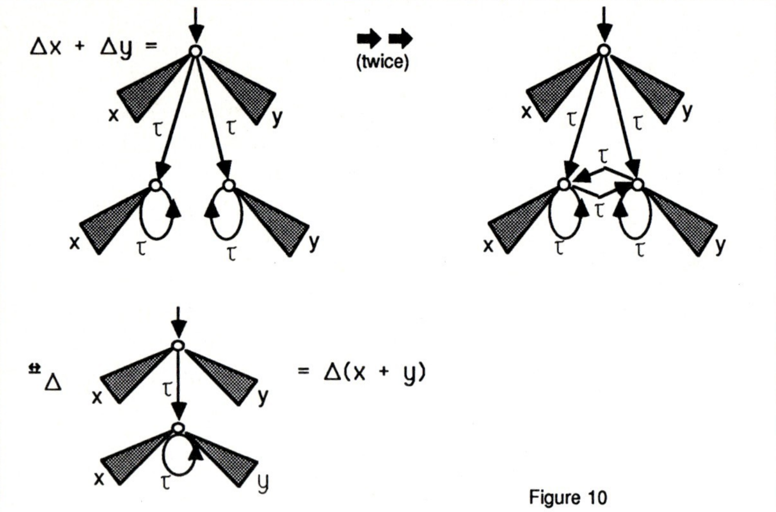

Figure 10

5. Failure Semantics with Catastrophic Divergence: FS_χ

We now come to the main point of our question: can, as in bisimulation semantics BS_Δ, the divergence Δ be abstracted away? Let us try the axiom

$$\Delta = \tau$$

that yields Koomen's Fair Abstraction Rule KFAR when added to BS_Δ. Surprisingly, we can use the linearity of Δ to obtain:

PROPOSITION 6. *The system* $FS_\Delta + (\Delta = \tau)$ *is trace inconsistent.*

PROOF. By Proposition 5, $\Delta = \tau$ implies $\tau(x + y) = \tau x + \tau y$ which is trace inconsistent analogously to Proposition 3. □

Another trace inconsistency of failure semantics directly with KFAR instead of DE_∞ and $\Delta = \tau$ is shown in [BKO].

So how did Brookes, Hoare and Roscoe [BHR], the inventors of failure semantics, manage? They treated divergence as being "catastrophic": all processes with an infinite τ-sequence from the root are identified with the wholly arbitrary process, called CHAOS. We can express their solution by adding to FS_Δ the axiom

$$\Delta\delta = \Delta$$

which states that Δ never terminates. Call the resulting system FS_χ (χ for CHAOS).

PROPOSITION 7. (i) $FS_\chi \vdash \Delta x = \Delta$ (ii) $FS_\chi \vdash \Delta + x = \Delta$.

PROOF. $\Delta + x = \Delta\delta + x =$ [Prop. 5]
$\Delta x = \Delta\delta x =$ [A7]
$\Delta\delta = \Delta$. □

The equations (i) and (ii) characterise Δ as the process CHAOS of [BHR] that makes any distinction of the subsequent or alternative process behaviour impossible.

As a model $\mathcal{A}(FS_\chi)$ for FS_χ essentially the original failure model in [BHR, BR] or the equivalent ("must"-version of) acceptance model in [dNH] suffices.

6. Failure Semantics with Fair Abstraction of Unstable Divergence: FS

6.1. Fair Abstraction.

Thus failure semantics seems unfit for fair abstraction and to point to CHAOS. Also the different versions of acceptance semantics of [dNH, He] do not help here. Nevertheless there is a surprising solution. We can formulate a restricted fair abstraction principle:

$$\Delta\tau = \tau.$$

This axiom says that a process will never stay forever in a cycle of internal τ-steps if it can be exited by another internal τ-step. Since in $\Delta\tau$ the status of being divergent is itself unstable due to the τ we refer to $\Delta\tau$ as *unstable divergence* and to $\Delta\tau = \tau$ as abstraction of unstable divergence.

Let FS be the axiom system $FS_\Delta + (\Delta\tau = \tau)$. In FS the following Fair Abstraction Rule of Unstable Divergence $KFAR^-$ is derivable:

$$\frac{\forall k \in \mathbb{N}:\quad x_k = i_k.x_{k+1} + y_k,\quad i_k \in I \qquad \exists k \in \mathbb{N}\ \exists i \in I\ \exists z:\ y_k = i.z}{\tau_I(x_0) = \tau.\tau_I(\Sigma_{k\in\mathbb{N}}\ y_k)} \qquad KFAR^-$$

PROOF. Applying the rule DE_∞ of FS_Δ to the first premise of $KFAR^-$ yields

$$\tau_I(x_0) = \Delta.\tau_I(\Sigma_{k\in\mathbb{N}}\ y_k).$$

Using the second premise of KFAR⁻ and the failure specific axioms T4 and R1 (more precisely its consequence stated in Proposition 4) we derive further

$$\tau_I(x_0) = \Delta\tau.\tau_I(\Sigma_{k\in\mathbb{N}}\ y_k).$$

A final application of $\Delta\tau = \tau$ yields the consequence of KFAR⁻. □

6.2. Protocol Verification in FS.

An inspection of the algebraic verification of the Alternating Bit [BK 3] and Sliding Window Protocols [Va], which was done in the setting of bisimulation semantics using KFAR, shows that this verification is also possible in the system FS with KFAR⁻. Thus KFAR⁻ is an interesting alternative to KFAR.

We demonstrate this here for the idealised protocol P of Section 3.2. Recall that P satisfies the equations

$$\begin{aligned} P &= send?.P_0 \\ P_0 &= \underline{in}.P_1 \\ P_1 &= \underline{error}.P_0 + \underline{out}.rec!.\underline{ack}.P \end{aligned}$$

and that in order to complete the verification it suffices to show

(*) $\tau_I(P) = send?.rec!.\ \tau_I(P)$

where I := {in, error, out, ack}.

Consider the equations for P_0 and P_1. Since the second summand of P_1 starts with the action $\underline{out} \in I$, the rule KFAR⁻ is applicable and yields:

$$\tau_I(P_0) = \tau.\tau_I(\underline{out}.rec!.\underline{ack}.P).$$

Now we can continue as in Section 3.2:

$$\begin{aligned} \tau_I(P) &= send?.\ \tau_I(P_0) \\ &= send?.\ \tau.\tau_I(\underline{out}.rec!.\underline{ack}.P) \\ &= send?.rec!.\ \tau_I(P). \end{aligned}$$

Hence (*) holds in the axiom system FS.

6.3. A Model for FS.

We first introduce a failure semantics $\mathcal{F}^*$ that assigns to every process graph $g \in \mathbb{G}$ a set

$$\mathcal{F}^*[g] \subseteq A^* \times \wp(A \cup \{\surd\}) \ \cup\ \{\tau\}\ \cup\ A^*.\{\surd\}\ \cup\ A^*.$$

Compared with $\mathfrak{F}_\Delta[g]$ no divergence elements $\sigma\Delta$ appear; instead all (partial) traces $\sigma \in A^*$ are recorded. $\mathfrak{F}^*[g]$ is defined as the least set satisfying the conditions F1-3 of $\mathfrak{F}_\Delta[g]$ but with F4 replaced by the new condition

(F4*) $\quad \sigma \in \mathfrak{F}^*[g] \qquad$ if $r \Longrightarrow^{\sigma}_{g} s$ for the root r and some node s of g.

Defining the new failure equivalence $\equiv^*$ on the graph domain $\mathfrak{G}$ by

$$g \equiv^* h \text{ iff } \mathfrak{F}^*[g] = \mathfrak{F}^*[h],$$

we take as model $\mathcal{A}(FS) = \mathfrak{G}/\equiv^*$.

THEOREM 3. (i) $\equiv^*$ *is a congruence on* $\mathfrak{G}$, (ii) $\mathcal{A}(FS) \models FS$.

We show only, in Figure 11, how the crucial laws $\Delta\tau = \tau$ and $\Delta \neq \tau$ are realised in $\mathcal{A}(FS)$.

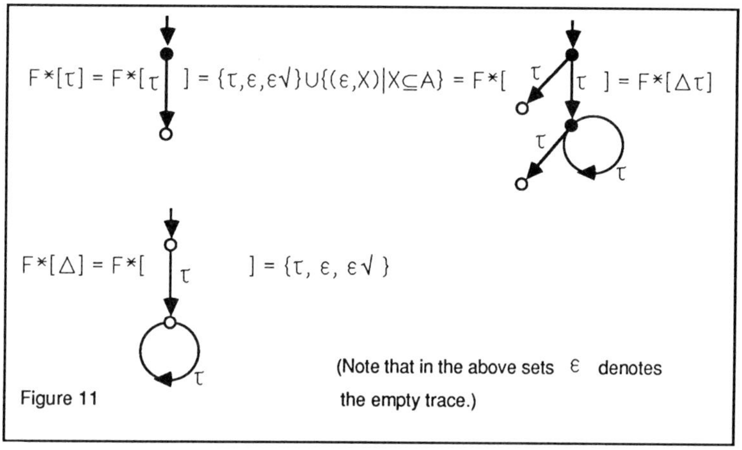
F*[τ] = F*[τ] = {τ,ε,ε√}∪{(ε,X)|X⊆A} = F*[τ τ τ τ] = F*[Δτ]
F*[Δ] = F*[τ τ] = {τ, ε, ε√ }
(Note that in the above sets ε denotes the empty trace.)
Figure 11

Clearly, these laws are not realised in the failure semantics of [BHR, BR] or any of the acceptance semantics of [dNH, He].

7. Conclusion

The axiom systems BS and FS appear to be attractive for algebraic process verification. The advantage of the "branching system" BS is that the full abstraction rule KFAR is available. On the other hand, verifications in BS can be very tedious because so many distinctions are made -

unnecessarily many the supporters of the "linear approach" FS might say. The simplicity of FS over BS is best illustrated by looking at the set Char of finite process terms which are built exclusively from the characteristic processes ε, δ, τ, Δ by means of . and +.

PROPOSITION 8 [KV]. *Under the bisimulation semantics* BS *with fair abstraction* Char *contains infinitely many semantically different processes.*

PROPOSITION 9. *Under the failure semantics* FS *with fair abstraction of unstable divergence every process in* Char *is semantically equal to one of the seven processes:* δ, ε, $\Delta\delta$, Δ, τ, $\tau\delta$, $\tau+\tau\delta$. *These seven processes cannot be collapsed any further without introducing a trace inconsistency.*

A disadvantage of the above axiom systems BS_Δ, BS, FS_Δ, FS_χ and FS is that each of them treats all occurrences of divergence Δ in a process in the same way. Consequently the fairness assumptions represented by KFAR or $KFAR^-$ are only of global nature; in a process built up from several components it is not clear which one is responsible for this global fairness. In our future work we intend to investigate axiom systems where different forms of divergence coexist. An interesting question is whether this idea allows us to deal purely algebraically, i.e. by means of equations only, with local fairness assumptions. If so, this approach would be complementary to the work of Parrow where local fairness is expressed using temporal logic formulas in addition to the algebraic framework [Par].

Acknowledgement. We would like to thank R. van Glabbeek for pointing out to us the difference between our bisimilarity with explicit divergence and the related notion of Milner in [Mi 2].

References

[BBK 1] J.C.M. Baeten, J.A. Bergstra, J.W. Klop, *Syntax and defining equations for an interrupt mechanism in process algebra*, Rep. CS-R8503, CWI, Amsterdam 1985.

[BBK 2] J.C.M. Baeten, J.A. Bergstra, J.W. Klop, *On the consistency of Koomen's Fair Abstraction Rule*, Rep. CS-R8511, CWI, Amsterdam 1985.

[BMOZ] J.W. de Bakker, J.-J.Ch. Meyer, E.-R. Olderog, J.I. Zucker, *Transition systems, infinitary languages and the semantics of uniform concurrency*, in: Proc. 17th ACM STOC, Providence, R.I., 1985.

[BK 1] J.A. Bergstra, J.W. Klop, *Algebra of communicating processes*, to appear in: J.W. de Bakker, M. Hazewinkel, J.K. Lenstra, Eds., Proc. CWI Symp. Math. and Comp. Sci., North-Holland, Amsterdam.

[BK 2] J.A. Bergstra, J.W. Klop, *Process algebra for synchronous communication*, Inform. and Control 60 (1984) 109-137.

[BK 3] J.A. Bergstra, J.W. Klop, *Verification of an alternating bit protocol by means of process algebra*, Rep. CS-R8404, CWI, Amsterdam 1984.

[BK 4] J.A. Bergstra, J.W. Klop, *Algebra of communicating processes with abstraction*, TCS 37 (1985) 77-121.

[BKO] J.A. Bergstra, J.W. Klop, E.-R. Olderog, *Readies and failures in the algebra of communicating processes*, Rep. CS-R8523, CWI, Amsterdam 1985.

[vB] G. v. Bochmann, *Concepts of distributed systems design*, (Springer-Verlag, Berlin, 1983).

[Br] S.D. Brookes, *On the relationship of CCS and CSP*, in: J. Díaz, Ed., Proc. 10th ICALP, Springer-LNCS 154 (1983) 83-96.

[BHR] S.D. Brookes, C.A.R. Hoare, A.W. Roscoe, *A theory of communicating sequential processes*, J.ACM 31 (1984) 560-599.

[BR] S.D. Brookes, A.W. Roscoe, *An improved model for communicating sequential processes*, in: S.D. Brookes, A.W. Roscoe, G. Winskel, Eds., Proc. NSF-SERC Seminar on Concurrency, Springer-LNCS 197 (1985).

[Ha] B. Hailpern, *Verifying concurrent processes using temporal logic*, Springer-LNCS 129, 1982.

[He] M. Hennessy, *Acceptance trees*, J.ACM 32 (1985).

[Ho] C.A.R. Hoare, *Communicating sequential processes*, (Prentice-Hall, London, 1985).

[Ko] C.J. Koomen, *Algebraic specification and verification of communication protocols*, SCP 5 (1985) 1-36.

[KV] C.P.J. Koymans, J.L.M. Vrancken, personal communication.

[Mi 1] R. Milner, *A calculus of communicating systems*, Springer-LNCS 92, 1980.

[Mi 2] R. Milner, *A modal characterisation of observable machine-behaviour*, in: E. Astesiano, C. Böhm (Eds.), Proc. 6th CAAP, Springer-LNCS 112 (1981) 25-34.

[Mi 3] R. Milner, *Calculi for synchrony and asynchrony*, TCS 25 (1983) 267-310.

[dNH] R. de Nicola, M. Hennessy, *Testing equivalences for processes*, TCS 34 (1984) 83-134.

[OH] E.-R. Olderog, C.A.R. Hoare, *Specification-oriented semantics of communicating processes*, Acta Informatica 23 (1986) 9-66.

[Pa] D. Park, *Concurrency and automata on infinite sequences*, in: P. Deussen, Ed., Proc. 5th GI Conf. on Theoret. Comp. Sci., Springer-LNCS 104 (1981).

[Par] J. Parrow, *Fairness properties in process algebra - with applications in communication protocol verification*, Ph.D. thesis, Dept. of Comp. Sci., Uppsala Univ., 1985.

[Pn] A. Pnueli, *Linear and branching structures in the semantics and logics of reactive systems*, in: W. Brauer, Ed., Proc. 12th ICALP, Springer-LNCS 194 (1985) 15-32.

[Ta] A.S. Tanenbaum, *Computer networks*, (Prentice-Hall, Englewood Cliffs, NJ, 1981).

[Va] F. Vaandrager, *Verification of two communication protocols by means of process algebra*, Rep. CS-R8608, CWI, Amsterdam 1986.

QUESTIONS AND ANSWERS

Lauer: Do you speak about local fairness?

Olderog: We consider global fairness. For a process built up from several components I cannot say in this approach which component is responsible for the global fairness.

Pnueli: Can you think of a system in which some of the occurring nondeterminisms would be fair and some of the others will not and perhaps have an axiom similar to $\Delta\tau = \tau$ that will apply only to the fair kinds of nondeterminism and not to the unfair ones?

Olderog: That would be one of the things one should try whether several copies of delay can coexist; so that you have one version of divergence which would be treated in a fair manner (if that is what you are referring to) and other versions which would just stay as signally delayed. I am also considering of using this model for a predicate approach to process verification where I can more easily express (at least for me at the moment) that actually the medium is responsible for fairness. I don´t see at the moment how one could do it algebraically. One would hope that one just could state one more equation which involves symbols dealing with infinitary objects so that it can only be applied to divergences whose origin comes from this medium. At the moment everything is treated in the same manner in all these models. But I look for more distinctions.

de Roever: In the intermission I was talking with a few colleagues about your results. One of them signals that there is something funny going on. You have a nice model obtained by algebraic means. The original model with chaos came out of the goal to make a number of operators consistent with a hiding operator and I believe that this was the original motivation of Tony Hoare and his group in Oxford to introduce this model. You are familiar with this model. You have been in Oxford for a long time. Could you somehow say or does anybody of you have thought whether there is also a denotational model for the operators you study in this paper?

Olderog: I think, for the last model with fair abstraction rules a denotational model can be given. It is just a very simple extension of the trace model with upper inclusion as ordering on which I add information about deadlocks. So I think, what has been done is a sort of separation, that the phenomenon of deadlock is separated from the phenomenon of divergence. And I think, in the original figures about semantics these things were mixed together. So the denotational semantics would be a very minor extension of the trace model with the same sort of ordering: set inclusion. The least element would be the empty trace. It would correspond to a fully divergent process which never gets into stability.

Wirsing: What is the right formalism for program development and systems construction for distributed systems: first-order predicate calculus or the algebraic, equational approach?

Olderog: I sometimes ask myself why is so much done using the algebraic approach? I entered this club to learn about this approach. I think, one of the reasons is that the algebraic approach seems so conceptually simple. You just have to state very few notions (equations, signatures) and then you can start. Moreover, Jos Baeten said it also: there are no hidden assumptions. This seems to be attractive. Every step of the verification has to be done explicitly. However, this is also a disadvantage because you have to do every small step. One has to elaborate a lot to get over all these little steps. And I think, maybe, that by using predicates we could in one description cover more and that some descriptions would be simpler than in the algebraic approach.

Apt: The disadvantage of algebraic approach which I see is a confusing variety of semantics. The point is that, and I think your paper is a good example of these difficulties, that if one wants to use this approach to verify some particular problems then the first issue is with respect to which semantics. Your paper is a case in point that one can use a simpler semantics with respect to which you prove correctness. On the other hand, there is still one hidden assumption why this semantics is sufficient for our purposes, and in this variety of semantics, it is not easy to find a way through.

Olderog: For choosing the right semantics I would always hope that you use some principles like agreeing on a very simple notion of equivalence and then work out the fully abstract model for all the operators. That would be a convincing approach to a model for me. The first equivalence has to be very simple like trace equivalence or saying, I am not interested in processes which diverge. I have to be convinced that some model is good; so one has to start with very few principles and then use some machinery to produce the model which could have more properties because of the context conditions. Then I would be convinced, but otherwise I also would not easily like to use a model which has some nice properties but which you don´t overlook very easily. It´s always the case that, when changing little details in these models, it usually breaks down, an experience, most people have made.

Pnueli: Just a very short comment. I don´t think, this is a disadvantage especially of the algebraic method. In the predicate approach you have exactly the same problem: many models and many different semantics. The logic that we impose is just supposed to characterize a particular model. So I think, the problem of variety and of choosing the semantics is equally bad in both approaches.

Formal Description of Programming Concepts - III
M. Wirsing (Editor)
Elsevier Science Publishers B.V. (North-Holland)
IFIP, 1987

OBSERVATIONAL EQUIVALENCES FOR CONCURRENCY MODELS

*Pierpaolo Degano**, *Rocco De Nicola*+ *and Ugo Montanari**

* Dipartimento di Informatica, Università di Pisa
Corso Italia, 40 – I-56100 PISA, Italy

+ Istituto di Elaborazione dell'Informazione del CNR
Via S. Maria, 46 – I-56100 PISA, Italy

Certain node-labelled trees, called NMS's, are introduced as a framework for dealing with various observational equivalences for concurrent systems. An NMS consists of the finite and infinite computations (ordered by prefix) of a transition system. The label of a node is the observation performed on the corresponding computation. A notion of NMS observational equivalence is introduced as the maximal bisimulation. Depending on the labels we can capture different equivalences. Milner's CCS is used as a test case for our approach. Both an *interleaving* and a *partial ordering observation* for CCS computations are defined, thus inducing two equivalences on CCS agents. In the former case the induced equivalence coincides with Milner's observational equivalence, while in the latter case it is finer exactly in that it distinguishes interleaving of sequential nondeterministic processes from their concurrent execution.

1. INTRODUCTION

In many cases it is useful to have theories for establishing whether two systems are equivalent. For instance, if both the specifications of a system and its implementation are written in the same formalism, then we can use theories based on equivalences to prove that the latter meets the former.

Not surprisingly, many different equivalences have been proposed in the literature for models which are intended to describe and reason about nondeterministic concurrent systems [1, 2, 4, 11, 12]. This is mainly due to the large number of properties which may be relevant to the analysis of such systems. Nevertheless, almost all the equivalences are based on the idea of considering two systems as equivalent whenever no external observation can distinguish them. Most of these equivalences are based on Milner's observational equivalence [16] and defined for (sub-)classes of labelled transition systems [13]. Conceptually, the behaviour of a system is represented by a tree, called *synchronization tree,* the arcs of which are labelled by actions and which can be seen as the unfolding of the transition system itself. Equivalences are based on testing whether, given two trees, pairs of branches can be found which are labelled by the same sequences of actions and end up in related subtrees.

One of the critical issues in defining observations is how the causal/temporal ordering of events is dealt with [7, 14, 15, 20, 21, 22]. Many authors assume that observers are intrisically sequential, and thus describe the occurrence of concurrent events by the set of their nondeterministic interleavings. Even when concurrent observers are assumed, usually only temporal dependencies among (possibly set of contemporary) events are captured, and causal dependencies are lost. When dealing with distributed systems, seen as a collection of spatially distributed processes, causal dependencies play a crucial rôle in defining important properties. In fact it is quite difficult, if at all possible, to recover causal dependencies from temporal dependencies when needed, and the treatment of properties such as fairness or starvation freedom may be awkward.

A straightforward solution to the above problem is to assume that causal dependencies are directly observable. A natural representation is in this case obtained using *partial orderings of events*, where ordered events are causally related and unordered events are concurrent/independent.

It is tempting to refine the various proposed equivalences to deal with observations consisting of partial orderings instead of sequences of events. However, a severe difficulty now arises, since synchronization trees become inadequate. Actually, it is not clear at all how to recover from a path in the given tree the information which is necessary for constructing the partial ordering observation. In fact, whenever two consecutive events are considered, there is no way to know whether they are causally related or concurrent.

In the paper a new class of trees called *Nondeterministic Measurement Systems* (*NMS*'s) is introduced. Given a transition system T, its derived NMS is the tree consisting of the (finite and infinite) computations of T ordered by prefix, labelled with *observations* taken from a set D. Depending on the set D (e.g. sequences, partial orderings, etc.) and the labelling function, we can capture different notions of observation. As done for synchronization trees, various equivalences on NMS's can be defined. Following Park [18] and Milner [17], in this paper we introduce a notion of *NMS observational equivalence* as the maximal bisimulation.

NMS's are a useful tool for dealing with partial orderings, since they allow to define observations directly from computations, instead of composing them from the observations of the single steps. Another advantage is that NMS's possess limit points on their infinite branches, with observations on them; it is thus possible to deal naturally with non-continuous properties, e.g. fairness.

In the paper, Milner's Calculus of Communicating Systems (CCS) is used as a test case for our approach. We use the techniques developed in [5] for definining a new transition system for CCS, D_{CCS}, whose states are sets of sequential processes (obtained from CCS agents via a decomposition function) and whose transitions are defined via a set of inference rules in the usual SOS style [19]. The initial state of the transition system is the decomposition of a given CCS agent. Then, by specializing [10], we define both an *interleaving* and a *partial ordering observation* for computations of D_{CCS}. This association induces an *interleaving* and a *partial ordering NMS observational equivalence* on the set of CCS agents. We show that in the former case, i.e. if NMS's are labelled by sequences of actions, the induced equivalence coincides with Milner's observational equivalence ($\approx$); and that in the latter case, when NMS's are labelled by partial orderings of actions, the induced equivalence is finer than $\approx$ exactly in that it distinguishes interleaving of sequential nondeterministic processes from their concurrent execution.

The paper is organized as follows. Section 2. contains a brief survey of CCS syntax and operational semantics and an introduction to the notion of observational equivalence via bisimulation. Section 3. contains the definition of NMS's and of an observational equivalence over them. It is also shown that observation of Milner's transition system leads to an equivalence over CCS agents which coincides with $\approx$. In Section 4. D_{CCS}, the new transition system for CCS, is introduced, and interleaving and partial ordering observations over it are defined. In the same section also the two equivalences for CCS obtained via the two kind of observations are contrasted and related.

2. CCS

This section contains a brief survey of CCS's syntax and semantics. First, we shall recall the main operators of the calculus, then we will present the traditional interleaving semantics and the observational equivalence of [16].

The concrete syntax of "pure" CCS is defined as follows.

Definition 2.1. (*agents*)
Let

- $\Delta = \{\alpha, \beta, \gamma \dots\}$ be a fixed set and $\Delta^- = \{\alpha^- \mid \alpha \in \Delta\}$;
- $\Lambda = \Delta \cup \Delta^-$ (ranged over by λ) be the set of *visible actions*;
- $\tau \notin \Lambda$ be a distinguished *invisible action*, and $\Lambda \cup \{\tau\}$ be ranged over by μ.

The CCS agents are closed terms (i.e. terms without free variables) which can be generated by the following BNF-like grammar

$$E ::= x \mid NIL \mid \mu E \mid E\backslash\alpha \mid E[\phi] \mid E + E \mid E|E \mid rec\ x.\ E,$$

where x is a variable and ϕ is a permutation of Λ which preserves τ and the operation $^-$ of complementation.
We will let *PROC* denote the set of all CCS agents, ranged over by E. ♦

CCS has a two level semantics: the first level describes the behaviour of agents through an abstract machine and the second level forgets their internal structure by identifying those machines which all exhibit the same external behaviour.

The first level, i.e. the interleaving operational semantics, is based on labelled transition systems, the transition relation of which is defined by a set of transition rules over agents. A relation $—\mu\rightarrow$, called *derivation relation*, is defined, with the intuition that agent E_1 may evolve to become agent E_2 either by reacting to a λ-stimulus from its environment ($E_1—\lambda\rightarrow E_2$) or by performing an internal action which is independent of the environment ($E_1—\tau\rightarrow E_2$).

Definition 2.2. (*transitions*)
Milner's derivation relation $E_1—\mu\rightarrow E_2$ is defined as the least relation satisfying the following axiom and inference rules.

Act) $\mu E—\mu\rightarrow E$

Res) $E_1—\mu\rightarrow E_2$ **implies** $E_1\backslash\alpha—\mu\rightarrow E_2\backslash\alpha, \quad \mu \notin \{\alpha,\alpha^-\}$

Rel) $E_1—\mu\rightarrow E_2$ **implies** $E_1[\phi]—\phi(\mu)\rightarrow E_2[\phi]$

Sum) $E_1—\mu\rightarrow E_2$ **implies** $E_1+E—\mu\rightarrow E_2$ **and** $E+E_1—\mu\rightarrow E_2$

Com) $E_1 \text{—}\mu\text{→} E_2$ **implies** $E_1|E \text{—}\mu\text{→} E_2|E$ **and** $E|E_1 \text{—}\mu\text{→} E|E_2$

$E_1 \text{—}\lambda\text{→} E_2$ **and** $E'_1 \text{—}\lambda^{-}\text{→} E'_2$ **implies** $E_1|E'_1 \text{—}\tau\text{→} E_2|E'_2$

Rec) $E_1[\text{rec } x.\ E_1/x] \text{—}\mu\text{→} E_2$ **implies** $\text{rec } x.\ E_1 \text{—}\mu\text{→} E_2$. ♦

Hereto, we will use the following conventions to talk about sequences of actions and sequences of visible actions:

- $E = \varepsilon => E'$, ε being the null string of Λ^*, stands for $E \text{—}\tau^n\text{→} E'$, $n \geq 0$;
- $E = \lambda => E'$, stands for there exist E_1 and E_2 such that

  $E = \varepsilon => E_1 \text{—}\lambda\text{→} E_2 = \varepsilon => E'$;
- $E = s => E'$, $s = \lambda_1 \ldots \lambda_n \in \Lambda^+$, stands for there exist E_i, $0 < i < n$, such that

  $E = E_0 = \lambda_1 => E_1 = \lambda_2 => \ldots = \lambda_n => E_n = E'$;
- the relation $=s=>$, $s \in \Lambda^*$ will be referred as *many step derivation.*

The derivation relation of Definition 2.2. completely specifies the operational semantics of CCS; the second level of CCS semantics is obtained by abstracting from unwanted details. To this purpose, a notion of observational equivalence is introduced which is based on the notion of bisimulation [18] and which improves upon the notion of observational equivalence proposed in [16]. Below we introduce the notion of bisimulation by following [17].

Definition 2.3. (*bisimulation and observational equivalence*)

1. If $\mathfrak{R}$ is a relation over CCS agents, then Ψ, a function from relations to relations, is defined as follows

   $<E_1, E_2> \in \Psi(\mathfrak{R})$ if, for all $s \in \Lambda^*$,

   i) whenever $E_1 = s => E'_1$ then there exists E'_2, $E_2 = s => E'_2$ and $<E'_1, E'_2> \in \mathfrak{R}$

   ii) whenever $E_2 = s => E'_2$ then there exists E'_1, $E_1 = s => E'_1$ and $<E'_1, E'_2> \in \mathfrak{R}$.
2. A relation $\mathfrak{R}$ is a *bisimulation* if $\mathfrak{R} \subseteq \Psi(\mathfrak{R})$.
3. Relation $\approx$, defined as $\approx\, = \cup \{\mathfrak{R} \mid \mathfrak{R} \subseteq \Psi(\mathfrak{R})\}$, is called *observational equivalence.* ♦

Proposition 2.1.

- Function Ψ is monotonic on the lattice of relations under inclusion.
- Relation $\approx$ is a bisimulation.
- Relation $\approx$ is an equivalence relation.

Loosely speaking, two agents E_1 and E_2 are considered as equivalent, written $E_1 \approx E_2$, iff there exists a relation $\mathfrak{R}$, called *bisimulation,* which contains the pair $<E_1, E_2>$ and guarantees that E_1 and E_2 must be able to perform equal sequences of visible actions evolving to equal (up to $\mathfrak{R}$) agents.
Below we propose two pairs of equivalent processes. The first shows that the bisimulation based

equivalence succeeds in ignoring the internal structure of agents; the second shows that concurrent and nondeterministic processes are sometimes identified.

Example 2.1.

a. $\alpha(\beta NIL + \tau\gamma NIL) + \alpha\gamma NIL \approx \alpha(\beta NIL + \tau\gamma NIL)$;

b. $\alpha NIL \mid \beta NIL \approx \alpha\beta NIL + \beta\alpha NIL$ (see also Figure 3.1.a)).

Here, the relevant bisimulations are

a. $\{\langle\alpha(\beta NIL + \tau\gamma NIL) + \alpha\gamma NIL, \alpha(\beta NIL + \tau\gamma NIL)\rangle\} \cup ID$

b. $\{\langle\alpha NIL \mid \beta NIL, \alpha\beta NIL + \beta\alpha NIL\rangle, \langle NIL \mid \beta NIL, \beta NIL\rangle, \langle\alpha NIL \mid NIL, \alpha NIL\rangle,$
$\langle NIL \mid NIL, NIL\rangle\} \cup ID$,
where $ID = \{\langle E, E\rangle\}$. ♦

3. TRANSITION SYSTEMS AND EQUIVALENCES

We first give some simple notions about transition systems; then we define our observation device on them.

Definition 3.1. (*transition systems*)
A *transition system* is a quadruple $<Q, T, c, q_0>$ where

- Q is a countable set of *states*;
- T is a countable set of *transitions*;
- $c : T \rightarrow Q \times Q$ is a function giving for every transition its *initial* and its *final* state;
- $q_0 \in Q$ is the *initial* state.

A *computation* is a finite or infinite path (understood as a sequence of **occurrences** of both states and transitions) starting from q_0. ♦

A transition system is a purely operational, intensional model. To make transition systems more extensional, we may simply define an equivalence relation on them. To this purpose it is convenient to derive from a transition system a device called Nondeterministic Measurement System.

Definition 3.2. (*observation function*)
Given a transition system T, an *observation function* **o** is a function from the computations of T to a set D, called *observations*. ♦

Definition 3.3. (*from transition systems to NMS's*)
Given a transition system T and an observation function **o** from its computations to a set D, the *derived Nondeterministic Measurement System* (*NMS*) is the node-labelled tree consisting of the computations of T ordered by prefix, labelled via **o**.
An *fd-subtree* of an NMS t is an NMS t' consisting of a node of t at finite depth, together with all its descendents. Sometimes we identify a subtree with its root. ♦

Here, the purpose of the observation function is to abstract out the relevant information from the computation.

Note that NMS's may have an uncountable number of nodes, since they contain the limit points on their infinite branches. Note also that NMS's are cpo's.

Next step addresses the definition of equivalence relations on NMS's having the same set of observations.

Definition 3.4. (*NMS observational equivalence*)

1. If $\Im$ is a relation over NMS's, then Φ, a function from relations to relations, is defined as follows: $<t, u> \in \Phi(\Im)$ if
   - i) the labels of the roots of t and u are the same;
   - ii) for every fd-subtree t' of t there exists an fd-subtree u' of u such that $<t',u'> \in \Im$;
   - iii) for every fd-subtree u' of u there exists an fd-subtree t' of t such that $<t',u'> \in \Im$;
2. A relation $\Im$ is a *bisimulation* if $\Im \subseteq \Phi(\Im)$.
3. Relation $\cong$, defined as $\cong \; = \; \cup \{\Im \mid \Im \subseteq \Phi(\Im)\}$, is called *NMS observational equivalence.* ♦

Proposition 3.1.

- Function Φ is monotonic on the lattice of relations under inclusion.
- Relation $\cong$ is a bisimulation.
- Relation $\cong$ is an equivalence relation.

Of course many other equivalence relations, both finer and coarser, can be defined. For instance, we can define equivalence relations based on NMS isomorphism or based on the equality of the sets of observations of terminal computations (trace equivalence). Another example is testing equivalence [11], which requires for NMS's to be equivalent that they have the same sets of labels and have the successors of every set of nodes with the same label in a certain relation (must–may). We have considered $\cong$ because we want to directly compare our NMS observational equivalence with Milner's. As proved by Theorem 3.1. below, the two equivalences coincide when the transition system and the observation function are defined in the obvious way.

Definition 3.5. (*the classical transition system for CCS*)

Given a CCS agent E, the transition system $T_{CCS}(E)$ for CCS is $<Q, T, c, q_0>$ where

- Q = PROC;
- $T = \{E_1 \overset{\mu}{\longrightarrow} E_2\}$;
- $c(E_1 \overset{\mu}{\longrightarrow} E_2) = <E_1, E_2>$;
- $q_0 = E$. ♦

Definition 3.6. (*observation function for CCS*)

Given a finite computation of $T_{CCS}(E_1)$ corresponding to $E_1 \overset{s}{\Longrightarrow} E_2$, its observation, through the observation function ***obs***, is the string s.

The observations of infinite computations are irrelevant. ♦

In Figure 3.1. below, we show the synchronization tree (part **a**)) and the NMS derived via **obs** (part **b**)) of the CCS agent $\alpha\beta NIL + \beta\alpha NIL$ of Example 2.1.b).

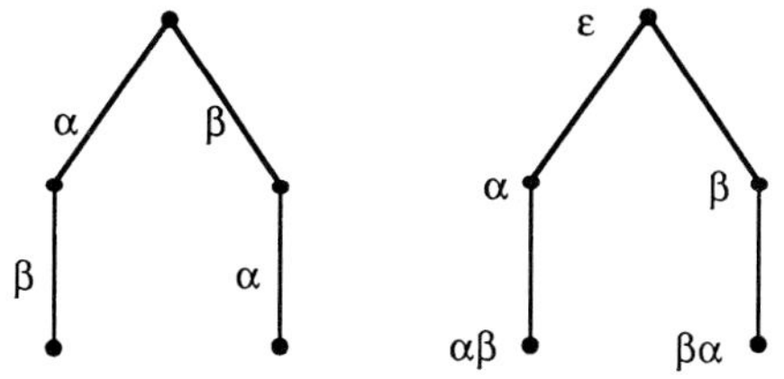

Figure 3.1. The synchronization tree (part **a)**) and the NMS derived via **obs** (part **b)**) of the CCS agent αβNIL + βαNIL.

Definition 3.7. (*NMS observational equivalence via **obs** for CCS*)
Given two CCS agents E_1 and E_2, E_1 is *observationally equivalent* to E_2 *via **obs***, written $E_1 \cong_{\mathbf{obs}} E_2$, whenever the NMS's derived from $T_{CCS}(E_1)$ and $T_{CCS}(E_2)$ via **obs** are in ≅. ♦

Theorem 3.1. (*NMS observational equivalence via **obs** is Milner's observational equivalence*)
Given two CCS agents E_1 and E_2, $E_1 \approx E_2$ if and only if $E_1 \cong_{\mathbf{obs}} E_2$.

Proof. The proof relies on three propositions which follow from Definition 3.4. . Let **pref**(s,t) be a function which, given a finite string s and an NMS t, prefixes with s all the strings labelling the nodes of t. Below t(E) will denote the derived NMS (via **obs**) of $T_{CCS}(E)$.

i) If $\mathfrak{I}$ is an NMS bisimulation then also
$$\mathfrak{I}_1 = \mathfrak{I} \cap \{<\mathbf{pref}(s, t(E_1)), \mathbf{pref}(s, t(E_2))> \mid s \in \Lambda^* \text{ and } E_1, E_2 \in \text{PROC}\})$$
is an NMS bisimulation;

ii) If E_1=s=>E'_1 then there exists a subtree t of $t(E_1)$ such that t = **pref**(s, $t(E'_1)$);

iii) If t is a subtree of $t(E_1)$ such that its root is labelled by s then there exists E'_1 such that E_1=s=>E'_1 and t = **pref**(s, $t(E'_1)$).

We prove that ≈ implies $\cong_{\mathbf{obs}}$. It suffices to show that given any bisimulation relation $\mathfrak{R}$ such that $<E_1, E_2> \in \mathfrak{R}$, it is possible to define a new relation $\mathfrak{I}$ such that $<t(E_1), t(E_2)> \in \mathfrak{I}$ and $\mathfrak{I} \subseteq \Phi(\mathfrak{I})$. Indeed if we let
$$\mathfrak{I} = \{<\mathbf{pref}(s, t(E_1)), \mathbf{pref}(s, t(E_2))> \mid s \in \Lambda^* \text{ and } <E_1, E_2> \in \mathfrak{R}\})$$
the claim follows from (iii) above.

We prove that $\cong_{\mathbf{obs}}$ **implies ≈.** Similarly, given an NMS bisimulation $\mathfrak{I}$ such that $<t(E_1), t(E_2)> \in \mathfrak{I}$, we can use (i) above to define a bisimulation $\mathfrak{I}_1$ which contains only pairs of NMS's which correspond to CCS agents and which is such that $<t(E_1), t(E_2)> \in \mathfrak{I}_1$. We can then use $\mathfrak{I}_1$ to define an $\mathfrak{R}$ such that $<E_1, E_2> \in \mathfrak{R}$ and $\mathfrak{R} \subseteq \Psi(\mathfrak{R})$. Indeed (ii) above guarantees that
$$\mathfrak{R} = \{<E_1, E_2> \mid s \in \Lambda^* \text{ and } <\mathbf{pref}(s, t(E_1)), \mathbf{pref}(s, t(E_2))> \in \mathfrak{I}\}$$
is the wanted bisimulation. ♦

According to our definition, NMS's contain their limit points as well. However, the previous application to CCS (and also the rest of the paper) does not take any advantage of them in defining the observational equivalence, since only fd-trees are considered and limit points are always ignored.

On the contrary, limit points are needed for defining equivalences which take into account non-continuous properties of computations. A tipical example is fairness. In order to deal with this property, it is sufficient to define an observation which distinguishes fair infinite computations from unfair ones. The following example applies this approach to CCS.

Example 3.1.

Let $\cong_{\mathbf{f\_obs}}$ be defined as $\cong_{\mathbf{obs}}$, except that

- **f_obs** is defined on infinite computations yielding 'fair' ('unfair'), according to a given definition (e.g. [3]);
- in the definition of the NMS observational equivalence relation $\cong$, subtrees are considered instead of fd-subtrees.

Consider for instance the following CCS agents

E_1 = (rec x. αx) | rec x. αx

E_2 = ((rec x. αβx) | rec x. αβ¯x)\β.

We have that $E_1 \approx E_2$, but not that $E_1 \cong_{\mathbf{f\_obs}} E_2$. ♦

4. A CASE STUDY: INTERLEAVING AND PARTIAL ORDERING NMS OBSERVATIONAL EQUIVALENCES FOR CCS

4.1. D_{CCS}: a new transition system for CCS

The operational semantics for CCS presented in Section 2 does not consider the operator "|" for parallel composition of processes as primitive: given any finite agent containing |, there always exists another agent without | which exhibits the same behaviour. In this section we present a new operational semantics for CCS essentially borrowed from [5], which allows to consider the parallel operator as a first class one. Again, the SOS approach of [19] is taken, but a different notion of *partial ordering transition* is defined which relates parts of CCS agents, rather than whole global states. CCS agents are decomposed into sets of sequential processes, called grapes, and the new transition relation not only tells the actions an agent E may perform, but also tells the parts of E which move and the parts which stay idle when a transition occurs. This operational semantics has also been used as the starting point for defining a translation of general CCS agents into certain Petri Nets [6].

Definition 4.1. (*defining CCS sequential processes*)
A *grape* is a term defined by the following BNF-like grammar

$G ::= E \mid id|G \mid G|id \mid G\backslash\alpha \mid G[\phi]$

where E, $\backslash\alpha$, $[\phi]$ have the standard CCS meaning. ♦

Intuitively speaking, a grape represents a subterm of a CCS agent, together with its access path. A CCS agent can be decomposed by function dec into a set of grapes.

Definition 4.2. (*decomposing a CCS agent into its sequential processes*)
The function dec decomposes a CCS agent into a set of grapes and is defined by structural induction as follows:

$dec(x) = \{x\}$

$dec(NIL) = \{NIL\}$

$dec(\mu E) = \{\mu E\}$

$dec(E\backslash\alpha) = dec(E)\backslash\alpha$

$dec(E[\phi]) = dec(E)[\phi]$

$dec(E_1+E_2) = \{E_1+E_2\}$

$dec(E_1|E_2) = dec(E_1)|id \cup id|dec(E_2)$

$dec(rec\ x.\ E) = \{rec\ x.\ E\}$. ♦

We understand constructors as extended to operate on sets, e.g. $I\backslash\alpha = \{g\backslash\alpha \mid g \in I\}$. Note that the decomposition stops when an action, a sum or a recursion is encountered, since these are considered as atomic sequential processes.

Example 4.1.

$dec((((recx.\ \alpha x+\beta x) \mid recx.\ \alpha x+\gamma x) \mid recx.\ \alpha^{-}x)\backslash\alpha) = \{p_0, p_1, p_2\}$, where

$p_0 = (((recx.\alpha x+\beta x)|id)|id)\backslash\alpha;$

$p_1 = ((id|recx.\ \alpha x+\gamma x)|id)\backslash\alpha;$

$p_2 = (id|recx.\ \alpha^{-}x)\backslash\alpha.$ ♦

Example 4.2.

$dec(\alpha NIL \mid (\beta^{-}NIL \mid \gamma(\beta\beta NIL \mid \delta NIL))) = \{g_0, g_1, g_2\}$, where

$g_0 = \alpha NIL|id;$

$g_1 = id|(\beta^{-}NIL|id);$

$g_2 = id|(id|\gamma(\beta\beta NIL \mid \delta NIL)).$ ♦

Definition 4.3.

A set I of grapes is *complete* if there exists a CCS agent E such that dec(E)=I. ♦

Property 4.1.

Function dec is injective and thus defines a bijection between CCS agents and complete sets of grapes.

Proof. Immediate by induction. ♦

Note that the inverse function of dec is standard unification, provided that distinct variables are substituted for each occurrence of id, and $\{\mu E\}$, $\{E_1+E_2\}$ and {rec x. E} are considered atomic. In other words, the most general unifier of a complete set of grapes I is the CCS agent of which I is the decomposition.

The new transitions have the form $I_1-[\mu, I_3]\rightarrow I_2$, whose intuitive meaning is that the set of grapes I_1 may become the set I_2 by performing the action μ, while the grapes in I_3, a subset of I_1 and I_2, stay idle. It should be noted that the new axioms and inference rules are in direct correspondence with those of Section 2.

Definition 4.4. (*partial ordering derivation relation*)

The *partial ordering derivation relation* $I_1 \text{—}[\mu,I_3]\rightarrow I_2$ is defined as the least relation satisfying the following axiom and inference rules.

act)	$\{\mu E\}\text{—}[\mu,\Phi]\rightarrow dec(E)$		
res)	$I_1\text{—}[\mu,I_3]\rightarrow I_2$	**implies**	$I_1\backslash\alpha\text{—}[\mu,I_3\backslash\alpha]\rightarrow I_2\backslash\alpha,\quad \mu\notin\{\alpha,\alpha^{-}\}$
rel)	$I_1\text{—}[\mu,I_3]\rightarrow I_2$	**implies**	$I_1[\phi]\text{—}[\phi(\mu), I_3[\phi]]\rightarrow I_2[\phi]$
sum)	$dec(E_1)\text{—}[\mu,I_3]\rightarrow I_2$	**implies**	$\{E_1+E\}\text{—}[\mu,\Phi]\rightarrow I_2$
		and	$\{E+E_1\}\text{—}[\mu,\Phi]\rightarrow I_2$

com) $I_1 —[\mu,I_3]\rightarrow I_2$

implies $I_1|id \cup id|dec(E) —[\mu,I_3|id \cup id|dec(E)]\rightarrow I_2|id \cup id|dec(E)$

and $id|I_1 \cup dec(E)|id —[\mu, id|I_3 \cup dec(E)|id]\rightarrow id|I_2 \cup dec(E)|id$

$I_1 —[\lambda,I_3]\rightarrow I_2$ **and** $I'_1 —[\lambda^-,I'_3]\rightarrow I'_2$

implies $I_1|id \cup id|I'_1 —[\tau,I_3|id \cup id|I'_3]\rightarrow I_2|id \cup id|I'_2$

rec) $dec(E_1[rec\ x.\ E_1/x]) —[\mu,I_3]\rightarrow I_2$ **implies** $\{rec\ x.\ E_1\} —[\mu,\Phi]\rightarrow I_2$. ♦

We can now shortly comment about our axiom and rules. In axiom **act**), a single grape is rewritten as a set of grapes, since the firing of the action makes explicit the (possible) parallelism of E. A move generated by the rule **sum**) can be understood as consisting of two steps. Starting from the singleton $\{E_1+E\}$ or $\{E+E_1\}$ a first step discards alternative E and decomposes E_1 into I_1 while a second step (the condition of the inference rule) rewrites I_1 as I_2, where I_3 stays idle. The net effect of the two steps, however, is to rewrite the singleton $\{E_1+E\}$ or $\{E+E_1\}$ into the set I_2 with no idle grapes. The first rule for **com**) can be read as follows. If we have a move where I_1 is rewritten as I_2 while I_3 stays idle, we can add in parallel to I_1 and I_2 a complete set of grapes dec(E) which stays idle. The second rule for **com**) is the synchronization rule.

The above rules are essentially the same as in [5]. The main difference is that here I_1 and I_2 are the sets of all sequential processes involved, while in [5] they are only the sets of the active ones; furthermore, in [5] the rules are parametrized with respect to the synchronization algebra. More precisely, if $I_1 —[\mu,I_3]\rightarrow I_2$ is the relation defined here and $I'_1 —[L',I'_3]\rightarrow I'_2$ is the relation defined in [5] (with syn(L') $\neq$ synerror), we have μ=syn(L'); $I_3=I'_3$; $I'_1=I_1-I_3$; and $I'_2=I_2-I_3$, where syn is the synchronization function of CCS. The reason of the main change is that in [5] the underlying model was a rewriting system, while here it is a transition system.

Property 4.2.

Given a quadruple $I_1 —[\mu,I_3]\rightarrow I_2$

i) I_1 and I_2 are complete sets of grapes;

ii) $I_3 \subset I_1$ and $I_3 \subset I_2$;

iii) I_1-I_3 contains either one or two grapes.

Proof. The proof of items (i) and (ii) is immediate by induction; that of (iii) follows from the synchronization algebra of CCS. ♦

The direct correspondence between Milner's derivation relation and the above defined one is stressed by the following theorem.

Theorem 4.1. (*correspondence between Milner's and partial ordering derivations*)

We have a derivation $E_1 —\mu\rightarrow E_2$ iff there exists a set of grapes I_3 such that

$dec(E_1) —[\mu,I_3]\rightarrow dec(E_2)$.

Proof. Given a derivation, use the structure of its deduction to obtain the other derivation. ♦

The theorem below, which will be useful in successive proofs, throws light on the asynchronous nature of our partial ordering derivation relation for CCS.

Theorem 4.2. (*idle processes can always be added*)
Given a quadruple $H \cup I_3$—$[\mu,I_3]$→$T\cup I_3$ in the partial ordering derivation relation, and a set I'_3 such that $H\cup I'_3$ is complete, also $H\cup I'_3$—$[\mu,I'_3]$→ $T\cup I'_3$ is in the partial ordering derivation relation.

Proof. The proof is by induction on the deduction structure of the quadruple. The base step is when the quadruple has been obtained by **act**) and is trivial, since $I'_3=I_3=\Phi$. Also if the deduction step is an inference of type **sum**) or **rec**), the inductive step is trivial, since $I'_3=I_3=\Phi$. If the quadruple has been derived using **res**), let I_3 by inductive hypothesis be the most general set of grapes completing both H and T. Then, the most general I'_3 which completes both $H\backslash\alpha$ and $T\backslash\alpha$ is exactly $I_3\backslash\alpha$. The same argument holds in case of **rel**). Let us consider now the first **com**) rule. The most general I'_3 completing H|id and T|id is the union of I_3|id (I_3 completes by hypothesis H and T) and of id|dec(E). The proof of the remaining two **com**) rules is similar. ♦

As for Milner's derivation rules, we can use Definition 4.4 to obtain a new transition system for CCS which now contains also information about the moves of the single sequential processes.

Definition 4.5. (*from CCS agents to the new transition systems*)
Given a CCS agent E, let $D_{CCS}(E) = <Q, T, c, q_0>$ be its *associated* transition system, where:

- the states in Q are the complete sets of grapes;
- $T = \{I_1$—$[\mu,I_3]$→ $I_2\}$;
- $c(I_1$—$[\mu,I_3]$→ $I_2) = <I_1,I_2>$;
- $q_0 = dec(E)$. ♦

Example 4.3. Let us consider the CCS agent of Example 4.1.

$E = (((recx.\ \alpha x+\beta x)\ |\ recx.\ \alpha x+\gamma x)\ |\ recx.\ \bar{\alpha} x)\backslash\alpha$.

The transition system $D_{CCS}(E) = <Q, T, c, dec(E)>$ has as reachable state only the initial state

$q_0 = \{p_0, p_1, p_2\}$, where

$p_0 = (((recx.\alpha x+\beta x)|id)|id)\backslash\alpha$;

$p_1 = ((id|recx.\ \alpha x+\gamma x)|id)\backslash\alpha$;

$p_2 = (id|recx.\ \bar{\alpha} x)\backslash\alpha$;

and the following four transitions

$u_0 : q_0$—$[\tau,\{p_1\}]$→q_0;

$u_1 : q_0$—$[\beta,\{p_1, p_2\}]$→q_0;

$u_2 : q_0$—$[\gamma,\{p_0, p_2\}]$→q_0;

$u_3 : q_0$—$[\tau,\{p_0\}]$→q_0. ♦

4.2. Observations

4.2.1. Interleaving Observations

Given a computation in D_{CCS}, we define its interleaving observation to be the string consisting of the (labels of) the occurred visible events.

Definition 4.6. (*interleaving observation function*)
Given a finite computation

$\xi = \{I_0\ I_0 —[\mu_1,I_{1,3}]\rightarrow I_1\ I_1 \ldots\ I_{n-1} —[\mu_n,I_{n,3}]\rightarrow I_n\ I_n\}$

of the transition system $D_{CCS}(E) = <Q, T, c, dec(E)>$ associated to the CCS agent E, its *interleaving observation* is just the sequence of its visible actions, i.e. it is the sequence obtained through the following observation function **int**.

$\mathbf{int}(\varepsilon) = \varepsilon$

$\mathbf{int}(I_i\ I_i —[\tau,I_{i+1,3}]\rightarrow I_{i+1}\ I_{i+1} \ldots\ I_{n-1} —[\mu_n,I_{n,3}]\rightarrow I_n\ I_n) =$
$\mathbf{int}(I_{i+1} \ldots\ I_{n-1} —[\mu_n,I_{n,3}]\rightarrow I_n\ I_n)$

$\mathbf{int}(I_i\ I_i —[\lambda,I_{i+1,3}]\rightarrow I_{i+1}\ I_{i+1} \ldots\ I_{n-1} —[\mu_n,I_{n,3}]\rightarrow I_n\ I_n) =$
$\lambda\ \mathbf{int}(I_{i+1} \ldots\ I_{n-1} —[\mu_n,I_{n,3}]\rightarrow I_n\ I_n)$

The observations of infinite computations are irrelevant. ♦

Definition 4.7. (*NMS interleaving equivalence for CCS*)
Given two CCS agents E_1 and E_2, E_1 is *NMS observationally equivalent* to E_2 *via* ***int***, written $E_1 \cong_{\mathbf{int}} E_2$, whenever the NMS's derived from $D_{CCS}(E_1)$ and $D_{CCS}(E_2)$ via **int** are in $\cong$. ♦

Lemma 4.1. (*Milner's many step derivations are interleaving observations*)
Given a CCS agent E and its associated transition system $D_{CCS}(E)$, we have that E=s=>E' iff there exists a computation ξ of $D_{CCS}(E)$ ending at dec(E') such that $\mathbf{int}(\xi) = s$.

Proof. Given a sequence of derivations $E=E_0 —\mu_1\rightarrow E_1 \ldots E_{n-1} —\mu_n\rightarrow E_n=E'$ such that E=s=>E', a corresponding computation of $D_{CCS}(E)$ can be found having as transitions (with $dec(E_i)$ and $dec(E_{i+1})$ as initial and final states) the partial ordering derivations $dec(E_i) —[\mu_{i+1},I_{i+1}]\rightarrow dec(E_{i+1})$ by Theorem 4.1.; and viceversa. Since **int** and =s=> simply forget τ's, the thesis follows. ♦

Theorem 4.3. (NMS *interleaving equivalence corresponds to Milner's observational equivalence*)
Given two CCS agents E_1 and E_2, $E_1 \approx E_2$ if and only if $E_1 \cong_{\mathbf{int}} E_2$.

Proof. Given a CCS term E, by Lemma 4.1. the NMS derived from $T_{CCS}(E)$ via **obs** and the NMS derived from $D_{CCS}(E)$ via **int** are isomorphic. The thesis follows from Theorem 3.1.. ♦

4.2.2. Partial Ordering Observations

In this subsection we define partial orderings observations for computations of D_{CCS}. We generate from a computation the events together with their complete causal dependencies. Observations are obtained in three steps: first an event is associated to every transition; then the grapes (of two successive states) which stay idle in a transition are identified; and finally all grapes are removed to be left with a causal relation between events.

Definition 4.8. (*partial ordering of events*)
Let A be a countable set of *event labels*.
A *partial ordering of events* $h \in H$ is a triple $<S, l, \leq>$, where

- S is a set of *events*;
- $l : S \to A$ is a *labelling function*;
- $\leq$ is a partial ordering relation on S, called *causal relation.*

In the following only finite partial orderings of events will be considered.
Two events e_1 and e_2 are *concurrent* if neither $e_1 \leq e_2$ nor $e_2 \leq e_1$.
Two partial ordering of events will be identified if *isomorphic*, i.e. if there is a label- and order-preserving bijection between their events. ♦

Figure 4.2. shows a partial ordering of events, with the conventions that events are represented by circles with their labels inside, and that the partial ordering $\leq$ is represented by its Hasse diagram growing downwards. So, we have that event labelled by α has no relation with the other three events, thus is concurrent with them all. Event labelled by γ dominates, i.e. *causes* both the remaining events, which in turn are concurrent.

Definition 4.9. (*partial ordering observation function*)
Given a finite computation ξ of the transition system $D_{CCS}(E)$ associated to CCS agent E,

$$\xi = \{I_0\ I_0 \text{—}[\mu_1, I_{1,3}] \rightarrow I_1\ I_1 \ldots I_{n-1} \text{—}[\mu_n, I_{n,3}] \rightarrow I_n\ I_n\},$$

its *partial ordering observation* is the partial ordering of events defined by the following procedure which implements the observation function **po**.

1. For every transition occurrence $I_i \text{—}[\mu, I_{i+1,3}] \rightarrow I_{i+1}$ in computation ξ, generate an event e_{i+1} labelled by μ, consider the grapes in state occurrences I_i and I_{i+1}, and let
   $(I_i - I_{i+1,3}) \leq e_{i+1} \leq (I_{i+1} - I_{i+1,3})$
   (understanding e_{i+1} larger/smaller than all grapes in $(I_i - I_{i+1,3})$ / $(I_{i+1} - I_{i+1,3})$);
2. identify those grapes of I_i and I_{i+1} which occur in $I_{i+1,3}$;
3. close transitively $\leq$;
4. restrict $\leq$ on the events not labelled by τ.

The observations of infinite computations are irrelevant. ♦

Definition 4.10. (*generation ordering*)

Let

$\xi = \{I_0\ I_0 \text{—}[\mu_1, I_{1,3}] \rightarrow I_1\ I_1 \ldots I_{n-1} \text{—}[\mu_n, I_{n,3}] \rightarrow I_n\ I_n\}$

be a computation of the transition system $D_{CCS}(E)$, associated to CCS agent E, having as observation the partial ordering of events $<S, 1, \leq>$.

The computation ξ induces on S the total ordering <, called *generation ordering*, where

$e_i < e_j,\quad 0<i<j\leq n$

being e_{i+1} the event generated by transition $I_i \text{—}[\mu, I_{i+1,3}] \rightarrow I_{i+1}$, $0\leq i<n$ (Step 1. of the Procedure in Def. 4.9.). ♦

The following example shows a computation of the transition system associated to the agent in Example 4.2.; Figure 4.2. shows its partial ordering observation; and Figure 4.2. shows an intermediate step of the Procedure in Def. 4.9. .

Example 4.4.

Let

$E = \alpha NIL \mid (\beta^- NIL \mid \gamma(\beta\beta NIL \mid \delta NIL)$

be the agent of Example 4.2., and let

$g_0 = \alpha NIL|id;$ $\qquad g_1 = id|(\beta^- NIL|id);$

$g_2 = id|(id|\gamma(\beta\beta NIL)|\ \delta NIL));$ $\qquad g_3 = NIL|id;$

$g_4 = id|(id|(\beta\beta NIL|id));$ $\qquad g_5 = id|(id|(id|\delta NIL));$

$g_6 = id|(NIL|id);$ $\qquad g_7 = id|(id|(\beta NIL|id));$

$g_8 = id|(id|(id|NIL));$ $\qquad g_9 = id|(id|(NIL|id)).$

Finally, let

$I_0 = \{g_0, g_1, g_2\}$ $\qquad I_1 = \{g_3, g_1, g_2\}$

$I_2 = \{g_3, g_1, g_4, g_5\}$ $\qquad I_3 = \{g_3, g_6, g_7, g_5\}$

$I_4 = \{g_3, g_6, g_7, g_8\}$ $\qquad I_5 = \{g_3, g_6, g_9, g_8\}$

The following is a computation of $D_{CCS}(E)$:

$\{I_0\ I_0 \text{—}[\alpha, \{g_1, g_2\}] \rightarrow I_1\ I_1\ I_1 \text{—}[\gamma, \{g_3, g_1\}] \rightarrow I_2\ I_2\ I_2 \text{—}[\tau, \{g_3, g_5\}] \rightarrow I_3$

$I_3\ I_3 \text{—}[\delta, \{g_3, g_6, g_7\}] \rightarrow I_4\ I_4\ I_4 \text{—}[\beta, \{g_3, g_6, g_8\}] \rightarrow I_5\ I_5\}.$

Its partial ordering observation is $h = (S, 1, \leq)$, where

- $S = \{e_1, e_2, e_4, e_5\};$
- $1(e_1) = \alpha,\ 1(e_2) = \gamma,\ 1(e_4) = \delta,\ 1(e_5) = \beta;$
- $e_2 \leq e_4,\ e_2 \leq e_5.$

Figure 4.2. shows h and Figure 4.1. shows an intermediate snapshot in getting the observation (after the execution of step 3. of the Procedure in Def. 4.9.), in which also grapes are depicted. Note that only the Hasse diagram is shown, instead of the full partial ordering ≤, thus e.g. the arc between events e_2 and e_5 is not drawn. The generation ordering of the above computation is

$e_1 < e_2 < e_4 < e_5.$ ♦

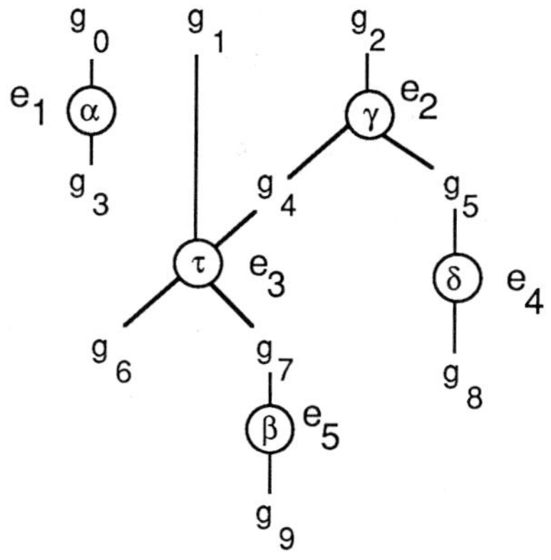

Figure 4.1. An intermediate step in getting the partial ordering observation of the computation of Example 4.4. .

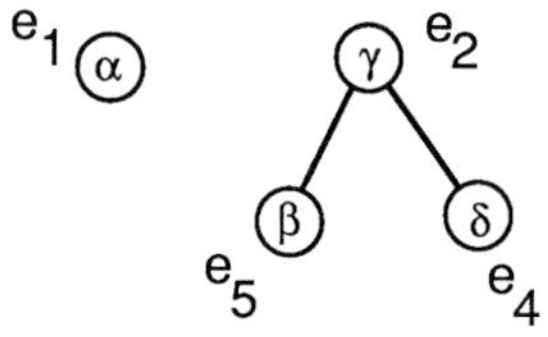

Figure 4.2. The partial ordering observation of the computation of Example 4.4. .

Definition 4.11. (*NMS partial ordering equivalence for CCS*)
Given two CCS agents E_1 and E_2, E_1 is *NMS observationally equivalent* to E_2 *via* ***po***, written $E_1 \cong_{\mathbf{po}} E_2$, whenever the NMS's derived from $D_{CCS}(E_1)$ and $D_{CCS}(E_2)$ via **po** are in $\cong$. ♦

4.3. Relationships among NMS interleaving and partial ordering equivalences and Milner's observational equivalence

In Section 4.2.1. we have shown that Milner's many step derivations coincide with our interleaving observations. In this section we relate them to partial ordering observation. Indeed we show that the interleavings of partial ordering observations are Milner's many step derivations. This result and the fact that both NMS interleaving equivalence and NMS partial ordering equivalence are based on bisimulation permits then to prove that the latter is coarser than the former.

Theorem 4.4. (*generation orderings are interleaving observations*)
Given a CCS agent E and a computation ξ of $D_{CCS}(E)$, let

- $h = \langle S, l, \leq \rangle$ be its partial ordering observation, and
- $e_0 < e_1 \ldots < e_n$, $e_i \in S$, be its generation ordering.

The interleaving observation of ξ is $l(e_0)\, l(e_1) \ldots l(e_n)$.
Proof. Obvious. ♦

Theorem 4.5. (*interleavings of partial ordering observations are generation orderings*)
Given a CCS agent E, and given a partial ordering of events $h = \langle S, l, \leq \rangle$ observed out of a computation of $D_{CCS}(E)$, let Ξ be the set of all the computations of $D_{CCS}(E)$ having h as partial ordering observation.
$D_{CCS}(E)$ is *completely concurrent*, i.e. the partial ordering $\leq$ is the intersection (in set-theoretical sense) of all the generation orderings imposed by the computations in Ξ on the events of h. ♦

Proof Outline. Complete concurrency is guaranteed by a commutativity condition (Theorem 3.3. [10]) which $D_{CCS}(E)$ enjoys, for every E (Theorem 6.4. [10]). Here, we summarize the proofs given there which require a couple of pages.
Commutativity ensures that, whenever two transitions u_1 and u_2 are such that the final state of the former is the initial state of the latter and they originate under **po** two concurrent events, there exists a pair of transitions u'_2 and u'_1, the observations of which are the same of u_2 and u_1, such that the final state of the former is the initial state of the latter. This is the case for $D_{CCS}(E)$, since we can single out in the initial state of u_1 those grapes which produce μ_1, those which produce μ_2 and those which stay idle in both transitions. Thus, we can write

u_1: $H_1 \cup H_2 \cup I —[\mu_1, H_2 \cup I] \rightarrow T_1 \cup H_2 \cup I$ and
u_2: $T_1 \cup H_2 \cup I —[\mu_2, T_1 \cup I] \rightarrow T_1 \cup T_2 \cup I$.

Then, the existence of the required pair of transitions

u'_2: $H_1 \cup H_2 \cup I —[\mu_2, H_1 \cup I] \rightarrow H_1 \cup T_2 \cup I$ and
u'_1: $H_1 \cup T_2 \cup I —[\mu_1, T_2 \cup I] \rightarrow T_1 \cup T_2 \cup I$

is guaranteed by Theorem 4.2..
The next step exploits commutativity: two concurrent events, generated by two successive transitions in the given computation (observed as the partial ordering of events h), can be generated in the inverse order by another computation, also observed as h. Finally, this result is extended to every pair of concurrent events, thus establishing complete concurrency. ♦

Corollary 4.1. (*interleavings of partial ordering observations are Milner's many step derivations*)

i) Given a CCS many step derivation $E_1 =s=> E_2$, there exists a computation ξ of the associated transition system $D_{CCS}(E_1)$ ending at $dec(E_2)$ with partial ordering observation $\mathbf{po}(\xi) = \langle S, l, \leq \rangle$, such that s is *compatible* with $\leq$, i.e. s is the sequence of the labels of a total ordering of events which is smaller than or equal to $\leq$ in the set-theoretical sense.

ii) Given a computation ξ of the transition system $D_{CCS}(E_1)$, associated to a CCS agent E_1, ending at $dec(E_2)$ with partial ordering observation $\mathbf{po}(\xi) = <S, l, \leq>$, for every total ordering s compatible with $\leq$, E_1=s=>E_2.

Proof. Follows from Theorems 4.4., 4.5. and by Lemma 4.1. . ♦

Theorem 4.6. (*partial ordering equivalence is finer than interleaving equivalence*)
Given two CCS agents E_1 and E_2, $E_1 \cong_{\mathbf{po}} E_2$ implies $E_1 \cong_{\mathbf{int}} E_2$, but not viceversa.

Proof. The proof relies on crucial properties of NMS's and bisimulations reported below. We will use $t_{int}(E)$ ($t_{po}(E)$) to denote the NMS derived via interleaving (partial ordering) observations of $D_{CCS}(E)$. Let $T_{po} = \{t \mid t$ is an fd-subtree of $t_{po}(E)$, $E \in$ PROC$\}$. We have that the following properties hold.

i) If $\mathfrak{I}_{po}$ is a **po** labelled NMS bisimulation then also

$$\mathfrak{I}'_{po} = \mathfrak{I}_{po} \cap T_{po} \times T_{po}$$

is an NMS bisimulation.

ii) Given a $t \in T_{po}$, it is possible to **uniquely** determine the generation ordering of any partial ordering labelling a node of t.

To show that $\cong_{\mathbf{po}}$ implies $\cong_{\mathbf{int}}$ it suffices to prove that given any bisimulation relation $\mathfrak{I}_{po}$ such that $<t_{po}(E_1), t_{po}(E_2)> \in \mathfrak{I}_{po}$ it is possible to define a new relation $\mathfrak{I}_{int}$ such that $<t_{int}(E_1), t_{int}(E_2)> \in \mathfrak{I}_{int}$ and $\mathfrak{I}_{int} \subseteq \Phi(\mathfrak{I}_{int})$.

Let $\mathfrak{I}_{int} = \{<t_1, t_2> \mid$ a. $<t'_1, t'_2> \in \mathfrak{I}'_{po}$;

b. t_i is isomorphic to t'_i, $i = 1, 2$;

c. the label of the root of both t_1 and t_2 is a total ordering compatible with the label of the root of t'_1 (or t'_2);

d. the other labels of t_1 and t_2 are obtained by prefixing the label of their immediate predecessor to the last label generated according to the generation ordering as determined by (ii) above.$\}$.

Now (i) above guarantees that $\mathfrak{I}'_{po}$ is a bisimulation and Theorems 4.4 and 4.5. guarantee that if $\mathfrak{I}'_{po}$ is a bisimulation then also $\mathfrak{I}_{int}$ is a bisimulation and the claim follows.

The viceversa does not hold as shown by the following counterexample. We have that

$$\alpha NIL \mid \beta NIL \cong_{\mathbf{int}} \alpha\beta NIL+\beta\alpha NIL$$

but not that

$$\alpha NIL \mid \beta NIL \cong_{\mathbf{po}} \alpha\beta NIL+ \beta\alpha NIL$$

as shown by Figure 4.3. below. ♦

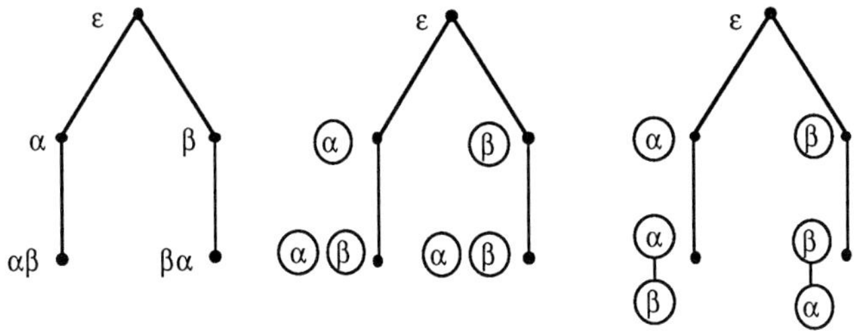

a) b) c)

Figure 4.3. **a)** The NMS derived via **int** for αNIL | βNIL and αβNIL + βαNIL; **b)** and **c)** The NMS's derived via **po** of α.NIL | β.NIL and of αβNIL + βαNIL.

Corollary 4.2. (*partial ordering equivalence is finer than observational equivalence*)
Given two CCS agents E_1 and E_2, $E_1 \cong_{\mathbf{po}} E_2$ implies $E_1 \approx E_2$, but not viceversa.

Proof. $E_1 \cong_{\mathbf{po}} E_2$ implies $E_1 \cong_{\mathbf{int}} E_2$ (by Theorem 4.4.) which coincides with $E_1 \approx E_2$ (by Theorem 4.3.). ♦

Figures 4.4. and 4.5. show that some relevant identifications induced by $\approx$ are preserved by $\cong_{\mathbf{po}}$ as well. Actually, we have that

i) $\alpha\text{NIL} \cong_{\mathbf{po}} \alpha\tau\text{NIL}$;
ii) $\alpha\text{NIL} \cong_{\mathbf{po}} \tau\alpha\text{NIL}$;
iii) $\alpha(\beta\text{NIL} + \tau\gamma\text{NIL}) + \alpha\gamma\text{NIL} \cong_{\mathbf{po}} \alpha(\beta\text{NIL} + \tau\gamma\text{NIL})$.

being (i) and (iii) instantiations of two τ-laws [16]. In passing, note that (ii) is not preserved by +-contexts, hence also $\cong_{\mathbf{po}}$ is not a congruence for CCS.

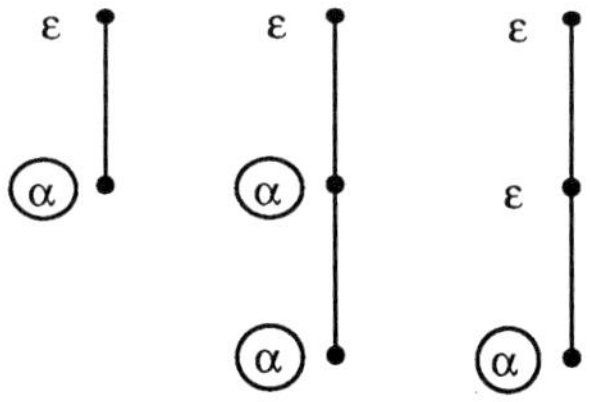

a) b) c)

Figure 4.4. The NMS's derived via **po** of αNIL, ατNIL and ταNIL (in **a)**, **b)** and **c)** respectively), showing that $\alpha\text{NIL} \cong_{\mathbf{po}} \alpha\tau\text{NIL} \cong_{\mathbf{po}} \tau\alpha\text{NIL}$.

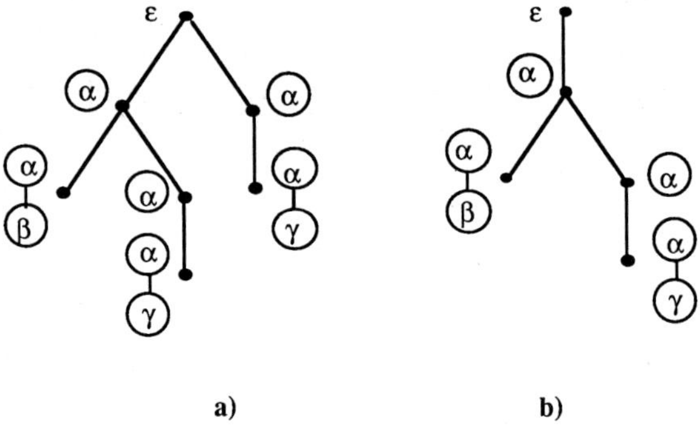

Figure 4.5. The NMS's derived via **po** of $\alpha(\beta NIL + \tau\gamma NIL) + \alpha\gamma NIL$ (in part **a**)) and $\alpha(\beta NIL+\tau\gamma NIL)$ (in part **b**)), showing that $\alpha(\beta NIL + \tau\gamma NIL) + \alpha\gamma NIL \cong_{\mathbf{po}} \alpha(\beta NIL+\tau\gamma NIL)$.

Theorem 4.7. (*partial ordering equivalence and observational equivalence coincide on sequential processes*)

Let PROC' be the set of CCS agents in which | does not occur.

The restriction of $\cong_{\mathbf{po}}$ to PROC'×PROC' coincide with the restriction of ≈ to PROC'×PROC'.

Proof. If E_1 is in PROC' and $E_1{=}s{=}{>}E_2$, then $dec(E_1)$ is a singleton; all partial ordering observations of $D_{CCS}(E)$ are total orderings; and $E_1 \cong_{\mathbf{po}} E_2$ iff $E_1 \cong_{\mathbf{int}} E_2$. ♦

5. CONCLUSIONS

Nondeterministic Measurement Systems were introduced as a framework for dealing with various notions of observation for concurrent systems. An NMS observational equivalence was defined on them as the maximal bisimulation.

As a case study, two equivalences were defined for the Calculus of Communicating Systems, the first based on interleaving observations, the second on partial ordering observations. The first equivalence coincides with Milner's observational equivalence, while the second is finer exactly in that it distinguishes interleaving of sequential nondeterministic processes from their concurrent execution.

In the paper, the partial ordering observation of a given computation is a partial ordering of *events*. These observations completely abstract out of the initial and the final states of computations, aiming at achieving a level of abstraction comparable with Milner's. A consequence is that observations of computations must be defined directly, instead of composing them from the observations of single steps. Moreover, some useful properties of computations, e.g. deadlock freedom, starvation freedom and fairness, cannot be recovered from these observations.

When also initial and final states are observed (as sets of processes), the observations are Concurrent Histories, a model for distributed concurrent systems introduced in [8, 9] and used in [5] to define partial ordering computations for CCS. Concurrent histories can be concatenated, thus growing the observation of the whole computation incrementally. Furthermore, concurrent histories and their limits in metric spaces have been used to characterize infinite computations and their liveness properties [8, 10].

We think that NMS's are a rather general tool for comparing behaviours of concurrent systems. They can be instantiated in many ways by defining either different observation functions or different equivalences. Examples of the former are given in the paper; the definition of alternative equivalences, especially for treating non-continuous properties, may be the subject of future work.

When dealing with models for concurrent systems composed through operators one should consider congruences rather than simply equivalences. There is no reason, *a priori*, for an observational equivalence defined independently of language operators to be preserved by them. In fact the three equivalences on CCS agents discussed in the paper are not congruences. Nevertheless, the coarsest congruence finer than the given equivalence can always be taken. On a case-by-case basis one may also try to refine the observational mechanism in order to obtain the desired observational congruence directly.

REFERENCES

1. Brookes,S.D., Hoare,C.A.R. and Roscoe,A.D. A Theory of Communicating Sequential Processes, *Journal of the A.C.M., 31* (1984), 560-599.

2. Brookes,S.D. On the Relationship between CCS and CSP, Proc. 10th ICALP (J. Diaz Ed.), LNCS 154, Springer-Verlag, 1983, pp. 83-96.

3. Costa,G. and Stirling,C. A Fair Calculus of Communicating Systems, *Acta Informatica 31* (1984), 417-441.

4. Darondeau,Ph. An Enlarged Definition and Complete Axiomatization of Observational Congruence of Finite Processes, Proc. 5th Int. Symposium on Programming (M. Dezani-Ciancaglini and U. Montanari Eds), LNCS 137, Springer-Verlag, 1982, pp. 47-62.

5. Degano,P., De Nicola,R. and Montanari,U. Partial Ordering Derivations for CCS, Proc. FCT '85 (L. Budach Ed.), LNCS 199, Springer Verlag, Heidelberg, 1985, pp.520-533.

6. Degano,P., De Nicola,R. and Montanari,U. CCS is an (Augmented) Contact-free C/E System, submitted for publication.

7. Degano,P. and Montanari,U. A Model for Distributed Systems Base on Graph Rewriting, Note Cnet 111 (1983), University of Pisa, to appear in *Journal of the A.C.M.*.

8. Degano,P. and Montanari,U. Liveness Properties as Convergence in Metric Spaces, Proc. 16th ACM SIGACT Symposium on Theory of Computing '84,1984, pp. 31-38.

9. Degano,P. and Montanari,U. Distributed Systems, Partial Orderings of Events and Event Structures, in *Control Flow and Data Flow: Concepts of Distributed Programming* (M. Broy Ed.) NATO ASI Series F, Vol. 14, Springer Verlag, Heidelberg, pp. 7-106.

10. Degano,P. and Montanari,U. Concurrent Histories – A Basis for Observing Distributed Systems, to appear in *Journal of Computer and System Sciences.*

11. De Nicola,R. and Hennessy,M. Testing Equivalences for Processes, *Theoretical Computer Science 34* (1984), 83-133.

12. Hennessy,M. and Milner,R. Algebraic Laws for Nondeterminism and Concurrency, *Journal of the A.C.M. 32* (1985), 137-161.

13. Keller,R. Formal Verification of Parallel Programs, *Journal of the A.C.M. 19* (1976), 561-572.

14. Lauer, P.E., Torrigiani,P.R. and Shields,M.W. COSY: A Specification Language Based on Path Expressions, *Acta Informatica 12* (1979), 109-158.

15. Mazurkiewicz,A. Concurrent Program Schemas and Their Interpretation, Proc. Aarhus Workshop on Verification of Parallel Programs, 1977.

16. Milner,R. *A Calculus of Communicating Systems*, LNCS 92, Springer Verlag, Heidelberg, 1980.

17. Milner,R. Notes on a Calculus for Communicating Systems, in: *Control Flow and Data Flow: Concepts of Distributed Programming* (M. Broy Ed.), NATO ASI Series F: Vol. 14, Springer Verlag, 1985, pp. 205-228.

18. Park,D. Concurrency and Automata on Infinite Sequences, Proc. Theoretical Computer Science (P. Deussen Ed.), LNCS 104, Springer Verlag, Heidelberg, 1981, pp.167-183.

19. Plotkin,G. A Structural Approach to Operational Semantics, Lecture Notes, Aarhus University, (1981).

20. Reisig,W. *Petri Nets: An Introduction*, EACTS Monographs on Theoretical Computer Science, Springer Verlag, 1985.

21. Winkowski,J. Behaviours of Concurrent Systems, *Theoretical Computer Science 12* (1980), 39-60.

22. Winskel,G. Event Structure Semantics for CCS and Related Languages, Proc. 9th ICALP (M. Nielsen and E. M. Schmidt Eds), LNCS 140, Springer Verlag, 1982, pp. 561-567.

QUESTIONS AND ANSWERS

Best: Are you restricting yourself implicitly to finite processes because your generation orders are only defined for finite processes?

Degano: The fact is that technically we need total orders which are finitely preceeded. That means, every element has only a finite number of predecessors. The theorem holds in general.

Best: But, is it true that you stated the theorem only for finite processes?

Degano: Yes, because we deal only with finite computations.

Darondeau: How would you define an equivalence for distributed linear time rather than for distributed branching time?

Degano: I don´t know (laughter). I have no answer up to now. I´m sorry! It´s a very good question (laughter)!

Wirsing: It´s more a comment than a question. I cannot agree that equivalences are better than congruences. If I deal with a language and if I want to reason about programs, I need a congruence.

Degano: If you have a language, I agree, you need a congruence. But apart from the CCS-example I do not have any language, so no congruence either.

Wirsing: But in all your examples, if you want to apply a theorem you get a language because you get at least a signature, the language of your example, and then you can speak about several congruences.

Degano: I agree! In that case we can talk either about a general way of taking the quotient, the congruence closure, or you just use some trick. I have sketched it for CCS by distinguishing the first occurrence of τ.

Wirsing: So, what you say, is that you have a simple way of defining the observational equivalence and afterwards, if you are interested, then you are considering the observational congruence.

de Nicola: Milner´s approach consists in defining observational equivalence of processes and then to close with respect to contexts in order to get a congruence. We do exactly the same. But moreover with these NMS we can also define other notions of observation. For example, consider the following kind of tricky observation where we observe whether there is a τ at the beginning of a process; we observe the first τ and forget about the rest. In this paper we want to stress the point that we can define a general method for finding observational equivalences which would respect concurrency. The matter of congruences is about languages, it is not about this general mechanism of finding the equivalence.

Degano: This is the core of the paper.

Bougé: I have a question about your labels. It seems that most of the syntax of the terms is encapsulated into the labels. Does that mean that for eample ´p | q´ and ´q | p´ can induce different label conditions.

Degano: No, that´s not true.

Bougé: Suppose that you have a term that can make a transition. Now, you encapsulate this term very deeply into a very large one, then the very large one cannot make exactly the same transition. I feel, it is somehow disturbing since the labels have to encapsulate the syntax of the terms. A great advantage of Milner´s transition system is its independence from the depth of nesting of the active term.

Degano: The great disadvantage of Milner´s approach is that he cannot recover concurrency explicitly. Exactly what we did is to bring this structure to a ´first class´ level so that concurrency can be explicitly represented.

Bougé: Could you please compare your approach with the recent attempt by Boudol and Castellani, for a partial order semantics for CCS.

Degano: I know some work of Gerard Boudol and some work of Ilaria Castellani, but I do not know about their joint work. [G. Boudol, I. Castellani: On the semantics of concurrency: Partial orders and transition systems. In: CAAP 87, Pisa, Lecture Notes in Computer Science 249, Berlin: Springer, 1987]

de Bakker: Maybe we should have a last question, if there is one.

Degano: May I show you, how fairness works in our approach. It´s very simple. We observe the computations as in Milner´s transition system, just as strings, but define observation on infinite computations too. An infinite computation is observed as fair or unfair according to some definition of fairness. Then we consider all subtrees, also subtrees at infinite points are taken into account. As an example, consider two agents which are perfectly observationally equivalent with respect to the finite behaviour but which are not equivalent according to fairness: one of them may perform an infinite string of α's, but not the other [cf. example 3.1]. I just show you this example to give you an idea of how by defining suitable observation functions one can capture different notions of equivalence and deal with different semantics of a language. This example is very special because of the noncontinuity of the observation function.

SESSION 3

Semantics

Chairman: A. Blikle

P.D. Mosses and D.A. Watt

The use of action semantics

S. Jagannathan

A Model of data backup and recovery in a computer system for functional programming

M. Felleisen and D.P. Friedman

Control operators, the SECD - machine, and the λ - calculus

Formal Description of Programming Concepts - III
M. Wirsing (Editor)
Elsevier Science Publishers B.V. (North-Holland)

© IFIP, 1987

THE USE OF ACTION SEMANTICS

Peter D. Mosses

Computer Science Department
Aarhus University
DK-8000 Aarhus C, Denmark

David A. Watt

Computing Science Department
University of Glasgow
Glasgow G12 8QQ, U.K.

Formal descriptions of semantics have so far failed to match the acceptance and popularity of formal descriptions of syntax. Thus, in current standards for programming languages, syntax is usually described formally but semantics informally, despite the greater danger of impreciseness in the description of semantics. Possible reasons for this state of affairs are discussed. Action Semantics, which has been developed from Denotational Semantics and Abstract Semantic Algebras, has some features that may make it more attractive than other semantic formalisms. This paper describes and motivates Action Semantics, and gives some realistic examples of its use.

1. INTRODUCTION

For many years now, BNF (with minor variations) has been used for describing the context-free syntax of programming languages. It has been found to be generally acceptable and useful — to language designers and standardizers, to programmers and implementors, and in formal studies.

In contrast, there is no such consensus with semantic descriptions. There is a diversity of approaches, each having advantages for some applications, but also having disadvantages for others. In particular, none of the previous approaches to formal semantics seems to be appropriate for use in standards for programming languages, and standardizers have generally kept to informal, natural-language descriptions of semantics (*e.g.*, [1,2]). But it seems doubtful that informal descriptions of such complex artefacts as programming languages can ever be made sufficiently precise to rule out mis-interpretation by implementors and programmers; likewise, they cannot be used reliably in connection with program verification.

The main approaches to formal semantics are Denotational Semantics, Axiomatic Semantics and Operational Semantics. Let us look at them briefly in turn, and consider their strengths and weaknesses for describing conventional programming languages.

Denotational Semantics [22,25,23,11] is perhaps the main contender. It seems that it is able to cope with everything that language designers can come up with, and it is founded upon an elegant and powerful theory. But there are problems with the comprehensibility of denotational descriptions. This may be partly because the higher-order functions taken as denotations of phrases are unfamiliar objects to many. Moreover, the λ-notation used to express denotations has obscure operational implications, and it takes considerable time and effort to learn the various idioms of λ-programming (such as continuations) that are generally used in denotational descriptions. Lastly, little attention has been paid to modularization, so that, even in the absence of the other factors, larger descriptions would still be disproportionately difficult to grasp.

The Vienna Development Method (VDM) provides an alternative notation for denotational descriptions, usually referred to as "Meta-IV" [6]. In fact Meta-IV is an extension of λ-notation, incorporating a variety of familiar data types, such as trees, sets and mappings, and it even has imperative features. The operational implications of Meta-IV are more apparent than those of pure λ-notation, and there is less need to depend on idioms. However, the foundations of Meta-IV seem somewhat shaky, and there are the usual problems with the modularity and comprehensibility of large-scale descriptions.

The (largely) functional programming language ML [15] has also been tried as a meta-language for expressing denotational descriptions. The ML implementation enables the empirical testing of semantic descriptions (and rapid prototyping [26]). It is unclear how difficult it would be to reason about denotations expressed in ML.

It is also possible to use a general-purpose programming language as a meta-language: variants of Pascal, Algol68, C, and Ada have all been proposed for this purpose. This might seem attractive, due to the use of familiar notation, and the possibility (in some languages) of achieving modularity. However, such general-purpose programming languages, even when reduced to applicative subsets and extended to allow higher-order functions (which makes them less familiar!), turn out to be rather clumsy for expressing semantic descriptions. They also lack formal definitions themselves, making it impossible to reason about the semantics given to programs in the described language (especially with meta-circular descriptions!). Finally, it is not at all clear that it is desirable to reduce the semantics of new languages to the (often idiosyncratic) semantics of existing languages.

Axiomatic Semantics [12,3] is reasonably accessible to programmers and implementors, involving only assertions about the values of variables, and the basic notions of formal logic (axioms and inference rules). The main problems here are with generality and comprehensibility — some simple programming constructs, like procedures with parameters, have uncomfortably intricate descriptions — and with ensuring consistency. The published axiomatic description of Pascal [13] does not cover the full language, and its rules for function declarations give logical inconsistency [4].

By the way, the so-called "weakest precondition" semantics of [8] is not particularly axiomatic, even though it uses assertions: it is denotational in essence, and suffers from some of the pragmatic deficiencies of the usual denotational approach.

Operational Semantics [27] is just abstract programming of compilers and interpreters, and as such is quite easy for programmers and implementors to work with. However, operational descriptions of full-scale languages are rather voluminous documents, and little attention has been paid to modularity. There is a constant danger of operational specifications being biased towards particular implementation strategies, making it difficult to relate them to (real) implementations based on alternative strategies. Even when there is no bias towards a particular implementation strategy, there are certain to be details in the operational description that are of an implementation nature and not essential to an abstract understanding of the programming language's semantics. It is presumably this that accounts for the voluminousness of operational descriptions.

The Structural Operational Semantics approach [21,20,7] employs axiomatic descriptions of operational transitions. It can be used for static semantics and translation, as well as dynamic semantics. It has yet to be tried out "in the large", although a modified version, SMoLCS [5], is currently being used in an attempt to give a formal description of Ada. Both Structural Operational Semantics and SMoLCS seem to have some advantages over the pure axiomatic and operational approaches.

A significant weakness shared by *all* the above approaches is the lack of any explicit relation to familiar computational concepts, such as order of computation, scope rules, *etc.* The reader of the formal semantic description is forced to rediscover the concepts that were in the mind of the language designer in the first place. Informal semantic descriptions, when well-written, can avoid this problem, and possibly this is the major factor that causes programmers to prefer them to formal descriptions.

We are proposing a new approach to semantic description, one that attempts to avoid the pragmatic disadvantages of the approaches mentioned above. Our approach is still evolving, and we are currently conducting a large-scale experiment — a full semantic description of ISO Standard Pascal (Level 0) — to see how well it can cope with conventional programming languages. This experiment is nearing completion, and the results so far look promising [18].

The approach is called *Action Semantics*. It is based on "Abstract Semantic Algebras" [16,17], but the presentation of semantic descriptions has been significantly modified, with the aim of improving readability.

Action Semantics is *compositional*, like conventional Denotational Semantics (and Initial Algebra Semantics [10]), in that the semantics of each phrase is determined by the semantics of its subphrases. The difference is that the semantics of phrases (*i.e.*, their denotations) are no longer taken to be higher-order functions: they are "actions", which have (reasonably) simple operational interpretations, and quite nice algebraic properties.

In fact, Action Semantics may be regarded as "denotational", although taking actions as denotations generally gives a less "abstract" semantics than that obtained using higher-order functions — *i.e.*, fewer phrases are semantically-equivalent. (But note that "full abstractness" [19,14] is seldom achieved in conventional denotational descriptions, in practice.)

We consider actions in detail in the next section. The semantics of a wide class of programming languages (both functional and imperative) can, it seems, be given in terms of a fairly small number of *standard* primitive actions and action combinators. This gives the possibility of re-using parts of previous semantic descriptions when describing new languages, and facilitates the semantic comparison of languages. Moreover, actions enjoy a high degree of orthogonality, which gives good modifiability of semantic descriptions. (Note that modularity alone does *not* necessarily give good modifiablity.)

Our notation for actions is intentionally verbose and suggestive. This, we believe, makes it possible to gain a (broad) impression of a language's semantics from a casual reading of its action-semantic description — we hope that this will encourage the casual reader to become a serious reader! There seem to be substantial pragmatic advantages, both for the readers and the authors of semantic descriptions, in having a notation with a fair amount of redundancy. Our action notation mimics natural language, but remains completely formal. (Other, more "mathematical", representations of the notation could be adopted when conciseness is a primary concern.)

The formal interpretation of standard actions is specified by algebraic axioms. These axioms provide useful information about the properties of actions. Note that we do not expect the reader to acquire an intuitive grasp of actions just by gazing at the axioms for them; rather, the axioms are to be used to "fine-tune" a previously-established conceptual understanding (and for formal reasoning about actions, of course).

We shall not dwell on the algebraic specification of actions in this paper. We refer the reader to [17] for examples and a discussion of foundational aspects. But note that giving an algebraic specification of actions does not preclude supplementary specifications using other formalisms. For example, one could give a model for actions based on domains of higher-order functions — thus turning action-semantic descriptions into conventional denotational descriptions!

Preface		
1.	Standard Notation	
	1.1.	Sorts
	1.2.	Operations
2.	Abstract Syntax	
	2.1.	Abstract Phrase Sorts
	2.2.	Abstract Phrase Productions
3.	Static Semantics	
	3.1.	Special Sorts
	3.2.	Special Operations
	3.3.	Semantic Functions
4.	Dynamic Semantics	
	4.1.	Special Sorts
	4.2.	Special Operations
	4.3.	Semantic Functions
Appendices		
A.	Algebraic Axioms for Standard Notation	
X.	Explanation of Meta-Notation	

TABLE 1
Organization of an Action Semantics

Action Semantics was originally developed for use in specifying just the dynamic semantics of programming languages. Recently, we have become attracted by the idea of using it for expressing the checking of static constraints as well. Both the static and dynamic semantics are then specified as mappings from context-free abstract syntax to actions, using the same notation.

In the rest of the paper, we first indicate the meta-notation used in Action Semantics, and explain the concept of actions. Then we give some examples of the use of Action Semantics, taken from the current version of our Pascal semantic description. We conclude by sketching our intentions regarding the future development of Action Semantics.

2. NOTATION

The overall organization of action-semantic descriptions is indicated in Table 1. The remaining tables and the appendices illustrate the various parts of an action-semantic description with examples taken from our Pascal description [18]. In this section we explain the notation used, leaving discussion of the Pascal examples themselves to the following sections.

By the way, informal comments may be used throughout action-semantic descriptions. Each comment is initiated by an exclamation mark '!', and terminated by the end of the line. (In this paper, we give explanatory comments in the text, rather than incorporating them in the examples.)

The first section of an action semantics presents the *standard notation* for values and actions. The sorts (*i.e.*, types) and operations of the notation are introduced using something akin to the OBJ2 algebraic specification framework [9]. We differ from OBJ2 mainly in blurring the distinction between sorts and "objects".

The standard *sorts* of values and actions are listed first, see Table 2. As in OBJ2, sorts may be *subsorts* of other sorts. They may also be parameterized by sorts (or values). A parameterized sort is identified with the union (*i.e.*, least supersort) of all its instances.

After the sorts come the *operations* on values and actions. The sorts of the arguments and result of each operation are given in the usual way, see Tables 3 and 4. "Mixfix" notation for operations is specified, as in OBJ2, using underlines '_' to indicate argument positions (prefix notation is assumed otherwise). Optional bits of notation are enclosed in square brackets.

The *axioms* that formally specify the interpretation of the operations are deferred to an appendix (not illustrated in this paper). The form of the axioms is much as in OBJ2, allowing equations and positive conditional equations in terms over the operations and (sorted) variables.

The second section of an action semantics specifies the (context-free) *abstract syntax* of the programming language to be described. The style of presentation of abstract syntax is similar to that commonly used in conventional Denotational Semantics, *i.e.*, "abstract BNF". See Table 5 for an example. The *sorts* of abstract syntactic phrases are listed first, together with their relationship to the nonterminal symbols of the programming language's concrete grammar. (At present the relationship is stated only informally, by means of comments.) Then *productions* list the alternative constructions for each phrase sort, introducing sorted syntactic variables that are used as abstract nonterminals (these are later used also in the semantic equations). Note that the "abstract terminal symbols" used in abstract productions have no formal connection with concrete syntax: they are merely a suggestive means of distinguishing abstract constructs. Algebraically, each alternative of a production corresponds to the introduction of an operation with (possibly) mixfix syntax. Ambiguity in the abstract grammar is of no concern, as the grammar is not used for parsing strings of symbols, only for describing the (tree) structure of abstract phrases.

The remaining section (or sections) specifies the semantic functions for the programming language. As a prelude, *special sorts and operations* may be introduced (see Tables 6 and 7). As well as new sorts being introduced here, sort parameters of the standard notation are instantiated to unions of other sorts, effectively specializing the standard notation for the purpose of the semantics of the particular language to be described. (This is analogous to identifying the "characteristic domains" in conventional Denotational Semantics: the domains of denotable, storable and expressible values [24].)

The *semantic functions*, mapping abstract phrases to actions (or, occasionally, to values) are specified inductively by semantic equations. See the appendices for examples. The notation is just as in conventional Denotational Semantics.

The left hand side of each semantic equation is the application of a semantic function to a schematic abstract phrase construction. The phrase construction is indicated by abstract nonterminals and terminal symbols, enclosed in double square brackets. Primes and/or subscripts may be used on the nonterminals so as to identify different subphrases of the same sort.

The right hand side is any term built from the (standard and special) operations and from applications of semantic functions to subphrases of the phrase construction given in the left hand side. In practice, we may relax this strict "homomorphic" discipline and allow compound constructions on the right hand side, provided that this does not affect the well-foundedness of the inductive definition. This can be used to emphasize that one phrase is merely an abbreviation for another phrase in the language.

Defining several semantic functions on a single sort abbreviates defining a single semantic function mapping to tuples (of values or actions). This is especially convenient for factorization into *static semantics* and *dynamic semantics*, as there is often not much commonality between them. The total semantics of programs can then be defined as a particular combination of their static and dynamic semantics.

We now explain and motivate our *standard notation* for actions and values. The formal syntax of the notation is given in Tables 2–4.

An *action*, conceptually, is just an entity that can be performed so as to process information. In general, the outcome of a performance may be *completion* (normal termination), or *escape* (exceptional termination), or *divergence* (non-termination), or *failure*.

When performed, actions operate on named values, cells of storage, and bindings for tokens. It is useful to consider separately various *facets* of actions: in the *functional* facet, actions receive and produce sets of named values; in the *imperative* facet, actions receive and may change the contents of cells in storage (they may also create and destroy cells); in the *binding* facet, actions receive and produce sets of bindings of tokens to values.

The various facets are *orthogonal*, in that operations in one facet do not interfere with operations in the other facets. For example, storing a value in a cell of storage does not produce new bindings for tokens; binding a token to a value does not cause any change to storage.

This separation of facets is closely related to the distinct uses in conventional Denotational Semantics of arguments, states, and environments. In the action notation, however, we do not refer explicitly to such data structures, in the interests of modifiability.

Each facet has rather different characteristics with respect to the propagation of information. In the functional facet, values are *transient*, and are "forgotten", unless explicitly copied. In the imperative facet, in contrast, the values stored in cells are *stable*, remaining constant until new values are stored there (or the cells are destroyed). In the binding facet, the bindings are established for a particular *scope*, and earlier bindings get re-established when performance leaves a scope.

The consideration of facets of actions has guided the design of the standard action notation. Each primitive action is generally concerned with one particular facet, and does not produce information in the other facets. Likewise, each action combinator is essentially a tuple of basic single-faceted combinators, and usually one or more of these are neutral, not restricting the flow of information either into or out of sub-actions.

There are various standard *sorts* in the action notation. These are listed in Table 2. First of all, there are the usual sorts of mathematical values, such as `Boolean` and `Natural`. For any sort of values `S`, the sort `List(S)` is standard; also `Set(S)`, when `S` has an equality operation.

For each sort of values `S`, the sort `S?` is the union of `S` with the sort `Undefined`, whose only value is "`undefined`". (Note that "`undefined`" is essentially an "error value" — it does *not* represent non-termination!)

Then there are the sorts `Name`, `Cell`, and `Token`. Names are used for referring to previously-computed values in actions (like bound variables in λ-notation). Cells are the identities (addresses, locations) of *potential* bits of storage; we assume that storage management is implementation-dependent, so the action that creates a cell may choose any cell that is not part of the current storage. Tokens are syntactic items such as identifiers and labels, to which values may be bound.

Boolean	Natural	List(S)	Set(S)
Value	Name(S)	Adjective	Term(S)
Storable	Cell(S)	Bindable	Token(S)
Undefined	S ?	Abstraction	Action

TABLE 2
Standard Sorts

Associated with Name, Cell, and Token are the sorts Value, Storable, and Bindable, respectively. These sorts are not further specified in the standard notation, they are essentially parameters that can be instantiated with whatever particular (unions of) sorts are required for the semantics of a particular programming language.

It is convenient to assume subsorts Name(S), Cell(S), and Token(S) corresponding to the subsorts (S) of Value, Storable, and Bindable, respectively. Note that the subsorts Name(S) do not inherit the subsort relation of Value: in fact they are *disjoint*. Nevertheless, a name in Name(S) may still refer to a value that is in a subsort of S, as such a value is also of sort S.

The sort Term provides the means for actions to use operations on values. Terms may contain references to named values, the contents of cells, and the bindings of tokens — note that these references are *not* regarded as separate actions, in contrast to earlier versions of the action notation [16]. For each value sort S, Term has a subsort Term(S), consisting of terms that yield values of sort S (or the value "undefined").

Finally, there are the standard sorts Action and Abstraction. Actions are not themselves values, but they can be encapsulated in *abstractions* (which *are* values) and subsequently enacted.

Now for the standard *operations*. The operations on values are listed in Table 3, and the suggestive words used in the operation symbols are intended to make further informal explanation superfluous.

The standard notation for names in Name(S) is to use the lower-case spelling "s" of the sort S, *e.g.*, "boolean" of sort Name(Boolean). Different names of the same sort are formed by prefixing adjectives, such as "1st", "2nd", "other" — adjectives should not clash with other symbols in the notation, but are otherwise arbitrary. When S is an instantiation of a parameterized sort, *e.g.*, List(Boolean), we allow the spelling of the parameter to prefix the spelling of the parameterized sort, *e.g.*, "boolean-list" (instead of "list(boolean)").

References to the values of names in terms are made by use of the definite article, "the". Thus "the boolean" in a term yields the value named by "boolean", if there is one; otherwise it yields the value "undefined". Analogously, "contents-of" yields the value stored in a cell, *e.g.*, "contents-of(the boolean-cell)"; and "binding-of" yields the value bound to a token, *e.g.*, "binding-of(*I*)", where *I* is an (identifier) token.

Value operations used in terms are strict in "undefined", so that the evaluation of a term containing references to undefined names, *etc.*, always yields "undefined".

We defer the explanation of the operations that involve abstractions until the end of the section.

Now for the standard primitive actions and action combinators. There is insufficient space here for full details; we consider only the main features of each form of action, ignoring the special cases that arise when actions are used in "unintended" ways. (To prohibit the unintended uses of actions syntactically would involve the use of a cumbersome notation for subsorts of actions, which we currently prefer to avoid.) The syntax of the standard action notation is given in

```
undefined          :                                → Undefined

true               :                                → Boolean
false              :                                → Boolean
complement         : Boolean                        → Boolean
disjunction        : Boolean, Boolean               → Boolean
conjunction        : Boolean, Boolean               → Boolean

0                  :                                → Natural
_ + 1              : Natural                        → Natural
 ...

empty-list         :                                → List(S)
only               : S                              → List(S)
join               : List(S), List(S)               → List(S)
first-of           : List(S)                        → S?
rest-of            : List(S)                        → List(S)?
length             : List(S)                        → Natural

empty-set          :                                → Set(S)
singleton          : S                              → Set(S)
union              : Set(S), Set(S)                 → Set(S)
difference         : Set(S), Set(S)                 → Set(S)
intersection       : Set(S), Set(S)                 → Set(S)
is-equal           : Set(S), Set(S)                 → Boolean
is-subset          : Set(S), Set(S)                 → Boolean
is-contained       : S, Set(S)                      → Boolean

s                  :                                → Name(S)
s1-s2              :                                → Name(S2(S1))
_ _                : Adjective, Name(S)             → Name(S)

the _              : Name(S)                        → Term(S)
contents-of _      : Term(Cell(S))                  → Term(S)
binding-of _       : Term(Token(S))                 → Term(S)
op                 : Term(S1), ..., Term(Sn)        → Term(S)

abstraction _      : Action                         → Term(Abstraction)
_ with the _       : Term(Abstraction), Name        → Term(Abstraction)
_ importing all    : Term(Abstraction)              → Term(Abstraction)
```

TABLE 3
Standard Operations on Values and Terms

Table 4.

The number of primitives and combinators in the standard notation may seem rather large — in fact there are 25 of them in all. But the conceptual complexity of the action notation is much less than this might suggest, thanks to the orthogonality (and commonality) of the various facets. Indeed we claim that all the actions express familiar computational notions. In any case, the aim is for the same action notation to be used in the semantic descriptions of many different programming languages, which may compensate for the effort of learning it.

Below, *N* stands for an arbitrary name, *T* for a term, *V* for a value, and *A* for an action (all with optional subscripts). Note that the square brackets used are not symbols themselves, they

```
obtain a[n] _ from _     : Name(S1), Term(S2)        → Action
check _ is _             : Term(S1), Term(S2)        → Action
copy the _               : Name(S)                   → Action
copy all                 :                           → Action
skip                     :                           → Action
fail                     :                           → Action
create a[n] _            : Name(Cell(S))             → Action
destroy _                : Term(Cell(S))             → Action
store _ in _             : Term(S), Term(Cell(S))    → Action
bind _ to _              : Term(Token(S)), Term(S)   → Action
[either] _ or _          : Action, Action            → Action
[preferably] _ else _    : Action, Action            → Action
[both] _ and _           : Action, Action            → Action
[first] _ then _         : Action, Action            → Action
_ before _               : Action, Action            → Action
_ within _               : Action, Action            → Action
block _                  : Action                    → Action
enact _                  : Term(Abstraction)         → Action
_ where □ is _           : Action, Action            → Action
□                        :                           → Action
recursively _            : Action                    → Action
escape                   :                           → Action
_ then exceptionally _   : Action, Action            → Action
_ and exceptionally _    : Action, Action            → Action
error                    :                           → Action
```

TABLE 4
Standard Operations on Actions

merely enclose optional symbols.

Except where stated otherwise:

- actions complete (*i.e.*, terminate normally);
- the values, storage, and bindings received by actions are propagated to their component actions and terms;
- escapes, divergence and failures propagate;
- primitive actions produce no values, make no changes to storage, and produce no bindings.

"`obtain a[n]` *N* `from` *T*" names the value of *T* by *N*, if that value is of the sort indicated by *N*; otherwise it fails. *Usage:* Naming values for later reference, renaming values to avoid name clashes, and checking that values belong to particular subsorts.
Example: `obtain a boolean from contents-of(the cell) .`

"`check` T_1 `is` T_2" completes if the value of T_1 is the same as the value of T_2; otherwise it fails. *Usage:* Checking for a particular value, and guarding alternative actions.
Example: `check the boolean is true .`

"`copy the` *N*" copies only the value named *N*. *Usage:* Propagating values.
Example: `copy the 1st boolean .`

"`copy all`" copies all the named values.

"`skip`" simply completes, forgetting all the named values.

"`fail`" simply fails.

"`create a[n]` *N*" creates a cell whose contents are initially "`undefined`". The sort of the contents is indicated by *N*. *Usage:* Allocating storage for (simple) variables.

Example: `create a boolean-cell .`

"`destroy` *T*" destroys the cell given by the value of *T*. *Usage:* Re-allocating storage.

Example: `destroy the boolean-cell .`

"`store` T_1 `in` T_2" stores the value of T_1 in the cell given by the value of T_2. *Usage:* Assigning to (simple) variables.

Example: `store true in the boolean-cell .`

"`bind` T_1 `to` T_2" binds the token given by the value of T_1 to the value of T_2. *Usage:* Declaring identifiers and formal parameters.

Example: `bind id` *I* `to the boolean-cell .`

"`[either]` A_1 `or` A_2" may choose between performing A_1 or performing A_2; but if the chosen action fails, it performs the other action instead. *Usage:* Combining alternative actions with exclusive guards, and implementation-dependent (non-deterministic) choice.

Example:
```
either
     check the boolean is true then A'
  or check the boolean is false then A" .
```

"`[preferably]` A_1 `else` A_2" performs A_1; but if A_1 fails, it performs A_2 instead. *Usage:* Combining alternative actions with non-exclusive guards.

Example:
```
preferably
       obtain a boolean from the value then A'
  else error .
```

"`[both]` A_1 `and` A_2" performs A_1 and A_2 together, combining any values and bindings that they produce, and interleaving any changes to storage that they make. *Usage:* Implementation-dependent combination of interfering actions, and ordinary combination of independent actions.

Example:
```
both obtain a boolean from first-of the boolean-list
and  obtain a boolean-list from rest-of the boolean-list .
```

"`[first]` A_1 `then` A_2" performs A_1, followed by A_2 (if A_1 completes). The only values produced by the whole action are those produced by A_2, and the only values received by A_2 are those produced by A_1. *Usage:* Sequential composition of actions.

Example:
```
first create a boolean-cell
then  bind id I to the boolean-cell .
```

"A_1 `before` A_2" performs A_1, followed by A_2 (if A_1 completes). In contrast to "A_1 `then` A_2", both A_1 and A_2 receive the values received by the whole action, and the whole action produces all the values produced by A_1 and A_2 (as in "A_1 `and` A_2"). The bindings produced by the whole action are those produced by A_1, overridden by those produced by A_2, which itself receives the bindings received by the whole action overridden by those produced by A_1. *Usage:* Sequential composition of declarations, and sequential evaluation of expressions.

Example:
```
bind id I1 to the 1st value before
bind id I2 to the 2nd value .
```

"A_1 `within` A_2" performs A1, followed by A_2 (if A_1 completes). This is like "A_1 `before` A_2", except that bindings are composed differently: the only bindings produced by the whole action are those produced by A_2, and the only bindings received by A_2 are those produced by A_1. *Usage:* Restricting the scopes of declarations.

Example:
```
bind id I1 to the 1st value within
bind id I2 to the 2nd value .
```

"`block` A" performs A, but then discards any bindings produced by A. *Usage:* Localizing the scopes of declarations in block structure.

Example:
```
block A'
      before A" .
```

"A_1 `where` □ `is` A_2" performs A_1. Whenever the performance reaches an occurrence of the dummy action "□", A_2 is performed in place of "□". This corresponds to performing the action given by replacing the occurrences of "□" in A_1 with the (perhaps infinite) action obtained by unfolding A_2 at "□". Note that "`where`" can be nested; but there does not seem to be a need for more than the one dummy action, "□". *Usage:* Iterating actions.

Example:
```
first obtain a natural from 42
then  □
where □ is
      preferably
            check the natural is 0 and copy the natural
      else  first obtain a natural from the natural - 1
            then  □
            then  obtain a natural from the natural + 1 .
```

"`recursively` A" performs A, which must complete, producing only bindings: no values, no changes to storage. The action A receives the bindings received by the whole action, overridden by those produced by A itself. *Usage:* Making declarations recursive.

Example:
```
block recursively A'
      before A" .
```

"`escape`" simply escapes, producing all the received values. *Usage:* Raising exceptions, and performing jumps.

Example: `copy the value then escape .`

"A_1 `then exceptionally` A_2" performs A_1 first. If A_1 escapes, then A_2 is performed as well, the only values received being those produced by A_1, and the escape is not propagated. *Usage:* Handling exceptions and jumps to labelled statements.

Example:
```
A' then exceptionally
preferably check the value is 0 else escape .
```

"A_1 `and exceptionally` A_2" performs A_1 first. If A_1 escapes, then A_2 is performed as well, the only values received being those received by the whole action, and the escape is propagated, producing all the values produced by A_1 and A_2. *Usage:* Adding further values to escapes.

Example:
```
A' and exceptionally
first copy the extra value
then  escape .
```

"`error`" escapes, not producing any values. *Usage:* Dynamic error conditions causing premature termination of programs.

Now we consider abstractions. The term "`abstraction` A" yields a value of sort `Abstraction`, encapsulating the action A. The action "`enact` T" performs the action encapsulated in the abstraction value given by evaluating *T*. The encapsulated action does *not* receive the values and bindings received by "enact *T*", although it does receive the storage.

Such simple abstractions could be used for parameterless procedures *without* non-local references to bindings (there being then no distinction between static and dynamic scope rules).

In order to deal with parameter-passing, we use the term "*T* with the *N*", where *T* yields an abstraction. The value of this term is an abstraction that encapsulates the same action that the value of *T* encapsulates, except that the action now receives the value named by *N* — the same value as received by "*T* with the *N*" — when enacted. Thus the value named by *N* is "frozen" into the abstraction given by "*T* with the *N*".

Further named values can be supplied to the abstraction given by "*T* with the *N*" in the same way, but of course the value of *N* cannot be altered. This is adequate for dealing with the concept of partial application used in various programming languages. Note that normal (total) application is expressed by "enact *T* with the *N*", where *N* names a previously-computed list of actual parameter values.

Similarly, to specify whether static or dynamic scopes are to be used for non-local references to bindings in abstractions, we use the term "*T* importing all". This gives an abstraction in which all the bindings received by this term are also received by the encapsulated action. So "(abstraction *A*) importing all" gives an abstraction with static scopes, whereas "enact *T* importing all" gives dynamic scopes for the abstraction yielded by *T*, in general.

There does not seem to be much use for abstractions like "*T* with all" and "T_1 importing T_2" (where the value of T_2 is a token), but they could easily be incorporated in the full standard notation.

A final point about the notation, concerning disambiguation: It would be intolerable to insist on full parenthesization of actions, as the plethora of parentheses would greatly hinder the fluent reading of the notation. On the other hand, it would be just as unreasonable to expect the reader to remember an elaborate operator precedence.

Our solution is to use *indentation* as a suggestive way of indicating grouping. The main rule is that each (maximal) indented sequence of lines is always a complete action — this can be formalized by means of an attribute grammar, with an inherited attribute corresponding to indentation level. Within a sequence of lines at the same level of indentation, combinators associate to the left. By the way, *all* the combinators in the action notation are associative, so repeated combinations involving the same combinator do not need grouping at all.

When the nesting gets too deep for indentation, as it does occasionally in our Pascal semantics, we resort to punctuation: an operator preceded by a comma has lower precedence than any operator without punctuation marks, and higher precedence than operators preceded by semicolons (as in ordinary English sentence structure). We reserve parentheses for use in terms occurring in actions.

3. DYNAMIC SEMANTICS

In this section we discuss some examples of dynamic semantics. These examples are all taken from the current version of our action-semantic description of ISO Standard Pascal (Level 0) [18].

Table 5 gives our abstract syntax for some typical expressions, statements, and declarations in Pascal. The relation between this abstract syntax and the standard concrete syntax of Pascal is

```
          Identifier              !  identifier
          Unsigned-Integer        !  unsigned-integer
          Expression              !  expression | variable-access |
                                  !  actual-parameter
          Expression-List         !  expression { , expression}
          Dyadic-Operator         !  adding-operator | ...
          Statements              !  statement | statement-sequence
          Block                   !  block
          Procedure-and-Function-Declaration-Part
                                  !  procedure-and-function-declaration-part
          Formal-Parameter-Part
                                  !  [formal-parameter-list]
          Formal-Parameter-Sections
                                  !  formal-parameter-section {;
                                  !        formal-parameter-section}
          Identifier-List         !  identifier-list

     I :  Identifier              !  productions omitted
    UI :  Unsigned-Integer        !  productions omitted
     E :  Expression            ::=  I | UI | E DO E | ...
    DO :  Dyadic-Operator       ::=  + | ...
     S :  Statements            ::=  E := E | S ; S | if E then S else S
                                  |  while E do S | I ( EL ) | ...
    EL :  Expression-List       ::=  E | E , EL
     B :  Block                 ::=  ... PFDP begin S end
  PFDP :  Procedure-and-Function-Declaration-Part
                                ::=  procedure I FPP ; B ; | PFDP PFDP | ...
   FPP :  Formal-Parameter-Part
                                ::=  ( FPS ) | EMPTY
   FPS :  Formal-Parameter-Sections
                                ::=  IL : I | var IL : I | FPS ; FPS | ...
    IL :  Identifier-List       ::=  I | IL , IL
```

TABLE 5

Some of the Pascal Abstract Syntax

quite straightforward: the abstract syntax essentially just ignores those details of concrete syntax that have no semantic significance, *e.g.*, whether an expression *E* is a term or a factor.

Before the action notation can be used to specify the denotations of the abstract phrases of Pascal, it needs to be specialized with respect to the sorts of values that actions process. Table 6 gives the special sorts appropriate for Pascal. (Actually, a few sorts are omitted in Table 6 — they will be discussed at the end of this section.)

Some of the sorts in Table 6 are parameterized by sorts (ranged over by `S`) or integers (ranged over by `M`, `N`).

The sorts `Character`, `Integer`, and `Real` are all "implementation-defined", and they are parameters of the whole semantic description. (The constraints on their associated operations are to be specified formally in an appendix.)

```
     Character          Enumerand(N)      Integer
     Real               String(N)         Array(N,N',S)        Record
     Pointer(S)         File(S)           Variable(S)          Type(S)
     Procedure          Function          Active-Function      Formal-Mode

Ordinal                = Boolean, Character, Enumerand, Integer
Storable               = Boolean, Character, Enumerand, Integer,
                         Real, Set, Pointer
Assignable             = Boolean, Character, Enumerand, Integer,
                         Real, Set, String, Array, Record, Pointer, File
Identifiable           = Boolean, Character, Enumerand, Integer,
                         Real, String, Variable, Type,
                         Procedure, Function, Active-Function
Token(Identifiable)    = Identifier
Bindable               = Identifiable, ...
Operand                = Boolean, Character, Enumerand, Integer,
                         Real, Set, String, Pointer
Operator-Result        = Boolean, Integer, Real, Set
Argument               = Boolean, Character, Enumerand, Integer,
                         Real, Set, String, Array, Record, Pointer,
                         Variable, Procedure, Function
Function-Result        = Boolean, Character, Enumerand, Integer,
                         Real, Pointer
Constant               = Boolean, Character, Enumerand, Integer,
                         Real, String
Result                 = Boolean, Character, Enumerand, Integer,
                         Real, Set, String, Array, Record, Pointer,
                         Variable, Procedure, Function, Active-Function
Value                  = ...
```

TABLE 6

Some Special Sorts for the Pascal Dynamic Semantics

Enumerand(N) is essentially a copy of the integers 0,...,N-1. String(N) has the same values as Array(1,N,Character), where Array(M,N,S) is the sort of tuples indexed by the integers M, ..., N, with components of sort S. Record values are essentially mappings from (field-)identifiers to component values.

Variable(S) is rather like the standard sort Cell(S), but it is generalized to deal with compound variables that may share cells in storage. Values of sort Type(S) merely give adequate structural information for allocating elements of Variable(S).

Procedure and Function values are really just pairs with components of sorts List(Formal-Mode) and Abstraction. The Formal-Mode values indicate whether coercions are to be applied to actual parameters. Each value of sort Active-Function consists of an ordinary Function value paired with a result-variable.

The remaining sorts are just unions of the above sorts. The sort Ordinal corresponds to the Pascal notion of ordinal values. Storable indicates what Cell values may contain, and Assignable does the same for Variable. Identifiable values can be bound to Pascal identifiers (the other sorts of Bindable values in the full Pascal semantics will be discussed later).

Operand values are operated upon by relational, Boolean and arithmetic operators, yielding values of sort Operator-Result. Similarly, Argument values are passed to procedures and

```
zero                   :                                    → Integer
maximum-integer        :                                    → Integer
negation               : Integer                            → Integer
sum                    : Integer, Integer                   → Integer?
ordinal-number         : Ordinal                            → Integer
float                  : Integer                            → Real?
negation               : Real                               → Real
sum                    : Real, Real                         → Real?

procedure              : List(Formal-Mode), Abstraction     → Procedure
body-of                : Procedure                          → Abstraction
formal-mode-list-of    : Procedure                          → List(Formal-Mode)
function               : List(Formal-Mode), Abstraction     → Function
body-of                : Function                           → Abstraction
formal-mode-list-of    : Function                           → List(Formal-Mode)
active-function        : Function, Variable                 → Active-Function
function-of            : Active-Function                    → Function
result-variable-of     : Active-Function                    → Variable
value-mode             :                                    → Formal-Mode
variable-mode          :                                    → Formal-Mode
procedural-mode        :                                    → Formal-Mode
functional-mode        :                                    → Formal-Mode

allocate a[n] _ of _   : Name(Variable), Term(Type)         → Action
assign _ to _          : Term(Assignable), Term(Variable)   → Action
access a[n] _ in _     : Name(Assignable), Term(Variable)   → Action
coerce a[n] _ from _   : Name(S1), Term(S2)                 → Action

coerce a[n] N from T =

     preferably
          obtain a[n] N from T
     else obtain an integer from T then coerce a[n] N from the integer
     else obtain a variable from T then access a[n] N in the variable
     else ...
```

TABLE 7

Some Special Operations for the Pascal Dynamic Semantics

functions as the values of actual parameters, and function activations (may) yield values of sort Function-Result. Result encompasses all the values that can be yielded by expression[1] evaluation in Pascal; likewise Constant for constant values. Value is the union of all the (standard and special) value sorts, and indicates what can be referred to by names in the action notation.

A closer inspection of Table 6 reveals that no two of the various union sorts coincide! This indicates a certain semantic irregularity in Pascal, presumably due to implementation considerations and incidental syntactic restrictions — although it seems strange that Set values may be operands, operator-results, or arguments, but not function-results!

A few of the operations associated with the special sorts are listed in Table 7. Note particularly that some names (for instance, "procedure"), are overloaded and used as constructor operations.

[1]In our abstract syntax, expressions include variable-accesses and actual-parameters.

The special operations "allocate", "assign", and "access" are generalizations of the Cell operations "create", "store", and "contents-of", respectively, to cope with compound variables. But note that "access" is an *action*, rather than a Term constructor: we do not assume that obtaining the value of a compound variable is an indivisible action. Formally, "allocate", "assign", and "access" are to be specified as abbreviations for compound standard actions involving (multiple) operations on cells.

Also, "coerce *N* from *T*" is an abbreviation for a compound action: it is just the same as "obtain *N* from *T*" when *T* yields a value of the same sort as the name *N*; otherwise, "coerce" performs Pascal-specific actions in order to get a value of the desired sort. Some of the possibilities are floating an integer to a real number, accessing the value of a variable, or calling a parameterless function. "coerce" is widely used in the Pascal action semantics.

We hope that the reader will now find it possible to get the gist of the semantic equations given in Appendix A — or even the full Pascal description. Even though the accuracy of the reader's understanding of the action notation may be poor to start with, it should increase rapidly by considering the actions corresponding to familiar Pascal constructs. Ultimately, points of doubt about the intended interpretation of the action notation are to be resolved by study of its algebraic axioms.

To help the reader, we provide the following comments on the semantic functions used in Appendix A.

For identifiers, "id *I*" is just *I* with all letters converted to lower case. Almost as trivial are the denotations of unsigned integer literals: "valuation *UI*" is the corresponding integer value. These denotations do not involve actions at all.

Expressions are more interesting. There are several reasons for letting the denotations of expressions be actions, rather than mere values. First, we wish to indicate explicitly that the order of evaluation of sub-expressions in Pascal is implementation-dependent; with actions, this is done by using the combinator "and".[2] (If evaluation of expressions were sequential, we would use "before" instead.) Next, function activations in expressions require the use of actions — and may have side-effects. Finally, our algebraic framework is first-order, so the denotations of operators occurring in expressions cannot be operations (on values), whereas they can be actions.

Anyway, "evaluate *E*" is an action that computes the *uncoerced* value of *E*, naming it "result". For dyadic operators, "operate *DO*" is an action that receives two values named "1st operand" and "2nd operand", and produces a value named "operator-result".

The denotations of statements, given by "execute *S*", are actions that neither receive nor produce named values.

The evaluation of actual parameters by "evaluate-arguments *EL*" receives a list of formal mode values, and produces a list of argument values.

For blocks, "activate *B*" executes the declarations and statements of *B*, using "establish *PFDP*" to bind the declared procedure and function identifiers to appropriate values. (For brevity, we are ignoring other kinds of declarations occurring in blocks.) Finally, for formal parameters, "formal-modes-of *FPP*" is the list of their modes (value, variable, *etc.*) — this is not an action, as it does not involve any processing of computed information — and "establish-formals *FPP*" binds the identifiers in *FPP* to the components of the argument-list received.

Finally, we consider how to deal with the action-semantic description of some of the "nastier"

[2]Actually, the Standard Pascal allows the evaluation of sub-expressions to be omitted (when their values are irrelevant) or to be done "in parallel"; but it is not clear to us exactly what that might mean.

features of Pascal: forward procedure declarations, variant records, and jumps. Lack of space prohibits us from giving the formal description of these constructs here, the energetic reader is referred to [18].

Note, by the way, that we do *not* consider it to be a disadvantage of Action Semantics that it is able to cope with nasty, as well as nice, features of programming languages. The nastier a construct, the more it needs a formal description! However, we do hope that language designers might be discouraged from including nasty constructs by the complexity of their action-semantic descriptions. Approaches to formal semantics that lack generality and prohibit various features run the risk of alienating language designers, and could delay the development of new programming concepts.

Now for forward procedure declarations. These allow procedure headings to be declared separately from (but before) the corresponding procedure bodies. A heading declaration is an ordinary procedure declaration where the body is replaced by the symbol **forward**. In the body declaration, the procedure heading is abbreviated by leaving out the formal parameters. (Similarly for forward function declarations.)

The idea of forward declarations is to permit mutually recursive procedures while keeping to a "declaration-before-use" discipline. There is no problem in expressing mutual recursion in action semantics, the only difficulty is in reconstituting complete procedures from the separate headings and bodies.

Of course, one could just regard forward declarations as something to be eliminated in going from concrete syntax to abstract syntax. But that is not as trivial as it might sound, and cannot easily be separated from static semantics. Anyway, we prefer to treat the entire Pascal language in the dynamic semantics, rather than insisting that the reader be aware of various syntactic transformations and checks that are to be applied to programs before taking their semantics.

Briefly, our semantics for a forward-declaration of a procedure identifier *I* binds a token "`forward-id` *I*" to a value of sort `Procedure-Head`, consisting of a `Formal-Mode-List` value and an abstraction. The action encapsulated in the abstraction binds the formal-parameters of the procedure-heading to the arguments it receives, but there is no body yet to be the scope of these bindings. Subsequently, the body declaration for *I* binds "`id` *I*" to a normal `Procedure` value whose abstraction component is supplied with the abstraction component of the procedure head. The insertion of "`recursively`" in the semantic equation for block activation then gives the required mutual recursion between bindings for "`id` *I*".

An inspection of the semantic equations for forward declarations given in [18] indicates that this feature complicates the semantics of procedure declaration about threefold.

As for variant records, we hide most of the gory details in the special actions "`allocate`", "`assign`", and "`access`". The main idea is to represent fields of a variant record by abstractions which, when enacted, perform the required checks on the associated selector variable of the variant. Note that the Pascal with-statement rules out handling variant field accesses in the semantics of field-designator expressions, as it causes field identifiers to be bound directly to component variables. When changing variants, the old variant part gets destroyed, and the new variant part is created.

Finally, jumps and labels. In conventional Denotational Semantics, the idiom of "continuations" is used to express sequential performance. This allows labels to be bound to continuations that represent "the rest of the computation" from the label onwards. Denotations of statements, *etc.*, take continuations as arguments, and the goto-statement merely ignores its continuation argument and applies the continuation bound to the label. This is not possible in the standard action-notation, where sequencing is expressed directly, rather than by means of idioms.

Instead, we bind labels to dynamically-generated values of sort `Jump-Point`. The only feature of these values is that they can be tested for equality. The execution of a goto-statement just escapes with the jump-point bound to the label. The semantics of block activation is extended to include, after the execution of the statements of the block, the exceptional performance of an auxiliary semantics of statements. This handles any escapes with those jump-points that are bound to the labels in the statements. (This has to be iterated, using the "`where`" notation, to cater for subsequent jumps at the same block-level.) The idea of using escapes instead of continuations has been exploited in VDM [6]; we were led to it by consideration of the algebraic properties of actions.

An alternative approach to jumps and labels would be to let the jump-points include abstractions that encapsulate the performance of the rest of the statements in the block. Then a jump escapes to the activation level indicated by the jump-point, executes the (recursively-bound) abstraction and finally terminates the block. But this turns out to be even more complicated to specify than the approach sketched above.

For more examples of Pascal nasties, see [18]!

4. STATIC SEMANTICS

Action Semantics was designed originally to describe the *dynamic semantics* of (conventional) programming languages — witness the terminology 'action' and the selection of standard actions (Table 4). In developing our action-semantic description of Pascal, however, we have found that Action Semantics is quite suitable for describing *static semantics* too.

Because the standard actions are worded as imperative verbs and conjunctions, the dynamic semantic description reads like a set of instructions stating what has to be done when each program phrase is 'executed'. The static semantic description reads like a set of instructions stating what has to be done to check whether each program phrase is well-formed or not (in a context-sensitive sense).

Of course, there are important differences between the static and dynamic semantic descriptions of (conventional) programming languages. In the Pascal description we find the following differences:

- The values processed by the dynamic semantics are integers, reals, sets, pointers, variables, procedures, functions, and so on. The values processed by the static semantics are constants, types, 'variable-modes', 'procedure-modes', 'function-modes', and so on. Consider variables, for example: the dynamic semantics is concerned principally with the storage cell(s) occupied by each variable; whereas the static semantics is concerned principally with its type, and sometimes with whether it is a component of a packed structure. We use the term 'mode' for the statically-known properties of an entity such as a variable, procedure, function, or formal parameter.

  Some values are common to the dynamic semantics and the static semantics, such as constants and types — although types are used for type-checking in the static semantics but only for storage allocation of variables in the dynamic semantics.
- Actions concerned with storage — namely "`create`", "`destroy`" and "`store`" — are not ordinarily used in the static semantics. To that extent, the entire imperative facet of actions is redundant in the static semantics. (One exception is mentioned later in this section.)
- Iteration and escapes are never used in the static semantics, so the actions "_ `where` □ `is` _", "`escape`", "_ `then exceptionally` _" and "_ `and exceptionally` _" are not needed.

A consequence of the last point is that no action in the Pascal static semantics ever diverges or escapes; the only possible outcomes are completion and failure. We adopt the following

Integer	Real	String	Packing
Integer-Type	Set-Type	Array-Type	Pointer-Type
Data-Mode	Procedure-Mode	Function-Mode	Active-Function-Mode

Constant	=	Boolean, Character, Enumerand, Integer, Real, String
Ordinal-Type	=	Boolean-Type, ..., Integer-Type
Structured-Type	=	Set-Type, Array-Type, ...
Operand-Type	=	Boolean-Type, ..., Integer-Type, ..., Pointer-Type
Operation-Result-Type	=	Boolean-Type, Integer-Type, ...
Function-Result-Type	=	Ordinal-Type, Real-Type, Pointer-Type
Type	=	Ordinal-Type, Real-Type, Structured-Type, Pointer-Type
Formal-Mode	=	Formal-Value-Mode, Formal-Variable-Mode, ...
Variable-Mode	=	Entire-Variable-Mode, Component-Variable-Mode, ...
Result-Mode	=	Constant, Data-Mode, Variable-Mode, Procedure-Mode, Function-Mode
Identifiable	=	Constant, Type, Variable-Mode, Procedure-Mode, Function-Mode
Token(Identifiable)	=	Identifier
Bindable	=	Identifiable, ...
Value	=	...

TABLE 8
Some Special Sorts for the Pascal Static Semantics

convention: if the denotation of a phrase is an action that completes, that phrase is well-formed; if the denotation of a phrase is an action that fails, that phrase is ill-formed.

In the static semantics of Pascal, the denotation of a program *P* is "constrain *P*", which completes if and only if *P* is well-formed. In the dynamic semantics, the denotation of *P* is "run *P*", which when performed will produce some changes in storage (*i.e.*, the storage where the external entities are held). These are composed to form the complete semantics of Pascal as follows, with the "then" combinator ensuring that "run *P*" is not performed if "constrain *P*" fails:

"constrain *P* then run *P*"

Now let us examine in more detail the static semantics of parts of Pascal whose abstract syntax is shown in Table 5. Some, but not all, of the standard sorts and operations (Tables 2-4) are used in the static semantics.

Some of the special sorts required by the Pascal static semantics are shown in Table 8, and some of the special operations in Table 9.

Sorts such as Integer-Type, Set-Type, and Pointer-Type correspond to the various type classes of Pascal. Some of these type classes contain a single type, *e.g.*, "integer-type" of sort Integer-Type. For each other type class an appropriate constructor operation is defined, *e.g.*, "set-type". Type is defined to be the union of all the type classes, and Ordinal-Type, Structured-Type, *etc.*, are defined to be unions of certain type classes only. Operations such as "is-numeric" and "assignment-compatible" correspond to the various predicates on types required in the static semantics.

Other sorts in Table 8 correspond to the various mode classes of Pascal. For example, Procedure-Mode is the sort of 'procedure-modes', each of which is constructed from a list

```
integer-type            :                                          → Integer-Type
real-type               :                                          → Real-Type
set-type                : Type-Name, Packing, Ordinal-Type         → Set-Type
is-numeric              : Type                                     → Boolean
assignment-compatible   : Type, Type                               → Boolean
data-mode               : Type                                     → Data-Mode
procedure-mode          : List(Formal-Mode)                        → Procedure-Mode
type-of                 : Data-Mode                                → Type
type-of                 : Variable-Mode                            → Type
formal-modes-of         : Procedure-Mode                           → List(Formal-Mode)
formal-modes-of         : Function-Mode                            → List(Formal-Mode)
result-type-of          : Function-Mode                            → Function-Result-Type

coerce a[n] _ from _    : Name(Data-Mode), Term(Result-Mode)       → Action
```

TABLE 9
Some Special Operations for the Pascal Static Semantics

of 'formal-modes' by the operation "procedure-mode". Our phrase sort Expression covers not only ordinary expressions (whose modes are of sort Data-Mode), but also variable-accesses (Variable-Mode), procedure identifiers (Procedure-Mode), and function identifiers (Function-Mode). The sort Result-Mode is defined to be the union of all these sorts. The operation "type-of" is overloaded on various mode classes such as Variable-Mode and Data-Mode.

Identifiable is instantiated for the Pascal static semantics to be the union of Constant, Type, Variable-Mode, Procedure-Mode, and Function-Mode. These are the 'values' to which identifiers are bound in the static semantics. Compare the instantiation of Identifiable in the dynamic semantics (Table 6).

Some semantic equations of the Pascal static semantics are shown in Appendix B.

For expressions, "infer-mode *E*" is an action that infers the (uncoerced) mode of *E*, naming it "result-mode", if *E* is well-formed — otherwise it fails. The action "typify-result *DO*" checks the application of *DO* to two operands; it receives values named "1st operand-type" and "2nd operand-type", and produces a value named "operation-result-type" (unless it fails).

For statements, "constrain *S*" is an action that simply completes if *S* is well-formed — otherwise it fails. Its semantic equations illustrate the basic techniques of using Action Semantics to describe static semantics.

The denotations of blocks and declarations in Appendix B show how we enforce the language's scope rules. Declarations in Pascal are essentially sequential, so the combinator "before" is suitable in the way it accumulates bindings. However, no identifier *I* may be declared twice in the same block, nor may *I* be used in a block before its declaration (even if *I* is also declared in an enclosing block). Our solution deals with both constraints at once. The denotation (component) "hide-locals *B*" produces a binding of *I* to "undefined" for every identifier *I* declared in block *B*. Moreover, it fails if any identifier is declared more than once in *B*. Wherever "declare-and-constrain *B*" is performed, "hide-locals *B*" is performed beforehand. This prevents duplicate declarations of *I*. It also ensure that "binding-of (id *I*)" is "undefined" throughout the part of *B* that precedes the declaration of *I*.

For procedure and function declarations, "declare *PFDP*" binds all the identifiers declared in *PFDP* to their modes; "produce-formal-mode-list *FPP*" checks the formal-parameter-part *FPP* and deduces its formal-mode-list; and "`declare-formals` *FPP*" binds the formal parameters of *FPP*, in sequence, to the received formal-mode-list, for the purpose of checking whether the corresponding procedure body is well-formed.

The parts of the Pascal static semantics that we have illustrated are fairly straightforward. Some other aspects of Pascal, such as the restrictions on mutual recursion of types, forward procedures and functions, and scopes of labels, make the static semantic equations messy but are quite tractable.

One problem that is fairly troublesome is Pascal's name-equivalence rule for types. This requires a unique "type-name" to be generated for each anonymous type-denoter in the program. This is why (surprisingly) we do use the imperative facet in the Pascal static semantics. We can treat a type name as a kind of storage cell, whose content is an (unchanging) type. (Alternatively, we could let `Cell(Undefined)` be a subsort of `Token`, and bind type names to types.) Something of the sort would seem to be needed to formalize the name-equivalence rule in any denotational framework.

5. CONCLUSION

Action Semantics is a novel and (at least for the authors) exciting approach to the formal description of programming languages. Its novelty lies mainly in the standard notation for actions — hence the name. Other significant innovations are the use of formalized naturalistic language in the meta-notation, and the modular organization of action-semantic descriptions.

Action Semantics combines several techniques. The denotational technique is used to express the semantics of program phrases in terms of actions. The (algebraic) axiomatic technique is used to specify the intended interpretation of actions formally, but this is supplemented by an informal operational description of actions. We claim that this makes the most appropriate use of the various techniques: for instance, it would not be appropriate to try to give algebraic axioms for unruly programming languages, nor would it give much insight into actions to reduce them to higher-order functions.

By the way, although we hope that the standard action notation will remain stable for some time to come, it may be useful to isolate special-purpose sub-notations, e.g., for use in static semantics. Note also that there is no guarantee that our action combinators can express all possible ways of combining actions: it may be necessary to add new ones, perhaps corresponding to concepts that we have overseen, or else just different ways of combinbing single-faceted combinators.

How do action-semantic descriptions compare to the usual *informal* semantic descriptions used in standard documents and reference manuals for programming languages? Well, despite the fact that informal semantic descriptions often use a rather legalistic and stilted language, we have to admit that they still *read* more fluently than our action notation. But on the other hand, when it comes to *understanding* the consequences of semantic descriptions, the informal reader of an action semantics should benefit from its compositional structure and uniformity of notation.

It will be interesting to see whether or not the programming community does find Action Semantics sufficiently useful to attract it away from informal descriptions. It seems to have become firmly established that formal semantics is generally incomprehensible to the average programmer. Action Semantics has tried to find a "middle way" between the rigours of formalism and the pitfalls of informal descriptions — but without abandoning formality! Instead of insisting that programmers should get to know an unfamiliar semantic universe of higher-order functions, we have tried to formalize *their* universe of actions, in the hope of a reconciliation between theory and practice.

We have worked out one large-scale example of the use of Action Semantics: a description of ISO Standard Pascal. We intend to provide other examples in the near future, such as Standard ML, in order to demonstrate that action-semantic descriptions are not particularly biased towards any one style of language — only towards good design and semantic regularity!

If there is sufficient interest in action-semantic descriptions for sequential languages, it will encourage us to extend actions with a communication facet, with a view to describing languages involving concurrency. Other action-semantics-based projects include compiler-generation and program development. But these may not be worthwhile unless Action Semantics becomes rather popular.

We appeal for reactions to Action Semantics: please let us know what could be improved, preferably with concrete examples. Also we would welcome collaboration in giving action-semantic descriptions of various programming languages. If there is enough interest, PDM will maintain a mailing list of "activists". By the way, our electronic addresses are: `pdm@daimi.uucp`, and `daw@cs.glasgow.ac.uk`.

ACKNOWLEDGMENTS

We thank our colleagues at home and abroad for encouragement during the early days of Action Semantics. The diverse comments from the referees on our extended abstract helped us to decide the contents of the full paper.

REFERENCES

[1] *The Pascal Standard, ISO 7185*. 1982. See [28].

[2] *Reference Manual for the Ada Programming Language, ANSI/MIL-STD 1815 A*. 1983.

[3] K. R. Apt. Ten years of Hoare's logic: A survey. In *Proc. 5th Scand. Logic Symp.*, Aalborg Univ. Press, 1979.

[4] E. A. Ashcroft, M. Clint, and C. A. R. Hoare. Remarks on 'Program proving: Jumps and functions, by M. Clint and C. A. R. Hoare'. *Acta Inf.*, 6:317–318, 1976.

[5] E. Astesiano et al. On parameterized algebraic specification of concurrent systems. In *Proc. CAAP-TAPSOFT 85*, Springer-Verlag, 1985. LNCS 185.

[6] D. Bjørner and C. B. Jones. *Formal Specification and Software Development*. Prentice-Hall, 1982.

[7] D. Clement, J. Despeyroux, et al. *Natural Semantics on the Computer*. Rapport de Recherche No. 416, INRIA, 1985.

[8] E. W. Dijkstra. Guarded commands, non-determinacy, and formal derivations of programs. *Commun. ACM*, 18:453–457, 1975.

[9] K. Futatsugi, J. A. Goguen, et al. Principles of OBJ2. In *Proc. POPL'84*, ACM, 1984.

[10] J. A. Goguen, J. W. Thatcher, E. G. Wagner, and J. B. Wright. Initial algebra semantics and continuous algebras. *J. ACM*, 24:68–95, 1977.

[11] M. J. C. Gordon. *The Denotational Description of Programming Languages*. Springer-Verlag, 1979.

[12] C. A. R. Hoare. An axiomatic basis for computer programming. *Commun. ACM*, 12:576–580, 1969.

[13] C. A. R. Hoare and N. Wirth. An axiomatic definition of the programming language PASCAL. *Acta Inf.*, 2:335-355, 1973.

[14] R. Milner. Fully abstract models of typed lambda-calculus. *Theoretical Comput. Sci.*, 1-22, 1977.

[15] R. Milner. The standard ML core language. *Polymorphism*, II(2), 1985.

[16] P. D. Mosses. Abstract semantic algebras! In *Proc. IFIP TC2 Working Conference on Formal Description of Programming Concepts II (Garmisch-Partenkirchen, 1982)*, North-Holland, 1983.

[17] P. D. Mosses. A basic abstract semantic algebra. In *Proc. Int. Symp. on Semantics of Data Types (Sophia-Antipolis)*, Springer-Verlag, 1984. LNCS 173.

[18] P. D. Mosses and D. A. Watt. Pascal: Action semantics. August 1986. Draft, Version 0.3.

[19] G. D. Plotkin. LCF considered as a programming language. *Theoretical Comput. Sci.*, 5:223-255, 1977.

[20] G. D. Plotkin. An operational semantics for CSP. In *Proc. IFIP TC2 Working Conference on Formal Description of Programming Concepts II (Garmisch-Partenkirchen, 1982)*, North-Holland, 1983.

[21] G. D. Plotkin. *A Structural Approach to Operational Semantics.* DAIMI FN-19, Computer Science Department, Aarhus University, 1981.

[22] D. S. Scott and C. Strachey. *Towards a Mathematical Semantics for Computer Languages.* Tech. Mono. PRG-6, Programming Research Group, Oxford University, 1971.

[23] J. E. Stoy. *The Scott-Strachey Approach to Programming Language Theory.* MIT Press, 1977.

[24] C. Strachey. *The Varieties of Programming Language.* Tech. Mono. PRG-10, Programming Research Group, Oxford University, 1973.

[25] R. D. Tennent. The denotational semantics of programming languages. *Commun. ACM*, 19:437-453, 1976.

[26] D. A. Watt. Executable semantic descriptions. *Software: Practice and Experience*, 16:13-43, 1986.

[27] P. Wegner. The Vienna definition language. *ACM Comput. Surv.*, 4:5-63, 1972.

[28] I. R. Wilson and A. M. Addyman. *A Practical Introduction to Pascal — with BS 6192.* Macmillan, 1982.

APPENDIX A. SOME DYNAMIC SEMANTIC FUNCTIONS FOR PASCAL

```
id: Identifier → Identifier
```

...

```
valuation: Unsigned-Integer → Integer
```

...

```
evaluate: Expression → Action
```

```
evaluate [[ I ]] =
      obtain a result from binding-of (id I)
```

```
evaluate [[ UI ]] =
      obtain a result from valuation UI


evaluate [[ E1 DO E2 ]] =
      first both  evaluate E1 then
                  coerce a 1st operand from the result
            and   evaluate E2 then
                  coerce a 2nd operand from the result
      then  operate DO
      then  obtain a result from the operator-result
```

```
operate: Dyadic-Operator → Action
```

```
operate [[ + ]] =
      preferably
            obtain a 1st integer from the 1st operand and
            obtain a 2nd integer from the 2nd operand, then
            obtain an operator-result from
                  sum (the 1st integer, the 2nd integer)
            else  error
      else  coerce a 1st real from the 1st operand and
            coerce a 2nd real from the 2nd operand, then
            obtain an operator-result from
                  sum (the 1st real, the 2nd real)
            else  error
      or    obtain a 1st set from the 1st operand and
            obtain a 2nd set from the 2nd operand, then
            obtain an operator-result from
                  union (the 1st set, the 2nd set)
```

```
execute: Statements → Action
```

```
execute [[ E1 := E2 ]] =
      first both  evaluate E1 then
                  obtain a variable from the result
            and   evaluate E2 then
                  coerce an assignable from the result
      then  assign the assignable to the variable


execute [[ S1 ; S2 ]] =
      first execute S1 then execute S2
```

```
execute [[ if E then S1 else S2 ]] =

      evaluate E then
      coerce a boolean from the result then
      either
            check the boolean is true then
            execute S1
      or    check the boolean is false then
            execute S2


execute [[ while E do S ]] =

      □ where □ is
            evaluate E then
            coerce a boolean from the result then
            either
                  check the boolean is true then
                  execute S then □
            or    check the boolean is false then skip


execute [[ I ( EL ) ]] =

      first obtain a procedure from binding-of (id I)
      then  both  obtain an abstraction from body-of (the procedure)
            and   obtain a formal-mode-list from
                        formal-mode-list-of (the procedure) then
                  evaluate-arguments EL
      then  enact the abstraction with the argument-list
```

evaluate-arguments: Expression-List → Action

```
evaluate-arguments [[ E ]] =

      first evaluate E and
            obtain a formal-mode from first-of (the formal-mode-list)
      then  either
                  check the formal-mode is value-mode and
                  coerce an assignable from the result, then
                  obtain an argument from the assignable
            or    check the formal-mode is variable-mode and
                  obtain a variable from the result, then
                  obtain an argument from the variable
            or    ...
      then  obtain an argument-list from only (the argument)


evaluate-arguments [[ E , EL ]] =

      both  obtain a formal-mode-list from
                  only (first-of (the formal-mode-list)) then
            evaluate-arguments [[ E ]] then
            obtain an argument from first-of (the argument-list)
      and   obtain a formal-mode-list from
                  rest-of (the formal-mode-list) then
            evaluate-arguments EL
      then  obtain an argument-list from
                  join (only (the argument), the argument-list)
```

```
activate: Block → Action

activate [[ ... PFDP begin S end ]] =

      block ... before
                establish PFDP
            before
                execute S


establish: Procedure-and-Function-Declaration-Part → Action

establish [[ procedure I FPP ; B ; ]] =

            recursively
            bind id I to procedure (
                  formal-modes-of FPP,
                  abstraction (
                        block establish-formals FPP before
                              activate B
                              ) importing all )


establish [[ PFDP1 PFDP2 ]] =

      establish PFDP1 before
      establish PFDP2


formal-modes-of: Formal-Parameter-Part → List(Formal-Mode)

...


establish-formals: Formal-Parameter-Part → Action

establish-formals [[ ( FPS ) ]] =

      establish-formals FPS


establish-formals [[ EMPTY ]] =

      skip


establish-formals: Formal-Parameter-Section → Action

establish-formals [[ I : I' ]] =

      first both  obtain an assignable from first-of (the argument-list)
            and   obtain a type from binding-of (id I') then
                  allocate a variable of the type
      then  both  bind id I to the variable
            and   assign the assignable to the variable
      and   obtain an argument-list from rest-of (the argument-list)
```

```
establish-formals [[ IL₁ , IL₂ : I' ]] =
      establish-formals [[ IL₁ : I' ; IL₂ : I' ]]

establish-formals [[ var I : I' ]] =
      first obtain a variable from first-of (the argument-list)
      then  bind id I to the variable
      and   obtain an argument-list from rest-of (the argument-list)

establish-formals [[ var IL₁ , IL₂ : I' ]] =
      establish-formals [[ var IL₁ : I' ; var IL₂ : I' ]]

establish-formals [[ FPS₁ ; FPS₂ ]] =
      establish-formals FPS₁ then
      establish-formals FPS₂
```

APPENDIX B. SOME STATIC SEMANTIC FUNCTIONS FOR PASCAL

```
infer-mode: Expression → Action

infer-mode [[ I ]] =
      obtain a result-mode from binding-of (id I)

infer-mode [[ E₁ DO E₂ ]] =
      both  infer-mode E₁ then
            coerce a data-mode from the result-mode then
            obtain a 1st operand-type from type-of (the data-mode)
      and   infer-mode E₂ then
            coerce a data-mode from the result-mode then
            obtain a 2nd operand-type from type-of (the data-mode)
      then  typify-result DO
      then  obtain a result-mode from data-mode (the operation-result-type)
```

```
typify-result: Dyadic-Operator → Action

typify-result [[ + ]] =
      preferably
            check the 1st operand-type is integer-type and
            check the 2nd operand-type is integer-type, then
            obtain an operation-result-type from integer-type
      else  check is-numeric (the 1st operand-type) is true and
            check is-numeric (the 2nd operand-type) is true, then
            obtain an operation-result-type from real-type
      or    ...
```

```
constrain: Statements → Action
```

```
constrain [[ E1 := E2 ]] =
      both  infer-mode E1 then
            obtain a variable-mode from the result-mode then
            obtain a 1st type from type-of (the variable-mode)
      and   infer-mode E2 then
            coerce a data-mode from the result-mode then
            obtain a 2nd type from type-of (the data-mode)
      then  check assignment-compatible (the 1st type, the 2nd type) is true

constrain [[ S1 ; S2 ]] =
      both  constrain S1
      and   constrain S2

constrain [[ while E do S ]] =
      both  infer-mode E then
            coerce a data-mode from the result-mode then
            check type-of (the data-mode) is boolean-type
      and   constrain S

constrain [[ I ( EL ) ]] =
      obtain a procedure-mode from binding-of (id I) then
      obtain a formal-mode-list from formal-modes-of (the procedure-mode) then
      modulate EL
```

```
modulate: Expression-List → Action
```

...

```
declare-and-constrain: Block → Action
```

```
declare-and-constrain [[ ... PFDP begin S end ]] =
      ... before
      declare PFDP before
      constrain S
```

```
declare: Procedure-and-Function-Declaration-Part → Action
```

```
declare [[ procedure I FPP ; B ; ]] =
      first produce-formal-mode-list FPP
      then  bind id I to procedure-mode (the formal-mode-list) before
            block hide-locals B before
                  declare-formals FPP before
                  declare-and-constrain B

declare [[ PFDP1 PFDP2 ]] =
      declare PFDP1 before
      declare PFDP2
```

```
hide-locals: Block → Action
```

hide-locals [[... ***PFDP* begin *S* end**]] =
    ... and hide-locals ***PFDP***

```
hide-locals: Procedure-and-Function-Declaration-Part → Action
```

hide-locals [[**procedure *I FPP* ; *B* ;**]] =
    bind id ***I*** to undefined

hide-locals [[$PFDP_1$ $PFDP_2$]] =
    hide-locals $PFDP_1$ and hide-locals $PFDP_2$

```
produce-formal-mode-list: Formal-Parameter-Part → Action
```

...

```
declare-formals: Formal-Parameter-Part → Action
```

...

QUESTIONS AND ANSWERS

Takasu: Your approach to semantics seems to be adapted to the semantics of compilers? I think that the semantics of a programming language is quite different from the semantics of a compiler.

Mosses: This is, I think, a matter of what the reader of a semantics description wants to know about the language. I can agree that a mathematician might regard the phrases of a programming language as denoting higher order functions in the traditional way of denotational semantics and thereby understand the semantics in that way. But I think that such a semantics which is remote from the operational concerns that pervade compilers and implementations is inappropriate for the general public, the programming community, programmers, implementors. What they want is the operational information about the order of computation, or whether there is no intended order. And they want to know information about scope rules and bindings and data flow. We think that we provide that in the denotations.

Takasu: Computer science is concerned with efficient algorithms and mathematical theory. The mathematics which is adequate for programming languages is a theory of data domains.

Mosses: It seems to me that there is considerable antipathy in the programming community to that abstract way of thinking in higher order functions. What we are trying to do here is to bridge the gap between theory and practice by providing a theory for the objects which are in the minds already of the practitioners, rather than insisting that practitioners come to Mohammed and see the real truth of higher order functions.

Apt: I think, the semantic description should allow us to identify dubious programming language constructions. Do you think that Action Semantics can help in this respect?

Mosses: Yes, I think that Action Semantics can help. Action Semantics means to reduce the programming language to combinations of rather regular action combinators and primitive actions. Our experience is that, at least in the case of PASCAL, the messy features of the language do in fact show up in the size of these constructs. There is not something that pervades the whole semantic description that suddenly makes every semantic equation messier. It is something that one can identify locally in the semantic description. You have one little construct and its description needs a lot of action notation. I think, we can document this in PASCAL that there is some semantic irregularity in the language, if we have to do quite a lot of work to represent it in the action notation. Whether the action notation will ensure language design that is good in any other sense than just regular, is less certain. We hope that it will encourage with language design, but we have not designed it specifically for that purpose and it remains to be seen whether it is practical or not.

Friedman: My feeling is that the modularity question is probably the most significant of your unanswered questions and that, once again, I think we´ll have an opportunity to learn from the success of our artificial intelligence colleagues. They have developed the ´flavor´ system that has done wonders for keeping structures very modular and very easy to modify [cf. e.g. D. Weinreb, D. Moon: Flavors - Message passing in the LISP machine. AI Memo, MIT AI Lab., Cambridge 1980]. I would highly recommend that you look into picking some of the good ideas of flavors.

Blum: When you made your first slide, you have phrased initial algebra semantics. I got the idea that this approach was the foundation for the Action Semantics. I am having trouble to see where the initial algebra plays a role in the Action Semantics now.

Mosses: In the standard notation, the action notation, these actions are specified formally not by giving a model in terms of some domain although they could be specified in that way. But we prefer for reasons concerning modularity that these operations on actions are specified by giving their algebraic properties: for instance, associativity of nondeterministic choice, commutativity and several kinds of distributivity that hold between those operations. There is almost a semi-ring structure in the various action notations, for example, ´and´ which is something like a product and the ´or´ which is something like a sum. And when one takes those general properties together with some perhaps more concrete axioms relating to how storage propagates or how bindings can be substituted in other actions, then one ends up with a limiting complete specification which is sufficient to do symbolic computation using the axioms as rewriting rules [P.D. Mosses, G. Plotkin: On proving limiting completeness. Åarhus University, Tech. Rep. DAIMI PB-188, 1985].

Blum: Are the axioms equational formulas?

Mosses: Conditional equational formulas.

Olderog: You mention that your action semantics is less abstract than the usual denotational semantics, so I expect, it is more difficult to use your semantics for verification of programs. How would you go about to make it more abstract in a pragmatic way?

Mosses: Well, one could wave the magic of finality over it and say: we take final algebra semantics instead. But that means just that one knows that certain terms get identified, and that there exist some observer operations that can distinguish those terms which are provably different. So it doesn´t really help you in proving equations. On the other hand, with continuous initial algebra semantics something like Scott - induction holds which allows to show properties of iterations and also of recursions. I don´t see at the moment how I can get further than that - maybe by adding more axioms that correspond to program transformations.

Bjørner: It seems to me that, when you have worked on abstract semantic algebras, the motivation then was to liberate yourself from having to be concerned with particular domains whether they be direct semantics or continuation semantics. Now, the shift that you are telling us, is to Action Semantics. It appears to me that the emphasis now is on the proper set of actions.

Mosses: Yes, I think, the two things go together. You noticed from the example that there is no mention of continuations, or stores or anything else. One could give both a continuation based interpretation of the example or a direct interpretation of the notation used in the example. That might induce a corresponding semantics for the λ-calculus. I think the fact that we don´t explicitly refer to continuations and other such items here (as in the abstract semantics algebra approach we avoid doing that), is an inherited part of an action notation that is going to have modifiability properties and could allow pragmatic properties like comprehensibility.

Bjørner Is your set of actions particularly polished to programming language semantics or could it be used for other things like formalizing database systems or other systems?

Mosses: I would not like to make definite claims in that direction, but I have no doubt to believe, it couldn´t be used in that way. (laughter)

Bjørner: Your answer to Ed Blum´s question on the algebraic semantics seems to differ a little bit from a statement in your talk, namely that you have not actually written down the axioms of your system yet. Have I disturbed you?

Mosses: For an earlier version of the action notation you can find reasonably complete examples of the axioms [see references [16] and [17] of the paper]. That was a very symbolic version of the notation which means that it is difficult to relate it for readers to the version of the action notation here. But within six months we hope to bring that up to date.

Jones: One of the advantages of formal methods is that the person who writes the definition of a language gets a better understanding in the process of what he is doing. Christopher Strachey in the old days was mentioning that especially the process of formulating the domain definitions of a language gives considerable insight into a language. What bothers me a little bit here is that somehow the domains seem to be a bit lost. This process of formulating domain equations, and in particular the difference, between let´s say a function abstraction and a thunk is very hard to see here. If you write domain equations for them, there are quite different objects.

Mosses: If I may interprete what Strachey said, that was in the context of the differences between the domains of denotable and storable values, not the differences between direct semantics and continuation semantics. The domains, you have in mind, are those that are also here as unions of sorts in the specialization of the standard notation to a particular language. So, I think, the domains that Strachey was talking about, were the characteristic domains that give useful information about the language, they are still here. What we have chosen to do here with functions and thunks is to keep those sorts of values abstract and provide constructor and selector functions on them rather than representing them in terms of giving standard sorts of values like abstractions or pairs. This has a slide overhead; we have to introduce these extra operations and you can´t so immediately see precisely what are the components of such values. On the other hand, it does have some pragmatical value with respect to modifiability and modularity. It´s not something that we think is the essential part of action semantics, precisely whether we want to choose the representation up to data level. What we think is important, is that we don´t have to choose models and representations at the action level.

Jones: But then the difference between, say, functions and thunks is more implicit. It is expressed by the operators one uses to model them in these semantics.

Mosses: As in the usual techniques of abstract data types. You are right.

Formal Description of Programming Concepts - III
M. Wirsing (Editor)
Elsevier Science Publishers B.V. (North-Holland)
© IFIP, 1987

A Model of Data Backup and Recovery in a Computer System for Functional Programming[1]

Suresh Jagannathan
Massachusetts Institute of Technology
Cambridge, MA 02139
USA

Abstract: We present a formal operational model of an abstract data flow interpreter for an applicative programming language. This model serves as a precise specification of an idealized implementation for the VIM computer system, an experimental system under development at M.I.T. intended to examine the efficient implementation of functional languages using data flow principles. The correctness of any implementation of VIM can be verified by showing that it preserves all the invariants specified by this abstract model. To demonstrate this technique, we present an extension of this idealized system which contains backup and recovery facilities to guarantee the security of all online data against loss or corruption as a result of hardware malfunction. To show that the augmented system correctly preserves the system state, we use a simple inductive proof technique that establishes the equivalence of the behaviour of the two systems. Our specification language is a simple applicative language augmented with operations to perform first-order existential and universal quantification.

1 Introduction

The VIM (VAL Interpretive Machine) [2][3][13] is an experimental project under development at M.I.T. intended to examine the efficient implementation of functional languages using the principles of data flow computation. VIM is an outgrowth of our efforts in the construction of computer systems using the principles of language-based design. The project is unique in striving for a system that will serve multiple users with a degree of semantic coherence well beyond what contemporary systems are able to offer.

Programs to be run on VIM are expressed using the applicative language VIMVAL, an exposition on which can be found in [3] and [13]. VIMVAL programs are translated into a data flow graph representation which can then be executed by the VIM interpreter. The base language of VIM comprises a set of data flow operators and rules for connecting these operators to form a data flow graph.

VIM includes several mechanisms which we believe are useful in supporting efficient execution of functional programs on data flow machines. It provides support for implementation of higher-order functions; and structure types such as arrays and records are supported at the base language level [6]. A mechanism called *early-completion* allows the implementation of deferred reads, and the *suspension* mechanism allows stream structures to be evaluated in a demand-driven manner. In addition, there are provisions in the base language to support tail-recursion.

VIM is a multi-user computer system in which users share access to all online information through a universal referencing mechanism. An important consequence of this property is that

[1]This work was developed with funding provided in part by the National Science Foundation #NSF DCR-7915255 and the Department of Energy, #DOE DE-AC02-79ER 10473

there is no need to maintain any distinction between *files* and *data* – the principal units of storage allocation are the the conceptual units of data that the programmer manipulates ,*i.e.*, instructions, scalar values, and structures. This homogeneous representation for both data and programs will allow us to design a backup and recovery system closely integrated with the VIM Interpreter.

This paper is divided into two parts. In the first part, we present a subset of a formal operational model of an idealized implementation of VIM which gives a precise definition of the base language and interpreter. This model provides a rigorous specification of the system; any implementation of VIM must satisfy these specifications. Our model views VIM as a state transition system in which the interpreter for the base language ,*i.e.*, the language of data flow graphs, specifies the state transition function. Our specification language is a simple applicative language augmented with features for set abstraction. In addition to being easily understood and semantically sound, we feel these specifications can be suitably refined to be easily translatable into machine or micro-code. In this respect, we agree with Turner [14] on the suitability of applicative languages as executable specifications. In the second part of the paper, we develop backup and recovery algorithms for VIM that guarantee the security of all online information in the system from loss or corruption as a result of some hardware malfunction. We exploit the power of the applicative base language by distributing the logic of these algorithms among the relevant base language instructions. This approach will allow us to achieve a measure of data security far greater than is possible in more conventional systems. The algorithms we present are simple and efficient and require no user guidance to perform their task. We can verify the correctness of these algorithms by showing that the behaviour of the system with these added facilities in the presence of failures is equivalent to the behaviour of the idealized system in a fault-free universe. Our operational model greatly facilitates the proof of equivalence.

2 The VIM Computer System

There are three major components in the VIM system: a system Shell, the VIM Interpreter and the system State. We describe each of these components below.

2.1 The VIM Shell

Users communicate with the VIM system through a system *Shell.* The shell is responsible for accepting user commands, translating them into the appropriate base language representations and then invoking the interpreter to execute this program. A user session typically consists of the user communicating with the shell in an interactive mode, inputing shell commands whose results are subsequently output to the user. Every user executes in a unique *environment.* A VIM environment relates symbolic names to values and acts as a repository for all long-lived objects. Users specify that a particular $< name, value >$ pair is to be placed in the current environment through a BIND command:

$$\text{BIND } name := < expression >$$

that binds the value of the expression to the name specified. In addition to the BIND command, there is also a DELETE command that, when given a name, removes the $<$

name, *value* > binding from the users's environment. For simplicity, we assume that there is a single user and environment; extending the model for multiple users is straightforward, but does involve introducing a non-determinate *merge* operator.

2.2 The VIM Interpreter and Base Language

The abstract architecture of VIM uses data-driven program execution. Each VIMVAL function is translated into a base language representation which is an acyclic, directed data flow graph. The nodes of the graph are base-language instructions and the arcs between the nodes specify the data dependencies among them. Arcs connecting two nodes may be of two types – *value arcs* and *signal arcs*. Values are carried on *tokens* along the directed value arcs of the graph. Signal arcs may be used to place constraints, in addition to those imposed by data dependencies, on the order in which the instructions within a graph may be executed.

The data flow graph corresponding to a function definition in VIM is called a *function template*. Each instruction within a function template is uniquely identified by an integer, called its *index*. An instruction consists of an opcode, operand slots, counters to indicate the number of operands and signals yet to be received, and a list of destinations. A destination is a triple $< destindex, destcond, desttype >$; *destindex* is the index of the instruction that is to receive the result, *destcond* is a flag which is used to send results conditionally, and *desttype* indicates whether the destination instruction is to receive a value or a signal. The destination list only references instructions within the template of the sending instruction. Sending results to other activations is done through the function call and return mechanism described below.

Every function application uses a fresh copy of the graph represented by the function template, the copy being called an *activation*. The use of graph copying coupled with the fact that all base language graphs are acyclic ensures that each value or signal arc in an activation is used at most once. Informally, the only difference between a function definition and its corresponding activation is that the latter represents a piece of executable code, while the former is an immutable data structure like any other on the heap.

An instruction in an activation is *enabled*, or ready for *firing*, when a value is available on each input value arc and a signal has been received on each signal arc. Only an enabled instruction can be executed, and the interpreter is free to execute enabled instructions in any order. The ability of the interpreter to execute many enabled instructions simultaneously is a source of concurrency in the system.

A distinctive feature of VIM is the *heap* which holds all structure values that are used by user programs. Scalar values are stored in the operand fields of the instructions and are passed around among the instructions on tokens. The kinds of objects held by the heap include function templates, closures, early-completion queues (described below) and data structures (arrays, records, streams etc.). Each object on the heap has a unique identifier (*uid*) which permits its selection from among all objects in the heap. Conceptually, the heap is a multi-rooted, directed acyclic graph in which an arc signifies that the target object is a component of its superior. Activations in the system are distinguished from each other by being associated with unique identifiers also.

VIM contains a number of mechanisms designed to support aspects of the VIMVAL language; in particular, these include support for function application, tail recursion and computations on streams. In the next section, we give a formal description of the interpreter and some relevant base language instructions that highlight the role of these mechanisms in the system. For a more detailed exposition on various aspects of the base language, the reader should see [3].

3 An Operational Model for VIM

The VIM system has four major components: a function *Interp*, a function *Shell*, a system *State* and an alphabet, Σ, which is the alphabet of the applicative source language. The state embodies all the current information in the system ,*i.e.*, heap, activations, enabled instructions, the user environment, and the set of unique identifiers available for activations and the heap. The *Interp* function takes as arguments a *State* and an enabled instruction and returns a new *State* of the machine. The interpreter is a non-deterministic state transition function; the choice of which enabled instruction to execute in any given state is the source of this non-determinancy. It should be noted that the overall behaviour of the system is still determinate since, from any initial state, the same final state will be reached regardless of the particular transition sequence chosen.

The following notation is used below. Sets are denoted in **bold font**, elements of sets (which themselves may be sets) are denoted in *italics*, tags and names are indicated using script characters and instructions are referred to using SMALL CAPITALS. Our specification language is a simple applicative language extended to include operations on sets. Elements within angled brackets indicates tuples. We shall use dot notation to refer to components of a tuple.

The VIM System is a four-tuple:

VIM *System* = <*Shell*, *Interp*, **State**, Σ > where
Shell: **Session** × **State** → **State**
Interp : **State** × **EIS** → (**State** × ($\mathbf{U_H}$ ∪ **Scalar**))
Σ = the source language alphabet
State = < **Act** × **H** × **EIS** × **Env** × $\mathbf{U_{FA}}$ × $\mathbf{U_H}$ >
Session = **Command***
Command = < **C** × **Name** × Σ* >
C = { BIND, DELETE}
Act = $\mathbf{U_{FA}}$ → **ActivationTemplate**
ActivationTemplate = **N** → **Instruction**
H = $\mathbf{U_H}$ → **ST**
$\mathbf{U_{FA}}$ = the set of all unique identifiers for the activations
$\mathbf{U_H}$ = the set of all unique identifiers for structures on the heap
EIS = $\mathcal{P}$(**EI**)
EI = < $\mathbf{U_{FA}}$ × **N** >
Env = Σ* → $\mathbf{U_H}$ ∪ **Scalar**

A *session* is a stream of shell commands that are input to the system. A shell *command* is simply the operation to be performed, either BIND or DELETE, the identifier in the environment being operated upon, and the text of the expression that is to be evaluated.

For a BIND command, the shell translates the command into its base language data flow graph representation. This data flow graph augments the current set of activations and the enabled instructions in this activation are subsequently executed by the interpreter. The result of this execution is returned by the interpreter to the shell which then binds this result to the NAME associated with the command; this binding is then added to the user environment. We can view the shell as the top-level function in VIM – it continues to call the interpreter so long as there are commands to be processed; the result returned by the shell is the state of the system after all commands have been completely evaluated. Because of the presence of early completion structures (described below), there is a potential for much overlap between the operation of the shell and interpreter.

There are six components in the VIM state – a set of activations *Act*, a heap *H*, the set of enabled instructions *EIS*, the user environment, *Env*, and the set of available unique identifiers that can be used to identify activations and data structures, U_{FA} and U_H resp. *Act* defines a mapping from activation uids to activation templates that represents the collection of activations in the system. An *activation template* is a function mapping from natural numbers to instructions and represents the code of an activation. The heap, *H*, is modeled similarly as a function from unique identifiers to structure types, **ST** defined below. The structure of the heap is determined from the mapping defined by the heap function. Scalar values are not represented on the heap; such values are transmitted directly along the value arcs in the graph. The set of enabled instructions is a collection of pairs $< u, i >$, where u is the uid of an activation template and i is the index of the instruction in the template. A more detailed description of these domains follows.

Scalars = **Integers** ∪ **Reals** ∪ **Booleans** ∪ **Character** ∪ **Null**
Integers = ({*undef*} ∪ the set of all integers)
Reals = ({*undef*} ∪ the set of all reals)
Booleans = {*true*, *false*, *undef*}
Character = {*undef*} ∪ the set of characters in the machine.
Null = {*nil*, *undef*}

3.1 Elements of the Heap

The set **ST** describes the components of the heap.

ST = **Array** ∪ **Record** ∪ **Oneof** ∪ **Function** ∪ **ECQ** ∪ **Closure**
Array = [**Z** → ($\mathbf{U_H}$ ∪ **Scalars** ∪ **SUSP** ∪ {*undef*})] **Z** being the set of Integers.
Record = [**N** → ($\mathbf{U_H}$ ∪ **Scalars** ∪ **SUSP** ∪ {*undef*})] **N** being the set of natural numbers.
Oneof = [**N** → ($\mathbf{U_H}$ ∪ **Scalars** ∪ **SUSP** ∪ {*undef*})] **N** being the set ot natural numbers.
Function = [**N** → **Instruction**], **N** being the set of natural numbers.

The set of structure types includes arrays, records, and oneofs. Arrays are modeled as functions from integers to either unique identifiers of structures on the heap, suspensions, or scalar values. Records and oneofs are modeled similarly. Oneof's are discriminated unions similar to CLU oneof's or Algol68 union's.

Note also that the set of functions is also included among the elements of the structure types in the system. This is consonant with our treatment of functions as first class citizens. An element of type **Function** is a mapping from natural numbers to instructions just as elements of the set of activations are.

A function closure is a special record used in function application. It completely defines the execution environment for the invoked function. It has two components: the first component is the uid of the function which is to be applied; the second component is the list of values used by the activation to bind its free variables. The closure of the function must be defined before the function can be applied. The definition of a closure is given formally as:

$$\textbf{Closure} = < \mathbf{U_H} \times (\mathbf{N} \rightarrow (\mathbf{U_H} \cup \textbf{Scalar})) >$$

3.2 Early Completion

To allow greater concurrency of operation without incurring potential read-before-write problems, VIM provides a special mechanism called *early-completion* which permits structures to be created before the values of all its components are available[2].

The early-completion mechanism is comprised of a special data structure called an early-completion queue (EC-queue) and a set of instructions which manipulate it. An EC-queue is a collection of instruction addresses, each of which is a pair consisting of the uid of the activation template and the index of the instruction in the template. The MAKERECORDEC instruction creates the shell of an array in which all the elements are EC-queues, all initially empty. This shell is passed onto consumers of the data structure, and also to producers which replace the EC-queues by values using the RSET instruction. If a RSELECT instruction tries to access an element which is an EC-queue, its address is added to the EC-queue and the instruction is removed from the set of enabled instructions. Eventually, a RSET instruction will replace the EC-queue by a value and will add the addresses of the instructions in the EC-queue to the set of enabled instructions. When these instructions are executed again, they would read the value, as desired.

The early-completion mechanism makes it possible to allow function activations to begin execution before the values of all their arguments have been computed. This is done by packaging the arguments into a record, each of whose elements is an EC-queue. Similarly, the result values may be returned as a structure whose elements are EC-queues, thus allowing the caller to access some of the results before all of them have been evaluated.

Formally, an early completion element (EC-element)is a tuple $< u, i >$ where u is the uid of a function activation and i is the index of an instruction in the activation; an early completion queue is a collection of such EC-elements.

$$\begin{aligned} \textbf{ECE} &= < \mathbf{U_{FA}} \times \mathbf{N} > \\ \textbf{ECQ} &= \mathcal{P}(\textbf{ECE}) \end{aligned}$$

[2]Early Completion structures are similar to the I-structure proposed by Arvind[1]

3.3 Suspensions

A *stream* is a data type provided in the VIMVAL language to allow users to express history-sensitive computation. A stream is a potentially infinite sequence of values all of the same type. VIM uses *suspensions* to implement demand-driven evaluation of streams [4][7]. A stream element is translated into a record of two fields: the first field contains the value of the stream element and the second field contains either a suspension or a pointer to the next stream element. In VIM, a suspension contains the address of an instruction. When a RSELECT instruction tries to access a structure element which is a suspension, the suspension is replaced by an EC-queue containing the address of the RSELECT. A signal is then sent to the instruction whose address is found in the suspension. The signalled instruction eventually causes the execution of a RSET instruction which replaces the EC-queue by a value. Suspensions can also be used to advantage for evaluating the elements of other data types such as arrays or general records in a demand-driven manner. The main benefit in doing this would be that structure elements which are never read need not be computed, thus reducing the amount of computation performed. Thus, it is possible for an implementor to build a fully lazy version of VIM without having to devise a different instruction set or computation model; only the implementation of the VIMVAL compiler need be changed.

The suspension structure is a pair $<u, i>$ which represents the address in the stream producer that is to be signalled when the suspension is accessed. Formally, this is specified by :

$$\mathbf{SUSP} = < \mathbf{U_{FA}} \times \mathbf{N}>$$

3.4 Instructions

A base language instruction is an eight-tuple consisting of an *opcode*, a *type field*, three operand fields (not all need be used), an *operand count* used to indicate how many operands are yet to arrive, a *signal* count used to indicate how many signals must be still received, and a destination record containing the list of destinations for this instruction. The set of opcodes we will be considering in our operational model will include structure operations, function application instructions, and operations on early completion elements.

$$\begin{aligned}
&\mathbf{Instruction} = < \mathbf{OPS} \times \mathbf{VimTypes} \times (\mathbf{U_H} \cup \mathbf{Scalars} \cup \mathbf{ReturnLink})^3 \\
&\qquad\qquad \times \mathbf{N} \times \mathbf{N} \times \mathbf{Dests}> \\
&\mathbf{VimTypes} = \mathbf{Scalars} \cup \mathbf{Array} \cup \mathbf{Record} \cup \mathbf{Oneof} \ \mathbf{Function} \cup \mathbf{Closure} \\
&\mathbf{ReturnLink} = < \mathbf{U_{FA}} \times \mathbf{Dests} >
\end{aligned}$$

A destination of an instruction consists of the address of the instruction to which the result is to be sent, and the operand which is to receive the result value. op1, op2 and op3 denote the first, second, and third operand fields in an instruction, respectively. If the result is a signal, then no operand number is required. The destination also specifies if the result is to be sent unconditionally or conditionally. For all instructions except the conditional branch operator which is used for conditional branching, the results of instructions (both values and signals) are sent to the destinations unconditionally. Whenever a result is sent to an instruction, either its operand count or signal count field is decremented appropriately. Note that because all destinations of an instruction are within the same activation template, there is no need to have the uid of the activation template as part of the destination information.

$$\mathbf{Dests} = \mathcal{P}(\mathbf{D})$$
$$\mathbf{D} = \langle \{\ \mathsf{unconditional},\ \mathsf{true},\ \mathsf{false}\} \times \mathbf{N} \times \{\ \mathsf{op1},\ \mathsf{op2},\ \mathsf{op3},\ \mathsf{signal}\} \rangle$$

An enabled instruction is an element of $\mathbf{EI} = \langle \mathbf{U} \times \mathbf{N} \rangle$. An instruction *I* becomes enabled only when *I*.opcnt and *I*.sigcnt both become zero. The set of enabled instructions describes the collection of instructions which are ready to be executed because they have received an operand on each of the operand arcs and a signal on each of the signal arcs. Any enabled instruction can be executed by the interpreter.

4 A Formal Description of the VIM Shell

The formal definition of the VIM shell is given below. It takes as input a stream of shell commands and a VIM state and returns a new VIM state which is the result of evaluating these commands. It uses several auxiliary functions which we do not describe formally. The *Translate* function maps a source language program into its base language representation. The *ChooseToExecute* function determines whether the shell should continue processing further shell commands or whether the system should execute more enabled instructions and the *AddToEnv* and *DelEnv* functions add and remove a $< name, value >$ pair to and from the current environment respectively. The *Execute* and *NewAct* functions as well as the *Choice* operator are described below.

```
Shell : Session × State → State

Function Shell(Session, State)
    let <Act, H, EIS, Env, U_FA, U_H > = State
        NewState =
          if ChooseToExecute(State, Session)
                    then Shell (Session, Execute (State, Choice(EIS)))
                    elseif empty (Session)
                        then State
                        else let c = first (Session)
                                in if c.C = DELETE
                                       then <Act, H, EIS, DelEnv(Env, Name) >
                                       elseif c.C = BIND
                                           then let
                                             FA = Translate (c)
                                             u_FA, U_FA = GetNewUid (U_FA)
                                             Act ' = NewAct(Act, u_FA, FA)
                                             NewEIS = EIS ∪ {< u_FA, i> | FA(i).opcnt = 0
                                                         ∧ FA(i).sigcnt = 0}
                                             State ' = < Act ', H, NewEIS, Env>
                                             State ' ' , v = Interp (State ', Choice (NewEIS))
                                           <Act ' ' , H ' , NewEIS ', Env, U'_FA, U'_H > = State '
                                             Env ' = AddtoEnv (Env, c.name, v)
                                             in
                                                <Act ' ', H ' , NewEIS ', Env ', U'_FA, U'_H >
                                             endlet
                                       endif
                                endlet
                    endif
    in
      if empty (Session)
          then if EIS ' ≠ {}
                    then Shell (Session, Execute(Newstate, Choice(EIS ')))
                    else Newstate
          else Shell ( rest(Session), Newstate)
      endif
    endlet
endfun
```

5 A Formal Description of the VIM Interpreter

The VIM instruction interpreter, *Interp* is a state transition function from states and enabled instructions to new states and values. *Interp*, when given as input a VIM state, non-deterministically executes enabled instructions in this state until a TERMINATE instruction is chosen for execution. The TERMINATE instruction becomes enabled when the value which is to be bound to the name associated with the current shell BIND command being processed becomes known. In this sense, the TERMINATE instruction serves as a synchronization mechanism between the interpreter and shell.

```
Interp : State × EI → State × ( U_H ∪ Scalar)

Function Interp(State, EI)
    let
        <Act, H, EIS, Env, U_FA, U_H > = State
        <u_FA, k_FA> = EI,  % the address of the enabled instruction
        FA = Act (u_FA),       % the function activation
        I =  FA (k_FA)       % the instruction
        Newstate = Execute ( State, EI )
        < Act', H', EIS', Env, U'_FA, U_H  > = Newstate
    in
        if FA( I ). opcode = TERMINATE
                then Newstate, FA( i ). opnum1
                else Interp ( Newstate, Choice ( EIS' ))
        endif
    endlet
endfun
```

The *Choice* operator non-deterministically chooses an instruction in the set of enabled instructions from a VIM state for the interpreter to execute. We assume that *Choice* is *fair* in choosing from the set of enabled instructions; this assumption is necessary to guarantee termination of the *Interp* function. Note that the interpreter only returns its result when the TERMINATE instruction is chosen for execution. The function *Execute* contains the definitions of all the base language primitive instructions. Its definition is given below:

```
Execute : State ×  (EIS) → State

Function Execute(State, EI)
    let
        <u_FA, k_FA> = EI,  % the address of the enabled instruction
        FA = Act (u_FA),       % the function activation
        I =  FA (k_FA)       % the instruction
    in
        if I. opcode = SET  then SetOp(State, EI, I)
        elseif I. opcode = APPLY  then ApplyOp(State, EI, I)
            .
            .
            .
        endif
    endlet
endfun
```

In the following sections, we present the formal definitions of some of the VIM base language instructions. The instructions we describe are particularly relevant in the design of our backup and recovery algorithms that we give in Section 6. Among those instructions which operate on data structures, the RSET and RSUSP instructions are of greatest interest to us and among the instructions manipulating activations, the APPLY, RETURN and TAILAPPLY, STREAMTAIL operators are used in our algorithms. The reader is referred to [5] for a formal description of the remainder of the VIM instruction set. Throughout the following definitions, we make use of several auxiliary functions – *SendSignal*, and

SendValue are called whenever a value or signal is to be sent to destination instructions, respectively. The functions, *NewHeap* and *NewAct* when given a current heap/activation, a uid, and a value, return a new heap/activation reflecting the new structure of the respective components.

5.1 Structure Operations

The RSET instruction takes three arguments, a structure R, whose element with index i is an EC-queue, and a value, v. It replaces the EC-queue with v. Moreover, all the elements in the EC-queue are added to the enabled instruction set since the value which these instructions initially requested is now available. The RSET instruction does not cause a new version of the structure to be created. Instead, the early completion structure is replaced with the value *in situ*. This does not violate the applicative nature of the base language because no instruction is allowed to read a field which is an EC-queue. RSET sends only signals to its destinations.

```
SetOp: State × EI × Instruction → State
Instruction = { RSET} × VimTypes × U_H × Z ×[ U_H ∪ Scalars] × N^2 × Dests

Function SetOp(<Act, H, EIS, Env, U_FA, U_H >, <u_FA, k_FA>, I)
    let
        u1 = I. op1,
        R = H(u1),
        i = I. op2,
        v = I. op3,
        t = R(i),
        NewEis = EIS - {<u_FA, k_FA>}
        A' = a function such that
            ∀ j ∈ N
                    A'(j) = A(j) if i = j
                          = v otherwise
        Act', NewEis' = SendSignal (Act, NewEis, u_FA, I. dests)
        H' = NewHeap (H, u, A ')
    in
        if t ∈ ECQ
            then
                <Act ', H ',
                NewEis ' ∪ {t},
                Env, U_FA, U_H >
            else
                <Act ', H, NewEis ', Env, U_FA, U_H >
            endif
    endlet
endfun
```

The next instruction we present is RSETSUSP which is used to set a suspension in a VIM record representing a stream element. A suspension is a two-tuple of the uid u of some function activation, and the index i of an instruction in that activation. RSETSUSP takes three arguments : a record A, an integer v_1 which is an index of the structure, and another integer v_2 which is the index of an instruction in the template of the RSETSUSP instruction. RSETSUSP sets the v_1^{th} element of the structure to a suspension of the form (u_{FA}, v_2) where u_{FA} is the uid of the activation template of the RSETSUSP. This element *must* be an EC-queue. RSETSUSP sends signals to its destinations.

```
RsuspOp: State × EIS × Instruction → State
Instruction = { RSETSUSP} × VimTypes × U_H × N^2 × N^2 × Dests

Function RsuspOp(<Act, H, EIS, Env, U_FA, U_H >, <u_FA, k_FA>, I)
  let
      u = I. op1,
      A = H(u),
      v1 = I. op2,
      v2 = I. op3,
      NewEis = EIS   {< u_FA, k_FA >}
      Act', NewEis' =
            SendSignal (Act, NewEis, u_FA, I. dests)
      A ' = a function such that
              ∀ x ∈ N
                   A'(x) = A(x) if x ≠ v1
                         = MakeSusp (< u_FA, k_FA >)
  in
      if A(f) ∈ U_H ∧ H(A(f)) ∈ ECQ ∧ |H(A(f))| = 0
            % If there are no waiting instructions on this EC-queue then
            % replace it by a suspension. Otherwise, send a signal
            % to the suspended instruction.
      then
          <Act ',
          AddtoHeap (H, u, A '),
          NewEis ', Env, U_FA, U_H >
      else
          let
              Act '', NewEis '' =
                   SendResult( Act', EIS', u_FA,
                          ( unconditional, v2, signal), signal)
          in
              <Act '', H, NewEis '', Env, U_FA, U_H >
          endlet
      endif
  endlet
endfun
```

5.2 Function Operators

There are four instructions in VIM which deal with function application and return: APPLY, TAILAPPLY, STREAMTAIL and RETURN. APPLY is the instruction for standard function application; it takes a function closure and an argument record and constructs a new activation template for this function. In our model of VIM, the first operand of the first instruction in the activation receives the closure of the function, the first operand of the second instruction receives the argument record, and the first operand of the third instruction receives the addresses of instructions to which the result of this activation is to be sent. The **type** field is ignored by the APPLY and RETURN instructions. The auxillary function, *GetNewUid*, given a set of uid's (presumably infinite) returns one element in that set as well as a new uid set identical to the old one except for the absence of the element returned.

```
ApplyOp: State × EIS × Instruction → State
Instruction = { APPLY} × VimTypes × U_H^2 × Null × N^2 × Dests

Function ApplyOp(<Act, H, EIS, Env, U_FA, U_H¿, ¡u_FA, k_FA>, I)
    let
        C   = I. op1,
        arg = I. op2,
        <u_f, free> = H(C),
        u ', U'_FA  = GetNewUid(U_FA),
        Act'  = NewAct(Act, u ', H(u_f)),
        NewEis = EIS   {<u_FA, k_FA>}
        Act' ', NewEis'  =
            SendResult(
                SendResult(
                    SendResult(
                        Act', NewEis, u ', < uncond, 1, op1>, C),
                            u ' , < uncond, 2, op1>, arg)
                                u ' , < uncond, 3, op1>, <u_FA, k_FA>)
    in
        <Act ' ', H, NewEis ', Env, U'_FA, U_H >
    endlet
endfun
```

In many cases the value returned by a function *f* is computed directly by a tail-recursive application of *f*. In this situation, the result to be returned by the caller is exactly that returned from the callee, and the reactivation of the caller is unnecessary. The TAILAPPLY instruction in VIM implements this idea. Like the APPLY, it also creates a function activation but differs in that it has an extra operand, a return link, which it passes to the callee. The TAILAPPLY instruction does not receive any result from the callee; after it fires, it sends signals to its target instructions. Note that in contrast to the APPLY operator, the target instructions of TAILAPPLY receive results as soon as the instruction fires, and need not wait for the called activation to return a value. The compiler can use this mechanism to arrange graphs so that the tail-recursive activations can be released before the computation of their callees terminate.

We exploit the presence of a special operator for tail-recursion by treating iteration in VIMVAL as tail-recursion. The use of tail-recursion allows multiple invocations of the loop body to be active simultaneously; this mechanism is expected to increase the amount of concurrency that can be exploited by VIM.

The STREAMTAIL operator is another instruction for function application and is used for tail-recursive evaluation of streams. It takes three arguments – a function closure which contains the stream producer, a record which contains the last element of the stream, and the argument record. It differs from the APPLY instruction in that it has a third operand, which is a stream record that serves as a return link. Using a stream record as a return link allows the stream producer to link all elements of a stream together as successive demands are made. The TAILAPPLY operator is very similar to STREAMTAIL and we omit its formal description here.

```
StreamTailOp: State × EIS × Instruction → State
Instruction = { STREAMTAIL} × VimTypes × U_H^3 × N^2 × Dests

Function StreamTailOp(<Act, H, EIS, Env, U_FA, U_H >, <u_FA, k_FA>, I)
    let
        C  = I. op1,
        arg = I. op2,
        returnlink = I. op3,
        NewEis = EIS − {<u_FA, k_FA>},
        <u_f , free> = H(C),
        u ',U'_FA  = GetNewUid(U_FA),
        Act'  = NewAct (Act, u ', H(u_f))
        Act' ', NewEis'  =
            SendResult(
                SendResult(
                    SendResult(
                        Act', NewEis, u ', < uncond, 1, op1>, C),
                            u ', < uncond, 2, op1>, arg)
                                u ', < uncond, 3, op1>, returnlink),
        Act' ' ', NewEis ' ' =
            SendSignal (Act' ', NewEis ', u_FA, I. dests)
    in
        < Act' ' ', H, NewEis' ', Env, U'_FA, U_H >
    endlet
endfun
```

The last instruction we present is the RETURN instruction which takes as input two arguments, a return link and a value. It sends the value to addresses specified in the return link and then sends signals to target instructions within its own activation.

```
ReturnOp: State × EIS × Instruction → State
Instruction = { RETURN} × VimTypes × ReturnLink ×[ U_H ∪ Scalar] × N^2 × Dests

Function ReturnOp(<Act, H, EIS, Env, U_FA, U_H >, <u_FA, k_FA>, I)
    let
        < u_c, i_c >  = I. op1,        % The return link
        returnvalue = I. op2,          % The return value
        NewEis = EIS - {<u_FA, k_FA>},
        Act', NewEis' =
            SendValue(Act, EIS, u_c, i_c, returnvalue),
                        % Send the result using the return link
        Act '', NewEis '' =
            SendSignal(Act, EIS, u_FA, I. dests)
                        % Send signals to its targets in this activation
    in
        <Act '', H, NewEis '', Env, U_FA, U_H >
    endlet
endfun
```

With this introduction to VIM, we turn to the problem of incorporating backup and recovery procedures into the system. In the following section, we describe our failure model and give a high-level description of our algorithms.

6 A Backup and Recovery Technique

Many of the decisions that are made in the design of the backup and recovery system follow from the failure model that is assumed. A failure model is a specification of hardware behaviour characterizing the type of faults expected and the interaction between failed and non-failed components in the machine. Some of the factors which will influence the design of the backup and recovery algorithms that are described by the failure model include the frequency of failures in the system and the level of hardware error detection capability that is provided.

VIM is not a fault-tolerant system and, therefore, there will be faults that are not masked which will cause the system to behave erroneously. It is unreasonable to expect, however, that there will be no fault coverage in the system at all; like many conventional systems, VIM is expected to provide enough fault coverage to correct many common errors arising from minor transient faults. Correction of single bit errors in memory, for example, is a feature which is found in many commercially available memory units and, thus, the services of the recovery utility should not be required when such an error is detected. In this paper, we assume that the recovery utility is invoked only when errors cause information found on main memory or secondary store to be lost or corrupted. Power outage, short circuits, a malfunctioning disk head etc. are some examples of the type of faults which lead to such errors.

We do not expect that such faults will occur frequently; hardware is assumed to be reliable most of the time. We do make the assumption, however, that invalid information created because of an error is detected when it is accessed. For example, if a faulty disk head causes data to be written incorrectly onto disk, then when the data is read at some future time, the error will be detected. This assumption is important because it means that any information which the backup system observes will either be correct or detected as being erroneous – invalid data is never manipulated by the backup utility.

The data found on the VIM heap and environment may be classified into two categories: *quiescent* and *transitional*, the former corresponding to the result values of computations associated with BIND commands that have been bound to a name in the user environment and the latter representing those values that are either part of an active computation or result values of a computation that have not yet been bound to a name in the environment[3].

If the recovery utility is invoked, it will need to reconstruct the system state based on the information preserved by the backup facility. During this period, another failure may occur; the recovery facility must be robust enough to correctly restore the system state even following such circumstances. As computations complete, causing values to be bound within some environment, the backup facility preserves these bindings on the backup storage medium. In addition, there will also be many active computations in progress. The backup facility maintains information about these computations in two structures. The first structure is called a *command log* and is simply a log of all outstanding shell commands input by the user whose results have not yet been reflected in the user environment. Every command log entry denotes some active computation in the system. Information about these computations is embodied in a *computation record* that is used by the recovery procedures to avoid needless reexecution of activations which have already produced their result before the failure. When the recovery system is invoked, it first restores all quiescent data found on the backup store. It then uses the computation records to restore the remaining part of the state. The state after recovery is complete will be equivalent to the state which existed prior to the failure insofar as the structure and information content of both states will be the same. The states need not be identical, however, because the uid's associated with activations and structures may be different. The reason why the states would not be identical is that the order in which enabled instructions are chosen for execution may be different during the recovery process than before the failure. This does not compromise the correctness of the recovered state because of the applicative nature of VIM – no side-effects occur and, thus, no explicit ordering on instruction execution needs to be adhered to. We illustrate the operation of the system in Fig. 1.

Our algorithms are considerably different from other proposals to guarantee data security both for conventional single-processor systems [12] as well as distributed ones [10]. In systems which use a checkpoint strategy to achieve data security, the presence of a file system makes it impossible for the backup system to immediately discern when useful information has been created (or modified) and to reflect this change on the backup state. The end result is a computer system which cannot guarantee full data security without incurring excessive overhead. Our approach also differs from distributed transaction systems which are based on an updatable memory model. Such systems either require user guidance to specify the objects that are to survive a failure or must resort to expensive synchronization protocols such as two-phase commit or distributed checkpointing to ensure the security of the information on individual processors.

[3] A computation consists of the collection of activations and data created during the evaluation of a shell command.

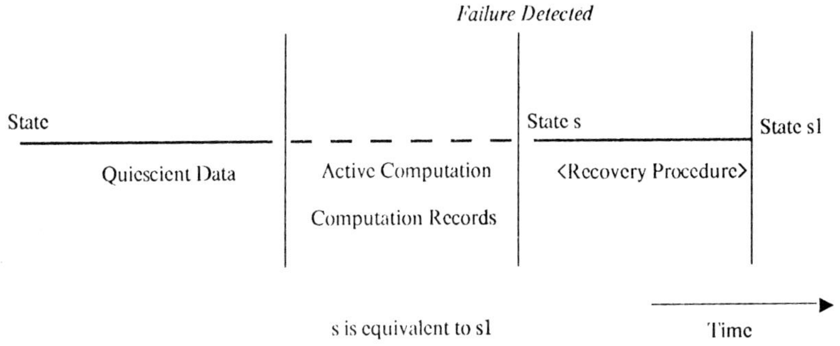

Figure 1 : System Operation

A computation record maintains information about the progress of active computations in the system. We can represent such a record as a directed tree where nodes in the tree denote activations and edges signify caller/callee relationships. The base language instructions are responsible for constructing this tree. A node in the computation tree is known as an *activation descriptor entry* (*ADE*) and embodies information about a particular activation. When an activation is instantiated, a new descriptor entry is placed in the computation tree and an edge is added from the caller to this new entry. When the result of an activation becomes known, it replaces this node in the tree. It should be noted that there is very little cost involved in building the tree; the only instructions which actually transmit data to the backup state are RETURN and RSET. All the other relevant instructions convey information about the progress of a computation; this information is used by the recovery procedures to significantly reduce the recovery process.

Quiescent data is never updated by the backup procedures and, therefore, can be kept on an inexpensive non-volatile storage device such as tape. The computation records associated with active computations and the command log, however, do need to be accessed and augmented relatively frequently. These records will, therefore, need to be held on a fail-safe storage device from which information may be easily accessed, updated and deleted. We call a device with such properties a *stable storage* device[9]. We expect that most computation records will be relatively short-lived and, thus, will not occupy stable storage for any significant amount of time. The final value of a computation record is quiescent and can be migrated onto tape, allowing the space used by the computation record to be reclaimed. It is expected that stable storage will always be able to support all computation records in the system because of their short lifetime. When the recovery system is invoked after a failure is detected, it first reads from the tape the quiescent data and restores as much of the environment image as possible from this. Volatile shell commands are then executed from the command log in the order in which they were originally input. The computation records found on stable store are used to reduce the overall reexecution time

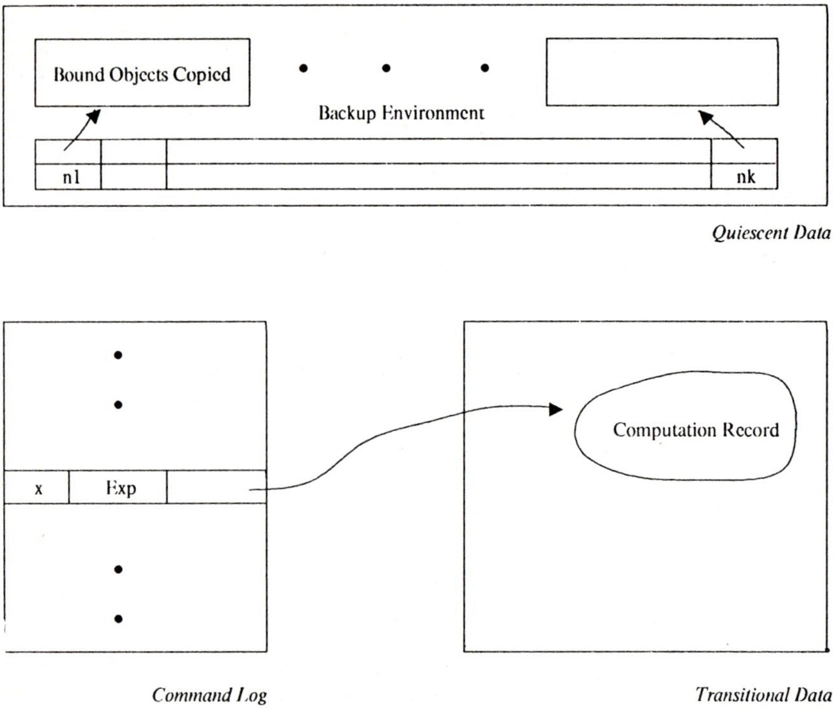

Figure 2 : High Level Organization of the Backup Store

during this phase. When this phase is complete, the system can proceed with normal operation. The high-level organization of the backup store is depicted in Fig 2.

During recovery, after all quiescent data is restored, the recovery system begins reexecution of all computations using the command log found on stable storage. Whenever a new activation is to be instantiated, the corresponding activation descriptor entry is consulted; if that entry contains a result, then that value is used directly and the new activation is not instantiated. Viewed in this way, one can treat functions which have the results of their various activations recorded on a computation record as being *memoized*; reinstantiation of the activation will not cause any recomputation. The recovery system is itself just another version of the interpreter with function application instructions modified to first examine the backup state to see if the value of the activation that is to be instantiated has already been recorded. Thus, the logic of the recovery system can be completely integrated within the definitions of the base language instructions and interpreter.

<table>
<tr><td rowspan="2">uid
of
activation</td><td></td><td></td><td>offsets</td><td></td><td rowspan="2">type</td><td rowspan="2">value</td></tr>
<tr><td></td><td></td><td>edges to descendent ADE's</td><td></td></tr>
</table>

Figure 3 : Structure of an Activation Descriptor Entry

An edge in an activation descriptor entry is a two-tuple $< offset, uid >$ where offset represents the offset in the activation array of a function application instruction which instantiates the activation and *uid* represents the uid of the activation descriptor associated with the called activation. The offset component uniquely identifies the activation being instantiated. The *ADE* to be examined is determined from the current point in the computation tree by noting the index of the APPLY, TAILAPPLY or STREAMTAIL instruction in the activation template that instantiated the corresponding activation. For example, if there is an APPLY instruction at index i in activation α, then the entry in the *ADE* corresponding to α that is of the form $< i, \beta >$ indicates that β is the uid of the *ADE* corresponding to the activation that the APPLY originally instantiated.

Most *ADE*'s are constructed using just the APPLY and RETURN instructions – the former builds the tree and the latter replaces nodes in the tree with the value of the activation that the node represents. There are simple optimizations that can be performed to reduce the size of the computation tree in many instances. One commonly occuring case is tail recursive functions. The TAILAPPLY instruction avoids building new activation descriptors on backup store by reusing the same *ADE* associated with the top-level activation of the tail-recursion.

The technique for maintaining a history of active computations on a reliable backup storage medium given above is a very general scheme that is easy to incorporate into the interpreter. Unfortunately, there are several program structures found in VIM whose behaviour is not efficiently captured using just the procedures given above; we briefly discuss two of them, the early completion mechanism and the stream structure.

6.1 Early Completion Structures

As we had mentioned earlier, to increase concurrency of operation, it will commonly be the case that the result of a function will be an early completion record. Keeping early completion records as part of the backup state does not provide any useful information to the recovery system since it only indicates there exists an activation that will produce a value for this structure but gives no information on the value of the structure itself. To handle EC-structures, the RETURN instruction, whenever it receives an early completion structure as the return value, records in the value field of the *ADE* the special tag, *ec-value* and records in the early completion structure a flag indicating that the structure is a result value of an activation. The RSET instruction, which fills in the value for the early completion field, becomes responsible for augmenting the computation tree appropriately.

6.2 Stream Structures and Demand Driven Evaluation

Because streams in VIMVAL are lazy, it is not possible to record the value returned by a stream producer onto the backup image without generating the entire stream; this would be clearly impractical. It is important that demand-driven evaluation of a stream structure can proceed after the recovery process completes. To do this involves modifying the operation of the RSETSUSP and STREAMTAIL instructions. Because the RSETSUSP instruction has as input the last stream record created by the stream producer, it can augment the *ADE* of the stream producer activation with this record. In addition to recording the stream elements produced, we also use the STREAMTAIL operator to note the argument records of each activation of the stream producer onto the backup image. The <value, argument> pair is referred to as a *stream coordinator record* and is built jointly by the RSETSUSP and STREAMTAIL operators. During recovery, this information will be used to allow demand-driven evaluation of the stream to resume from the stream image recorded on the backup medium as follows: Let $< x_1, x_2, \ldots, x_n >$ be the stream elements recorded. Then, during recovery, the first j elements, $j \leq n$ are restored where x_j is the greatest element for which the argument record needed to create the next element has been recorded. A skeleton activation is created to yield the $j + 1^{st}$ element when a demand for it is made.

In the following section, we describe extensions to the model to include the backup algorithms described informally above.

7 Enhancing the Model to Include a Backup State

Formally, the VIM system is now treated as a five-tuple:

VIM *System* = <*Shell, Interp,* **State**, **BackupState**, Σ > where
State = {< **Act** × **H** × **EIS** × **Env** × $\mathbf{U_{FA}}$ × $\mathbf{U_H}$ >} ∪ { **failed**}
BackupState = < **Log** × **BHeap** × **BEnv** × $\mathbf{U_B}$ >

The **Act, H, EIS, Env**, $\mathbf{U_{FA}}$ and $\mathbf{U_H}$ components of the **State** were given earlier. A failure in the system is modeled by having the current *State* take on the value **failed**. All information found on the heap, environment and activation components as well as the uid sets are presumed "lost" in this case. The domain **BackupState** is defined as a four-tuple where the first component in the tuple, **Log**, represents the command Log of all volatile Shell commands. The domain equation for **BEnv** is the same as that for the environment component in the VIM State, namely,

BEnv = $\Sigma^* \rightarrow$ ($\mathbf{U_H}$ ∪ **Scalar**)

Note that the same uid's for structures are used regardless of whether they are referenced from within the backup environment or the normal environment. Associating a structure with at most one uid simplifies the specification of the extended system. The **Log** is a two-tuple, consisting of a function mapping from natural numbers to log entries and a size component indicating the size of the log. New log entries are appended to the end of the log. The domain, $\mathbf{U_B}$, denotes the set of uid's used exclusively on the backup state; this is used to reference structures not found on the heap ,*e.g.*, computation records etc.

Log = < (**N** → **LogEntry**) × **N** >
LogEntry = < **Command** × $\mathbf{U_B}$ >
$\mathbf{U_B}$ = the set of uid's used for computation records.

As new Shell commands are input to the system, the text of the command is copied by the backup procedures onto the log. This text corresponds to the **Command** component of the **Logentry**. The second component in a log entry is a reference to the root of the computation tree associated with this computation. This computation tree will reside on the backup heap.

There are three types of elements on the heap: structures which are normal VIM structures discussed previously, activation descriptor entries, and stream coordinator records that are used to package information about a stream activation. Every *ADE* on the backup heap will either be referenced by some other *ADE* in the computation tree or will be referenced from a command log entry if it is the initial *ADE* in the computation tree.

BHeap = ($\mathbf{U_H}$ ∪ $\mathbf{U_B}$) → (**ST** ∪ **ADE** ∪ **StreamRec**)
StreamRec = < **Val** × **Arg** × **Link** >
ADE = < $\mathbf{U_A}$ × **AdeEntry** × **AdeType** × **Result** >
Val, Arg = $\mathbf{U_H}$ ∪ **Scalar** ∪ *undef*
Link = $\mathbf{U_B}$ ∪ *undef*
AdeEntry = **N** → $\mathbf{U_B}$
AdeType = { apply, tailapply, stream, value}
Result = $\mathbf{U_H}$ ∪ **Scalar** ∪ *undef*

An activation descriptor entry is a structure of four components. The first component is the uid of the activation being represented. This field is used to identify the activation descriptor so that the result of the activation can be properly forwarded to the *ADE* when it becomes known. The second component, the **AdeEntry**, is a function mapping from natural numbers to backup uids. The domain of the function is the set of all instruction numbers in the corresponding activation which are either APPLY, TAILAPPLY, or STREAM-TAIL operations. The range denotes the uid's of the *ADE*'s in the *BHeap* corresponding to these activations. Thus, if j was the instruction number in some activation α corresponding to an APPLY instruction, then *AdeEntry*(j) would be the uid of the *ADE* associated with the activation created by this APPLY instruction. The third component in the *ADE* contains the type of the descriptor. There are two main *ADE* types: apply *ADE*'s which represent activations for which a result is not yet known and value *ADE*'s which contain the result of the activation. In addition to these two types of descriptors, there are also special descriptors for tail recursive activations and stream producers which we described earlier. The fourth field represents the result of the activation. It can either be a scalar or a uid which references a VIM structure. We shall use dot notation to refer to components of an activation descriptor.

Early completion structures in this enhanced model are now denoted as follows:

ECQ = $\mathcal{P}$ (**ECE**)
ECE = {< $\mathbf{U_H}$ × **N** >} ∪ { back}

back is a special flag which indicates that an early completion structure is part of a larger structure which needs to be placed on the backup heap.

7.1 Describing the Shell and Interpreter in this Model

The *Shell* and *Interpreter* are both key functions in the backup and recovery scheme given above. The *Shell* is responsible for recording the stream of shell commands input onto the command log and augmenting the set of quiescent data on the backup image whenever a new $< name, value >$ binding is added to the user environment. We introduce the notion of a failure within the *Interpreter* through a non-determinate primitive, *Failure*, that given a *State*, returns back that state or returns a failed state.

The formal description of the *Shell* now reads as follows:

```
Shell : Session × State × BackupState → State × BackupState

Function Shell(Session, State, BackupState)
    let <Act, H, EIS, Env, U_FA, U_H > = State
      NewState =
        if ChooseToExecute(State, Session)
              .
              .    % same specification as given originally
              .
            elseif c.C = BIND
                then let
                       .
                       .
                       u, U'_B = GetnewUid (U_B)
                       NewAde = < u_FA, φ, apply,undef >  % φ is the null function
                       BHeap ' = NewBHeap (BHeap, u, NewAde)
                       LogEntry = < c, u >
                       NewLog = AddLog (Log, LogEntry)
                       BackupState ' = < NewLog, Bheap ', BEnv, U'_B >
                           State '' ,BackupState '', v = Interp (State ', BackupState ', Choice
(NewEIS))
                       <Act '' , H ' , NewEIS ', Env, U'_FA, U'_H > = State ''
                       < NewLog, BHeap '', BEnv > = BackupState '
                       BEnv ' = Env ' = AddtoEnv ( Env, c.name, v )
                 in
                     <<Act '' , H ' , NewEIS ', Env ', U'_FA, U'_H >,
                       < NewLog, BHeap '', BEnv ' >>
                 endlet
              .
              .
              .
    endlet
endfun
```

The definition of the *Interpreter* now cognizant of failures in the system is given in Fig. 7.1.

```
Interp : State × BackupState × EI → State × BackupState × ( U_H ∪ Scalar)

Function Interp(State, BackupState, EI)
    let
        < Act, H, EIS, Env, U_FA, U_H > = State
        <u_FA, k_FA> = EI,  % the address of the enabled instruction
        FA = Act (u_FA),        % the function activation
        I = FA (k_FA)        % the instruction
        State ', BackupState ' = Execute ( State, BackupState, EI )
        State ' ' = Failure (State ')
        < Act', H', EIS', Env, U'_FA, U_H > = State ' '
    in
         if failed? (State ' ')
             then   Recovery (BackupState ')
             elseif FA( I ). opcode = TERMINATE
                           then State ' ', BackupState ', FA( i ). opnum1
                           else Interp ( State ' ', BackupState ', Choice ( EIS' ))
         endif
    endlet
endfun
```

Our specification of the interpreter reveals some of the premises of our fault model; in particular, no error is ever propogated onto the backup image. Failures are only manifested in between instruction execution cycles and, thus, it is not possible for any instruction to write illegal data onto the backup image within this model. If a failure is detected, the recovery system is invoked. The main functions in the recovery system are a boot function which restores the quiescent data found on the backup environment and the recovery interpreter which is identical to the normal interpreter except that the definition for APPLY, TAILAPPLY and STREAMTAIL now can refer to the computation records on the backup state before constructing new activations. The formal definitions of the base language instructions that operate on the backup state are a simple extension of the original definitions given above and are not presented here. The interested reader is referred to [8] for more details.

7.2 Showing the Correctness of the Algorithms

One of the purposes served by having a precise description of the operation of a computer system is that it allows properties of the system to be inferred using formal proof techniques. In our model, we can use a simple inductive proof to demonstrate that the algorithms described above correctly preserve and restore the correct system state. Our approach is to compare the behaviour of the ideal system in which no faults arise with the enhanced version that is susceptible to failures but which also manipulates a backup state. Correctness in this context involves showing that no computation which executes after the recovery process is complete ,*i.e.*, after all entries in the command log are processed, should be able to discern that a failure occured before. The key observation is that computations only observe the effects of other computations through the VIM environment structure. Thus, to show that the backup and recovery algorithms are correct reduces to the problem of showing that the VIM environment structure after the recovery process completes is equivalent to the environment structure that would have been constructed in the ideal system where no failures occur. The basic flavour of our approach is very similar to that of the two machine proof technique proposed by McGowan [11].

To establish that environment equivalence is preserved, we examine the state transitions produced by the system when interpreting the command log during recovery and compare it with the state transitions that result when executing the same commands in the fault-free system. The proof involves showing that if environment equivalence holds between a state S in a recovery state transition sequence and a state T in the corresponding ideal recovery sequence, then if $S \vdash S'$, there exists a state transition sequence, $T \overset{*}{\vdash} T'$. We omit the details of the proof here; the interested reader is referred to [8]. Our operational model allows us to treat VIM as a state transition system in which the interpreter is the state transition function. Showing that extensions to the system still preserve the properties desired is done by establishing the equivalence of the state transition sequences produced by the interpreter in the idealized model and the interpreter of the extended system.

8 Conclusion

The motivation for describing a computer system through a formal operational model as outlined in this paper is two-fold. The first is that such a model provides a precise description of the behaviour of the system. In this respect, it serves as a expressive medium through which the designer can communicate all relevant aspects of the intended behaviour of the system to the implementor. Secondly, such a model serves as a specification which, through a process of successive refinement, can be translated into a machine executable form. The correctness of successive stages can be demonstrated by establishing equivalence of behaviour of the corresponding models. The simplicity of the model presented here makes the task of providing such proofs a straightforward one.

This paper has developed a formal operational model for the interpreter and shell of the VIM applicative computer system and has presented a backup and recovery scheme that guarantees the security of all online data in this system. We first presented an ideal model of the system; this model contained no concept of hardware failures. We then enhanced the model to include a backup state and imbued the notion of failure in the new interpreter.

We believe that the formal description techniques as presented here can be used to specify a large class of possible extensions to the VIM system. Enhancing the model to include a backup state allowed us to reason about the correctness of our algorithms using very simple proof techniques. The correctness of the procedures which implement these extensions can be established by demonstrating the equivalence of the operation of the extended system with the ideal one. In another related effort, Guharoy[6] has described, using a technique similar to ours, a model of VIM which includes the notion of hierarchical memory in which data structures have a concrete storage representation.

Acknowledgements

The author would like to thank Prof. Jack Dennis for many invaluable suggestions and criticisms. Much of the idealized model of VIM was developed jointly with Bhaskar Guharoy.

References

[1] Arvind and R. E. Thomas. *I-Structures: An Efficient Data Type for Functional Languages.* Technical Report TM-178, Laboratory for Computer Science, MIT, Cambridge, Mass., September 1980.

[2] J. B. Dennis. *Data Should Not Change: A Model for a Computer System.* Technical Report 209, Computation Structures Group, Laboratory for Computer Science, MIT, Cambridge, Mass., July 1981.

[3] J. B. Dennis, J. E. Stoy, and B. Guharoy. *VIM: An Experimental Multi-User System Supporting Functional Programming.* In *1984 Conference on High-Level Architecture,* 1984.

[4] D. P. Friedman and D. S. Wise. Cons should not evaluate its arguments. In *Automata, Languages, and Programming,* pages 257–284, unknown, 1976.

[5] B. Guharoy and S Jagannathan. An operational model for an applicative computer system. In preparation.

[6] Bhaskar Guharoy. *Data Structure Management in a Data Flow Computer System.* Master's thesis, Massachusetts Institute Technology, 1985.

[7] P. Henderson. *Functional Programming: Application and Implementation.* Prentice/Hall International, Englewood Cliffs, New Jersey, 1980.

[8] Suresh Jagannathan. *Data Backup and Recovery in a Computer Architecture for Functional Programming.* Master's thesis, Massachusetts Institute Technology, 1985.

[9] B.W. Lampson and H. E Sturgis. *Crash Recovery in a Distributed Data Storage System.* Technical Report, Xerox PARC, 1979. Internal draft.

[10] B. Liskov and R. Scheifler. *Guardians and Actions: Linguistic Support for Robust, Distributed Programs.* Technical Report 210-1, Computation Structures Group, Laboratory for Computer Science, MIT, Cambridge, Mass., Novemeber 1981.

[11] C. McGowan. An inductive proof technique for interpreter correctness. In *Courant Institute Symposium on Formal Semantics of Programming Languages,* 1970.

[12] J. A Stern. *Backup and Recovery of Online Information in a Computer Utility.* Technical Report TR-116, Laboratory for Computer Science, MIT, Cambridge, Mass., 1974.

[13] J. E. Stoy. *VIM: A Dynamic Dataflow Implementation of VAL. TOPLAS.* To appear in ACM Transactions On Programming Languages And Systems.

[14] D. A. Turner. Programs as executable specifications. In *Mathematical Logic and Computer Programs,* 1985.

QUESTIONS AND ANSWERS

Blikle: What sort of software support are you using for the application of your system? Do you have any?

Jagannathan: We have a functional shell, a compiler and a parallel interpreter. Our goal is to design a computing system based on multiprogramming ideas.

Formal Description of Programming Concepts - III
M. Wirsing (Editor)
Elsevier Science Publishers B.V. (North-Holland)

© IFIP, 1987

Control Operators, the SECD-Machine, and the λ-Calculus

Matthias Felleisen, Daniel P. Friedman

Indiana University, Lindley Hall 101, Bloomington, IN 47405, USA

Abstract

Control operators like J and *call/cc* are often found in implementations of the λ-calculus as a programming language. Their semantics is always defined by the evaluation function of an abstract machine. We show that, given such a machine semantics, one can derive an algebraic extension of the λ_v-calculus. The extended calculus satisfies the diamond property and contains a Church-Rosser subcalculus. This underscores that the interpretation of control operators is to a certain degree independent of a specific order of evaluation.

1. The control problem of the λ-calculus

The λ-calculus is a natural basis for a programming language. Recognition of this fact led Landin to use it as a meta-language to study programming language features [9, 10]. Since the purely functional basis was insufficient to transliterate jumps and labels directly, Landin extended the language with the non-functional control operator **J**[9]. Others who used similar languages for ordinary applications followed and also added control operators. Notably all the Scheme dialects include control facilities which are equal in power to **J**, *e.g.* *catch* and *throw* [17] and *call-with-current-continuation* (abbreviated *call/cc*) [13]. Common Lisp [16] is equipped with a less powerful version of *catch* and *throw*. Label values in GEDANKEN [14] and escape functions [15] are related to **J**, but more traditional in nature.

The general advantage of non-functional control operators is that they "provide a way of pruning unnecessary computation and allow certain computations to be expressed by more compact and conceptually manageable programs." [18, p.16] They enhance the expressive power of a language and give the programmer a conceptual handle for the specification of control. Some examples will support our case.

Suppose a function $\Sigma_0^\bullet$ is required which maps a tree of numbers to the sum of the numbers if there is no 0 in the tree and otherwise returns a 0. A tree is either an empty tree or it is a node which contains a number and two (sub-) trees. If the specification did not include the 0-exception clause, the function could be written in the ordinary, recursive style. In the λ-value-calculus it would be expressed by:

$$\begin{aligned}\Sigma^\bullet \equiv \mathbf{Y}_v(&\lambda s.\lambda t.\\ &\quad(\mathbf{if}\,(\mathbf{mt?}\,t)\,\ulcorner 0 \urcorner\\ &\qquad(+(\mathbf{num}\,t)(+(s(\mathbf{lson}\,t))(s(\mathbf{rson}\,t))))))\end{aligned}$$

This material is partly based on work supported by the National Science Foundation under grants DCR 85-01277 and DCR 85-03279.

where $\mathbf{Y}_v$ is the call-by-value recursion operator, **if** is syntactic sugar for a branching construct, and **mt?**, **num**, **lson**, and **rson** are combinators to deal with number trees.

Given continuation-operators like **J** and *call/cc*, we can solve the problem by modifying the recursive function. For example, with *call/cc* we could write:

$$
\begin{aligned}
\Sigma_0^{\bullet} \equiv \lambda t.\mathit{call/cc}(\lambda \kappa.&\\
&\mathbf{Y}_v(\lambda s.\lambda t.\\
&\quad (\mathbf{if}\,(\mathbf{mt?}\,t)\,\ulcorner 0 \urcorner\\
&\qquad (\mathbf{if}\,(\mathbf{zero?}\,(\mathbf{num}\,t))\,(\kappa \ulcorner 0 \urcorner)\\
&\qquad\quad (+(\mathbf{num}\,t)(+(s(\mathbf{lson}\,t))(s(\mathbf{rson}\,t)))))))\\
&t).
\end{aligned}
$$

With **J** the definition becomes $\lambda t.(\lambda k.\ \ldots)(\mathbf{J}\lambda x.x)$ [15]. When $\Sigma_0^{\bullet}$ is applied to an argument, the operator *call/cc* applies its argument to a representation of the current continuation, *i.e.*, κ becomes bound to a function-like abstraction of the rest of the program. Then the recursive tree traversal begins. If there is a 0 in the tree, $\Sigma_0^{\bullet}$ sooner or later visits that node and can then invoke the continuation on 0. The program evaluation continues as if $\Sigma_0^{\bullet}$ had returned a value. The advantage of this approach is clear: the function differs from the purely recursive summation function only to the extent to which the two specifications differ. The modification is simple and, we believe, easy to understand. The function definition is in no way obscured by auxiliary expressions. We classify this kind of continuation as an ***escape*** continuation.

When continuations can be passed around freely as first-class objects, like in Scheme and ISWIM, they may be used to implement more interesting control strategies. A classical example is the coroutine facility. There are numerous situations when a program is best expressed as two or more coroutines which simultaneously analyze input and synthesize output files [7]. If a programming language does not have a coroutine mecahnism but has continuation operators, this behavior can easily be achieved by passing around the current control state in the form of a continuation [18]. The advantage of continuations is even more apparent when bi-directional communication among the coroutines is required [5].

First-class continuations are also useful when multi-valued functions or relations are needed in a functional language. A (functional representation of a) relation generally produces more than one result for a given argument. To this end, it can return a result with a continuation. If more results are required, the calling function can reinvoke the continuation. With this technique it becomes possible to implement a Landin-style embedding of logic languages [2, 6]. Intelligent backtrack strategies are realized in a similar manner by retaining a store of appropriate continuations [4]. There are many other examples of advantageous uses of continuation operators, but an introduction to the techniques of programming with continuations is not our concern here.

Although this is well-recognized and control operators are heavily used in practical programming, non-functional operators are regarded with skepticism among language theoreticians. The imperative character of these operations is suspicious. Programs using them are difficult to prove correct. Whereas function application is modeled by the β-rule, which allows for algebraic manipulations of programs, there is nothing in the λ-calculus for reasoning about non-functional control.

This difficulty was overcome when we showed in a companion paper [3] that the λ_v-calculus [12] can incorporate axioms for general control operators. The development of this extension was rather *ad hoc*. The new axioms were based on our intuition about programming with continuations. The formal, operational semantics of the control operators had no direct influence on our work. Consequently, it was rather hard to connect the two systems. It finally turned out that the standard reduction semantics disagreed with the machine semantics. If the result contains continuations, the respective continuations can differ by huge pieces of dead code, *i.e.*, subterms which never play a role in an evaluation.

In this paper we show that there is a (more) systematic way to derive a calculus for a given machine. The approach generalizes Plotkin's way of deriving the λ_v-calculus from the SECD-machine. The main idea is to gradually eliminate components of the machine by merging them into the program component. The outcome is a program rewriting system. This in turn can be taken as the specification of a standard reduction function. The transition from it to a reduction system is easy.

In the next section we define our extended programming language and its meaning. For the latter part we revise Landin's SECD-machine. The third section contains a derivation of a program-oriented rewriting system from the original machine. The reduction system is presented in Section 4. For this we assume some general knowledge of the notation and terminology of the classical λ-calculus [1, Ch. 2, 3]. Our calculus is an extension of Plotkin's λ_v-calculus since our machine defines a call-by-value semantics for applications. It differs slightly from the one presented in our companion paper but we can still prove variations of the Church-Rosser Theorem and the Curry-Feys Standardization Theorem. In the fifth section we demonstrate in what sense the calculus corresponds to the machine. The standard reduction function does not simulate the machine evaluation function, but the difference is irrelevant. For the rest of the section we follow Plotkin's programme for the investigation of the λ_v-calculus. The last section is a brief discussion of our results.

2. The extended programming language

The traditional term set of the pure λ-calculus is the basis of our programming language. It includes two new types of applications: $\mathcal{C}$- and $\mathcal{A}$-applications. For the sake of simplicity we omit constant and function symbols, but they could easily be added. The formal syntax specification is shown in Definition 1. In what follows we liberally omit parentheses wherever it is unambiguous.

The notion of free and bound variables in a term M, $FV(M)$ and $BV(M)$, respectively, carries over directly from the *pure* λ-calculus under the provision that $\mathcal{C}$ and $\mathcal{A}$ are symbols which are neither free nor bound. Terms with no free variables are called *closed terms* or *programs*. Since we want to avoid syntactic issues, we adopt Barendregt's convention of identifying terms that are equal except for some renaming of bound variables and his hygiene condition which says that *in a discussion, free variables are assumed to be distinct from bound ones*. Furthermore, we extend Barendregt's definition of the substitution function, $M[x := N]$, to Λ_c in the natural way: $\mathcal{C}$- and $\mathcal{A}$-applications are treated like applications where the function part is simply ignored.

The intuitive meaning of the traditional constructs is approximately the same. A variable represents a value. An abstraction roughly corresponds to a function. An $\mathcal{A}$-application

Definition 1: The term sets Λ_c and Λ

The improper symbols are λ, (,), ., $\mathcal{C}$, and $\mathcal{A}$. *Var* is a countable set of variables. The symbols $x, \kappa, f, v, \ldots$, range over *Var* as meta-variables but are also used as if they were elements of *Var*. The *term set* Λ_c contains

- *variables:* x if $x \in Var$;
- *abstractions:* $(\lambda x.M)$ if $M \in \Lambda_c$ and $x \in Var$;
- *applications:* (MN) if $M, N \in \Lambda_c$; M is called the function, N is called the argument;
- *$\mathcal{C}$-applications:* $(\mathcal{C}M)$ if $M \in \Lambda_c$; M is called the $\mathcal{C}$-argument;
- *$\mathcal{A}$-applications:* $(\mathcal{A}M)$ if $M \in \Lambda_c$; M is called the $\mathcal{A}$-argument.

The union of variables and abstractions is referred to as the set of *values*. Λ, the term set of the traditional λ-calculus, stands for Λ_c restricted to variables, applications, and abstractions.

aborts the current computation and begins a new one with its argument as the starting point. A $\mathcal{C}$-application captures the current continuation of the program and passes it as a function-like abstraction to its argument. An application invokes a function or a continuation on an argument.

For historical reasons we use an abstract machine to formally define the semantics of Λ_c-programs. The machine is derived from Reynolds' extended interpreter IV [15]. It is similar to Landin's SECD-machine [8] but closer to denotational semantics and, hopefully, easier to understand. The machine works on states which are triples composed of a control string, an environment, and a continuation code; it is accordingly referred to as the CEK-machine.

A *control string* is either the symbol "$\ddagger$" or a Λ_c-expression. *Environments* are finite maps from the set of variables *Var* to the set of *semantic values*, that is, the union of closures and continuation points. If ρ is an environment, then $\rho[x := V]$ is the environment which is like ρ except for the point x where it is V. A *closure* is an ordered pair composed of an abstraction and an environment whose domain contains the free variables of the abstraction. A closure $\langle M, \rho \rangle$ is called *continuation-free* iff for all free x in M, $\rho(x)$ is a continuation-free closure. *Continuation points* are tagged structures of the form $\langle \mathbf{p}, \kappa \rangle$ where κ is a continuation code.

A *continuation code* represents the remainder of the computation, *i.e.*, it encodes what the machine has left to do when the current control string is evaluated. The representation is defined in two stages. If N is a Λ_c-term, ρ is an environment such that $FV(N) \subseteq Dom(\rho)$, and V is a semantic value, then a $\mathbf{p}$-continuation has one of the following forms:

$$(\mathbf{stop}),\ (\kappa\,\mathbf{cont}),\ (\kappa\,\mathbf{arg}\ N\rho),\ (\kappa\,\mathbf{fun}\ V),$$

where κ is a $\mathbf{p}$-continuation. A $\mathbf{ret}$-continuation is of the form

$$(\kappa\,\mathbf{ret}\ V)$$

where κ is a $\mathbf{p}$-continuation and V is a semantic value.

Table 1: The CEK-transition function

(1)	$\langle x, \rho, \kappa\rangle \overset{CEK}{\longmapsto} \langle \ddagger, \emptyset, (\kappa\, \mathbf{ret}\ \rho(x))\rangle$
(2)	$\langle \lambda x.M, \rho, \kappa\rangle \overset{CEK}{\longmapsto} \langle \ddagger, \emptyset, (\kappa\, \mathbf{ret}\ \langle \lambda x.M, \rho\rangle)\rangle$
(3)	$\langle MN, \rho, \kappa\rangle \overset{CEK}{\longmapsto} \langle M, \rho, (\kappa\, \mathbf{arg}\ N\, \rho)\rangle$
(4)	$\langle \ddagger, \emptyset, ((\kappa\, \mathbf{arg}\ N\, \rho)\, \mathbf{ret}\ F)\rangle \overset{CEK}{\longmapsto} \langle N, \rho, (\kappa\, \mathbf{fun}\ F)\rangle$
(5)	$\langle \ddagger, \emptyset, ((\kappa\, \mathbf{fun}\ \langle \lambda x.M, \rho\rangle)\, \mathbf{ret}\ V)\rangle \overset{CEK}{\longmapsto} \langle M, \rho[x := V], \kappa\rangle$
(6)	$\langle \mathcal{C}M, \rho, \kappa\rangle \overset{CEK}{\longmapsto} \langle M, \rho, (\kappa\, \mathbf{cont})\rangle$
(7)	$\langle \ddagger, \emptyset, ((\kappa\, \mathbf{cont})\, \mathbf{ret}\ \langle \lambda x.M, \rho\rangle)\rangle \overset{CEK}{\longmapsto} \langle M, \rho[x := \langle \mathrm{p}, \kappa\rangle], (\mathbf{stop})\rangle$
(8)	$\langle \ddagger, \emptyset, ((\kappa\, \mathbf{cont})\, \mathbf{ret}\ \langle \mathrm{p}, \kappa_0\rangle)\rangle \overset{CEK}{\longmapsto} \langle \ddagger, \emptyset, (\kappa_0\, \mathbf{ret}\ \langle \mathrm{p}, \kappa\rangle)\rangle$
(9)	$\langle \ddagger, \emptyset, ((\kappa\, \mathbf{fun}\ \langle \mathrm{p}, \kappa_0\rangle)\, \mathbf{ret}\ V)\rangle \overset{CEK}{\longmapsto} \langle \ddagger, \emptyset, (\kappa_0\, \mathbf{ret}\ V)\rangle$
(10)	$\langle \mathcal{A}M, \rho, \kappa\rangle \overset{CEK}{\longmapsto} \langle M, \rho, (\mathbf{stop})\rangle$

A CEK-*machine state* is either a triple of the form $\langle \ddagger, \emptyset, \kappa\rangle$ where κ is a **ret**-continuation or a triple of the form $\langle M, \rho, \kappa\rangle$ where M is a Λ_c-term, ρ is an environment with $FV(M) \subseteq Dom(\rho)$, and κ is a **p**-continuation. Machine states of the form $\langle M, \emptyset, (\mathbf{stop})\rangle$ are the *initial* states; for all semantic values V, $\langle \ddagger, \emptyset, ((\mathbf{stop})\, \mathbf{ret}\ V)\rangle$ is a *terminal* state.

The state transition function is displayed in Table 1. We use $\overset{CEK^+}{\longmapsto}$, $\overset{CEK^*}{\longmapsto}$, and $\overset{CEK}{\longmapsto}_=$ to denote the transitive, transitive-reflexive, and reflexive closure, respectively. The rules (CEK1) through (CEK5) correspond to an evaluator for the λ-value-calculus, *e.g.*, the classical SECD-machine. The rules (CEK6) to (CEK8) define the operations of a $\mathcal{C}$-application: the current continuation is marked, the $\mathcal{C}$-argument is evaluated, and, eventually, the continuation point is passed to the evaluated argument. The last step in this sequence also replaces the current continuation by the initial one. This is where *call/cc* and $\mathcal{C}$ differ: *call/cc* is equivalent to $\lambda f.\mathcal{C}\lambda\kappa.\kappa(f\kappa)$. Rule (CEK9) shows that the invocation of a continuation removes the current continuation, and moves the former one in its place. The invocation argument is placed on the stack. According to rule (CEK10), an $\mathcal{A}$-application ignores the continuation and starts the evaluation of the $\mathcal{A}$-argument.

In order to evaluate a program M, the machine is started in the initial state $\langle M, \emptyset, (\mathbf{stop})\rangle$. Then the machine moves into the next legal state according to the transition function. This is repeated until a terminal state is reached. When the machine reaches a terminal state, it stops and returns the value on the stack as the answer. We summarize the evaluation process in the following:

$$eval_{CEK}(M) = V \text{ iff } \langle M, \emptyset, (\mathbf{stop})\rangle \overset{CEK^+}{\longmapsto} \langle \ddagger, \emptyset, ((\mathbf{stop})\, \mathbf{ret}\ V)\rangle.$$

Since the transition function is clearly defined on all legal states except for terminal ones, the machine, when started in a legal state, either halts in a terminal state or never terminates.

The evaluation function returns semantic values. A continuation-free closure can be mapped to a Λ_c-term by substituting all free variables by the terms which correspond to their environment values. A continuation point does not have an obvious association. We accept this and do not define an unload function for the CEK-machine until later.

Convention. M, N, P, Q are variables ranging over terms in control string position. U, V, and F stand for values. The letters s, c, ρ, and κ denote machine states, control strings, environments, and continuation codes, respectively. We use similar conventions throughout the sequel (*proviso quod* the appropriate changes). **End of Convention**

Given the CEK-machine, one can theoretically reason about programs with non-functional control [18], but it is rather awkward. What a programmer really wants is a rewriting system that allows him to think about programs in terms of program code and related notions. In the next section, we show how to derive such a term rewriting system from the machine definition.

3. From the CEK-machine to a term rewriting system

The CEK-machine uses environments and continuations in addition to terms for the evaluation of programs. Hence, if we want to have a pure term rewriting system, we need to eliminate environments and continuations. We perform this transformation in three steps. The first step results in a machine with two state components: control strings and continuation codes. The second step is an intermediary which introduces a less machine-oriented encoding for continuations. The last one incorporates the two remaining components into a single one.

3.1 The CK-machine

Environments in the CEK-machine are merely a functional representation of substitutions. It is quite natural to replace environments by substitutions which are performed at the appropriate place. The resulting machine is called the CK-machine.

The CK-machine has control string-continuation pairs as states. The definition of control terms needs to be adjusted. They now include continuation points at the base case. Continuation codes contain control strings where they formerly had closures or term-environment pairs, *e.g.* $(\kappa\, \mathbf{arg}\ M\rho)$ becomes $(\kappa\, \mathbf{arg}\ N)$ for some control string N. We leave it at these informal revisions and define the CK-transition function in Table 2.

The substitution function is extended in the obvious way to work on control strings and semantic values. All other definitions of the CEK-machine are applied to the CK-machine *mutatis mutandis*.

For the transition from CEK-states to CK-states we adopt Plotkin's function *Real* to work on the entire control string domain:

$$\begin{aligned}
\mathcal{R}(\langle M, \rho\rangle) &\equiv M[x_1 := \mathcal{R}(\rho(x_1))]\ldots[x_n := \mathcal{R}(\rho(x_n))] \\
&\quad\text{where } FV(M) = \{x_1, \ldots, x_n\} \\
\mathcal{R}(\langle \mathbf{p}, \kappa\rangle) &= \langle \mathbf{p}, \mathcal{K}(\kappa)\rangle \\
\mathcal{R}(\langle \ddagger, \rho\rangle) &= \ddagger.
\end{aligned}$$

Table 2: The CK-transition function

(1)	$\langle\langle \mathbf{p}, \kappa_0\rangle, \kappa\rangle \overset{CK}{\longmapsto} \langle \ddagger, (\kappa\,\mathbf{ret}\,\langle \mathbf{p}, \kappa_0\rangle)\rangle$
(2)	$\langle \lambda x.M, \kappa\rangle \overset{CK}{\longmapsto} \langle \ddagger, (\kappa\,\mathbf{ret}\,\lambda x.M)\rangle$
(3)	$\langle MN, \kappa\rangle \overset{CK}{\longmapsto} \langle M, (\kappa\,\mathbf{arg}\,N)\rangle$
(4)	$\langle \ddagger, ((\kappa\,\mathbf{arg}\,N)\,\mathbf{ret}\,F)\rangle \overset{CK}{\longmapsto} \langle N, (\kappa\,\mathbf{fun}\,F)\rangle$
(5)	$\langle \ddagger, ((\kappa\,\mathbf{fun}\,\lambda x.M)\,\mathbf{ret}\,V)\rangle \overset{CK}{\longmapsto} \langle M[x := V], \kappa\rangle$
(6)	$\langle \mathcal{C}M, \kappa\rangle \overset{CK}{\longmapsto} \langle M, (\kappa\,\mathbf{cont})\rangle$
(7)	$\langle \ddagger, ((\kappa\,\mathbf{cont})\,\mathbf{ret}\,\lambda x.M)\rangle \overset{CK}{\longmapsto} \langle M[x := \langle \mathbf{p}, \kappa\rangle], (\mathbf{stop})\rangle$
(8)	$\langle \ddagger, ((\kappa\,\mathbf{cont})\,\mathbf{ret}\,\langle \mathbf{p}, \kappa_0\rangle)\rangle \overset{CK}{\longmapsto} \langle \ddagger, (\kappa_0\,\mathbf{ret}\,\langle \mathbf{p}, \kappa\rangle)\rangle$
(9)	$\langle \ddagger, ((\kappa\,\mathbf{fun}\,\langle \mathbf{p}, \kappa_0\rangle)\,\mathbf{ret}\,V)\rangle \overset{CK}{\longmapsto} \langle \ddagger, (\kappa_0\,\mathbf{ret}\,V)\rangle$
(10)	$\langle \mathcal{A}M, \kappa\rangle \overset{CK}{\longmapsto} \langle M, (\mathbf{stop})\rangle.$

The auxiliary function $\mathcal{K}$ maps CEK-continuation codes to CK-continuation codes:

$$\begin{aligned}
\mathcal{K}((\mathbf{stop})) &= (\mathbf{stop}) \\
\mathcal{K}((\kappa\,\mathbf{cont})) &= (\mathcal{K}(\kappa)\,\mathbf{cont}) \\
\mathcal{K}((\kappa\,\mathbf{arg}\,N\rho)) &= (\mathcal{K}(\kappa)\,\mathbf{arg}\,\mathcal{R}(\langle N, \rho\rangle)) \\
\mathcal{K}((\kappa\,\mathbf{fun}\,F)) &= (\mathcal{K}(\kappa)\,\mathbf{fun}\,\mathcal{R}(F)) \\
\mathcal{K}((\kappa\,\mathbf{ret}\,V)) &= (\mathcal{K}(\kappa)\,\mathbf{ret}\,\mathcal{R}(V)).
\end{aligned}$$

With these functions we can now express in what sense the CEK-machine is equivalent to the CK-machine:

Theorem 3.1 (CK-simulation). *For any program M, $\mathcal{R}(eval_{CEK}(M)) = eval_{CK}(M)$.*

Proof. The clauses of the two transition functions obviously correspond to each other. The CK-machine has no variables in control string position, but will always contain a value in the respective place. Thus, rule (CK1) provides the means to return a continuation point as did (CEK1) in the CEK-machine. More formally, one can show that

$$\langle c_1, \rho_1, \kappa_1\rangle \overset{CEK}{\longmapsto} \langle c_2, \rho_2, \kappa_2\rangle$$

implies

$$\langle \mathcal{R}(\langle c_1, \rho_1\rangle), \mathcal{K}(\kappa_1)\rangle \overset{CK}{\longmapsto} \langle \mathcal{R}(\langle c_2, \rho_2\rangle), \mathcal{K}(\kappa_2)\rangle.$$

This in turn says that, if the CEK-machine halts in $\langle \ddagger, \emptyset, ((\mathbf{stop})\,\mathbf{ret}\,V)\rangle$, the CK-machine reaches the state $\langle \ddagger, ((\mathbf{stop})\,\mathbf{ret}\,\mathcal{R}(V))\rangle$. On the other hand, if the CEK-machine loops forever on a program M, then so does the CK-machine. There are no other cases and this concludes the proof. □

This first transition leaves us with a machine that works with control strings and continuation codes. The expected next step would be to incorporate continuation codes into the term components. We have found, however, that the notion of continuation codes is too machine-oriented for a smooth transition. The next step is a replacement of continuation codes by a more familiar concept. The final step is then quite natural.

3.2 The CC-machine

An inspection of some sample evaluations on the CK-machine reveals that the machine repeats a two-phase procedure. In the first phase the control string is searched for either an application of the form (FV), a $\mathcal{C}$-application, or an $\mathcal{A}$-application. When one of these subterms is found, the machine performs a computation step proper. This may either be a substitution, the labeling of a continuation, or the throwing away of a continuation. Then the machine re-enters the search phase.

During the search phase the machine unravels the control string and shifts term components to the continuation part of the state. These program parts are saved for later use, *i.e.*, the continuation code memorizes the textual context of the next "good" application. The term **(stop)** in continuation position simply means that nothing has to be remembered; the machine is about to begin an evaluation and when this continuation is ever looked at again, the evaluation stops. A continuation like $(\kappa\,\mathbf{arg}\ N)$ recalls that the machine had found an application with argument part N, that the context of this application was encoded in κ, and that the machine is currently evaluating the function part. Conversely, $(\kappa\,\mathbf{fun}\ F)$ indicates that the function part is evaluated and that the argument part is directing the evaluation. A continuation of the type $(\kappa\,\mathbf{cont})$ originates from a $\mathcal{C}$-application. The continuation code was marked and the $\mathcal{C}$-argument determines the further course of the evaluation. The machine acts as if it had encountered an application at the root of a term. The argument is the current continuation; the $\mathcal{C}$-argument stands for the function part. **ret**-continuations finally express that a value has been found and that the machine has to inspect the continuation code—or, control memory—to find out what to do next.

With this description we are now in a position to design a term-like representation of continuation codes. The notion of a textual context is captured in the concept of a term context. For our special case we need contexts with one hole and, furthermore, the path from the root to the hole may only lead through applications. However, the machine not only needs to know the context, but it also needs to remember which part of an application it has already seen. To this end we introduce labeled applications and labeled sk-contexts. If M and N are Λ_c-terms, then $M \bullet N$ is a *labeled application* of M to N; MN is the corresponding unlabeled application. *Labeled sk-contexts* are defined inductively as follows:

(skC1) $[\ ]$ is a labeled sk-context,

(skC2) $C[\ ]P$ is a labeled sk-context if $C[\ ]$ is a labeled sk-context and P is a Λ_c-term,

(skC3) $P \bullet C[\ ]$ is a labeled sk-context if $C[\ ]$ is a labeled sk-context and P is a value.

Unlabeled sk-contexts are defined in the same way except that unlabeled applications are used in the third clause. If $C[\ ]$ is an sk-context, then $C[M]$ is the term where the hole is filled with the term M; $C[C'[\ ]]$ is the sk-context where the hole is filled with the sk-context $C'[\ ]$. The important connection between contexts and control strings $M \in \Lambda_c$ is captured in:

Lemma (Unique context). *For all control strings M there is a unique (labeled or unlabeled) sk-context $C[\ ]$ such that, if M is not a value, then $M \equiv C[FV]$ or $M \equiv C[\mathcal{C}N]$ or*

$M \equiv C[\mathcal{A}N]$ (or $M \equiv C[F \bullet V]$, for labeled sk-contexts).

Proof. A straightforward induction on the structure of M. □

The above description of the function of particular control codes leads to the following definition for a morphism $\mathcal{C}$ from continuation codes to sk-contexts:

$$\left.\begin{array}{r}\mathcal{C}((\mathbf{stop})) = [\ ] \\ \mathcal{C}((\kappa\,\mathbf{arg}\ N)) = C[[\ ]\mathcal{S}(N)] \\ \mathcal{C}((\kappa\,\mathbf{fun}\ F)) = C[\mathcal{S}(F) \bullet [\ ]] \\ \mathcal{C}((\kappa\,\mathbf{cont})) = [\ ] \bullet \langle \mathbf{p}, C[\ ]\rangle \\ \mathcal{C}((\kappa\,\mathbf{ret}\ V)) = C[\mathcal{S}(V)]\end{array}\right\} \text{ where } \mathcal{C}(\kappa) = C[\ ].$$

$\mathcal{S}$ replaces codes in continuation points by contexts:

$$\mathcal{S}(\langle \mathbf{p}, \kappa\rangle) = \langle \mathbf{p}, \mathcal{C}(\kappa)\rangle,\ \mathcal{S}(\ddagger) = \ddagger,\ \mathcal{S}(x) = x,$$
$$\mathcal{S}(MN) = \mathcal{S}(M)\mathcal{S}(N),\ \mathcal{S}(\lambda x.M) = \lambda x.\mathcal{S}(M),$$
$$\mathcal{S}(\mathcal{C}M) = \mathcal{C}\mathcal{S}(M),\ \mathcal{S}(\mathcal{A}M) = \mathcal{A}\mathcal{S}(M).$$

The new CC-machine works on states which combine control strings and labeled sk-contexts. Control strings contain sk-contexts where they used to contain continuation codes. The initial state of the machine is $\langle M, [\ ]\rangle$; the machine stops when it reaches the state $\langle \ddagger, V\rangle$ for some value V. The CC-transition function is shown in Table 3. All other notions, in particular the one for the eval-function, are adapted in the appropriate way.

Table 3: The CC-transition function

(1)	$\langle\langle \mathbf{p}, C_0[\ ]\rangle, C[\ ]\rangle \overset{CC}{\longmapsto} \langle \ddagger, C[\langle \mathbf{p}, C_0[\ ]\rangle]\rangle$
(2)	$\langle \lambda x.M, C[\ ]\rangle \overset{CC}{\longmapsto} \langle \ddagger, C[\lambda x.M]\rangle$
(3)	$\langle MN, C[\ ]\rangle \overset{CC}{\longmapsto} \langle M, C[[\ ]N]\rangle$
(4)	$\langle \ddagger, C[VN]\rangle \overset{CC}{\longmapsto} \langle N, C[V \bullet [\ ]]\rangle$
(5)	$\langle \ddagger, C[(\lambda x.M) \bullet V]\rangle \overset{CC}{\longmapsto} \langle M[x := V], C[\ ]\rangle$
(6)	$\langle \mathcal{C}M, C[\ ]\rangle \overset{CC}{\longmapsto} \langle M, [\ ] \bullet \langle \mathbf{p}, C[\ ]\rangle\rangle$
(7)	$\langle \ddagger, (\lambda x.M) \bullet \langle \mathbf{p}, C[\ ]\rangle\rangle \overset{CC}{\longmapsto} \langle M[x := \langle \mathbf{p}, C[\ ]\rangle], [\ ]\rangle$
(8)	$\langle \ddagger, \langle \mathbf{p}, C_0[\ ]\rangle \bullet \langle \mathbf{p}, C[\ ]\rangle\rangle \overset{CC}{\longmapsto} \langle \ddagger, C_0[\langle \mathbf{p}, C[\ ]\rangle]\rangle$
(9)	$\langle \ddagger, C[\langle \mathbf{p}, C_0[\ ]\rangle \bullet V]\rangle \overset{CC}{\longmapsto} \langle \ddagger, C_0[V]\rangle$
(10)	$\langle \mathcal{A}M, C[\ ]\rangle \overset{CC}{\longmapsto} \langle M, [\ ]\rangle.$

From the definition of the CC-transition function it follows that labeled applications are only needed to make the CC-transition relation into a proper function. Even though there is only one unique context surrounding the "good" subterm, the machine could still take two different paths in case $M \equiv C[(\lambda x.P)V]$, *i.e.*, in the absence of labels it may either use (CC4) or (CC5). A labeled application means the machine has evaluated the function *and* the argument part. It is then safe to perform a computation step. Furthermore, this device makes the CC-machine reflect the CK-machine on a rule-by-rule basis:

Theorem 3.2 (CC-simulation). *For any program M,* $\mathcal{S}(eval_{CK}(M)) = eval_{CC}(M)$.

Proof. Again, we can show that every CK-step is reflected by a CC-transition move, *i.e.*

$$\langle c_1, \kappa_1\rangle \overset{CK}{\longmapsto} \langle c_2, \kappa_2\rangle \text{ implies } \langle \mathcal{S}(c_1), \mathcal{C}(\kappa_1)\rangle \overset{CC}{\longmapsto} \langle \mathcal{S}(c_2), \mathcal{C}(\kappa_2)\rangle.$$

Hence, if the CK-machine returns a value V, then the CC-machine returns the value $\mathcal{S}(V)$. Otherwise, both machines loop forever. □

Before we end this subsection we note that not all of the rules are necessary. The first two transitions may be merged into a single rule:

$$\langle V, C[\ \ ]\rangle \overset{CC}{\longmapsto} \langle \updownarrow, C[V]\rangle.$$

Rule (CC5) subsumes (CC7) and rule (CC9) subsumes (CC8). Furthermore, the first four rules are simply bookkeeping rules which allow the machine to remember which part of the term it has visited. For a pure rewriting system they may be eliminated.

3.3 The C-rewriting system

The key idea for the third and last transition step is simple. It eliminates the bookkeeping machinery of the CC-machine and directly relates control strings to each other. Every state in the CC-machine already corresponds to a control string. If all labels are removed from control strings and contexts, a state of the form $\langle \updownarrow, M\rangle$ stands for M and a state like $\langle M, C[\ \ ]\rangle$ represents $C[M]$. This translation does not map continuation points to terms; the result is like a Λ_c-term possibly containing contexts. The precise definition of the term set Λ_p is given in Definition 2. Given a function $\mathcal{I}$ which removes all the labels from applications including those that occur within continuation contexts, the morphism $|\cdot|$ from CC-states to Λ_p-terms is formalized by:

$$|\langle \updownarrow, M\rangle| = \mathcal{I}(M)$$
$$|\langle M, C[\ \ ]\rangle| = \mathcal{I}(C[M]).$$

As this correspondence is not one-to-one, the CC-transition function only induces a relation. This is easily remedied by throwing out all the rules that just keep track of what the machine has already seen. Together with the simplifications at the end of the previous subsection we get the control string rewriting function as shown in Table 4. The "Unique context"-Lemma assures that this is indeed a well-defined function.

The transition function induces the usual evaluation function:

$$eval_C(M) = N \text{ iff } M \overset{C}{\longmapsto}{}^{*} N \text{ such that } N \text{ is a value.}$$

With this eval-function we can state our final simulation theorem.

Definition 2: The term set Λ_p

The *term set* Λ_p and the set of sk-contexts are defined by mutual induction. Given $x \in Var$ and a Λ_p-sk-context $C[\ ]$,

$$x \text{ and } \langle \mathbf{p}, C[\ ]\rangle \text{ are in } \Lambda_p.$$

If M and N are in Λ_p, then, for any x,

$$\lambda x.M, MN, \mathcal{C}M, \text{ and } \mathcal{A}M \text{ are in } \Lambda_p.$$

Variables, continuation points, and abstractions are referred to as values. The set of Λ_p-*sk-contexts* contains

$$[\ ], \text{ and,}$$

if $C[\ ]$ is a Λ_p sk-context, P is a Λ_p-term, and Q is a Λ_p-value, then

$$C[\ ]P \text{ and } QC[\ ] \text{ are } \Lambda_p\text{-sk-contexts.}$$

Table 4: The C-transition function

(1)	$C[(\lambda x.M)V] \overset{C}{\longmapsto} C[M[x := V]]$
(2)	$C[\mathcal{C}M] \overset{C}{\longmapsto} M\langle \mathbf{p}, C[\ ]\rangle$
(3)	$C[\langle \mathbf{p}, C_0[\ ]\rangle V] \overset{C}{\longmapsto} C_0[V]$
(4)	$C[\mathcal{A}M] \overset{C}{\longmapsto} M.$

Theorem 3.3 (C-simulation). *For any program M,* $\mathcal{J}(eval_{CC}(M)) = eval_C(M)$.

Proof. The proof is similar to the previous ones. The major difference is that the C-rewriting system does not mirror all CC-moves directly. One can only prove that if $s_1 \overset{CC}{\longmapsto} s_2$ then $|s_1| \overset{C}{\longmapsto}_= |s_2|$. This is not surprising since the C-transition function was obtained from the CC-machine by *dropping* all the bookkeeping rules. □

The three simulation theorems immediately imply:

Theorem 3.4. *For any program M,* $\mathcal{J}(\mathcal{S}(\mathcal{R}(eval_{CEK}(M)))) = eval_C(M)$.

From a different point of view this theorem stipulates that $eval_{CEK}$ should be redefined. Instead of returning a semantic value, the function should unload the machine with the function $\mathcal{J} \circ \mathcal{S} \circ \mathcal{R}$. Since $\mathcal{J}$ and $\mathcal{S}$ behave like the identity function on Λ_c, this would certainly make sense for continuation-free results. The results are Λ_c-terms; the unload function is equal to $\mathcal{R}$ which, when restricted to Λ, is the unload function for the SECD-machine [12].

The case when the result of a program contains a continuation needs some further consideration. Continuations represent machine behavior. It is therefore not clear what it means when a *batch* computation returns a continuation as a (part of the) result. One naturally wants to interpret results as numbers, truth values, *etc.* On the other hand, if a machine is used for *interactive* computations where intermediate results can be saved, the user or programmer can only be interested in getting a continuation back for potential future use. He is then quite satisfied just to see the word "CONTINUATION." If he wants to know more, contexts tell him more than continuation codes. We can thus define:

$$eval_{CEK}(M) = \mathcal{I}(\mathcal{S}(\mathcal{R}(V))) \text{ iff } \langle M, \emptyset, (\mathbf{stop})\rangle \overset{CEK}{\longmapsto} \langle \ddagger, \emptyset, ((\mathbf{stop})\ \mathbf{ret}\ V)\rangle$$

and, hence, we can consider $eval_{CEK}$ and $eval_C$ to be the same function.

The C-rewriting system is certainly easier to understand than the CEK-machine. But we have not yet achieved our goal of expressing all the rewriting rules within the programming language Λ_c. We still need the notion of a context in order to capture the concept of a continuation. Although we feel that contexts are naturally related to terms and that it is rather intuitive to reason with them, the rewriting system is not a calculus. It neither explicitly defines program equivalences nor justifies local transformations. What we really aim for is an equational system which gives a programmer the same power over programs as the pure λ-calculus. This is the topic of the next section.

4. The λ_c-calculus

The traditional λ-calculus can be perceived as an axiomatic theory as well as a reduction system. The two views are equivalent. The theory can only prove terms equal that are equal under the congruence relation generated from the β-reduction. From an operational or computational viewpoint the reduction system is more attractive since it exposes the rule character of the λ-calculus. Reductions also lead in a straightforward way to the standard reduction function. Thus, it is quite natural when we go the inverse direction in this section, taking the specification of the C-transition function as the point of departure and deriving the reduction system.

We clearly need the β-value reduction:

$$(\lambda x.M)N \xrightarrow{\beta_v} M[x := N] \text{ provided that } N \text{ is a value.} \qquad (\beta_v)$$

It completely captures (C1) and the underlying λ_v-calculus.

Next we turn our attention to $\mathcal{A}$-applications. According to (C4), an $\mathcal{A}$-application removes its *sk*-context. A case analysis of sk-contexts leads to appropriate *notions* of reduction. If an $\mathcal{A}$-application $\mathcal{A}M$ is within an sk-context $C[\ ]$ and to the left of some arbitrary term N, then first the N must be thrown away and, second, the rest of the context must be removed. This is a recursive problem: $C[\ ]$ can be eliminated in favor of M by simply placing $\mathcal{A}M$ in the hole. Thus, the relation should state that $C[(\mathcal{A}M)N]$ goes to $C[\mathcal{A}M]$. Since this is independent of the sk-context, we can formulate our first notion of reduction for $\mathcal{A}$-applications:

$$(\mathcal{A}M)N \xrightarrow{\mathcal{A}_L} \mathcal{A}M. \qquad (\mathcal{A}_L)$$

The second possible case, where $\mathcal{A}N$ is to the right of a value M, is treated symmetrically:

$$M(\mathcal{A}N) \xrightarrow{\mathcal{A}_R} \mathcal{A}N \text{ provided that } M \text{ is a value.} \qquad (\mathcal{A}_R)$$

This covers all but the *base* case of sk-contexts.

The case of the empty context requires special treatment. An occurrence of $\mathcal{A}M$ at the root of a term must evaluate to M, but this cannot be a proper reduction. One can only apply this rule when the $\mathcal{A}$-application is not embedded in a term. Otherwise the reduction system becomes inconsistent. Consider, for example, the expression $(\mathcal{A}\mathbf{I})\mathbf{K}$. Applying the $\mathcal{A}_L$-step results in $\mathcal{A}\mathbf{I}$; the top-level rule then leads to $\mathbf{I}$. When the top-level relation is first applied to the embedded $\mathcal{A}$-application, we get: $(\mathcal{A}\mathbf{I})\mathbf{K}$ goes to $\mathbf{IK}$ which, in turn, results in $\mathbf{K}$. $\mathbf{I}$ would equal $\mathbf{K}$ and this is inconsistent with the λ-calculus. We therefore introduce this top-level relation as a *computation rule* and use a $\triangleright$ instead of $\rightarrow$:

$$\mathcal{A}M \triangleright_{\mathcal{A}} M. \qquad (\mathcal{A}_T)$$

When we build the calculus later, care must be taken to add this computation rule at the right place.

The considerations for $\mathcal{C}$-applications move along the same line. We need to satisfy equations (C2) and (C3). Again, (C2) specifies that the context of a $\mathcal{C}$-application must be removed. So we expect that the $\mathcal{C}$-reduction rules must be designed according to the position of $\mathcal{C}M$ in an sk-context and that they must be similar to $\mathcal{A}$-reductions. For example, the expression $(\mathcal{C}M)N$ must relate to a term $\mathcal{C}X$ for some term X.

For the correct design of X we appeal to the intended semantics of the $\mathcal{C}$-application. The $\mathcal{C}$-application must capture the current continuation and supply it to its argument. Hence, if X is the next $\mathcal{C}$-argument, it will be applied to the continuation which stands for the rest of the context. This continuation must be passed on to the original $\mathcal{C}$-argument M. Furthermore, M's context also includes an application with N as the argument. In other words, if we let f be the function to which N must be applied, then the continuation of $\mathcal{C}M$ could be characterized by $\kappa(fN)$ where κ stands for the continuation of $\mathcal{C}X$. Since the continuation gets the function when it is invoked, it must be an abstraction whose parameter is f: $\lambda f.\kappa(fN)$. The term X, on the other hand, must be a function which accepts the continuation κ and passes it to M via $\lambda f.\kappa(fN)$. A first approximation of X is hence $\lambda\kappa.M(\lambda f.\kappa(fN))$. This satisfies (C2) since it removes the context of a $\mathcal{C}$-application and applies its argument to some encoding of the context. But continuations also need to respect (C3).

The rewriting rule (C3) demands that, when a continuation is invoked, the current context is removed. This reflects the fact that upon a continuation invocation, the CEK-machine ignores the current continuation. It means for our Λ_c-continuations that the first action must be an *abort* action to remove the curent context. Hence, $\lambda f.\mathcal{A}(\kappa(fN))$ is the correct continuation for M. The symmetric case where $\mathcal{C}N$ is to the right of a value M is treated in a similar way and so we define the two notions of reduction for the $\mathcal{C}$-application by:

$$(\mathcal{C}M)N \xrightarrow{\mathcal{C}_L} \mathcal{C}\lambda\kappa.M(\lambda f.\mathcal{A}(\kappa(fN))) \qquad (\mathcal{C}_L)$$

$$M(\mathcal{C}N) \xrightarrow{\mathcal{C}_R} \mathcal{C}\lambda\kappa.N(\lambda v.\mathcal{A}(\kappa(Mv))) \text{ provided that } M \text{ is a value.} \qquad (\mathcal{C}_R)$$

We still need to investigate the case of the empty context, *i.e.*, the occurrence of a $\mathcal{C}$-application at the root of a term. The $\mathcal{C}$-argument M must now be applied to a function which simulates the continuation-point $\langle \mathbf{p}, [\ ] \rangle$. The natural choice is $\lambda x.\mathcal{A}x$. Again, this relation is not a proper notion of reduction but a computation rule:

$$\mathcal{C}M \triangleright_{\mathcal{C}} M(\lambda x.\mathcal{A}x). \qquad (\mathcal{C}_T)$$

With this last rule we have derived all the reduction and computation rules that are intuitively needed for a standard reduction function equivalent to $\overset{C}{\longmapsto}$.

Defining notions of reduction is only the first step on the way to a reduction system. The next one is to build a one-step reduction relation. A ***one-step reduction relation*** is the extension of a notion of reduction to a relation which is compatible with the syntactic constructors. In other words, the extended relation connects terms which are the same except for two subterms related by a reduction rule. In our case four syntactic constructions must be considered: abstraction, application, $\mathcal{C}$-application, and $\mathcal{A}$-application. The two computation rules cannot be included in this step since they are not applicable to nested subterms. Definition 3 contains a formal description of the one-step reduction relation $\rightarrow_c$.

The last step in the development of a calculus is to make a congruence relation out of the reduction relation, *i.e.*, an equivalence relation which respects the syntactic constructors. Conforming to tradition, we do this in two stages: $\twoheadrightarrow_c$ is the transitive-reflexive closure of $\rightarrow_c$; its respective equivalence relation is $=_c$. This, however, is not yet the final goal. We still need to build in the computation rules. Without computation rules it is impossible to find a standard reduction function which simulates the machine evaluation: occurrences of $\mathcal{C}$- and $\mathcal{A}$-applications at the root of a term cannot be removed. We extend the reduction relation $\twoheadrightarrow_c$ to a computation relation $\triangleright_k$ by adding the top-level relations. Forming the symmetric, reflexive, and transitive closure of $\triangleright_k$ results in an equivalence relation $=_k$ which establishes equality among terms according to reductions ***and*** computations. All these concepts are summarized in Definition 3.

The relation $=_k$ determines the λ_c-calculus and we write $\lambda_c \vdash M =_k N$ if the terms M and N are equal under $=_k$. This calculus is not traditional in the sense that it uses incompatible relations. The congruence relation $=_c$ is somewhat weaker but more traditional and we consider it as a subcalculus. We also write $\lambda_c \vdash M =_c N$ when we refer to proofs within the subcalculus.

The preceding derivation of the λ_c-calculus has produced a system which is similar to the one described in our earlier paper [3]. The C-rewriting system and the previous experience directed our search this time. The important difference is that the invocation of a continuation immediately removes the current context. The correspondence of the λ_c-calculus to the real machine is almost built-in. Before we can discuss this issue further, we need to recall some earlier results on the logical properties of the calculus.

For the next section two questions are of importance:

- Are the relations $\overset{c}{\rightarrow}$ and $\triangleright_k$ Church-Rosser?, and
- Is there a standard reduction function?

Since the relation $\triangleright_k$ is not a compatible relation, it is clear that it cannot be Church-Rosser in the classical sense, but that we have to check whether it satisfies the diamond property. The reduction relation $\twoheadrightarrow_c$ can be treated in a more conventional manner. The following theorem states our version of the CR-theorem for the λ_c-calculus:

Definition 3: The λ_c-calculus

Let $\xrightarrow{c} = \xrightarrow{\mathcal{C}_L} \cup \xrightarrow{\mathcal{C}_R} \cup \xrightarrow{\mathcal{A}_L} \cup \xrightarrow{\mathcal{A}_R} \cup \xrightarrow{\beta_v}$. Then define the ***one-step C-reduction*** $\rightarrow_c$ as the compatible closure of $\xrightarrow{c}$:

$$M \xrightarrow{c} N \Rightarrow M \rightarrow_c N;$$
$$M \rightarrow_c N \Rightarrow \lambda x.M \rightarrow_c \lambda x.N;$$
$$M \rightarrow_c N \Rightarrow ZM \rightarrow_c ZN, MZ \rightarrow_c NZ \quad \text{for } Z \in \Lambda_c;$$
$$M \rightarrow_c N \Rightarrow \mathcal{C}M \rightarrow_c \mathcal{C}N;$$
$$M \rightarrow_c N \Rightarrow \mathcal{A}M \rightarrow_c \mathcal{A}N.$$

The *C-reduction* is denoted by $\twoheadrightarrow_c$ and is the transitive-reflexive closure of $\rightarrow_c$. We denote the smallest congruence relation generated by $\twoheadrightarrow_c$ with $=_c$ and call it *C-equality*.
The *computation* $\triangleright_k$ is defined by: $\triangleright_k = \triangleright_{\mathcal{C}} \cup \triangleright_{\mathcal{A}} \cup \twoheadrightarrow_c$. The relation $=_k$ is the smallest equivalence relation generated by $\triangleright_k$. We refer to it as *computational equality* or just *K-equality*.
The left-hand side of the reduction and computation rules are called *C-redexes*. A *C-normal form* M is a term that does not contain a C-redex. A term M *has a C-normal form* N if $M =_k N$ and N is in C-normal form.

Theorem 4.1 (Church-Rosser).

(i) *The relation* $\xrightarrow{c}$ *is Church-Rosser.*

(ii) *The computation relation* $\triangleright_k$ *satisfies the diamond property, i.e., if* $M \triangleright_k N$ *and* $M \triangleright_k L$ *then there exists a* K *such that* $N \triangleright_k K$ *and* $L \triangleright_k K$.

(iii) *If* $M =_c N$ *then there exists an* L *such that* $M \twoheadrightarrow_c L$ *and* $N \twoheadrightarrow_c L$.

(iv) *If* $M =_k N$ *then there exists an* L *such that* $M \triangleright_k^* L$ *and* $N \triangleright_k^* L$.

The proof of this theorem is a modification of the one for the traditional λ-calculus [3].

We also need to show the existence of a standard reduction function. A standard reduction function is *the* function which reduces a term to a value by performing outermost-leftmost reductions or computation steps. It is defined in two stages. First, the relation $\xrightarrow{c}$ is extended to a function which works on all sk-contexts. Second, the computation steps are added. Definition 4 contains the formal specification. The respective theorem is:

Theorem 4.2. *$M \triangleright_k^* N$ for some value N iff $M \mapsto_{sk}^* N'$ for some value N'.*

In other words, if a program can be interpreted as a value, then the standard reduction function will produce a value. The theorem is a direct consequence of the Curry-Feys Standardization Theorem for the λ_c-calculus [3]. The next question is whether the value of a program produced by the machine is equivalent to the value produced by the standard reduction function. This is a part of the correspondence problem discussed in the next section.

Definition 4: Standard reduction sequences and functions

Given an sk-context $C[\ ]$ and $M \xrightarrow{c} N$, then the ***standard reduction function***, $\longmapsto_{sc}$, *for* $\xrightarrow{c}$ maps $C[M]$ to $C[N]$:

$$C[M] \longmapsto_{sc} C[N].$$

The *standard reduction function for* $\triangleright_k$ extends $\longmapsto_{sc}$ to computations:

$$\longmapsto_{sk} = \triangleright_{\mathcal{C}} \cup \triangleright_{\mathcal{A}} \cup \longmapsto_{sc}.$$

$\longmapsto_{sk}^{+}$ and $\longmapsto_{sk}^{*}$ stand for the transitive and transitive-reflexive closure of $\longmapsto_{sk}$, respectively; $\longmapsto_{sk}^{i}$ indicates i applications of $\longmapsto_{sk}$.

5. The machine-calculus correspondence

In order to prove the equivalence of the machine semantics with the operational rewriting semantics of λ_c we need to show that the standard reduction function simulates the rules (C1) through (C4). As in the previous transition steps, we must construct a morphism from Λ_p to Λ_c since the two functions work on different term sets.

The only real task of the morphism between Λ_p and Λ_c is to encode continuation points—or sk-contexts—as terms. We had the same goal when we designed the notions of reduction for $\mathcal{C}$-applications, so we can use these relations as an orientation.

The empty context in a continuation point means that the continuation was captured with a $\mathcal{C}$-application at the root of the term. Hence, $[\ ]$ maps to $\lambda x.\mathcal{A}x$. If the hole is to the left of some arbitrary term P in some context $C[\ ]$, then a $\mathcal{C}$-application would use $\mathcal{C}_L$ to construct the next piece of the continuation. This new piece would look like $\lambda f.\mathcal{A}(\kappa(fP))$ where κ stands for the encoding of $C[\ ]$ and so we are led to the following inductive definition of the map $[\![\cdot]\!]_c$ from contexts to terms:

$$[\![[\ ]]\!]_c \equiv \lambda x.\mathcal{A}x$$
$$[\![C[[\ ]P]]\!]_c \equiv \lambda f.\mathcal{A}([\![C[\ ]]\!]_c(f\overline{P}))$$
$$[\![C[V[\ ]]]\!]_c \equiv \lambda v.\mathcal{A}([\![C[\ ]]\!]_c(\overline{V}v)).$$

The map from Q to $\overline{Q}$ replaces continuation points in Q by terms:

$$\overline{\langle \mathbf{p}, C[\ ]\rangle} \equiv [\![C[\ ]]\!]_c,\ \overline{x} \equiv x,\ \overline{\lambda x.M} \equiv \lambda x.\overline{M},\ \overline{MN} \equiv \overline{M}\,\overline{N},\ \overline{\mathcal{C}M} \equiv \mathcal{C}\overline{M},\ \overline{\mathcal{A}M} \equiv \mathcal{A}\overline{M}.$$

Given this morphism, we could now attempt to prove a simulation theorem similar to the ones in Section 3. The β_v-step, *i.e.* (C1), is clearly reflected in the definition of $\longmapsto_{sk}$. It is also easy to see that the two C-transition rules (C2) and (C4) are simulated by the standard reduction function. Both rules were a major guide in the derivation of the reduction system and the map $[\![\cdot]\!]_c$ was designed according to the resulting notions of reduction:

Lemma 5.1. *For any sk-context* $C[\ ]$,

(i) $C[\mathcal{C}M] \longmapsto_{sk}^{+} M[\![C[\ ]]\!]_c$, and

(ii) $C[\mathcal{A}M] \mapsto_{sk}^{+} M$.

Proof. Both statements are proved by an induction on the depth of the redex in the context [3]. □

We are, however, unable to show that the standard reduction function satisfies rule (C3). This transition rule requires that a continuation invocation removes the current context and that it continues as if the old context—filled with the argument—were the new term. The first condition is clearly implemented since continuations immediately perform an $\mathcal{A}$-application. The second one causes problems. In the λ_c-calculus continuations are constructed to ***simulate*** the behavior of contexts, but in the machine continuations ***are*** contexts. Thus, when a continuation is to be captured after another one was invoked, the transition in the machine and the one via the sk-function diverge. The machine simply labels the current context which contains the old continuation context; the sk-reduction sequence encodes for a second time the term which simulates the former continuation.

The nature of the problem is best illustrated with an example. Suppose $\langle \mathbf{p}, C[[\ ]V]\rangle$ is invoked on the value F: $\langle \mathbf{p}, C[[\ ]V]\rangle F \overset{C}{\longmapsto} C[FV]$. Furthermore, assume that the application FV evaluates to $D[\mathcal{C}P]$ after some β_v-steps. Then the C-reduction sequence reaches the term $P\langle \mathbf{p}, C[D[\ ]]\rangle$. According to Lemma 5.1, if $K_c \equiv [\![C[\ ]]\!]_c$, the corresponding reduction sequence in the λ_c-calculus begins with:

$$[\![C[[\ ]V]]\!]_c \overline{F} \mapsto_{sk}^{+} K_c(\overline{F}\,\overline{V}).$$

The next few β_v-steps for $\overline{F}\,\overline{V}$ are correctly performed by the sk-function:

$$K_c(\overline{F}\,\overline{V}) \mapsto_{sk}^{+} K_c\overline{D}[\mathcal{C}\overline{P}].$$

This last term also constructs a continuation—just like its correspondent $C[D[\mathcal{C}P]]$—, but the continuation encodes the term K_c instead of the context $C[\ ]$:

$$K_c\overline{D}[\mathcal{C}\overline{P}] \mapsto_{sk}^{+} \overline{P}[\![K_c\overline{D}[\ ]]\!]_c.$$

One readily sees that $[\![C[D[\ ]]]\!]_c$ is not equal to $[\![K_c\overline{D}[\ ]]\!]_c$. This means that a naïve version of the simulation theorem fails. The best we can hope for is that the sk-simulation of the C-transition function preserves a relation between continuation points and terms.

From the above lemma and the example one could suspect that a continuation point like $\langle \mathbf{p}, C[D[\ ]]\rangle$ is related to the terms $[\![C[D[\ ]]]\!]_c$ and $[\![[\![C[\ ]]\!]_c D[\ ]]\!]_c$. However, the situation in our example could recur many times. Instead of having two contexts composing a new one, we would then have several of them. In fact, we have to take into account all possible finite decompositions of a given context into smaller contexts, including the empty one. Each sub-context can be encoded as a term by itself; each of these encoded contexts can be a part of a bigger context which is being encoded. We have formalized this relation in Definition 5.

The relation $\approx_p$ in Definition 5 is implicit. It is well-suited to capture the different continuation representations from the example, but it does not expose the structure of the terms which stand for continuation points. A brief investigation reveals that these terms are rather similar and that they share another important attribute: they are behaviorally indistinguishable with respect to β_v-steps in standard reduction sequences. Empty contexts

Definition 5: The continuation point correspondence

The relation $\approx_p$ relates terms of Λ_p and Λ_p-sk-contexts to terms in Λ_c and sk-contexts. It is defined inductively by:

$\langle \mathbf{p}, C[\ ]\rangle \approx_p K_c$ iff

for some finite number of sk-contexts $C_1[\ ], \ldots, C_n[\ ]$ such that $C[\ ] \equiv C_1[C_2[\ldots C_n[\ ]\ldots]]$ the term K_c is determined by:

$$K_c \equiv [\![\ldots [\![[\![\overline{C}_1[\ ]]\!]_c \overline{C}_2[\ ]]\!]_c \ldots \overline{C}_n[\ ]]\!]_c$$

where $C_i[\ ] \approx_p \overline{C}_i[\ ]$ for all i.

If $P \approx_p \overline{P}$ and $Q \approx_p \overline{Q}$, then, for all x

$$x \approx_p x,\ \lambda x.P \approx_p \lambda x.\overline{P},\ PQ \approx_p \overline{P}\,\overline{Q},\ \mathcal{C}P \approx_p \mathcal{C}\overline{P},\ \mathcal{A}P \approx_p \mathcal{A}\overline{P}.$$

For sk-contexts we have to add

$$[\ ] \approx_p [\ ].$$

Note, we use the notation $\overline{P}$ ambiguously for both the result of mapping P to $\overline{P}$ and a term in Λ_c that is related to a term P in Λ_p via $\approx_p$.

in the partitioning of a continuation-point context add an extra $\lambda x.\mathcal{A}x$ to its representation. On the other hand, if there is a proper term contained in the context, exactly one of the subcontexts will cover it. Therefore, each subterm appears exactly once in the representation. Putting this together, we see that the terms that are related to a continuation point are the same modulo some occurrences of $\lambda x.\mathcal{A}x$:

Lemma 5.2. *Define $K_{i+1} \equiv \lambda x.\mathcal{A}((\lambda x.\mathcal{A}x)(K_i x))$ to be a term sequence which is parameterized with respect to its first element K_1. Then the relation of a continuation point to a term is characterized by exactly one of the following three statements:*

(i) $\langle \mathbf{p}, [\ ]\rangle \approx_p K_i$ *where* $K_1 \equiv \lambda x.\mathcal{A}x$, *or*

(ii) $\langle \mathbf{p}, C[[\ ]P]\rangle \approx_p K_i$ *where* $K_1 \equiv \lambda f.\mathcal{A}(K_c(f\overline{P}))$, $\langle \mathbf{p}, C[\ ]\rangle \approx_p K_c$, *and* $P \approx_p \overline{P}$, *or*

(iii) $\langle \mathbf{p}, C[U[\ ]]\rangle \approx_p K_i$ *where* $K_1 \equiv \lambda v.\mathcal{A}(K_c(\overline{U}v))$, $\langle \mathbf{p}, C[\ ]\rangle \approx_p K_c$, *and* $U \approx_p \overline{U}$.

Furthermore, we can generalize this to

$$\langle \mathbf{p}, C[D[\ ]]\rangle \approx_p [\![K_c D[\ ]]\!]_c \text{ iff } \langle \mathbf{p}, C[\ ]\rangle \approx_p K_c.$$

Proof. First note that (i), (ii), and (iii) cover all possible cases of sk-contexts. One of them must match a particular sk-context. Furthermore, the proof of all three statements is naturally divided into two parts: one for $i = 1$ and one for $i > 1$. The latter is the same in all cases. For the former we demonstrate how to prove case (ii) as a typical example.

From the definition of $\approx_p$ we know that for any context $C[[\ ]P]$ and finite number of contexts $C_i[\ ]$ which compose $C[[\ ]P]$, we have

$$\langle \mathbf{p}, C[[\ ]P]\rangle \approx_p [\![\ldots [\![[\![\overline{C}_1[\ ]]\!]_c \overline{C}_2[\ ]]\!]_c \ldots \overline{C}_n[\ ]]\!]_c.$$

For the base case we assume that $C_n[\ ] \not\equiv [\ ]$. Then, in (ii), $C_n[\ ] \equiv D[[\ ]P]$ for some context $D[\ ]$ since P is the term next to the hole in the continuation-point context. This implies that

$$[\ldots[[\overline{C}_1[\ ]]_c\overline{C}_2[\ ]]_c\ldots\overline{D}[[\ ]\overline{P}]]_c \equiv \lambda f.\mathcal{A}([\ldots[[\overline{C}_1[\ ]]_c\overline{C}_2[\ ]]_c\ldots\overline{D}[\ ]]_c(f\overline{P})).$$

On the other hand, $C[\ ] \equiv C_1[\ldots D[\ ]\ldots]$ and thus

$$\langle \mathbf{p}, C[\ ]\rangle \approx_p [\ldots[[\overline{C}_1[\ ]]_c\overline{C}_2[\ ]]_c\ldots\overline{D}[\ ]]_c.$$

This proves the case for $i = 1$.

For the case where $i > 1$ assume that the last few, say $j \geq 1$, contexts in this sequence are empty, *i.e.* equal to $[\ ]$. By factoring out the first one, we get

$$\begin{aligned}[\ldots[[\overline{C}_1[\ ]]_c\overline{C}_2[\ ]]_c\ldots[\ ]]_c &\equiv \lambda x.\mathcal{A}([[\ ]]_c([\ldots[[\overline{C}_1[\ ]]_c\overline{C}_2[\ ]]_c\ldots]_c x)) \\ &\equiv \lambda x.\mathcal{A}((\lambda x.\mathcal{A}x)([\ldots[[\overline{C}_1[\ ]]_c\overline{C}_2[\ ]]_c\ldots]_c x)).\end{aligned}$$

Thus we see that, as mentioned above, every empty context adds one term $\lambda x.\mathcal{A}x$. Hence, $\langle \mathbf{p}, C[[\ ]P]\rangle \approx_p K_{j+1}$ and this concludes the proof.

The generalization follows immediately. □

Lemma 5.2 verifies our claim about the behavior of the terms in the representation set of $\langle \mathbf{p}, C[\ ]\rangle$. They invoke a continuation and, since continuations always remove the current context, none of the $\lambda x.\mathcal{A}x$ will ever play a role in an evaluation.

Proposition 5.3. *Define three series K_i as in Lemma 5.2. with the initial terms $\lambda x.\mathcal{A}x$, $\lambda f.\mathcal{A}(K_c(f\overline{P}))$, and $\lambda v.\mathcal{A}(K_c(\overline{U}v))$. Then we can show:*

$$\begin{aligned} K_i &\twoheadrightarrow_c \lambda x.\mathcal{A}\ldots(i\text{-times})\ldots x, \\ K_i &\twoheadrightarrow_c \lambda f.\mathcal{A}\ldots(i\text{-times})\ldots(K_c(f\overline{P})), \\ K_i &\twoheadrightarrow_c \lambda v.\mathcal{A}\ldots(i\text{-times})\ldots(K_c(\overline{U}v)),\end{aligned}$$

respectively.

Remark. If we had formalized standard reduction *sequences*, we could replace $\twoheadrightarrow_c$ by standard reduction steps. **End of Remark**

Proof. Clearly, $K_i \equiv \lambda x.\mathcal{A}M_i^x$ for some (open) term M_i^x. Hence,

$$\begin{aligned} K_{i+1} &\twoheadrightarrow_c \lambda x.\mathcal{A}((\lambda x.\mathcal{A}x)((\lambda x.\mathcal{A}M_i^x)x)) \\ &\twoheadrightarrow_c \lambda x.\mathcal{A}((\lambda x.\mathcal{A}x)(\mathcal{A}M_i^x[x := x])) \\ &\twoheadrightarrow_c \lambda x.\mathcal{A}(\mathcal{A}M_i^x).\end{aligned}$$

But, the three M_i^x's for the base cases are x, $(K_c(x\overline{P}))$, and $(K_c(\overline{U}x))$, respectively. □

All continuations that are related to a continuation point behave similarly when invoked; the difference is the number of abort operations. Thus, we can show that evaluations via $\mapsto_{sk}$ and $\overset{C}{\longmapsto}$ only differ in their outcome. First, we prove that $\mapsto_{sk}$ mirrors C-transition steps as long as no continuation is invoked:

Lemma 5.4. *Assume $C[\ ] \approx_p \overline{C}[\ ]$, $P \approx_p \overline{P}$, and $U \approx_p \overline{U}$. The simulation of the rules (C1), (C2), and (C4) via $\mapsto_{sk}$ respects $\approx_p$:*

(i) if $C[(\lambda x.P)U] \overset{C}{\longmapsto} C[P[x := U]]$ then $\overline{D}[(\lambda x.\overline{P})\overline{U}] \mapsto_{sk} \overline{D}[\overline{P}[x := \overline{U}]]$ for any sk-context $\overline{D}[\ ]$;

(ii) if $C[\mathcal{A}P] \overset{C}{\longmapsto} P$ then $\overline{C}[\mathcal{A}\overline{P}] \mapsto_{sk}^{+} \overline{P}$;

(iii) if $C[\mathcal{C}P] \overset{C}{\longmapsto} P\langle \mathbf{p}, C[\ ]\rangle$ then $\overline{C}[\mathcal{C}\overline{P}] \mapsto_{sk}^{+} \overline{P}[\![\overline{C}[\ ]]\!]_c$.

Proof. The first statement reiterates that β-steps are simulated independently of the context. Points (ii) and (iii) are consequences of Lemma 5.1. □

Things get more complicated when a continuation is invoked. The sk-reduction sequence contains a series of auxiliary moves in order to simulate the jump to a different context in the C-reduction sequence. Since proper simulation steps are interspersed in this detour, it is impossible to prove a corresponding lemma for (C3). However, a direct proof that continuation invocations are correctly implemented by $\mapsto_{sk}$ is possible:

Lemma 5.5. *Suppose* $\langle \mathbf{p}, C_0[\ ]\rangle \approx_p K_0$, $V \approx_p \overline{V}$, *and* $U \approx_p \overline{U}$. *Then,*

$$C[\langle \mathbf{p}, C_0[\ ]\rangle V] \overset{C}{\longmapsto}^{+} U \text{ iff } \overline{C}[K_0\overline{V}] \mapsto_{sk}^{+} \overline{U}.$$

Proof. The condition $C[\ ] \approx_p \overline{C}[\ ]$ is unnecessary for the antecedent since a continuation immediately performs some $\mathcal{A}$-applications.

The equivalence is proved by an induction on the unique number of steps, n, in the $\overset{C}{\longmapsto}$-reduction sequence from $C[\langle \mathbf{p}, C_0[\ ]\rangle]$ to U. We proceed by a case analysis on the structure of $C_0[\ ]$:

(skC1) $C_0[\ ] \equiv [\ ]$: This case is trivial. It implies that

$$K_0 \equiv K_1 \equiv \lambda x.\mathcal{A}x \text{ or}$$
$$K_0 \equiv K_2 \equiv \lambda x.\mathcal{A}((\lambda x.\mathcal{A}x)((\lambda x.\mathcal{A}x)x)), \textit{etc.}$$

In any case, we have

$$\langle \mathbf{p}, C_0[\ ]\rangle V \overset{C}{\longmapsto} V \text{ and } K_0\overline{V} \mapsto_{sk}^{+} \overline{V}.$$

(skC2) $C_0[\ ] \equiv D[[\ ]P]$ for some Λ_p-sk-context and term P. Now we know from Lemma 5.2 that

$$K_0 \equiv K_1 \equiv \lambda f.\mathcal{A}(K_D(f\overline{P})), \text{ or}$$
$$K_0 \equiv K_2 \equiv \lambda x.\mathcal{A}((\lambda x.\mathcal{A}x)(K_1 x)), \textit{etc.}$$

where $\langle \mathbf{p}, D[\ ]\rangle V \approx_p K_D$ and $P \approx_p \overline{P}$. The two reduction sequences start out with

$$C[\langle \mathbf{p}, C_0[\ ]\rangle V] \overset{C}{\longmapsto} D[VP]$$

and

$$\overline{C}[K_0\overline{V}] \mapsto_{sk}^{+} K_D(\overline{V}\,\overline{P}).$$

Next, we consider the possible evaluations of VP and $\overline{V}\,\overline{P}$. The previous lemma reassures us that as long as the rule (C1) is used the context plays no role and, more importantly, the relation $\approx_p$ is preserved. The first transition step which does not conform to (C1) is the distinguishing criteria for the rest of the reduction sequence. Since this sequence is finite, four cases must be analyzed:

a) $VP \overset{C}{\longmapsto}^{+}_{(C1)} W$ where W is a value. This means that $\overline{V}\,\overline{P} \mapsto_{sk}^{+} \overline{W}$ and we have the following development for the C-transition:

$$D[VP] \overset{C}{\longmapsto}^{+} D[W].$$

For the one according to $\mapsto_{sk}$ we get

$$K_D(\overline{V}\,\overline{P}) \mapsto_{sk}^{+} K_D\overline{W}.$$

By assumption we know that

$$D[W] \overset{C}{\longmapsto}^{m} U \text{ with } m \leq n-2.$$

From the definition of $\overset{C}{\longmapsto}$ we see that, $D[W] \overset{C}{\longmapsto}^{m} U$ iff $\langle \mathbf{p}, D[\;\;]\rangle W \overset{C}{\longmapsto}^{m+1} U$. Thus, we can safely replace $D[W]$ by $\langle \mathbf{p}, D[\;\;]\rangle W$ since $m+1 \leq n-1$. But note, $\langle \mathbf{p}, D[\;\;]\rangle \approx_p K_D$ and so, by inductive hypothesis, we get the desired conclusion.

b) $VP \overset{C}{\longmapsto}^{*}_{(C1)} E[\mathcal{A}Q]$ and $\overline{V}\,\overline{P} \mapsto_{sk}^{*} \overline{E}[\mathcal{A}\overline{Q}]$ for some term Q and sk-context $E[\;\;]$. Comparing the two reduction sequences

$$D[VP] \overset{C}{\longmapsto}^{*} D[E[\mathcal{A}Q]] \overset{C}{\longmapsto} Q$$

and

$$K_D(\overline{V}\,\overline{P}) \mapsto_{sk}^{*} K_D\overline{E}[\mathcal{A}\overline{Q}] \mapsto_{sk}^{*} \overline{Q},$$

we see that both continue with related terms. From this point on, two developments are possible: the rest of the sequence either uses the (C3) rule or it doesn't:

b1) If $Q \overset{C}{\longmapsto}^{*} U$ does not use (C3), then according to Lemma 5.4 $\overline{Q} \mapsto_{sk}^{*} \overline{U}$ is immediate.

b2) Suppose (C3) is used a first time. That means, that $Q \overset{C}{\longmapsto}^{*} F[\langle \mathbf{p}, F_0[\;\;]\rangle W]$ and also by Lemma 5.4 that $\overline{Q} \mapsto_{sk}^{*} \overline{F}[K_F\overline{W}]$ such that $\langle \mathbf{p}, F_0[\;\;]\rangle \approx_p K_F$. Since the reduction sequence is at least one step shorter, we can now apply our inductive hypothesis and this finishes case b).

c) $VP \overset{C}{\longmapsto}^{*}_{(C1)} E[\mathcal{C}Q]$ and $\overline{V}\,\overline{P} \mapsto_{sk}^{*} \overline{E}[\mathcal{C}\overline{Q}]$. The reduction sequence according to $\mapsto_{sk}$ continues as:

$$K_D(\overline{V}\,\overline{P}) \mapsto_{sk}^{*} K_D\overline{E}[\mathcal{C}\overline{Q}] \mapsto_{sk}^{+} \overline{Q}[\![K_D\overline{E}[\;\;]]\!]_c.$$

The transition rule (C2) accomplishes the capturing of this continuation in one step:

$$D[VP] \overset{C}{\longmapsto}^{*} D[E[\mathcal{C}Q]] \overset{C}{\longmapsto} Q\langle \mathbf{p}, D[E[\;\;]]\rangle.$$

By assumption $\langle \mathbf{p}, D[\;\;]\rangle \approx_p K_D$ and, hence, $\langle \mathbf{p}, D[E[\;\;]]\rangle \approx_p [\![K_D\overline{E}[\;\;]]\!]$ by Lemma 5.2. The rest of this subcase is as in b).

d) $VP \overset{C}{\longmapsto}^{*}_{(C1)} E[\langle \mathbf{p}, E_0[\;\;]\rangle W]$ and $\overline{V}\,\overline{P} \mapsto_{sk}^{*} \overline{E}[K_E\overline{W}]$ such that $\langle \mathbf{p}, E_0[\;\;]\rangle \approx_p K_E$. This is an instance of the inductive hypothesis and the case (skC2) is finished.

(skC3) $C_0[\ ] \equiv D[P[\ ]]$ for some Λ_p-sk-context and value P. Again, the respective continuations are characterized by $K_1 \equiv \lambda v.\mathcal{A}(K_D(\overline{P}v))$, *etc.* The two reduction sequences immediately arrive at the same constellation as in (skC2):

$$C[(\mathbf{p}, C_0[\ ])V] \overset{c}{\longmapsto} D[PV]$$

and

$$\overline{C}[K_0\overline{V}] \mapsto_{sk}{}^{+} K_D(\overline{P}\,\overline{V}).$$

The rest is analogous to the previous case. □

Putting the previous two lemmas together, the following theorem is obvious:

Theorem 5.6 (Sk-simulation). *For any program $M \in \Lambda_c$, values V, $\overline{V}$ such that $V \approx_p \overline{V}$*

$$M \overset{c}{\longmapsto}{}^{+} V \text{ iff } M \mapsto_{sk}{}^{+} \overline{V}.$$

Since $V \approx_p \overline{V}$ implies $V \equiv \overline{V}$ for $V \in \Lambda_c$, the theorem can be specialized:

Corollary 5.7. *For any program $M \in \Lambda_c$ whose result V is continuation-free,*

$$M \overset{c}{\longmapsto}{}^{+} V \text{ iff } M \mapsto_{sk}{}^{+} V.$$

Finally, we can note that $eval_{CEK}$ is only defined if the program is equivalent to a value:

Corollary 5.8. *There exists a value N such that $\lambda_c \vdash M =_k N$ iff $eval_{CEK}(M)$ is defined.*

Informally, these results mean that the CEK-machine is characterized by a standard reduction function (and sequence) of a calculus modulo some syntactic difference. In order to eliminate this difference, we would have to change the standard reduction function in such a way that a term $K(\mathcal{C}M)$ evaluates to MK for a continuation K. From the above definition of $[\![\cdot]\!]_c$ one can see that recognizing terms as continuations is possible. But, a user could easily construct such a term K and then the normal evaluation sequence would be preferable: without knowing the history of a term, it is impossible to know when to apply the new rule.

Although the difference cannot be eliminated, it is not stringent. Since—as dicussed after Theorem 3.4—the result of a computation is generally considered to be some kind of ground value, *e.g.* number, boolean value, tree, list, *etc.*, and not a continuation, we are safe. Corollary 5.8 assures us that we get the correct result back if we encode ground values in Λ_c or even better in Λ. If continuations are a legitimate part of the result, then it is their potential behavior that is interesting. In this case we are safe because of Proposition 5.3. All terms that are related to a continuation point are behaviorally equivalent. Thus, we can indeed assume that $eval_{CEK}$ and the operational semantics of λ_c are equivalent.

A disadvantage of the above theorem and corollaries is their dependence on the standard reduction function of the calculus. One would prefer to interpret terms in a less operational way using $=_k$ instead. Traditionally, one thinks of terms as functions from some set of basic constants to basic constants. Since we have neither a model for our calculus nor constant names in our language, we follow Morris's example [11] and define the set of ***basic values*** to be the set of closed normal forms in Λ. This definition is not restrictive because ground values can all be encoded in a normal-form representation, and on the other hand, it allows us to compare values syntactically.

Next we define two interpretations of terms [11, 12]. For all $n \geq 0$, the ***calculus interpretation*** of a term M is the function $\mathcal{I}^n_M = \{\langle N_1, \ldots, N_n, U\rangle | \lambda_c \vdash MN_1 \ldots N_n =_k U\}$ where the N_i and U are basic values. The ***machine interpretation*** of a term M is the function $\mathcal{M}^n_M = \{\langle N_1, \ldots, N_n, U\rangle | eval_{CEK}(MN_1 \ldots N_n) \equiv U\}$.

With these interpretations we can show that the correspondence of the CEK-machine to the λ_c-calculus is independent of a standard reduction function:

Theorem 5.9. *For any program M in Λ_c, its calculus and machine interpretation are the same for all $n \geq 0$:*

$$\mathcal{I}^n_M = \mathcal{M}^n_M.$$

Proof. The proof is a straightforward consequence of the Church-Rosser Theorem, Corollary 5.7, and Corollary 5.8. □

Theorem 5.9 essentially says that the machine and the calculus interpret a program as the same function. Given that the classical λ-calculus is for reasoning about the equivalence of these functions, the question naturally arises what proofs in λ_c ***mean***.

Since the relation $=_k$ is not a congruence relation, it is clear that $M =_k N$ does *not* mean that $\mathcal{M}^n_M = \mathcal{M}^n_N$ for any $n > 0$. The relation $=_k$ only compares programs that are already supplied with all their input arguments. Intuitively, the equivalence relation $=_k$ is equating the global control intentions of programs. The subrelation $=_c$ is more like $=_{\beta_v}$: it compares the functionality and *local* control structure of terms.

The question can also be generalized to what equality in λ_c means for open expressions. In Morris's words, we ask whether equality is preserved under all possible interpretations; for Plotkin it is the question if equations in λ_v are true with respect to the machine. For this last step in our investigation we adapt Morris's $\simeq$ and Plotkin's $\approx_V$ relation. M is *operationally equivalent* to N, $M \simeq_{CEK} N$, if for any program context $C[\ ]$—a term with one hole at an arbitrary position—, $C[M]$ and $C[N]$ are programs, $eval_{CEK}$ is undefined for both, or, if it is defined for both programs, it produces the same basic value. From the above discussion about $=_k$ and $=_c$, we know that only $=_c$ implies operational equivalence. For $=_k$ we need to make sure that the terms behave equivalently in all cases, then it also implies operational equivalence:

Theorem 5.10. *For M, N in Λ_c,*

(i) if $\lambda_c \vdash M =_c N$, then $M \simeq_{CEK} N$, and

(ii) if $\lambda_c \vdash C[M] =_k C[N]$ for all sk-contexts $C[\ ]$, then $M \simeq_{CEK} N$.

Proof. The proof of (i) is easy. It is essentially a transcription of Plotkin's corresponding proof for the λ_v-calculus.

Part (ii) deserves some elaboration. Assume the hypothesis and w.l.o.g. assume that M and N are in Λ_c proper. Let $D[\ ]$ be a context such that $D[MN]$ is closed. Now, suppose that $eval_{CEK}(D[M])$ is defined and, furthermore, that it is a basic constant. By Theorem 4.2 and Corollary 5.8

$$\lambda_c \vdash D[M] =_k eval_{CEK}(D[M]).$$

Depending on the role of the fill-in term during the evaluation, we have to distinguish two cases. It is possible that the term in the hole is never a direct component of an sk-redex. Then it gets thrown away since the result is a basic constant. The conclusion is immediate.

Otherwise, at some point a closed form of M or N is an immediate component of some sk-redex in some sk-context. But note, $\lambda_c \vdash C[M] =_k C[N]$ clearly implies $\lambda_c \vdash C[M[x := L]] =_k C[N[x := L]]$ for all values L. Therefore, with the necessary generalization to multiple substitutions, we have

$$\lambda_c \vdash eval_{CEK}(D[M]) =_k eval_{CEK}(C[M[\vec{x} := \vec{L}]]) =_k eval_{CEK}(C[N[\vec{x} := \vec{L}]]).$$

Hence, by the Church-Rosser theorem, $D[M]$ and $D[N]$ produce the same basic value. □

The inverse of both statements is false. This is inherited from the λ_v-calculus for which Plotkin has already shown that it is consistent but not complete with respect to $\approx_V$.

The second point of Theorem 5.10 is important. Although $=_k$ is only an equivalence relation it induces a natural, consistent extension of $=_c$. Instead of requiring $C[M] =_k C[N]$ for *any* context in the antecedent, sk-contexts are sufficient. Since sk-contexts represent control contexts and nothing else, this statement reaffirms that $=_k$ compares control intentions in programs.

6. Discussion

In the preceding sections we have demonstrated how a calculus can be derived from an operational semantics of a programming language. Our particular example involved the derivation of a calculus for a language with non-functional control operators.

Two points deserve mentioning. First, the derivation produced a symbolic evaluation function which works on the level of programs and related concepts. This is an important tool when tracing of programs is required. Until now programs with control operators could only be understood in terms of machine implementations. Second, the existence of a calculus which corresponds to the machine stipulates that many aspects of control are independent of a particular evaluation order. The two-part definition of the calculus expresses the fact that the imperative nature of our operators only shows up at isolated points. These results also encourage us to continue our research on other, seemingly imperative programming constructs.

Acknowledgement. We thank Carolyn Talcott for her careful reading of an earlier draft. Her comments led to a simplification in the presentation of the proofs of Theorem 3.1 and Theorem 3.2.

References

1. BARENDREGT, H.P. *The Lambda Calculus: Its Syntax and Semantics*, North-Holland, 1981.
2. CARLSSON, M. On implementing Prolog in functional programming, *New Generation Computing* **2**, 1984, 347–359.
3. FELLEISEN, M., D.P. FRIEDMAN, E. KOHLBECKER, B. DUBA. Reasoning with Continuations, *Proc. Symp. Logic in Computer Science*, 1986, 131–141; also available in extended form as Technical Report No. 191, Indiana University Computer Science Department, 1986.
4. FRIEDMAN, D.P., C.T. HAYNES, E. KOHLBECKER. Programming with continuations, in *Program Transformations and Programming Environments*, P.Pepper (Ed.), Springer-Verlag, 1985, 263–274.
5. HAYNES, C.T., D.P. FRIEDMAN, M. WAND. Obtaining coroutines from continuations, *Computer Languages*, to appear.
6. HAYNES, C. T. Logic continuations, Technical Report No. 183, Indiana University Computer Science Department, to appear in the proceedings of the *Third International Conference on Logic Programming,* London, Springer-Verlag, 1986.
7. JACKSON, M. A. *Principles of Program Design*, Academic Press, New York, 1975.
8. LANDIN, P.J. The mechanical evaluation of expressions, *Computer Journal* **6**(4), 1964, 308–320.
9. LANDIN, P.J. A correspondence between ALGOL 60 and Church's lambda notation, *Comm. ACM,* **8**(2), 1965, 89–101; 158–165.
10. LANDIN, P.J. A formal description of ALGOL 60, in *Formal Language Description Languages for Computer Programming*, T.B. Steel (Ed.), 1966, 266–294.
11. MORRIS, J.H. *Lambda-Calculus Models of Programming Languages*, Ph.D. Thesis, Project MAC, MAC-TR-57, MIT, 1968.
12. PLOTKIN, G. Call-by-name, call-by-value, and the λ-calculus, *Theoretical Computer Science* **1**, 1975, 125–159.
13. REES, J. (Ed.) The revised^3 report on Scheme, Joint Technical Report Indiana University and MIT Laboratory for Computer Science, 1986, to appear in *SIGPLAN Notices*.
14. REYNOLDS, J.C. GEDANKEN—A simple typeless language based on the principle of completeness and the reference concept, *Comm. ACM* **13**(5), 1970, 308–319.
15. REYNOLDS, J.C. Definitional interpreters for higher-order programming languages, *Proc. ACM Annual Conference*, 1972, 717–740.
16. STEELE, G. *COMMON LISP—The Language*, Digital Press, 1984.
17. SUSSMAN G.J., G. STEELE. Scheme: An interpreter for extended lambda calculus, Memo 349, MIT AI-Lab, 1975.
18. TALCOTT, C. *The Essence of Rum—A Theory of the Intensional and Extensional Aspects of Lisp-type Computation*, Ph.D. dissertation, Stanford University, 1985.

QUESTIONS AND ANSWERS

Jouannaud: If you introduce the notion of procedure in your language is it true that you cannot have separate compilation because your original relation is not congruential?

Felleisen: There is a problem because one may not have a congruence at all places. Instead of using these relations we establish an operational equivalence relation in our paper. In order to reason about these operational equivalences one embeds everything in applicative contexts. If one can show a property for all applicative contexts one gets around the problem of saying: you can only do it at the top level. The loop exit for example works for all applicative contexts. So I can involve this special function, which is a loop exit function, in all places. I can embed it in any program context. It is true: one has to be careful to reason about. But once the theorem that is in this paper is established, one does not lose too much.

Mosses: You base this on call-by-value λ-calculus. Would it work also for call-by-name λ-calculus?

Felleisen: I think, it should be possible, but it may be that you get a different behaviour of continuations.

Mosses: That brings me to a supplementary question. Your goal, I think, was to provide a means for reasoning about these programs. What I would question is whether the way you have now described this language explicates the language in a way that is easy to understand for somebody wanting to understand the language. I am not sure that being able to reason technically about the language is the same as having insight into the language.

Felleisen: Since I have only four rules in the transition system to understand the entire language as opposed to ten rules originally, or six equations in denotational semantics, I think, I have a better chance. At the moment it is an unusual notion to talk about applicative contexts. But I think, people will get used to applicative contexts like they did to environment continuations in denotational semantics or in action semantics. The last point: you see that we agree on a basic notion of evaluation of instructions. There are four possibilities: two are already explicitly in the λ-calculus, namely normal termination of expressions and infinite evaluation of expressions. But, in action semantics you also have an escape of an expression (this is a continuation) and you can fail with an expression. So the four concepts that you can find in our control-calculus are exactly the concepts for defining your action semantics. They may be spelled out differently, but these are the same concepts.

Möller: Plotkin gives translations between the call-by-value and the call-by-name calculus [see reference in the paper]. I would like to know whether there is a translation of your calculus into the λ_v-calculus?

Felleisen: Yes, there is a translation in a continuation passing style, and we can show that this is sound [see reference [3] of the paper]. But the soundness of the translation does not imply a correspondence theorem because in our old calculus we have a lot of dead code. The continuations may contain subterms which never play a role in an evaluation.

SESSION 4

Term Rewriting and Logic Programming

Chairman: K. R. Apt

J.P. Jouannaud and B. Waldmann
Reductive conditional term rewriting systems

S.K. Debray and P. Mishra
Denotational and operational semantics for PROLOG

J. Jaffar, J. - L. Lassez and M.J. Maher
PROLOG - II as an instance of the logic programming language scheme

Formal Description of Programming Concepts - III
M. Wirsing (Editor)
Elsevier Science Publishers B.V. (North-Holland)
IFIP, 1987

Reductive conditional term rewriting systems

Jean Pierre JOUANNAUD*
Bernard WALDMANN

CRIN, BP239
54506 Vandoeuvre-les-Nancy

ABSTRACT

Conditional Term Rewriting Systems (CTRS in short) have been investigated these past years, but no practical completion procedure had ever been given. This is because of many difficulties including: confluence results for terms with variables, irrelevant critical pairs, new possibilities of looping when deciding if a critical pair is relevant or not, etc... This paper describes a completion procedure that solves these problems for the case of reductive CTRS, a class even larger than hierarchical or simplifying CTRS as considered in the current literature. This completion procedure is implemented in the REVE system.

CONTENTS

*) present address: Université de Paris XI, LRI, batiment 490, 91405 Orsay Cedex

1. Introduction

In algebraic specification languages like OBJ2 [F&al 85], rewriting techniques are used to execute the specification on given inputs as well as to make proofs on it. It would be interesting to use conditional rewriting in order to allow axioms like:

$$x/y \rightarrow div(x,gcd(x,y))/\ div(y,\ gcd(x,\ y))\ \textbf{if}\ gcd(x,\ y) \neq 1$$

to normalize the rational numbers.

In a CTRS, we use rules of the form $G \rightarrow D$ **if** C where C is a boolean expression. We could read such a rule: "If the precondition C evaluates to true, then the term G can be rewritten into the term D."

Hierarchical systems

Following [PEE 82], [Rém 82] and [R&Z 84] propose, **hierarchical conditional term rewriting systems**, in which a function symbol can be used in the precondition of a rule only if it has been defined at a lower level of the hierarchy; of course, the starting level permits non-conditional rules only, and rules at a given level of the hierarchy must be terminating.

The following specification of ordered lists, where el stands for the empty list, is hierarchical:

$$R = \{\ r_1:\ ins(el,a) \rightarrow ajt(el,a),$$
$$r_2:\ ins(ajt(l,a),b) \rightarrow ajt(l,a)\ \textbf{if}\ a = b,$$
$$r_3:\ ins(ajt(l,a),b) \rightarrow ajt(ajt(l,a),b)\ \textbf{if}\ (a \neq b) \wedge (a \leqq b),$$
$$r_4:\ ins(ajt(l,a),b) \rightarrow ajt(ins(l,b),a)\ \textbf{if}\ (b \leqq a)\}$$

But these systems present two major drawbacks: first, many systems are not hierarchical; second, the confluence results obtained are available for ground terms only (i.e. without any variable).

Simplifying systems

[Kap 84] obtains results of confluence for non-ground terms by considering what he calls **simplifying conditional term rewriting systems**:

a) preconditions are conjunctions of equalities of the form:

$$\wedge_i (u_i = v_i)$$

and checking a precondition (assuming confluence) is done by testing for each equality $u_i = v_i$ that u_i and v_i have the same normal form.

b) each variable in the precondition or right hand side of a rule must belong to the corresponding left hand side

c) There exists a simplification ordering $>$ (i.e $>$ satisfies the subterm property: $f(\ldots t \ldots) > t$, and is compatible: if $t > t'$ then $f(\ldots t \ldots) > f(\ldots t' \ldots)$) such that for any rule $G \to D$ **if** $\wedge_i u_i = v_i$ and for any substitution σ:

$$\sigma(G) > \sigma(D),\ \sigma(G) > \sigma(u_i) \text{ and } \sigma(G) > \sigma(v_i).$$

This specification of integers with $\leqq$ is simplifying:

$$R = \{r_1:\ s(p(x)) \to x,$$
$$r_2:\ p(s(x)) \to x,$$
$$r_3:\ 0 \leqq 0 \to \text{true},$$
$$r_4:\ 0 \leqq p(0) \to \text{false},$$
$$r_5:\ 0 \leqq s(x) \to \text{true } \textbf{if } (0 \leqq x) = \text{true},$$
$$r_6:\ 0 \leqq p(x) \to \text{false } \textbf{if } (0 \leqq x) = \text{false},$$
$$r_7:\ (s(x) \leqq y) \to x \leqq p(y),$$
$$r_8:\ (p(x) \leqq y) \to x \leqq s(y)\}$$

Kaplan gives a rough sketch of a completion procedure. However, it turns out that his procedure cannot handle most practical examples, because non-simplifying equations are generated by the completion process. For example, the following critical pair between rules r_1 and r_5 is not simplifying:

$$\langle 0 \leqq x,\ \text{true}\rangle \textbf{ if } (0 \leqq p(x)) = \text{true}$$

Reductive systems

To improve Kaplan's results, we introduce the notion of **reductive conditional term rewriting systems** in which the rules verify Kaplan's conditions a) and b) and the following one (weaker than c):

c') There exists a reduction ordering > (i.e. > is compatible and well founded) such that $\sigma(G) > \sigma(u_i)$ and $\sigma(G) > \sigma(v_i)$ for all substitutions σ and $\sigma(G) > \sigma(D)$ for all substitutions σ such that $\sigma(C)$ evaluates to true.

In this paper, we show that rewriting with reductive CTRS terminates and we give first, a confluence theorem, then a Knuth-Bendix like procedure. Moreover we discuss the problem of R-unification in a reductive CTRS which is crucial for our completion procedure. At last, we introduce an inductive completion method.

Remark

The notations used in this paper follow [H&O 80]; for example, $t\downarrow$ stands for "the normal form of t" and $t[\omega \leftarrow D]$ means "the term t in which the subterm at occurrence ω had been substituted by D".

2. Termination

The problem of termination is more complicated with CTRS than usually: we must, of course, prove that any rewriting issued from a term has a finite length but we must also prove that the evaluation of the precondition will not induce an infinite recursive call.

To prove that rewriting with a reductive CTRS R terminates, we use an ordering denoted by **st>** which is the transitive closure of the relation (**st** ∪ >) where **st** is the strict subterm ordering and > is the reduction ordering associated with the system R. This ordering is well-founded [J&K 84].

Theorem

If R is a reductive CTRS then it terminates.

Proof

We show by noetherian induction on **st>** that rewriting terminates, i.e. if any rewriting issued from a term t' smaller than t terminates then any rewriting issued from t terminates.

Let us assume that there exists a rule G $\rightarrow$ D **if** C, a substitution σ and an occurrence ω of t which satisfy

$$t|_{\omega} = \sigma(G)$$

then we have to rewrite the terms $\sigma(u_i)$ and $\sigma(v_i)$ to check whether $\sigma(C)$ evaluates to true. Since R is reductive, these terms are smaller than $\sigma(G)$ w.r.t. > then they are smaller than t w.r.t. **st>** since $\sigma(G)$ is a subterm of t, so rewriting stops for them.

Let us assume that $\sigma(C)$ evaluates to true, then:

$$t \rightarrow t' = t[\omega \leftarrow \sigma(D)]$$

we can see that t > t' (by compatibility), so rewriting stops for t' and then also for t.

3. Confluence

3.1. Critical pair

Before giving a confluence result, we first recall the notion of critical pair for the CTRS.

Definitions [Kap 84]

Given two rules r: G $\rightarrow$ D **if** C, r': G'$\rightarrow$ D' **if** C' of a CTRS R, if there exist a substitution σ and an occurrence ω of G such that:

$$\sigma(G|_{\omega}) = \sigma(G')$$

then we have the **contextual critical pair** (CCP):

$$<\sigma(G[\omega \leftarrow D']), \sigma(D)> \textbf{ if } \sigma(C) \wedge \sigma(C').$$

If there exists a substitution ρ such that $\rho(\sigma(C) \wedge \sigma(C'))$ evaluates to true then the CCP is **solvable**.

3.2. Confluence theorem

Theorem

A reductive CTRS R is confluent if and only if:

_ for all solvable CCP <P, Q> **if** C

_ for all substitutions σ such that $\sigma(C)$ evaluates to true

we have:

$$\sigma(P)\downarrow_R = \sigma(Q)\downarrow_R.$$

Proof

The confluence of R implies of course the confluence of CCPs.

The converse is proved by noetherian induction on **st>.** The proof is done in two steps:

i) we prove the local confluence for t assuming confluence for term strictly smaller than t.

ii) then we prove confluence for t assuming local confluence for t and confluence for terms strictly smaller than t.

Let us start with ii) whose proof is a classical one [New 42]; The basic scheme of the proof is the following:

Let us assume that there exist t_1 and t_2 such that:

$$t \to t_1 \quad \text{and} \quad t \to t_2$$

the local confluence hypothesis implies that there exists t' such that:

$$t_1 \xrightarrow{*} t' \quad \text{and} \quad t_2 \xrightarrow{*} t'.$$

The confluence hypothesis for terms smaller than t implies that if there exists t'_1 such that:

$$t_1 \xrightarrow{*} t'_1$$

then there exists t''_1 such that:

$$t'_1 \xrightarrow{*} t''_1 \quad \text{and} \quad t' \xrightarrow{*} t''_1$$

A second induction with t''_1, t_2 and t'_2 shows that the following diagram is closed:

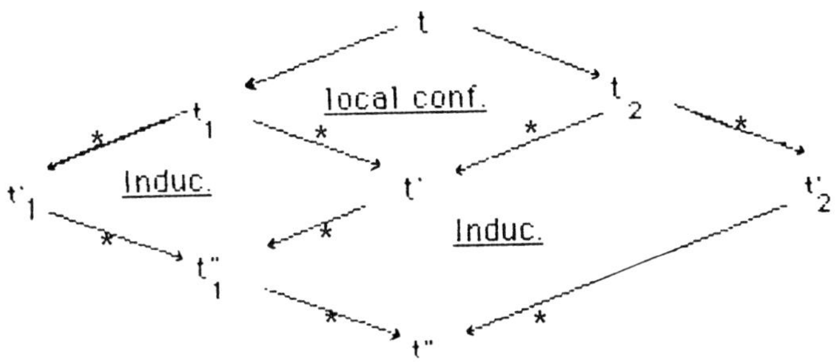

then we can deduce that we have confluence for t.

Let us now prove i): given a term t, two rules r: $G \rightarrow D$ **if** C and r': $G' \rightarrow D'$ **if** C' such that there exist occurrences ω and ω' and substitutions σ and σ' which satisfy:

_ $t|_\omega = \sigma(G)$ and $t|_{\omega'} = \sigma'(G')$

_ σ(C) and σ'(C') evaluate to true

We call t_1, t_2 the following terms:

$$t_1 = t[\omega \leftarrow \sigma(D)] \qquad t_2 = t[\omega' \leftarrow \sigma'(D')]$$

There are three cases:

i) If ω and ω' are disjoint then confluence for t is straightforward.

ii) There is a CCP $\langle\theta(D'), \theta(G[\omega \leftarrow D])\rangle$ **if** $\theta(C \wedge C')$ between the two rules and there is a substitution ρ such that $\sigma = \rho\theta$ for the variables of C and $\sigma' = \rho\theta$ for the variables of C'. The result $t_1{\downarrow}_R = t_2{\downarrow}_R$ follows classically from the critical pair lemma and the confluence hypothesis for solvable CCPs [Hue 80].

iii) There is no CCP and, without loss of generality, ω' is smaller than ω. This situation is described by the following pictures:

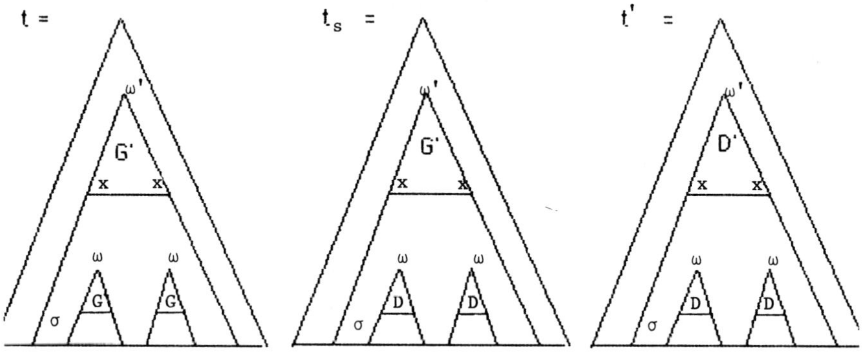

where the terms t_s and t' are obtained by rewriting t_1 and t_2 as many times as possible with the rule r, this is legal since $\sigma(C)$ evaluates to true. We can see on the picture that the rule $G' \rightarrow D'$ reduces t_s into t' when instanciated by σ'' defined as follows:

$$\sigma''(x) = \sigma'(x)[\omega \leftarrow \sigma(D)]$$

$$\sigma''(y) = \sigma'(y) \text{ for } y \neq x$$

However, we must now prove that $\sigma''(C')$ evaluates to true.

We know that the terms $\sigma'(u'_i)$ and $\sigma'(v'_i)$ have the same normal form u. From the definition of σ'', we also get:

$$\sigma'(u'_i) \xrightarrow{*} \sigma''(u'_i) \quad \text{and} \quad \sigma'(v'_i) \xrightarrow{*} \sigma''(v'_i)$$

and we want to prove that $\sigma''(u'_i)\downarrow = \sigma''(v'_i)\downarrow$.

Since R is reductive, we have:

$$\sigma'(G') > \sigma'(u'_i) \quad \text{and} \quad \sigma'(G') > \sigma'(v'_i)$$

On the other hand, t_s is greater than $\sigma'(G)$ w.r.t. **st**; therefore:

$$t \textbf{ st>} \sigma'(u'_i) \quad \text{and} \quad t \textbf{ st>} \sigma'(v'_i).$$

The confluence hypothesis for terms smaller than t implies that there exists a term w such that u and $\sigma''(u'_i)$ can be rewritten into w. Similarly, there exists a term for u and $\sigma''(v'_i)$. The confluence hypothesis is again applied to w and w' to close the diagram as shown on the picture.

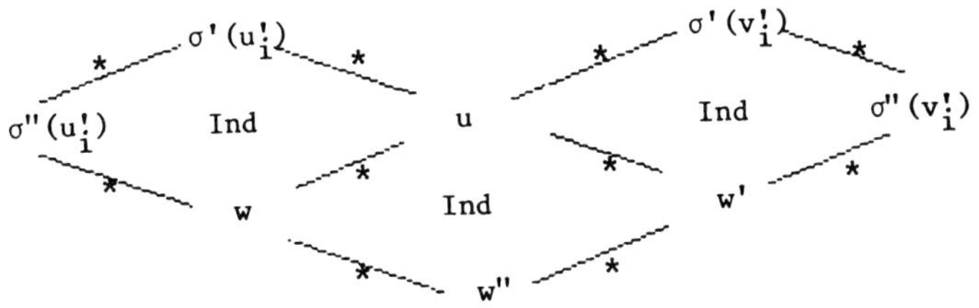

Hence, for each i, $\sigma''(u_i') = \sigma''(v_i')$ is a theorem of R.

4. Completion procedure

As usual, our confluence results can be extended into a completion procedure by orienting non-confluent critical pairs.

4.1. The procedure

To obtain a complete set of rules R which is equivalent to the initial set of equations E_1, we consider the following Knuth-Bendix like procedure. The differences with the usual one are discussed later on.

```
Completion (E1, E2, R, n, >);
IF E1 ≠ ø THEN
   Take an equation e in E1
   Gn → Dn if Cn := orientation (e, >)
   R := R ∪ {Gn → Dn if Cn }
   Normalize the right member and precondition of the rules in R
   Move the rules whose left hand side is reducible from R to E1
   Completion (E1, E2, R, n+1, >)
ELSEIF there is an unmarked rule ri in R THEN
  Mark ri
  E2 := E2 ∪ {CCP of ri with the rules of number j ≤ i}
  Completion ( E1, E2, R, n, >)
ELSEIF E2=ø THEN RETURN (R)
ELSE
   WHILE E2 ≠ ø and E1 = ø DO
     Bound := Bound + 1
     FOR each equation <p, q> if C in E2 DO
         IF Solvable (C, R, Bound ) THEN
            move <p, q> if C from E2 to E1
   Completion ( E1, E2, R, n, >)
END Completion
```

4.2. Unsolved critical pairs

The problems with the usual Knuth-Bendix completion procedure are the following:

i) It may run forever, computing new critical pairs.

ii) It may fail inside the orientation procedure because of an unorderable equation.

Moreover, with CTRS, the computation of CCPs may generate unsolvable conditional equations simply called equations hereafter. For example, if we consider a specification of integers with the two predicates "even" and "odd":

$$\begin{aligned} R = \{\ & r_1: \text{even}(0) \to \text{true}, \\ & r_2: \text{even}(s(0)) \to \text{false}, \\ & r_3: \text{even}(s(s(x)) \to \text{even}(x), \\ & r_4: \text{odd}(x) \to \text{false } \mathbf{if} \text{ even}(x) = \text{true}, \\ & r_5: \text{odd}(x) \to \text{true } \mathbf{if} \text{ even}(x) = \text{false}\} \end{aligned}$$

the completion procedure will compute the following CCP between rules r_4 and r_5:

$$\langle \text{true}, \text{false} \rangle \ \mathbf{if}\ (\text{even}(x) = \text{true}) \wedge (\text{even}(x) = \text{false}).$$

To prevent the procedure of looping or failing while computing such CCPs only, we chose to consider two sets: E_1, the set of solvable equations and E_2, the set of unsolved equations (we do not know yet if they are solvable or not). The conditional completion procedure works the following way:

i) new CCPs are added to E_2.

ii) when E_1 becomes empty and all rules in R are marked, the procedure stops only if E_2 is empty; else, it checks E_2 for solvable equations and moves them to E_1.

Unfortunately, the feasibility of a CCP is a semi-decidable property when R is Church-Rosser. However, many practical cases (the previous example) can be decided by simple means such as normalization with Hsiang's TRS for boolean algebras [Hsi 85]. In the following, we describe a procedure based on more general techniques.

5. R-unification

The technique used to solve equations is based on narrowing, a complete procedure if the system R is Church-Rosser. A narrowing procedure was already used in [Kap 84]. Our procedure however is different and solves the two following problems which are not solved by [Kap 84]:

i) The system is not yet Church-Rosser.

ii) It is a semi-decidable procedure and we must prevent it from running forever since we use it while running the completion procedure.

For these reasons, we perform what we call **bounded narrowing**.

5.1. Narrowing

Definition

A term t is **narrowable** into a term t' if and only if there exist a rule $r: G \to D$, an occurrence ω of t and a substitution σ such that:

i) σ is a most general unifier for $t|_\omega$ and G

ii) $t' = \sigma(t[\omega \leftarrow D])$

We note this relation:

$$t \xrightarrow{v}_{[\sigma,\ \omega,\ r]} t'$$

Lifting lemma

The completeness property of narrowing is based on the lifting lemma [Hul 80] which says that a derivation issued from $s_0 = \sigma(t_0)$ can be associated to every narrowing derivation issued from t_0 where $\sigma = \sigma_n \ldots \sigma_0$:

$$\sigma(t_0) = s_0 \to_{[r_0,\ \omega_0]} s_1 \to_{[\ldots]} \cdots \to_{[r_n,\ \omega_n]} s_{n+1}$$

$$t_0 \xrightarrow{v}_{[\sigma_0, r_0, \omega_0]} t_1 \xrightarrow{v}_{[\ldots]} \cdots \xrightarrow{v}_{[\sigma_n, r_n, \omega_n]} t_{n+1}$$

Narrowing tree

To solve an equation $u_0 = v_0$, i.e. to get an R-unifier for u_0 and v_0, we compute a **narrowing tree** in the following way:

_ its root is labeled by the couple (u_0, v_0)

_ if (u_i, v_i) labels one of its nodes and if $u_i \text{-v}\!\rightarrow_{[\sigma_i, r_i, \omega_i]} u_{i+1}$ and $v_{i+1} = \sigma_i(v_i)$ then (u_{i+1}, v_{i+1}) labels one of the sons of this node. (The roles of u_i and v_i may be reversed).

If u_n and v_n are unifiable by a most general unifier θ, then the substitution $\sigma = \theta\sigma_n \ldots \sigma_0$ is an R-unifier for u_0 and v_0.

5.2. Conditional narrowing

Conditional narrowing is defined the same way, but we must also be sure that $\sigma(C_i)$ evaluates to true for all the preconditions of the rules $G_i \rightarrow D_i$ **if** C_i. In other words, if we just take θ as a most general unifier for u_n and v_n like [Kap 84], we are not guaranteed to produce only R-unfiers even when all the $\theta\sigma_n \ldots \sigma_0(C_i)$ are solvable, θ must also be a common R-unifier of each $\sigma_n \ldots \sigma_0(C_i)$, hence, we can say that $\sigma(C_i)$ evaluates to true.

To solve this problem, we shall collect the preconditions of the rules applied during the narrowing process together with the equality $u = v$ (or the precondition) to be solved: the narrowing process will narrow at the same time the starting equality (or precondition) and the preconditions of the already applied rules! Therefore, the nodes of the narrowing tree will now be labeled by conditions interpreted as sets of equalities. This is done by the following definition of the conditional narrowing.

Definition

Given a CTRS R, a precondition C is **narrowable** into a precondition C' if and only if there exist a rule r: $G_r \rightarrow D_r$ **if** C_r, an occurrence ω of C and a substitution σ such that:

i) σ is a most general unifier for G_r and $C|_\omega$

ii) $C' = \sigma(C[\omega \leftarrow D_r]) \wedge \sigma(C_r)$

This definition is inspired by [D&P 85a] and [D&P 85b]. It allows us to compute a substitution σ which is a solution of C and of all the C_is appearing during the narrowing process without having to verify recursively at the end of the narrowing process that $\sigma(C_i)$ evaluates to true. On the other hand [Kap 84]'s narrowing procedure does not work by collecting preconditions with the equality to be solved: as a consequence, it is not guaranteed to produce an R-unifier even if there exists one.

5.3. Bounded narrowing

There are still three problems to be solved:

_ First, the narrowing tree may be infinite. In that case, the procedure should be fair, i.e., find a solution in a finite time if there is one. This is classically achieved by searching the tree breadthfirst.

_ Second, there might be no solution at all and as already said, we do want to stop eventually in this case too.

_ Third, the narrowing tree may be incomplete because R is not yet Church-Rosser.

These two last points are solved by using bounded narrowing, i.e. we look at a finite number of nodes in the tree, the bound first ones. Since a precondition may need more than the computation of bound nodes of the tree, bound is increased at each call of the narrowing procedure by the completion procedure, hence we are sure that a solvable precondition will eventually be solved. Moreover, as the rewriting system R may change between two calls of the narrowing procedure, we do not keep the narrowing tree from one call to the next one.

5.4. Procedure of bounded-narrowing

The next procedure will be used in the completion procedure to know whether the precondition "Cond", can be solved in less than "Bound" steps with the CTRS "R".

```
Solvable (Cond, R, Bound)
F := empty_fifo
Push Cond on to F
FOR i = 1 TO Bound DO
   C := the top of F
   Pop F
   IF there exists σ such σ(C) evaluates to true
   THEN RETURN (TRUE)
   ELSE FOR G → D if C' IN R DO
            FOR ω occurrence of C such that σ (C|ω)= σ(G) DO
                Push (σ(C[ω ← D]) ∧  σ(C')) on to F
            END FOR
        END FOR
        IF F is empty THEN RETURN (failure1)
END FOR
RETURN (failure2)
END Solvable
```

The difference between "failure1" and "failure2" is the following: the first means that we are not able to solve the precondition with the system R while the second means that we are not able to do it in less than "Bound" steps. Moreover, if R is Church-Rosser, then "failure1" does not only mean that we are not able to solve it, it also means that it is really unsolvable.

6. Main theorem

Given our narrowing procedure, we have the following result:

Theorem

The completion procedure leads to one of the following situations:

_ it terminates with a confluent reductive CTRS equivalent to the set of axioms.

_ it fails inside the orientation procedure.

_ it generates an infinite set of rules; in that case, it is a semi decision procedure.

_ it runs forever with unsolvable CCP in E_2 and an empty E_1. In this case, the finite set of rules is Church-Rosser (but we do not know it). However, we can also use it as a semi decision procedure.

Proof

It is similar to Huet's one, in [Hue 81], except for the problem of fairness which is solved thanks to the following lemma:

Lemma

If e:<P, Q> **if** $C \in E_1 \cup E_2$ at step i and if the precondition C is solvable then there exists a step j > i such that e is chosed for orientation into a rule.

Proof

i) if $e \in E_1$, since the procedure does not loop while orienting the equations, then there is a step j such that e will be ordered into a rewrite rule.

ii) If $e \in E_2$ and is solvable, then it will eventually be moved into E_1 and we are back to case i) this is so because the bound of narrowing is increased at each call.

7. Inductive Completion

A major use of the completion procedure is the proof of inductive theorems, that is theorems valid in the initial algebra of the specification (the kind of conditional specification we consider admits always an initial algebra [TWW 76]). Our approach is based on the concept of inductive reducibility. This concept was first suggested by [Der 81] in a seminar paper, then (but independently) by Kounalis in the context of decision procedures for sufficient completeness [K&Z 85]. It was further developed by [J&K 86] as the adequate tool for inductive completion. Let us recall the basic principles of this approach:

Definition

A term t is inductively reducible by a term rewriting system R if and only if every ground instance of t is reducible by R.

The inductive completion procedure is nothing but the usual one, plus a check that the left hand side of every added rule is inductively reducible. Starting from a confluent set of rules R and an equation s=t to be proved an inductive theorem of R, the answer is yes if the completion succeeds or runs forever and no if the inductive reducibility check ever fails. Assume we modify our completion procedure for conditional specifications to include the inductive reducibility check on left hand sides. Then, we get the following result:

Theorem

Assume R is a confluent CTRS and s=t a non-conditional equation. If Inductive-completion (R, s = t) returns a convergent set of rules or runs forever, then s=t is an inductive theorem of R. Nothing can be said if Inductive-completion fails, either when orienting an equation or when checking a left hand side for inductive reducibility.

Proof:

The proof is based on the property that the set of ground normal forms remains the same all along the inductive completion process. This is due to the fact that all added rules have a left hand side which is inductively reducible [J&K 86]. When the inductive reducibility check fails for a rule $G \rightarrow D$ **if** C, this means that some ground instance $\sigma(G)$ of G is a ground normal form. This does not mean however that this ground normal form becomes reducible, since we are not guaranteed that $\sigma(C)$ evaluates to true. Only if we are sure that $\sigma(C)$ evaluates to true, can we conclude that s=t if C was not an inductive theorem. We are left to solve two different problems:

i) checking for inductive reducibility in presence of conditional rules. This is needed to apply our inductive completion procedure.

ii) check if all ground instances of G, a left hand side of a rule $G \rightarrow D$ **if** C, that satisfy C are reducible. This is needed to extend our inductive completion procedure, and be able to disprove theorems when the check fails.

Unfortunately, we are not even able to solve the first of them.

8. Conclusion

In this paper, we have extended the use of the CTRSs by giving a completion procedure to transform a non confluent CTRS into a confluent one. We believe that the scheme of our completion procedure is the right one. However, there still exist systems that terminate but that are not reductive; for example, the following one (with only one rule):

$$f(x) \rightarrow a \textbf{ if } f(f(x)) = f(x)$$

Of course, it is not a practical one, but it shows that the condition c' of our definition is not necessary.

Let us now discuss another (more practical) example which also fails and indicates directions for further research:

$$R = \{\ r_1\text{: } EQ\ (x\ ,\ x) \rightarrow \text{true},$$
$$r_2\text{: } x \in \emptyset \rightarrow \text{false},$$
$$r_3\text{: } x \in z \cup \{y\} \rightarrow \text{true } \mathbf{if}\ EQ\ (x,\ y) = \text{true},$$
$$r_4\text{: } x \in z \cup \{y\} \rightarrow x \in z\ \mathbf{if}\ EQ\ (x,\ y) = \text{false},$$
$$r_5\text{: } z \cup \{x\} \rightarrow z\ \mathbf{if}\ x \in z = \text{true}\ \}$$

The completion procedure generates the following CCP between the rules r_3 and r_5:

$$\langle\ x \in z,\ \text{true}\rangle\ \mathbf{if}\ (y \in z = \text{true}) \wedge\ (EQ\ (x,\ y) = \text{true})$$

where the variable y appears in the precondition but in none of the members of the equation.

This problem can be solved by using narrowing instead of rewriting in the evaluation process of the precondition. However, this is rather a problem of logical programming and we think, for efficiency reasons, that before dealing with it, it would be interesting to extend basic narrowing and narrowing with normalization to CTRSs.

The problem encountered with simplifying CTRS that generates non-simplifying CCPs still remains with reductive CTRS. However, we think that the completion procedure could be improved by eliminating, in a purely syntactical way, some of these CCPs. In the example of the introduction, we can see that the generated CCP is an instance of a rule modulo R. More precisely, the precondition C of the rule r_5 is a σ-instance of the precondition C' of the CCP and the equational part of the CCP is a σ'-instance of the equational part of the rule r_5 and σ and σ' are such that:

$$C \Rightarrow \sigma(\sigma'(C')) =_R C$$

so, we have $\sigma\sigma' \geqq_R$ **Id** where **Id** stands for the identity substitution. This mechanism should be further investigated.

References

[Der 81] **N. Dershowitz**, Applications of the Knuth-Bendix Procedure, actes du séminaire d'informatique theorique du LITP, 1981

[D&P 85a] **N. Dershowitz, D-A. Plaisted**, Logic Programming cum Applicative Programming, IEEE proceedings of the Symposium on Logic Programming, Boston (Massachusetts USA)

[D&P 85b] **N. Dershowitz, D-A. Plaisted**, Equational Programming, to appear in Machine Intelligence 11

[F&al 85] **K. Futatsugi, J.A. Goguen, J.P. Jouannaud, J. Meseguer**, Principles of OBJ2, To appear, Proceedings, 1985 Symposium on Principles of Programming Langages

[Hsi 85] **J. Hsiang**, Refutational Theorem Proving using Term Rewriting Systems, To appear in artificial intelligence journal

[Hue 80] **G. Huet**, Confluent Reductions: Abstract Properties and Applications to Term Rewriting Systems, Journal of the association for computing machinery 27 (1980)

[Hue 81] **G. Huet**, A Complete Proof of Correctness of the Knuth-Bendix Completion Algorithm, J.C.S.S. 23, 1, pp 11-21 (1981)

[H&O 80] **G. Huet, D.C. Oppen**, Equations and Rewrite Rules: a Survey, Formal Langages: Perspectives and Open Problems, Ed. Book R. Academic Press (1980)

[Hul 80] **J-M. Hullot**, Compilation de Formes Canoniques dans les Théories Equationnelles, Thèse de 3eme cycle, Université de Paris sud, Orsay (1980)

[J&K 84] **J.P. Jouannaud, H. Kirchner**, Completion of a Set of Rules modulo a Set of Equations, Proceedings of the 11 ACM Conference on Programming Langages, Salt Lake City (Utah USA)

[J&K 86] **J.P. Jouannaud, E. Kounalis**, Proofs by Induction in Equational Theories without Constructors, Proceedings of the 1st IEEE Symposium on Logic in Computer Science, Cambridge, Massachussets.

[Kap 84] **S. Kaplan**, Fair Conditional Term Rewriting Systems: Unification, Termination and Confluence, Laboratoire de Recherche Informatique, Université d'Orsay

[K&B 70] **D. Knuth, P. Bendix**, Simple Word Problems in Universal Algebra, Computational Problems in Abstract Algebra, Ed. Leech J. Pergammon press

[K&Z 85] **E. Kounalis, H. Zhang**, A General Completeness Test for Equational Specifications, Proceedings of the Hungarian Conference of Computer Science, 1985, Budapest (Hungary)

[New 42] **M.H.A. Newman**, On Theories with a Combinatorial Definition of Equivalence, Annals of Mathematics, 43, 2, p 223-243, 1942

[PEE 82] **U. Pletat, G. Engels, H.D. Ehrich**, Operational Semantics of Algebraic Specifications with Conditional Equations, 7eme C.A.A.P., Lille 1982

[Rém 82] **J-L. Rémy**, Etude de la Réécriture Conditionnelle et de ses Applications à la Spécification, à l'Implémentation et à la Certification des Types Abstraits Algébriques, Thèse d'état, Université de Nancy I

[R&Z 84] **J-L. Rémy, H. Zhang**, Reveur4: A System for Validating Conditional Algebraic Specification of Parametrized Abstract Data Types, Proceedings of the second ECAI Conference, Pisa 1984

[TWW 76] **J.W. Thatcher, E.G. Wagner, J.B. Wright**, Specification of Abstract Data Types Using Conditional Axioms, Ibm Research Report Rc 6214, 1976

QUESTIONS AND ANSWERS

Ganzinger: I have two questions: I found that in practice there are many specifications that are not confluent on all terms, but confluent on ground terms only. Is there any way to modify your completion procedures so that they can handle these situations? The second question is the following: in the framework of conditional equational specifications one would be interested in inductive proofs for conditional equations and not for equations only. Is there any way to extend these induction principles to that case?

Jouannaud: For the first question: my answer is a feeling, I would say ´yes´. The idea would be to mix techniques used in this framework and techniques used by Jean Luc Rémy in his hierarchical framework [see reference [Rém 82] of the paper]. And I think, we could be able to design procedures to check ground confluence. The problem is that in Rémy´s framework the ground confluence check does not give rise to a completion procedure because it computes some very complicated objects which he calls ´contextual sets of normal forms´. And from these sets of normal forms you don´t really know how to get a completion procedure. So, maybe at least you can have a check of ground confluence and I am not sure whether you will be able to derive a completion procedure for ground confluence. Now, for the second question: the answer is here [the theorem of section 7]. This will enable you to prove conditional equations as well. The problem will be that defining inductive reducibility is a little more complicated. You will have to check whether ground instances of ´t´ are reducible, but you will restrict ground instances to those instances that satisfy the precondition. To do that, you will need to solve the precondition in the equational theory which means computing a complete set of most general unifiers. From this set instantiate ´t´ and check for inductive reducibility. Thus you need the unification algorithm in the theory.

Orejas: What are your results with experimentation?

Jouannaud: The answer is not simple. First of all, what we have implemented is Kaplan´s method [see reference [Kap 84] of the paper]. It´s when we saw all problems with Kaplan´s method that we decided to study whether it was possible to expand the method. The main problem is that in many experiments you don´t get at the end of the completion because rules are generated that do not belong to the class. So the experiments fail in some way. It is hard to speak about efficiency. The experiments usually fail very quickly. (laughter)

Felleisen: What kinds of examples can you do in your system that you could not do in Kaplan´s system?

Jouannaud: Very few. Most of them were toy examples. We had one real example. Most examples failed exactly for the same reason because when Kaplan´s method fails what is generated is not even a reductive rule. Some theory is terminating but not reductive. Now, actually I must confess that there is a possibility to get around that which I have indicated here, but we did not implement it for the moment. We must improve the completion procedure because what happens is that, when a so called ´contextual critical pair´ is computed, the preconditions are accumulated. The precondition part becomes bigger and bigger. On the other hand, every critical pair is reduced as much as possible. What happens then is that the left-hand side becomes smaller than the precondition. What is needed is an algorithm for reducing preconditions, in particular a reduction algorithm in Boolean algebras. I must say that in many cases where the completion algorithm failed it was because we were not reducing the preconditions. If we had an algorithm to reduce them then the completion would succeed much more often, but it has not yet been implemented.

Ganzinger: Just a remark about the example of lists: I believe that, if you add to this list for example the maximum function of natural numbers, then there is no chance to get it complete because it is not confluent on all terms. You can only make it confluent on ground terms.

Jouannaud: I agree.

Blum: Are there any complexity results?

Jouannaud: I know that Kaplan has been working about two years ago on complexity results, about the complexity of the normalization function. He has some results about average complexity. But these results have not been published. This is the only complexity result, I am aware of.

Orejas: Have you tried examples for which Rémy proved confluence using his hierarchical approach? Have you checked, if your system fails in these examples?

Jouannaud: There are some examples where our system fails, for the reason indicated by Harald Ganzinger: it is fairly possible that a set of rules is ground confluent, but not confluent.

Formal Description of Programming Concepts - III
M. Wirsing (Editor)
Elsevier Science Publishers B.V. (North-Holland)

© IFIP, 1987

Denotational and Operational Semantics for Prolog

Saumya K. Debray† *Prateek Mishra*

Department of Computer Science
State University of New York at Stony Brook
Stony Brook, NY 11794

The semantics of Prolog programs is usually given in terms of the model theory of first order logic. However, this does not adequately characterize the computational behaviour of Prolog programs. Prolog implementations typically use a sequential evaluation strategy based on the textual order of clauses and literals in a program, as well as non-logical features like "cut". In this work we develop a denotational semantics that expresses the computational behaviour of Prolog. We present a semantics for "cut-free" Prolog, which is then extended to Prolog with cut. For each case we develop a congruence proof that relates the semantics to an abstract interpreter. As an application of our denotational semantics, we show the correctness of some standard "folk" theorems regarding transformations on Prolog programs.

1. Introduction

Any attempt at formulating a semantics for the programming language Prolog must cope with a certain schizophrenia. From one perspective the question is simply closed, as programs in Prolog are statements in the Horn clause fragment of first-order logic. The semantics of Prolog can therefore be stated in terms of the model theory of first order logic [1, 13]. This is usually referred to as the *declarative* or *logical* semantics of Prolog. From a computational point of view, this formulation is inadequate as it ignores several behavioural aspects of Prolog programs. These include termination, use of a sequential depth-first search strategy as well as methods for controlling search such as *cut*. Further, in practice, Prolog seems to be used more as a language for defining computations over sequences of substitutions than as a language for asserting the truth of certain formulae.

In this work we develop a denotational semantics [12] for Prolog that can express behavioural properties of interest. The semantics incorporates the sequential evaluation strategy used by standard Prolog evaluators and can express the effect of the *cut* operator. A natural consequence is that the meaning of a predicate is a function from substitutions, to a (potentially) infinite sequence of substitutions rather than a set of ground atoms, as is classical. The reasonableness of the denotational semantics is demonstrated

This work was supported in part by the National Science Foundation under grant number DCR-8407688.

† Present Address: Department of Computer Science, University of Arizona, Tucson, AZ 85721

by developing a congruence proof that relates it to an operational interpreter for Prolog.

The motivation for our work comes from the need to verify various optimizing transformations on Prolog programs. The literature contains various references to folk theorems as the basis for such transformations [3, 7]. Many such theorems entail reasoning about the computational behaviour of Prolog programs: e.g., reasoning about termination owing to the insertion or removal of cuts or about the behaviour of predicates when viewed as substitution sequence transformers. In Section 5 we use our semantics to give simple proofs for two nontrivial theorems regarding program transformations involving cuts. We are currently using our denotational semantics to validate sophisticated static analysis schemes such as mode inference and determinacy inference.

Proofs of semantic equivalence are traditionally unreadable, and need be developed with care to possess even a modest degree of versimilitude. The key issue in our proof is reconciling a compositional denotational semantics with an operational semantics that is much more oriented towards "literal-at-a-time" processing. For the cut-free case we reconcile the two semantic specifications by developing a set of theorems that support a modular decomposition of interpreter states. Unfortunately, for full Prolog such a straightforward decomposition is not possible and the proof is instead expressed as an invariant relating the interpreter state to the denotational semantics (Section 4). For the sake of continuity, the proofs of theorems have been relegated to the appendix.

Related work on the denotational treatment of the semantics of logic programming languages includes that of Frandsen [4, 5] and Jones and Mycroft [6]. Frandsen treats "pure" programs and ignores Prolog's sequential nature of computation, which makes it difficult to use his semantics to explain behavioural aspects of programs. There are a number of differences between our work and that of Jones and Mycroft. Our semantic definitions are motivated by the need to justify program analysis and transformation methods, whereas their definitions are driven by the goal of generating correct Prolog interpreters. In contrast to their direct semantics wherein "cut" is a modelled by means of a special token, we give a continuation semantics that models "cut" in a more intuitively accessible manner. In final contrast, we provide a congruence proof relating operational and denotational semantics, and use the semantics to validate two nontrivial optimizing transformations of Prolog programs.

The remainder of this paper is organized as follows: Section 2 discusses some basic notions, and develops the notation used in the rest of the paper. Section 3 is concerned with the semantics of cut-free Prolog. Section 4 discusses the semantics of Prolog with cut. Section 5 applies the semantics to validate two optimizing transformations of Prolog programs, and Section 6 concludes the paper. The appendix contains outlines of the proofs of equivalence between the denotational and operational semantics for the cut-free and the cut cases respectively; details of proofs may be found in [2].

2. Preliminaries

2.1. SLD-resolution

A term in Prolog is either a variable, a constant or a compound term $f(t_1, ..., t_n)$ where f is an n-ary function symbol and the t_i, $1 \leq i \leq n$, are terms. The set of variables, function symbols and predicate symbols will be denoted by **Var**, **Func** and **Pred** respectively. The set of terms will be denoted **Term**. A substitution is an idempotent mapping from **Var** to **Term** which is the identity mapping at all but finitely many points. The set of substitutions will be denoted by **Subst**. Given substitutions σ_1 and σ_2, σ_1 will be said to be *more general* than σ_2 if there is a substitution θ such that $\sigma_2 = \theta \circ \sigma_1$. Two terms t_1 and t_2 are said to be *unifiable* if there exists a substitution σ such that $\sigma(t_1) = \sigma(t_2)$; in this case, the substitution σ is said to be a *unifier* for the terms. If two terms t_1 and t_2 have a unifier, then they have a *most general unifier* mgu(t_1, t_2), which is unique up to variable renaming.

A Prolog program consists of a set of predicate definitions. A predicate definition consists of a sequence of clauses. Each clause is a sequence of literals, which are either atomic goals or negations of atomic goals. Prolog clauses are generally constrained to be definite Horn, i.e. have exactly one positive literal. The positive literal is called the *head* of the clause, and the remaining literals, if any, constitute the *body* of the clause; a clause with only negative literals is referred to as a *negative clause* or *goal*. We will adhere to the syntax of DEC-10 Prolog and write clauses in the form

p :- $q_1, \ldots, q_n$.

which can be read as "p *if* q_1 *and* . . . *and* q_n".

The evaluation strategy used by Prolog is an instance of a more general theorem proving procedure called SLD-resolution [1]. An SLD-derivation with respect to a set of clauses P is a sequence $N_0, N_1, ...$ of negative clauses such that for each i, if $N_i = a_1, ..., a_n$, then

$$N_{i+1} = \theta(a_1, ..., a_{k-1}, (b_1, ..., b_m), a_{k+1}, ..., a_n)$$

satisfying:

(1) $1 \leq k \leq n$.

(2) b :- $b_1, ..., b_m$ is a clause in P, appropriately renamed to have no variables in common with those in N_i.

(3) $\theta(a_k) = \theta(b)$ where θ is a substitution.

A program $\langle P;$:- $q\rangle$ is a set of definite clauses P togther with a goal clause :- q. Given a program $\langle P;$:- $q\rangle$, an SLD-tree consists of nodes labelled with negative or empty clauses. If node N has label $a_1, ..., a_k$ then a selected atom a_m is designated, $(1 \leq m \leq k)$. Further N has exactly one son for each clause a' :- b' of P such that a_m unifies with

a' after appropriate renaming of the variables in the latter clause, this son being labelled with the resulting resolvent. The sons are ordered according to the textual order in which the clauses appear in P. The root is labelled q.

An SLD-tree represents a collection of SLD-derivations all starting with q. An execution of a program can be thought of as a traversal of an SLD-tree for that program searching for refutations, i.e. paths that terminate in the empty clause. It can be shown that that the existence of a node labelled by the empty clause in any SLD-tree for a program implies the existence of a node labelled by the empty clause in every SLD-tree for that program [1]. Hence in solving for a refutation it suffices to search any one SLD-tree.

2.2. Sequential Prolog

Prolog implementations incorporate a sequential evaluation strategy that is a depth-first traversal of the "leftmost" SLD-tree, i.e., the SLD-tree formed by consistently choosing the leftmost literal for expansion. In such an evaluation, an invocation of a Prolog predicate (unitary goal) is handled by unifying it with the appropriate clauses chosen in sequence. This can result in programs that are declaratively identical but computationally distinct. As an example, consider the following definitions of the reverse function:

```
append([],X,X).
append([A|B],Y,[A|D]) :- append(B,Y,D).

rev1([],[]).
rev1([A|X],Y) :- rev1(X,Z),append(Z,[A],Y).

rev2([],[]).
rev2([A|X],Y) :- append(Z,[A],Y),rev2(X,Z).
```

The reader can verify that the goal *rev1*([1,2],X) terminates with X bound to [2,1], whereas the goal *rev2*([1,2],X) yields one solution and then goes into an infinite loop.

2.3. On the Observable Behaviour of Prolog Programs

An aspect of Prolog that has attracted much attention is its ability to define computations over substitutions. A naive semantic definition of the substitution generated by evaluating a goal is to compose the substitutions generated in going from one node in the SLD-tree to the next until an empty clause is encountered. This neglects the fact that the only ***observable*** aspect of a computation generated by a Prolog predicate is in terms of the variables contained in the top-level goal. Our semantic definitions incorporate this notion of observability and project out unnecessary information from substitutions. As an example, the predicates *foo1* and *foo2* have identical meaning in our formulation:

```
foo([],[]).

foo1(X,Y) :- foo(X,Z).
```

foo2([],Y).

2.4. Definitions and Notation

Given a (countable) set S, the set of finite and (ω-)infinite sequences of elements of S will be denoted by S^∞. The set of finite sequences of elements of a set S will be denoted by $S*$. If the first element of a sequence is a and the sequence formed by the second element onwards is L, it will sometimes be written $a :: L$; the empty sequence will be denoted by *nil*. Given two sequences S_1 and S_2, their concatenation will be denoted by $S_1 \lozenge S_2$. Let $\perp$ denote the undefined sequence. Then, $\lozenge$ is defined as follows:

$$\perp \lozenge L = \perp;$$
$$nil \lozenge L = L;$$
$$(a :: L_1) \lozenge L_2 = a :: (L_1 \lozenge L_2).$$

An n-tuple of objects $a_1, ..., a_n$ will be denoted by $\langle a_1, ..., a_n \rangle$. Where there is no need to distinguish between the elements of a tuple, we will sometimes write the tuple with a bar, e.g. $\bar{t}$.

A common operation on sequences is to apply a function to each element of the sequence, and collect the results in order. This operation (also referred to as *apply to all* in [2]) is denoted by '||':

$$f || \perp = \perp;$$
$$f || nil = nil;$$
$$f || (a :: L) = f(a) :: f || L.$$

Finally, we define an operator to "collect" the results of applying a sequence-valued function to the elements of a sequence of values. Let $f : S \to S^\infty$ be such a function, and $s \in S^\infty$ a sequence of S-objects. We wish to apply f to each element of s in order, and concatenate the resulting sequences together to produce the output. This operation is denoted by $\bigcirc$:

$$f \bigcirc \perp = \perp;$$
$$f \bigcirc nil = nil;$$
$$f \bigcirc a :: L = f(a) \lozenge (f \bigcirc L).$$

The syntactic categories of Prolog are as follows:

Variable ::= **Var**;
Functor ::= **Func**;
Predicate ::= **Pred**;
Term ::= *Variable* + *Functor*($Term_1$, ..., $Term_n$);
Atom ::= *Predicate*($Term_1$, ..., $Term_n$);
Literal ::= *Atom* + '!';
Goal ::= $Literal^+$;
Clause ::= *Atom* :- *Goal*.

Recall that a substitution is an idempotent, almost-identity mapping from **Var** to **Term**. Given a substitution σ, we will usually wish to know the effect of σ on some finite set of variables only, which are of interest to us. For this, we define the set

FSubst to be the set of *finite substitutions*, which are mappings from **Var** to **Term** with finite domain and range. It is convenient to require that any variable "mentioned" in a finite substitution be in its domain. Thus, we have the following definition:

Definition: A *finite substitution* ϕ is a mapping from a finite set of variables V to a finite set of terms T, such that for any v in V, $vars(\phi(v)) \subseteq V$.

The domain of a finite substitution ϕ will be written $dom(\phi)$. Given a finite substitution ϕ and a set of variables V containing $dom(\phi)$, the *extension* of ϕ to V, written $\phi\uparrow V$, is the mapping with domain V which is the same as ϕ on $dom(\phi)$, and the identity mapping on $V \setminus dom(\phi)$. In the limit, the extension of a finite substitution to the set of all variables **Var** yields a substitution. Where the kind of mapping being referred to in the discussion that follows is clear from the context, we will sometimes not distinguish between finite substitutions and substitutions. Given two finite substitutions θ and σ, their composition is defined as follows:

Definition: Given θ, $\sigma \in$ **FSubst**, if $\sigma : V_\sigma \rightarrow T_\sigma$ and $\theta : V_\theta \rightarrow T_\theta$, then their composition $\theta \circ \sigma$ is a finite substitution $\theta \circ \sigma : V_{\theta \circ \sigma} \rightarrow T_{\theta \circ \sigma}$ such that for any v in $V_{\theta\circ\sigma}$, $(\theta \circ \sigma)(v) = (\theta \uparrow V_{\theta\circ\sigma})(\sigma \uparrow V_{\theta\circ\sigma})(v)$, where $V_{\theta\circ\sigma} = V_\theta \cup V_\sigma$ and $T_{\theta\circ\sigma} = T_\theta \cup T_\sigma$.

The set of finite substitutions is closed under finite composition; however, it is not closed under infinite composition.

The function $unify$: **Term** $\times$ **Term** $\rightarrow$ (**FSubst** $\cup$ $\{fail\}$) returns the most general unifier of two terms, if it exists, and the token *fail* otherwise. It extends in the natural way to atoms. The function $vars$: **Term** $\rightarrow 2^{\mathbf{Var}}$ yields the set of variables occurring in a term. The function $rename$: **Term** $\times\ 2^{\mathbf{Var}} \rightarrow$ **Term** takes a term t and a set of variables V and yields a term t' identical to t but with its variables consistently replaced by "new" variables not occurring in V. (We assume that the set of variables **Var** is a countably infinite set $v_1, v_2, \ldots$ indexed by the natural numbers; and that given any finite set of variables V such that $v_k \in V$ has the largest index of any element in V, it is possible to effectively find v_m with $m > k$, so that $v_m \notin V$. We do not elaborate the nature of *rename* further.) When referring to $rename(t, V)$, we will say that t has been "renamed with respect to V". The functions *vars* and *rename* extend naturally to atoms, goals and clauses.

In the denotational treatment of Prolog that follows, will be interested in the set $\mathbf{FSubst}^\infty$, the set of finite and infinite sequences of finite substitutions. Elements of **FSubst** will be written as lower case Greek letters σ, θ, ϕ, ..., while elements of $\mathbf{FSubst}^\infty$ will be written as upper case Greek letters Σ, Θ, Φ, ... The finite substitution with domain V which is the identity mapping on its domain will be written ϵ_V.

Let V be the set of variables occurring in a goal G. If θ is an "answer substitution" for G, then we are interested only in the part of θ dealing with variables in V. Another way of saying this is the observation that since θ is an answer substitution, any instance of $\theta(G)$ is refutable from the program, which implies that for any substitution θ' that agrees with θ on elements of V, $\theta'(G)$ is also refutable from the program. The "interesting" part of θ is therefore the part dealing with V. We use the projection function $\downarrow$: $\mathbf{FSubst} \times 2^{\mathrm{Var}} \rightarrow \mathbf{FSubst}$ to restrict a finite substitution to a set of variables:

Definition: Given a finite substitution $\phi : V \rightarrow T$, and $W \subseteq V$, the *projection* of ϕ on W, written $\phi \downarrow W$, is the finite substitution with domain $V_1 = W \cup (\bigcup_{v \in W} vars(\phi(v)))$, such that for any v in V_1, $(\phi \downarrow W)(v) =$ *if* $v \in W$ *then* $\phi(v)$ *else* v.

We assume we have available a function *dom* : $\mathbf{FSubst} \rightarrow 2^{\mathrm{Var}}$ which returns the domain of a finite substitution. From the definition, it follows that any variable mentioned by a finite substitution ϕ is present in $dom(\phi)$.

3. Semantics of Prolog without Cut

3.1. Denotational Semantics for Cut-free Prolog

In our semantics, the meaning of a predicate definition is a function that maps terms to sequences of finite substitutions. The set of finite and infinite sequences of finite substitutions, $\mathbf{FSubst}^{\infty}$, is a complete partial order under the standard prefix ordering. Predicate symbols are associated with their meanings in the usual way, using environments. Intuitively, an environment would map identifier names to functions from terms to substitution sequences. It turns out, however, that for technical reasons (renaming of variables before resolution) it is also necessary to dynamically propagate the set of variables encountered during execution. This is done by passing in, as an argument, the appropriate finite substitution, and performing renaming with respect to the domain of this substitution. We therefore have

$$Env = Predicate \rightarrow Term \rightarrow \mathbf{FSubst} \rightarrow \mathbf{FSubst}^{\infty}.$$

Environments will typically be denoted as ρ, ρ_0, ρ_1, ... The act of binding an identifier Id to an object Obj in an environment will be indicated by $Id \leftarrow Obj$. Given an environment ρ, the environment $\rho[p \leftarrow f]$ will denote the environment which is the same as ρ except for the value of p, which is f.

The process of defining the denotational semantics of a program can be seen as consisting of two parts. First, the semantic function $\mathbf{D}[[\ ]]$ defines the meaning of a sequence of clauses to be a function over environments. Given a sequence of clauses C^* and an environment ρ, $\mathbf{D}[[C^*]]\rho$ gives the new environment obtained by elaborating the clause sequence C^* in environment ρ. Second, the meanings of goals must be specified.

This is done using the semantic function **G**[[ ]]: given a sequence of literals G, an environment ρ and an input substitution σ, **G**[[G]]$\rho\,\sigma$ gives the output substitution sequence obtained by evaluating $\sigma(G)$ in environment ρ. We use two auxiliary functions, **C**[[ ]], which gives the meaning of a single clause, and **L**[[ ]], which gives the meaning of a single literal.

The function **D**[[ ]] takes a clause sequence and an environment and returns a new environment. This can be written in curried form as

$$\mathbf{D}[[\ ]] : Clause^{*} \rightarrow Env \rightarrow Env.$$

The function **G** takes a sequence of literals, an environment defining the meanings of various predicates, a substitution and a set of variables, and returns a sequence of substitutions. In curried form, this is

$$\mathbf{G}[[\ ]] : Goal \rightarrow Env \rightarrow \mathbf{FSubst}^{\infty} \rightarrow \mathbf{FSubst}^{\infty}.$$

The semantic functions are summarized in Figure 1. Below, we briefly describe each clause.

(D1.1) An empty sequence of clauses defines the null environment.

(D1.2) For a sequence of clauses $c_0 :: C$, according to Prolog's computation strategy, all the answers that can be generated using clause c_0 are generated before any of the clauses C are attempted. Thus, if the substitution sequence obtained using only cl_0 is s_0, and that obtained using clauses C is s_1, then the resuting substitution sequence is $s_0 \lozenge s_1$.

(C1.1) The meaning of a single clause is a function that takes a tuple of terms $\overline{Y}$ and a finite substitution σ, and returns a sequence of substitutions. The idea is to first rename variables in the clause uniformly, such that none of the new variables used appear in $dom(\sigma)$; then unify the tuple of terms $\sigma(\overline{Y})$ with the tuple of terms appearing in the head of the clause; evaluate the body of the clause after applying the resulting substitution to it; and finally, project each substitution in the resulting sequence on the set of variables $dom(\sigma)$ that the clause was called with.

(G1.1) The empty goal represents a successful computation, and in this case the substitution stream returned is the input stream.

(G1.2) The meaning of a sequence of literals $L :: G$ is the stream of substitutions obtained by first solving L with the input stream of substitutions, and using the resulting substitution stream as the input for G.

(L1.1) The meaning of a single literal $p(\overline{T})$ in an environment ρ, given a finite substitution σ, is the substitution sequence Θ obtained by calling the corresponding predicate in that environment for each substitution in the input stream, and concatenating the resulting substitution streams in order.

Let '$fix\ x.f(x)$' denote $\bigsqcup_n f^n(\bot)$. The meaning of a program $\langle C, G\rangle$, where C is a sequence of clauses and G a goal, is then defined to be

$\mathbf{D}[[\ ]] : Clause^{*} \rightarrow Env \rightarrow Env.$

(D1.1) $\mathbf{D}[[nil]]\rho = \lambda x \lambda y \lambda z.nil.$
(D1.2) $\mathbf{D}[[c_0 :: C]]\rho = \lambda x \lambda y \lambda z.[(\mathbf{C}[[c_0]]\rho\, x\, y\, z) \lozenge (\mathbf{D}[[C]]\rho\, x\, y\, z)]$

$\mathbf{C}[[\ ]] : Clause \rightarrow Env \rightarrow Env.$

(C1.1) $\mathbf{C}[[\mathrm{p}(\overline{T}_0) :- G_0]]\rho =$

$$\mathrm{p} \leftarrow \lambda \overline{S} \lambda \sigma.[let\ (\mathrm{p}(\overline{T}_1) :- G_1) = \mathrm{rename}((\mathrm{p}(\overline{T}_0) :- G_0),\ dom(\sigma));$$
$$\theta = unify(\sigma(\overline{S}),\ \overline{T}_1);$$
$$in$$
$$\text{if } \theta = fail \text{ then } nil \text{ else } (\lambda x.x \downarrow dom(\sigma))\ ||\ \mathbf{G}[[G_1]]\rho(\theta \circ \sigma :: nil)].$$

$\mathbf{G}[[\ ]] : Literal^{*} \rightarrow Env \rightarrow \mathbf{FSubst}^{\infty} \rightarrow \mathbf{FSubst}^{\infty}.$

(G1.1) $\mathbf{G}[[nil]]\rho\Theta = \Theta.$
(G1.2) $\mathbf{G}[[L :: G]]\rho\Theta = \mathbf{G}[[G]]\rho(\mathbf{L}[[L]]\rho\Theta).$

$\mathbf{L}[[\ ]] : Literal \rightarrow Env \rightarrow \mathbf{FSubst}^{\infty} \rightarrow \mathbf{FSubst}^{\infty}.$

(L1.1) $\mathbf{L}[[\mathrm{p}(\overline{T})]]\rho\Theta = (\rho(\mathrm{p})(\overline{T}))\bigcirc\Theta.$

FIGURE 1: The semantic functions $\mathbf{D}[[\ ]]$ and $\mathbf{G}[[\ ]]$ for Cut-free Prolog

$$\mathbf{G}[[G]]\rho_0\,(\epsilon_V :: nil),$$

where ρ_0 is essentially $fix\ \rho.\mathbf{D}[[C]]\rho$, and $V = vars(G)$. To define the limit environment ρ_0 precisely, it is necessary to distinguish between the bottom substitution sequence $\perp$, which denotes nontermination, and the bottom environment $\perp_{\mathrm{Env}}$, which maps every predicate defined in the program to $\lambda y.\lambda y.\perp$, and any predicate not defined in the program to $\lambda x.\lambda y.nil$. This is because in typical Prolog systems, execution fails if it encounters a predicate not defined in the program. Then, the limit environment defined by a program P is defined to be $\rho_0 = \bigsqcup_n \mathbf{D}^n[[P]]\perp_{\mathrm{Env}}$. Notice that since **G** and **D** are both defined by the composition of continuous functions and (in the case of **G**) simple recursion, they are continuous (see [12]), and hence the fixpoint ρ_0 exists.

3.2. Operational Semantics for Cut-free Prolog

The operational semantics is given by an interpreter that repeatedly transforms a state encoding a depth-first backtracking traversal of a "leftmost" SLD-tree. A state of the interpreter consists of a runtime stack describing the state of the computation, and the list of clauses comprising the program. The stack is a list of records, each record describing a path from the root of the SLD-tree to some node in the tree. Each such record is a triple $\langle FrameList,\ Subst,\ Clauses\rangle$, where *FrameList* is a sequence of *Frames*, and each *Frame* represents a goal to be solved; *Subst* is the current (finite) substitution, being developed incrementally; and *Clauses* is a tail segment of the program, with respect to which the leftmost literal is being solved. A *Frame* is a pair consisting of a goal (which is either the user's query or the right hand side of some clause used to solve the query) and a set of variables Var_P, which is the set of variables the parent of the goal is interested in. Any substitution resulting from the computation of the goal is projected on the variables in Var_P before being returned.

$Frame ::= \langle Atom^*,\ Var_P \rangle$
$FrameList ::= nil \mid Frame :: FrameList$
$Stack ::= nil \mid \langle FrameList,\ Subst,\ Clause^* \rangle :: Stack$
$State ::= Stack.$

The interpreter is defined by the function *interp*, which maps a state to a (possibly infinite) sequence of substitutions. It carries around the sequence of clauses that define the predicates in the program:

$interp : State \times Clause^* \rightarrow \mathbf{FSubst}^{\infty}.$

The interpreter is summarized in Figure 2. Below we briefly describe each clause in its definition.

(I1.1) Execution terminates when the runtime stack becomes empty.

(I1.2) When the goal to be solved in the current forward execution component becomes empty, a solution has been found. The current substitution is therefore returned, and execution backtracks to search for other solutions.

(I1.3) If there are no more program clauses to match against a (non-empty) goal, execution fails and backtracking takes place.

(I1.4) Given a non-empty goal and a non-empty sequence of clauses, the interpreter tries to solve the leftmost literal in the goal with respect to those clauses. If the head of the first clause, after appropriate renaming of clause variables, unifies with the leftmost literal, the frame list is extended with a frame describing the subgoal consisting of the body of that clause. The original goal, together with the untried clauses, is saved on the stack so that alternative solutions may be found on backtracking.

(I1.5) If the head of the first clause does not unify with the leftmost literal, the clause is discarded and the process repeated with the remaining clauses.

(I1.6) When the goal in a frame becomes empty (there may still be other goals to be solved in the current forward execution path), the current substitution is appropriately projected and computation continues with this projected substitution and the remaining framelist. This corresponds to a return from a procedure. Since new variables may have been introduced in the computation from which the return is being made, any such variables occurring in the projected substitution must be taken into account for renaming purposes as far as the rest of the forward computation is concerned.

Evaluation of a goal G with respect to a clause sequence C that defines the relevant predicates is defined by the expression

$interp(\langle\langle G, V\rangle :: nil, \epsilon_V, P\rangle :: nil\rangle, P)$,

where $V = vars(G)$ and ϵ_V is the identity finite substitution with domain V.

3.3. Equivalence of Denotational and Operational Semantics

In this section we show that the meaning given to predicates, atoms and goals by the abstract interpreter described above is in fact that specified by the semantic functions described earlier. Before proceeding with the proof of equivalence, however, we require some structural lemmas regarding the behaviour of the abstract interperter.

The first lemma states that given an interpreter stack $F :: St$, the component F encodes the current forward computation, while the remainder of the stack, St, encodes the remaining portion of the SLD-tree that has to be searched:

Lemma 3.1: For any stack frame F and stack St,

$interp(F :: St, P) \equiv interp(F :: nil, P) \lozenge interp(St, P)$.

Proof: By structural induction on *interp*. □

The next two lemmas state that the interpreter carries out a tuple at a time computation, solving the literals in a goal in their left to right order. First, we show that the tuple at a time computation proceeds with the frames in the current forward computation component of the stack being processed in their LIFO order:

$interp : State \times Clause^* \rightarrow \mathbf{Subst}^\infty$.

(I1.1) $interp(nil, P) = nil$.

(I1.2) $interp(\langle nil, \phi, C\rangle :: St, P) = \phi :: interp(St, P)$.

(I1.3) $interp(\langle F_0 :: F_1, \phi, nil\rangle :: St, P) = interp(St, P)$.

(I1.4) $interp(\langle\langle L :: G, V_P\rangle :: F_0, \phi, (H_0 \text{ :- } B_0) :: C\rangle :: St_0, P) =$

$interp(\langle F_2 :: F_1 :: F_0, \theta \circ \phi, P\rangle :: St_1, P)$, where

$H_1 \text{ :- } B_1 = rename((H_0 \text{ :- } B_0), dom(\phi))$;

$\theta = unify(\phi(L), H_1) \quad (\neq fail)$;

$V_P{}' = dom(\phi)$;

$F_2 = \langle B_1, V_P{}'\rangle$; $F_1 = \langle G, V_P\rangle$;

$St_1 = \langle\langle L :: G, V_P\rangle :: F_0, \phi, C\rangle :: St_0$.

(I1.5) $interp(\langle\langle L :: G, V_P\rangle :: F_0, \phi, (H_0 \text{ :- } B_0) :: C\rangle :: St_0, P) =$

$interp(\langle\langle L :: G, V_P\rangle :: F_0, \phi, C\rangle :: St_0, P)$, where

$H_1 \text{ :- } B_1 = rename((H_0 \text{ :- } B_0), dom(\phi))$, and $unify(\phi(L), H_1) = fail$.

(I1.6) $interp(\langle\langle nil, V_P\rangle :: F_0, \phi, C\rangle :: St, P) = interp(\langle F_0, \phi \downarrow V_P, P\rangle :: St, P)$.

FIGURE 2: Abstract Interpreter for Cut-free Prolog

Lemma 3.2: For any frame F, framelist F_1, substitution ϕ, and program P and clause list C,

$$interp(\langle F :: F_1,\ \phi,\ C\rangle :: nil,\ P) \equiv$$
$$[\lambda\theta.interp(\langle F_1,\ \theta,\ P\rangle :: nil,\ P)] \bigcirc interp(\langle F :: nil,\ \phi,\ C\rangle :: nil,\ P).$$

Proof: By structural induction on *interp*. □

The next lemma states that computation of the literals within a frame proceds a tuple at a time, in their left to right order:

Lemma 3.3: For any goal $L :: G$, set of variables V_P, framelist F, substitution ϕ, clause list C, and program P,

$$interp(\langle\langle L :: G,\ V_P\rangle :: F,\ \phi,\ C\rangle :: nil,\ P) \equiv$$
$$[\lambda\theta.interp(\langle\langle G,\ V_P\rangle :: F,\ \theta,\ P\rangle :: nil,\ P)] \bigcirc$$
$$interp(\langle\langle L :: nil,\ dom(\phi)\rangle :: nil,\ \phi,\ C\rangle :: nil,\ P).$$

Proof : By structural induction on *interp*. □

Our final lemma concerns the projection away of extraneous substitutions at the return from a call in the interpreter. The lemma states that this can be done in two steps. This is a purely technical lemma necessary for the proof of equivalence of the denotational and operational semantics.

Lemma 3.4: For any goal G, substitutions θ and ϕ, stack component St and program P with tail C,

$$interp(\langle\langle G,\ dom(\phi)\rangle :: nil,\ \theta \circ \phi,\ C\rangle :: St,\ P) \equiv$$
$$(\lambda\sigma.\sigma \downarrow dom(\phi)) \ || \ interp(\langle\langle G,\ dom(\theta \circ \phi)\rangle :: nil,\ \theta \circ \phi,\ C\rangle :: St,\ P)$$

Proof: By structural induction on G, and observing that $dom(\phi) \subseteq dom(\theta \circ \phi)$. □

Finally, consider the effect of failures on substitution sequences. If a goal fails, it returns the empty substitution sequence. As mentioned in the previous section, given a goal $L :: G$, if the literal L fails, then the entire goal fails. This is expressed by the following theorem:

Theorem 3.1: For any goal G and environment ρ, $\mathbf{G}[[G]]\ \rho\ nil = nil$.

Proof: By structural induction on G. □

We are now in a position to prove the main result of this section:

Theorem 3.2: For any goal G, literal L, program P with tail C, and substitution stream Θ,

$$\mathbf{G}[[G]]\ \rho_0\ (\mathbf{L}[[L]]\ \mathbf{D}[[C]]\ \rho_0\ \Theta) \equiv \lambda\sigma.interp(\langle\langle L :: G,\ dom(\sigma)\rangle :: nil,\ \sigma,\ C\rangle :: nil,\ P)\bigcirc\Theta.$$

Proof: By fixpoint induction on **G**[[ ]], **D**[[ ]] and *interp*. □

Corollary (Equivalence of Denotational and Operational Semantics): For any goal G and program P, and substitution sequence Θ,

$$\mathbf{G}[[G]]\rho_0\ \Theta \equiv \lambda\sigma.interp(\langle\langle G,\ dom(\sigma)\rangle :: nil,\ \sigma,\ P\rangle :: nil,\ P)\bigcirc\Theta.$$

4. Semantics of Prolog with Cut

4.1. The "Cut" Construct

One problem that can arise with the simple control strategy of the Prolog interpreter given earlier is that execution may backtrack exhaustively through subtrees of the search tree that cannot contribute to a solution (in extreme cases, exhaustive search through an infinite tree can lead to nontermination of logically correct programs). The *cut* construct returns some control over this backtracking behaviour to the user.

Operationally, the effect of a cut is to discard certain backtrack points, so that execution can never backtrack into them. The behaviour of cut is not universally agreed upon in all contexts [10]. In practice, however, cuts are most frequently encountered in one of two static contexts: as part of the top-level conjunction in a clause, or within a disjunction in a clause, i.e. either in a context

```
p :- . . .
p :- . . ., !, . . .
p :- . . .
```

or in a context

```
p :- . . .
p :- . . ., ( ( . . . !, . . . ) ;
              ( . . . )
            ), . . .
p :- . . .
```

Most current implementations of Prolog behave similarly in their treatment of cut in these contexts. The expected behaviour here is that the backtrack points discarded by a cut will consist of: all those set up by literals to the left of the cut all the way to the beginning of the clause; and the backtrack point for the parent predicate whose definition includes the clause containing the cut, i.e. all remaining alternative clauses for this predicate. Cuts exhibiting this behaviour are sometimes referred to as *hard* cuts; this is to distinguish them from cuts which discard the backtrack points set up by literals to the left of the cut in the clause but not the alternative clauses for the predicate, and are referred to as *soft* cuts. We will restrict our attention to cuts that occur statically in the above contexts, and assume them to be hard.

4.2. Denotational Semantics for Prolog with Cut

Since the effect of a cut is to modify the "rest of the computation", it is naturally modelled using a continuation semantics. As before, each literal in the body of a clause acts as a transformer on streams of substitutions: each literal receives a substitution stream from those on its left, and in turn feeds a substitution stream to those on its right. The action of a cut is to discard all but the first substitution from the sequence received from its left. However, this is not enough to model the effect of a cut with respect to the clauses that follow. To express the notion of "remaining clauses", we introduce *declaration continuations, DCont.*

A declaration continuation is similar to an environment in that given an identifier (i.e. a predicate name), it returns a function that, if called with a tuple of terms and a substitution, returns a sequence of substitutions. It differs from the environment in which a goal is evaluated in that while the environment reflects the meaning of the "current" list of clauses to solve the goal with, the continuation gives the meaning of the "remaining" clauses, i.e. the alternatives that would be tried were execution to backtrack from the first clause of the list.

Each literal now yields a boolean "cut flag", indicating whether a cut was encountered in that goal. For non-cut literals, the flag remains unchanged, while a cut sets the flag to true. As before, semantic functions **D**[[ ]] and **G**[[ ]] give the meanings of clause and literal sequences respectively, with the auxiliary functions **C**[[ ]] and **L**[[ ]] giving the meanings of individual clauses and literals; they are now extended to incorporate cut flags. The semantic functions are summarized in Figure 3. We briefly describe those clauses which differ from the corresponding clauses in the cut-free case.

In clause D2.2, given a clause sequence $c_0 :: C$, an environment ρ and continuation δ, we first find the meaning ρ_1 of C in the environment ρ and continuation δ. The environment ρ_1 thus represents the solutions that would be found for any predicate were we to use only the clauses C, using environment ρ to solve for literals in the bodies of these clauses. Thus, ρ_1 represents the "rest of the program" as far as c_0 is concerned.

The semantic function **G**[[ ]] gives the meaning of a goal. It takes as arguments an environment in which to look up predicate meanings for the literals in its body, and a pair consisting of a substitution sequence (corresponding to the substitutions generated by literals to the left of the goal being evaluated) and a boolean flag, the "cut flag". It returns a pair consisting of a substitution sequence (those generated by the literals to its left and the goal itself) and a boolean, which has the value **t** if a cut has been encountered in the goal, **f** otherwise.

For a single literal, the interesting case is dealing with a cut. There are two possibilities in clause L2.1: an empty input substitution stream means that execution has failed for some literal to the left of the cut, so the cut is not, in fact, executed, and has no effect. In this case, clearly, execution would have continued by trying the remaining clauses. Thus, the empty substitution sequence is returned, together with the input cut flag. The cut becomes meaningful only if the input substitution sequence is nonempty. In this case, the output substitution sequence is the singleton list consisting of the first element of the input stream. Also, since the remaining clauses are discarded, the output cut flag is **t**.

The limit environment ρ_0 is now defined as $\bigsqcup_n \mathbf{D}^n[[P]]\langle \bot_{\mathrm{Env}}, \mathit{ncont}\rangle$, where $\mathit{ncont} = \lambda x \lambda y \lambda z.\mathit{nil}$ is the null continuation.

4.3. Operational Semantics for Prolog with Cut

The interpreter has to be modified slightly to deal with cut. Since the effect of a cut is to discard certain choice points, and choice points are maintained on the stack, the interpreter now has to maintain pointers into the stack, at each level, to the point to cut back (i.e. discard choice points) to if a cut is encountered. The *Frame* component is therefore extended with an additional *Stack* element, which we will refer to as the *dump*.

$$\mathit{DCont} = \mathit{Predicate} \rightarrow \mathit{Term} \rightarrow \mathbf{FSubst} \rightarrow \mathbf{FSubst}^{\infty}.$$

$\mathbf{D}[[\ ]] : \mathit{Clause}^* \rightarrow (\mathit{Env} \times \mathit{DCont}) \rightarrow \mathit{Env}$

(D2.1) $\mathbf{D}[[\mathit{nil}]]\langle \rho, \delta\rangle = \lambda x \lambda y \lambda z.\mathit{nil}.$

(D2.2) $\mathbf{D}[[c_0 :: C]]\langle \rho, \delta\rangle = \mathbf{C}[[c_0]]\ \langle \rho, (\mathbf{D}[[C]]\langle \rho, \delta\rangle)\rangle.$

$\mathbf{C}[[\ ]] : \mathit{Clause} \rightarrow (\mathit{Env} \times \mathit{DCont}) \rightarrow \mathit{Env}$

(C2.1) $\mathbf{C}[[p(\overline{T}) \text{ :- } B_0]]\langle \rho, \delta\rangle = \rho[p \leftarrow f]$, where

$f = \lambda \overline{S} \lambda \sigma.[\text{let } (p(\overline{T}_1) \text{ :- } B_1) = \mathit{rename}(\ (p(\overline{T}_0) \text{ :- } B_0),\ \mathit{dom}(\sigma));$

$\theta = \mathit{unify}(\sigma(\overline{S}),\ \overline{T}_1);$

in

if $\theta = \mathit{fail}$ then $(\delta(p)\overline{Y})(\sigma)$

else $([\lambda x.x \downarrow \mathit{dom}(\sigma)]\ ||\ \Phi)\ \lozenge$ (if cflag then nil else $\delta(p)\overline{Y})(\sigma))$,

where $\langle \Phi,\ \mathit{cflag}\rangle = \mathbf{G}[[B_1]]\rho\ \langle(\theta \circ \sigma :: \mathit{nil}),\ \mathbf{f}\rangle]$.

$\mathbf{G}[[\ ]] : \mathit{Literal}^* \rightarrow \mathit{Env} \rightarrow (\mathbf{FSubst}^{\infty} \times \mathbf{Bool}) \rightarrow (\mathbf{FSubst}^{\infty} \times \mathbf{Bool})$

(G2.1) $\mathbf{G}[[\mathit{nil}]]\rho\ \langle \Theta,\ \mathit{cflag}\rangle = \langle \Theta,\ \mathit{cflag}\rangle.$

(G2.2) $\mathbf{G}[[L :: G]]\rho\ \langle \Theta,\ \mathit{cflag}\rangle = \mathbf{G}[[G]]\rho\ (\mathbf{G}[[L]]\rho\ \langle \Theta,\ \mathit{cflag}\rangle.$

$\mathbf{L}[[\ ]] : \mathit{Literal} \rightarrow \mathit{Env} \rightarrow (\mathbf{FSubst}^{\infty} \times \mathbf{Bool}) \rightarrow (\mathbf{FSubst}^{\infty} \times \mathbf{Bool})$

(L2.1) $\mathbf{L}[[\ !\ ]]\rho\ \langle \Theta,\ \mathit{cflag}\rangle = \text{if } \Theta = \mathit{nil} \text{ then } \langle \mathit{nil},\ \mathit{cflag}\rangle \text{ else } \langle \mathit{head}(\Theta),\ \mathbf{t}\rangle.$

(L2.2) $\mathbf{L}[[\mathrm{p}(\overline{T})]]\rho\ \langle \Theta,\ \mathit{cflag}\rangle = \langle \Phi,\ \mathit{cflag}\rangle$, where $\Phi = (\rho(\mathrm{p})(\overline{T}))\bigcirc\Theta.$

FIGURE 3: Semantic Functions for Prolog with Cut

$Frame ::= \langle Atom^*,\ V_P,\ Stack\rangle.$
$FrameList ::= nil \mid Frame :: FrameList.$
$Stack ::= nil \mid \langle FrameList,\ Subst,\ Clause^*\rangle :: Stack.$

The actions of the interpreter also have to be modified slightly. There are two main points to note. First, observe that when a cut is encountered when evaluating the body of a clause, only those choice points set up *during* and *after* the call that led to that clause will be discarded. Therefore in any invocation of a predicate, it is enough to pass the stack component just before the call is made, into the call as the dump component of the callee. The second is that when a cut is encountered, the backtrack stack should be set to the current dump component, thereby resulting in some choice points at the top of the stack being discarded. The resulting interpreter is summarized in Figure 4.

4.4. Equivalence of Denotational and Operational Semantics

In this section, we show that the meaning given to programs by the abstract interpreter defined above, in the case of Prolog with cut, is the same as that given by the semantic functions. Top level goals are evaluated through the auxiliary semantic function $\hat{\mathbf{G}}$, which is similar to $\mathbf{G}[[\ ]]$ except that it takes as argument two environments – one to evaluate the leftmost literal of the goal in, and the other to evaluate the rest of the goal in.

$$\hat{\mathbf{G}}[[\ ]] : Literal^* \rightarrow Env \rightarrow Env \rightarrow (\mathbf{FSubst}^\infty \times \mathbf{Bool}) \rightarrow (\mathbf{FSubst}^\infty \times \mathbf{Bool})$$

$$\hat{\mathbf{G}}[[L :: G]]\rho_1\ \rho_2\ \langle\Phi,\ b\rangle = \mathbf{G}[[G]]\rho_1\ (\mathbf{L}[[L]]\rho_2\ \langle\Phi,\ b\rangle).$$
$$\hat{\mathbf{G}}[[nil]]\rho_1\ \rho_2\ \langle\Phi,\ b\rangle = \mathbf{G}[[nil]]\rho_2\ \langle\Phi,\ b\rangle.$$

(I2.1) $interp(nil,\ P) = nil.$

(I2.2) $interp(\langle nil,\ \phi,\ C\rangle :: St,\ P) = \phi :: interp(St,\ P).$

(I2.3) $interp(\langle F_0 :: FRest,\ \phi,\ nil\rangle :: St,\ P) = interp(St,\ P).$

(I2.4) $interp(\langle\langle ! :: A,\ V_P,\ D\rangle :: F_0,\ \phi,\ C\rangle :: St,\ P) = interp(\langle\langle A,\ V_P,\ D\rangle :: F_0,\ \phi,\ P\rangle :: D,\ P).$

(I2.5) $interp(\langle\langle L :: G,\ V_P,\ D\rangle :: F_0,\ \phi,\ (H_0 \text{ :- } B_0) :: C\rangle :: St_0,\ P) =$
$interp(\langle F_2 :: F_1 :: F_0,\ \theta\circ\phi,\ P\rangle :: St_1,\ P)$, where $L \neq$ '!';
$H_1 \text{ :- } B_1 = rename((H_0 \text{ :- } B_0),\ dom(\phi));$
$\theta = unify(\phi(L),\ H_1) \qquad (\neq fail);$
$F_2 = \langle B_1,\ dom(\phi),\ St_0\rangle;\ \ F_1 = \langle G,\ V_P,\ D\rangle;$
$St_1 = \langle\langle L :: G,\ V_P,\ D\rangle :: F_0,\ \phi,\ C\rangle :: St_0.$

(I2.6) $interp(\langle\langle L :: G,\ V_P,\ D\rangle :: F_0,\ \phi,\ (H_0 \text{ :- } B_0) :: C\rangle :: St_0,\ P) =$
$interp(\langle\langle L :: G,\ V_P,\ D\rangle :: F_0,\ \phi,\ C\rangle :: St_0,\ P)$, where
$L \neq$ '!',
$H_1 \text{ :- } B_1 = rename((H_0 \text{ :- } B_0),\ dom(\phi))$, and $unify(\ \phi(L),\ H_1\ ) = fail.$

(I2.7) $interp(\langle\langle nil,\ V_P,\ D\rangle :: F_0,\ \phi,\ C\rangle :: St,\ P) = interp(\langle F_0,\ \phi\downarrow V_P,\ P\ \rangle :: St,\ P).$

FIGURE 4 : Abstract Interpreter for Prolog with Cut

Unfortunately, unlike the case of Prolog without cut, the non-local effects of cut preclude simple structural decompositions, and make the proof more complex. Instead of a direct proof of equivalence, we now have to resort to an intermediate function, ***tran***, that mediates between the denotational and the operational semantics. This is very similar to *interp*, except that while the interpreter only works on one substitution at a time, and encodes the other computation paths in a rather complicated manner in its stack, *tran* works on substitution sequences. This function is illustrated in Figure 5.

In order to prove the equivalence of the denotational and operational semantics, it is necessary to state some structural lemmas regarding $\mathbf{G}[[\ ]]$ and *tran*. If a sequence A_1 is a prefix of a sequence A_2, we will write $A_1 \leq A_2$. It is easy to show that $\mathbf{G}[[\ ]]$ is monotonic with respect to $\leq$:

Lemma 4.1: If $\Phi_1 \leq \Phi_2$, $\langle \Psi_1, cf_1 \rangle = \mathbf{G}[[G]]\rho\ \langle \Phi_1, cf_0 \rangle$, and $\langle \Psi_2, cf_2 \rangle = \mathbf{G}[[G]]\rho\ \langle \Phi_2, cf_0 \rangle$, then $\Psi_1 \leq \Psi_2$.

Proof: By structural induction on G. □

Lemma 4.2: Let $\langle \Psi_0, cf_0 \rangle = \mathbf{G}[[G]]\rho\ \langle \Phi_1 \between \Phi_2, \mathbf{f} \rangle$, and $\langle \Psi_1, cf_1 \rangle = \mathbf{G}[[G]]\rho\ \langle \Phi_1, \mathbf{f} \rangle$. Then, if cf_1 is false, then $\Psi_0 = \Psi_1 \between \mathbf{G}[[G]]\rho\ \langle \Phi_2, \mathbf{f} \rangle$.

Proof: By structural induction on G. □

Lemma 4.3: Let $\langle \Psi_0, cf_0 \rangle = \mathbf{G}[[G]]\rho\ \langle \Phi_1 \between \Phi_2, \mathbf{f} \rangle$, and $\langle \Psi_1, cf_1 \rangle = \mathbf{G}[[G]]\rho\ \langle \Phi_1, \mathbf{f} \rangle$. Then, if cf_1 is true and $\Psi_1 \neq nil$, then $\Psi_0 = \Psi_1$.

Proof: By structural induction on G. □

Theorem 4.2: For any framelist F, substitution sequence $\Phi_1 \between \Phi_2$, stack component St and program P, $tran(\langle F, \Phi_1 \between \Phi_2, P \rangle :: St, P) = tran(\langle F, \Phi_1, P \rangle :: \langle F, \Phi_2, P \rangle :: St, P)$.

(T2.1) $tran(nil, P) = nil$.
(T2.2) $tran(\langle nil, \Phi, C \rangle :: St, P) = \Phi \between tran(St, P)$.
(T2.3) $tran(\langle F :: FRest, \Phi, nil \rangle :: St, P) = tran(St, P)$.
(T2.4) $tran(\langle\langle G_1 \between G_2, V_P, D \rangle :: FRest, \Psi, C \rangle :: St, P) =$
  let $\langle \Phi, cflag \rangle = \hat{\mathbf{G}}[[G_1]]\rho_0\ (\mathbf{D}[[C]]\langle \rho_0, ncont \rangle)\ \langle \Psi, \mathbf{f} \rangle$ in
  if $\Phi = nil$ then
    $tran($ (if $cflag$ then D else St), $P)$;
  if $\Phi \neq nil$ then
    $tran(\langle\langle G_2, V_P, D \rangle :: FRest, \Phi, P \rangle ::$ (if $cflag$ then D else St), $P)$.
(T2.5) $tran(\langle\langle nil, V_P, D \rangle :: FRest, \Phi, C \rangle :: St, P) =$
  $tran(\langle FRest, (\lambda x.x \downarrow V_P) \parallel \Phi, P \rangle :: St, P)$.

FIGURE 5 : The *tran* function

Proof: By structural induction on F. □

The equivalence of the denotational and operational semantics is then asserted by the following theorem:

Theorem 4.3: For any framelist F, substitution θ, clause list C, stack component St and program P, $interp(\langle F, \theta, C\rangle :: St, P) \equiv tran(\langle F, \theta :: nil, C\rangle :: St, P)$.

Proof: By fixpoint induction on *interp*, *tran*, **G**[[ ]] and **D**[[ ]]. □

Corollary (Equivalence of Denotational and Operational Semantics): If $\Phi = interp(\langle\langle G, dom(\theta), nil\rangle :: nil, \theta, P\rangle :: nil, P)$, then $\langle \Phi, ncont\rangle = \mathbf{G}[[G]]\rho_0 \langle \theta :: nil, \mathbf{f}\rangle$ where $\rho_0 = fix\ \rho.\ \mathbf{D}[[P]]\langle \rho, ncont\rangle$.

5. Applications

A central motivation for developing a denotational semantics for Prolog has been the need to justify the correctness of transformations on Prolog programs. Typically, such justification is useful for validating transformations used in optimizing compilers. And while there are plenty of "folk theorems", such as that contiguous cuts are idempotent, i.e. 'L_1, !, !, L_2' ≡ 'L_1, !, L_2', none are firmly based on a semantics that describes the computational behaviour of programs. The need for a denotational formulation of the semantics follows from its ability to support reasoning about the *strong* correctness of transformations. This is particularly important in the case of Prolog, since many transformations involve the insertion of cuts [3, 5, 9, 11], which may change the termination behaviour of programs.

As an example, we prove the correctness of two transformations involving the manipulation of cuts. The first involves the removal of cuts in certain contexts to minimize unnecessary state saving. The second involves the insertion of cuts to constrain the search space.

A predicate (clause, literal) is *determinate* in a program if any call to it in that program yields at most one substitution, i.e. the output sequence has length at most 1. By 'P_q' we mean a sequence of clauses without any clause defining q.

The first theorem we prove states that if a cut appears as the last literal in the last clause of a predicate, and that clause is determinate independently of the cut, then the cut can be discarded without affecting the semantics of the program.

Theorem 5.1: Let P and Q be the programs

$$P = (p(\overline{T}_{11}) :\!-\ q_1(\overline{T}_{12}) :: nil)) :: \ldots :: (p(\overline{T}_{n1}) :\!-\ q_n(\overline{T}_{n2}) :: ! :: nil) :: P_p, \text{ and}$$

$$Q = (p(\overline{T}_{11}) :\!-\ q_1(\overline{T}_{12}) :: nil)) :: \ldots :: (p(\overline{T}_{n1}) :\!-\ q_n(\overline{T}_{n2}) :: nil) :: P_p.$$

If q_n is determinate in both P and Q, then for any tuple of terms $\overline{T}$ and substitution sequence Θ,

$$\mathbf{L}[[p(\overline{T})]]\rho_0 \langle \Theta,\ ncont\rangle \equiv \mathbf{L}[[p(\overline{T})]]\rho_0' \langle \Theta,\ ncont\rangle,$$

where $\rho_0 = fix\ \rho.\mathbf{D}[[P]]\langle \rho,\ ncont\rangle$ and $\rho_0' = fix\ \rho.\mathbf{D}[[Q]]\langle \rho,\ ncont\rangle$.

Proof Outline: The proof is by fixpoint induction, showing $\rho_0(r)\ \overline{T}\ \theta \equiv \rho_0'(r)\ \overline{T}\ \theta$ for arbitrary r, $\overline{T}$ and θ. □

We have considered the case where the last clause for p has a single atom in its body, but the generalization to a list of atoms is obvious. The practical utility of this result is that it makes possible the elimination of some redundant cuts, which in turn leads to improved space utilization because opportunities open up for tail recursion optimization (in general, last goal optimization). For example, the predicate

```
append1([],L,L).
append1([H|L1],L2,[H|L3]) :- append1(L1,L2,L3), !.
```

is not tail recursive, and needs linear space to concatenate two lists. On the other hand, the predicate

```
append2([],L,L).
append2([H|L1],L2,[H|L3]) :- append2(L1,L2,L3).
```

which, by the theorem above is equivalent to *append1*/3, is tail recursive, and can concatenate two lists using constant space.

The second transformation we validate involves the insertion of cuts in determinate predicates to reduce the amount of search. Similar transformations have been proposed by several researchers [5, 9, 11], but none, to our knowledge, have been formally validated.

Theorem 5.2: Let P and Q be the programs

$P = (p(\overline{T}_{11}) \text{ :- } q_1(\overline{T}_{12}) :: nil)) :: (p(\overline{T}_{21}) \text{ :- } q_2(\overline{T}_{22}) :: nil) :: \ldots :: (p(\overline{T}_{n1}) \text{ :- } q_n(\overline{T}_{n2})$
$:: nil) :: P_{p'}$

$Q = (p(\overline{T}_{11}) \text{ :- } q_1(\overline{T}_{12})) :: ! :: nil) :: (p(\overline{T}_{21}) \text{ :- } q_1(\overline{T}_{22}) :: nil) :: ! :: nil)) :: \ldots ::$
$(p(\overline{T}_{n1}) \text{ :- } q_n(\overline{T}_{n2}) :: nil) :: P_p.$

If p is determinate in both P and Q, then for any tuple of terms $\overline{T}$ and substitution sequence Θ,

$$\mathbf{L}[[p(\overline{T})]]\rho_0 \langle \Theta,\ ncont\rangle \sqsubseteq \mathbf{L}[[p(\overline{T})]]\rho_0' \langle \Theta,\ ncont\rangle,$$

where $\rho_0 = fix\ \rho.\mathbf{D}[[P]]\langle \rho,\ ncont\rangle$ and $\rho_0' = fix\ \rho.\mathbf{D}[[Q]]\langle \rho,\ ncont\rangle$.

Proof Outline: The proof is by fixpoint induction, showing $\rho_0(r)\ \overline{T}\ \theta \sqsubseteq \rho_0'(r)\ \overline{T}\ \theta$ for arbitrary r, $\overline{T}$ and θ. □

Notice that the insertion of cuts can change the termination behaviour of programs, so that an otherwise nonterminating program may terminate once cuts have been inserted.

6. Conclusions

The semantics of Prolog has traditionally been given in terms of the model theory of first order logic. However, such a semantics is often inadequate for reasoning about Prolog programs, and validating the strong correctness of transformations on them, since it does not allow us to reason about the computational behaviour of such programs. The problem becomes even more serious if we wish to deal with programs that contain "impure" features such as *cut*.

In this paper, we gave a denotational and operational semantics for Prolog, both with and without cut; proved the congruence of these semantics; and demonstrated the utility of such a semantics by validating two optimizing transformations on Prolog programs. We believe that while the model theoretic semantics is very useful for understanding Prolog programs, it is necessary to resort to a denotational description such as this in order to reason about tools that manipulate and transform Prolog programs.

7. References

1. K. R. Apt and M. H. van Emden, "Contributions to the Theory of Logic Programming", *J. ACM*, **29**, 3 (July 1982), 841-862.

2. J. Backus, "Can Programming be Liberated from the von Neumann Style? A Functional Style and Its Algebra of Programs", *Comm. ACM*, **21**, 8 (Aug. 1978), .

3. S. K. Debray, "Towards Banishing the Cut from Prolog", in *Proc. 1986 Int. Conf. on Computer Languages*, IEEE Computer Society, Miami Beach, Florida, Oct. 1986. To appear.

4. S. K. Debray and P. Mishra, "Denotational and Operational Semantics for Prolog", Technical Report #86/15, Department of Computer Science, SUNY at Stony Brook, Stony Brook, NY 11794, July 1986.

5. S. K. Debray and D. S. Warren, "Detection and Optimization of Functional Computations in Prolog", in *Proc. Third Int. Conf. on Logic Programming*, London, July 1986.

6. G. Frandsen, "Logic Programming, Substitutions and Finite Computability", DAIMI PB-186, Computer Science Department, Aarhus University, Denmark, Jan. 1985.

7. G. Frandsen, "Logic Programming and Substitutions", in *Proc. International Conference on Fundamentals of Computation Theory*, Springer-Verlag, , 146-158. LNCS v. 199.

8. N. D. Jones and A. Mycroft, "Stepwise Development of Operational and Denotational Semantics for PROLOG", in *Proc. 1984 Int. Symp. on Logic Programming*, IEEE Computer Society, Atlantic City, New Jersey, Feb. 1984,

289-298.

9. C. S. Mellish, "Some Global Optimizations for a Prolog Compiler", *J. Logic Programming*, **2**, 1 (Apr. 1985), 43-66.

10. C. Moss, "Results of Cut Tests", in *Prolog Electronic Digest, Vol. 3, No. 42*, Oct 9, 1985.

11. H. Sawamura and T. Takeshima, "Recursive Unsolvability of Determinacy, Solvable Cases of Determinacy and Their Applications to Prolog Optimization", in *Proc. 1985 Symposium on Logic Programming*, Boston, July 1985, 200-207.

12. J. E. Stoy, *Denotational Semantics: The Scott-Strachey Approach to Programming Language Theory*, MIT Press, Cambridge, Mass., 1977.

13. M. H. van Emden and R. A. Kowalski, "The Semantics of Predicate Logic as a Programming Language", *J. ACM*, **23**, 4 (Oct. 1976), .

Appendix: Proofs of Equivalence

Theorem 3.1: For any goal G and environment ρ,

$$\mathbf{G}[[G]]\ \rho\ nil = nil.$$

Proof: By structural induction on G. □

To simplify the notation in the proof of the next theorem, if an expression E_0 reduces to an expression E_1 by application of rule R, we will write this as

$$E_0 \Rightarrow_R E_1.$$

Thus, for example, if E_0 reduces to E_1 from clause G1.1 of the definition of $\mathbf{G}[[\ ]]$ and clause D1.2 of that of $\mathbf{D}[[\ ]]$, we will write

$$E_0 \Rightarrow_{(\text{G1.1, D1.2})} E_1.$$

Where the source of the reduction is obvious, these annotations will sometimes be omitted.

Theorem 3.2: For any goal G, literal L, program P with tail C, and substitution stream Θ,

$$\mathbf{G}[[G]]\ \rho_0\ (\mathbf{L}[[p(\overline{T})]]\ \mathbf{D}[[C]]\ \rho_0\ \Theta) \equiv$$
$$\lambda\sigma.interp(\langle\langle p(\overline{T}) :: G,\ dom(\sigma)\rangle :: nil,\ \sigma,\ C\rangle :: nil,\ P) \bigcirc \Theta.$$

Proof: By fixpoint induction on $\mathbf{G}[[\ ]]$, $\mathbf{D}[[\ ]]$ and *interp*. There are six relevant cases:

Case 1: $G = nil$, $C = nil$.

Case 2: $G = nil$, $C = c_0 :: C'$, unification of $p(\overline{T})$ with the head of c_0 succeeds.

Case 3: $G = nil$, $C = c_0 :: C'$, unification of $p(\overline{T})$ with the head of c_0 fails.

Case 4: $G \neq nil$, $C = nil$.

Case 5: $G \neq nil$, $C = c_0 :: C'$, unification of $p(\overline{T})$ with the head of c_0 succeeds.

Case 6: $G \neq nil$, $C = c_0 :: C'$, unification of $p(\overline{T})$ with the head of c_0 fails.

The proof proceeds as follows:

Case 1: Straightforward.

Case 2: The left hand side is

$$\mathbf{G}[[nil]]\ \rho_0\ (\mathbf{L}[[p(\overline{T})]]\ \mathbf{D}[[(H_0 :- B_0) :: C']]\ \rho_0\ \Theta)$$
$$\Rightarrow_{(G1.1,\ D1.2)}\ \mathbf{L}[[p(\overline{T})]]\ (\lambda x \lambda y \lambda z.(\mathbf{C}[[H_0 :- B_0]]\rho_0\ x\ y\ z \between \mathbf{D}[[C']]\rho_0\ x\ y\ z))\ \Theta)$$
$$\Rightarrow_{C1.1}\ \lambda z.((\lambda x.x{\downarrow}dom(z))\ ||\ \mathbf{G}[[B_1]]\rho_0\ \theta \circ z :: nil) \between (\mathbf{D}[[C']]\rho_0\ p\ \overline{T}\ z) \bigcirc \Theta, \text{ where}$$
$$H_1 :- B_1 = rename((H_0 :- B_0),\ dom(z)),\ H_1 = p(\overline{S}), \text{ and}$$
$$\theta = unify(z(\overline{T}),\ \overline{S}). \qquad (1)$$

The right hand side is

$$\lambda\sigma.interp(\langle\langle p(\overline{T}) :: nil,\ dom(\sigma)\rangle :: nil,\ \sigma,\ (H_0 :- B_0) :: C'\rangle :: nil,\ P) \bigcirc \Theta$$
$$\Rightarrow_{I1.4}\ \lambda\sigma.interp(\langle\langle B_1,\ dom(\sigma)\rangle :: \langle nil,\ dom(\sigma)\rangle :: nil,\ \theta\circ\sigma,\ P\rangle :: St,\ P) \bigcirc \Theta, \text{ where}$$
$$H_1 :- B_1 = rename((H_0 :- B_0,\ dom(\sigma)),\ H_1 = p(\overline{S}),$$
$$\theta = unify(\sigma(\overline{T}),\ \overline{S}),$$
$$St = \langle\langle p(\overline{T}) :: nil,\ dom(\sigma)\rangle :: nil,\ \sigma,\ C'\rangle :: nil.$$
$$\Rightarrow_{\text{Lemmas 3.1, 3.2}}\ \lambda\sigma.[((\lambda\psi.interp(\langle\langle nil,\ dom(\psi)\rangle :: nil,\ \psi,\ P\rangle :: nil,\ P) \bigcirc$$
$$interp(\langle\langle B_1,\ dom(\sigma)\rangle :: nil,\ \theta\circ\sigma,\ P\rangle :: nil,\ P)) \between$$
$$interp(\langle\langle p(\overline{T}) :: nil,\ dom(\sigma)\rangle :: nil,\ \sigma,\ C'\rangle :: nil,\ P)] \bigcirc \Theta$$
$$\Rightarrow_{I1.6}\ \lambda\sigma.[(\lambda\psi.\psi{\downarrow}dom(\sigma)\ ||\ interp(\langle\langle B_1,\ dom(\sigma)\rangle :: nil,\ \theta\circ\sigma,\ P\rangle :: nil,\ P)) \between$$
$$interp(\langle\langle p(\overline{T}) :: nil,\ dom(\sigma)\rangle :: nil,\ \sigma,\ C'\rangle :: nil,\ P)] \bigcirc \Theta$$
$$\Rightarrow\ \lambda\sigma.[(\lambda\psi.\psi{\downarrow}dom(\sigma)\ ||$$
$$(\lambda\phi.interp(\langle\langle B_1,\ dom(\phi)\rangle :: nil,\ \phi,\ P\rangle :: nil,\ P) \bigcirc \theta\circ\sigma :: nil)) \between$$
$$(\lambda\phi.interp(\langle\langle p(\overline{T}) :: nil,\ dom(\phi)\rangle :: nil,\ \phi,\ C'\rangle :: nil,\ P) \bigcirc \sigma :: nil))] \bigcirc \Theta \qquad (2)$$

If $B_1 = nil$, then this yields

$$\Rightarrow_{I1.6}\ \lambda\sigma.[(\lambda\psi.\psi{\downarrow}dom(\sigma)\ ||\ (\sigma{\downarrow}dom(\sigma) :: nil)) \between$$
$$(\lambda\phi.interp(\langle\langle p(\overline{T}) :: nil,\ dom(\phi)\rangle,\ \phi,\ C'\rangle :: nil,\ P) \bigcirc \sigma :: nil)] \bigcirc \Theta$$
$$\Rightarrow\ \lambda\sigma.[(\lambda\psi.\psi{\downarrow}dom(\sigma)\ ||\ (\theta\circ\sigma :: nil)) \between$$
$$(\lambda\phi.interp(\langle\langle p(\overline{T}) :: nil,\ dom(\phi),\ C'\rangle :: nil,\ P) \bigcirc \sigma :: nil)] \bigcirc \Theta$$

Now we have $\lambda x.x{\downarrow}dom(y)\ ||\ \mathbf{G}[[B_1]]\rho_0\ (\theta\circ\sigma :: nil)$

$$\Rightarrow\ \lambda x.x{\downarrow}dom(y)\ ||\ \mathbf{G}[[nil_1]]\rho_0\ (\theta\circ\sigma :: nil)$$
$$\Rightarrow\ \lambda x.x{\downarrow}dom(y)\ ||\ (\theta\circ\sigma :: nil)$$

and from the induction hypothesis, $interp(\langle\langle p(\overline{T}) :: nil,\ dom(\phi)\rangle :: nil,\ \phi,\ C'\rangle :: nil,\ P)$

$$\Rightarrow\ \mathbf{G}[[nil]]\rho_0(\mathbf{L}[[p(\overline{T})]]\ \mathbf{D}[[C']]\rho_0\ \Theta)$$
$$\Rightarrow_{G1.1}\ \mathbf{L}[[p(\overline{T})]]\ \mathbf{D}[[C']]\rho_0\ \Theta\ \Rightarrow_{L1.1}\ (\mathbf{D}[[C']]\rho_0\ p\ \overline{T}) \bigcirc \Theta$$

whence (1) $\equiv$ (2), and the theorem holds.

When $B_1 \neq nil$, assume $B_1 = R :: B_2$. From the induction hypothesis, (2) reduces to $\lambda\sigma.[(\lambda\psi.\psi{\downarrow}dom(\sigma)\ ||\ \mathbf{G}[[B_2]]\ \rho_0\ \mathbf{L}[[R]]\ \mathbf{D}[[P]]\rho_0\ \theta\circ\sigma :: nil) \between$

$$(\mathbf{G}[[nil]]\rho_0\ \mathbf{L}[[p(\overline{T})]]\ \mathbf{D}[[C']]\rho_0\ \sigma :: nil)] \bigcirc \Theta$$

where $\rho_0 = \mathbf{D}[[P]]\rho_0$ (being the fixpoint). This can therefore be rewritten, using G1.1, L1.1, as $\lambda\sigma.[(\lambda\psi.\psi\downarrow dom(\sigma)\ ||\ \mathbf{G}[[R :: B_2]]\rho_0\ \sigma :: nil)\ \Diamond\ (\mathbf{D}[[C']]\rho_0\ p\ \overline{T}\ \sigma)] \bigcirc \Theta$, which is the left hand side.

Case 3: Here, unification of the literal with the head of the first clause fails. The left hand side is

$$\mathbf{G}[[G]]\ \rho_0\ (\mathbf{L}[[p(\overline{T})]]\ \mathbf{D}[[C]]\ \rho_0\ \Theta)$$
$$\Rightarrow_{(G1.1,\ D1.2)}\ \lambda z.[(\mathbf{C}[[H_0 :- B_0]]\rho_0\ p\ \overline{T}\ z)\ \Diamond\ (\mathbf{D}[[C']]\rho_0\ p\ \overline{T}\ z)] \bigcirc \Theta$$
$$\Rightarrow_{C1.1}\ \lambda z.[nil\ \Diamond\ (\mathbf{D}[[C']]\rho_0\ p\ \overline{T}\ z)] \bigcirc \Theta.$$
$$\Rightarrow\ \lambda z.[\mathbf{D}[[C']]\rho_0\ p\ \overline{T}\ z] \bigcirc \Theta.$$

The right hand side is

$$\lambda\sigma.interp(\langle\langle p(\overline{T}) :: nil,\ dom(\sigma)\rangle :: nil,\ \sigma,\ (H_0 :- B_0) :: C'\rangle :: nil,\ P) \bigcirc \Theta$$
$$\Rightarrow_{I1.5}\ \lambda\sigma.interp(\langle\langle p(\overline{T}) :: nil,\ dom(\sigma)\rangle :: nil,\ \sigma,\ C'\rangle :: nil,\ P) \bigcirc \Theta$$

which reduces, from the inductive hypothesis, to $\mathbf{G}[[nil]]\rho_0\ (\mathbf{L}[[p(\overline{T})\ \mathbf{D}[[C']]\rho_0\ \Theta)$

$$\Rightarrow_{G1.1,\ C1.1)}\ \lambda z.[\mathbf{D}[[C']]\rho_0\ p\ \overline{T}\ z] \bigcirc \Theta.$$

Case 4: Straightforward.

Case 5: The left hand side is $\mathbf{G}[[L :: G_1]]\rho_0\ (\mathbf{L}[[p(\overline{T})]]\ \mathbf{D}[[(H_0 :- B_0) :: C']]\rho_0\ \Theta)$

$$\Rightarrow_{(G1.2,\ D1.2,\ C1.1)}\ \mathbf{G}[[G_1]]\rho_0\ (\mathbf{L}[[L]]\rho_0\ (\lambda z.[(\lambda x.x\downarrow dom(z)\ ||$$
$$\mathbf{G}[[B_1]]\rho_0\ \theta \circ z :: nil)\ \Diamond\ (\mathbf{D}[[C']]\rho_0\ p\ \overline{T}\ z)] \bigcirc \Theta)),\ \text{where}$$
$$H_1 :- B_1 = rename((H_0 :- B_0);\ dom(z));\ H_1 = p(\overline{S}),\ \text{and}\ \theta = unify(z(\overline{T}),\ \overline{S}).$$

The right hand side is

$$\lambda\sigma.interp(\langle\langle p(\overline{T}) :: L :: G_1,\ dom(\sigma)\rangle :: nil,\ \sigma,\ (H_0 :- B_0) :: C'\rangle :: nil,\ P) \bigcirc \Theta$$
$$\Rightarrow_{I1.4}\ \lambda\sigma.interp(\langle\langle B_1,\ dom(\sigma)\rangle :: \langle L :: G_1,\ dom(\sigma)\rangle :: nil,\ \theta \circ \sigma,\ P\rangle :: St,\ P),\ \text{where}$$
$$H_1 :- B_1 = rename((H_0 :- B_0),\ dom(z));\ H_1 = p(\overline{S}),;\ \theta = unify(\sigma(\overline{T}),\ \overline{S});\ \text{and}$$
$$St = \langle\langle p(\overline{T}) :: nil,\ dom(\sigma)\rangle :: nil,\ \sigma,\ C'\rangle :: nil.$$

That the theorem holds now follows from Lemmas 3.1, 3.2, 3.3 and the inductive hypothesis.

Case 6: Here, unification of the leftmost literal of the goal with the head of the first clause fails. The left hand side is $\mathbf{G}[[L :: G_1]]\rho_0\ (\mathbf{L}[[p(\overline{T})]]\ \mathbf{D}[[(H_0 :- B_0) :: C']]\rho_0\ \Theta)$

$$\Rightarrow_{(G1.2,\ D1.2,\ L1.1)}\ \mathbf{G}[[G]]\rho_0\ (\lambda y.[\mathbf{D}[[C']]p\ \overline{T}\ y] \bigcirc \Theta)).$$

The right hand side is

$$\lambda\sigma.interp(\langle\langle p(\overline{T}) :: L :: G_1,\ dom(\sigma)\rangle :: nil,\ \sigma,\ (H_0 :- B_0) :: C'\rangle :: nil,\ P) \bigcirc \Theta$$
$$\Rightarrow_{I1.4}\ \lambda\sigma.interp(\langle\langle p(\overline{T}) :: L :: G_1,\ dom(\sigma)\rangle :: nil,\ \sigma,\ C'\rangle :: nil,\ P) \bigcirc \Theta$$

and the theorem now follows from Lemma 3.3 and Case 3 above. □

Corollary (Equivalence of Denotational and Operational Semantics): For any goal G and program P, and substitution sequence Θ,

$$\mathbf{G}[[G]]\rho_0\ \Theta \equiv \lambda\sigma.interp(\langle\langle G,\ dom(\sigma)\rangle :: nil,\ \sigma,\ P\rangle :: nil,\ P) \bigcirc \Theta.$$

Proof: The case where $G = nil$ follows directly from the definitions of **G**[[]] and *interp*. The case where $G \neq nil$ follows from Theorem 3.2, with $C = P$. $\quad\square$

Theorem 4.1: For any goal G, $\mathbf{G}[[G]]\langle nil, ncont\rangle = \langle nil, ncont\rangle$.

Proof: Similar to Theorem 3.1. $\quad\square$

Theorem 4.2: For any framelist F, substitution sequence $\Phi_1 \lozenge \Phi_2$, stack component St and program P,

$$tran(\langle F, \Phi_1 \lozenge \Phi_2, P\rangle :: St, P) = tran(\langle F, \Phi_1, P\rangle :: \langle F, \Phi_2, P\rangle :: St, P).$$

Proof: By structural induction on F. $\quad\square$

Theorem 4.3: For any framelist F, substitution θ, clause list C, stack component St and program P,

$$interp(\langle F, \theta, C\rangle :: St, P) \equiv tran(\langle F, \theta :: nil, C\rangle :: St, P).$$

Proof: By fixpoint induction on *interp*, *tran*, **G**[[]] and **D**[[]]. The base case, where both *tran* and *interp* have empty stacks, follows from their definitions. The inductive step has five cases:

 Case 1: $F = nil$.

 Case 2: $F \neq nil$, $C = nil$.

 Case 3: $F = \langle G, V_P, D\rangle :: FRest$, $C \neq nil$, $G = \text{'!'} :: G'$.

 Case 4: $F = \langle G, V_P, D\rangle :: FRest$, $C \neq nil$, $G = p(\overline{T}) :: G'$, unification of $p(\overline{T})$ with the first clause of C fails.

 Case 5: $F = \langle G, V_P, D\rangle :: FRest$, $C \neq nil$, $G = p(\overline{T}) :: G'$, unification of $p(\overline{T})$ with the first clause of C succeeds.

The proof proceeds as follows:

Case 1, 2: Straightforward.

Case 3: The left hand side, from I2.4, is $\Rightarrow_{I2.4}$ $interp(\langle\langle G, V_P, D\rangle :: FRest, \theta, P\rangle :: D, P)$. On right hand side, we have $\langle \Phi, cflag\rangle = \hat{\mathbf{G}}[[! :: nil]]\rho_0 (\mathbf{D}[[C]]\langle\rho_0, ncont\rangle) \langle\theta :: nil, \mathbf{f}\rangle$

$\Rightarrow_{(G2.2, L2.2)}$ $\langle\Phi, cflag\rangle = \langle\theta :: nil, \mathbf{t}\rangle$

From this, the right hand side reduces to $tran(\langle\langle G, V_P, D\rangle :: FRest, \theta :: nil, P\rangle :: D, P)$, and from the induction hypothesis, we are done.

Case 4: $F = \langle p(\overline{T}) :: G, V_P, D\rangle :: FRest$, $C = (H_0 :- B_0) :: C'$,

$$H_1 :- B_1 = rename((H_0 :- B_0), dom(\theta)), \text{ and } unify(\theta(p(\overline{T})), H_1) = fail.$$ The left hand side is $interp(\langle\langle p(\overline{T}) :: G, V_P, D\rangle :: FRest, \theta, (H_0 :- B_0) :: C'\rangle :: St, P)$

$\Rightarrow_{I2.6}$ $interp(\langle\langle p(\overline{T}) :: G, V_P, D\rangle :: FRest, \theta, C'\rangle :: St, P)$

$\Rightarrow_{\text{Induction Hypothesis}}$ $\mathit{tran}(\langle\langle p(\overline{T}) :: G,\ V_P,\ D\rangle :: \mathit{FRest},\ \theta :: \mathit{nil},\ C'\rangle :: St,\ P)$.

$\Rightarrow_{\text{T2.4}}$ let $\langle\Phi,\ \mathit{cflag}\rangle = \hat{\mathbf{G}}[[p(\overline{T}) :: \mathit{nil}]]\rho_0\ (\mathbf{D}[[H_0 :- B_0 :: C']]\langle\rho_0,\ \mathit{ncont}\rangle)\ \langle\theta :: \mathit{nil},\ \mathbf{f}\rangle$
in if $\Phi = \mathit{nil}$ then tran(if cflag then D else St, P)
else $\mathit{tran}(\langle\langle G,\ V_P,\ D\rangle :: \mathit{FRest},\ \Phi,\ P\rangle ::$ (if cflag then D else St), P) (1)

Now $\langle\Phi,\ \mathit{cflag}\rangle = \hat{\mathbf{G}}[[p(\overline{T}) :: \mathit{nil}]]\rho_0\ (\mathbf{D}[[H_0 :- B_0 :: C']]\langle\rho_0,\ \mathit{ncont}\rangle)\ \langle\theta :: \mathit{nil},\ \mathbf{f}\rangle$

$\Rightarrow_{\text{D2.2}}$ $\hat{\mathbf{G}}[[p(\overline{T}) :: \mathit{nil}]]\rho_0\ (\mathbf{C}[[H_0 :- B_0]]\langle\rho_0,\ \mathbf{D}[[C']]\langle\rho_0,\ \mathit{ncont}\rangle\rangle)\ \langle\theta :: \mathit{nil},\ \mathbf{f}\rangle$

$\Rightarrow_{\text{(L2.2, C2.1)}}$ $\langle((\mathbf{D}[[C']]\langle\rho_0,\ \mathit{ncont}\rangle)\ p\ \overline{T}\ \theta),\ \mathbf{f}\rangle$

and since $\mathit{cflag} = \mathbf{f}$, (1) reduces to

if $\Phi = \mathit{nil}$ then $\mathit{tran}(St,\ P)$ else $\mathit{tran}(\langle\langle G,\ V_P,\ D\rangle :: \mathit{FRest},\ \Phi,\ P\rangle :: St,\ P)$.

The right hand side is $\mathit{tran}(\langle\langle p(\overline{T}) :: G,\ V_P,\ D\rangle :: \mathit{FRest},\ \theta :: \mathit{nil},\ H_0 :- B_0) :: C'\rangle :: St,\ P)$

$\Rightarrow_{\text{T2.4}}$ let $\langle\Phi,\ \mathit{cflag}\rangle = \hat{\mathbf{G}}[[p(\overline{T}) :: \mathit{nil}]]\rho_0\ (\mathbf{D}[[H_0 :- B_0 :: C']]\langle\rho_0,\ \mathit{ncont}\rangle)\ \langle\theta :: \mathit{nil},\ \mathbf{f}\rangle$
in if $\Phi = \mathit{nil}$ then tran(if cflag then D else St, P);
else $\mathit{tran}(\langle\langle G,\ V_P,\ D\rangle :: \mathit{FRest},\ \Phi,\ P\rangle ::$ (if cflag then D else St), P)

which, from the above, is precisely the left hand side, so we are done.

Case 5: $F = \langle p(\overline{T}) :: G,\ V_P,\ D\rangle :: \mathit{FRest},\ C = (H_0 :- B_0) :: C'$,

$H_1 :- B_1 = \mathit{rename}((H_0 :- B_0),\ \mathit{dom}(\theta)),\ \phi = \mathit{unify}(\theta(p(\overline{T})),\ H_1) \neq \mathit{fail}$. On the right hand side, we have $\langle\Phi,\ \mathit{cflag}\rangle = \hat{\mathbf{G}}[[p(\overline{T}) :: \mathit{nil}]]\rho_0\ (\mathbf{D}[[C]]\langle\rho_0,\ \mathit{ncont}\rangle)\ \langle\theta :: \mathit{nil},\ \mathbf{f}\rangle$

$\Rightarrow_{\text{(D2.2, C2.1, L2.2)}}$ $\langle$if cflag then $\lambda x.x\!\downarrow\!\mathit{dom}(\theta) \parallel \Psi$ else $(\lambda x.x\!\downarrow\!\mathit{dom}(\theta) \parallel \Psi)\ \lozenge\ \Theta,\ \mathbf{f}\rangle$
where $\langle\Psi,\ \mathit{cflag}_0\rangle = \mathbf{G}[[B_1]]\rho_0\ \langle\phi \circ \theta :: \mathit{nil},\ \mathbf{f}\rangle$; $\Theta = (\mathbf{D}[[C']]\langle\rho_0,\ \mathit{ncont}\rangle)\ p\ \overline{T}\ \theta$ (2)

Since $\mathit{cflag} = \mathbf{f}$, the right hand side therefore reduces to

if $\Phi = \mathit{nil}$ then $\mathit{tran}(St,\ P)$ (3)
else $\mathit{tran}(\langle\langle G,\ V_P,\ D\rangle :: \mathit{FRest},\ \Phi,\ P\rangle :: St,\ P)$. (4)

The left hand side is $\mathit{interp}(\langle\langle p(\overline{T}) :: G,\ V_P,\ D\rangle :: \mathit{FRest},\ \theta,\ C\rangle :: St,\ P)$

$\Rightarrow_{\text{I2.5}}$ $\mathit{interp}(\langle\langle B_1,\ \mathit{dom}(\theta),\ St\rangle :: \langle G,\ V_P,\ D\rangle :: \mathit{FRest},\ \phi \circ \theta,\ P\rangle :: St',\ P)$
where $St' = \langle\langle p(\overline{T}) :: G,\ V_P,\ D\rangle :: \mathit{FRest},\ \theta,\ C'\rangle :: St$.

$\Rightarrow_{\text{Inductive Hypothesis}}$ let $\langle\Psi,\ \mathit{cflag}_0\rangle = \mathbf{G}[[B_1]]\rho_0\ \langle\phi \circ \theta :: \mathit{nil},\ \mathbf{f}\rangle$ in
if $\Psi = \mathit{nil} \wedge \mathit{cflag}_0$ then $\mathit{tran}(St,\ P)$ (A)
else if $\Psi = \mathit{nil} \wedge \neg\mathit{cflag}_0$ then $\mathit{tran}(St',\ P)$ (B)
else if $\Psi \neq \mathit{nil} \wedge \mathit{cflag}_0$ then
$\mathit{tran}(\langle\langle \mathit{nil},\ \mathit{dom}(\theta),\ St\rangle :: \langle G,\ V_P,\ D\rangle :: \mathit{FRest},\ \Psi,\ P\rangle :: St,\ P)$ (C)
else if $\Psi \neq \mathit{nil} \wedge \neg\mathit{cflag}$ then
$\mathit{tran}(\langle\langle \mathit{nil},\ \mathit{dom}(\theta),\ St\rangle :: \langle G,\ V_P,\ D\rangle :: \mathit{FRest},\ \Psi,\ P\rangle :: St',\ P)$ (D)

We therefore have four subcases to consider:

(*i*) $\Psi = \mathit{nil} \wedge \mathit{cflag}_0$: Then, $\Phi = \mathit{nil}$, and (3) = (A). The theorem holds.

(*ii*) $\Psi = \mathit{nil} \wedge \neg\mathit{cflag}_0$: (B) is, from the definition of St',

$\mathit{tran}(\langle\langle p(\overline{T}) :: G,\ V_P,\ D\rangle :: \mathit{FRest},\ \theta :: \mathit{nil},\ C'\rangle :: St,\ P$.

Let $\langle\Xi,\ \mathit{cflag}_1\rangle = \hat{\mathbf{G}}[[p(\overline{T}) :: \mathit{nil}]]\rho_0\ (\mathbf{D}[[C']]\langle\rho_0,\ \mathit{ncont}\rangle)\ \langle\theta :: \mathit{nil},\ \mathbf{f}\rangle$

$$= \langle((\mathbf{D}[[C']]\langle\rho_0, ncont\rangle)\ p\ \overline{T}\ \theta), \mathbf{f}\rangle.$$

Observe that $\Xi = \Theta$. We therefore have, if $\Theta = nil$, that $[\Psi = nil \land \neg cflag_0 \land \Theta = nil]$ implies $\Phi = nil$ and (B) reduces to $tran(St, P)$, which is the same as (3). On the other hand, if $\Theta \neq nil$, then $[\Psi = nil \land \neg cflag_0 \land \Theta \neq nil]$ implies $\Phi \neq nil$ and (B) reduces to $tran(\langle\langle G, V_P, D\rangle :: FRest, \Phi, P\rangle :: St, P)$ which is equal to (3). Thus, the theorem holds.

(*iii*) $\Psi \neq nil \land cflag_0$: Then, from (T2.5) in the definition of *tran*, (C) reduces to

$$tran(\langle\langle G, V_P, D\rangle :: FRest, ((\lambda x.x{\downarrow}dom(\theta)) \,||\, \Psi), P\rangle :: St, P).$$

Observe that if $cflag_0 = \mathbf{t}$ then, from (2), we have $\Phi = (\lambda x.x{\downarrow}dom(\theta)) \,||\, \Psi$, so that this becomes $tran(\langle\langle G, V_P, D\rangle :: FRest, \Phi, P\rangle :: St, P)$, which is the same as (4). Thus, the theorem holds.

(*iv*) $\Psi \neq nil \land \neg cflag_0$: Then, from (T2.5) in the definition of *tran*, (D) reduces to

$$tran(\langle\langle G, V_P, D\rangle :: FRest, ((\lambda x.x{\downarrow}dom(\theta)) \,||\, \Psi), P\rangle :: St', P).$$

That the left and right hand sides are equal now follows from Theorem 4.2. □

The paper has been presented by Neil Jones who also is the answerer to the questions.

QUESTIONS AND ANSWERS

Lassez: What has been described here is PROLOG defined in ´72. There has been a lot of work since and I would like to know how the methods of the paper could be extended. One very important point, which is not addressed here but which makes me not quite sure that we are talking about real PROLOG programming, is that there is no mention at all of negation. The other one concerns the work by Colmerauer and others where instead of substitutions tree rewriting systems and equations are used. The third question is about various aspects of parallelism: ´and parallelism´ and ´or parallelism´.

Jones: This is a big question. In the first place this work really concerns just the very core of PROLOG, as you say. It probably could be painful to include the more general control of procedures. The reason for it would be that: this semantics and our own [see reference in the paper] are really not very abstract. Debray and Mishra are mostly concerned with describing control structure which is tricky in PROLOG. I´m describing it in a fairly concrete way, for example with interpreters, components and so on. Ideally what one should have is some basic, you might say,

´actions´ in Peter Mosses sense that could describe these control possibilities in a more abstract way without the messy details. In that case, if you could find such a more abstract description of these then, I think, it will be fairly easy to modify and take the same components and put them together in that way. As for parallelism, I don´t think I or Debray and Mishra could claim to get a good semantics for some parallelism in PROLOG, partly because the problem of semantics for parallelism in general is very hard.

Pnueli: Well, I would like to extend the list of people who are frustrated by this paper, not because it´s bad but because it´s good. I wish I would have written it. Nissim Francez, Shmuel Katz and myself we have developed a proof theory which is based on the same semantics. But we think there are some basic questions that maybe you could help us in evaluating. Something else need to be done: this is essentially the question of abstractness of their semantics which we claim there are some improvements. The question is what should we consider really to be a criterion for full abstractness, if you ever wanted to have this, and we suggest one criterion here which again can be disputed. The criterion is the following: as Debray and Mishra suggest the semantics of a PROLOG program is a sequence of substitutions. Now, we suggest that two programs should be considered inequivalent, if there exists some context such that if you plug those programs in that context then the result will be distinguished by just looking at the first component of the sequence of substitutions. This is our criterion for full abstractness; the equivalence should be declared whenever there is no context such that the results differ in the first component. I can show why this forces you - if you want a congruence - to look beyond the first component even though the definition says just this is the first. Suppose, you have two programs that are identical in the first component but differ in the second component then it is very easy to define a context that will fail on the first component and the first substitution and then to filter that out and the only remaining component would be the second. I have another remark: consider two PROLOG programs for which, according to the denotational semantics defined here, the resulting semantics will be different. One would have a sequence of two elements as result, the other would have a sequence of three elements containing the same substitutions where one element has been repeated. So my observation is: maybe you want to identify such sequences - and it is my feeling that those programs should be equivalent - and whenever somebody presented the second program the compiler should have the liberty to throw away this duplication. If you agree with me so far, that means that semantics should not be just a sequence without duplications, but a sequence of unique substitutions. What you really want are ordered sets, you don´t want a set element to be repeated twice. Now, there are some further identifications that one could make. Not only duplications should be eliminated but we could have some relative inclusions between subsequent substitutions, one of them being stronger than the other.

Bjørner: I have an observation and a request. The observation is: I think that the semantics we have been given has been labeled ´denotational´ but the denotations, I believe, are rather syntactic than conventional mathematical in the sense that when we define denotational semantics of PASCAL we think of denotations being functions on semantic domains, but there are really no semantic domains here. We are fideling around with substitutions which are syntactic objects in a sense. Amir Pnueli is proposing different equivalence classes that filter out various kinds of substitutions. Perhaps my observation is wrong - but if it is right then my question is: are we using the entirely wrong mechanism for talking about semantics? The denotational style seems to be appropiate when denotations are mathematical functions. My request is that perhaps the authors or perhaps Neil Jones could comment on the relationship between this paper and the work by one of my colleagues, Jørgen Fischer Nilsson, who has published in a book similar models also dealing with negation [J. Fischer Nilsson: Formal Vienna-Definition-Method models of PROLOG. In: J.A. Campbell (ed.): Implementations of PROLOG. New York: John Wiley, 1984, 281-308].

Jones: I will do what I can. I am not familiar in detail with Fischer Nilsson´s paper, but I have looked at it and I remember the semantics is not so much different in nature from this one. Having negations or not is simply a matter of extending the denotational functions. Getting back to the first problem: there I disagree; I think that substitutions are not syntactical in nature. I think that a substitution is the most natural generalization of a store. In PASCAL the store is a mapping of the variables to their correct values and to describe the meaning of a PASCAL program you describe it by store transformations. The natural analogy to ´store´ in PROLOG is ´substitution´. Substitutions say what the values of the variables are: for some of them explicitly, for some of them in terms of other variables. Moreover, the effect of satisfying an atom or a law is to transform one substitution into another. So, a denotation is a substitution transformation which is exactly the analogy to the store transformation in PASCAL.

Bjørner: You are using words "the most natural analog is so and so", but I thought you started off by saying that you were trying to derive the semantics of your language from mathematics. I also object completely to your first statement when you opened your talk by saying that there is some kind of ´ad hoc-ness´ about programming languages.

Tennent: The treatment of backtracking uses two continuations and that is I think very much clear in what we see here. Is it possible that this would simplify at least the control structure aspects as well ?

Jones: I don´t know. It might. I am aware there are these two continuations but I didn´t compare them.

Felleisen: When doing a cut, one simply has to duplicate continuations and this is much easier than passing around tokens as in the original paper by you and Mycroft. Because one just passes around cut information as it is. There is no technical trick to get into that place, it´s always there.

Tennent: Perhaps a comment for those who want to see that. It is in my book, sketched briefly.

Mosses: Slight comment that Gudmund Frandsen has got almost full abstractness for a denotational semantics of logic programming not taking into account sequentiality perhaps [see references in the paper]. The only way he fails to be fully abstract is in that the function from environments to environments of which you take a big point could be applied to environments that cannot be expressed by logic programs and that is the only source of a lack of abstractness.

Jones: Yes, it is a very nice piece of work.

Formal Description of Programming Concepts - III
M. Wirsing (Editor)
Elsevier Science Publishers B.V. (North-Holland)

© IFIP, 1987

PROLOG-II as an instance of the Logic Programming Language Scheme

Joxan Jaffar, Jean-Louis Lassez and Michael J. Maher

IBM Thomas J. Watson Research Center, P.O. Box 218,
Yorktown Heights, NY 10598, U. S. A.

There already is a logical basis for establishing the soundness of successful PROLOG-II derivations. Many other results remain to be established, such as the existence of least fixed point and least model semantics, completeness of successful derivations, soundness and completeness for finite failure, and soundness and completeness of the negation as failure rule. We show how all these results may be obtained by regarding PROLOG-II as an instance of the logic programming language scheme proposed earlier by the authors. Essentially, all that is required is to establish some elementary properties of an underlying equality theory.

1. Introduction

A number of extensions to PROLOG are now proposed. In order to provide greater versatility and expressive power, some versions allow functional programming features. Others such as PROLOG-II use different forms of unification. In [Jaffar et al. 85], we addressed the problem of the preservation, in the extensions, of the semantic properties of definite clause logic programs. The main properties are: the existence of a least model and its least fixpoint characterization [Van Emden and Kowalski 76], soundness and completeness of SLD-resolution [Apt and van Emden 82], soundness and completeness of fair SLD-resolution for finite failure [Lassez and Maher 83], and soundness and completeness of the negation as failure rule [Jaffar et al. 83, 84].

We proposed a logic programming language scheme, call it LP(X). When the parameter X is instantiated by a unification complete equality theory the resulting instance of the scheme provides us with a formal basis for a logic programming language which possesses all the previously mentioned semantic properties. Here we illustrate how the scheme can be applied, choosing PROLOG-II as an example.

The formal basis for PROLOG-II is a rewriting system over the domain of infinite trees [Colmerauer 82]. As PROLOG stands for "Programmer en logique", this departure from logic as a foundation was somewhat surprising. Hansson and Haridi [81] and, independently, Van Emden and Lloyd [84], provided a logical basis to establish the soundness of successful PROLOG-II derivations with respect to a certain equality theory. Our approach is more comprehensive and systematic; it has the added advantage of being readily applicable to other extensions. Essentially, it consists in finding an equality theory whose standard model is the intended domain and which is unification-complete.

In a preliminary section we provide the necessary notations and definitions relating to logic programs with equality and PROLOG-II. In the following section, the domain of rational trees is modelled in a natural way by an equality theory E_0. We then transform E_0 (by Skolemization) into an equality theory E to which the scheme can be applied. The two main results in that section are the Isomorphism Lemma, stating that the domain of rational trees is isomorphic to the least model of E, and a theorem which establishes that a given completion E* of E is unification complete. In the fourth section, the soundness and completeness of the reduction process in PROLOG-II for the computation of E-mgu's, and the equivalence between PROLOG-II derivations and (P, E)-derivations are proven.

By now, all the results needed in order to apply the scheme have been established. In the last section we list all the theorems that are obtained as a consequence of this study, and provide a logical foundation for PROLOG-II which is essentially the same as the one for PROLOG once the differences in unification algorithms have been abstracted.

2. *Preliminaries*

We use the symbols Σ, Π and V to denote our denumerable collections of functors, predicate symbols and variables respectively. $\tau(\Sigma)$ and $\tau(\Sigma \cup V)$ denote, respectively, the (ground, finite) trees and the (finite) terms. We extend this notation to (ground) infinite trees and infinite terms with $\tau^{\times}(\Sigma)$ and $\tau^{\times}(\Sigma \cup V)$ respectively. Subsets of these, $\tau^{r}(\Sigma)$ and $\tau^{r}(\Sigma \cup V)$ denoting the *rational trees* and *rational terms* respectively, contain those trees and terms which have a finite number of subtrees and subterms respectively (see e.g. [Courcelle 83]). An *atom* is of the form $p(t_1, \ldots, t_m)$ where p is an m-ary symbol in Π and $t_i \in \tau(\Sigma \cup V)$, $1 \leq i \leq m$. Similarly, *rational atoms* contain rational terms. *Equations* are of the form $s = t$, where s and t are finite terms. A *system* is then defined to be a finite set of equations.

A *program* (over the alphabets Π and Σ) is a finite collection of *clauses* of the form

$$A \leftarrow B_1, B_2, \dots, B_n$$

where $n \geq 0$ and A and B_i, $1 \leq i \leq n$, are finite atoms (over the alphabets Π and Σ).

The following notational conventions are adopted for notational convenience and ease of proofs. Unless otherwise stated, the predicate and function symbol alphabets at hand will be Π and Σ respectively. We use symbols i, j, k, n and m to denote numbers. We use possibly subscripted symbols w, x, y and z to denote variables, s and t to denote terms, and A, B, C and D to denote atoms. We use p and q to denote predicate symbols and f and g to denote functors. We use the symbol $\sim$ to denote finite sequences of objects such as terms, atoms, clauses, etc. Thus, for example, $\tilde{s} = \tilde{t}$ may denote the finite system of equations $\{s_1 = t_1, \dots, s_m = t_m\}$, and $\tilde{\exists}$ is used for existential closure. $\tilde{x}$ denotes a sequence of distinct variables.

A *Horn equality theory* E is a (finite or infinite) collection of *Horn equality clauses*, this last being of the form

$$e \leftarrow e_1, e_2, \dots, e_n, \text{ or}$$
$$\leftarrow e_1, e_2, \dots, e_n$$

where $n \geq 0$ and e and e_i, $1 \leq i \leq n$, are equations. When E is consistent, it gives a finest congruence on $\tau(\Sigma)$ and we call the collection of E-classes the *E-universe*; notationally, we use $\tau(\Sigma)/E$. The *E-base* is $\{p(\tilde{d})$: $p \in \Sigma$, p is n-ary, $\tilde{d} \in (\tau(\Sigma)/E)^n\}$. *E-interpretations* are functions from E-base to {true, false} and are represented by the subset of the E-base whose elements map to true. An *E-model* of a program P is an E-interpretation under which P evaluates to true. Where S is a set of ground atoms, [S] denotes the set of E-equivalence classes of these atoms, the corresponding subset of the E-base.

An *E-substitution* θ is a finite set $\{x_1/t_1, \dots, x_n/t_n\}$ where the x_i's are distinct variables and the t_i's are terms, not containing occurrences of x_i's. The natural extensions of this function to map terms to terms, atoms to atoms, formulas to formulas etc. are again denoted by θ. We associate a substitution $\theta = \{x_1/t_1, \dots, x_n/t_n\}$ with a system of equations, denoted $\hat{\theta}$, as follows: $\hat{\theta} = \{x_1 = t_1, \dots, x_n = t_n\}$.

Composition of substitutions is defined in the usual manner, modulo the use of equality defined by E (rather than syntactic identity), and an E-substitution α is *more general than* β (denoted $\alpha \leq_E \beta$) if there is an E-substitution γ such that $\beta = \alpha\gamma$. An E-substitution θ is an *E-unifier* of e iff $E \models e\theta$. A set of E-unifiers Θ of an equation e is *complete* if, for every E-unifier α of e, some θ in Θ is more general than α. A complete set of E-unifiers Θ is *minimal* if no E-unifier in Θ is less general than some other E-unifier in Θ. E-unifiers in a minimal complete set are called *maximally general E-unifiers*. An E-unifier which is more general than every E-unifier is called a *most general E-unifier*.

We now recall the core concepts about the logic programming language scheme whose instances are obtained by a given equality theory satisfying the "unification-complete" property defined below. Let P and E respectively denote a program and Horn equality theory. We begin with the operational concepts:

A *(P, E)-derivation sequence* for G_0 is a (finite or infinite) sequence of triples $<G_i, \tilde{C}_i, \theta_i>$ such that (a) the *goal* G_i is a sequence of zero or more atoms

$$A_1, A_2, \ldots, A_m,$$

(b) $\tilde{C}$ is a collection of m variants (containing new variables) of clauses in P

$$B_1 \leftarrow \tilde{D}_1$$
$$B_2 \leftarrow \tilde{D}_2$$
$$\ldots$$
$$B_m \leftarrow \tilde{D}_m$$

(c) when it exists, θ_i is a E-unifier of the equations

$$A_1 = B_1, \ldots, A_m = B_m,$$

and finally (d) when θ_i exists, G_{i+1} is

$$(\tilde{D}_1, \tilde{D}_2, \ldots, \tilde{D}_m)\theta_i.$$

θ_i will not exist if $\{A_1 = B_1, \ldots, A_m = B_m\}$ is not unifiable. For technical convenience we assume that, at each step, all atoms in the goal are chosen for rewriting. It is not difficult to show that this is equivalent to the choice of a single atom at each step, provided that the choice of atom is *fair*, that is no atom is ignored infinitely often.

A (P, E)-derivation sequence is *successful* if some G_i is empty. A (P, E)-derivation sequence is *finitely failed* with length i if θ_i cannot be formed. If a (P, E)-derivation sequence is neither successful nor finitely failed, then it is *infinite*. A finite (P, E)-derivation sequence which can be extended to form a (P, E)-derivation sequence is called a *partial* (P, E)-derivation sequence.

Where A denotes a ground atom, we define

SS(P, E) = {A: there exists a successful (P, E)-derivation for A}

FF(P, E) = {A: all (P, E)-derivation sequences for A are finitely failed
with length $\leq$ n for some n}

GF(P, E) = {A: all (P, E)-derivation sequences for A are finitely failed}

We note here that FF(P, E) = GF(P, E) if E is such that there exists a *finite* set of maximally general E-unifiers for any equation e. This is the case, for example, in (pure) PROLOG and PROLOG-II. Next is the definition of the "immediate consequence" function $T_{(P, E)}$ which maps from and into subsets of the E-base:

$T_{(P, E)}(I) = \{A \in$ E-base:
there exists a clause
$A' \leftarrow B_1, B_2, \ldots, B_n$
in P and a ground E-substitution θ such that
(a) $E \models (A = A'\theta)$, and
(b) $\{B_1\theta, \ldots, B_n\theta\} \subseteq I\}$

For brevity, let us write T in place of $T_{(P,E)}$. Now such functions T are monotonic (using the $\subseteq$ ordering) and so we can build, in a natural way, the following kinds of sets: where α is a (not necessarily finite) ordinal,

$T\uparrow 0 = \phi$;
$T\uparrow\alpha = T(T\uparrow(\alpha\text{-}1))$ if α is a successor ordinal;
$T\uparrow\alpha = \bigcup_{\beta<\alpha} T\uparrow\beta$ if α is a limit ordinal;

Similarly,

$T{\downarrow}0 = \text{E-base};$

$T{\downarrow}\alpha = T(T{\downarrow}(\alpha\text{-}1))$ if α is a successor ordinal;

$T{\downarrow}\alpha = \bigcap_{\beta<\alpha} T{\downarrow}\beta$ if α is a limit ordinal;

Where lfp(T) and gfp(T) respectively denote the least and greatest fixpoints of the function T, it is known that

$\text{lfp}(T) = T{\uparrow}\omega$, and

$\text{gfp}(T) = T{\downarrow}\alpha \subseteq T{\downarrow}\omega$ for some ordinal $\alpha \geq \omega$.

We finally deal with *complete logic programs* P* corresponding to programs P and *unification complete equality theories* E* corresponding to Horn equality theories E. Essentially, P* contains formulas of the form

$$p(\tilde{x}) \leftrightarrow \begin{bmatrix} \exists\tilde{y}_1(\tilde{x} = \tilde{t}_1 \ \& \ \tilde{A}_1) \\ \vee \ \exists\tilde{y}_2(\tilde{x} = \tilde{t}_2 \ \& \ \tilde{A}_2) \\ \ldots \\ \vee \ \exists\tilde{y}_n(\tilde{x} = \tilde{t}_n \ \& \ \tilde{A}_n) \end{bmatrix}$$

corresponding to the collection of all clauses in P with p in the heads:

$$\begin{array}{c} p(\tilde{t}_1) \leftarrow \tilde{A}_1 \\ p(\tilde{t}_2) \leftarrow \tilde{A}_2 \\ \ldots \\ p(\tilde{t}_n) \leftarrow \tilde{A}_n \end{array}$$

where $\tilde{y}_i$ denotes the variables in the ith clause above. The formal definition may be obtained from [Jaffar et al. 84].

E* bears a relationship to E similar to that between P* and P. We require that for every equation e,

$$E^* \models e \leftrightarrow (\hat{\theta}_1 \vee \hat{\theta}_2 \vee \ldots \vee \hat{\theta}_\alpha)$$

where $\alpha \in \{1, 2, \ldots, \omega\}$ and $\{\theta_1, \theta_2, \ldots, \theta_\alpha\}$ is a collection of maximally general E-unifiers for e. Note that this implies that $E^* \models \neg\tilde{\exists}e$ if it is not the case that $E \models \tilde{\exists}e$. We say that such equality theories E* are *unification-complete*.

The rest of this section recalls some basic properties of PROLOG-II. Firstly, we describe the heart of this programming system – its equation system reduction algorithm. Each of the following five steps, defined in [Colmerauer 82], may be used to transform an equation system e into another:

(1) Delete from e an equation of the form x = x.

(2) If the equation x = y appears in e, where x and y are different, and x appears elsewhere in e, then replace all other occurrences of x in e by y.

(3) Replace an equation in e of the form t = x by x = t where t is not a variable.

(4) Replace two equations in e of the form x = t and x = u by the equations x = t and t = u where t is the smaller (in terms of symbols) of the two terms t and u.

(5) Replace an equation in e of the form $f(\tilde{t}) = f(\tilde{u})$ by the equations $\tilde{t} = \tilde{u}$.

It is well known that any system e can be reduced, using these five steps, into one of the two forms: *reduced form*, that is, e is of the form

$$x_1 = t_1(\tilde{x}, \tilde{y})$$
$$x_2 = t_2(\tilde{x}, \tilde{y})$$
$$\ldots$$
$$x_k = t_k(\tilde{x}, \tilde{y})$$

where the $\tilde{x}$ contain only distinct variables, or *contradictory form*, that is, e contains an equation of the form

$$f(\tilde{t}) = g(\tilde{u})$$

where f and g are different. Furthermore, e has a reduced form iff e cannot be reduced into a contradictory form.

A $\tau^r(\Sigma)$*-valuation* v of a system e maps each variable in e into $\tau^r(\Sigma)$ such that, when v is extended to map terms, the term $v(f(\tilde{t}))$ is the tree with f at the root and $v(t_i)$ in the ith subtree. A $\tau^r(\Sigma)$*-solution* of a system e is a $\tau^r(\Sigma)$*-valuation* of e which maps each pair of terms in each equation in e to the same tree.

The following are some fundamental results about systems.

Proposition 1.

(a) A system e has a $\tau^r(\Sigma)$-solution iff e has a reduced form.

(b) A system e in reduced form has exactly one $\tau^r(\Sigma)$-solution if each variable on the right hand sides in e appears in the left hand sides. ◊

Using the notation $e_1 ==> e_2$ to denote that e_2 is obtained from e_1 by applying one of the five steps above, we also have

Proposition 2. Where $e_1 ==> e_2$, an $\tau^r(\Sigma)$-solution for one of these two systems is an $\tau^r(\Sigma)$-solution for the other. ◊

We use the term *goal* once again to define *P-rewrites* in PROLOG-II. A goal is of the form $(e \mid \tilde{A})$ where e has a reduced form. A P-rewrite maps a goal $(e_1 \mid \tilde{A}_1)$ into another goal $(e_2 \mid \tilde{A}_2)$ such that there is a collection of m variants of clauses in P,

$$\begin{array}{c} B_1 \leftarrow \tilde{C}_1 \\ B_2 \leftarrow \tilde{C}_2 \\ \cdots \\ B_m \leftarrow \tilde{C}_m \end{array}$$

where m is the number of atoms in $\tilde{A}_2$, and e_2 is $e_1 \cup \{\tilde{A}_1 = \tilde{B}\}$ and $\tilde{A}_2$ is $\tilde{C}_1, \tilde{C}_2, \ldots, \tilde{C}_m$.

Note that, as for (P, E)-derivations, we assume that all atoms in the current goal are chosen for rewriting. Again this is for technical convenience and is equivalent to the fair choice of a single atom at each step. A P-rewrite sequence is a sequence of goals $G_0, G_1, \ldots$ such that G_{i+1} is a P-rewrite of G_i. Such a sequences is *successful* if the last goal in the sequence contains no atoms; it is *finitely failed* if no goal is P-rewritable from the last goal in the sequence. All other sequences are *infinite*.

3. The Equality Theory for PROLOG-II

The underlying equality theory for the Herbrand universe is the empty theory, which corresponds to syntactic identity. Clark [78] has used a stronger axiomatization to cater for negation-as-failure. In [Jaffar et al. 85], we remarked that the semantic properties of definite clause logic programs depend only on some properties of this theory, which can be easily abstracted. The first property is the existence of a least model for the equality theory which is isomorphic to the domain under consideration. The second property is unification-completeness. It states that every solution of an equation in a model of the equality theory is the composition of some unifier and a valuation. In particular, if two terms do not unify, then they are unequal in every model.

In this section, we provide such an equality theory for the domain of rational trees. Specifically, we show both (a) an isomorphism between the least model of E and the intended domain of discourse, the rational trees, and (b) that E*, a simple extension of E, is a unification-complete theory.

It is known (see e.g. [Courcelle 83]) that any $\tau^r(\Sigma_0)$ solution of a system of equations in reduced form

$$\begin{aligned} x_1 &= t_1(\tilde{x}, \tilde{y}) \\ x_2 &= t_2(\tilde{x}, \tilde{y}) \\ &\dots \\ x_k &= t_k(\tilde{x}, \tilde{y}) \end{aligned} \qquad (3.1)$$

where $\tilde{x}$ and $\tilde{y}$ are disjoint and each $t_i(\tilde{x}, \tilde{y})$ is a finite term containing no variables other than these, is such that any choice of values for $\tilde{y}$ determines uniquely the values of $\tilde{x}$. (Such "eliminable" variables $\tilde{x}$ are discussed in [Colmerauer 84].) This, then, is the main motivation for considering the conjunction of all the following formulas as our equality theory E_0:

$$\forall \tilde{x} \exists ! \tilde{y} \begin{bmatrix} x_1 = t_1(\tilde{x}, \tilde{y}) \\ \& \; x_2 = t_2(\tilde{x}, \tilde{y}) \\ \cdots \\ \& \; x_k = t_k(\tilde{x}, \tilde{y}) \end{bmatrix} \tag{3.2}$$

The quantifier $\exists!$ can be regarded as an abbreviation: $\exists! x\, P(x) \leftrightarrow \exists x\, (P(x) \wedge \forall z (P(z) \rightarrow x = z))$. However, the framework as presented in [Jaffar et al. 85] requires Horn equality theories. We thus work hereafter with the following theory E which is a Skolemised version of E_0. Let Σ denote the set Σ_0 augmented with an infinite set of Skolem functors. E contains all the axioms of the form

$$\forall \tilde{x} \forall \tilde{y} \begin{bmatrix} x_1 = t_1(\tilde{x}, \tilde{y}) \\ \& \; x_2 = t_2(\tilde{x}, \tilde{y}) \\ \cdots \\ \& \; x_k = t_k(\tilde{x}, \tilde{y}) \end{bmatrix} \leftrightarrow \begin{bmatrix} x_1 = c_1(\tilde{y}) \\ \& \; x_2 = c_2(\tilde{y}) \\ \cdots \\ \& \; x_k = c_k(\tilde{y}) \end{bmatrix} \tag{3.3}$$

where each symbol $c_i \in (\Sigma - \Sigma_0)$ appears in at most one such axiom. Intuitively, these new functors c_i are used as names for rational terms. Note that E can be straightforwardly re-written into definite clause form.

For notational convenience we assume that a variable appears in at most one axiom. Thus for each Skolem functor c_i there is a single corresponding variable x_i and vice versa. Clearly there is also a corresponding equation system (3.1) for each c_i.

As mentioned above, the rational trees $\tau^r(\Sigma_0)$ form a model for E_0. It is straightforward to extend this result to:

Lemma 1: E has a $\tau^r(\Sigma_0)$-model.

Each system (3.1) has a $\tau^r(\Sigma_0)$ model (see e.g. Courcelle 83]) such that there is exactly one $\tau^r(\Sigma_0)$-valuation on $\tilde{x}$ for each valuation on $\tilde{y}$. In other words, this model for each system (3.1) defines $\tilde{x}$ as a ($\tau^r(\Sigma_0)$ valued) function of $\tilde{y}$. Now each axiom (3.3) is associated with exactly one system (3.1). We can thus extend this model to (3.3) by assigning to the Skolem functor $\tilde{c}$, the same function as given for $\tilde{x}$.

Using the kind of model mentioned above, we can construct the intended model for E. By means of a function Ψ, we can associate a rational tree in the original language of E_0 to each ground term of our extended language:

$$\Psi : \tau(\Sigma) \rightarrow \tau^r(\Sigma_0)$$

The formal definition of the function Ψ is given as follows. We first define a method of transforming a system of equations containing Skolem functors into another such that the new system contains one less occurrence of a Skolem functor than the orginal system.

Let the original system e contain an occurrence of a term $c_i(\tilde{u})$ where $\tilde{u}$ has no Skolem functors. Now c_i appears in exactly one axiom (3.3) of E; let e' denote the equation system of the form (3.1) corresponding to the left hand side of this axiom. We simultaneously rename $\tilde{x}$ to variables $\tilde{z}$ not appearing in e and replace $\tilde{y}$ by $\tilde{u}$ in e' to obtain e''. Finally, we replace the occurrence in e of $c_i(\tilde{u})$ by z_i (the ith variable in $\tilde{z}$) and conjoin e with the equations in e''. This system of equations is the result of the transformation on e. (Intuitively, we have replaced the functor c_i by a new variable z_i and then augmented e with system which constrains z_i to be the desired rational term.)

Let $t \in \tau(\Sigma)$ and e_0 be the equation $x_0 = t$ where x_0 is a variable. By applying the above transformation zero or more times, we can obtain the system

$$x_0 = t' \; \& \; e_1 \; \& \; e_2 \; \& \ldots \& \; e_k \qquad (3.4)$$

which contains no Skolem functors. It is easily verifiable that this system is in reduced form and thus, by Proposition 1(a), has a $\tau^r(\Sigma_0)$ solution. Furthermore, every variable appearing therein appears in the left hand side of some equation. Thus, by Proposition 1(b), (3.4) has precisely one $\tau^r(\Sigma_0)$-solution; the solution for x_0 is then the definition of $\Psi(t)$.

It is not hard to see that this transformation results in an equivalent equation system in the following sense: where e is transformed into e' and $\tilde{z}$ are variables appearing in e' but not in e, we have

Lemma 2. E $\models$ (e $\leftrightarrow$ $\exists\tilde{z}$(e')). ◊

Now we require that Ψ forms a basis for our intended model. Therefore, ground terms which are equal under our theory E must be mapped by Ψ to the same element of the intended domain of discourse, $\tau^r(\Sigma_0)$; similarly, ground terms which are not provably equal under E must be mapped by Ψ to different trees. Furthermore, Ψ must be surjective. These three properties of Ψ are proven now in the following two lemmas:

Lemma 3. If $\tilde{s}$ and $\tilde{t}$ are ground then E $\models$ $(\tilde{s} = \tilde{t})$ iff $\Psi(\tilde{s}) = \Psi(\tilde{t})$.

Proof. We do this proof for the case where the lengths of $\tilde{s}$ and $\tilde{t}$ is one, i.e. $\tilde{s}$ = s and $\tilde{t}$ = t. The appropriate generalisation is easy.

($\rightarrow$) Let the result of the above transformation on $\{x_0 = s\}$ and $\{x_0 = t\}$ be of the forms

$$x_0 = s' \;\&\; e_1 \text{ and}$$
$$x_0 = t' \;\&\; e_2$$

respectively. Clearly we may take it these two systems have no variable in common except x_0. Now, by Lemma 2 above, E $\models$ (s = t) implies that

$$E \models \tilde{\exists}(x_0 = s' = t' \;\&\; e_1 \;\&\; e_2).$$

This in turn means that

$$x_0 = s' = t' \;\&\; e_1 \;\&\; e_2 \tag{3.5}$$

is E-unifiable and hence has a $\tau^r(\Sigma_0)$-solution. Such a solution must solve each of the systems

$$x_0 = s' \;\&\; e_1 \text{ and}$$
$$x_0 = t' \;\&\; e_2$$

which, as noted in the definition of Ψ, have unique solutions. Thus these solutions are the same and $\Psi(s) = \Psi(t)$.

($\leftarrow$) $\Psi(s) = \Psi(t)$ implies that there is a $\tau^r(\Sigma_0)$ solution of (3.5). Hence (3.5) has a reduced form e and since E $\models \tilde{\exists}e$, we get

$$E \models \tilde{\exists}(s' = t' \;\&\; e_1 \;\&\; e_2)$$

By Lemma 2, E $\models$ (s = t) and we are done. ◊

Lemma 4. Ψ maps onto $\tau^r(\Sigma_0)$.

Proof. From [Courcelle 83], to every $t \in \tau^r(\Sigma_0)$ corresponds an equation system e of the form (3.1):

$$\begin{aligned} x_1 &= t_1(\tilde{x}) \\ x_2 &= t_2(\tilde{x}) \\ &\cdots \\ x_k &= t_k(\tilde{x}) \end{aligned}$$

such that the one and only $\tau^r(\Sigma_0)$-solution is such that $x_1 = t$. There is exactly one axiom (3.3) in E whose left hand side corresponds to the above system. It is now a matter of verification that that $\Psi(c_1) = t$. ◊

As a consequence of these two lemmas we obtain one of the main results of this section:

Isomorphism Lemma: Ψ is an isomorphism between $\tau(\Sigma)/E$ and $\tau^r(\Sigma_0)$. ◊

Before obtaining a unification-complete equality theory from E, we first prove the following technical lemma, to be used in the next section.

Lemma 5. Where $\tilde{s}$ and $\tilde{t}$ are ground and $f \in \Sigma_0$,

(a) $\Psi(f(\tilde{s})) = \Psi(f(\tilde{t}))$ iff $\Psi(\tilde{s}) = \Psi(\tilde{t})$.

(b) $E \models (f(\tilde{s}) = f(\tilde{t}))$ iff $E \models (\tilde{s} = \tilde{t})$.

Proof. (a) For any t_i in $\tilde{t}$, it is clear that the equation systems (3.4) corresponding to $f(\tilde{t})$ and t_i are of the form

$$x_0 = f(\tilde{u}) \;\&\; e_1 \;\&\; e_2 \;\&\; \dots \;\&\; e_k$$

and

$$x_0 = u_i \;\&\; e_1 \;\&\; e_2 \;\&\; \dots \;\&\; e_k$$

respectively. In other words, where n is the arity of f, $\Psi(f(\tilde{t}))$ is a tree with root label f and whose descendents are $\Psi(t_i)$, $1 \leq i \leq n$. The rest of the proof is straightforward.

(b) By the Isomorphism Lemma above, $\Psi(f(\tilde{s})) = \Psi(f(\tilde{t}))$ iff $E \models (f(\tilde{s}) = f(\tilde{t}))$, and $\Psi(\tilde{s}) = \Psi(\tilde{t})$ iff $E \models (\tilde{s} = \tilde{t})$. By (a) we are done. ◊

The final result of this section is a necessary prelude to characterising finitely failed P-rewrite sequences in terms of logical consequence and the *negation* of a goal. Since definite clauses do not explicitly provide negative information, we use complete logic programs (P*, E*) where E* is the set obtained by augmenting E with all (Horn) formulas of the form

$$f(\tilde{x}) \neq g(\tilde{y}), \tag{3.6}$$

$$h(\tilde{z}) = h(\tilde{w}) \rightarrow \tilde{z} = \tilde{w} \tag{3.7}$$

where $f, g, h \in \Sigma_0$.

Unification-Completeness Lemma: E* is unification-complete.

Proof. Let e be any equation system. Using the transformation described in Section 3 we obtain e′ which has the property $E \models (e \leftrightarrow \exists\tilde{z}(e'))$ (Lemma 2). Let $c' = e_0 ==> e_1 ==> \dots ==> e_k$ so that e_k is either a reduced form of e or it contains an equation of the form $f(\tilde{t}) = g(\tilde{u})$ where f and g are distinct functors in Σ_0. We first show that $E^* \models (e_i \leftrightarrow e_{i+1})$, for $0 \leq i < k$. This is trivially true if e_{i+1} is not obtained from e_i using step (5) in Section 2. Otherwise, e_i contains an occurrence of an equation $h(\tilde{t}) = h(\tilde{u})$ and e_{i+1} is obtained from e_i by replacing this occurrence with $\tilde{t} = \tilde{u}$. Clearly $E^* \models (e_i \leftrightarrow e_{i+1})$, by virtue of an axiom of the form (3.7).

We now consider two cases: suppose firstly that e' has no reduced form, i.e. e_k contains an equation of the form $f(\tilde{t}) = g(\tilde{u})$ where f and g are distinct functors in Σ_0. Clearly $E^* \models \neg\tilde{\exists} e_k$ by virtue of an axiom of the form (3.6). Since $E^* \models (e_i \leftrightarrow e_{i+1})$, for $0 \leq i < k$ and $E \models (e \leftrightarrow \exists\tilde{z}(e'))$ we have $E^* \models \neg e$ as desired.

If, on the other hand, e' has a reduced form e_k, let e_k be of the form (3.1):

$$\begin{aligned} x_1 &= t_1(\tilde{x}, \tilde{y}) \\ x_2 &= t_2(\tilde{x}, \tilde{y}) \\ &\dots \\ x_k &= t_k(\tilde{x}, \tilde{y}) \end{aligned}$$

Since E contains an axiom of the form (3.3):

$$\forall\tilde{x}\forall\tilde{y} \begin{bmatrix} x_1 = t_1(\tilde{x}, \tilde{y}) \\ \& \; x_2 = t_2(\tilde{x}, \tilde{y}) \\ \dots \\ \& \; x_k = t_k(\tilde{x}, \tilde{y}) \end{bmatrix} \leftrightarrow \begin{bmatrix} x_1 = c_1(\tilde{y}) \\ \& \; x_2 = c_2(\tilde{y}) \\ \dots \\ \& \; x_k = c_k(\tilde{y}) \end{bmatrix}$$

we can let θ denote the substitution

$$\{ x_1 / c_1(\tilde{y}), x_2 / c_2(\tilde{y}), \dots , x_k / c_k(\tilde{y}) \}$$

so that $E \models (e_k \leftrightarrow \hat{\theta})$. Since $E^* \models E$ and $E^* \models (e_i \leftrightarrow e_{i+1})$, for $0 \leq i < k$, we have $E^* \models (e' \leftrightarrow \hat{\theta})$. From the form of e', the variables $\tilde{z}$ are contained in $x_1, \dots, x_n$ and so there is a subset α of θ such that $E \models \exists\tilde{z}(\hat{\theta}) \leftrightarrow \hat{\alpha}$. Consequently $E^* \models (e \leftrightarrow \hat{\alpha})$. ◊

4. Logic Programming Derivations for PROLOG-II

The previous section has provided us with an unification-complete equality theory E* for the rational trees. Consequently, we have the foundation for a logic programming language over the domain of rational trees. Programs in this language differ from Prolog II in that they use E-unifiers in the derivations instead of reduced forms of systems of equations. We show in this section that these two operational notions are equivalent, i.e., (P, E)-derivation sequences are, in some sense, isomorphic to the P-rewrite sequences of Prolog II. The precisions follow:

Let

$$(e_0 \mid \tilde{B}_0),\ (e_1 \mid \tilde{B}_1),\ \ldots\ ,\ (e_i \mid \tilde{B}_i),\ \ldots$$

be a finite or infinite P-rewrite sequence and let

$$(\tilde{B}_0\alpha_0),\ (\tilde{B}_1\alpha_1),\ \ldots\ ,\ (\tilde{B}_i\alpha_i),\ \ldots$$

be a finite or infinite (P, E)-derivation sequence. We say these two sequences *correspond* to each other if $\alpha_0\ \alpha_1\ \ldots\ \alpha_i$ is an E-mgu of e_i for every i. The following preliminary result is easy to verify:

Proposition 3: Let e and e′ denote two systems of equations.

(a) If $e \cup e'$ has a $\tau^r(\Sigma_0)$-solution and θ is an E-mgu of e, then $e'\theta$ has an E-mgu.

(b) If θ is an E-mgu of e and γ is an E-mgu of $e'\theta$, then $\theta\gamma$ is an E-mgu of $e \cup e'$. ◊

The following result connects the operational concept of reduced form and the equality theory concept of mgu:

MGU Lemma: An equation system e in Σ_0 has an E-mgu θ iff e has a reduced form e′ with E-mgu θ.

Proof. We first observe that if e ==> e′, then an E-unifier for one system is also an E-unifier for the other. If e′ is obtained from e by means of steps 1, 2, 3 or 4 in Section2, then clearly E $\models$ (e $\leftrightarrow$ e′) and so the result is clear. If, however, e′ is obtained from e by means of step 5, then the result can be obtained from Lemma 5(b). The rest of the proof is given by the observation that a system in contradictory form has no E-unifier. ◊

We come now to the central lemma of this section which establishes the desired connection between (P, E)-derivations and P-rewrites:

Corresponding Derivations Lemma: Let e be an equation system with E-mgu α.

(a) Every P-rewrite sequence on (e | A) has a corresponding (P, E)-derivation sequence on Aα.

(b) Every (P, E)-derivation sequence on Aα has a corresponding P-rewrite sequence on (e | A).

Proof. (a) We proceed by induction on the length of the P-rewrite sequence. The base case clearly holds. For the induction step let (e_i | $\tilde{B}_i$), i = 0, 1, ... , k, denote the first k+1 goals in the P-rewrite sequence. By the induction hypothesis there is a (P, E)-derivation sequence $\tilde{B}_i\alpha_i$, i = 0, 1, ... , k−1, corresponding to the first k goals in the above P-rewrite sequence. Let $\tilde{C}$ denote the heads of the input clauses used to obtain the k+1th goal in the P-rewrite sequence. Thus $e_k = e_{k-1} \cup \{\tilde{B}_{k-1} = \tilde{C}\}$ and $\tilde{B}_k$ is given by the bodies of these input clauses. By Proposition 3(a) and the induction hypothesis that $\alpha_0\, \alpha_1 \ldots \alpha_{k-1}$ is an E-mgu of e_{k-1}, the equations $\{\tilde{B}_{k-1} = \tilde{C}\}\, \alpha_0\, \alpha_1 \ldots \alpha_{k-1}$ is E-unifiable. By suitable variable renaming, none of $\alpha_0, \alpha_1, \ldots, \alpha_{k-1}$ substitute variables in $\tilde{C}$ and none of $\alpha_0, \alpha_1, \ldots, \alpha_{k-2}$ substitute variables in $\tilde{B}_{k-1}$. Thus the E-unifiable system $\{\tilde{B}_{k-1} = \tilde{C}\}\, \alpha_0\, \alpha_1 \ldots \alpha_{k-1}$ is the same as $\{\tilde{B}_{k-1}\, \alpha_{k-1} = \tilde{C}\}$. Letting α_k be the mgu of this system it follows that $\tilde{B}_k\, \alpha_k$ can be the next goal in the (P, E)-derivation sequence. We finish off by showing that the induction hypothesis continues to hold. Since $\alpha_0\, \alpha_1 \ldots \alpha_{k-1}$ is an E-mgu of e_{k-1} and α_k is an E-mgu of $\{\tilde{B}_{k-1} = \tilde{C}\}\, \alpha_0\, \alpha_1 \ldots \alpha_{k-1}$, we have, by using Proposition 3(b), that $\alpha_0\, \alpha_1 \ldots \alpha_{k-1}\, \alpha_k$ is an mgu for e_k.

(b) We proceed by induction on the length of the (P, E)-derivation sequence. Once again, the base case is straightforward. For the induction step, let $\tilde{B}_i\alpha_i$, $0 \leq i \leq k$, denote the first k+1 goals in the derivation and there is a P-rewrite sequence (e_i | $\tilde{B}_i$), $0 \leq i < k$ corresponding to the first goals in the (P, E)-derivation. Let $\tilde{C}$ denote the heads of the input clauses used to obtain the k+1th goal in the (P, E)-derivation sequence. Thus α_k is an E-mgu of $\tilde{B}_{k-1}\alpha_{k-1}$ and $\tilde{C}$, and $\tilde{B}_k$ is given by the bodies of these input clauses. It suffices to show that $e_k = e_{k-1} \cup \{\tilde{B}_{k-1}\alpha_{k-1} = \tilde{C}\}$ has a reduced form.

As in part (a) above, $\{\tilde{B}_{k-1}\ \alpha_{k-1} = \tilde{C}\}$ is the same as $\{\tilde{B}_{k-1} = \tilde{C}\}\ \alpha_0\ \alpha_1 \ldots \alpha_{k-1}$. Thus the latter system also has an E-mgu α_k. Using the induction hypothesis and Proposition 3(b), e_k has an E-mgu $\alpha_0\ \alpha_1 \ldots \alpha_{k-1}\ \alpha_k$. The Mgu Lemma can now be used to show that this system has a reduced form. ◇

The above lemma shows a one-one association between P-rewrite sequences and (P, E)-derivation sequences. We thus have the following relationship between successful P-rewrite sequences and (P, E)-derivation sequences, and between the two forms of finitcly failed sequences.

Corollary: Let e be an equation system with E-mgu α. Then

(a) (e | A) has a successful P-rewrite iff $A\alpha$ has a successful (P, E)-derivation.

(b) (e | A) has only finitely failed P-rewrites iff $A\alpha$ has only finitely failed (P, E)-derivations. ◇

5. *Instantiating the Scheme*

The previous two sections have provided the proofs for the following results which amount to a logical foundation for PROLOG-II. Let E and E* be the equality theories given above; let A, B, e and P respectively denote any ground atom from Σ, collection of atoms from Σ_0, collection of equations from Σ_0, and program respectively. Then:

Theorem 1.

There is a least E-model of P, lm(P, E), and

$(P^*, E^*) \models A$ iff $(P, E) \models A$ iff $[A] \in lm(P, E)$. ◇

Theorem 2.

$lm(P, E) = lfp(T_{(P, E)})$. ◇

Theorem 3.

$\mathrm{lfp}(T_{(P,E)}) = T_{(P,E)}\uparrow\omega = [SS(P, E)]$. ◊

Theorem 4.

(a) $A \in SS(P, E)$ iff $(P^*, E^*) \models A$. ◊

(b) Let e be an equation system with E-mgu α.
Then (e | B) has a successful P-rewrite sequence iff $(P, E) \models \tilde{\exists} B\alpha$ iff $(P^*, E^*) \models \tilde{\exists} B\alpha$. ◊

Theorem 5.

$[A] \notin T_{(P,E)}\downarrow\omega$ iff $A \in FF(P, E)$. ◊

Theorem 6.

(a) $A \in FF(P, E)$ iff $(P^*, E^*) \models \neg A$. ◊

(b) Let e be an equation system with E-mgu α. Then (e | B) has only finitely failed P-rewrite sequences iff $(P^*, E^*) \models \neg\tilde{\exists} B\alpha$. ◊

The Isomorphism Lemma shows that we can regard [SS(P, E)] and [FF(P, E)] as sets of ground rational atoms, and regard $T_{(P,E)}$ as a function over such sets. Consequently Theorems 2, 3 and 5 can be understood without knowledge of E and the Skolem functions. We can achieve the same effect for Theorems 4(b) and 6(b) by "de-Skolemizing" E* to E_0*. E_0 * consists of all axioms of the forms (3.2), (3.6) and (3.7).

Theorem 7.

(a) (e | B) has a successful P-rewrite sequence iff $(P, E_0) \models \tilde{\exists}(e \wedge B)$ iff $(P^*, E_0^*) \models \tilde{\exists}(e \wedge B)$.

(b) (e | B) has only finitely failed P-rewrite sequences iff $(P^*, E_0^*) \models \neg\tilde{\exists}(e \wedge B)$. ◊

References

[Apt and van Emden 82]
K.R. Apt and M.H. van Emden, "Contributions to the Theory of Logic Programming", *Journal of the ACM*, 29(3), pp. 841-862, July 1982.

[Clark 78]
K.L. Clark, "Negation as Failure", in *Logic and Databases*, H. Gallaire and J. Minker (Eds), Plenum Press, New York, pp. 293-322, 1978.

[Colmerauer 82]
A. Colmerauer, "PROLOG II - Reference Manual and Theoretical Model", Internal Report, Groupe Intelligence Artificielle, Universite Aix-Marseille II, October 1982.

[Colmerauer 82]
A. Colmerauer, "Prolog and Infinite Trees", in *Logic Programming*, K.L. Clark and S-A. Tarnlund (Eds), Academic Press, New York, 1982.

[Colmerauer 84]
A. Colmerauer, "Equations and Inequations on Finite and Infinite Trees", *Proc. 2nd. Int. Conf. on Fifth Generation Computer Systems*, Tokyo, pp. 85-99, November 1984.

[Courcelle 83]
B. Courcelle, "Fundamental Properties of Infinite Trees", *Theoretical Computer Science*, 25(2), pp. 95 - 169, March 1983.

[Van Emden and Kowalski 76]
M.H. Van Emden and R.A. Kowalski, "The Semantics of Predicate Logic as a Programming Language", *Journal of the ACM*, 23(4), pp. 733-742, October 1976.

[Van Emden and Lloyd 84]
M.H. van Emden and J.W. Lloyd, "A Logical Reconstruction of PROLOG-II", *Proc. 2nd Int. Conf. on Logic Programming*, Uppsala, pp. 35-40, July 1984.

[Hansson and Haridi 81]
A. Hansson and A.S. Haridi, "Logic Programming in a Natural Deduction Framework", Workshop on Functional Languages and Computer Architecture, Goteburg, 1981.

[Jaffar et al. 83]
J. Jaffar, J-L. Lassez and J.W. Lloyd, "Completeness of the Negation-as-Failure Rule", *Proceedings 8th IJCAI*, Karlsruhe, pp. 500-506, August 1983.

[Jaffar et al. 84]
J. Jaffar, J-L. Lassez and M.J. Maher, "A Theory of Complete Logic Programs with Equality", *Journal of Logic Programming*, 3, pp. 211-233, 1984.

[Jaffar et al. 85]
J. Jaffar, J-L. Lassez and M.J. Maher, "A Logic Programming Language Scheme", in *Logic Programming: Relations, Functions and Equations*, D. DeGroot and G. Lindstrom (Eds), Prentice-Hall, pp. 441-467, 1985.

[Lassez and Maher 83]
J-L. Lassez and M.J. Maher, "Closures and Fairness in the Semantics of Programming Logic", *Theoretical Computer Science*, 29, pp. 167-184, 1984.

QUESTIONS AND ANSWERS

Jouannaud: There is an alternative approach to the one you use by embedding the unification algorithm into PROLOG: to use SLD-resolution plus paramodulation. This is a very general framework. In your framework I am afraid you use only very special equational theories because only very few of them have unification complete algorithms.

Maher: No, we show that for equality theories with rational solutions one can construct corresponding unification-complete equality theories. Hence, PROLOG II fits into the logic programming scheme LP(X). The problem of inequalities [in PROLOG II] cannot be accomodated by this scheme.

Jouannaud: My comment is really to what you said at the end about inequalities. There has been a quite recent work by Hubert Comon from Grenoble. He was using a concept he was calling ´anti-unification´ which was just reasoning with inequalities and computing substitutions for solving inequality problems [H. Comon: Sufficient completeness, term rewriting systems and "anti-unification". In: J. Siekmann (ed.): 8th Int. Conference on Automated Deduction. Lecture Notes in Computer Science 230. Springer: Berlin, 1986, 128-140]. This might be helpful for your problem in your case.

Lassez: When we have inequalities sometimes you can represent them by a finite number of substitutions, sometimes you can not. Hubert Comon is looking at this problem; I think that we have a solution with the constraints where we completely avoid this problem but that will be in the next talk [J.-L. Lassez, J. Jaffar: Constraint logic programming. Talk at IFIP WG 2.2. Meeting of August 1986, Ebberup, Denmark. Paper in: 14th ACM Symposium on Principles of Programming Languages, Munich, 1987, 111-119]. So a complete and hopefully satisfactory answer to your question will be given later. You were mentioning ´putting equalities´ and ´using paramodulation´. There is one point which is very important. We just don´t want to put any equality, we don´t want to do only theorem proving. The keypoint in our approach is, we want to preserve in the PROLOG extension all the semantic properties of definite clause logic programs. If you put any equality theory, in general, not all these properties are preserved. You are going to lose all these properties of at least half of them. What we want to have is a formal semantics which is *the* formal semantics of logic programs, so we can´t fool around too much with equality theories.

Wirsing: PROLOG II seems to me a first step in the direction of having a structured way of logic programming. Most of the logic programs, I know, are unstructured; they consist of a bunch of rules. But for verifying programs I need structuring. So, in terms of abstract data types what you did is saying: I consider a parameterized PROLOG specification where the parameter is an equality theory. This parameterization could be a starting point for structuring PROLOG programs. Did you do work in that direction?

Maher: No, we have not done any concrete work in that direction. One of the problems is that, although the abstract data type approach fits naturally into this framework, for abstract data types in general the unification problem will be undecidable. That means when you are writing a program using abstract data types you have to be very careful that you do not create an undecidable problem for the interpreter. Lots of times this can be avoided simply by delaying a goal, but in general it would not be possible. Still I believe that it is better to keep this approach.

Wirsing: It is not necessary to include abstract data types there. I would only like to have a structured language for logic programs - logic programming modules.

Maher: Our approach is basicly describing a two-step modularization. It isn´t really addressing the problem of modularization in full detail.

Apt: I have just one thing to say, to complete your presentation, it is said in the paper but perhaps it should also be stated here: the theory of rational trees which you use is based on results of Courcelle. He studied the subject extensively.

SESSION 5

Concurrency II

Chairman: A. Pnueli

Formal Description of Programming Concepts - III
M. Wirsing (Editor)
Elsevier Science Publishers B.V. (North-Holland)

© IFIP, 1987

INTERLEAVING AND PARTIAL ORDERS IN CONCURRENCY: A FORMAL COMPARISON

Eike Best[1] and Raymond Devillers[2]

ABSTRACT

Two ways of describing the behaviour of concurrent systems have widely been suggested: arbitrary interleaving and partial orders. Sometimes the latter has been claimed superior because concurrency is represented in a 'true' way; on the other hand, some authors have claimed that the former is sufficient for all practical purposes. Petri net theory offers a framework in which both kinds of semantics can be defined formally and hence compared with each other. Occurrence sequences correspond to interleaved behaviour while the notion of a process is used to capture partial order semantics.

This paper aims at obtaining formal results about the relationship between processes and occurrence sequences in net theory. We shall compare an axiomatic approach to the definition of processes with an inductive approach which relates processes to occurrence sequences. It will be shown that, in general, axiomatic process semantics is more powerful than inductive semantics using occurrence sequences. However, in an interesting special case, an equivalence result exists. The structure of the relation between sequences and processes will be explored, exhibiting two simple meaningful equivalence relations, one on the sequences and one on the processes, whose classes correspond to each other bijectively. We shall apply and simplify the theory to 1-safe nets.

1 Introduction

The semantics of concurrent systems can be, and have been, described by different means, notably by so-called arbitrary interleaving and by partial ordering (of atomic actions). The problem of determining which ones of these means is either absolutely adequate, or more adequate than the other(s), has been very widely discussed, often on an informal basis. This paper presents a partial formal answer in terms of Petri nets. This is *not* a too restricted view because our considerations and results can be transferred with slight changes to concurrent programs, either centralised ones or distributed ones [1,2].

Petri nets are an appropriate formalism to start with because there exists an easily definable interleaving semantics (in terms of 'occurrence sequences' or the well known 'firing sequences') as well as a partial order semantics (in terms of a special class of nets called 'occurrence nets' or sometimes also 'causal nets' [11]). The partially ordered behaviours of Petri nets are usually called 'processes' [8]; mathematically speaking they are occurrence nets with a labelling. Processes are defined independently of occurrence sequences by means of a 'reasonable' set of axioms which has evolved through the discussion in [11,8,9,7,1]. Hence a formal comparison is possible.

[1]Institut für methodische Grundlagen, Gesellschaft für Mathematik und Datenverarbeitung, 5205 St.Augustin, Fed. Rep. Germany

[2]Laboratoire d'Informatique Théorique, Université Libre de Bruxelles, Campus Plaine, 1050 Bruxelles, Belgium

In [2] we have conducted a rather general study, allowing infinite (but countable) Petri nets. This study has revealed that there are indeed cases in which interleaving semantics is strictly less powerful than partial order (i.e. process) semantics. The example which shows this will be reproduced below. Furthermore, we have shown that within a certain class of nets (those of finite synchronisation, also to be defined below), such examples may not occur. More precisely, if synchronisation is finite then every process (i.e. partially ordered behaviour) of a Petri net can be linearised in such a way that it corresponds to an occurrence sequence (i.e. an interleaved behaviour).

In the present paper we concentrate on nets of finite synchronisation. Such nets are still very general; they include all finite nets and hence the practically interesting cases. Although, in this case, every process corresponds to at least one occurrence sequence (in general, to many of them, namely to all appropriate linearisations), there is a sense in which a partial order contains *more* information than any of its associated occurrence sequences, viz. the partial ordering aspect (and with it, the concurrency aspect). An interesting question is: exactly *what* information is gained if one switches from occurrence sequences to processes? Conversely, every occurrence sequence corresponds to at least one partial order (in general, to many of them, except for 1-safe nets, as will be seen later), so that there is surely also a sense in which an occurrence sequence abstracts away from some details present in partial orderings. Now the question arises: which details, and what is the exact structure of the relation between occurrence sequences and partial orderings in net theory? To answer these questions is the main objective of this paper.

When this work was begun in [1], the idea was that one could find a general result along the lines that a process corresponds more or less uniquely to a certain equivalence class of occurrence sequences which is induced by exchanging neighbouring concurrent transitions. However, this is by no means true in general: [1] manages to prove only one direction, namely that the linearisations of a process arise from each other by such exchanges; however, the other half of the statement had to be left open. This paper fills the gap. Essentially, the solution is that a certain equivalence relation has to be defined on the set of processes also, based on the *swap* relation which will be introduced in this paper. It is then possible to establish a bijection between equivalence classes of sequences and equivalence classes of processes — but no more, since in general the *swap* relation does not reduce to identity. There is an interesting class of nets, namely the 1-safe nets, for which *swap* does equal identity. We will prove these results and illustrate their consequences.

In section 2 we provide the definitions of nets, their occurrence sequence and process semantics and further necessary definitions such as that of 1-safeness. In section 3 we define the class of nets of finite synchronisation and we show in what sense occurrence sequences describe the same behaviours as processes within that class. Section 4, the core of this paper, contains the definitions of the two equivalence relations mentioned above, one on the set of occurrence sequences and one on the set of processes, and the formulation and proof outline of the corresponding equivalence results. In section 5, the theory will be applied to 1-safe nets. Section 6 addresses the question whether or not one can reconstruct processes from occurrence sequences only; it also gives some examples which show why the general theory of section 4 has to be so relatively complicated.

Since this paper is a sequel to [1], sections 2 and 3 partially overlap with the earlier paper. However, we preferred to make the present paper self-contained by giving all necessary definitions. Because the proofs of section 4 are rather long, they cannot be included in full; the interested reader is referred to [2] which supplies the details.

2 Basic Definitions

Net theory stipulates that a concurrent system be described by two kinds of objects, state-like objects S (sometimes called places) and action-like objects T (sometimes called transitions). The idea is that state objects may 'hold' (to make up a certain state) and that transitions may 'occur' (and thus change the state). Thus, state objects and transitions are interconnected in an alternating fashion, which in net theory is captured by an interconnection relation F (for 'flow') defined as a subset of $(S \times T) \cup (T \times S)$.

Definition 2.1 *Petri nets*

(i) (S, T, F) *is a net iff* S *and* T *are disjoint sets and* $F \subseteq (S \times T) \cup (T \times S)$.

(ii) (S, T, F) *is a* T*-restricted net iff it is a net and* $T \subseteq dom(F) \cap cod(F)$. □ 2.1

From a formal point of view it is advantageous to interpret the relation F as a function

$$F: (S \times T \cup T \times S) \to \{0, 1\}$$

with the convention $(x, y) \in F \Leftrightarrow F(x, y) \neq 0$. We will sometimes make use of this view in order to shorten formulae. Moreover, this allows to extend very easily the whole theory to nets with weighted arrows; one simply has to replace $\{0, 1\}$ by the set $\mathbf{N} = \{0, 1, 2, \ldots\}$ of natural numbers.

Net theory employs the concept of a marking in order to describe state holdings, while the state changes effected by a transition occurrence are described by the transition rule. In general, state objects are allowed to hold several times, for example representing the presence of several similar resources.

Definition 2.2 *System nets*

(i) M *is a marking of* (S, T, F) *iff* $M: S \to \mathbf{N}$;

(ii) $\Sigma = (S, T, F, M_0)$ *is a system net (or place/transition net) iff* (S, T, F) *is a countable* T*-restricted net and* M_0 *is a marking (called the initial marking of* Σ*).* □ 2.2

M_0 represents the initial state of the system net described by Σ. Sometimes, an upper limit is required for the markings on the places. Such limits introduce difficulties in the interpretation of processes, as do non-T-restricted or uncountable nets. The reader is referred to [4] where it is indicated how the process notion could be extended to allow upper limits.

The transition rule specifies under which conditions a marking M enables a transition t, and how the occurrence of t changes M into a new marking M'.

Definition 2.3 *Transition rule*

Let (S, T, F) *be a net,* M *a marking and* $t \in T$.

(i) M *enables* t *iff* $\forall s \in S: F(s, t) \leq M(s)$.

(ii) M' *is produced from* M *by the occurrence of* t *(in symbols:* $M[t\rangle M'$*) iff* M *enables* t *and* $\forall s \in S: M'(s) = M(s) - F(s, t) + F(t, s)$. □ 2.3

Note that this definition ensures that M' is again a marking.

Definition 2.4 *Occurrence sequence semantics of nets*

Let $\Sigma = (S, T, F, M_0)$ *be a system net, let* $M_1, M_2, \ldots$ *be markings of* Σ *and let* $t_1, t_2, \ldots \in T$.

(i) $\sigma = M_0 t_1 M_1 \ldots t_n M_n$ *is a (finite) occurrence sequence of* Σ *iff* $\forall i, 1 \leq i \leq n: M_{i-1}[t_i\rangle M_i$;
$\sigma = M_0 t_1 M_1 t_2 \ldots$ *is an (infinite) occurrence sequence of* Σ *iff* $\forall i, 1 \leq i: M_{i-1}[t_i\rangle M_i$.

(ii) For finite σ *we define its length* $|\sigma|$ *by* n*, that is the number of transitions (not necessarily distinct) in* σ*; this includes the case* $\sigma = M_0$ *for which* $|\sigma| = 0$*; we also define* $last(\sigma) = M_{|\sigma|}$ *as the last marking of* σ*. If* σ *is finite and* σ' *is an occurrence sequence of* $(S, T, F, last(\sigma))$ *then the catenation* $\sigma'' = \sigma\sigma'$ *is defined and is an occurrence sequence of* Σ*;* σ *is called a prefix of length* $|\sigma|$ *of* σ''.

(iii) $[M_0\rangle = \{M \mid \exists \sigma: M_0 = first(\sigma) \wedge M = last(\sigma)\}$ *(the set of markings reachable from* M_0 *by successive occurrences of single transitions).* □ 2.4

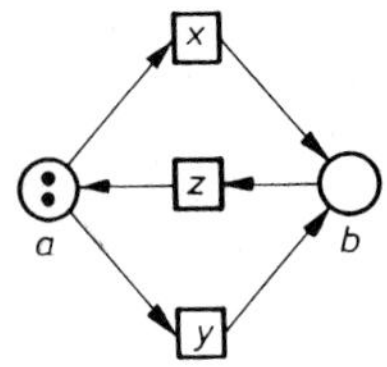

(i) A system net

$$\begin{pmatrix}a\\a\end{pmatrix} x \begin{pmatrix}a\\b\end{pmatrix} y \begin{pmatrix}b\\b\end{pmatrix} z \begin{pmatrix}a\\b\end{pmatrix} y \begin{pmatrix}b\\b\end{pmatrix}$$

(ii) An occurrence sequence of (i)

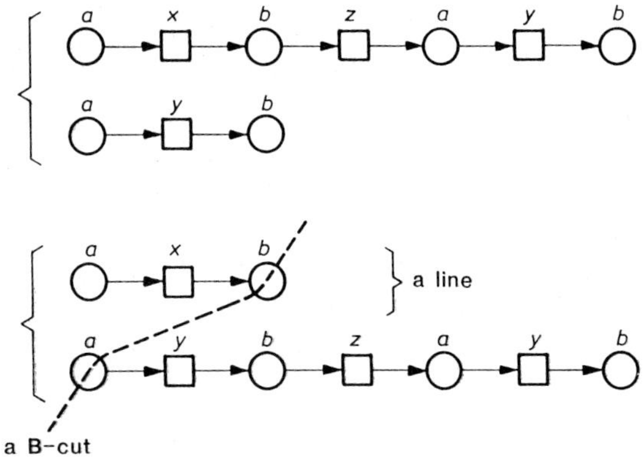

(iii) Two occurrence nets describing processes of (i)

Figure 1: A Simple Example

Definition 2.4 specifies the interleaved semantics of Petri nets. Often in the literature, instead of the full occurrence sequences defined in 2.4.2.4, one may find their restrictions to $T^\star \cup T^\omega$ (where $T^\star$ and T^ω are the sets of finite and infinite sequences over T, respectively):

$$\sigma = M_0 t_1 M_1 t_2 \ldots \longrightarrow \sigma_T = t_1 t_2 \ldots$$

The restricted sequences have often been called 'firing sequences' or 'transition sequences'. From a restricted sequence σ_T, the initial marking M_0 and the flow relation F, one may uniquely reconstruct the corresponding full occurrence sequence.

Pictorially, the S-elements of a net are represented by circles, the T-elements are represented by boxes, and the F relation is represented by arrows from boxes to circles or the other way round. Markings M are represented by placing $M(s)$ 'tokens' (black dots) on the place s. Figure 1 gives a simple example illustrating the main notions introduced so far (as well as anticipating the process notion).

The places 'a' and 'b' in Figure 1(i) might represent the 'free' state and the 'used' state, respectively, of a stock of resources. x and y then represent two (possibly conflicting) acts of claiming a resource for use, while z describes the freeing of a resource. The initial marking indicates that initially two resources are free and none is used. The occurrence sequence in Figure 1(ii) and the processes 1(iii) describe the (concurrent) claiming of the two resources and the freeing and re-claiming of one of them.

The events (labelled boxes) of the processes shown in Figure 1(iii) correspond to the transitions in the occurrence sequence σ of Figure 1(ii), so that they represent, in a sense, the same behaviour. However, in the processes some of the events are concurrent (unordered) and others are not, while in σ all transitions are ordered, so that no information concerning concurrency can be extracted from σ. The next definition specifies the additional information that may be used as an indication of concurrency; this will be made precise below.

Definition 2.5 *Concurrent enabling of transitions*

> *Let $N = (S, T, F, M_0)$ be a system net, M a reachable marking and t_1, t_2 two transitions. t_1 and t_2 are concurrently enabled under M iff $\forall s \in S$: $F(s,t_1) + F(s,t_2) \leq M(s)$.* □ 2.5

For instance, the initial marking of the net shown in Figure 1(i) concurrently enables x and y, although x and y appear sequentially in σ of Figure 1(ii). The clause $F(s,t_1) + F(s,t_2) \leq M(s)$ means that the input places of t_1 and t_2 must carry enough tokens. We do not require t_1 and t_2 to be different, so that a transition may be concurrently enabled to itself (an example being the transition z at the third marking of σ in Figure 1(ii)).

We also define an important systems property which will be needed later:

Definition 2.6 *1-safeness*

Let $\Sigma = (S, T, F, M_0)$ *be a system net.* Σ *is 1-safe iff* $\forall s \in S\ \forall M \in [M_0\rangle : M(s) \leq 1$.

□ 2.6

We now turn to the definition of the process semantics of Petri nets. This uses a special class of nets which we will introduce next, defining some useful notation first.

Notation 2.7 *Pre-sets and post-sets*

For $x \in S \cup T$, *we define* ${}^\bullet x = \{y \in T \cup S \mid (y, x) \in F\}$ *(the pre-set of x)* *and* $x^\bullet = \{y \in T \cup S \mid (x, y) \in F\}$ *(the post-set of x).*
For $Y \subseteq S \cup T$ *we define* ${}^\bullet Y = \bigcup_{x \in Y} {}^\bullet x$ *and* $Y^\bullet = \bigcup_{x \in Y} x^\bullet$.

□ 2.7

Definition 2.8 *Occurrence nets*

A net (S, T, F) *is an occurrence net iff*

(i) $\forall s \in S : |{}^\bullet s| \leq 1 \wedge |s^\bullet| \leq 1$, *and*

(ii) $F^\star$ *is acyclic, i.e.* $\forall x, y \in S \cup T : (x, y) \in F^\star \wedge (y, x) \in F^\star \Rightarrow x = y$ *(where* $F^\star$ *is the reflexive and transitive closure of F).*

□ 2.8

The S-elements of an occurrence net are usually called conditions and denoted by B. Conditions will be used to represent state holdings. The T-elements of an occurrence net are usually called events and denoted by E. They will be used to represent transition occurrences. 2.8(i) means that an occurrence net contains no non-deterministic choices, the idea being that all choices are resolved at the behaviour level. 2.8(ii) means that an occurrence net contains no cycles, the idea being that all loops are unfolded at the behaviour level. Because of 2.8(ii), the structure $(X, \preceq)$ derived from an occurrence net (B, E, F) by putting $X = B \cup E$ and $\preceq = F^\star$ is a partially ordered set (a poset).

Definition 2.9 *Lines and cuts*

Let $(X, \preceq)$ *be the poset derived from an occurrence net* $N = (B, E, F)$.

(i) $\prec = (\preceq \setminus id_X)$, $li = (\preceq \cup \succeq)$, $co = (X \times X \setminus li) \cup id_X$.

(ii) $l \subseteq X$ *is a li-set (chain) iff* $\forall x, y \in l : (x, y) \in li$;
$l \subseteq X$ *is a line iff l is a li-set and* $\forall z \in X \setminus l\ \exists x \in l : (x, z) \notin li$ *(i.e. l is maximal w.r.t. li);* $L(N)$ *is the set of lines of N.*

(iii) $c \subseteq X$ *is a co-set (antichain) iff* $\forall x, y \in c : (x, y) \in co$;
$c \subseteq X$ *is a cut iff c is a co-set and* $\forall z \in X \setminus c\ \exists x \in c : (x, z) \notin co$ *(i.e. c is maximal w.r.t. co); a cut c will be called a B-cut iff* $c \subseteq B$.

□ 2.9

The relations li and co denote sequentiality (ordering) and concurrency (absence of ordering), respectively. Lines may be interpreted as the 'sequential subprocesses' of (B, E, F) while cuts may be interpreted as the 'states' of (B, E, F). In particular, the B-cuts are related to the markings of a system net under a process labelling [2].

Notation 2.10 *Initial and final elements, intervals, upsets and downsets*

Let $N = (B, E, F)$ *be an occurrence net and let* $(X, \preceq)$ *be the associated poset.*

(i) $Min(N) = \{x \in X \mid {}^\bullet x = \emptyset\}$ *(the set of initial elements of N);*
$Max(N) = \{x \in X \mid x^\bullet = \emptyset\}$ *(the set of final elements of N);*
let us notice that $Min(N)$ *and* $Max(N)$ *are co-sets since* $b \prec b'$ *implies that* b' *has an input arc and b has an output arc.*

(ii) For co-sets $c_1, c_2 \subseteq X$: $[c_1, c_2] = \{z \in X \mid \exists x \in c_1 \exists y \in c_2 : x \preceq z \preceq y\}$ *(the interval between* c_1 *and* c_2*); for* $x \in X$ *we write* $[c_1, x]$ *and* $[x, c_2]$ *instead of, respectively,* $[c_1, \{x\}]$ *and* $[\{x\}, c_2]$.

(iii) For $A \subseteq X$, $\downarrow A = \{x \in X \mid \exists a \in A : x \preceq a\}$ *and* $\uparrow A = \{x \in X \mid \exists a \in A : a \preceq x\}$.

□ 2.10

To formulate the process definition we first need the following property defined for occurrence nets.

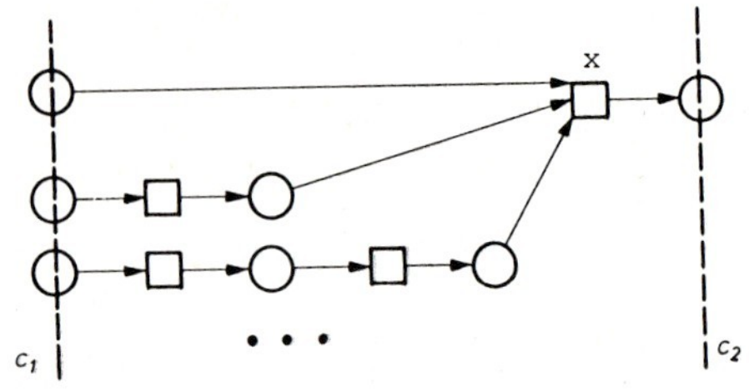

Figure 2: An occurrence net which is c_2-discrete but not c_1-discrete

Definition 2.11 *Discreteness with respect to a cut*

Let $N = (B, E, F)$ be an occurrence net and let c be a cut of N.
N is c-discrete iff $\forall x \in B \cup E\ \exists n = n(x) \in \mathbf{N}: \forall l \in L(N): |[c, x] \cap l| \le n$ and $|[x, c] \cap l| \le n$.
□ 2.11

The c-discreteness property requires that all elements of N have a 'finite distance' to c. Figure 2 illustrates this definition. To see that the net shown in Figure 2 is not c_1-discrete, consider the event x; for any $n \in \mathbf{N}$ a line l can be found such that $|[c_1, x] \cap l| > n$.

We shall now define processes formally. Mathematically speaking, they are labelled occurrence nets where the labelling specifies a relationship between the conditions and the events of the occurrence net and the places, the markings and the transitions of a given system net.

Definition 2.12 *Process axioms*

Let $\Sigma = (S, T, F, M_0)$ be a system net, $N = (B, E, F')$ an occurrence net and $p: B \cup E \to S \cup T$ a labelling of N. The pair $\pi = (N, p) = (B, E, F', p)$ is called a process of Σ iff

(i) $Min(N)$ *is a B-cut of* N.

(ii) N *is* $Min(N)$*-discrete.*

(iii) $p(B) \subseteq S$, $p(E) \subseteq T$.

(iv) $\forall e \in E\ \forall s \in S: F(s, p(e)) = |p^{-1}(s) \cap {}^\bullet e|$ *and* $F(p(e), s) = |p^{-1}(s) \cap e^\bullet|$.

(v) $\forall s \in S: M_0(s) = |p^{-1}(s) \cap Min(N)|$. □ 2.12

It may be noticed that the axioms 2.12(i) and (ii) only concern the occurrence net N, while the other axioms concern the labelling function p (and hence Σ and N). Axiom 2.12(iii) means that the conditions of N represent holdings of the places of Σ and that the events of N represent occurrences of the transitions of Σ. Axiom 2.12(i) means that N has a true 'starting point' (everything is accessible from $Min(N)$), and axiom 2.12(v) specifies that this initial cut corresponds to the initial marking of Σ in the sense that every condition in $Min(N)$ represents some token of M_0. Axiom 2.12(ii) requires that all elements of N are finitely reachable from $Min(N)$, in the sense that no ever-increasing li-sets are between $Min(N)$ and x. The intuitive significance of this axiom should be clear from the definition of c-discreteness. In section 3 below, we will show that this axiom allows a correspondence between processes and occurrence sequences to be established. Finally, axiom 2.12(iv) expresses the local conformity of N and Σ with respect to p: transition environments are respected. This encodes the transition rule 2.3(ii): the set ${}^\bullet e$ ($e^\bullet$) models the tokens consumed (produced, respectively), by the occurrence of the transition $p(e)$. The axioms are independent of each other, except for (i) which is a necessary precondition for (ii) and $p(E) \subseteq T$ which is a necessary precondition for (iv).

[2] shows that processes of (countable) system nets are again countable. Moreover, axiom 2.12(iv) together with the T-restrictedness of system nets implies that the occurrence nets of processes are also T-restricted, so that $Min(N) \subseteq B$ and $Max(N) \subseteq B$, justifying the fact that we consider only B-cuts in 2.12(i).

Processes may be finite or infinite; the following is a reasonable notion of finiteness:

Definition 2.13 *Event-finiteness and reachable B-cuts*

Let $\pi = (B, E, F, p)$ be a process of $\Sigma = (S, T, F, M_0)$.

(i) π is **event-finite** *iff $|E| \in \mathbf{N}$.*

(ii) A B-cut c of π is **reachable** *iff $|E \cap \downarrow c| \in \mathbf{N}$.* □ 2.13

Event-finiteness corresponds to the finiteness of occurrence sequences as has been defined in 2.4(i). The reachable B-cuts of π correspond to the markings that may occur in the sequences corresponding to π [2].

There is also the notion of an initial part, or prefix, of a process which is analogous to what has been defined in 2.4(ii) for occurrence sequences. Given a cut c of a process, we may define the portions below c and above c of the process:

Notation 2.14 $\Downarrow(c, \pi)$ *and* $\Uparrow(c, \pi)$

Let $\pi = (B, E, F, p)$ be a process of Σ and let c be a B-cut of π.

(i) $\Downarrow(c, \pi) = (B \cap \downarrow c, E \cap \downarrow c, F' \cap (\downarrow c \times \downarrow c), p|_{(\downarrow c)})$.

(ii) $\Uparrow(c, \pi) = (B \cap \uparrow c, E \cap \uparrow c, F' \cap (\uparrow c \times \uparrow c), p|_{(\uparrow c)})$. □ 2.14

It is routine to check that $\Downarrow(c, \pi)$ is again a process of Σ (if π is).

When considering a process π of a system Σ, we shall not be interested in the exact nature of the sets used to define the conditions and the events of π. Rather, we are only interested in their interconnections and in the labelling which relates π to Σ. Hence we may assume the conditions and the events of all processes we shall henceforth consider to be taken from a (large enough) fixed common set. Furthermore, processes which are isomorphic in the following sense shall not be distinguished because they represent the same interconnection and labelling patterns:

Definition 2.15 *Isomorphism of processes*

Let $\pi_1 = (B_1, E_1, F_1, p_1)$ and $\pi_2 = (B_2, E_2, F_2, p_2)$ be two processes of Σ.
π_1 and π_2 are isomorphic (in symbols: $\pi_1 \cong \pi_2$) iff there is a bijection β: $B_1 \cup E_1 \rightarrow B_2 \cup E_2$ such that:

(i) $\forall x \in B_1 \cup E_1$: $p_1(x) = p_2(\beta(x))$

(ii) $\forall x_1, x_2 \in B_1 \cup E_1$: $x_1 \prec_1 x_2 \Leftrightarrow \beta(x_1) \prec_2 \beta(x_2)$ □ 2.15

Clearly, $\cong$ is an equivalence relation. From now on, whenever we speak of two different processes we mean two non-isomorphic processes.

3 Finite Synchronisation

In the last section, the notion of a process was introduced axiomatically. Since processes are intended to capture the behaviour of a system, it should be possible to define them, in some way, operationally or inductively. One may think of a process being generated by applying the transition rule several times in succession. For example, the processes shown in Figure 1(iii) may be related to the occurrence sequence shown in Figure 1(ii) in the sense that both may be generated from that sequence. The next definition formalises this idea.

Definition 3.1 *Associating processes to occurrence sequences*

Let $\Sigma = (S, T, F, M_0)$ be a system net and let $\sigma = M_0 t_1 M_1 \ldots$ be an occurrence sequence of Σ. To σ we associate a set $\Pi(\sigma)$ of (what will turn out to be) processes of Σ by defining a construction to produce the elements $\pi = (N, p)$ of $\Pi(\sigma)$.
To this end, we construct successively embedded labelled occurrence nets $(N_i, p_i) = (B_i, E_i, F_i, p_i)$ where $p_i\colon B_i \cup E_i \to S \cup T$, by induction on i.

$i = 0$: *Define $E_0 = F_0 = \emptyset$ and B_0 as containing, for each $s \in S$, $M_0(s)$ distinct conditions b with $p_0(b) = s$ (this defines p_0 as well).*

$i \to i+1$: *Suppose $(N_i, p_i) = (B_i, E_i, F_i, p_i)$ to be constructed.*
For each $s \in {}^\bullet t_{i+1}$ we choose a condition $b(s) \in Max(N_i) \cap p_i^{-1}(s)$; then we add a new event e with $p_{i+1}(e) = t_{i+1}$ and $(b(s), e) \in F_{i+1}$ for all $s \in {}^\bullet t_{i+1}$.
Also, for each $s \in t_{i+1}^\bullet$ we add a new condition $b'(s)$ with $p_{i+1}(b'(s)) = s$ and $(e, b'(s)) \in F_{i+1}$.
For $x, y \in B_i \cup E_i$, $p_{i+1}(x) = p_i(x)$ and $(x,y) \in F_i \Leftrightarrow (x,y) \in F_{i+1}$.

If σ is finite then the construction stops at $i = |\sigma|$, and we put $\pi = (N_{|\sigma|}, p_{|\sigma|})$.
If σ is infinite then we put $\pi = (N, p)$ with $N = (\bigcup_i B_i, \bigcup_i E_i; \bigcup_i F_i)$ and $p = \bigcup_i p_i$.
Finally, $\Pi(\sigma) = \{\pi \mid \pi$ may be constructed as above $\}$. □ 3.1

In order to show that this construction makes sense, we have to show that for every $i \geq 0$ and $s \in {}^\bullet t_{i+1}$ there is always at least one $b(s)$ in $Max(N_i) \cap p_i^{-1}(s)$. However, this easily follows from the construction as shown in [2].

The construction is non-deterministic because, in general, there may be more than one $b \in Max(N_i) \cap p_i^{-1}(s)$. For example, both processes shown in Figure 1(iii) are in $\Pi(\sigma)$ (in fact, they constitute $\Pi(\sigma)$) if σ is the occurrence sequence shown in Figure 1(ii).

The consistency of the process axioms with respect to definition 3.1 may be expressed as follows:

Theorem 3.2 *Consistency of the process axioms w.r.t. occurrence sequences*

All $\pi \in \Pi(\sigma)$ satisfy the process axioms 2.12.

Proof: Easy; see [2]. □ 3.2

The converse of this theorem will be dealt with later. We define the 'inverse' of the Π operator:

Definition 3.3 *The Lin-set of a process*

Let π be a process of Σ. $Lin(\pi) = \{\sigma \mid \sigma$ is an occurrence sequence of Σ and $\pi \in \Pi(\sigma)\}$. □ 3.3

Next we will investigate construction 3.1 for the important case of 1-safe nets.

Theorem 3.4 *The special case of 1-safe nets*

Let Σ be a 1-safe system net and let σ be an occurrence sequence of Σ.
Then all processes in $\Pi(\sigma)$ are isomorphic to each other.

Proof: The construction in definition 3.1 is in this case deterministic (up to the choice of nodes), since $M_i(s) \leq 1$ (by 1-safeness) implies $|Max(N_i) \cap p_i^{-1}(s)| \leq 1$.
Hence π that may be constructed from σ is unique (up to isomorphism). □ 3.4

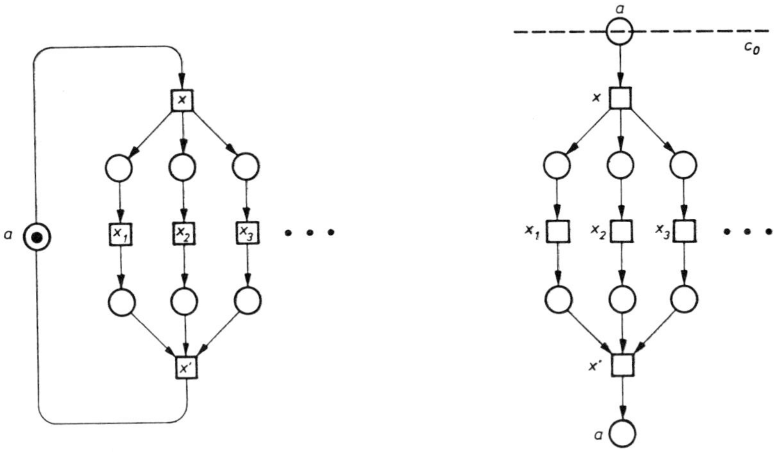

(i) A system net (ii) A process of (i)

Figure 3: A process which cannot be generated by occurrence sequences

We may remark that when isomorphic processes are identified, the statement of theorem 3.4 may be expressed more simply as $|\Pi(\sigma)| = 1$. In other words, for 1-safe nets, every occurrence sequence has one and only one associated process.

We now turn to the converse of theorem 3.2: are all objects satisfying the process axioms 2.12 producible by means of construction 3.1? First we turn to a counterexample. Figure 3 shows an infinite system net (3(i)) and a labelled occurrence net (3(ii)) which satisfies all of the process axioms 2.12.

There is clearly no occurrence sequence which can generate the process shown in Figure 3(ii); for example, an attempt $xx_1x_2\ldots$ (markings omitted) will fail to include the transition x'. On the other hand, one may argue that the process shown in Figure 3(ii) does describe a meaningful 'behaviour' of the system shown in Figure 3(i). (The interpretation of such a behaviour is also examined in [2].) This example shows that, in general, processes describe 'more' behaviour than do occurrence sequences. However, there is a large and practically interesting class of system nets for which a converse of theorem 3.2 holds true:

Definition 3.5 *Finite synchronisation*

A net (S,T,F) is of finite synchronisation iff $\forall t \in T: |{}^\bullet t| < \infty \wedge |t^\bullet| < \infty$. □ 3.5

The name 'finite synchronisation' arises from the similarity of this property to the more well known property of 'bounded nondeterminism' (or better: 'finite nondeterminism') [6].

Then we have the following:

Theorem 3.6 *Completeness of the process axioms w.r.t. occurrence sequences*

Let Σ be a system net of finite synchronisation and let π be a process of Σ according to definition 2.12. Then there is an occurrence sequence σ of Σ such that $\pi \in \Pi(\sigma)$.

Proof: [2]. □ 3.6

We may remark that the essential consequence of finite synchronisation, together with axiom 2.12(ii), is the fact that E can be linearised in an appropriate way, i.e. such that the resulting linear order is both compatible with the given partial order and order-isomorphic to the natural numbers or to an initial segment thereof. The remaining part of 3.6 consists of a standard construction of suitable B-cuts of π corresponding to the intermediate markings, so that, by axiom 2.12(iv), the alternate sequence of markings and transitions corresponding to (any) such linearisation indeed is an occurrence sequence from which π may be reconstructed. Axiom 2.12(ii), together with finite synchronisation, is only a sufficient (not a necessary) condition for the possibility of linearising E suitably. The exact conditions have been investigated in [2].

Systems of finite synchronisation (which include, of course, all finite systems) are really the main cases of practical interest. Occurrence sequences are the appropriate semantics of a concurrent system if one assumes the presence of a central scheduling mechanism; hence theorem 3.6 can be interpreted as stating that for systems of finite synchronisation, central scheduling is (in principle) sufficient to generate all interesting behaviours. However, it is also clear that a process of a system net contains 'more information' than does any of its corresponding occurrence sequences, even if the system is of finite synchronisation. Exactly *what* is lost if one switches from processes to occurrence sequences will be studied in the next section.

4 An Equivalence Result

Thus far, the relationship between occurrence sequences and processes was investigated in a general way. There is a sense in which the class of behaviours defined by occurrence sequences is more restricted than the class of behaviours defined by the process axioms. This was shown by Figure 3, the essential idea being that the poset shown there cannot be linearised order-isomorphically to the set of natural numbers. In the presence of finite synchronisation, no examples of this nature can be found. That is to say, every process of a system of finite synchronisation has at least one linearisation which is an occurrence sequence.

However, these results leave open several questions concerning the details of the relationship between processes and occurrence sequences. For instance, we may observe that a process determines a partial ordering on the set of its events while an occurrence sequence determines a linear ordering on the set of the transition (positions) it contains. Hence a process contains concurrency information which is absent in any single associated occurrence sequence. Construction 3.1 reflects this by the fact that it depends, in addition to a given occurrence sequence, on the F relation of the original net. It may be asked, however, whether a process is in some way determined by the *set* of all of its occurrence sequence linearisations. More generally, one might also enquire whether the set af all processes is in some way reconstructible from the set of all occurrence sequences, and vice versa.

We will start by observing that there are two main differences between a process π and an occurrence sequence in $Lin(\pi)$. The first difference is the partial ordering aspect already mentioned. The second difference is the fact that in π, the individualities of several tokens on the same place may be distinguished while an occurrence sequence provides no means to distinguish tokens on the same place. Construction 3.1 reflects this by the fact that it is non-deterministic. Consequently, different processes may correspond to the same sequence, as illustrated by Figure 1. Other examples, to be given later in this paper, show that two processes which correspond to a single sequence may be very gravely different.

Let us study these two points of difference between occurrence sequences and processes in more detail. Obviously, we will have to restrict our discussion to system nets of finite synchronisation, since no general connection between sequences and processes could otherwise be assumed.

Notation 4.1 *Restriction to countable system nets of finite synchronisation*

> *Throughout sections 4 to 6, $\Sigma = (S, T, F, M_0)$ will denote a countable T-restricted system net of finite synchronisation.* □ 4.1

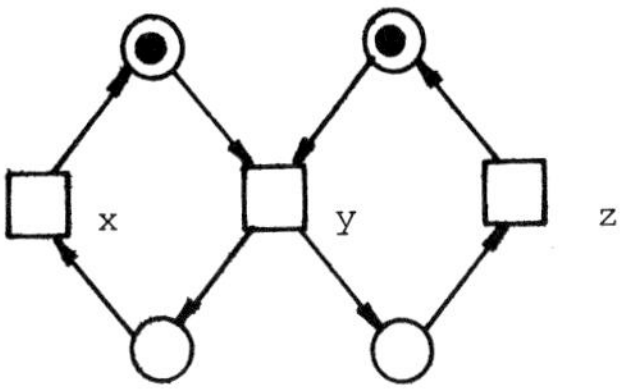

(i) A system net

$\sigma_1 = yxzyxz$

$\sigma_2 = yzxyxz$

$\sigma_3 = yzxyzx$

(ii) Three occurrence sequences (markings omitted)

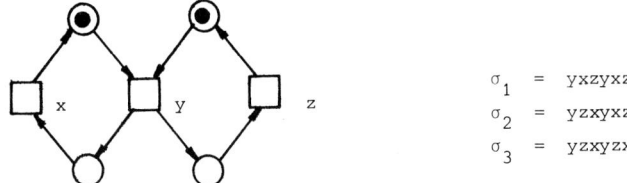

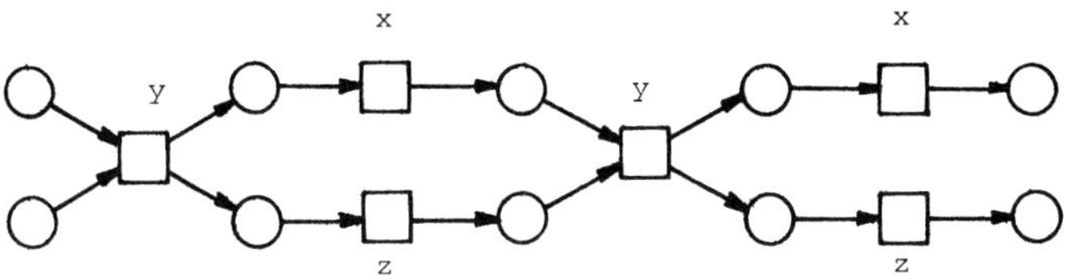

(iii) A process

Figure 4: Illustrating the meaning of $\equiv_0^\star$

If a process π of Σ contains two concurrent events then one may find two sequences in $Lin(\pi)$ in which two transitions corresponding to these two events appear as neighbours in different order and are concurrently enabled by the marking preceding them (the two sequences may be equal if the two events have the same label). This suggests to investigate occurrence sequences which differ only in the order of neighbouring concurrently enabled transitions.

Definition 4.2 *The relation $\equiv_0$ on occurrence sequences*

Let σ_1, σ_2 be occurrence sequences of Σ.
Then $\sigma_1 \equiv_0 \sigma_2$ iff $\sigma_1 = \sigma_{11} t M_1 t' \sigma_{12}$ and $\sigma_2 = \sigma_{21} t' M_2 t \sigma_{22}$ such that $\sigma_{11} = \sigma_{21}$, $\sigma_{12} = \sigma_{22}$, and $last(\sigma_{11}) = last(\sigma_{21})$ concurrently enables t and t'. □ 4.2

In some way, the relation $\equiv_0$ is intended to capture the concurrency which is absent in the occurrence sequences; $\equiv_0$-related sequences could be interpreted as denoting 'a same concurrent behaviour'. Consider Figure 4; all three occurrence sequences shown in Figure 4(ii) are related to the same concurrent behaviour, namely the process shown in Figure 4(iii). The sequences σ_1 and σ_3 shown in Figure 4(ii) differ not in one but in two $\equiv_0$- exchanges. In general, therefore, one is interested in the reflexive and transitive closure $\equiv_0^\star$ of $\equiv_0$.

However, the reflexive and transitive closure of $\equiv_0$ may be insufficient for infinite occurrence sequences. To appreciate this problem, consider Figure 5. The two occurrence sequences σ_1, σ_2 of Figure 5(ii) should intuitively be $\equiv_0^\infty$-related because they arise from each other through exchanging neighbouring concurrently enabled transitions (and have a common associated process, as shown in Figure 5(iii)). However, a finite number of exchanges is not enough to transform σ_1 into σ_2 or conversely. We should like to iterate $\equiv_0$-exchanges 'infinitely often', but in a 'fair' way in order not to lose transitions; for instance, in the example shown in Figure 5, we do not wish to push away the y's infinitely far so as to obtain a sequence with only x's. In order to express this in terms of finite applications of $\equiv_0$ we propose the definition which follows.

Definition 4.3 *The equivalence $\equiv_0^\infty$ on sequences*

Let σ_1 and σ_2 be occurrence sequences of Σ.

(i) A system net

σ_1 = xyxyxy ...
σ_2 = yxyxyx ...

(ii) Two infinite occurrence sequences (markings omitted)

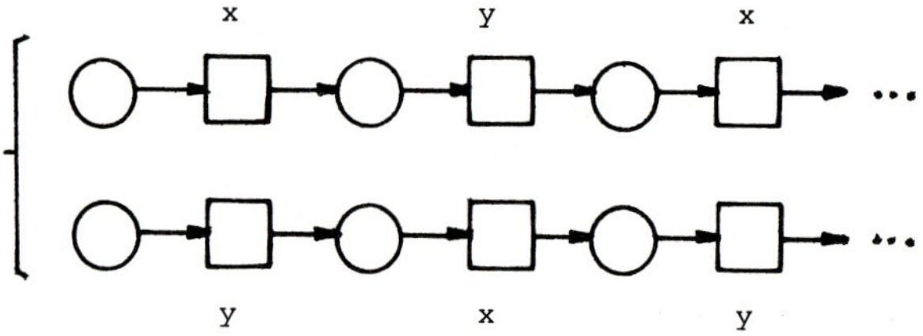

(iii) A process of (i) contained in $\Pi(\sigma_1) \cap \Pi(\sigma_2)$

Figure 5: Illustrating the definition of $\equiv_0^\infty$

(i) Let $n \in \mathbf{N}$; then $\sigma_1 \,{}_n\!\!= \sigma_2$ iff $\sigma_1 = \sigma_2$ or $\exists \sigma, w_1, w_2$: $|\sigma| = n$ and $\sigma_1 = \sigma w_1$ and $\sigma_2 = \sigma w_2$ and w_1, w_2 are either both infinite or have the same finite length. (This means that σ_1, σ_2 have equal lengths and agree on the prefix of length n; if they are shorter than n then they must be equal altogether.)

(ii) $\sigma_1 \equiv_0^\infty \sigma_2$ iff $\forall n \in \mathbf{N}$: $\exists \sigma_1', \sigma_2'$: $(\sigma_1 \equiv_0^\star \sigma_1'$ and $\sigma_1' \,{}_n\!\!= \sigma_2$ and $\sigma_2 \equiv_0^\star \sigma_2'$ and $\sigma_2' \,{}_n\!\!= \sigma_1)$.

□ 4.3

In other words, $\sigma_1 \equiv_0^\infty \sigma_2$ iff for any arbitrarily long prefix, σ_1 can be $\equiv_0^\star$-transformed into another sequence σ_1' that agrees with σ_2 on that prefix, and vice versa. When applied to finite sequences, $\equiv_0^\infty$ comes to the same as $\equiv_0^\star$.

It may be mentioned that this definition is not the only possible one; [1] discusses another attempt which looks easier but fails because of the lacking transitivity. For 4.3 we have transitivity:

Theorem 4.4 *Correctness of definition* 4.3

> $\equiv_0^\infty$ *is an equivalence on the set of occurrence sequences of* Σ.

Proof: [1]. □ 4.4

So far in our examples, two sequences were $\equiv_0^\infty$-related whenever they were contained in the *Lin*-set of some common process. We shall see below that this is always true. However, the *Lin*-sets of processes by no means coincide with the $\equiv_0^\infty$-equivalence classes. To see this we may consider Figure 6.

Figure 6(iii,iv) depicts two processes π_1, π_2 whose *Lin*-sets overlap. Furthermore, the $\equiv_0^\infty$-equivalence class shown in Figure 6(ii) agrees neither with $Lin(\pi_1)$ nor with $Lin(\pi_2)$, nor is it the *Lin*-set of any other process. Hence there is no obvious relationship between processes, their *Lin*-sets and the $\equiv_0^\infty$-equivalence classes.

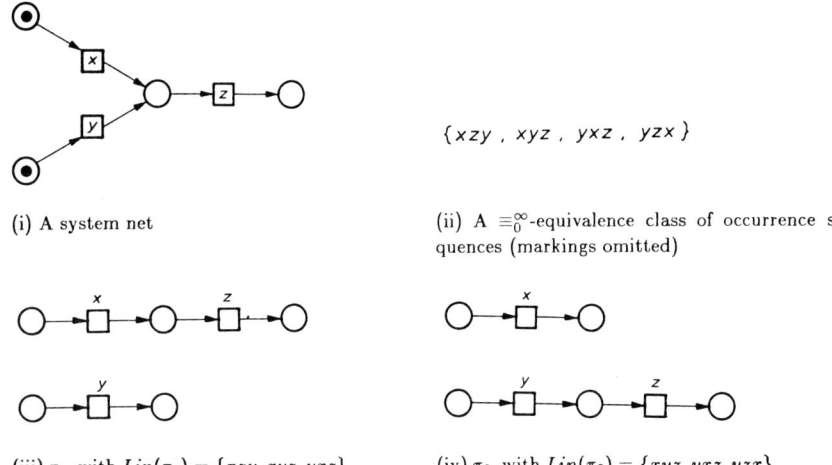

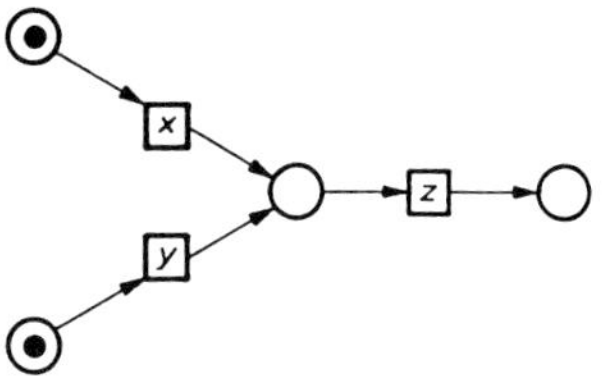

(i) A system net

$\{xzy\ ,\ xyz\ ,\ yxz\ ,\ yzx\}$

(ii) A $\equiv_0^\infty$-equivalence class of occurrence sequences (markings omitted)

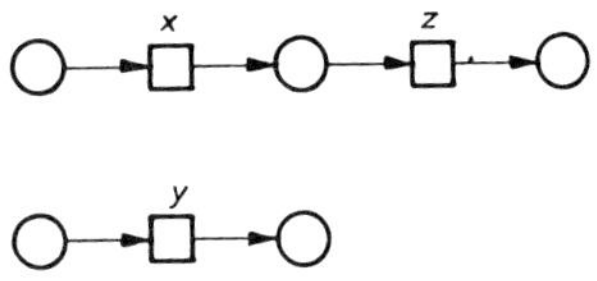

(iii) π_1, with $Lin(\pi_1) = \{xzy, xyz, yxz\}$

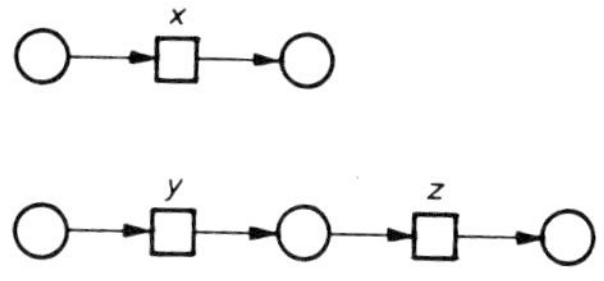

(iv) π_2, with $Lin(\pi_2) = \{xyz, yxz, yzx\}$

Figure 6: Two processes whose Lin-sets overlap and are not $\equiv_0^\infty$-equivalence classes

Now, in order to discover why distinct processes may have a common linearisation, let us have a closer look at why construction 3.1 may lead to π_1 and π_2 in Figure 6 from their common occurrence sequence xyz: the divergence occurs when adding an event labelled by z since then we have the choice between two conditions labelled c to connect it to. This means that besides the partial ordering aspect, one of the main differences between sequences and processes is that processes distinguish the individualities of several tokens on the same place while occurrence sequences consider them as indistinguishable. The $\equiv_1^\infty$ relation on processes will be introduced to abstract from this distinction. Its basic building block is a *swap* transformation which swaps the forward rôle of two conditions with the same label.

Definition 4.5 *The swap transformation*

Let $\pi = (N,p) = (B,E,F',p)$ be a process of Σ and let b_1, b_2 be two conditions of N with the same label: $p(b_1) = p(b_2)$.
We define $swap(\pi, b_1, b_2) = \hat{\pi} = (B, E, \hat{F}', p)$ where $\forall b \in B\ \forall e \in E$:

$$\hat{F}'(e,b) = F'(e,b) \text{ and}$$

$$\hat{F}'(b,e) = \begin{cases} F'(b,e) & \text{if } b_1 \neq b \neq b_2 \\ F'(b_2,e) & \text{if } b = b_1 \\ F'(b_1,e) & \text{if } b = b_2 \end{cases}$$

□ 4.5

Schematically, this corresponds to the transformation shown in Figure 7.

We may observe that *swap* does not always give rise to a process. Rather, the following is true:

Theorem 4.6 *Characterisation of swap*

Let $\pi = (N,p)$ be a process of Σ and b_1, b_2 two conditions of N with $p(b_1) = p(b_2)$.
Then $swap(\pi, b_1, b_2)$ is a process of $\Sigma \iff b_1$ and b_2 are co-related in N.

Proof: From the acyclicity of processes [2]. □ 4.6

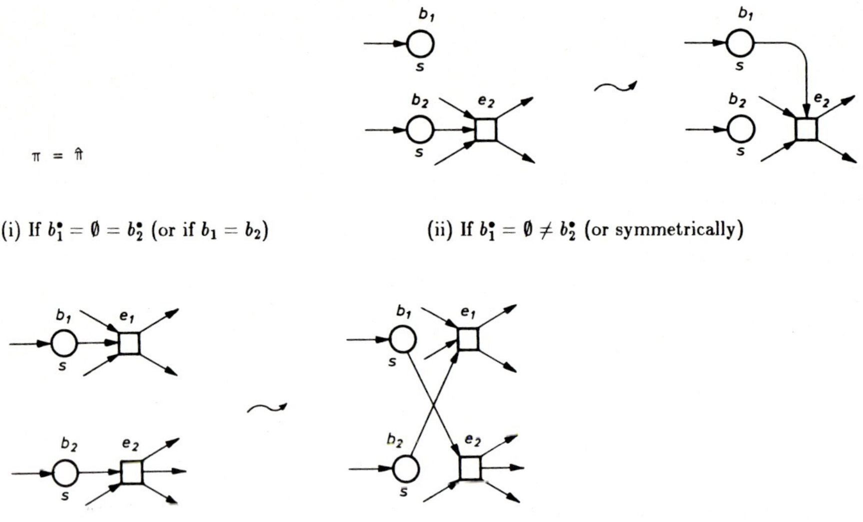

(i) If $b_1^\bullet = \emptyset = b_2^\bullet$ (or if $b_1 = b_2$)

(ii) If $b_1^\bullet = \emptyset \neq b_2^\bullet$ (or symmetrically)

(iii) If $b_1^\bullet \neq \emptyset \neq b_2^\bullet$

Figure 7: The *swap* transformation

We may also observe that *swap* is symmetric in b_1 and b_2:

$$swap(\pi, b_1, b_2) = swap(\pi, b_2, b_1),$$

and that it is involutive: applying it twice with the same conditions b_1, b_2 reconstructs the original process:

$$swap(swap(\pi, b_1, b_2), b_1, b_2) = \pi.$$

We may now define:

Definition 4.7 *The relation $\equiv_1$ for processes*

Let π_1, π_2 be two processes of Σ.
We shall say that $\pi_1 \equiv_1 \pi_2$ iff $\exists b_1, b_2$ conditions in π_1 with the same label such that π_2 is (isomorphic to) $swap(\pi_1, b_1, b_2)$. □ 4.7

Due to the fact that *swap* is involutive, it may easily be seen that the relation $\equiv_1$ is symmetrical: $\pi_1 \equiv_1 \pi_2 \iff \pi_2 \equiv_1 \pi_1$. As usual, $\equiv_1^\star$ will denote the reflexive and transitive closure of $\equiv_1$.

The discussion on Figure 6 suggests that there should be a strong relationship between the fact that two processes are $\equiv_1^\star$-related and the fact that their compatible occurrence sequences are the same, or $\equiv_0^\star$-related. To consolidate this intuition, we first have to generalise the $\equiv_1^\star$ relation to infinite processes. This can be done in the same way as $\equiv_0^\star$ has been generalised to infinite sequences in definition 4.3 and is achieved by the next definition.

Definition 4.8 *The $\equiv_1^\infty$ relation for processes*

Let π_1, π_2 be two processes of Σ.

$\pi_1 \equiv_1^\infty \pi_2$ *iff* $\forall$ *reachable B-cut* c_2 *of* π_2 $\exists$ *process* π_1' *of* Σ $\exists$ *reachable cut* c_1' *of* π_1' *such that* $\pi_1 \equiv_1^* \pi_1' \wedge \Downarrow(c_1', \pi_1') \cong \Downarrow(c_2, \pi_2)$.

and $\forall$ *reachable B-cut* c_1 *of* π_1 $\exists$ *process* π_2' *of* Σ $\exists$ *reachable cut* c_2' *of* π_2' *such that* $\pi_2 \equiv_1^* \pi_2' \wedge \Downarrow(c_2', \pi_2') \cong \Downarrow(c_1, \pi_1)$. □ 4.8

That is, $\pi_1 \equiv_1^\infty \pi_2$ iff π_2 can be derived from π_1 by applying the *swap* operation, possibly 'infinitely often', in succession. Clearly, $\equiv_1^\infty$ reduces to $\equiv_1^*$ for finite processes.

Notice that the definition of $\equiv_1^\infty$ on processes is formally similar to the definition of $\equiv_0^\infty$ on sequences. There is also a similar result:

Theorem 4.9 *Correctness of definition* 4.8

$\equiv_1^\infty$ *is an equivalence relation on the processes of* Σ.

Proof: The proof is a technical exercise; it is given in [2]. □ 4.9

Being an equivalence, $\equiv_1^\infty$ partitions the set of processes of Σ into equivalence classes. We will now prove the main result of this section which states that the $\equiv_0^\infty$-classes of occurrence sequences and the $\equiv_1^\infty$-classes of processes of a given system Σ are in bijection with each other. More precisely, we intend to show that if π_1 and π_2 are processes of Σ and $\sigma_1 \in Lin(\pi_1)$, $\sigma_2 \in Lin(\pi_2)$ then

$$\sigma_1 \equiv_0^\infty \sigma_2 \text{ iff } \pi_1 \equiv_1^\infty \pi_2.$$

The proof of this result requires several auxiliary results all of which are symmetrical with respect to $\equiv_0$ and $\equiv_1$. The first of these results states that finite occurrence sequences which have a common associated process are $\equiv_0^*$-related, and similarly that event-finite processes which have a common linearisation are $\equiv_1^*$-related.

Theorem 4.10 *Common processes or sequences imply* $\equiv$

(i) If σ_1 *and* σ_2 *are finite occurrence sequences of* Σ *with* $\Pi(\sigma_1) \cap \Pi(\sigma_2) \neq \emptyset$, *then* $\sigma_1 \equiv_0^* \sigma_2$.

(ii) If π_1 *and* π_2 *are event-finite processes of* Σ *with* $Lin(\pi_1) \cap Lin(\pi_2) \neq \emptyset$, *then* $\pi_1 \equiv_1^* \pi_2$.

Proof: The proof of (i) can be found in [1]; it works by constructing an appropriate sequence of $\equiv_0$-exchanges of σ_1 (or of σ_2) directly.
(ii), on the other hand, is a consequence of the way π_1 and π_2 may be (re)constructed from a common σ by construction 3.1: at each step, up to an isomorphism, the two constructions may only differ by the choice of the input conditions for the new events. Since the system is of finite synchronisation, this means that there is a finite set of *swaps* that leads from one construction to the other. The property then results from the finite number of steps due to the finiteness of σ. □ 4.10

Theorem 4.10 extends to infinite occurrence sequences and infinite processes. However, this extension will be implied by the main result of this section, so that we do not need to prove it here. The converses of theorem 4.10 are not true. Figure 6 shows a counterexample to the converse of 4.10(i) while Figure 8 shows a counterexample to the converse of 4.10(ii).

Despite these counterexamples, there exists a partial converse of the previous theorem:

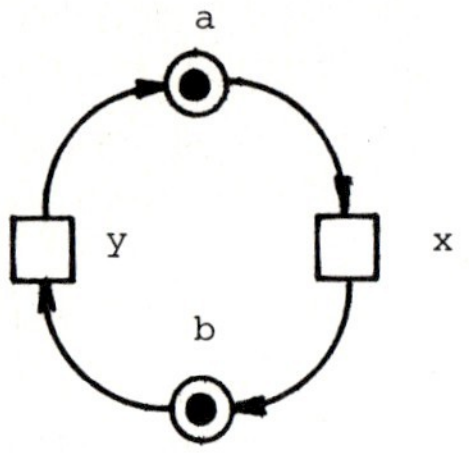

(i) A system net

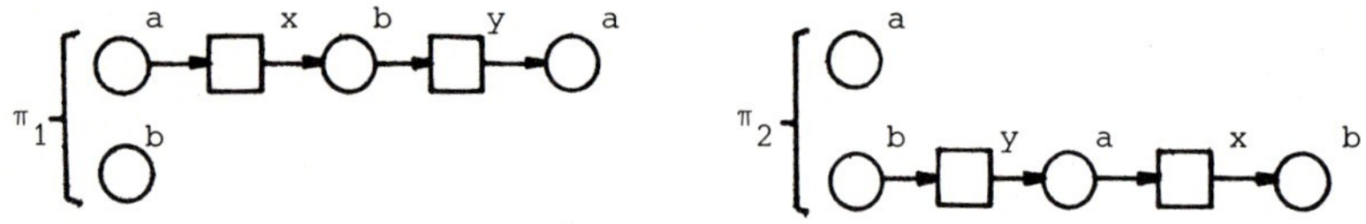

(ii) Two processes of (i) which are $\equiv_1^2$-related but have no common linearisation

Figure 8: Processes which are $\equiv_1^\star$-related but have no common linearisation

Theorem 4.11 *Partial converse of* 4.10

> *(i) If σ_1, σ_2 are occurrence sequences of Σ and $\sigma_1 \equiv_0 \sigma_2$ then $\Pi(\sigma_1) \cap \Pi(\sigma_2) \neq \emptyset$.*
>
> *(ii) If π_1, π_2 are processes of Σ and $\pi_1 \equiv_1 \pi_2$ then $Lin(\pi_1) \cap Lin(\pi_2) \neq \emptyset$.*

Proof: (i) simply follows from construction 3.1: if M concurrently enables two transitions then we may add the corresponding labelled events in such a (separate) way that the order of their incorporation makes no difference.
To prove (ii), theorem 4.6 is needed to show that two equally labelled conditions whose rôles are swapped are concurrent; a result from [2] can then be used to show that the two conditions are contained in some reachable B-cut. An occurrence sequence leading up to this cut can be extended to be compatible with both π_1 and π_2. □ 4.11

The last result may, in fact, be used to prove the following stronger version of itself:

Theorem 4.12 *Stronger version of* 4.11

> *(i) If σ_1, σ_2 are occurrence sequences of Σ, $\sigma_1 \equiv_0 \sigma_2$, and $\pi_1 \in \Pi(\sigma_1)$ then $\exists \pi_2 \in \Pi(\sigma_1) \cap \Pi(\sigma_2)$: $\pi_1 \equiv_1^\star \pi_2$.*
>
> *(ii) If π_1, π_2 are processes of Σ, $\pi_1 \equiv_1 \pi_2$, and $\sigma_1 \in Lin(\pi_1)$ then $\exists \sigma_2 \in Lin(\pi_1) \cap Lin(\pi_2)$: $\sigma_1 \equiv_0^\star \sigma_2$.*

Proof: (i) can be proved by applying 4.11(i) in combination with 4.10(ii);
(ii) can be proved by applying 4.11(ii) in combination with 4.10(i). See [2]. □ 4.12

Theorem 4.12(i) is stronger than 4.11(i) in the sense that for any given $\pi_1 \in \Pi(\sigma_1)$, the $\pi_2 \in \Pi(\sigma_1) \cap \Pi(\sigma_2)$ can be chosen in a particular way, namely such that $\pi_1 \equiv_1^\star \pi_2$ holds true. 4.12(ii) is stronger than 4.11(ii) in a similar sense. We are now prepared to state the main result of this section:

Theorem 4.13 *Equivalence between $\equiv_1^\infty$-classes of processes and $\equiv_0^\infty$-classes of sequences*

> *Let σ_1, σ_2 be occurrence sequences of Σ and let $\pi_1 = (B_1, E_1, F_1, p_1)$ and $\pi_2 = (B_2, E_2, F_2, p_2)$ be processes of Σ such that $\pi_1 \in \Pi(\sigma_1)$ and $\pi_2 \in \Pi(\sigma_2)$. Then $\sigma_1 \equiv_0^\infty \sigma_2$ iff $\pi_1 \equiv_1^\infty \pi_2$.*

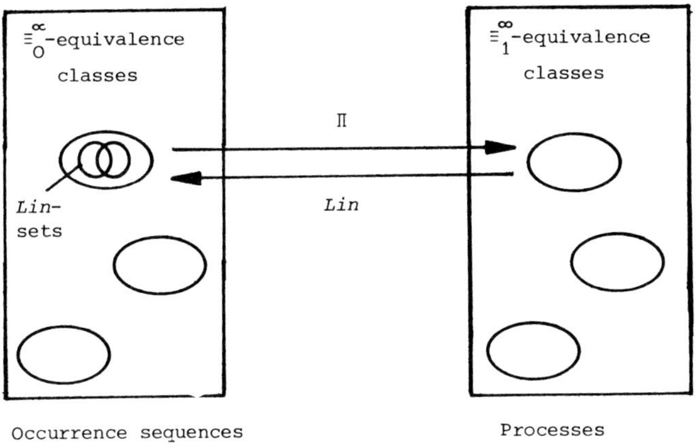

Figure 9: Correspondence between occurrence sequences and processes

Proof: To prove part ($\Rightarrow$) of this theorem, we assume c_2 to be a reachable B-cut of π_2 and we wish to construct a suitable process π_1' which satisfies the definition 4.8. To this end, we must take a large enough prefix of σ_2 (say, of length n) such that all events below c_2 are related to transitions of this prefix. Then using the definition of $\equiv_0^\infty$ and theorem 4.12(i) repeatedly, a process π' can be constructed which is 'almost' the desired one, except that it may fail to contain a B-cut c_1 with the desired properties. Hence π_1' must be glued together, using π_2 (up to position n) and π' (from position n onwards); it must be shown that this is possible and that the result is a process of the right kind.

To prove part ($\Leftarrow$), a similar (though somewhat more complicated) argument can be used [2]. □ **4.13**

Having proved these results clarifies the overall picture. The equivalences $\equiv_0^\infty$ and $\equiv_1^\infty$ partition the set of occurrence sequences and the set of processes, respectively, into equivalence classes such that the relations Π and *Lin* define a bijection on these classes (see Figure 9).

It may be asked whether the equivalences $\equiv_0^\infty$ and $\equiv_1^\infty$ are the finest equivalence relations which ensure this bijection. For finite sequences and processes, the answer is affirmative and results immediately from theorems 4.10 and 4.11: the finest equivalence relation on sequences which respects Π and *Lin* can be expressed as $(Lin \circ \Pi)^*$, but from 4.10(i) and 4.11(i) it is immediate that $(Lin \circ \Pi)^*$ equals $\equiv_0^*$. Conversely, $(\Pi \circ Lin)^*$ equals $\equiv_1^*$ from 4.10(ii) and 4.11(ii), that is, $\equiv_1^*$ is the finest equivalence relation on (finite) processes which respects *Lin* and Π. The corresponding question for infinite sequences and processes is still open.

5 1-Safe Systems

We shall now show that for 1-safe nets, the general theory just outlined becomes much simpler and more perspicuous. Since concurrent programs can be dealt with essentially in the same way as with 1-safe nets (see [2]), 1-safeness is of great practical importance.

First, we may recall from [10] that for 1-safe nets there exists a simple relation which (intuitively speaking) 'generates' concurrency and is expressible in terms of the structure of the original net only:

Definition 5.1 *The independence relation*

Let $\Sigma = (S, T, F, M_0)$ *and let* $t, t' \in T$. t *indep* t' *iff* $({}^\bullet t \cup t^\bullet) \cap ({}^\bullet t' \cup t'^\bullet) = \emptyset$. □ 5.1

Intuitively, t *indep* t' means that t and t' do not directly influence each other, their surroundings (in terms of places) being disjoint. If two such transitions are neighbours in an occurrence sequence then they can be $\equiv_0$-exchanged in that sequence. The converse of this statement is also true for 1-safe nets:

Theorem 5.2 *Correspondence between* $\equiv_0$ *and indep*

Let Σ *be 1-safe and let* $\sigma_1 = \sigma t M_1 t' \sigma'$ *and* $\sigma_2 = \sigma t' M_2 t \sigma'$ *be two occurrence sequences of* Σ. *Then* $\sigma_1 \equiv_0 \sigma_2$ *iff* t *indep* t'.

Proof: ($\Rightarrow$:) $\sigma_1 \equiv_0 \sigma_2$ means that $M = last(\sigma)$ concurrently enables $\{t, t'\}$, implying that ${}^\bullet t \cap {}^\bullet t' = \emptyset$.
Suppose $s \in {}^\bullet t \cap t'^\bullet$; by ${}^\bullet t \cap {}^\bullet t' = \emptyset$, $s \notin {}^\bullet t'$.
M enables t implies $M(s) = 1$, but since M enables t' as well, this contradicts 1-safeness.
Similarly, $s \in t^\bullet \cap {}^\bullet t'$ is impossible.
Finally, suppose that $s \in t^\bullet \cap t'^\bullet$ but $s \notin {}^\bullet t \cap t'^\bullet$ and $s \notin t^\bullet \cap {}^\bullet t'$.
Then $first(\sigma')(s) \geq 2$, contradicting 1-safeness.

($\Leftarrow$:) It is immediately clear that $last(\sigma)$ concurrently enables t and t'. □ 5.2

We may remark that it is immediate from 4.11(i) that $\sigma_1 \equiv_0 \sigma_2$ implies $\Pi(\sigma_1) \cap \Pi(\sigma_2) \neq \emptyset$ and hence, by theorem 3.4, $\Pi(\sigma_1) = \Pi(\sigma_2) \neq \emptyset$. The generalisation is:

Theorem 5.3 $\equiv_0^\infty$ *implies the existence of a common process*

Let Σ *be 1-safe and* σ_1, σ_2 *two occurrence sequences of* Σ. *Then* $\sigma_1 \equiv_0^\infty \sigma_2 \Rightarrow \Pi(\sigma_1) = \Pi(\sigma_2)$.

Proof: In the finite case, as $\equiv_0^\infty$ reduces to $\equiv_0^\star$, the property results from a repeated application of the preceding remark.
Let us suppose that σ_1 and σ_2 are infinite
and let $\Pi(\sigma_1) = \{\pi_1\} = \{(N_1, p_1)\}$ and $\Pi(\sigma_2) = \{\pi_2\} = \{(N_2, p_2)\}$.
Since $\sigma_1 \equiv_0^\infty \sigma_2$, $\forall n \in \mathbf{N}\ \exists \sigma_1' : \sigma_1' \equiv_0^\star \sigma_1$ and $\sigma_1'\ {}_n\!= \sigma_2$, and we see that $\Pi(\sigma_1) = \Pi(\sigma_1')$.
Consider the subprocess of π_1 corresponding to the common n-prefix of σ_1' and σ_2: since the system is 1-safe, this substructure is unique inside π_1 (its construction by means of 3.1 is deterministic).
Consequently, if n increases, we may construct a series of fixed successively embedded subprocesses of π_1, finally obtaining a process π_1' included in π_1 which is compatible with σ_2 and thus isomorphic to π_2. Symmetrically, π_1 is isomorphic to a process π_2' included in π_2.
We claim that $\pi_1' = \pi_1$ and $\pi_2' = \pi_2$.
Indeed, let $x \in \pi_1$ and $l = \{b_0, \ldots, x\}$ be any maximal chain from $Min(N_1)$ to x; then from the constructed isomorphisms, there is an isomorphic chain l' in π_2', and another one, say $l'' = \{b_0'', \ldots, x''\}$ in π_1'. From 1-safeness, $b_0'' = b_0$ and from then on, all the successive corresponding elements of the chains l and l'' are the same, so that finally $x = x'' \in \pi_1'$ and $\pi_1 = \pi_1'$; symmetrically, $\pi_2 = \pi_2'$. □ 5.3

This immediately leads to the fundamental property for 1-safe systems:

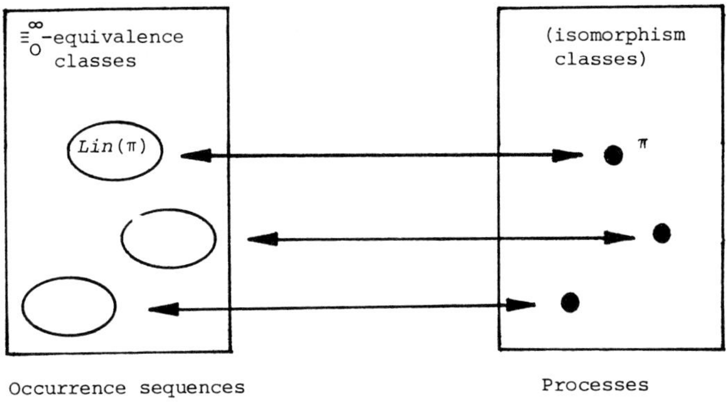

Figure 10: Correspondence between occurrence sequences and processes for 1-safe nets

Theorem 5.4 $\equiv_1^\infty$ *equals* $\cong$ *for 1-safe nets*

Let Σ *be 1-safe and let* π_1, π_2 *be processes of* Σ *and* σ_1, σ_2 *occurrence sequences of* Σ *such that* $\sigma_1 \in Lin(\pi_1)$ *and* $\sigma_2 \in Lin(\pi_2)$.
Then: $\pi_1 \equiv_1^\infty \pi_2 \iff \pi_1 \cong \pi_2 \iff \sigma_1 \equiv_0^\infty \sigma_2$.

Proof: This is an immediate consequence of 5.3 and 4.13. □ 5.4

Summarising the preceding results, we may simplify the relationship indicated in Figure 9 as follows (see Figure 10). For a 1-safe system, a process π corresponds uniquely to the set $Lin(\pi)$. Moreover, the Lin-sets of processes define a partitioning of the set of occurrence sequences, and each Lin-set is exactly one $\equiv_0^\infty$-class of sequences.

6 Information Carried by Sequences and Partial Orders

So far, we have analysed the expressive power of sequences and processes, and the structure of their relation. Another interesting problem is to determine exactly what type of information is inherently carried by some (family of) sequences and partial orders, and thus to determine what is lost and what can be reconstructed if one considers a type of behavioural description instead of another one. This is a vast question, however, and we shall only mention here some properties directly concerned with our previous considerations.

First, let us notice that from an alternating description, by dropping half of it, we may obtain a non-alternating one. For instance, if $\sigma = M_0 t_1 M_1 t_2 \ldots$ is an occurrence sequence of some system net $\Sigma = (S, T, F, M_0)$ and if we drop the intermediate markings then we get a transition (or firing) sequence $\sigma_T = t_1 t_2 \ldots$. Some information has been lost here, but it may be reconstructed if we know Σ; the problem is of course different if we do not know Σ (although there may be interesting information that may be deduced without knowing Σ, for instance on the class of systems that may generate the set of firing sequences, see [5]). Similarly, if we look at a process $\pi = (B, E, F', p)$ of Σ and if we drop the conditions then we get a partial order on the labelled events, say π_E. Here, however, we may no longer reconstruct π from π_E, even if we know Σ, as shown by the counterexample in Figure 11 which is taken from [13].

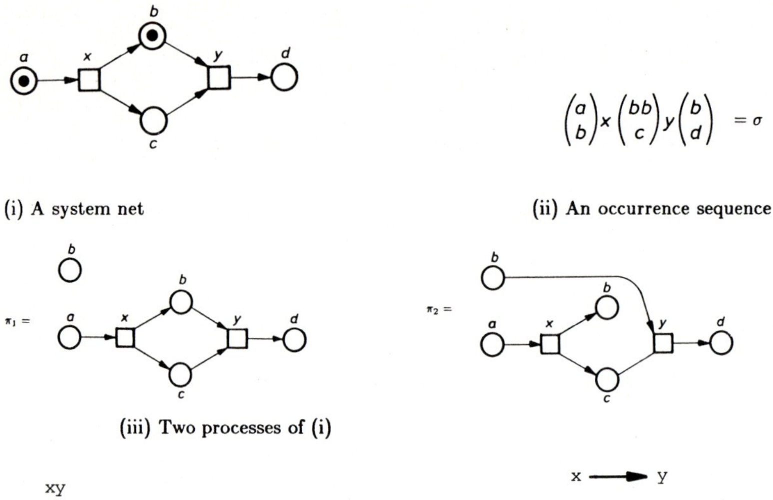

(i) A system net

$$\binom{a}{b} x \binom{bb}{c} y \binom{b}{d} = \sigma$$

(ii) An occurrence sequence of (i)

$\pi_1 =$ $\pi_2 =$(iii) Two processes of (i)

xy

x ⟶ y

(iv) A transition sequence of (i)

(v) A partial order on the labelled events, corresponding to both π_1 and π_2

Figure 11: Two processes with the same event ordering

This is again due to the distinction between token individualities made by the processes.

Now, it may be observed that if two processes have the same partial order on the sets of their events then they have the same linearisations:

$$\pi_E^1 = \pi_E^2 \;\Rightarrow\; Lin(\pi^1) = Lin(\pi^2).$$

One may wonder, therefore, whether it is possible to reconstruct a unique event order from the knowledge of a whole Lin-set. The answer is again negative, as exhibited by the example shown in Figure 12.

Simpler counterexamples may be found [2] but the one given here deserves special interest because it has no side conditions (see definition 6.1) and the partial orderings on the labelled events are incomparable; worse, the two processes do not have a common 'looser' process with the same Lin-set (the partial orderings are, in some sense, minimal, i.e. there exists no unique minimal element).

Definition 6.1 *Side condition*

Let $N = (S,T,F)$ be a net and $s \in S$, $t \in T$; s is called a side condition (of t) iff $t \in {}^\bullet s \cap s^\bullet$.
□ 6.1

One of the main interests of the process approach (as well as of the partial orders on events) is that it explicates the concurrency relation (by means of the co relation). In particular, it is possible to deduce the set of occurrence sequences from the set of processes only. Further, if we start with some process π, even if we do not know its originating system, we may define the *swap* operation and generate the whole \equiv_1^∞-class of π.

In order to do the same job with an occurrence sequence (or a transition sequence), we need the \equiv_0 relation but this is not as indigenous as \equiv_1; rather, it has to be imported from the system. One may

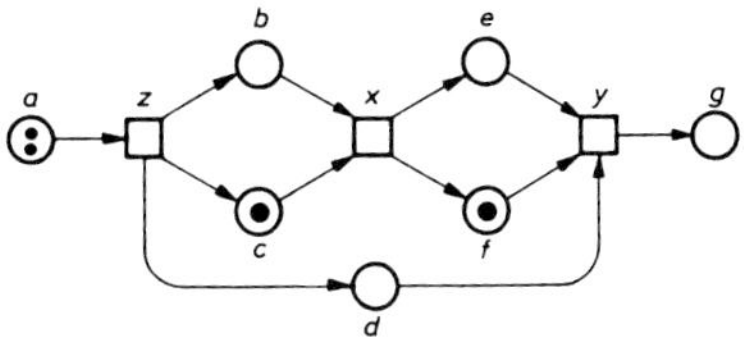

(i) A system net

$$
\begin{aligned}
\sigma_1 &= zzxxyy \\
\sigma_2 &= zzxyxy \\
\sigma_3 &= zxzxyy \\
\sigma_4 &= zxzyxy
\end{aligned}
$$

(ii) Four occurrence sequences of (i) (markings omitted)

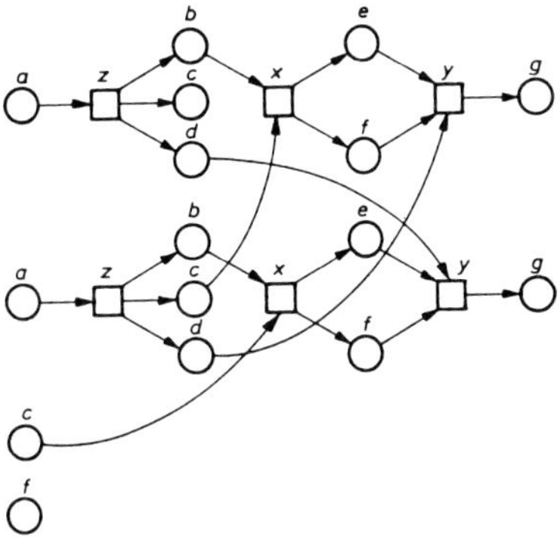

(iii) A process π_1 of (i) with $Lin(\pi_1) = \{\sigma_1, \sigma_2, \sigma_3, \sigma_4\}$

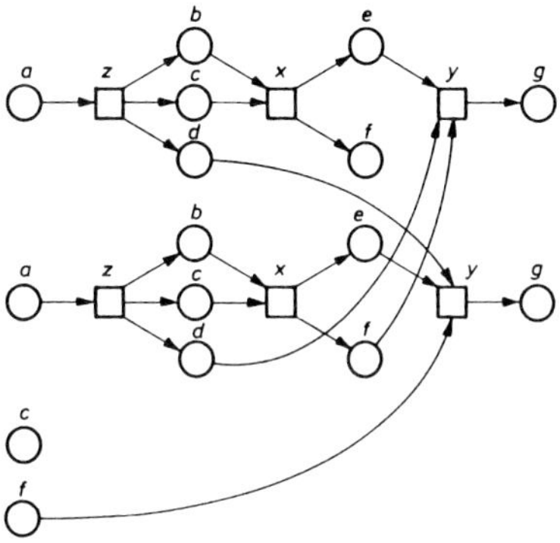

(iv) A process π_2 of (i) with $Lin(\pi_2) = \{\sigma_1, \sigma_2, \sigma_3, \sigma_4\}$

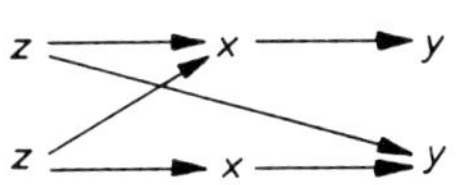

(v) The partial ordering on the labelled events of π_1

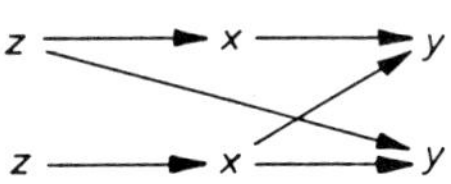

(vi) The partial ordering on the labelled events of π_2

Figure 12: Two processes which have the same *Lin*-set but different event orderings

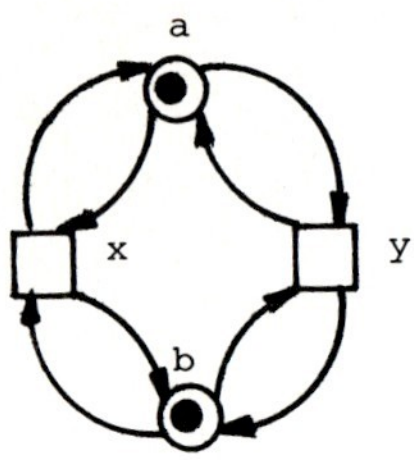

(i) A system net Σ_1

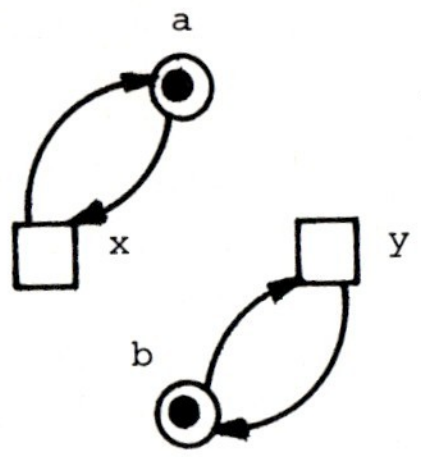

(ii) A system net Σ_2

$$\begin{pmatrix} a \\ b \end{pmatrix} \{ x \begin{pmatrix} a \\ b \end{pmatrix}, y \begin{pmatrix} a \\ b \end{pmatrix} \}^{\infty}$$

(iii) Occurrence sequences of Σ_1 and Σ_2

$\equiv_0$ for Σ_1: $\emptyset$

$\equiv_0$ for Σ_2: any permutation of successive distinct transitions

Figure 13: Two processes with the same occurrence sequences but different $\equiv_0$ relations

wonder whether $\equiv_0$ may be constructed from the whole set of occurrence (or transition) sequences, but the answer is negative even for 1-safe systems, as shown by the example of Figure 13.

The situation becomes different, however, if we exclude side conditions. Then the whole concurrency relation may be (re-)constructed from the set of occurrence sequences. This follows simply because from an occurrence sequence, if the system has no side condition, we may reconstruct the local environment of each transition which occurs in it: if $\ldots MtM' \ldots$ then for all $s \in S$:

$$F(s,t) = \max\{M(s) - M'(s), 0\}$$
$$F(t,s) = \max\{M'(s) - M(s), 0\},$$

and using the F relation the set of processes can be constructed using 3.1. The examples of Figure 13 again show that this does not hold in general. A process, on the contrary, always exhibits the local environment of each of its labelling transitions.

Even if one knows only the set of transition sequences (of a side-condition free system net) then one may partially reconstruct the concurrency relation. Namely, $\sigma_T t_1 t_2$ and $\sigma_T t_2 t_1$ are transition sequences iff t_1 and t_2 are concurrently enabled by the (unknown) marking resulting after σ_T (this includes the case that $t_1 = t_2$). Hence it is possible to derive the concurrency relation $\equiv_0$ (restricted to transition sequences) from the set of transition sequences only.

In conclusion, we may say that for the purposes just outlined, processes carry the most information. Partial orders on events still exhibit concurrency, and occurrence sequences exhibit transition environments up to side conditions; thus, concurrency may be reconstructed from occurrence sequences and even from transition sequences, but only if we know all of them and if there are no side conditions.

7 Conclusion

In this paper we have examined the interleaved (sequence) semantics and the partial order (process) semantics of Petri nets and the relationship between these semantics. The emphasis in our study was on identifying exactly the power of the respective approaches and the structure of their relationship.

We have based our considerations on existing definitions of sequences and processes, but in the existing literature there has been an evolution of these definitions. The transition rule, of course, is the basis of every semantics of nets. From the transition rule, the occurrence sequences are most easily defined; they denote nothing but a repeated successive application of that rule. The process axioms have evolved differently. At first (in [11] and in [8]) they were so general that an inductive interpretation could hardly be attached to them. They have arrived in the form given in definition 2.12 through the discussion in [9], [7] and [1].

Intuitively, it seems clear that processes should, in some way, be definable inductively, 'growing' from some initial (or otherwise well-chosen) cut. Thus the starting point of this research has been construction 3.1 which relates processes to sequences in an intuitive and inductive manner. The questions were then: (i) What are the 'good' process axioms? (ii) What is their behavioural expressive power? (iii) For which class of systems are the axiomatic and the inductive approaches exactly equivalent? (iv) What is the structure of the relationship between processes and occurrence sequences?

The results concerning the first three questions are sketched in sections 2 and 3. In particular, it has been mentioned that the situation is paticularly agreeable in the case of finite synchronisation. Systems of finite synchronisation include, of course, all finite systems as a special case. Since the practical interests clearly rest with finite systems and (a fortiori) with ones of finite synchronisation, it may be objected why we bother at all about the general infinite case. The answer is that the study of infinite nets may be interesting in a variety of ways. First, it may shed more light on the reasons why in the special cases some simplifications may be attained. For instance, the general statement (that can sometimes be heard) to the effect that 'by arbitrary interleaving, nothing essential is lost', is not true in cases of infinite synchronisation such as shown in Figure 3. The second motivation for studying infinite nets is that they may arise in various circumstances: if one translates unsafe nets into 1-safe infinite ones; when one deals with inhibitor arcs; and last but not least, when one translates concurrent programs into 1-safe nets [2].

For systems of finite synchronisation, occurrence sequences and processes define the same behaviour 'in principle'. This means that some important definitions, such as that of the set $[M_0\rangle$ (and all other definition based on this), are the same whether defined via occurrence sequences or via processes. This result does not imply, however, a complete equivalence between processes and occurrence sequences.

Firstly, as shown in section 4, if we desire a nice bijection between them then we need to introduce equivalence relations abstracting 'artificial details' from both occurrence sequences and processes, and confine our attention on the corresponding equivalence classes. For sequences, the detail is the total order arbitrarily chosen when operations are actually concurrent, which is abstracted from by the $\equiv_0$ relation; for processes, the detail is the token distinction exhibited by the process definition, which is abstracted from by the $\equiv_1$ relation. Quite nicely, these relations are both connected to the existence of a common corresponding representative of the other type, and they correspond to each other when one looks at the equivalence relations they generate.

Next, as exhibited in section 6, processes carry indigenously more information on concurrency and system structure than do sequences. Also, our study has shown that 1-safeness and side condition-freeness are important properties to make the general setup more perspicuous. Indeed, for 1-safe nets, the equivalence relation on processes reduces to identity, and each process may be identified uniquely with its corresponding class of sequences which is also its *Lin*-set. Also, for side condition free nets, some important properties of the system may be reconstructed from the knowledge of its sequences only.

References

[1] E.Best: Concurrent Behaviour: Sequences, Processes and Axioms. Proc. CMU Workshop on Concurrency, LNCS Vol.197, 221-245 (1985).

[2] E.Best and R.Devillers: Concurrent Behaviour: Sequences, Processes and Programming Languages. GMD-Studien No.99 (May 1985).

[3] W.Brauer (ed.): Net Theory and Applications. LNCS Vol.84 (1980).

[4] R.Devillers: The Semantics of Capacities in P/T-nets: a First Look. 6th Workshop on Petri Nets, Helsinki (1985).

[5] R.Devillers: The Expressive Power of Various Enabling Rules for P/T Nets. Technical Report LIT 161, ULB Bruxelles (1985).

[6] E.W.Dijkstra: A Discipline of Programming. Prentice Hall (1976).

[7] C.Fernández, M.Nielsen and P.S.Thiagarajan: A Note on Observable Occurrence Nets. Advances in Petri Nets 1984 (ed. G.Rozenberg), LNCS Vol.188, 122-138 (1985).

[8] H.J.Genrich, K.Lautenbach and P.S.Thiagarajan: Elements of General Net Theory. In: [3], 21-163.

[9] U.Goltz and W.Reisig: The Non-sequential Behaviour of Petri Nets. Information and Control 57, 125-147 (1983).

[10] A.Mazurkiewicz: Concurrent Program Schemes and their Interpretation. Århus University Computer Science Department, Report DAIMI-PB-78 (1977).

[11] C.A.Petri: Non-sequential Processes. GMD-ISF Report 77.05 (1977).

[12] W.Reisig: Partial Order Semantics versus Interleaving Semantics of CSP-like Languages and its Impact on Fairness. LNCS Vol.172, 403-413 (1984).

[13] W.Reisig: On the Semantics of Petri Nets. in Formal Models in Programming (ed: E.J.Neuhold and G.Chroust), North Holland, 347-372 (1985).

QUESTIONS AND ANSWERS

Apt: May I suggest a simpler definition of your first equivalence relation? The notion of permutation makes also sense if you apply it to infinite sequences. A permutation is simply a function which is 1-1 and onto. It seems to me that two sequences are equivalent in the sense you define, if one is a permutation of the other.

Best: But 1-1 and onto is not enough because then you might permute one element right to the front.

Apt: What is wrong with this?

Bednarczyk: Actually, there is essentially one more condition to be imposed, namely that there should be a condition that you can swap only independent actions. That makes sure this doesn´t happen.

Apt: But this definition here is a general definition which does not refer to dependency. So, my question was addressing exclusively this definition not the use of it.

Best: No, I have tried permutations first. If you actually go into details it becomes more complicated. I challenge you to try it.

Jouannaud: It does not work for technical reasons?

Best: Yes. (laughter)

De Roever: I would like to go back to the main subject (laughter). Can you translate or relate your results for Petri-Nets to programs in CSP or CCS because there, of course, one usually uses interleaving semantics ?

Best: I can do it at least for simple CSP programs and by simple I mean: no recursion, no nesting. For these programs I know that a 1-safe marked net can be associated with them. The net is 1-safe because it turnes out that every variable has always one value, every control point is always at one location. And it has the finite synchronization property because all communications have two partners or at most finitely many, you won´t admit infinitely many. All atomic actions have finitely many variables which could be the only source of infinite synchronization. So the net which is associated to these kind of programs satisfies the 1-safeness and the finite synchronization property although it could be infinite, but the two first points are enough to transfer the theory. In that case every process of such a program corresponds to an equivalence class of sequences.

De Roever: But my problem is: I´m always working these days with nesting, with recursion and recursive process creation. Do you think that the result is still the same? What´s your guess?

Best: My guess is yes, but my guess will take some time to prove.

Degano: You can take the old CCS and transform it to obtain a context-free condition in that system which is 1-safe. So you can carry all the results over for CCS. Does this answer your question?

De Roever: Yes, since (thanks to the recursion in CCS) you can build everything in CCS.

Formal Description of Programming Concepts - III
M. Wirsing (Editor)
Elsevier Science Publishers B.V. (North-Holland)

© IFIP, 1987

NOTIONS OF FAIRNESS FOR SYNCHRONOUS FORK JOIN NETS

M. CHADILI (*)

I. GUESSARIAN (*)

Abstract: Synchronous fork-join flow-diagrams are defined and their operational semantics is given using finite automata. Three notions of fairness are relevant: fairness regarding path-behavior, fairness regarding input-output behavior, and a combination of these two notions. Properties of nets and their fair computations are studied.

1. Introduction

In the present paper, we address fairness problems for synchronous fork-join parallelism. Fork-join parallelism is the most basic and lowlevel form of parallelism, where a process can fork - i.e. split - into two subprocesses which then proceed independantly : two processes can also join into a single one at some point, namely the final process waits for the results of the two processes racing to the join, and proceeds with the results of either one, non deterministically (cf. *fork* and *wait* statements in C, PL1, etc...). There is a major difference between our synchronous join and the asynchronous merge mostly studied in the literature (see e.g. [Boussinot]); data which do not find their way through the merge can wait for an arbitrary long time in infinite buffers, whereas data which do not pass through a join are irremediably lost, because we assume :

(1) that all processes are ruled by a global clock and take some action at every time unit

(2) that buffers are finite (or length 1 to simplify). These assumptions, to our sense, correspond more closely to "real life", but make fairness more difficult to study.

D. Benson gave an algebraic semantics for fork-join parallelism [Benson]; fairness, however, being an intrinsically operational phenomenon, does not seem to be easily expressible in that formalism. So, we first introduce an operational semantics for fork-join parallelism, using the notion of oracle [Boussinot], which then enables us to study fairness.

(*) L.I.T.P., Université Paris 7, 2 Place Jussieu, 75251 Paris Cedex 05.

Also, we allow explicitly for iteration in our formalism, whereas finite nets only are considered in [Benson], who leaves implicit the case of iterative nets, even though they might be studied by the same methods. We could also deal with recursive nets, but at the cost of heavier machinery, e.g. finite automata and transducers would not any more be sufficient, so we leave that case out of the present study.

Various notions of fairness naturally occur in the present formalism ; but they all pertain to the following intuitive notion : an event infinitely often possible does occur infinitely often, cf. the strong fairness of [Costa-Stirling, Darondeau, Hennessy].

We will study two main notions of fairness and the resulting properties for nets of processes.

1) Fairness with respect to path behavior : every finite path in the net must be executed infinitely often. This is a syntactic and global notion of fairness, well-suited to modelling e.g. fairness of hardware circuits, ensuring that no process will ever starve or get blocked. However, composing fair nets does not result in a fair net.

2) Fairness with respect to input-output behavior : every data item requesting infinitely often access through a join shall go through that join infinitely often. This is a semantic and local notion of fairness, which could model e.g. fairness in a message passing protocol. This second notion is stable by composition, but there exists no behavior globally fair with respect to all inputs.

Now, for the asynchronous case with infinite buffers, the first notion of fairness implies the second one. This is not true any more in the synchronous case, where the two notions are incomparable. Hence, we define a "strong" fairness by combining the two previous notions, and a notion of privilege-freeness which is a variant of strong fairness.

The paper is organized as follows : we first describe the semantics of fork-join nets and show it can be characterized by finite state transducers, which give a semantics in terms of infinitary languages. We then study various notions of fairness, their properties and relationships. Finally, we give in an appendix a few useful properties of infinitary languages. This paper has been written with a bias in favor of intuition in order to improve readability. Consequently, some formal definitions and proofs are skipped and replaced by examples. Proofs and technical details will be given in an extended version of the paper.

2. Fork-join nets

2.1 Fork-join nets and their semantics

Our nets will consist of three basic components, processes, forks and joins connected together in a finite flowdiagram organization.

A *process* is a one state transducer which transforms an infinite stream of data into an infinite stream of results ; processes will be considered as unary functions in the sequel.

The same results hold if we consider transducers with more than one state and more than one output stream. For simplicity and readibility of notations, however, we will treat the unary case only.

Example 2.1

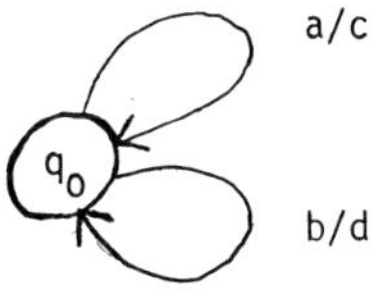

with input alphabet $\{a,b\}$ and output alphabet $\{c,d\}$ corresponds to the function

$$f(x) = \begin{cases} c & \text{if } x = a \\ d & \text{if } x = b \end{cases}$$

and will transform the input $(ab)^\omega$ into the output $(cd)^\omega$. □

A *fork* is an operator with one input channel and two output channels, which instantaneously duplicates the contents of its input channel into its output channels. A fork will be represented by the diagram :

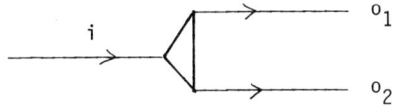

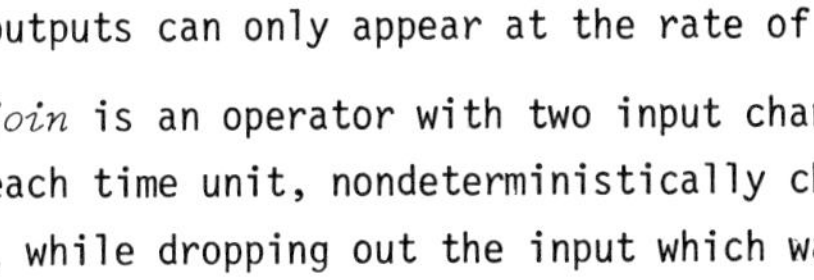

and will transform the input $(ab)^\omega$ into the outputs $((ab)^\omega,(ab)^\omega)$. However, since we will assume in the sequel that channels are length one buffers, both input and outputs can only appear at the rate of one per time unit.

A *join* is an operator with two input channels and one output channel, which, at each time unit, nondeterministically chooses one of its inputs and outputs it, while dropping out the input which was not chosen ; this whole process takes one time unit, contrary to the fork which was supposed to be instantaneous. A join will be depicted as follows :

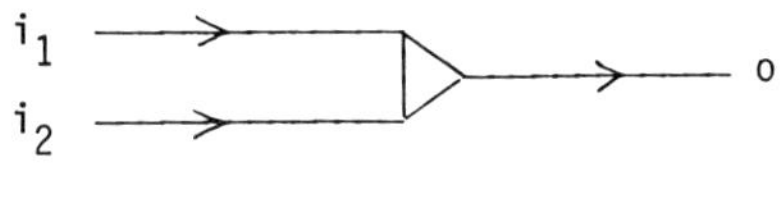

If we feed the previous join with inputs i_1 = ab i_2 = cd, the possible output will be one among {ab, cd, ad, cb}. In order to make deterministic the behavior of the join, we add a third, fictive, input, the *oracle* δ, which tells which input is picked, so that, e.g.

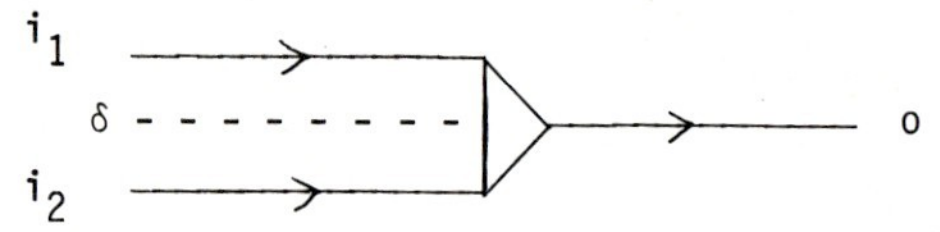

with $i_1 = (ab)^{\omega}$, $i_2 = (cd)^{\omega}$, $\delta = (01)^{\omega}$ will output $o = (ad)^{\omega}$.

The method of introducing oracles to deal with nondeterminism is also used for the asynchronous merge in [Boussinot, Park1].

Definition 2.2 : a *net* N is a finite flowdiagram built up from processes, forks and joins, which we represent as a quintuple :

N = <I, O, n, m, L>, where

- $I = (i_1,\ldots,i_k)$ is the vector of input channels
- $O = (o_1,\ldots,o_\ell)$ is the vector of output channels
- n is the number of joins
- m is the number of forks
- L is the set of all labels in the net. □

Example 2.3

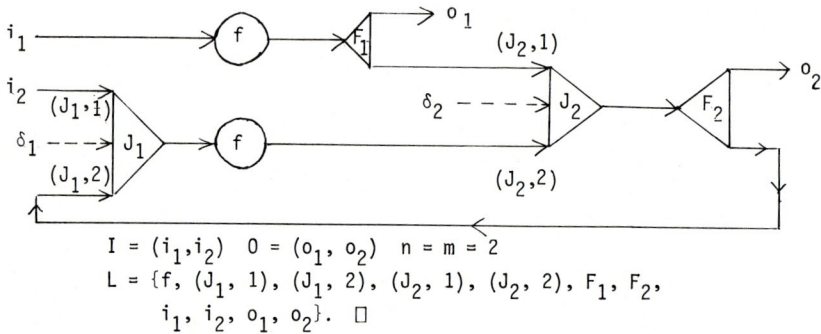

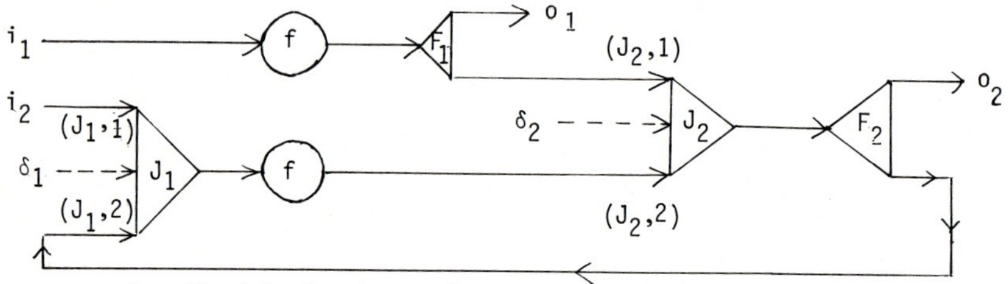

$I = (i_1,i_2)$ $O = (o_1, o_2)$ $n = m = 2$

$L = \{f, (J_1, 1), (J_1, 2), (J_2, 1), (J_2, 2), F_1, F_2, i_1, i_2, o_1, o_2\}$. □

Nets can thus be considered as finite state transducers with several input channels and several output channels, or as transition nets. An equivalent algebraic definition could be given, saying that nets are the least structure containing processes, fork, join, projections and closed under tupling, composition and iteration. The advantage of that second definition is that it can be more readily generalized to allow for recursion. However, the definition with transition nets presents the advantages of being more intuitive and more handy for describing the operational semantics of nets.

Since our main interest is fairness, which is intrinsically operational, we will use definition 2.2 only.

The operational semantics is based on Arnold's work [Arnold], and the following assumptions :

(i) nets are synchronous and there is a global clock : i.e. at each time unit, all operations advance by one step,

(ii) a letter takes one unit of time to go through a join, or to be transformed by a process,

(iii) a letter takes no time to go through a fork.

Modulo the above assumptions, a net can be considered as a transducer based on a finite automaton : it performs a transduction, transforming each vector I of infinite input words into a vector O of infinite output words : this transformation is by definition the semantics of the net.

More precisely, each oracle δ in $(\{0,1\}^n)^\omega$ determines a *computation* of the net for every input i in $(A^k)^\omega$: the result of this computation is an output o in $(T^\ell)^\omega$, where A is the input alphabet and T the output alphabet. The semantics of the net is the set of all pairs (i,o), for all possible inputs i and oracles δ.

<u>Proposition 2.4</u> : if the inputs and the oracle of a join are regular ω-languages, the output of the join is a regular ω-language.

Proof : A suitable product of the automata recognizing the inputs and the oracle gives an extended Büchi automaton recognizing the output. □

For the next proposition, we need to assume that the input and output alphabets of all processes in a net are finite, so that the net has only a finite number of possible behaviors for arbitrary inputs of bounded length ; then

<u>Proposition 2.5</u> if all inputs and oracles of a net with finite alphabets are regular ω-languages, then the outputs of the net are regular ω-languages too.

The proof proceeds on the same ideas as the previous proposition, except that one has to add one more component in the product automaton ; this new component simulates the behavior of the net. □

<u>2.2 Some examples of fork-join nets</u>

There are quite a few examples of such nets in the literature. One class of such examples are the systolic automata, which exhibit the same kind of synchronous behavior, though they are usually simpler since they normally do not include joins [Culik-Salomaa-Wood] ; systolic automata can thus be viewed as unwindings of nets. Other examples are the data flow programs, and more specifically nondeterminate networks of data flow operators [Dennis]. Apart from the merge which is intrinsically different from the join, since the former is asynchronous with infinite buffering while the latter is synchronous with finite buffering, data flow operators can be simulated with the join and a judicious choice of oracles. For instance, the true gate :

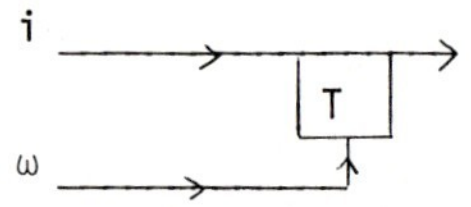

with input stream i and boolean stream ω, can be simulated by the following join :

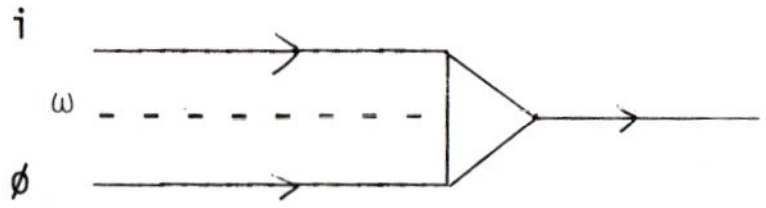

with input streams i and $\emptyset$ (the empty stream), and oracle ω. Hence a semantics for fork-join nets could help in giving a semantics for data flow nets.

These examples illustrate the two essential features of fork-join nets :

1 - fork-join nets have a synchronous behavior : i.e. all components are always enabled and take a step at each time unit as in systolic automata

2 - there is no infinite buffering ; together with synchronousness this implies that data which are not transmitted are lost ; this is a somehow stringent requirement which makes fairness much more difficult to study, but it reflects some aspects of realtime programming.

3. Fairness

3.1 Fairness with respect to path behavior

The first notion of fairness which we will study is a global notion, ensuring that a computation will go through every channel infinitely often. In order to express it easily, we introduce the notion of path in a net. To this end, we label the input channels with pairwise different names ; all other channels are implicitly distinguished by the labeling of the forks and joins (we could almost forget about the processes and keep only the fork-join structure of the net).

Equivalently, the first notion of fairness that we study is relative to streams of data of the form x_p^ω on input channel i_p, for every p.

Definition 3.1 A *path* in a net N is a word $w = w_1 \ldots w_n$ in L^+ such that $w_1 = i_j$, $w_n = o_i$, for some input channel i_j and output channel o_i and for each $p = 1,\ldots,n-1$, there is a channel linking directly w_p to w_{p+1}. P_N denotes the set of finite paths in the net N. □

Example 3.2 Let N be the net of example 2.3, then $i_1 f\ F_1 o_1$, $i_2 (J_1,1)\ f\ (J_2,2)\ F_2 (J_1,2)\ f\ (J_2,2)\ F_2 o_2$ are two paths in P_N. □

Proposition 3.3 The set P_N is a regular language. □

We now state intuitively the goal we wish to achieve with fairness with respect to path behavior. A computation is fair if condition (i) is satisfied.

(i) every input letter x_p, which could, after transformations in a path, arrive infinitely often to an output channel o_i, does arrive infinitely often to that output channel.

We will in the sequel give sufficient conditions for (i) to become true.

A path is *active* in a computation iff it is taken infinitely often during that computation. More formally, define for each net N the alphabetic morphism $\phi_N : L \rightarrow P(\{0,1\}^n)$ by $\forall x \in L$

$$\phi_N(x) = \begin{cases} \{\{b_1,\ldots,b_{i-1}, a-1, b_{i+1},\ldots,b_n\}, b_i \in \{0,1\}\} & \text{if } x = (J_i,a) \\ \{0,1\}^n & \text{if } x = f \text{ where } f \text{ is a process} \\ \emptyset & \text{otherwise} \end{cases}$$

ϕ_N is alphabetically extended to L^*.

Definition 3.4 (i) Let N be a net and δ an oracle in $(\{0,1\}^n)^\omega$; δ is *path-fair* iff for every path p in P_N, $|\delta|_{\phi_N(p)} = \omega$, where $|\delta|_B$ is the number of times words of B occur in δ.

(ii) a computation is path-fair iff the corresponding oracle is, or iff, equivalently, every path is active in that computation. □

For instance, let N be a net consisting of a single join, then e.g. $(01)^\omega$, $(100)^\omega$ are path-fair, whereas $(01)^n 1^\omega$ is not path-fair.

Proposition 3.5 : path-fairness implies condition (i). □

When the output alphabets of all processes in the net are finite, we can replace the previous notion of fairness by a weaker one, which nevertheless implies condition (i). Namely, instead of demanding that every finite path be active, it is enough to require that all paths in a finite set of finite paths be active.

Definition 3.6 a path $p = w_1 \ldots w_n$ with $w_1 = i_j$ and $w_n = o_i$ is *useful* iff $w_2 \ldots w_{n-1} = w'w^q w''$ for some q and $w = w_k \ldots w_\ell$ such that

(i) for all x in L, if x is not a process $\sup\{|w|_x, |w'|_x, |w''|_x\} \leq 1$

(ii) if $f_1, \ldots, f_r$ are the processes occurring in w, and n_i is the cardinal of the output alphabet of f_i, then $q \leq \inf\{n_i \;/\; i = 1, \ldots, r\}$. □

Intuitively, a useful path can go through a given loop at most q times, where q is the minimum of the cardinals of the output alphabets of the processes in that loop. Useful paths are sufficient to ensure that inputs will undergo all possible transformations before being output. Notice first that the set of useful paths is finite, hence this will lead to an effective notion of fairness.

Exemple 3.7 Let N be the following net

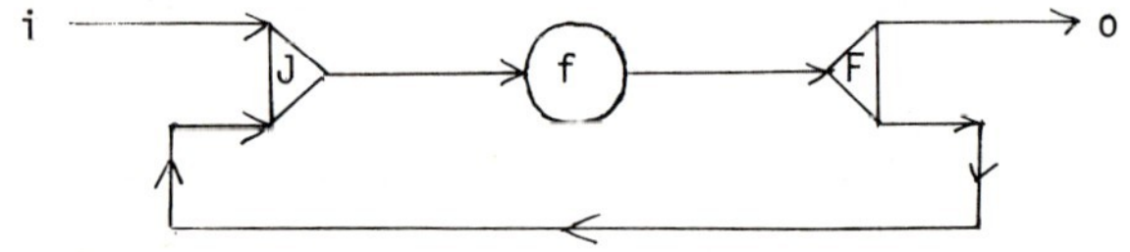

where f has input and output alphabets $A = \{a,b\}$ and is defined by $f(a) = b$ $f(b) = a$. Then, the set of useful paths in N is

$$P_u = \{i(J,1)\ f\ F\ w^\ell o, \text{ where } \ell = 0, 1, 2 \text{ and } w = (J,2)\ f\ F\}$$

Definition 3.8 A computation of a net N is *weakly path-fair* iff all useful paths are active. □

Proposition 3.9 If the output alphabets of all processes in a net are finite, then weak path-fairness implies condition (i). □

Proposition 3.10 Path-fairness (weak or not) is not closed under composition.

This is shown by the following example : let N be

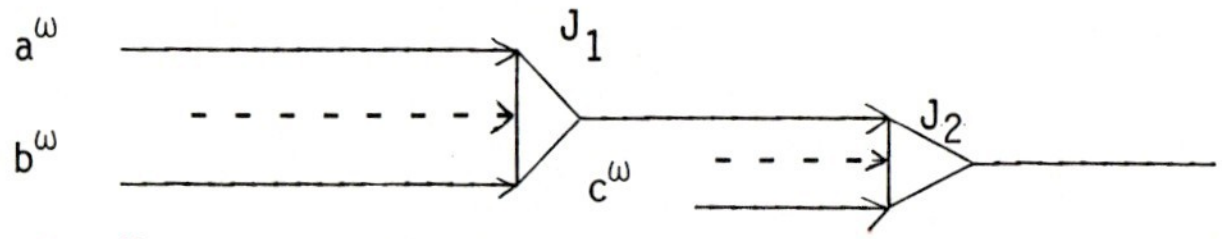

$\delta_1 = (01)^\omega$ and $\delta_2 = (10)^\omega$ are path-fair when we consider each join separately. But $\delta = ((0,1)(1,0))^\omega$ is not path-fair for the net N, because the path $p = (J_1,2)(J_2,1)$ will never be taken.

For that path, $\phi_N(p) = \{(1,x)(y,0) \mid x,y \in \{0,1\}\}$ and $|\delta|_{\phi_N(p)} = 0$. If the inputs are as shown in the picture, namely a^ω on $(J_1,1)$, b^ω on $(J_1,2)$, c^ω on $(J_2,2)$, the output will be $(ca)^\omega$. □

Our nets can be related to the probabilistic concurrent programs of [Lichtenstein-Pnueli-Zuck] by endowing each one of the two channels leading to a join with a probability 0·5. Then our notion of weak path-fairness can be compared to the α-fairness of [Lichtenstein-Pnueli-Zuck]. Recall that, roughly speaking, a computation c is α-fair iff every rational set of initial subcomputations of c goes infinitely often through each channel. Namely, α-fairness is a local notion, concerning each join individually ; weak path fairness, on the other hand, is a global notion, concerning finite sequences of joins ; weak path fairness is also weaker in the sense that it is concerned only with the computation c itself, disregarding its subcomputations.

In the rest of this section we will assume that all input and output alphabets are finite.

3.2 Fairness with respect to input-output behavior

Because of the synchronous behaviors of our nets, and of the lack of infinite buffers, path-fairness does not imply fairness with respect to input-output behavior as it does for the case of the asynchronous merge (cf. [Boussinot]). This is shown by the following :

Exemple 3.11 : N consists of a single join

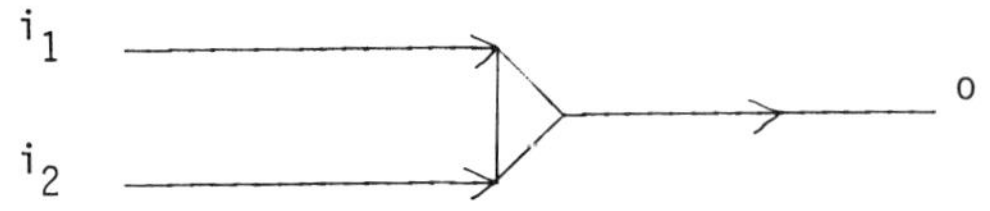

Then $\delta = (01)^{\omega}$ is path-fair ; however, if $x_1 = (ab)^{\omega}$ $x_2 = (cd)^{\omega}$, then the output is $(ad)^{\omega}$, and b and c will never go through the join. □

To remedy this drawback, we define a local notion of fairness with respect to input-output behavior, which ensures that, whenever a letter "knocks" infinitely often at the door of a join, coming from either channel, it will go through infinitely often.

Definition 3.12 A computation of a net N is *IO-fair* for input I iff, for each join in the net, every letter which comes infinitely often on either one of the input channels of the join goes also infinitely often through the output channel of that join. □

Remarks (i) in an IO-fair computation for every channel c of the net and every letter x, if x could go infinitely often through c, then x must go infinitely often through c.

(ii) IO-fairness is always relative to some input I.

Proposition 3.13 path-fairness and IO-fairness are incomparable.

Proof : Example 3.11 shows that path fairness does not imply IO-fairness ; the converse implication is also false as shown by the following example : let N be as in example 3.11 and $i_1 = i_2 = a^\omega$, $\delta = 0^\omega$. Then δ defines an IO-fair computation which is not path-fair, since the path $i_2(J_2,2)o$ is never taken.□

Definition 3.14 : Let $F_N(I)$ be the set of oracles which define IO-fair computations for input I. □

Proposition 3.15 : For all I, $F_N(I) \neq \emptyset$, i.e. for each input there exists at least one IO-fair computation.

Proof : we only have to ensure fairness at each join : this is done locally by endowing each join with an algorithm which defines the oracle at that join so that IO-fairness is guaranteed. The idea of the algorithm is as follows : if $(x_1,\ldots,x_q)$ are all the letters which could arrive at the join, we define a list $(n_1,\ldots,n_q)$ of integers where n_i gives the "priority" rank of letter x_i for going through the join : n_i simply counts the number of times letter x_i tried unsuccessfully access to the join. The oracle is then defined in order to let through the letter with the higher priority, while resetting the priority of that letter to 0. □

This algorithm in fact implements a scheduler for IO-fairness. The idea is to organize a queue of the letters waiting for each join; it is very similar to the scheduler for strong fairness of [Park2], but somehow different from the schedulers of [Apt-Olderog], which are intrinsically distributed, and do not use a queue but random assignments. If q is the number of different letters which can arrive at join J, the scheduler for that join has q! states which is the minimal number of storage states to be expected (cf. [Fischer-Paterson]).

Proposition 3.16 For every net N and inputs I, I', $F_N(I) \cap F_N(I') \neq \emptyset$.

Proof : let N be represented as follows :

and let $I = (x_1,\ldots,x_k)$, $I' = (x'_1,\ldots,x'_k)$

Define N' by

N' = 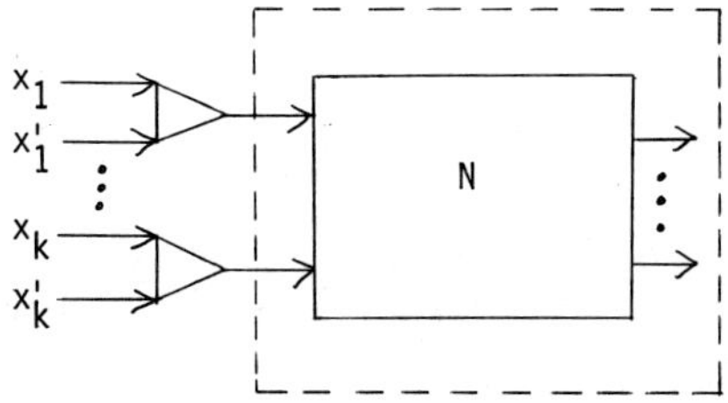

where the dotted square contains a copy of N

Then, every computation of N' which is IO-fair for the input $(x_1,x'_1,\dots,x_k,x'_k)$ defines by restriction to the subnet N, a computation of N which is fair with respect to both inputs I and I'. □

Corollary 3.17 For every finite set K of inputs, $K \subset A_1^\omega x \dots x A_k^\omega$, where A_j is the input alphabet for channel i_j, $\bigcap_{I \in K} F_N(I) \neq \emptyset$. □

The next proposition expresses that there is no oracle which is globally IO-fair with respect to all inputs.

Proposition 3.18 If at least one of the joins in a net N has an output alphabet containing at least two elements, then $\bigcap_{I \in A} F_N(I) = \emptyset$, where $A = A_1^\omega x \dots x A_k^\omega$, where A_j is the input alphabet for channel j.

Proof : We can then extract from N a join, possibly linked to input channels via processes but no loops, whose output, and hence input, alphabets contain at least two letters, say $\{a,b\}$. Let $\delta = 0^{i_1} 1^{j_1} 0^{i_2} 1^{j_2} \dots$ be an arbitrary oracle for that join J and consider the net N' consisting of the single join J. Then, letting $I = (x_1,x_2)$ with $x_1 = a^{i_1}b^{j_1}a^{i_2}b^{j_2} \dots$

$$\text{and } x_2 = \begin{cases} a^\omega & \text{if } |x_1|_b = \omega \\ a^q b^\omega & \text{if } x_1 = a^{i_1}b^{j_1}\dots a^{i_p}b^{j_p}a^\omega \text{ with } i_1+j_1+\dots+i_p+j_p \le q \end{cases}$$

δ is not IO-fair for I, since b will never be output. Hence, for subnet N', and also thus for net N, every oracle is IO-unfair for some input. □

Proposition 3.19 IO-fair computations are closed under composition.

Proof :

N" =

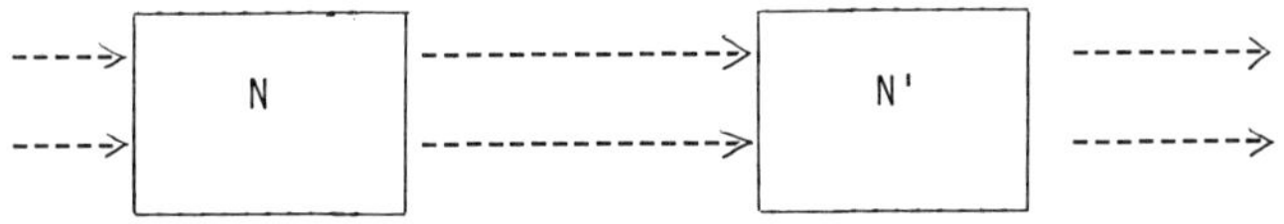

Let N, N' be two nets, and N'' be the net obtained by feeding the outputs of N as inputs to N'. Then, if δ is in $F_N(I)$ and δ' is in $F_{N'}(I')$, where I' is the output of the computation of N defined by δ, $\delta'' = \delta \times \delta'$ is in $F_{N''}(I)$, where, if $\delta = a_1a_2\dots \in (\{0,1\}^n)^\omega$ and $\delta' = a'_1a'_2 \dots \in (\{0,1\}^{n'})^\omega$ $\delta'' = (a_1a'_1)(a_2a'_2) \dots \in (\{0,1\}^{n+n'})^\omega$. □

Now, even though proposition 3.18 showed us that there is no oracle globally IO-fair for all inputs, we can show that there are oracles IO-fair with respect to classes of inputs. One such class is the class of ultimately periodic inputs.

Lemma 3.20 Let N be a net, $w = (w_1,\dots,w_k)$ a vector of finite input words such that $|w_1| = \dots = |w_k| = \ell$, and let w^ω be the infinite input $(w_1^\omega,\dots,w_k^\omega)$; let $(\sigma_1,\dots,\sigma_k)$ in Σ^k be arbitrary circular permutations of $\{1,\dots,\ell\}$ and let $\sigma(w)^\omega$ be the vector of inputs $(\sigma_1\,(w_1)^\omega,\dots,\sigma_k(w_k)^\omega)$. Then $\bigcap_{\sigma\in\Sigma^k} F_N(\sigma(w)^\omega)$ is non empty and contains an oracle δ of the form $\delta = \eta^\omega$.

Proof : as in proposition 3.16, we first construct a net N' with an input combining all the $\sigma(w)^\omega$, for σ in Σ^k : this is possible since there are at most ℓ^k such vectors $\sigma(w)$. We then use the algorithm in proposition 3.16 to compute a fair oracle : everything being periodic, the oracle will also be periodic. □

This lemma asserts that there exists a single periodic oracle IO-fair for all inputs of the form $\sigma(w)^\omega$. The restriction that all the w_i have the same length is inessential ; if the periods are different, it suffices to take as common period their least common multiple.

Lemma 3.21 Let $I = (x_1w_1^\omega,\dots,x_kw_k^\omega)$, where $w = (w_1,\dots,w_k)$, σ and δ are as in Lemma 3.20 ; then $\delta \in F_N(I)$.

Proof : Let $q = \max\{|x_i| \mid i = 1,\dots,k\}$ and let m be the first multiple of $|\eta|$ greater than q.

There exists $u = (u_1,\dots,u_k)$ and σ in Σ^k such that

$$\text{for } i = 1,\dots,k \quad |u_i| = m$$
$$I = (u_1\sigma_1(w_1)^\omega,\dots,u_k\sigma_k(w_k)^\omega) = u\,\sigma(w)^\omega$$

Notice now that $\eta^\omega = \delta \in F_N(\sigma(w)^\omega)$; moreover, fairness being concerned with infinitary behavior, we can forget about the first m components of I and δ, hence all oracles δ' in $\Delta = (\{0,1\}^n)^m\,\delta$ are in $F_N(I)$; in particular, δ itself being in Δ, is in $F_N(I)$. The following figure 1 representing the lengths of w, η and I might help. □

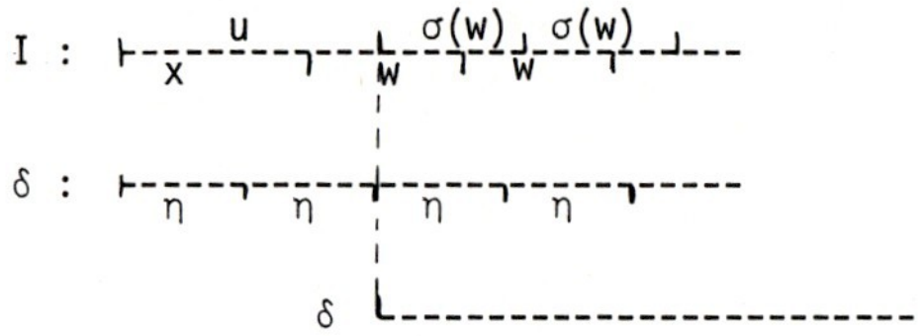

figure 1.

Theorem 3.22 : Let L be the set of inputs of the form $I = u.w^\omega$, where $u=(u_1,\dots,u_k)$ is an arbitrary k-tuple of finite words, and $w = (w_1,\dots,w_k)$ is a k-tuple of words such that $|w_1|=\dots=|w_k| = \ell$, then $\bigcap_{I\in L} F_N(I) \neq \emptyset$.

Proof : lemma 3.21 shows that δ is in $F_N(I)$ for each I in L. □

Note that

(i) we can relax the hypothesis that all w_i have the same length ℓ

(ii) we can, more generally, assume that w is an element of a finite set W of finite k-tuples $(w_1,\ldots,w_k)$, instead of w being always the same k-tuple.

The proof of lemma 3.20, and hence of the theorem, is the same under those weaker hypotheses.

Note finally that the oracles are perfectly effective, and might be called schedulers.

3.3 Strong fairness

We noticed in proposition 3.13 that both IO-fairness and path-fairness allow for some injustice (respectively for path-fairness and IO-fairness). In the present subsection, we will henceforth combine these two notions of fairness into a notion of strong fairness. Recall that all input and output alphabets are finite, so that path-fairness amounts to all useful paths being active. In order to define strong fairness we will keep track of the path a letter has gone through before arriving in a channel, as long as that path is a useful path or a prefix thereof.

Example 3.23 Let N be as in example 3.7, with input $(ab)^{\omega}$, oracle 001^{ω}. Then, the pairs (p,x) of the letter x which is in the channel [F,(J,2)] together with the prefix p of useful path x has already gone through, are as follows for the successive time units : at time 1, the channel is empty, so $(p,x) = \emptyset$

at time unit 2 : (i(J,1)fF,b)
at time unit 3 : (i(J,1)fF,a)
at time unit 4 : (i(J,1)fFw,a)
at time unit 5 : (i(J,1)fFw,b)
at time unit 6 : $(i(J,1)fFw^2,b)$
at time unit 7 : $(i(J,1)fFw^2,a)$

where w = (J,2) f F ;
at the subsequent time units, we no longer keep track of the path, because it is no more a useful path, hence the sequence of histories of that channel starting from time unit 8 and on will be $((*,a)(*,b)(*,b)(*,a))^{\omega}$, where $*$ replaces paths which are no more useful ; $*$ acts as a zero, or a sink. □

Definition 3.24 : Let N be a net, $P_u(N)$ the set of prefixes of useful paths in N, I an input. A computation is *strongly fair* with respect to I iff : for every channel c, and every history h = (p,x), where $p \in P_u(N) \cup \{*\}$ describes the portion of useful path already taken by letter x, if h could go infinitely often through channel c, then h must go infinitely often through channel c. Let $SF_N(I)$ be the set of oracles defining strongly fair computations for I. □

Example 3.23 (continued) : 001^ω is IO-fair for the input $(ab)^\omega$, but it is neither path-fair, nor strongly fair. The corresponding output is $b(a^2b^2)^\omega$. Now the oracle $\delta = (0^2 1^6)^\omega$ is strongly fair, path-fair and IO-fair ; the sequence of histories corresponding to channel [F, (J,2)] is $[(p,b)(p,a)(pw,a)(pw,b)(pw^2,b)(pw^2,a)(*,a)(*,b)]^\omega$, where p = i(J,1)fF and w = (J,2)fF as above ; the corresponding output is $(baabbaab)^\omega$. □

Basically all the propositions and theorems we proved for IO-fairness also hold for strong fairness with similar proofs. We state some of them.

Proposition 3.25 : for every net N and input I, $SF_N(I) \neq \emptyset$.

The proof is similar to the one for proposition 3.15 ; the algorithm for finding fair oracles now has to keep track not only of the number of times a letter tried to go through a join, but also of the previous history of that letter. Hence, instead of having n different algorithms, one for each join in the net, we have a single global algorithm, which chooses all the oracles in the net, while keeping track of all useful histories in its priority list. This list stays bounded because once a useful path is completed, the corresponding history becomes (*,a) and * acts as zero for path composition, i.e. extending * by any path again results in *. □

Proposition 3.26 : for every finite set K of inputs $\bigcap_{I \in K} SF_N(I) \neq \emptyset$.

Proposition 3.27 : a strongly fair computation is both IO-fair and weakly path-fair.

Since there are only a finite number of pairs h = (p,x), including the pairs (*,x), then :

(i) if a letter x comes infinitely often to a join, then some h = (p,x) (with possibly p = *), will also come infinitely often to that join, hence h will go through infinitely often because of strong fairness ; whence IO-fairness

(ii) assume now c is strongly fair but not weakly path-fair. Let p be a shortest useful path which is taken only finitely many times, p cannot be of length one, since inputs are infinite streams. Hence p is of the form $p = p'\phi$, where p' is taken infinitely often. p' can only output a finite number of different letters, hence for some letter x, $(p'\phi,x)$ is possible infinitely often, hence is taken infinitely often by the strong fairness assumption ; p is thus also taken infinitely often, a contradiction. □

Corollary 3.28 : (i) $\bigcap_{I \in A} SF_N(I) = \emptyset$, where A is the set of all possible inputs

(ii) strongly fair computations are not closed under composition.

Proof : (i) holds for IO-fair computations

(ii) see the counter example in remark 3.29 (i). □

Remark 3.29

(i) the converse of proposition 3.27 is false. Let N be the following net, with the indicated inputs and oracles

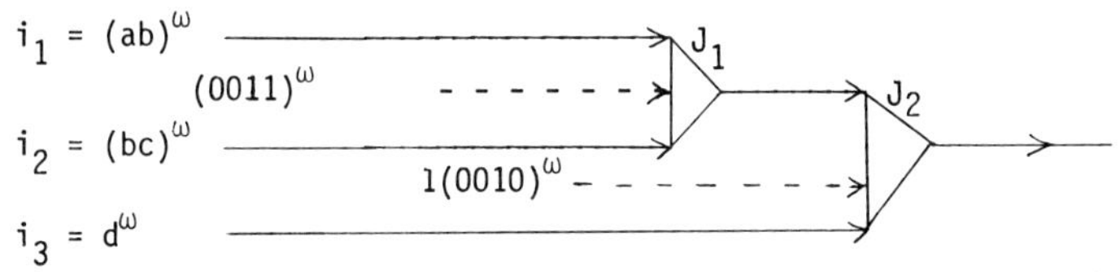

Then the output is $d(abdc)^\omega$ but the computation is not strongly fair, because the history $((J_1,2)(J_2,1), b)$ is never taken. Moreover the oracles define strongly fair computations if each join is considered as a separate net, but the composition is not strongly fair.

(ii) It is essential, in the definition of strong fairness, to demand that, if $(*,x)$ could go infinitely often through a channel c, then it must go infinitely often in that channel; if we relax that requirement, the following counter-example shows that strong fairness does not any more imply IO-fairness. Let N be

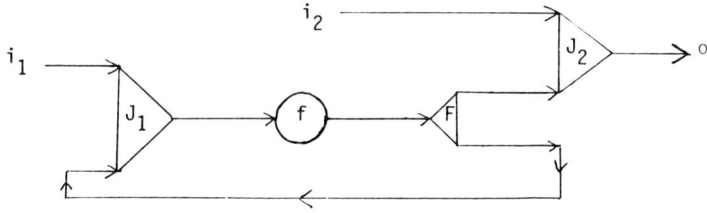

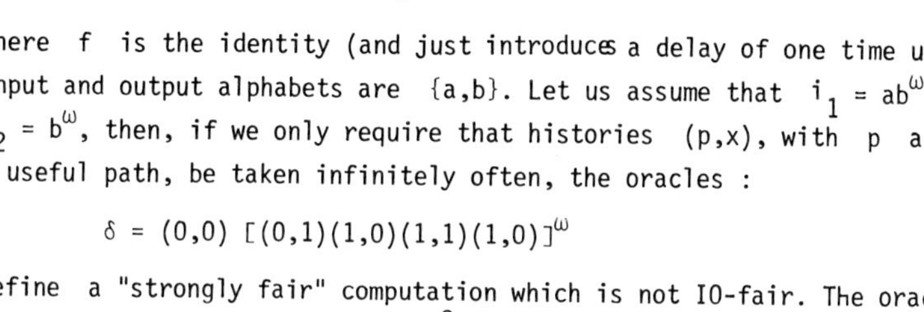

where f is the identity (and just introduces a delay of one time unit), and the input and output alphabets are {a,b}. Let us assume that $i_1 = ab^\omega$ and $i_2 = b^\omega$, then, if we only require that histories (p,x), with p a prefix of a useful path, be taken infinitely often, the oracles :

$$\delta = (0,0)\ [(0,1)(1,0)(1,1)(1,0)]^\omega$$

define a "strongly fair" computation which is not IO-fair. The oracle corresponding to the join J_1 is $0(01^3)^\omega$, corresponding to the output $\varepsilon^2(ab)^\omega$ on channel $[F, (J_2,2)]$. The oracle corresponding to join J_2 is $(01)^\omega$, corresponding to output b^{ω} on channel o, hence a will never pass join J_2 ; this is due to the fact that a arrives to that join with increasingly long histories of the form (pw^n,a), with $p = i_1(J_1,1)fF$, $w = (J_1,2)fF$ and $n = 0, 1, 2...$

(iii) a last remark is to note the essentiality of the synchronous behaviors of all operators : namely no process or join is ever blocked, and all operators take a step together at every time unit.

3.4 Privilege freeness

Even the notion of strong fairness allows for some privileges, or priorities : e.g. if a letter x has a priority over a letter y, each time x and y arrive together at a join, x will win the race and go through the join. The following definition excludes this kind of behavior.

Definition 3.30 Let N, I, h be as in definition 3.24, $h' = (p',x')$ be an history, J a join in N and $T(h, h', J)$ the set of time instants when h and h' arrive together at join J. A computation is *privilege-free* with respect to I iff for all h, h', J, both h and h' will infinitely often succeed to go through join J during the time units in $T(h, h', J)$. Let $PF_N(I)$ be the set of oracles defining privilege-free computations for I. □

Proposition 3.31 For every net N and input I, $PF_N(I) \neq \emptyset$.

Proof : We have to ensure privilege freeness at each join. This is again done locally by endowing each join with a scheduler which defines a privilege-free oracle for that join. The idea for building the scheduler is similar to the ones in propositions 3.15 and 3.25, but the scheduler now has two checklists. One list L keeps track of the priority rank of each $h = (p,x)$ arriving to the join, by counting the number of unsuccessful attempts to go through the join ; the other list L' keeps track of the privileges : namely, whenever a pair h, h' comes to the join, and h goes through, this is recorded in L', in order to choose h' the next time h and h' happen to race against each other again for that join. □

If we forget about paths, a privilege-free computation is also privilege-free with respect to data, namely if two letters x,y come together infinitely often at a given join, then both of them will win the race infinitely often. Since there are only finitely many paths, there exist histories (p,x), (q,y) which must also come together infinitely often at the same join, whence the result by privilege-freeness. Similarly, we can prove :

Proposition 3.32 (i) a privilege-free computation is strongly fair

(ii) $PF_N(I) \subsetneq SF_N(I)$

Proof : (ii) follows from (i) and the fact that, obviously, a strongly fair computation needs not be privilege-free.

(i) it suffices to check strong fairness at the joins. If a history h arrives infinitely often at a join, then there exists at least one h' which arrives at that join together with h infinitely often, since the set of histories is finite ; hence h will go through that join infinitely often. □

Corollary 3.33 (i) $\bigcap_{I \in A} PF_N(I) = \emptyset$, where A is the set of all possible inputs.

(ii) privilege-free computations are not closed under composition.

Proof : (i) otherwise, if $c \in \bigcap_{I \in A} PF_N(I)$, c would also be strongly fair for all inputs, thus contradicting Corollary 3.28.

(ii) take again the example of remark 3.29 (i). $(0011)^\omega$ is a privilege-free oracle for the inputs $(ab)^\omega$ and $(bc)^\omega$; $1(00101011)^\omega$ is a privilege free oracle for the inputs $\varepsilon(abbc)^\omega$ and d^ω, but the composition of the two is not even strongly fair for the composed net, again because the history $((J_1,2)(J_2,1), b)$ is never taken. □

Proposition 3.34 For every finite set K of inputs, $\bigcap_{I \in K} PF_N(I) \neq \emptyset$.

The idea of the proof is similar to the one of proposition 3.16. □

We thus note that only IO-fairness is closed under composition, and that all notions of fairness which take into account fairness with respect to path behavior are not closed under composition.

However, we can, by using a trick and coding the path together with the input, obtain notions of fairness which are closed under composition. For instance, we can modify the notion of privilege-freeness by feeding the net with histories, i.e. pairs consisting of a finite path together with an input, instead of single inputs ; we then require privilege-freeness with respect to streams of such histories. The subsequent notion of privilege-freeness will be closed under composition : this follows from the fact that when we compose two nets, the inputs to the second net will be histories consisting of one data output of the first net, together with the corresponding useful path ; since the second net must be privilege-free with respect to such inputs, the composed net will also be privilege-free. So, for instance, going back to corollary 3.33 (ii) and example 3.29, if we feed the histories $((\varepsilon,a)(\varepsilon,b))^\omega$ and $((\varepsilon,b)(\varepsilon,c))^\omega$ to the first join, the oracle $(0011)^\omega$ is privilege-free for these inputs ; the corresponding output can be represented as $w = ((1,a)(1,b)(2,b)(2,c))^\omega$, by denoting the path (J_1,i) by i, for $i = 1,2$. But now, the oracle $1(00101011)^\omega$ is no more privilege-free for $(\varepsilon,\varepsilon)w$ and $(\varepsilon,d)^\omega$.

Similarly, a notion of strong fairness which is closed under composition can be defined by incorporating the useful paths together with the inputs. Apart from closure under composition, this notion of fairness inherits all properties of strong fairness.

Conclusion

We have introduced fork-join nets, which give a model of synchronous low-level non determinism and parallelism. We studied various notions of fairness, of the strong fairness type, for such nets : a global and syntactic notion, related to the path behavior of the net, a local and more semantic notion, related to the IO behavior of the net, and combinations of the two previous notions. We show that local notions of fairness, relative to IO behavior are closed under composition, which is an essential property in a modular approach to programming. We use the theory of ω-regular languages to prove properties of fair computations. More should be done in that direction, in particular to find effective characterizations of all fair computations. The behavior of our nets can be related to systolic automata or data flow nets and we hope our study will help in giving tools and/or different viewpoints for these theories.

Acknowledgments

We thank the anonymous referees and Krzysztof Apt for helpful comments.

Appendix - Infinitary languages

We recall some definitions about regular ω-languages. Let A be a finite non empty alphabet, we consider an infinite word w over A as a map

$w : N \text{-------}> \Sigma$ such that

$w(i)$ is the ith letter of w

A^* : the set of finite words on A,
A^ω : the set of infinite words on A,
$A^\infty = A^* \cup A^\omega$ $A^+ = AA^*$

We denote $|w|_a$: the number of occurrences of a in w.

Definition A.1

A. *Büchi automaton* is a structure

$A = \langle Q, A, q_0, \delta, Q_{inf} \rangle$

- Q : the set of states (finite)
- A : finite alphabet
- $q_0 \in Q$: initial state
- δ : transition function
  $\delta : Q \times A \text{-----}> 2^Q$
- Q_{inf} : the set of infinitary states

Definition A.2

For $w \in A^{\omega}$, we call *computation* of A over w a map

$c : N \text{-----}> Q$ such that

(i) $c(o) = q_0$

(ii) $c(i+1) \in \delta(c(i), w(i))$

and a computation is successful iff $inf(c) \cap Q_{inf} \neq \emptyset$
$inf(c)$ is the set of states such that : $q \in inf(c)$ iff there exists an infinity of $i \in N$ such that $c(i) = q$.

For a Büchi automaton A, the set of all ω-words in A^{ω} such that there exists a successful computation of A over w, is denoted by $||A||$, and called the ω-language accepted by A. An ω-language is said to be *ω-regular* if it is accepted by some Büchi automaton.

Definition A.3

An *extended Büchi automaton* is a structure $A = <Q,A,q_0,\delta,Q_1,\ldots,Q_n>$ such that Q,A,q_0 and δ are as in Definition A.1 and $Q_1,\ldots,Q_n$ are sets of infinitary states.

Definition A.4

A computation of A is successful iff $\forall\ i = 1,\ldots,n\ inf(c) \cap Q_i \neq \emptyset$.

Property A.1

Büchi automata and extended Büchi automata accept the same class of languages.

References

[Apt-Olderog] K. Apt, E.-R. Olderog, Proof rules and transformations dealing with fairness, Science of Comp. Prog. 3 (1983), 65-100.

[Arnold] A. Arnold, Sémantique des processus communicants, RAIRO Informatique Théorique 15, (1981), 103-139.

[Benson] D. Benson, Studies in Fork-join parallelism, report CS-82-101 WSU (1982).

[Boussinot] F. Boussinot, Proposition de sémantique dénotationnelle pour des réseaux de processus avec mélange équitable, TCS 18 (1982), 173-206.

[Costa-Stirling] G. Costa, C. Stirling, Weak and strong fairness in CCS, MFCS 84, LNCS 176, Springer Verlag, Berlin (1984), 245-254.

[Culik-Salomaa-Wood] K. Culik II, A. Salomaa, D. Wood, Systolic tree acceptors, RAIRO Informatique Théorique 18 (1984), 53-69.

[Darondeau] P. Darondeau, About fair Asynchrony, TCS 37 (1985).

[Dennis] J. Dennis, Data flow computations, in Control Flow and Data Flow : Concepts of Distributed Programming (ed. M. Broy), NATO ASI Series, Vol. F14, Springer-Verlag, Amsterdam (1985), 345-398.

[Fischer-Paterson] M. Fischer, M. Paterson, Storage requirements for fair scheduling, Inf. Proc. Letters 17 (1983), 249-250.

[Hennessy] M. Hennessy, Modelling finite delay operators, rep. CSR 153-83 (1983).

[Lichtenstein-Pnueli-Zuck] O. Lichtenstein, A. Pnueli, L. Zuck, The glory of the past, in proceedings of Logics of Programs 1985, Springer Verlag Lecture Notes in Computer Science 193, (1985), 196-218.

[Park1] D. Park, The "fairness" problem and nondeterministic computing networks, in Foundations of Computer Science IV, Part 2 (eds. de Bakker, Leuwen), Mathematical Centre Tracts 159, Amsterdam (1983), 133-161.

[Park2] D. Park, A predicate transformer for weak fair iteration, in Proceedings of 6th IBM Symp. MFOCS (1981), 259-275.

QUESTIONS AND ANSWERS

Pnueli: Suppose you have the following very simple net:

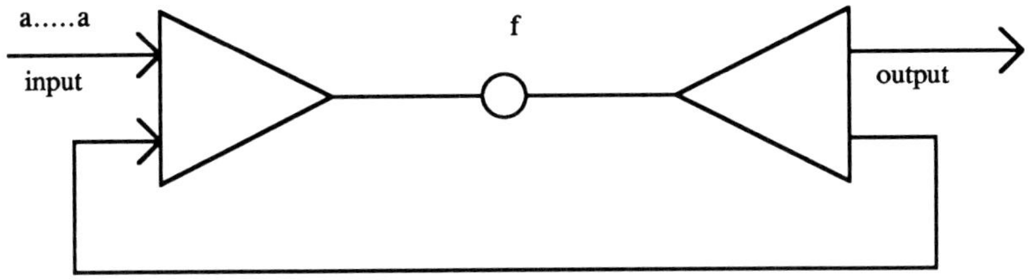

Moreover, suppose you have a sequence of just *a* 's coming in. Are you guaranteed to get $f^n(a)$ for any *n* in the output?

Chardili: Yes, if we take the first notion of fairness.

Pnueli: Have you thought about how to implement such a fairness? Because this notion is really similar to extreme fairness, it is very strong.

Chardili: No, I did not think about implementation. I agree, this notion is very strong.

Formal Description of Programming Concepts - III
M. Wirsing (Editor)
Elsevier Science Publishers B.V. (North-Holland)

© IFIP, 1987

A CCS Semantics for NIL

Scott A. Smolka[†]
Department of Computer Science
SUNY at Stony Brook
Stony Brook, NY 11794-4400
U.S.A.

Robert E. Strom
IBM T.J. Watson Research Center
P.O. Box 218
Yorktown Heights, NY 10598
U.S.A.

We present a syntax-directed translation of NIL, a high-level language for distributed systems programming, into CCS, Milner's Calculus of Communicating Systems. This translation presents unique problems because of NIL's highly dynamic nature, and makes full use of CCS's descriptive facilities. In particular, we consider NIL constructs for dynamic creation and deletion of processes and communication channels, queued synchronous and asynchronous message passing, nondeterministic message selection, and exception handling. A NIL implementation of a simple command shell is used to illustrate the translation procedure. We discuss various issues and open problems concerning the suitability of CCS as an abstract semantics for NIL.

1. Introduction

In this paper, we present a syntax-directed translation of NIL into CCS. NIL [SY83, SH84] is a high-level language for distributed systems programming developed at IBM Research, Yorktown Heights. CCS, Milner's Calculus of Communicating Systems [Mi80], is a calculus for the description and algebraic manipulation of concurrent communicating systems. Because of the existence of a formal (operational) semantics for CCS, the translation of NIL into CCS effectively gives NIL a formal semantics. However, much depends on the "adequacy" of the translation [HL83], a point we address when concluding this paper.

Our motivation for this work is multifold. First, we believe that a CCS semantics for NIL will enable people who know CCS to learn NIL and, conversely, enable people who know NIL to learn CCS. Secondly, we would like to prove properties of a NIL program by reasoning algebraically in terms of its CCS translation. Thirdly, we would like to prove that NIL program transformations, such as those proposed in [SY85a], are semantics preserving.

Milner, in Chapter 9 of [Mi80], illustrated the feasibility of using CCS as a semantics for programming languages by presenting a CCS translation of a simple parallel programming language. Other programming languages that have been given CCS semantics include Hoare's CSP [HLP81, AZ81], a subset of Ada [HL83], and Sticks and Stones [Ca81]. Furthermore, CCS has been used as a semantics for several programming systems including the ISO OSI [SW83] and the systems-calls level of UNIX

[†]Supported by NSF Grant DCR-8505873.

[DG83]. The sum of these efforts demonstrates the utility of CCS as a formal model for concurrent programming languages and systems.

Our translation of NIL into CCS differs from the above work in several respects. Unlike the static binding of Ada, communication ports are bound to a process dynamically in NIL. Also, the particular code body being executed by a NIL process is determined dynamically (see [SYW85] for a much more elaborate comparison of Ada and NIL). Our translation of NIL is inherently different from the [DG83] UNIX translation. In UNIX, process creation is at the "fork" level; its translation into CCS is thus primarily concerned with the copying and creation of memory segments. Interprocess communication is at the file level (i.e. pipes). The corresponding NIL constructs are at a much higher level of abstraction.

The structure of this paper is as follows: Sections 2 and 3 provide an overview of NIL and CCS, respectively. In Section 4, we present our translation of NIL into CCS. Some highlights of our translation are given in the beginning of Section 4.2. The translation procedure is illustrated in Section 5 using a NIL implementation of a simple command shell. Section 6 concludes with a discussion of some of the issues in using CCS as a semantics for NIL.

2. An Overview of NIL

NIL is a high-level systems programming language developed at T. J. Watson Research Laboratory. The single unit of abstraction in NIL is the *process*, which subsumes the notions of procedures, tasks, data abstraction, and others. Unlike abstract data types where the user of the type is actively making calls and the abstract data type module is passively accepting calls, the relationships between processes in NIL is symmetric.

Processes in NIL communicate only over *communication channels*; there is no sharing of data across processes. A unidirectional communication channel is created dynamically under program control by connecting an *input port* to an *output port*. A process, say P, can accomplish this through the statement "y = **outport of** x", where y is an output port and x is an initialized input port. P can initialize input port x using the statement "**initialize** x". By passing y to another process Q, P can give Q a *capability* to send messages to input port x.

NIL supports the standard control constructs of Algol-like imperative languages – sequential composition, **if** statements for alternation, and **while** statements for iteration. In addition, NIL supports exception handling. Each statement may result in a *normal* termination, which is followed by the execution of the next sequential statement, or an *exception* termination, in which case execution continues in an *exception handler* associated with the exception condition. The possible exception conditions which can be raised by a given statement are known statically: from the statement name for primitive statements, and from the port type definition for calls to programmer-defined ports.

All variables in NIL, including ports, are statically typed. A channel can connect only output ports and input ports of the same type. Several output ports may be connected to a single input port, but not vice versa. Messages arriving at an input port are enqueued. Processes use guarded commands similar to Ada **select** statements to selectively respond to communication on their input ports.

NIL supports both ***synchronous*** and ***asynchronous*** communication. Synchronous communication, designated by **call** and **accept**, involves the transmission of a *callrecord* (collection of actual parameters) and the suspension of the caller until the acceptor has processed and returned the callrecord. The **accept** operation removes a single callrecord from the input port, or waits until one is available. The acceptor can also **forward** the callrecord, and the responsibility of returning the callrecord to the caller, to another process. Asynchronous communication, designated by **send** and **receive**, does not cause the sender to wait. The **receive** operation causes a message to be dequeued from the input port, if one is present, and causes the receiver to wait if none is present. Successive messages sent over a single output port will be received in FIFO order, but no specific order other than a *fair merge* is guaranteed for messages sent over different output ports which arrive at the same input port.

Processes are created and destroyed dynamically. An object of type *process* is initialized by issuing a **create** operation, supplying as parameters the name of the file containing the compiled NIL program to be executed by the process, and a list of *creation-time parameters.* These parameters are used to pass initial data and capabilities to an initialization routine within the created process. Like any other NIL object, a process can be passed as a message from one process to another. This also effects a transfer of ownership of the object from the sending to the receiving process.

A process is destroyed when its owner issues a **cancel** operation. Canceling a process which has not already terminated causes that process to eventually enter the *canceled state*. A process in the canceled state will have a *CANCEL* exception raised as a result of issuing a subsequent waiting operation (**select**, **receive** or **call**), or on a subsequent loop iteration. The process is then permitted to perform "last wishes" by providing a handler for the *CANCEL* exception. However, the language rules stipulate that once a CANCEL exception has been raised, the process will terminate in a finite amount of time.

Unlike CCS, NIL has no concept of global time or simultaneity of events in distinct processes. There is only a partial order between the local times of each process as determined by causality of events: the event of a sender sending message M precedes the event at which the receiver receives M. Events which are not related by communication (either directly or indirectly) are incomparable.

A more complete summary of NIL can be found in [SY83] and a status report in [SY85b].

3. An Overview of CCS

Milner's CCS (Calculus of Communicating Systems) is a calculus for the description and algebraic manipulation of systems of communicating processes [Mi80]. Like NIL, communication in CCS is port-based. The *sort* of a process is the set of ports through which it can communicate with other processes. Unlike NIL, communication in CCS is unbuffered – the sender and receiver of a message must agree to synchronize at some point in time – and the sort of a process is fixed.

The semantics of concurrent composition in CCS is one of interleaved execution of the component processes, with simultaneous moves by two processes whenever they communicate (see Milner's "expansion theorem" [Mi80]).

We present the syntax and informal semantics of CCS with *value expressions* over a presupposed value domain D. We use $e_1, e_2, \cdots$ to denote expressions (e.g. function applications and constants) over D, and $x, y, \cdots$ to denote variables over D. A complete exposition on CCS including a formal (operational) semantics is given in [Mi80].

Input ports in CCS are denoted by *names* $\alpha, \beta, \cdots$, and output ports are denoted by *conames* $\overline{\alpha}, \overline{\beta}, \cdots$. (In practice, mnemonic English names are often used in place of small Greek letters.) A communication can take place only over *complementary* ports, e.g. α and $\overline{\alpha}$.

Names and conames will also be used to respectively denote input *actions* and output *coactions* taken by a CCS process. For example, $\alpha(x)$ is an action that inputs a value for x from port α, and $\overline{\alpha}(e)$ is a coaction that outputs the value of e over port $\overline{\alpha}$. In λ-calculus-like terms, the variable x is *bound* by α and the value expression e is *qualified* by $\overline{\alpha}$. Actions $\alpha(x)$ and $\overline{\alpha}(e)$ must occur simultaneously to effect a communication, the result of which is intuitively "$x := e$".

CCS programs, called *behavior expressions* by Milner, can be defined inductively as follow:

> *NIL* (not to be confused with the programming language) is a behavior expression which does absolutely nothing.

Let $\alpha(x)$ be an input action, $\overline{\alpha}(e)$ an output action, and B and C behavior expressions. Then

> $\alpha(x) . B$ is a behavior expression which first inputs some value v over port α and then behaves like B with all free occurrences of x bound to v.
>
> $\overline{\alpha}(e) . B$ is a behavior expression which first outputs the value of e over the port $\overline{\alpha}$ and then behaves exactly like B. Note that every variable in e must be bound for this coaction to make sense.
>
> $B + C$ is a behavior expression which nondeterministically behaves like B or C. The operator $+$ is the binary version of $\sum$.
>
> $B \mid C$ is a behavior expression which behaves as the concurrent composition of B and C. The operator $\mid$ is the binary version of $\prod$.
>
> $B \backslash \{\alpha_1, \cdots, \alpha_n\}$ is a behavior expression which behaves like B with the set of ports $\{\alpha_i, \overline{\alpha}_i \mid 1 \leq i \leq n\}$ deleted from its sort. $\backslash$ is called the *restriction*

operator and effectively hides all α_i-actions and $\overline{\alpha}_i$-coactions from B's outside world.

$B[\nu_1/\mu_1, \cdots, \nu_n/\mu_n]$ is a behavior expression which behaves like B with all actions/coactions μ_i *relabeled* as ν_i, $1 \leq i \leq n$.

if cond then B else C is a behavior expression which behaves like B if *cond* is true and like C otherwise.

$P(e_1, \cdots, e_k)$ is a ***behavior identifier*** with actual parameters $e_1, \cdots, e_k$. We write $P <= B$ to associate behavior identifier P with behavior expression B.

CCS also allows for parametric port names (e.g. α_x) and behavior identifiers (e.g. P_i). In fact, Milner shows in [Mi85] that the entire calculus with value expressions can be encoded into a simpler calculus devoid of value expressions using sets of parametric port names of the form $\{\alpha_d, \overline{\alpha}_d \mid d \in D\}$, where D is the value domain in question.

4. The Translation

In this section we present a syntax-directed translation of NIL into CCS, which will be given in terms of a set of translation rules (one for each construct). The translation rule for a given construct (syntactic unit) S of NIL yields a CCS behavior expression $[[S]]$. The translation is syntax-directed since $[[S]]$ is produced independently of the context of S. For example, $[[$if E **then** S **else** $S'\,]]$ will be derived uniquely from $[[E]]$, $[[S]]$, and $[[S'\,]]$.

Variables in NIL will be modeled as registers in CCS. The restriction operator is applied to prevent other processes from having access to the ports of the local variables of a particular process. However, NIL input and output ports will be modeled as globally accessible ports in the CCS translation.

4.1. Milner's Chapter 9

In Chapter 9 of [Mi80], Milner presents a translation of a simple parallel programming language into CCS. This work is fundamental to our own and we thus describe it here.

NIL programs, like programs from Milner's language, will be built from *declarations* D and *statements* S. Declarations in NIL associate variable names with types. Here we use type-free declarations whose syntax is $D \rightarrow$ **var**X; $\cdots$; **var** X, where X is a *program variable*.

Statements will be built from *expressions* E having syntax $E \rightarrow X \mid F(E, \cdots, E)$, where F is a *function symbol* standing for the built-in function f.

A variable X will be represented by a CCS behavior expression corresponding to a register with sort $\{write_X, \overline{read_X}\}$:

$$LOC_X <= write_X(x)\,.\,REG_X(x)$$
$$REG_X(y) <= write_X(x)\,.\,REG_X(x) + \overline{read_X}(y)\,.\,REG_X(y)$$

Note that X will be "born" as LOC_X and then become $REG_X(v)$ as soon as it inputs a value v. The set of ports needed to access LOC_X (the *access sort* of LOC_X) is $L_X = \{\overline{write_X}, read_X\}$.

Each n-ary function symbol F (denoting function f) will be represented by the behavior b_f which first inputs its n arguments, outputs the value of the corresponding application of f, and then dies:

$$b_f \;<=\; \rho_1(x_1)\,.\,\cdots\,.\,\rho_n(x_n)\,.\,\overline{\rho}(f(x_1,\cdots,x_n))\,.\,NIL$$

The translation rules for an expression E containing variables $X_1, \cdots, X_k$ will yield a behavior expression of sort $\{read_{X_1}, \cdots, read_{X_k}, \rho\}$. It uses port $read_{X_i}$ to read the value of X_i, and like function symbols, delivers its result at ρ and then dies.

Several translation rules (e.g. the one for assignment statements) will yield a behavior expression that is dependent on the result delivered by an expression. Thus, for some behavior expression B, Milner abbreviates the CCS expression $([\![E]\!] \mid \rho(x)\,.\,B)\backslash\rho$ as $[\![E]\!]$ *result* $(\rho(x)\,.\,B)$.

A statement S containing variables $X_1, \cdots, X_k$ will be represented by the behavior expression $[\![S]\!]$ whose sort includes the set $L_{X_1} \cup \cdots \cup L_{X_k} \cup \{\overline{\delta}\}$. The port $\overline{\delta}$ is used by $[\![S]\!]$ to signal its completion, and thus effect flow of control. Milner defines the following auxiliary behavior expressions in this light:

$done = \overline{\delta}\,.\,NIL$

B_1 *before* $B_2 = (B_1[\beta/\delta] \mid \beta\,.\,B_2)\backslash\beta$, where β is not in the sort of B_1 or B_2.

The following translation rules are for expressions [Mi80]:

$[\![X]\!] = read_X(x)\,.\,\overline{\rho}(x)\,.\,NIL$

$[\![F(E_1, \cdots, E_n)]\!] = ([\![E_1]\!][\rho_1/\rho] \mid \cdots \mid [\![E_n]\!][\rho_n/\rho] \mid b_f)\backslash\rho_1 \cdots \backslash\rho_n$

In the first rule, the value of X is read from its register and delivered as the result of the expression. In the second rule, the value of each expression is read by the behavior b_f, which then delivers the appropriate function application as its result.

What follows are the [Mi80] translation rules for assignment, sequential composition, conditional, iteration, and begin block statements. The NIL syntax of these statements can be seen on the left-hand side of the rules.

$[\![X := E]\!] = [\![E]\!]$ *result* $(\rho(x)\,.\,\overline{write}_X(x)\,.\,done)$

$[\![S;\, S'\,]\!] = [\![S]\!]$ *before* $[\![S'\,]\!]$

$[\![$**if** E **then** S **else** S' **end if**$]\!] = [\![E]\!]$ *result* $(\rho(x)\,.\,($*if* x *then* $[\![S]\!]$ *else* $[\![S'\,]\!]))$

$[\![$**while** E **do** S **end while**$]\!] = w$, where w is a new behavior identifier such that

$w \;<=\; [\![E]\!]$ *result* $(\rho(x)\,.\,$*if* x *then* $([\![S]\!]$ *before* $w)$ *else* *done*$)$

$[\![$**block declare var** $X_1; \cdots;$ **var** X_n; **begin** S **end block**$]\!] =$

$(LOC_{X_1} \mid \cdots \mid LOC_{X_n} \mid [\![S]\!])\backslash L_{X_1} \cup \cdots \cup L_{X_n}$

In the assignment statement rule, the result of evaluating E is stored in X's register. For sequential composition, the *before* operator ensures that $[\![S]\!]$ is executed before $[\![S'\,]\!]$. In the conditional statement rule, the result of evaluating E is used to determine whether to execute $[\![S]\!]$ or $[\![S'\,]\!]$. For the while statement, E is evaluated to determine whether to re-execute $[\![S]\!]$ or to deliver its *done* signal. Finally, for the begin statement, register behaviors for each declared variable are started up in parallel with $[\![S]\!]$. These variables are made local to the scope of the **begin** through restriction.

4.2. Translating the rest of NIL

In the previous subsection we consider the translation of expressions, assignment statements, sequential composition, if-then-else statements, while statements, and begin-block statements. Now we consider NIL constructs for dynamic creation and deletion of processes and ports, message passing, nondeterministic message selection, and exception handling. Some additional flow of control constructs are also considered.

NIL supports variables of type *inport* (*receiveport, acceptport*) and *outport* (*sendport, callport*). For example, statements such as $X := Y$ are permitted, where X and Y are outport variables. (After this statement is executed, X will be connected to the same inport as Y.) Also, inports and outports can be passed as messages.

In CCS there is no notion of port variable but only of port constant. The effect of port variables can be obtained in CCS through the use of an indexed set of ports [Mi85]. That is, we associate the CCS port $\overline{o}_{opid}$ with each instance of a NIL outport variable X, where *opid* (short for *outport id*) is a unique index. The outport X may now be referred to in the CCS translation by its index *opid*, which we store in a register associated with X. For example, X may be passed as a message by reading the value of *opid* from its register and then passing this value.

Similarly, we associate a CCS port ι_{ipid}, and a register in which to store the value of *ipid*, with each instance of a NIL inport variable. Note that under this convention, the sort of the CCS behavior expression resulting from the translation of a NIL process will include the set $\{\iota_j, \overline{o}_j \mid j \in I\}$.

To supply a source of ids in our translation, we define the following behavior expression:

$$IdGen(n) <= \overline{gen}(n) \,.\, IdGen(n+1)$$

Through relabeling we obtain a source for inport and outport ids: $IdGen(0)[igen/gen]$ and $IdGen(0)[ogen/gen]$, respectively. Note that both sources start with id 0. We will also need a source of process ids (see the translation of **create**) for which we use the behavior $IdGen(0)[pgen/gen]$.

As described in Section 2, message passing in NIL is completely asynchronous in that messages are queued at the receiving end, and the transit time of a message along a communication channel is indeterminate. To model this NIL asynchrony in CCS, where message passing is unbuffered and synchronous, we "attach" an infinite queue behavior to each of the $\iota_j, \overline{o}_j$ CCS ports used in the translation. The effect of a communication channel between outport $\overline{o}_{opid}$ and inport ι_{ipid} can then be obtained by diverting the output of the $\overline{o}_{opid}$ queue to the input of the ι_{ipid} queue. Note that it is necessary to attach an infinite queue to $\overline{o}_{opid}$ (as well as to ι_{ipid}) in order to "desynchronize" transmitting processes.

To illustrate, consider a NIL channel configuration consisting of outports X and Y connected to inport Z. Let $\overline{o}_{opid}$, $\overline{o}_{opid'}$, and ι_{ipid} be the respective CCS ports. Our translation would yield the following picture:

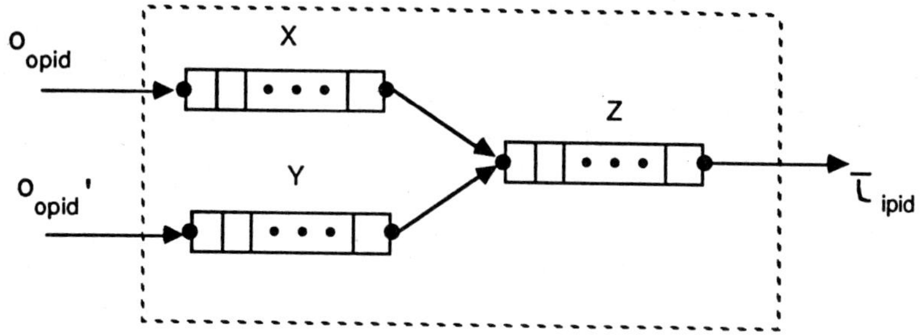

The access sort of this channel configuration is $\{\overline{o}_{opid}, \overline{o}_{opid'}, \iota_{ipid}\}$ as desired. If an infinite queue was not attached to each of ports o_{opid} and $o_{opid'}$, then the following scenario could occur: Let e be the event of transmitting message M over outport X, and let e' be the event of transmitting message M' over outport Y. If e precedes e' (in the partial order of events in a NIL system – see the end of Section 2), then M would necessarily be enqueued at inport Z before M', violating the indeterminate–transit–time aspect of NIL semantics.

What follows are the CCS behavior expressions for outport and inport queues. In each case, we first define a behavior that models an *empty queue*, which evolves into the behavior for a *nonempty queue* upon inputting a value. Of course, a nonempty queue becomes an empty queue after outputting its last value.

Outport queues are provided with a port $\overline{who}_{opid}$ which can be interrogated to determine the id of the inport to which it is connected. This feature is needed in translating outport assignment. Inport queues are provided with two auxiliary ports. Port $\overline{poll}_{ipid}$ can be queried to detect the current state of the queue, a feature needed in the translation of **select**. Port $make_{ipid}$ can be used to trigger the creation of an outport *opid* connected to inport *ipid*.

Empty Outport Queue:

$$outq(opid, ipid) \;\Leftarrow\; o_{opid}(x) \,.\, outq'(append\ x\ \epsilon, opid, ipid) + \overline{who}_{opid}(ipid) \,.\, outq(opid, ipid)$$

Nonempty Outport Queue:

$$\begin{aligned} outq'(s, opid, ipid) \;\Leftarrow\;& o_{opid}(x) \,.\, outq'(append\ x\ s, opid, ipid) + \\ & \overline{out}_{ipid}(first\ s) \,.\, if\,(rest\ s = \epsilon)\ then\ outq(opid, ipid) \\ & \quad else\ outq'(rest\ s, opid, ipid) \\ & + \overline{who}_{opid}(ipid) \,.\, outq'(s, opid, ipid) \end{aligned}$$

Empty Inport Queue:

$$inq\,(ipid) \;\Leftarrow\; out_{ipid}(x)\,.\,inq'\,(append\ x\ \epsilon,\ ipid) + \overline{poll}_{ipid}(\epsilon)\,.\,inq\,(ipid) + make_{ipid}(opid)\,.\,(inq\,(ipid) \mid outq\,(opid,\ ipid))\backslash out_{ipid}$$

Nonempty Inport Queue:

$$inq'\,(s,\ ipid) \;\Leftarrow\; out_{ipid}(x)\,.\,inq'\,(append\ x\ s,\ ipid) + \overline{i}_{ipid}(first\ s)\,.\ if\ rest\,(s) = \epsilon\ then\ inq\,(ipid)\ else\ inq'\,(rest\ s,\ ipid) + \overline{poll}_{ipid}(s)\,.\,inq'\,(s,\ ipid) + make_{ipid}(opid)\,.\,(inq'\,(s,\ ipid) \mid outq\,(opid,\ ipid))\backslash out_{ipid}$$

Notice the asymmetry in the definitions: *outq* (and *outq'*) names the inport queue to which it transmits messages, while *inq* (and *inq'*) receives messages anonymously. This parallels the situation in NIL where more than one outport may be connected to a single inport, but an outport may be connected to only one inport. Also note that port $\overline{out}_{ipid}$ in $outq\,(s,\ opid,\ ipid)$ complements out_{ipid} in $inq\,(s,\ ipid)$, thus effecting the connection. These ports are hidden for every inport–outport channel.

What follows are the translation rules for the rest of NIL. The formal syntax of each statement type is evident in the left–hand side of its corresponding translation rule. Comments about the semantics of each statement and its translation are included.

$[\![$**initialize** $X]\!] \;=\; igen\,(ipid)\,.\,\overline{write_X}(ipid)\,.\,(done \mid inq\,(ipid))$

Creates an initialized inport (i.e. capability) X. We note that another possibility for $(done \mid inq\,(ipid))$ is $\delta\,.\,inq\,(ipid)$. We view the former as an "optimization" of the latter.

$[\![Y :=$ **outport of** $X]\!] \;=\; ogen\,(opid)\,.\,\overline{write_Y}(opid)\,.\,read_X(ipid)\,.\,\overline{make}_{ipid}(opid)\,.\,done$

Creates a unidirectional channel from outport Y to inport X.

$[\![Y := X]\!] \;=\;$ (X, Y both outports)

$read_X(opid\,1)\,.\,who_{opid\,1}(ipid)\,.\,ogen\,(opid\,2)\,.\,\overline{write_Y}(opid\,2)\,.\,\overline{make}_{ipid}(opid\,2)\,.\,done$

Y becomes an outport connected to the same inport to which X is connected.

$[\![$**send**$(E_1, \cdots, E_n)$ **to** $Y]\!] \;=\; ([\![E_1]\!][\rho_1/\rho] \mid \cdots \mid [\![E_n]\!][\rho_n/\rho] \mid (\rho_1(x_1)\,.\,\cdots\,.\,\rho_n(x_n)\,.\,read_Y(opid)\,.\,\overline{o}_{opid}(x_1, \cdots, x_n)\,.\,done))\backslash\rho_1 \cdots \backslash\rho_n$

The values of expressions $E_1, \cdots, E_n$ are output to sendport Y. The sender does not wait for a reply.

$$[\![\textbf{receive}(X_1, \cdots, X_n)\ \textbf{from}\ Y]\!] = ready_Y(ipid)\,.\,\iota_{ipid}(x_1, \cdots, x_n)\,.\\ \overline{write}_{X_1}(x_1)\,.\ \cdots\ .\,\overline{write}_{X_n}(x_n)\,.\,done$$

Values are input into variables $X_1, \cdots, X_n$ from receiveport Y. The receiver must wait if Y's message queue is empty.

$$\begin{aligned}[\![\textbf{call}\ Y(X_1, \cdots, X_n)]\!] = {} & igen(ret\_ipid)\,.\,(done \mid inq(ret\_ipid))\\ & \quad before\\ & ogen(ret\_opid)\,.\,\overline{make}_{ret\_ipid}(ret\_opid)\,.\,done\\ & \quad before\\ & ([\![X_1]\!][\rho_1/\rho] \mid \cdots \mid [\![X_n]\!][\rho_n/\rho] \mid\\ & \rho_1(x_1)\,.\ \cdots\ .\,\rho_n(x_n)\,.\,ready_Y(opid)\,.\\ & \overline{o}_{opid}(x_1, \cdots, x_n, ret\_opid)\,.\,\iota_{ret\_ipid}(x_1', \cdots, x_n')\,.\\ & \overline{write}_{X_1}(x_1')\,.\ \cdots\ .\,\overline{write}_{X_n}(x_n')\,.\,done)\backslash \rho_1 \cdots \backslash \rho_n\end{aligned}$$

Like Ada's **call**, a *callrecord*, i.e. a list of actual parameters $X_1, \cdots, X_n$, is output to callport Y. The caller must wait for the return of the callrecord. NIL has a facility for returning an exception on a call, a facility we do not consider.

Regarding the translation, a communication channel for the return message is first created. The capability for this channel is passed along with the callrecord parameters to Y. All parameters are considered to be **in/out**, for **in** and **out** parameters are just special cases of **in/out**.

$$[\![\textbf{accept}\ CALLREC\ \textbf{from}\ Y]\!] = ready_Y(ipid)\,.\,\iota_{ipid}(callrec)\,.\\ \overline{write}_{CALLREC}(callrec)\,.\,done$$

Like Ada's **accept**, a callrecord is input from acceptport Y into variable $CALLREC$, a record having one field for each formal parameter. The acceptor must wait if Y's queue is empty. After dequeueing a callrecord, the acceptor is responsible for either forwarding or returning the callrecord.

Regarding the translation, the $n+1^{\text{st}}$ field of $CALLREC$ is the capability ret_opid to be used by a **return** statement to return $CALLREC$ to the caller.

$$[\![\textbf{return}\ CALLREC]\!] = [\![CALLREC]\!]\ result\ (\rho(callrec)\,.\\ \overline{o}_{callrec_{n+1}}(all\_but\_last\ \ callrec)\,.\,done)$$

$CALLREC$ is returned to the caller.

$$[\![\textbf{forward}\ CALLREC\ \textbf{to}\ Y]\!] = ready_Y(opid)\,.\,read_{CALLREC}(callrec)\,.\\ \overline{o}_{opid}(callrec)\,.\,done$$

$CALLREC$ is forwarded along sendport Y. The process that eventually receives $CALLREC$ assumes the responsibility of returning $CALLREC$ to the original caller or of reforwarding $CALLREC$.

$$
\begin{array}{l}
[[\textbf{select} \\
\quad \textbf{event}\ (X_1)\ \textbf{guard}\ (G_1)\ \ S_1 \\
\qquad \vdots \\
\quad \textbf{event}\ (X_n)\ \textbf{guard}\ (G_n)\ \ S_n \\
\textbf{end select}]] \quad = \quad (\prod_{1 \le i \le n} Watchdog_i \ \mid\ Controller) \backslash \{gotcha, stop_i, 1 \le i \le n\}
\end{array}
$$

where

$$
\begin{array}{rl}
Watchdog_i & <= \ read_{X_i}(ipid) \,.\, ([[G_i]]\ result\ (\rho(g_i) \,. \\
& \quad if\ g_i\ then\ W_i\ \ else\ stop_i \,.\, NIL))
\end{array}
$$

and

$$
\begin{array}{rl}
W_i & <= \ stop_i \,.\, NIL \ +\ poll_{ipid}(state) \,. \\
& \quad \text{if } state \ne \epsilon \ then\ (\overline{gotcha} \,.\, [[S_i]] \ \mid\ stop_i \,.\, NIL) + stop_i \,.\, NIL \\
& \quad else\ \ W_i
\end{array}
$$

and

$$
Controller \ <= \ (gotcha \,.\, \prod_{1 \le i \le n} \overline{stop_i} \,.\, NIL)\ before\ done
$$

Like Ada's **select**, one of the "open" statements S_i is nondeterministically chosen for execution. No fairness assumptions are made about the selection process. An S_i is open if the queue of its inport X_i is nonempty and its guard (Boolean expression) G_i is true. If none of the S_i are open, the process waits.

In the translation, $Watchdog_i$ continually polls the inport queue of X_i waiting for it to be non-empty. When this is the case and G_i is true (i.e. the i th alternative is open), it tries to get selected by signaling *Controller* with $\overline{gotcha}$. *Controller* will nondeterministically issue a complementary *gotcha* with one of the open alternatives and then kill all of the $Watchdog_i$. The signal $stop_i$ is needed in three different places in W_i to make sure it gets killed. (The killing of the $Watchdog_i$ is for the sake of cleanliness – we view processes as resources – it does not affect the semantics of the translation of **select**.)

$$
\begin{array}{rcl}
[[\textbf{create}(Q, NAME, X_1, \cdots, X_n)]] & = & igen(ipid) \,.\, (done \ \mid\ inq(ipid)) \\
& & \quad before \\
& & ogen(opid) \,.\, \overline{make_{ipid}}(opid) \,.\, done \\
& & \quad before \\
& & pgen(pid) \,.\, \overline{write_Q}(pid) \,.\, read_{NAME}(name) \,. \\
& & ([[\textbf{call}\ \text{"}opid\text{"}(X_1, \cdots, X_n)]] \ \mid\ P_{name}(ipid))
\end{array}
$$

Creates a process Q that executes the compiled NIL program contained in file *NAME*. Creation-time parameters $X_1, \cdots, X_n$ are passed to Q over its *initialization port*. A *process id* (*pid*) is returned as the value of Q, which the owner of Q can use to signal Q's termination (see the translation of the **cancel** operation and the Appendix).

This translation has the effect of starting up an instance of the parameterized behavior P_{name}, which will correspond to the created NIL process Q. P_{name} must have previously been defined through the translation of a process statement labeled *name*. Before that a channel is created for passing the creation–time parameters to Q. The parameter of P_{name} is the inport id for this channel, which P_{name} will refer to when doing an **accept** over its initialization port. Quoted arguments to translations (e.g. *opid* in [[**call** "*opid* "$(X_1, \cdots, X_n)$]]) are to be treated as constants, and thus no access to a register is required.*

[[**accept** *CALLREC* **from** Y]] $=$ (where Y is of type **initport**)
[[**accept** *CALLREC* **from** "*init_ipid* "]]

In the translation, *init_ipid* is the first parameter of the behavior currently being defined (see ahead for the translation of the **process** construct).

[[**cancel** Q]] $= \ read_Q(pid) \, . \, \overline{can}_{pid} \, . \, done$

The signal $\overline{can}_{pid}$ will invoke a cancel handler of Q (see the Appendix) if Q has not already terminated.

[[L: **block declare var** X_1; $\cdots$, **var** X_m;
begin
S_0;
on(EX_1) S_1;
.
.
.
on(EX_n) S_n;
end block]] $= \ ((LOC_{X_1} \mid \cdots \mid LOC_{X_m} \mid [[S_0]] \mid$

$$EX_1 \, . \, \overline{ex}_1 \, . \, NIL \mid \cdots \mid EX_n \, . \, \overline{ex}_n \, . \, NIL)\backslash L_{X_1} \cup \cdots \cup L_{X_m} \cup \{EX_1, \cdots, EX_n\}$$
$$\mid ex_1 \, . \, [[S_1]] \mid \cdots \mid ex_n \, . \, [[S_n]] \mid L \, . \, done)\backslash\{ex_1, \cdots, ex_n\} \cup \{L\}$$

The begin–block construct is enlarged to include the definition of a block label (L) and exception handlers: Statement S_i is executed whenever exception EX_i is raised during the execution of S_0 and is not handled by an exception handler of an inner begin block.

In the translation, identifiers EX_i are used as names of "exception ports". By restricting the names of these exception ports, an exception will activate the handler defined in the most closely surrounding block. The ex_i intermediate communications are used to ensure that exceptions raised within one of the handlers S_i, does not activate a handler S_j, $1 \leq i,j \leq n$, but rather a handler from a block surrounding L. When an exception is raised (see below for the translation of **raise**), [[S_0]] terminates without issuing a *done* signal; the *done* signal of the handler becomes the *done* signal of the block.

[[**raise** EX]] $= \ \overline{EX} \, . \, NIL$

Raises exception EX.

*This is strictly a notational convenience since we could factor out the accessing of the callport variable register from the translation of **call**. Similar comments apply to other uses of quoted arguments to translations.

[[**leave** L]] $= \bar{L} \,.\, NIL$

Compound statements (**begin**, **while**, and **select**) may have an optional label. The **leave** statement causes flow of control to be diverted to the point immediately following the compound statement labeled L, and must be nested within this compound statement.

A leave statement is translated as an exception with a null handler handled only by block L. (Refer to the behavior $L \,.\, done$ defined in connection with the translation of a block statement labeled L.) Leave statements that refer to other types of compound statements are translated similarly.

[[*Ident* : **process** D ;
  begin
    S ;
  end process]] $= P_{Ident}(init\_ipid)$

Ident is the name of the entry in the executable library which is created upon successful compilation of the NIL program (process) being defined. This name is used by a **create** statement to load the module at which time statement S is executed. As for a normal begin–block, exception handlers can be provided with the **process** construct. A default handler for the *CANCEL* exception is executed if no such handler is provided explicitly.

The CCS behavior P_{Ident} will be equal to the translation of a begin–block having declarations D and body S. The parameter $init\_ipid$ will correspond to the id of the initialization port for P_{Ident} (see also the translation of **create** and of **accept** over an initialization port).

To complete the translation, we present the CCS behavior corresponding to a NIL system generation. This behavior will initiate the generators for inport, outport, and process ids, and the translation of a special NIL process "*Init*", with predefined inports and outports. *Init* is supplied with (constant-valued) creation–time parameters.

$$IdGen(0)[igen/gen] \mid IdGen(0)[ogen/gen] \mid IdGen(0)[pgen/gen] \mid$$
$$[[\textbf{create}\,(Q\,,\ \text{“}Init\text{''}\,,\ E_1,\ \cdots\,,\ E_n)]].$$

In a typical NIL implementation, *Init* would start up the device drivers and then behave as a command shell.

5. An Example of the Translation

We present a NIL implementation of a simple command shell (interpreter) in order to illustrate our NIL–to–CCS translation. We believe that this example is small enough to be easily presented, yet large enough to highlight several interesting features of NIL and its translation into CCS.

Our shell repeatedly prompts the user for a command, waits until a command is input, and then creates a child process to perform the desired task. Our shell is simplistic in that background processing and I/O redirection are not provided, users cannot kill any processes created by the shell on their behalf, and command names are not checked for their legality.

Our NIL implementation of the shell uses the following variables:

StdIO is a record variable with component fields *StdIO.in*, a receiveport, and *StdIO.out*, a sendport.

initp is the shell's initport.

Child is a process variable and will correspond to the command that the shell is executing.

CmdName is a string variable and is the name of the program that the user would like executed.

Parms is a record variable and corresponds to the user-supplied parameters.

In our NIL implementation of the shell, user commands are processed within a while loop immediately following the shell's initial **accept**. This implementation is somewhat artificial in that there is no return from this accept.

What follows is our NIL program for the shell.

```
Shell: process
    declare
      var StdIO; var initp; var Child; var CmdName ; var Parms;
    begin
      accept(StdIO) from initp;
      while true do
        send('?') to StdIO.out;
        receive(CmdName, Parms) from StdIO.in;
        create(Child, CmdName, Parms);
      end while;
  end process
```

The CCS behavior expression resulting from our translation of *Shell* is now presented.

$$
\begin{array}{l}
P_{Shell}(\mathit{init\_ipid}) \quad <= \\
\quad (\ LOC_{StdIO} \ \mid\ LOC_{initp} \ \mid\ LOC_{Child} \ \mid\ LOC_{CmdName} \ \mid\ LOC_{Parms} \ \mid \\
\quad\quad (\ (\mathit{init\_ipid}(\mathit{callrec}) \ .\ \overline{\mathit{write}}_{StdIO}(\mathit{callrec}) \ .\ \mathit{done}\ ) \\
\qquad\qquad\qquad\qquad \mathit{before} \\
\qquad w \\
\quad\quad) \\
\quad)L_{StdIO} \cup L_{initp} \cup L_{Child} \cup L_{CmdName} \cup L_{Parms}
\end{array}
$$

where

$$
\begin{array}{l}
w \quad <= \\
\quad b_{TRUE} \quad \mathit{result} \\
\quad (\rho(x)\ . \\
\qquad \text{if } x \ \mathit{then} \\
\qquad\quad (b_{?}[\rho_1/\rho] \ \mid\ (\rho_1(x)\ .\ \mathit{read}_{StdIO.out}(\mathit{opid})\ .\ \overline{o}_{opid}(x)\ .\ \mathit{done}\ )\ )\backslash\rho_1 \\
\qquad\qquad\qquad\qquad \mathit{before} \\
\qquad\quad (\mathit{read}_{StdIO.in}(\mathit{ipid})\ .\ \iota_{ipid}(x_1, x_2)\ .\ \overline{\mathit{write}}_{CmdName}(x_1)\ .\ \overline{\mathit{write}}_{Parms}(x_2)\ .\ \mathit{done}\ ) \\
\qquad\qquad\qquad\qquad \mathit{before} \\
\qquad\quad (\ \mathit{igen}(\mathit{ipid})\ .\ (\mathit{done} \ \mid\ \mathit{inq}(\mathit{ipid})) \\
\qquad\qquad\qquad\qquad\qquad \mathit{before} \\
\qquad\qquad \mathit{ogen}(\mathit{opid})\ .\ \mathit{make}_{ipid}(\mathit{opid})\ .\ \mathit{done} \\
\qquad\qquad\qquad\qquad\qquad \mathit{before} \\
\qquad\qquad \mathit{pgen}(\mathit{pid})\ .\ \overline{\mathit{write}}_{Child}(\mathit{pid})\ .\ \mathit{read}_{CmdName}(\mathit{fn})\ . \\
\qquad\qquad (\ (\ (\mathit{igen}(\mathit{ret\_ipid})\ .\ (\mathit{done} \ \mid\ \mathit{inq}(\mathit{ret\_ipid})) \\
\qquad\qquad\qquad\qquad\qquad\qquad \mathit{before} \\
\qquad\qquad\qquad (\mathit{ogen}(\mathit{ret\_opid})\ .\ \mathit{make}_{ret\_ipid}(\mathit{ret\_opid})\ .\ \mathit{done} \\
\qquad\qquad\qquad\qquad\qquad\qquad \mathit{before} \\
\qquad\qquad\qquad (\ \ (\mathit{read}_{Parms}(x)\ .\ \overline{\rho}(x)\ .\ \mathit{NIL}\ )[\rho_1/\rho] \ \mid \\
\qquad\qquad\qquad\quad (\rho_1(x)\ .\ \overline{o}_{opid}(x,\ \mathit{ret\_opid})\ . \\
\qquad\qquad\qquad\qquad \iota_{ret\_ipid}(x')\ .\ \overline{\mathit{write}}_{Parms}(x')\ .\ \mathit{done}\ ) \\
\qquad\qquad\qquad)\backslash\rho_1 \\
\qquad\qquad\quad) \\
\qquad\qquad\quad \mid\ P_{fn}(\mathit{ipid}) \\
\qquad\qquad) \\
\qquad\quad) \\
\qquad\quad \mathit{before}\ w \\
\qquad \mathit{else}\ \mathit{done} \\
\quad)
\end{array}
$$

6. Discussion

The NIL and CCS models of concurrency share several fundamental principles: (1) Programs define dynamic systems of communicating, nondeterministic, sequential processes. (2) Message passing is the only means for processes to communicate. (3) The interface of a process to the rest of the system is the set of ports that it owns.

This commonality between NIL and CCS is certainly one of the reasons we chose CCS as a semantic model for NIL. Furthermore, the operation of restriction in CCS allowed us to model NIL's static scoping of variables and exception handlers.

NIL and CCS do not agree on the issues of synchronous vs. (buffered) asynchronous communication and dynamic port creation. However, these differences were reconcilable. To model the asynchronous communication of NIL, infinite–queue processes at both the transmitting and receiving ends were used in the CCS translation. NIL dynamic port creation was modeled in CCS using indexed sets of ports, a technique suggested by Milner in [Mi85] and applied in [DG83].

One of the primary concerns in giving a programming language a formal semantics is the level of *abstractness* of the semantics. In particular, the semantics should be abstract enough to allow all possible implementations. Otherwise, compilers for the language might be constrained to generate code that is less than ideal with respect to a particular target environment.

Our translations of NIL's **select** and **cancel** may not be abstract enough since they begin to suggest particular implementations, the use of watchdog processes for the former, and the "canceled state" approach for the latter (see the Appendix). For **cancel**, a truly abstract semantics would be a temporal statement of the form, "a canceled process eventually terminates." As such, *how* termination is obtained is left to the implementors and is not constrained by the semantics.

Our translation of NIL into CCS is from one (programming) language into another. One motivation behind this approach is to be able to use CCS to reason algebraically about NIL programs, e.g. to prove that NIL program transformations are semantics-preserving. Alternatively, we could directly give NIL a more abstract semantics such as archives [KP85], sets of infinite strings of input/output events. Archives are attractive as a semantics for NIL because they are very abstract and naturally allow one to express fairness. Future work will include using archives in this way.

Proof systems for CCS are based upon various equivalence notions, e.g. observation equivalence and strong congruence [Mi80]. When reasoning about NIL programs however, one typically wants to show that a program Q is a correct implementation of a program P, rather than equivalence of P and Q. Specifically, we would like Q to "satisfy" (or refine) P, i.e. every property true of P is true of Q but not necessarily vice versa (see also p. 22 of [Mi82]). Thus the addition to CCS of a proof system for satisfiability, along the lines of the [Mi82] proposal, would satisfy this desire.

In general, the concept of *fairness* is not directly expressible in CCS. For example, consider our CCS description of NIL inport queues, and let P and Q be two NIL processes having outports connected to a single inport X. A possible computation of our translation would allow the messages of P to be enqueued at X infinitely more often than the messages of Q, thereby violating the "fair–merge property" [Pa80]. In certain cases, however, fairness can be enforced in CCS by introducing additional "machinery". This is evidenced by our translation of **cancel** as described in the Appendix, which guarantees the eventual termination of the canceled process.

Fairness in CCS has been a subject of intense study in recent years [Mi82, He84, CS85 – to name only a few]. For our CCS translation of NIL, the work of [CS85] seems to be the most relevant. They propose to modify the basic operational semantics of CCS by introducing two rules (for both weak and strong fairness) that rule out unfair computations. Using this version of CCS would satisfy our fairness requirements.

A question one might ask of our translation of NIL into CCS is "How worthwhile is it"? In connection with their translation of a subset of Ada into CCS, Hennessy and Li [HL83] define what it means for a translation to be "adequate". They formulate this notion in terms of a set of properties that should be preserved by the translation, where a property X is preserved if whenever a program Pr possesses X, than so does $[\![Pr]\!]$. Hennessy and Li present an operational semantics for their Ada subset in order to evaluate the adequacy of their translation.

The work presented in this paper represents the first formal semantics for NIL. It would be interesting to also give NIL an operational semantics so that the adequacy of our translation of NIL into CCS could be judged in the Hennessy and Li style.

Acknowledgements: The authors are indebted to Rocky Bernstein, Alessandro Giacalone, Peter Wegner, and especially Shaula Yemini for many helpful discussions. They would also like to thank the referees for a careful reading of the paper that produced numerous comments/corrections. This work was initiated in the summer of 1984 when the first author was visiting IBM, Yorktown Heights as a faculty researcher. He is grateful for their support.

References

[AZ81] E. Astesiano, E. Zucca, "Semantics of CSP via Translation into CCS", in *Proc. 10th Symp. on Mathematical Foundations of Computing*, Lecture Notes in Computer Science 118, Springer-Verlag, pp. 172–182 (1981).

[Ca81] L. Cardelli, "Sticks and Stones: An Applicative VLSI Design Language", CSR-85-81, Dept. of Computer Science, Univ. of Edinburgh, Edinburgh, Scotland (1981).

[CS85] G. Costa, C. Stirling, "Weak and Strong Fairness in CCS", CSR-167-85, Dept. of Computer Science, Univ. of Edinburgh, Edinburgh, Scotland (Jan. 1985).

[DG83] T.W. Doeppner, Jr., A. Giacalone, "A Formal Description of the UNIX Operating System", *Proc. 2nd ACM Symp. on Principles of Distributed Computing*, Montreal, Quebec, Canada, pp. 241–253 (Aug. 1983).

[He84] M. Hennessy, "Axiomatising Finite Delay Operators", *Acta Informatica*, No. 21, pp. 61–88 (1984).

[HL83] M. Hennessy, W. Li, "Translating a Subset of Ada into CCS", *Proc. IFIP Conf. on Formal Description of Programming Concepts-II*, North Holland, pp. 227–247 (1983).

[HLP81] M. Hennessy, W. Li, G. Plotkin, "A First Attempt at Translating CSP into CCS", *Proc. 2nd IEEE Int. Conf. on Distributed Computing* (1981).

[KP85] R.M. Keller, P. Panangaden, "Semantics of Networks Containing Indeterminate Operators", *Proc. Seminar on Concurrency,* Lecture Notes in Computer Science 197, Springer Verlag, pp. 479–496 (1985).

[Mi80] R. Milner, *A Calculus of Communicating Systems,* Lecture Notes in Computer Science 92, Springer–Verlag (1980).

[Mi82] R. Milner, "A Finite–Delay Operator in Synchronous CCS", CSR–116–82, Dept. of Computer Science, University of Edinburgh, Edinburgh, Scotland (May 1982).

[Mi85] R. Milner, "Lectures on a Calculus for Communicating Systems", *Proc. Seminar on Concurrency,* Lecture Notes in Computer Science 197, Springer Verlag, pp. 197–220 (1985).

[Pa80] D. Park, *On the Semantics of Fair Parallelism,* Lecture Notes in Computer Science 86, Springer–Verlag, pp. 504–526 (1980).

[SH84] R.E. Strom, N. Halim, "A New Programming Methodology for Long–Lived Software Systems", *IBM Journal of Research and Development,* Vol. 28, No. 1, pp. 52–59 (Jan. 1984).

[SW83] M.W. Sheilds, M.J. Wray, "A CCS Specification of the OSI Network Service", CSR–136–83, Dept. of Computer Science, Univ. of Edinburgh, Edinburgh, Scotland (Aug. 1983).

[SY83] R.E. Strom, S. Yemini, "NIL: An Integrated Language and System for Distributed Programming", *Proc. SIGPLAN '83 Symp. on Programming Language Issues in Software Systems,* San Francisco, CA, pp. 73–82 (June 1983).

[SY85a] R.E. Strom, S. Yemini, "Synthesizing Distributed and Parallel Programs through Optimistic Transformations", *Proc. 1985 Int'l Conf. on Parallel Processing,* pp. 632–642 (Aug. 1985).

[SY85b] R.E. Strom, S. Yemini, "The NIL Distributed Systems Programming Language: A Status Report", *Proc. Seminar on Concurrency,* Lecture Notes in Computer Science 197, Springer Verlag, pp. 512–523 (1985).

[SY86] R.E. Strom, S. Yemini, "Typestate: A Programming Language Concept for Enhancing Software Reliability", *IEEE Trans. Software Eng.* (Jan. 1986).

[SYW85] R.E. Strom, S. Yemini, P. Wegner, "Viewing Ada from a Process Model Perspective", *Proc. AdaTec Symp. on the Ada Programming Language,* Paris, France (1985).

Appendix:
Semantics of Cancellation

Informal Semantics

Every process is the value of a variable of type *process* within its owner. The **create** P statement creates a new process and assigns it as the value of a process variable P; the **cancel** P statement causes the process designated by P to enter the *canceled state.* A process in the canceled state *may* execute some finite number of actions ("last wishes") before terminating, but is guaranteed to eventually terminate.

Processes may block indefinitely as a result of **while**, **select**, **receive**, **accept**, or **call** statements. It would be inconsistent for the semantics to both require that canceled processes always terminate and to have some statements not be live. Therefore, the above five statements are defined so that they may terminate by raising the *CANCEL* exception, as well as by normal termination. Normal termination will occur as defined in the main body of the paper. The exception termination must occur whenever normal termination is impossible and failure to terminate would result in the failure of a canceled process to terminate.

Derivation of the CCS specification

The CCS specification for termination of **while**, **select**, **receive**, or **accept** for canceled processes is relatively straightforward. If the process attempting to execute **while**, **select**, or **receive** is in the canceled state, then the statement may raise the *CANCEL* exception, or it may continue normal execution. For **receive/accept** and **select**, a blocked process will be waiting at ι_{ipid} or *gotcha* respectively; by waiting alternatively for a cancel "beacon" signal, these statements will be guaranteed to eventually become unblocked if the cancel signal is issued. For **while**, it is necessary to execute the loop in parallel with a behavior which waits for either the termination of the **while** or the cancel beacon. If the cancel beacon is sensed, then if the loop still does not terminate, a *stop* message is sent, forcing the loop to terminate.

The CCS specification for termination of **call** is more intricate as a result of the requirement that **call** must not terminate, even with an exception, without the callrecord being returned. Now it is necessary to require that the called process raise an exception if it does not make progress while holding a callrecord belonging to a canceled calling process.

A process under obligation to return its callrecord in order to allow some calling process to proceed towards cancellation is said to be *forced.* If a forced process is itself blocked because of a **call** statement, it may in turn cause the process it is calling to become forced. A forced process ceases to be forced after it has returned any callrecords it has accepted from canceled or forced processes. So long as a process is in the canceled state or is forced, attempts to execute otherwise non-terminating statements will terminate with an exception. Since in NIL, raising an exception always terminates the current block, eventually all blocks will terminate. The NIL *typestate rules* [SY86] guarantee that processes finalize all their variables before termination, and in particular that any accepted callrecords will be returned.

The CCS solution for **call** is as follows:

- Every process runs in parallel with a machine which tracks the canceled and forced states. When a *can* signal is received as a result of the owner canceling a process, the canceled state is entered. When a *force* signal is received as a result of another process discovering it is blocked waiting for this process to return its callmessage, the forced state is entered. A count is kept which is incremented each time the *force* signal is received, and decremented each time a callmessage from a canceled or forced process is returned. When canceled or forced, the cancelbeacon signal is repeatedly offered.
- A machine is provided which records the state of calls: either (a) no call is in progress; (b) a call is in progress to process *pid* but the caller has not yet tried to force the call to return; or (c) a call is in progress and another process has been put in the forced state because of the call.
- The call behavior is modified so that if the call does not return but the cancelbeacon is sensed, then a new state is entered which attempts to either receive the returned callrecord or force the current owner of the callmessage. The callrecord is augmented so that it includes the *pid* (process id) of the calling process.
- The return behavior is modified so that if the returning process has had its forced count incremented as a result of this callrecord, the forced count will be decremented.
- The forward behavior is modified so that if the forwarding process has had its forced count incremented as a result of this callrecord, the forward will be treated as a return, and if not, the calling process will be aware of the identity of the new owner of the callrecord.
- Output ports are modified so that the identity of the owner of the associated input port can be determined. (This modification is not shown here.)

Formal Definitions:

- $Who(pid) \;<=\; \overline{whoami}(pid) \,.\, Who(pid)$
- $Normal(pid) \;<=\; can_{pid} \,.\, Canceled(pid) + force_{pid} \,.\, Forced(1, pid)$
- $Canceled(pid) \;<=\; force_{pid} \,.\, Canceled(pid)$
  $+\; unforce_{pid} \,.\, Canceled(pid)$
  $+\; \overline{beacon} \,.\, Canceled(pid)$
- $Forced(i, pid) \;<=\; force_{pid} \,.\, Forced(i+1, pid)$
  $+\; unforce_{pid} \,.\, (\mathit{if}\ i-1 = 0\ \mathit{then}\ Normal\ \mathit{else}\ Forced(i-1, pid))$
  $+\; \overline{beacon} \,.\, Forced(i, pid)$
- $NotCalling(pid) \;<=\; call(pid2) \,.\, Calling(pid, pid2)$

- $Calling(pid, pid2) \Leftarrow returned . NotCalling(pid) +$
  $return_{pid} . Calling(pid, pid2)$
  $+ forward_{pid}(pid3, opid, callrec) . \overline{o}_{opid}(callrec) . Calling(pid, pid3)$
  $+ forcecallee . \overline{force_{pid2}} . Forcing(pid, pid2)$

- $Forcing(pid, pid2) \Leftarrow returned . NotCalling(pid)$
  $+ return_{pid} . \overline{unforce_{pid2}} . Forcing(pid, pid2)$
  $+ forward_{pid}(pid3, opid, callrec) . \overline{o}_{callrec_{n+1}}(all\_but\_last\_two\ callrec) .$
  $Forcing(pid, pid2)$

Translation of create: The last line of the translation of **create** given in Section 4.2 now reads:

$$([[\textbf{call}\ \text{``}opid\text{''}(X_1, \cdots, X_n)]] \mid$$
$$(P_{name}(ipid) \mid Who(pid) \mid Normal(pid) \mid NotCalling(pid))\backslash whoami \backslash call \backslash returned))$$

Translation of while: We define two new behaviors that will run in parallel with the translation of **while**.

$$Whilemonitor \Leftarrow check . Whilemonitor + stop . [[\textbf{raise}\ CANCEL]]$$
$$Cancelmonitor \Leftarrow \delta . done + beacon . (\delta . done + \overline{stop} . NIL)$$
$$[[\textbf{while}\ E\ \textbf{do}\ S\ \textbf{end while}]] = ((w \mid Whilemonitor)\backslash check \mid Cancelmonitor)\backslash \delta \backslash stop$$

where w is as in Section 4.1 but begins with a $\overline{check}$ action each time around.

Translation of receive: Nondeterministically or the behavior $beacon$. [[**raise** $CANCEL$]] to the translation of **receive** given in Section 4.2.

Translation of accept: Nondeterministically or the behavior $beacon$. [[**raise** $CANCEL$]] to the translation of **accept** given in Section 4.2.

Translation of call: The behavior immediately following the second *before* of the translation of **call** given in Section 4.2 now reads:

$$([[X_1]][\rho_1/\rho] \mid \cdots \mid [[X_n]][\rho_n/\rho] \mid$$
$$\rho_1(x_1) . \cdots . \rho_n(x_n) . ready_Y(opid) .$$
$$owner_{opid}(pid2) . call(pid2) . whoami(pid3) . \overline{o}_{opid}(x_1, \cdots, x_n, ret\_opid, pid3) .$$
$$(\iota_{ret\_ipid}(x_1', \cdots, x_n') . \overline{write_{X_1}}(x_1') . \cdots . \overline{write_{X_n}}(x_n') .$$
$$returned . done$$

$$+ \ beacon \ . (\iota_{ret\_ipid}(x_1' , \cdots, x_n') . \overline{write}_{X_1}(x_1') . \cdots . \overline{write}_{X_n}(x_n') .$$
$$returned \ . \ done)$$
$$+ \ \overline{forcecallee} . (\iota_{ret\_ipid}(x_1' , \cdots, x_n') . \overline{write}_{X_1}(x_1') . \cdots . \overline{write}_{X_n}(x_n') .$$
$$returned \ . (done + [\![\textbf{raise} \ CANCEL]\!])) \ ) \ )\backslash\rho_1\backslash \cdots \backslash\rho_n$$

Translation of return: Same as the translation given in Section 4.2 for **return** except insert the action $\overline{return}_{callrec_n+2}$ immediately before the $\overline{o}_{callrec_n+1}$ action.

Translation of forward: The translation of **forward** given in Section 4.2 now reads

$$ready_Y(opid) . read_{CALLREC}(callrec) . owner_{opid}(pid) .$$
$$\overline{forward}_{callrec_n+2}(pid , opid , callrec) . done$$

QUESTIONS AND ANSWERS

Mosses: As you say in the paper you could imagine giving different formal semantics of NIL in terms of other formalisms and I´m very glad that you say that because it seems to me that you give a rather difficult translation in terms of CCS for communication primitives in NIL that are rather simple to imagine how to implement. Another point in connection with that is that all these generators of identities of processes seem to imply some sort of central agent that is sychronizing the whole system and dealing with these unique identities all the time. Once this maybe a way of getting a semantics that allows you to reason about NIL. I think that the very complexity of this translation shows that this is perhaps not the right way, that there may be more direct ways of getting that power.

Smolka: I have two answers to that remark. One is: yes, it is indeed complex and if you really want to use it for proving something about your program, that will be difficult without mechanical systems dealing with manipulation and expansion in CCS terms. But a benefit of having done this translation is that the semantics of NIL is clearly defined even to look at. I think the translation is readable. Also the referees said that (laughter).

Bjørner: Who were the referees? (laughter)
How is your work related to de Boer's paper at this conference?

Smolka: Our work relates specifically to previous uses of CCS semantics. I should have stressed on that.

Bjørner: No, my point is what Peter Mosses was mentioning by the other kind of semantics. The dutch people seem to have a nice metric space (laughter) for that.

Smolka: I don't want to ignore their work. Rob Strom and I are both happy to see that a lot of work has been done on process creation and structuring of tasks.

de Nicola: I was a bit worried when you started saying that you were using Milner's 1980 version of CCS [see reference in the paper] and then I saw labels as parameters and maybe also subprocesses as parameters. Was that true? Were you passing labels as parameters?

Smolka: No, we only pass values as parameters. We just pass the index of the instance of the process variable or channel or port variable.

de Nicola: OK. Then I'm not worried anymore. I have another question to ask. Is there anything you have learned about CCS and about NIL while doing this work? Would you be prepared to change NIL after you have given this translation or would you suggest a change to CCS?

Smolka: That's a good question. NIL is changing as the result of this work. For the notion of cancellation, an alternative has been proposed which is called 'isolation' where instead of actually terminating the destinated process you simply cut away it's port connections from the rest of the system. So the process can go on on its own but it can no longer affect the rest of the system. This would have an easier semantics.

de Nicola: What about CCS?

Smolka: CCS is certainly not adequate for any change like this. It is not intended for liveness properties.

Bougé: For your translation you need to introduce some global objects such as identifier generators. I think that for the translation one would like to have some locality properties, for example that for the translation of a construct only such objects are needed which are local to this construct. Could it be possible to achieve such a local translation?

Smolka: It might be possible by using a kind of standard method; in particular, by using two port indices and generating them locally, but I haven´t really thought about this.

Bougé: Is there any other place where you use global objects, apart from generating identifiers?

Smolka: No just these three: input and output, port indices and process identifiers. That´s it.

Strom: In answer to the earlier question there is a paper that Van Nguyen and I have sketched out in the form of a couple of abstracts on a slight variant of NIL, called DNP - ´dynamic networks of processes´. It uses a behavioural trace semantics. One consequence of this work is that all of this operational complexity associated with cancellation where we essentially have to write three pages of CCS that look like assembly language goes away when we move over to this behavioural trace semantics because you can write a few global axioms that describe both, the fairness properties and the cancellation property. Moreover, when adding these properties it is not necessary to go back and revise the semantics of each individual statement to reflect those properties in. So, not only it is easier to give the semantics but it is easier to change individual properties - to change properties of the semantics like fairness properties or termination properties without having to change the meaning of all of the statements in the language.

de Nicola: What is this behavioural semantics?

Strom: It is based upon Van Nguyen´s thesis [V. Nguyen: A theory of processes. Ph.D. Thesis, Department of Computer Science, Cornell University, 1985] and a paper by Nguyen, Demers, Gries and Owicki that will appear in ´Distributed Computing´ [V. Nguyen, A. Demers, D. Gries, S. Owicki: A model and temporal proof system for networks of processes. Distributed Computing 1, 1986, 7-25].

Darondeau: If you give an operational definition of NIL, how can you show that it is correct with respect to your translation?

Smolka: One approach would be the one by Hennessy and Li in the previous working conference where one gives to the source language a purely operational semantics in Plotkin´s sense and then based on that one shows the equivalence to the CCS translation [M.C.B. Hennessy, W. Li: Translating a subset of ADA into CCS. In: D. Bjørner (ed.): Formal Description of Programming Concepts II. Amsterdam: North-Holland, 1983, 227-247].

Darondeau: What is the equivalence of NIL programs?

Smolka: That´s the source of a lot of debate. It is not observation equivalence because that is too strong.

Darondeau: So, you do not use the semantics of the translation? But what is the semantics of the translation?

Smolka: We don´t use observational equivalence, but we can use another (weaker) CCS equivalence or preorder notion.

Bednarczyk: May I try to raise the former problem once more, as it seems to me you are not quite right saying that your translation is based on CCS in the 1980 style because the language Milner gives in his book is finitary; for example the choice operator is a binary operation. But because of your coding, you have an infinite number of constants and of identifiers for channels. Using codes, you cannot avoid infinitary choice.

Smolka: Indeed I´m referring to the paper that Robin Milner presented in the 1984 CMU conference on concurrency [see reference in the paper]. There he shows how the 1980 CCS with values can be translated into a calculus with infinite summation.

Mosses: In connection with the remark of Marek Bednarczyk: I don´t see that is necessary having infinite choice for the generation of process identities and port identities. If all you want is an implementation in terms of CCS, you could just use some counter that delivers an integer and keep on counting up. So, I don´t think that it is necessary, but I agree it this is more abstract to express the implementation dependence in terms of an infinite choice.

Bednarczyk: I agree.

Smolka: No, I don´t.(laughter)

Bednarczyk: No, CCS is not dynamic. So, we just cannot use anything like that. The channels are constants.

Mosses: I thought that one was able to count in the 1980 version of CCS. If you are using numbers in place of channels then you pass those around rather then passing ports around explicitely. But you can´t count in 1980 CCS?

Bednarczyk: Well, of course you can almost simulate everything, but the problem is that you cannot dynamically choose which channels to be taken. The control structure of CCS programs is static, it is not dynamic. So, you cannot evolve during the time, you can´t expect anything like this.

de Niçola: This was my worry about sending ports around. Anyway, there are some good references with respect to passing channels in CCS. There is an Astesiano/Zucca paper [see reference in the paper] and there is also a very recent paper by Mogens Nielsen. He has added a new construct to CCS to be able to pass labels of ports and process names around, but you get a more complicated CCS semantics.

Smolka: May I also add: the Ph.D. thesis of Alessandro Giacalone (SUNY) deals with the same problem with a slightly different approach.

de Roever: This discussion is rather broke in my ears because this 1980 CCS which reflects the 1980 state of the art, although it has been well investigated, is not confronted with a slightly more evolved notion of concurrency. Today, you don´t have static networks, one thinks nowadays in terms of languages for - let´s say - object oriented programs in dynamically created networks, and those dynamically created networks are not only recursively created. But they can also be created just ´adhoc´ in a non-recursive way. Just like in PASCAL you can create objects and assign objects to the pointer type. That aspect is absent from CCS. Was Smolka and Strom have done is like - I hope the expression is the same in English - stretching their language on CCS´s. This fight with identifiers should neither be the idea of a paper nor the subject of a paper. This is a rather strange study because they want to have support of some formalism and they choose the formalism which is unfit to do the job. That is what we should basicly conclude from this discussion. What now happens is that the CCS-people say "Well, but in 1980 you didn´t have port variables nor syntactic structure". That is ridiculous and that is the point of this discussion. It just shows that CCS should by now be replaced. So we shouldn´t add a new statement to CCS to transmit labels; one should develop a new CCS in which this ´real-dynamic-process-creation´ for example could be naturally suggested: NIL! (laughter)

Apt: NIL is a proposal!

de Nicola: What would you propose? They have chosen CCS because it probably was the best formalism on the market at that time when they started their investigation. No one blamed them to do this. (laughter)

Løvengreen: Concerning the complexity of this translation: In NIL you do not have shared variables. Then passing the state around with a ´? signal´ instead of marking the variables by processes could simplify the translation.

Smolka: I think you are right. There might be a way to simplify the translation.

Degano: Why do you have chosen NIL as the name of the language? That´s a technical question! (laughter...)

Smolka: NIL means ´Network Implementation Language´.

SESSION 6

Higher Order Programming

Chairman: D. Bjørner

Formal Description of Programming Concepts - III
M. Wirsing (Editor)
Elsevier Science Publishers B.V. (North-Holland)
IFIP, 1987

TYPE-FREE COMPILING OF PARAMETRIC TYPES

Roberto Amadio Giuseppe Longo

Dipartimento di Informatica, Universita' di Pisa
Corso Italia 40, 56100 Pisa, Italia.

Introduction

The use of types as parameters in programming languages has been proposed following several approaches. The variety of view points has stimulated a very lively debate in theoretical as well as in practical computing. Indeed, languages which allow quantification over types and/or types as inputs present several mathematical and computational challenges.

In Logic and in Computer Science types allow an important, though partial, correctness verification by avoiding most logical paradoxes and frequent incorrectness in program writing. However, typed languages are too rigid: they require, say, that a different program is written in each type for the "same" intended function. Polymorphism introduced a more flexible programming style. First-order or implicit polymorphism, for example, is elegantly used in Edinburgh ML. Following early ideas of Curry, Hindley and Milner, ML programs may be written in an essentially type-free way and their consistency with respect to typing is automatically checked.

In this paper we deal with higher-order or explicit polymorphism. This logic or programming style originated in proof-theory by the work of Girard[1972] and Martin-Löf[1971] and in functional programming by the ideas in Reynolds[1974]. Its key features consist in the existence of type variables (as in ADA, Russell, CLU (Liskov&al.[1981])) and in the possibility of manipulating and calculating types explicitly, as part of the object language; moreover, this manipulation may be kept separated from the actual computation.

Note that these extra facilities do not need to rule out some important properties possessed by classically typed languages, such as typed λ-calculus. Namely, in Girard

---

Research partly supported by C.N.R. grant n. 85.02624.01 and, in part, by Min. P.I. (60%, Comitato per la Matematica).

and Reynolds' language (Λ_Δ), all computations terminate (strongly normalize), the equality of terms is decidable and, last but not least, it is decidable whether a term has a given type. The same holds for the stronger calculus of constructions (Λ_C) in Coquand&Huet[1985]. Both Λ_Δ and Λ_C do not consider Type, the collection of all types, as a type itself.

In contrast to this, several programming languages (e.g. Pebble, Burstall& Lampson[1984])) extend Λ_Δ in such a way to handle also Type as a type (Type:Type). The same holds for Martin-Löf 1971 approach to type theory. Let us shortly discuss the Type:Type issue, an highly debatable one both from a foundational perspective and a practical view point.

As one may expect from experience in classical Set Theory, the existence of a "universal set" leads to paradoxes. However, as unrestricted negation is not included in the language, there is no danger to incur Russell's paradox. Morever the collection or universe of all types (sets) may be classically considered a type (set) itself, as in program semantics there is no need to be committed to well-founded Set Theories (see Aczel[1985]). Indeed, the impossibility of finding a set-theoretical model for explicit polymorphism, where morphisms are all functions in classical Set Theory, is already due to the features in Λ_Δ (see Reynolds[1984]) and does not depend on the Type:Type assumption. By an heuristic observation, one may say that the assumption Type:Type is not the problem from the point of view of semantics as well known mathematical models of Λ_Δ and Λ_C posses a universal type, namely the various models where types are interpreted as classes of retractions over type-free structures (see Scott[1976,1980], MacCracken[1984], Bruce&Meyer[1984], Amadio&Bruce&Longo [1986]). However, an intuitionistic inconsistency is present in the early Martin-Löf's system (Girard[1972]). Namely, the expression $\forall t$:Type.t (≡ "all types are inhabited") is a type itself and there is a term of type $\forall t$:Type.t . In the perspective of types as formulae, terms are proofs of their types and, hence, there is a proof of the proposition which asserts that all intuitionistically acceptable formulae are provable. However, all terms of type $\forall t$:Type.t are provably with no normal form and, then, their metamathematical "meaning" should be explored as well as the computational relevance of the above intuitionistic inconsistency.

As already mentioned , there exist models of Λ_Δ and Λ_C where Type:Type is realized. How is this possible? The point is that Girard's paradox proves that, when Type:Type is assumed, the analogy between inhabited types and propositions, known as the "Curry-Howard isomorphism", fails, while nothing is said about the underlying equational theory. That is, the actual computations of programs, which are given by the equational theory of terms, may still form a consistent theory. The proof of this non-obvious fact is one of the merits of the various retraction models. In conclusion, the stimulating and important identification of types and logical formulae may be lost with no direct negative effect on the consistency of computations.

A similar pattern also occurs in classical or first order polymorphism. In this case, the Curry-Howard isomorphism relates inhabited types to propositions of positive (intuitionistic) propositional calculus. However, the most wellknown implemented version of first order polymorphism, Edinburgh ML, essentially uses a fixed point operator Y (or "let...rec..."), whose type-scheme, $(\sigma \rightarrow \sigma) \rightarrow \sigma$, is not a tautology; indeed, for any type σ , Y applied to the identity of type $(\sigma \rightarrow \sigma)$, gives a term of type σ , or any formula is proved. Thus, the Type:Type assumption provides a logical and computational challenge, which deserves climbing on the Capitol to "look in its eyes" (Curry&Feys[1958]) even if there may be some danger to "fall out of the Tarpean rock" (Girard[1985]).

Finally observe that, in the practice of computing, the introduction of Type:Type corresponds to the resonable desire of operating uniformly on every expressible entity. The advantages of such a strong claim are immediate. For example, using the greater flexibility in the programming style, one may easily write programs which compute types and the hierachy of levels required in Λ_Δ and Λ_C may be avoided. A computational drawback is surely given by the failure of all the three properties mentioned above on normalization and decidability; however, in some applications, the avalaibility of a stronger type-checker seems a reasonable price to be paid to the undecidability of typing as one may separate compiling from execution and use heuristic methods in a static type-checker (Cardelli[1986]). Moreover, the expressive power of the language allows a great simplicity in the recursive (equational) definition of data types (see Cardelli[1986] for some elegant examples). On the other hand, Meyer&Reinhold[1986] point out other negative effects of extending type theories with Type:Type by proving the failure of conservativity properties with respect to equational theories of the underlying base types.

In conclusion, different perspectives and applications suggested a variety of formalizations to parameterized typing. A uniform framework for dealing with all the various proposals is still missing. The design of such a framework is one of the purposes of the work sketched hereafter.

To this aim, we uniformly embed all extant approaches to typing in functional programming into a type-free language. By this we correlate the features of different programming styles and we provide a type-free (or Scheme-like) foundation to the higher order calculi, in particular to Pebble-like programming languages. An understanding of the relation between the various type disciplines and type-free λ-calculus is important insofar as computation (i.e. the operational side of λ-calculi) is an essentially type-free activity.

From a practical perspective this may be understood as follows. Usually, once types have been inferred or checked at compile time, the computation proceeds in a type-free way and all type information is lost. In this paper, we also compile types into the type-free language we deal with, so that the "untyped" computation may keep track of them.

Even though models are not discussed, the present work may be also viewed as a contribution to the model theory of higher order calculi, since the type-free λ–calculus axiomatized in §.3 formalizes properties of a large class of models and focuses, by this, their relevant structural attributes.

1. A simple variant of the calculus of constructions

Coquand[1985] and Coquand&Huet[1985] present an higher-order λ-calculus, Λ_C, where terms are typed with types which are themselves terms of the same nature. However, Λ_C is stratified in the sense that within the language one distinguishes between the various entities (programs, types , kinds...). By adding a name, Kind (see below), for the collection of all kinds, this may be represented as follows. The notation will be briefly reintroduced and simplified immediately afterwards.

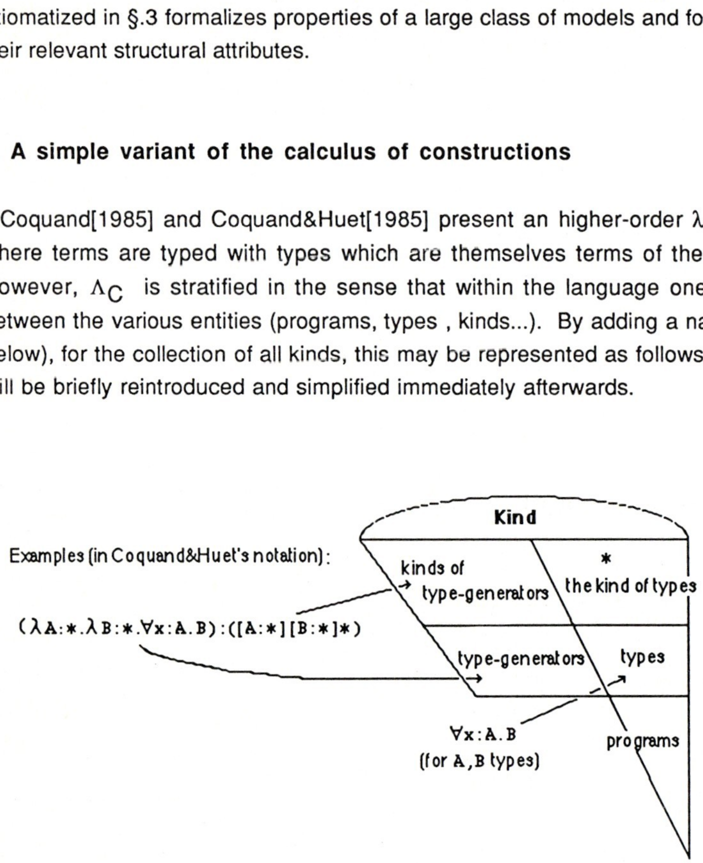

The purpose of this section is to rewrite Coquand and Huet calculus of constructions in such a way that it will be straightforward to embed it into the extension of Martin-Löf type theory in Cardelli[1986]. As already mentioned, our purpose is to get to a unified type-free perspective. As a side effect, the present rewriting answers a question in Cardelli[1986]. The translation simplifies the type assignment and stresses the elegance and expressiveness of Λ_C as a programming language (there already exists an implemented version of Λ_C in ML). The idea is to minimize the distinctions above by introducing an expression, Kind, the collection of all kinds, which is not a term (and, thus, not a kind). We use $*$ for the kind of all types (i.e. the term $*$ stands for Type in the introduction). Recently, Coquand[1986] rewrote the Coquand and Huet calculus in a way which is very similar to ours, except for the names of types and kinds.

Terms: $a ::= * \mid var \mid (aa) \mid (\lambda var{:}a.a) \mid (\forall var{:}a.a)$

Constructions: $\Gamma \vdash a : T$, where $T ::= a \mid Kind$ and $\Gamma = \{(var{:}T),\ldots,(var{:}T)\}$.

We write capital letters for terms which are types or kinds, i.e. for terms A such that for some assignment Γ, $\Gamma \vdash A : *$ or $\Gamma \vdash A : Kind$.

Well formed assignments: $\Gamma(x{:}A)$ stands for $\Gamma \cup \{(x{:}A)\}$, Γ is an ordered list.

ass.1 $\varnothing$ ok (the empty assignment is well formed)

ass.2
$$\frac{\Gamma\ ok,\ \Gamma \vdash A : Kind,\ x \notin dom(\Gamma)}{\Gamma(x{:}A)\ ok}$$

ass.3
$$\frac{\Gamma\ ok,\ \Gamma \vdash A : *,\ x \notin dom(\Gamma)}{\Gamma(x{:}A)\ ok}$$

From now on, we agree that $\Gamma \vdash \ldots$ implies that Γ is ok.

Typing rules: C.1 $\Gamma \vdash * : Kind$

C.2
$$\frac{(x{:}A) \in \Gamma}{\Gamma \vdash x : A}$$
(assumption or weakening)

C.3
$$\frac{\Gamma(x : A) \vdash B : Kind}{\Gamma \vdash \forall x : A . B : Kind}$$
(kinds' quantification)

C.4
$$\frac{\Gamma(x : A) \vdash B : *}{\Gamma \vdash \forall x : A . B : *}$$
(types' quantification)

C.5 $$\frac{\Gamma(x:A) \vdash a:B}{\Gamma \vdash (\lambda x:A\,.\,a) : \forall x:A\,.\,B}$$ (abstraction)

C.6 $$\frac{\Gamma \vdash a:\forall x:A\,.\,B, \quad \Gamma \vdash b:A}{\Gamma \vdash (ab) : [b/x]B}$$ (application)

C.7 $$\frac{\Gamma \vdash a:A \qquad \vdash A=B}{\Gamma \vdash a:B}$$ (conversion for types)

The congruence relation "=" above is derived by the following **conversion rules.**

(β) $$\frac{\Gamma \vdash (\lambda x:A\,.\,a)\, b : B}{\vdash (\lambda x:A\,.\,a)\, b = [b/x]a}$$

(η) $$\frac{\Gamma \vdash \lambda x:A\,.\,(ax) : B, \quad x \notin FV(a)}{\vdash \lambda x:A\,.\,(ax) = a\,.}$$

It is easy to prove that the above translation of Λ_C, which we still call Λ_C, preserves the normalizability and decidability properties of the original calculus. Moreover, as Kind is not a kind (nor a type, of course) its addition to the language does not change the class of models, provided that kinds are interpreted as sets in ZF set theory.

Remark 1.1 i) Λ_Δ is a subsystem of Λ_C. One may easely represent Reynolds' type $\Delta t.A$ by taking $A = *$ in C.4 above. Also de Bruijn[1980] Authomath can be subsumed in Λ_C.

ii) The calculus λ^Π in Meyer&Reinhold[1986], which is just an apparent extension of the classical typed λ-calculus, is immediately embedded into Λ_Δ by observing that their ($\Pi\beta$) + (λe) correspond to C.6 above (see figure at the end of §2).

2. Force Kind to be a type

This section is devoted to Cardelli's extension $\Lambda_{*:*}$ of the original Martin-Löf's type theory. Following Martin-Löf[1971], $* : *$ is assumed. Moreover, fixed point operators and existential quantification are added to the original calculus. As pointed out in Meyer&Reinhold[1986], one immediately obtains a very expressive calculus when adding $* : *$ even to the rather simple subsystem λ^{Π} of Λ_C.

With reference to Λ_C, $\Lambda_{*:*}$ is defined as follows.

Terms: a ::= Kind | $*$ | fst a | snd a | var | (aa) | <a,a> | (λvar:a.a)
| ($\forall$var:a.a) | (μx:a.a) | ($\exists$var:a.a)

Axiom $*$: Kind = $*$

Constructions: as for Λ_C.

Well formed assignments: as for Λ_C. (By Axiom $*$, ass.2 coincides with ass.3).

Typing rules: from $*$.1 to $*$.6 as for Λ_C, where C.3 = C.4 by Axiom $*$, that is

$*$.1 $\Gamma \vdash * : *$

$*$.2 $$\frac{(x:A) \in \Gamma}{\Gamma \vdash x : A}$$ (assumption or weakening)

$*$.3 $$\frac{\Gamma(x : A) \vdash B : *}{\Gamma \vdash \forall x : A . B : *}$$ (types' $\forall$-quantification)

$*$.4 $$\frac{\Gamma(x : A) \vdash a : B}{\Gamma \vdash (\lambda x : A . a) : \forall x : A . B}$$ (abstraction)

$*$.5 $$\frac{\Gamma \vdash a : \forall x : A . B, \quad \Gamma \vdash b : A}{\Gamma \vdash (ab) : [b/x]B}$$ (application)

$*$.6 $$\frac{\Gamma \vdash a : A \qquad \vdash A = B}{\Gamma \vdash a : B}$$ (conversion for types)

$*$.7 $$\frac{\Gamma(x:A) \vdash B : *}{\Gamma \vdash \exists x:A.B : *}$$ (types' $\exists$-quantification)

$$\star.8 \quad \frac{\Gamma \vdash a : A \qquad \Gamma \vdash b : [a/x]B}{\Gamma \vdash \langle a,b\rangle : \exists x{:}A.B} \quad \text{(pair)}$$

$$\star.9 \quad \frac{\Gamma \vdash c : \exists x{:}A.B}{\Gamma \vdash \text{fst } c : A \qquad \Gamma \vdash \text{snd } c : [\text{fst } c/x]B} \quad \text{(projections)}$$

$$\star.10 \quad \frac{\Gamma(x{:}A) \vdash a : A}{\Gamma \vdash (\mu x{:}A.a) : A} \quad \text{(fixed points)}$$

Conversion rules: (β) and (η) as for Λ_C ,

$$(\pi) \quad \frac{\Gamma \vdash \langle a,b\rangle : A}{\vdash \text{fst } \langle a,b\rangle = a \qquad \vdash \text{snd } \langle a,b\rangle = b}$$

$$(\sigma) \quad \frac{\Gamma \vdash a : \exists x{:}A.B}{\vdash \langle \text{fst } a, \text{snd } a\rangle = a}$$

$$(\mu) \quad \frac{\Gamma \vdash (\mu x{:}A.a) : B}{\vdash (\mu x{:}A.a) = [(\mu x{:}A.a)/x]a}$$

Remark 2.1 Assignment and equality in Λ_C and $\Lambda_{\star:\star}$ are soundly related:

i) $\Gamma \vdash_C a : A \;\Rightarrow\; \Gamma \vdash_{\star:\star} a : A$.

ii) $\vdash_C a = b \;\Rightarrow\; \vdash_{\star:\star} a = b$.

From now on we write $(\Gamma) \vdash$ .... for $(\Gamma) \vdash_{\star:\star}$ ..... . Indeed, the results below "a fortiori" apply to all the previous type assignment systems, each time the statement is applicable to the intended calculus (e.g. 2.2.i) and ii) clearly hold for Λ_C , while iii), iv) and v) do not make sense for Λ_C).

We omit the proof of the following proposition, which may be given by an easy inductive argument on the length of type assignment.

Proposition 2.2

i) Γ |— ab: A $\Rightarrow$ $\exists$B,C Γ |— a :$\forall$x:B.C , Γ |— b:B , |— A = [b/x]C .

ii) Γ |— λx:A.a:B $\Rightarrow$ Γ (x:A)|— a:C , |— $\forall$x:A.C = B .

iii) Γ |— <a,b>:A $\Rightarrow$ $\exists$B,C Γ |— a:B, Γ |— b:[a/x]C , |—A = $\exists$x:B.C.

iv) Γ |— fst c:A, Γ |— snd c:B $\Rightarrow$ Γ |— c: $\exists$x:C.D, |— C = A, |— B=[fst c/x]D.

v) Γ |— μx:A.a:B $\Rightarrow$ Γ (x:A) |— a:A , |— A=B .

Lemma 2.3 (Substitution) Γ (x:A)(y_1:B_1).....(y_n:B_n) |— a:C , Γ |— b:A $\Rightarrow$
Γ (y_1:[b/x]B_1).....(y_n:[b/x]B_n) |— [b/x]a:[b/x]C.

Proof. (By induction on the stucture of a) We just present some significant cases.

a $\equiv$ $\star$: Observe that Γ |— $\star$:A $\Rightarrow$ A$\equiv$ $\star$ and that Γ (y_1:[b/x]B_1).....(y_n:[b/x]B_n) is ok.

a $\equiv$ y : By the definition of an ok assignment and a case analysis: y $\equiv$ x , y $\equiv$ y_i...

a$\equiv$$\forall$y:B.C :

Γ(x:A)(y_1:B_1).....(y_n:B_n)(y:B) |— C:$\star$ $\Rightarrow$
Γ (y_1:[b/x]B_1).....(y_n:[b/x]B_n)(y:[b/x]/B) |— [b/x]C:$\star$,
by hypothesis. The result follows by $\star$.3 .

a$\equiv$$\lambda$y:B.a : By 2.2 , Γ (x:A)(y_1:B_1).....(y_n:B_n)(y:B) |— a:C $\Rightarrow$
Γ (y_1:[b/x]B_1).....(y_n:[b/x]B_n)(y:[b/x]/B) |— [b/x]a: [b/x]C . The result follows, by $\star$.4 .

a $\equiv$ cd : Γ(y_1:B_1).....(y_n:B_n)(x:A) |— cd:B $\Rightarrow$ Γ (y_1:B_1).....(y_n:B_n) (x:A) |— c:$\forall$y:B'.B",
Γ (y_1:B_1).....(y_n:B_n) (x:A) |— d:B' and |— [d/y]B"=B by proposition 2.2, for some B', B". By induction hypothesis, one has:
Γ (y_1:[b/x]B_1).....(y_n:[b/x]B_n) |— [b/x]c: [b/x]($\forall$y: B'. B") and
Γ (y_1:[b/x]B_1).....(y_n:[b/x]B_n) |— [b/x]d: [b/x]B' . Therefore,
Γ (y_1:[b/x]B_1).....(y_n:[b/x]B_n) |— [b/x] cd: [[b/x]d /y]([b/x]B") = [b/x]([d/y]B") = [b/x]B.

A typical case of the substitution lemma is the following:

Γ (x:A) |— a:C , Γ |— b:A $\Rightarrow$ Γ |— [b/x]a:[b/x]C.

Theorem 2.4 i) (Typing by types) Γ |— a : A $\Rightarrow$ Γ |— A: $\star$.

ii) |— a = b $\Rightarrow$ $\exists\Gamma$ ok , $\exists$A Γ |— a : A and, for each Γ ok,
if $\exists$A Γ |— a : A then Γ |— b : B and |— A = B.

Proof hint. (By combined induction on the length of the deduction) We just sketch some cases .

$\star$.5 : Apply 2.3: i.e. Γ(x:A) |— B:$\star$ $\Rightarrow$ Γ |— [b/x]B:$\star$.

$\star$.6 : Use combined induction on Γ |— a : B and |— B = A .

(β) : Apply again 2.3.

Corollary 2.5 i) (At most one type) $\Gamma \vdash a : A$ and $\Gamma \vdash a : B \Rightarrow \vdash A = B$.

ii) (Conversion preserves types) $\Gamma \vdash a : A$ and $\vdash a = b \Rightarrow \Gamma \vdash b : A$.

Proof. Straightforward application of 2.4.

The connections sketched so far may be summarized as follows, where λ^{τ} is the classically typed calculus and $\lambda^{\tau:\tau}$ is the $* : *$ extension of λ^{Π} in Meyer& Reinhold[1986].

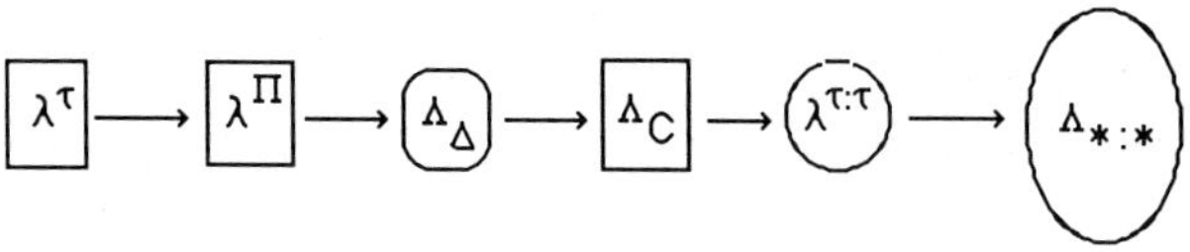

3. An extended calculus of retractions

In this section we define a type-free λ-calculus, for the purposes of the type-free foundation of types as parameters mentioned in the introduction. The idea is that types may be viewed as provable retractions in a type-free theory. (Recall that a retraction r is an idempotent $r \circ r = r$; thus, the fixed points of r are exactly the elements in the range of r). The extension we propose is meant to be rich enough to incorporate $\Lambda_{*:*}$. The language is that of type-free $\lambda\beta(\eta)$ plus an extra constant symbol p (and, possibly, pairing functions).

Conventions: as usual, set $Y \equiv \lambda f. (\lambda x.f(xx)) (\lambda x.f(xx))$ (fixed point operator) and let $[\_,\_]$ (pairings), fst, snd (projections) be defined terms (for example, $[\_,\_] \equiv \lambda yzx.xyz$, $fst \equiv \lambda x.xK$, $snd \equiv \lambda x.xO$) or added primitives satisfying the axioms 6 and 7 below. Set then

$$M \circ N \equiv \lambda x.M(Nx) \qquad x \notin FV(MN)$$

$$\forall x : N.M \equiv \lambda zt.(\lambda x.M) (Nt) (z(Nt)) \qquad z,t \notin FV(MN)$$

$$\exists x : N.M \equiv \lambda y. [N(fsty), (\lambda x.M) (N(fsty)) (sndy)] \qquad y \notin FV(MN) .$$

Remark 3.1. If $x \notin FV(M)$, set $N \to M \equiv \forall x : N. M$. Then $N \to M = \lambda z. M \circ z \circ N$. Similarly, one may set $N \times M \equiv \exists x{:}N. M$, when $x \notin FV(M)$ (see $*$.9 and Remark 3.9). Then $N \times M \equiv \lambda y. [N(fsty), M(sndy)]$. Reynolds' $\Delta t.M$ is $\forall t : p.M$, that is $\lambda zy.(\lambda t.M)(py) (z(py))$.

Definition 3.2. **$\lambda\beta(\eta)p$** is the $\lambda\beta(\eta)$ calculus extended by the following axioms.

1. $pp = p$
2. $(px) \circ (px) = px$
3. $p(\forall x : pN.pM) = \forall x : pN.pM$
4. $p(\exists x : pN.pM) = \exists x : pN.pM$
5. $pM(Y(pM \circ x \circ pM)) = Y(pM \circ x \circ pM)$

(If there is no ambiguity, we write $\ldots = \ldots$ for $\lambda\beta(\eta)p \vdash \ldots = \ldots$).

Note that 1+2 imply $p \circ p = p$. Thus p is a retraction, p is in its own range (1), all the elements in the range of p are retractions (2) and the range of p is closed under term formation by $\forall\ldots$, $\exists\ldots$(3+4). Finally, the intended meaning of (5) is that "functions" from the range of pM into the range of pM have fixed points in the range of pM, see 3.1 and 4.1(i).

By **$\lambda\beta(\eta)p$ + surj. pair.** we mean **$\lambda\beta(\eta)p$** plus fresh symbols [_ , _] , fst, snd satisfying:

6. fst[M,P] = M
7. snd[M,P] = P
8. [fstM,sndM] = M .

Clearly, if pairs and projections are defined by $[M,P] \equiv \lambda x.xMP$, $fst \equiv \lambda x.xK$ and $snd \equiv \lambda x.xO$, say, then, 6 and 7 follow from (β) ; however, no defined pairings may satisfy 6+7+8 (see Barendregt[1984]).

Note. A weaker axiomatization of a "calculus of retractions" was given in Amadio&Bruce&Longo[1985]. That was meant to deal only with Λ_Δ and the normalizability and decidabilty properties of Λ_Δ were an essential tool in the syntactic investigation of semantic equalities of types in models. Here, we look also at Λ_C and $\Lambda_{*:*}$ and a translation of polymorphic terms into type-free terms is given, see 3.5 below. The axiomatization in 3.2 has been explicitly borrowed by Cardelli[1986].

Theorem 3.3. $\lambda\beta\eta p$ + surj. pair. is consistent.

Proof reference: the closure model over $P\omega$ in Scott[1976] interprets $\lambda\beta p$ + surj. pair. A detailed computation may be found in Cardelli[1986], where $P\omega x P\omega \cong P\omega$ is used. Indeed, this isomorphism is the meaning of ax.6+7+8, surjective pairings. As for $\lambda\beta\eta p$, one needs to take a lattice L satisfying $LxL \cong L$ and $[L \to L] \cong L$, then the same computation applies.

Note that the theory of $\lambda\beta p$-conversion in 3.2 may be obtained from several distinct reduction systems. As we look at p as a (irreducible) constant, "natural" reduction systems for $\lambda\beta p$ are just based on two ways for deriving ax.2 from

2'. $px \circ px > px$ or

2". $px(pxz) > pxz$.

Note that 2" implies $px(pxz) = pxz$, which is sufficient for theorem 3.6; moreover, by (η), one obtains ax.2. There is little choice for the other axioms: reductions must go from left to right, in the way the axioms are formulated. Call $\lambda\beta p'$ and $\lambda\beta p''$ the extensions of $\lambda\beta p$ with axioms for reductions including 2' or 2" , respectively.

Proposition 3.4. i) $\lambda\beta p'$ and $\lambda\beta p''$ are not Church-Rosser.

ii) $\lambda\beta p$ + surj. pair is not Church-Rosser.

Proof hint: i) Let reductions be defined by taking 2' above. Then

$$(px \circ px)z > pxz \quad \text{and} \quad (px \circ px)z > px(pxz) .$$

Thus the sysyem is not even weakly Church-Rosser, i.e. it is not always the case that different one step reductions can be taken to a common reduct.

Consider now 2". Then the system is weakly Church-Rosser, but, by (a variant of) the result on δ-reductions in Klop[1980], the Church-Rosser property fails. Indeed, the following hint was suggeted by Klop in correspondence.

Write $\delta \equiv \lambda xy.\, px \circ py$. Then $\delta MMz >> pMz$, where $>>$ is the transitive closure of $>$. Further define, by Turing's fixed point operator, N and Q such that

$$Nx >> \delta x(Nx)I \quad \text{and} \quad Q >> NQ .$$

Then

(1) $Q >> NQ >> \delta Q(NQ)I >> \delta NQ(NQ)I >> p(NQ)I$,

and, hence, $NQ >> N(p(NQ)I)$, by prefixing N , and $NQ >> p(NQ)I$, by (1). With some case analysis, one can show that no reduct of $N(p(NQ)I)$ starts with p . Thus, $N(p(NQ)I)$ and $p(NQ)I$ have no common reduct.

ii) It is well known that $\lambda\beta$ + surj. pair is not Church- Rosser, moreover "p-reductions" do not interfere.

3.3 and 3.4 confirm the relevance of the model-theory in this matter.

We are now in the position to translate the previous higher order calculi into $\lambda\beta p$. The translation will be done at once for types and terms. However, as terms depend on type assignments, this will require some recursion (step1+2).

Definition 3.5. Let a be term of $\Lambda_{*:*}$ and Γ a type assignment. Define then $<a>^{\Gamma}$ in $\lambda\beta p$ as follows.

Step 1 ($\Gamma = \emptyset$) $<x> = x$

$<*> = p$

$$< \forall x{:}A.B > \; = \; \lambda zt.\,(\lambda x.\langle B\rangle)\,(\langle A\rangle t)\,(z(\langle A\rangle t)) \qquad z,t \;\notin FV(AB)$$
$$\langle \lambda x{:}A.b\rangle \; = \; (\lambda x.\langle b\rangle) \cdot \langle A\rangle$$
$$\langle ab\rangle \; = \; \langle a\rangle\,\langle b\rangle$$
$$\langle \exists x{:}A.B\rangle \; = \; \lambda y.\,[\langle A\rangle(\mathrm{fst}y),\ \langle \lambda x{:}A.B\rangle\,(\mathrm{fst}y)(\mathrm{snd}y)] \qquad y \notin FV(AB)$$
$$\langle \mu x{:}A.a\rangle \; = \; Y(\langle \lambda x{:}A.a\rangle)$$
$$\langle\langle a,b\rangle\rangle \; = \; [\langle a\rangle, \langle b\rangle]$$
$$\langle \mathrm{fst}\ a\rangle \; = \; \mathrm{fst}\ a$$
$$\langle \mathrm{snd}\ a\rangle \; = \; \mathrm{snd}\ a\,.$$

Step 2 For $\Gamma = \{(x_1{:}A_1), \ldots, (x_n : A_n)\}$ and $\Gamma_i = \{(x_1{:}A_1), \ldots, (x_{i-1}, A_{i-1})\}$, let $N_i \equiv \langle A_i\rangle^{\Gamma_i}\ x_i$. Then

$$\langle a\rangle^{\Gamma} = [N_1/x_1, \ldots, N_n/x_n]\,\langle a\rangle\ .$$

The intuition should be clear. Type, i.e. $*$, goes to p (see 3.6 below). When $\langle\lambda x{:}A.b\rangle$ is applied to a term, it coarses it first to be in the range of $\langle A\rangle$. $<\forall x{:}A.B>$ and $\langle\exists x{:}A.B\rangle$ express type dependence in product types and in types of pairs. Indeed, under the assumptions in 3.1, they represent function spaces and cartesian products in $\lambda\beta p$ (see 4.1).

Theorem 3.6 (Correctness) i) $\Gamma \vdash a : A \;\Rightarrow\; \lambda\beta p \vdash \langle a\rangle^{\Gamma} = \langle A\rangle^{\Gamma}\langle a\rangle^{\Gamma}$.

ii) $\vdash a = b \;\Rightarrow\; \exists\,\Gamma \vdash a : A$ and $\Gamma \vdash b : A$ and $\lambda\beta p \vdash \langle a\rangle^{\Gamma} = \langle b\rangle^{\Gamma}$.

Proof. The proof goes by some combined inductive work on the length of the deduction.

$*$.1. i) : by ax.1 in 3.2 , i.e. by the first axiom of $\lambda\beta(\eta)p$.

$*$.2 . i) : if $(x,A)\in\Gamma$ then $\Gamma \vdash A{:}*$ and, by induction, $p\langle A\rangle^{\Gamma} = \langle A\rangle^{\Gamma}$.

Hence by ax.2 in 3.2 we have, in $\lambda\beta(\eta)p$,

$\langle A\rangle^{\Gamma}\langle x\rangle^{\Gamma} = p\,\langle A\rangle^{\Gamma}(\,p\,\langle A\rangle^{\Gamma} x) = p\,\langle A\rangle^{\Gamma} x = \langle x\rangle^{\Gamma}$.

$*$.3 . i) : by induction, if $\Gamma(x{:}a) \vdash B{:}*$ then $p(\langle B\rangle^{\Gamma(x:a)}) = \langle B\rangle^{\Gamma(x:a)}$. Now, ax.3 in 3.2 applies, as $(\lambda x.\,\langle B\rangle^{\Gamma(x:a)})\,(\,\langle A\rangle^{\Gamma} t) = [\,\langle A\rangle^{\Gamma} t/x]\,\langle B\rangle^{\Gamma(x:a)}$ and this is equal to $\langle B\rangle^{\Gamma}$ if $x\notin FV(B)$ or to

$[\langle A\rangle^{\Gamma}(\,\langle A\rangle^{\Gamma} t)/x]\,\langle B\rangle^{\Gamma} = [\langle A\rangle^{\Gamma} t/x]\,\langle B\rangle^{\Gamma}$ if $x\in FV(B)$,

as $p\,\langle A\rangle^{\Gamma} = \langle A\rangle^{\Gamma}$ and by ax.2 .

$*$.4 . i) : $\langle\forall x{:}A.B\rangle^{\Gamma}\langle\lambda x{:}A.a\rangle^{\Gamma} =$

$= \lambda t.\,(\lambda x.\,\langle B\rangle^{\Gamma})(\langle A\rangle^{\Gamma} t)(\lambda x.\,\langle B\rangle^{\Gamma(x:A)}\,\langle a\rangle^{\Gamma(x:A)}(\,\langle A\rangle^{\Gamma} t))$

$= \lambda t.\,(\lambda x.\,\langle B\rangle^{\Gamma})(\langle A\rangle^{\Gamma} t)(\lambda x.\,\langle B\rangle^{\Gamma}\,\langle a\rangle^{\Gamma}(\,\langle A\rangle^{\Gamma} t))$

$= \lambda t.\,[\langle A\rangle^{\Gamma} t/x]\,\langle B\rangle^{\Gamma}(\,[\langle A\rangle^{\Gamma} t/x]\,\langle B\rangle^{\Gamma}[\langle A\rangle^{\Gamma} t/x]\,\langle a\rangle^{\Gamma})$

$= \lambda x.\,\langle B\rangle^{\Gamma(x:A)}\,\langle a\rangle^{\Gamma(x:A)} = \lambda x.\langle a\rangle^{\Gamma(x:A)} = \langle\lambda x{:}A.a\rangle^{\Gamma}$.

$*$.5 . i) : $\langle ab\rangle^{\Gamma} = \langle a\rangle^{\Gamma}\langle b\rangle^{\Gamma} =$

$= (\,\langle\forall x{:}A.B\rangle^{\Gamma}\langle a\rangle^{\Gamma}\langle b\rangle^{\Gamma})$

$= ((\lambda zt.(\lambda x.\,\langle B\rangle^{\Gamma})(\,\langle A\rangle^{\Gamma} t\,)(\,z(\langle A\rangle^{\Gamma} t\,)))\,\langle a\rangle^{\Gamma}\langle b\rangle^{\Gamma}\,)$

$$= ((\lambda x.\ \langle B\rangle^{\Gamma})(\langle A\rangle^{\Gamma}\langle b\rangle^{\Gamma})(\langle a\rangle^{\Gamma}(\langle A\rangle^{\Gamma}\langle b\rangle^{\Gamma})))$$
$$= ([\langle b\rangle^{\Gamma}/x]\langle B\rangle^{\Gamma}(\langle a\rangle^{\Gamma}\langle b\rangle^{\Gamma}))$$
$$= [\langle b\rangle^{\Gamma}/x]\langle B\rangle^{\Gamma}\langle ab\rangle^{\Gamma}.$$

$\star.6$. i) : easy, by induction on i) <u>and</u> ii).

$\star.7$. i) : just observe that $\langle \exists x{:}A.B\rangle^{\Gamma}$ is such that ax.4 in 3.2 applies.

$\star.8, \star.9$. i) : by a similar computation as for $\star.4$ and $\star.5$.

$\star.10$. i) : use ax.5 in 3.2.

Conjecture: the implications in 3.6 should be two ways.

Corollary 3.7 (Types go into the range of p). If $\Gamma \vdash A : \star$, then $\lambda\beta p \vdash \langle A\rangle^{\Gamma} = p\langle A\rangle^{\Gamma}$

Remark 3.8 Observe that translated typed terms into type-free terms satisfy axiom (η). Indeed, if $\Gamma \vdash \lambda x : A.(ax) : B$, with $x \notin FV(a)$, then $\Gamma \vdash a : (\forall x : A . B)$, by 2.2.i), and, thus, $\langle a\rangle^{\Gamma} = \langle \forall x{:}A.B\rangle^{\Gamma}\langle a\rangle^{\Gamma} = \lambda t.\ (\lambda x.\langle B\rangle^{\Gamma})(\langle A\rangle^{\Gamma} t)(\langle a\rangle^{\Gamma}(\langle A\rangle^{\Gamma} t))$. Therefore,

$\langle \lambda x : A.(ax)\rangle^{\Gamma} = \langle a\rangle^{\Gamma}$ holds, by (β), and the inference rule (η) is sound. By a similar proof, the classically defined pairing function in $\lambda\beta(\eta)$ turns out to be <u>surjective</u> on the traduction of typable terms (though it is not surjective on the whole universe of λ-terms). That is, define $[M,P] \equiv \lambda x.xMP$, $fst \equiv \lambda x.xK$ and $snd \equiv \lambda x.xO$, then ax.6 and 7 trivially hold and rule (σ) is sound too.

Remark 3.9 (On the meaning of "$\forall$" and "$\exists$") The definitions of "$\forall$" and "$\exists$" originate from elementary notions in Category Theory (see Scott[1976]). To explain this, we informally mix up syntax and semantics; $\lambda x.f(x)$ is the informal lambda notation for functions. The key point is that, in the interpretation of types as retractions, a:A is interpreted by $a \in range(A)$ or, equivalently, by $a = Aa$. Let' s then see how to obtain the higher types.

Recall that "$\to$" is just a special case of "$\forall$" , by 3.1. We discuss this simple case first. In a category **C**, an object c is a retract of d iff there exist $i \in \mathbf{C}[c,d]$ and $j \in \mathbf{C}[d,c]$ such that $j \circ i = id$. $i \circ j \in \mathbf{C}[d,d]$ is a retraction, or (i,j) is a retraction pair, as $i \circ j \circ i \circ j = i \circ j$. By this, c , as a "subtype" of d , may be identified with (i,j) or, by some abuse of language, since categories do not need to have points or elements, it may be identified with the fixed points of $i \circ j$ (the range of $i \circ j$).

Let d^{c} be the exponent in **C**, i.e. the object which represents $\mathbf{C}[c,d]$ in **C**, whenever it exists; then, if a is a retract of b by (i',j') and c is a retract of d via (i,j), one has

c^a is a retract of d^b via $(\lambda x.i \circ x \circ j', \lambda x.j \circ x \circ i')$.

Indeed, $(\lambda x.i \circ x \circ j') \circ (\lambda x.j \circ x \circ i')$ is a retraction and its fixed points may be identified with c^a as a subtype of d^b . In other words, if one writes $r = i \circ j$ and $s = i' \circ j'$, then c^a coincides with $\{x/ \ x = r \circ x \circ s \} = \text{range}(\lambda x.r \circ x \circ s)$, where r , s and $\lambda x.r \circ x \circ s$ are all retractions (cf. 3.1).

As for "$\forall$", recall that types are in the range of p , by 3.7, and that types are retractions, by ax.2 (but not necessarely all retractions are types, see 4.II). Consider rule $\star$.5 and assume, for the sake of simplicity, that $A = \star$ (i.e. A is the collection of types). The intuition is that a has type $\forall x{:}\star.B$ iff a is a function which takes any $b{:}\star$ into an element (ab) of type [b/x]B . By informally blending the notation for $\Lambda_{\star:\star}$ and $\lambda\beta p$, this means

$$ab = ([b/x]B)(ab) \text{ , by 3.6,}$$

as types are retractions. Thus, for all $b{:}\star$, one has $ab = (\lambda x.B)b(ab)$. By 3.7, this corresponds to, for all $b = pb$, $ab = (\lambda x.B)(pb)(a(pb))$, that is

$$a = \lambda t.(\lambda x.B)(pt)(a(pt)) \text{ ,}$$

if one loosely identifies a with $<a> = (\lambda x.<a'>) \circ p$, for the intended a' , see 3.5, line 4 of Step 1. Equivalently:

$$a = (\lambda zt.(\lambda x.B)(pt)(z(pt)))a \text{ .}$$

Indeed, $\lambda zt.(\lambda x.B)(pt)(z(pt))$ turns out to be a retraction, when B is a retraction. In conclusion, $\lambda zt.(\lambda x.B)(pt)(z(pt))$ soundly interprets $\forall x{:}\star.B$, as we derived it exactly from the intended meaning of the universal quantification over type variables (see the dependent product in Bruce&Meyer[1984]).

Existential quantification may be better understood by refering also to Intuitionistic Logic and to "types as propositions". A term of type

$$\exists x : N.M \equiv \lambda y. \ [N(fsty), (\lambda x.M) \ (N(fsty)) \ (sndy)]$$

is a pair [Q,R] such that Q = NQ is of type N and R is of type [NQ/x]M . That is, R is a proof that Q , of type N , is a witness for M .

Concluding remarks. In this paper, an implicit use of semantics has been made. Namely, the retraction models suggested a consistent extension of the pure type-free λ-calculus, which could bear enough information so as to encode higher order calculi. It is an open issue whether the interpretation of "$\forall$" in those models gives a significant interpretation to the parametric notion of polymorphism; indeed, the semantically not transparent or apparently "ad hoc" interpretation of "$\forall$" is simply due to the identification of a:A , $a \in \text{range}(A)$ and $Aa = a$, which comes from interpreting types as retractions. In any case, the formal theory of those models provides a simple and an elegant framework for a syntactic type-free translation of higher order type disciplines where computations may be uniformly carried on, as the operational side of λ-calculus is an essentially type-free activity.

Recall that this translation was made possible by the validity of the very strong assumption "Type:Type" in all retraction models, however good this may be for other purposes (see Introduction). Up to late 1985 these were the only known mathematical models of higher order calculi, including Λ_Δ . It should be noted, though, that in Girard[1972] and Troelstra[1973] a model for Λ_Δ was already presented, which did not realize Type:Type . The semantics for the crucial "∀" constructor was given by using intersection over quotient sets. Up to very recent times, this did not seem to be very satisfactory for the following reasons. First, terms were interpreted as elements of intersections by erasing all type information in them . For example, λt:Type.λx:t.x , the polymorphic identity, could be interpreted as an element of the intersection of all the interpretations of $t \to t$, by identifying it with λx.x . Second, the interpretation of "∀" as intersection may seem unsatisfactory, as a term depending on a type is better understood as a function from the collection of types into a specific type; this is exactly what is meant by dependent product in Bruce&Meyer[1984]. For example, the meaning of λt:Type.λx:t.x is a function which takes any type σ and gives as output the identity of type $\sigma \to \sigma$, see 3.9.

In a suitable categorical environment, though, well understood intersections over quotient sets and dependent products turn out to coincide. This is a simple consequence of a recent and original achievement of Eugenio Moggi who showed that the category **M** of partial equivalence relations over any partial combinatory algebra (the **modest** sets), which is a subCCC of the intended Effective Topos, may be also viewed as an object **m** , say, of that topos (as an internal category, to be precise). As **m** is not in **M**, Type: Type does not hold. However, quantification over **M**, the collection of all types, may be interpreted as a product indexed in **m**; this product happens to be an object of **M**. Moreover, in that framework, dependent products are sufficiently poor and intersections are sufficiently rich to be identified. Indeed, the Effective Topos has "few" morphisms, with respect to the classical category of sets, as it is a model of intuitionistic Set Theory. In other words, Moggi's result may be understood by rephrasing Reynolds[1984]: polymorphism is set-theoretic, provided that intuitionistic Set Theory is considered.

This elegant mathematical result seems to be immediately relevant to the current discussion on polymorphism in Computer Science. This should be clear by the newly established relation between intersections and products as well as by the following fact. All known models, including the recent models in Girard[1985], interpret "→" and "∀" by covariant functors, in the first argument (see 4.l). The above explanation of Girard-Troelstra model, based on a discussion on elettronic mail carried on by Moggi, Scott and Mitchell, provides a contravariant interpretation for "→" and "∀" . This seems to fit much better everyone's intuition on the possible connections between inheritance (subtypes) and explicit polymorphism.

4. Hints for further work

I - By similar computations as in Cardelli[1986], one could prove the consistency of $\lambda\beta\eta p$ also by the finitary retraction or the finitary projection models in Scott[1980], MacCracken[1984] and Amadio&Bruce&Longo[1986], respectively. In particular, the later models have some tecnical advantages. Recall that, in a Scott's domain U , a retraction r is a finitary projection ($r \in FP$) if $r \le id$ and range(r) is a Scott's domain. Then, for $r,s \in FP$, one has $r \ge s$ iff range(r) $\supseteq$ range(s) (see Amadio&Bruce&Longo[1986]), that is $r \ge s$ really seems to provide a sound interpretation for "s is a subtype of r". Moreover, by the following theorem, one may uniformely deal with subtypes.

Theorem 4.1 $\forall r \in FP\ \exists r' \in FP$ range(r') = $\{q \in FP\ /\ q \le r\}$.
<u>Proof</u>. Define $f_r(s) = \sup\{q \in FP\ /\ q \le r$ <u>and</u> $q \le s\}$. Then f_r is a continuous function whose representative r' in U is a finitary projection and satisfies range(r') = $\{q \in FP\ /\ q \le r\}$.

In other words, the collection of all subtypes of a type is a type. This strong property may suggest a way to formalize the relation between inheritance (subtypes) and explicit polymorphism. Namely, one may add axioms and inference rules for $\supseteq$ to Λ_C or $\Lambda_{\star:\star}$ as suggested by the model (which hold in the model). For example,

$$\frac{\Gamma \vdash A' \supseteq A \qquad \Gamma(x : A') \vdash B' \supseteq B}{\Gamma \vdash \forall x : A' .\ B' \supseteq \forall x : A .\ B} \qquad (\forall\text{-covariant})$$

is a sound rule when types are interpreted as finitary projections (see the concluding remark in §3).

II - The axiomatization of $\lambda\beta p$ is based on the existence of "some" classes of retractions each coinciding with the range of one of its elements and closed under type formation. The most natural axiomatization would be obtained from 3.2 by substituting ax.3 and ax.4 with the following rule

$$\frac{M \circ M = M}{pM = M} \qquad \text{(retractions are types)}$$

By this rule one may derive ax.3 and ax.4. Unfortunately, there is no model, up to now, of this strong and elegant calculus (see Barendregt[1984; p.492]) and a syntactic consistency proof would be very helpful, if any.

III - Category Theory is the basis or the hidden background for the present work, as category-theoretic notions inspired the "retraction models" for II-order λ-calculus in Scott[1976,1980], where types are interpreted as particular retractions (see 3.9). The above type-free axiomatization of various higher order calculi is directly derived from the core properties of those models. It is then sound to check that everything goes smoothly from the category-theoretic point of view.

Let $\{M\} = \{N \mid \lambda\beta(\eta)p \vdash N = M\}$ and $|\lambda\beta(\eta)p| = \{\{M\} \mid M \text{ is a term}\}$, the term model of $\lambda\beta(\eta)p$.

Theorem 4.2 (Type structures) .

i) The retractions in $|\lambda\beta(\eta)p|$ form a Cartesian Closed Category (CCC).

ii) range(p) is a full subCCC of the retractions in $|\lambda\beta(\eta)p|$.

iii) For each Γ ok, $\{\langle A\rangle^{\Gamma} \mid \Gamma \vdash A : *\}$ is a full subCCC of range(p) .

<u>Proof hint</u> : i) This is the Scott-Karoubi envelope (see Barendregt[1984]).

ii) + iii) By remark 3.1 and the axioms.

In a recent work Seely[1986] has related locally cartesian categories (lcc's) to models of Martin-Löf type theory. The categories over the term model in 4.2 are not lcc's, even though they provide models for the strong extension $\Lambda_{*:*}$ of Martin-Löf calculus. Does one obtain lcc's by taking more interesting models for $\lambda\beta(\eta)p$ than the term model? The connections between retraction models and lcc's should be explored, mostly because it may suggest interesting extensions of Λ_C or Martin-Löf calculus without assuming the strong $* : *$ hypothesis.

References

Aczel P. [1985] "Non-well founded sets" Lecture notes, CSLI Stanford.

Amadio R., Bruce K. B., Longo G. [1986] "The finitary projections model and the solution of higher order domain equations", **IEEE Symposium on Logic in Computer Science**, Boston, June 1986.

Barendregt, H. [1984], **The lambda calculus; its syntax and semantics**, revised edition, North Holland

Bruce K., Meyer A. [1984] "The semantics of second order polymorphic lambda-calculus", **Symposium on Semantics of Data Types** (Kahn, MacQueen, Plotkin eds.), LNCS 173, Springer-Verlag (pp. 131-144).

Burstall R.M., Lampson B. [1984] "A kernel language for abstract data types and modules", **Symposium on Semantics of Data Types** (Kahn, MacQueen, Plotkin eds.), LNCS 173, Springer-Verlag.

Cardelli L. [1986] "A polymorphic lambda-calculus with Type:Type", Preprint, Syst. Res. Center, Dig. Equip. Corp..

Coquand T. [1985] "Une théorie des constructions", Thèse de 3ème cycle, Université Paris VII.

Coquand T. [1986] "An analysis of Girard's paradox" , **IEEE Symposium on Logic in Computer Science**, Boston, June 1986.

Coquand T., Huet G. [1985] "A calculus of constructions", Preprint INRIA.

Curry H.B., Feys R. [1958] **Combinatory Logic I**, North-Holland.

De Bruijn, N. [1980], "A survey of the project AUTOMATH," in **To H.B. Curry: essays on Combinatory Logic, Lambda-Calculus and formalism**, Hindley, Seldin (eds.), Academic Press.

Girard, J. [1972] "Interpretation fonctionelle et elimination des coupure dans l'arithmetic d'ordre superieur," These de Doctorat d'Etat, Paris.

Girard, J. [1985] "The system F, fifteen years later" Preprint, Paris VII.

Klop J.W. [1980] "Combinatory reduction systems" Mathematical Center Tracts 129 , Amsterdam.

Liskov, B. et alii [1981] **CLU reference manual**, LNCS 114, Springer-Verlag.

Martin -Löf P. [1971] "A theory of types," **Report 71-3**, Dept of Mathematics, University of Stockholm, February 1971, revised October 1971.

Martin-Löf P. [1972] "An Intuitionistic Theory of Types" Report, Dept. of Mathematics, Univ. of Stockholm.

McCracken N. [1984] "A finitary retract model for the polymorphic lambda-calculus," **Information and Control** (to appear).

Meyer, A. R. Reinhold, M.B. [1986] "*Type* is not a type" (preliminary report), **Proc. Popl 86**, ACM.

Reynolds, J. [1974], "Towards a theory of type structures," **Colloque sur la Programmation**, LNCS 19, Springer-Verlag (pp. 408-425).

Reynolds, J. [1984], "Polymorphism is not set-theoretic," **Symposium on Semantics of Data Types**, (Kahn, MacQueen, Plotkin, eds.) LNCS 173, Springer-Verlag.

Scott D. [1976] "Data types as lattices," **SIAM Journal of Computing**, 5 (pp. 522-587).

Scott D. [1980] "A space of retracts" Manuscript, Bremen.

Seely R.A.G.[1986] "Categorical semantics for higher order polymorphic lambda calculus", preprint, Department of Mathematics , John Abbott College.

Troelstra A. [1973] **Metamathematical Investigation of Intuitionistic Arithmetic and Analysis**, LNM 344, Springer-Verlag.

QUESTIONS AND ANSWERS

Dezani: I have two questions. First, what happens with the translation if you add an existential quantifier to your language? And the second question is: You have a soundness theorem, do you also have a completeness theorem?

Longo: In the talk I have presented a restricted language, but in the paper a higher-order λ-calculus is presented with existential quantification and, following a suggestion of Luca Cardelli, with a fixed point operator. Concerning the second question: in the paper we present a conjecture and a student is trying to check it. For the translation, there is a completeness theorem on the syntactic level which does not hold in any specific model but which is true for the syntax.

Jones: I'll take the same risk that Krzysztof Apt took a little while ago revealing my own hatred to this field. You made an analogy in the beginning with physics that type-checking could be used to recognize inconsistencies. If you have an equation where the dimensions (which correspond to the types) don't match then you can recognize this by a fairly simple computation. The question is: what form does a type-inconsistency take in this framework? I'm concerned a little bit by the following: You do not observe a reference to an element which actually lies out of the type that a retraction defines.

Longo: The completeness theorem would give us a perfect correspondence between the inconsistency discovered in a type assignment and the equational inconsistency. So if we had a completeness theorem I could give an answer to you: no problem; if there are types not matching the type assignment I would get something which is not equated.

Jones: Do you then get something that you simply cannot prove, or do you get something more concrete? A concrete measure that there is an inconsistency.

Longo: No, something I cannot prove. The point is that by taking a type as a type assumption, you lose the decidability of type checking. That's the prize you have to pay for the sake of the form of the language.

Jouannaud: For the non-expert it's quite hard to understand why in some of these calculi such as in Huet and Coquand's calculus [see references in the paper] you still have the correspondence between types and propositions - and you have strong normalization; and why in other calculi you lose that. You suggest that it could come from some constructions which exist for example in ML. Could you be more explicit and explain why such constructions make this correspondence lost?

Longo: Well, it´s hard. This is based on a very nice result of Girard, namely Girard´s paradox for the original version of Martin Löf´s type theory [see references in the paper]. As all interesting theories, such as Frege´s [set] theory or the original version of λ-calculus, Martin Löf´s type theory was inconsistent. You have the type of all types and therefore you have the possibility of proving any type. This is comparable to Russel´s paradox of the set of all sets but it is not as easy as this because we don´t have negation in this language. So you lose the analogy with propositions. This is very much related to what happens in ML.

Mayoh: Last night we had a discussion about whether objects could have more than one type. For example, the expression ´x belongs to type A´ corresponds in your translation to ´x is a fixpoint of the retract for A´. In the same way it seems to me that your ´type is a type´-conjecture means that everything is a fixpoint of something. There is no objection in your theory for an object to be a fixpoint of several retracts. So that means that an object can have a large number of types.

Longo: First of all, of course, anything is a fixpoint of something - at least of the identity. But however, it´s not true that everything has more than one type, in the very precise sense that here we are translating a typed language; terms come together with their types. The second-order polymorphism turns things in a way that a metalinguistic notion of type scheme is a linguistic notion. For example, due to the universal quantification of types the polymorphic identity is just a term with a specific type. So, by applying the identity to any type you get a specific identity for a single type. But that´s a different step, you have to do an application to something.

Coppo: You said that you want to keep type information during computation. I want to ask: is this true and necessary? You can not separate type-checking and execution. The other question is: Can you have a translation of types and terms which use the same interpreter of the type free calculus to make type-checking?

Longo: Whether it is necessary or not I think it was a good thing to do because losing type information during computation is something very rare. The main point is your second question, namely computation of the interpreter. It works exactly the same way for terms and types; so, the interpreter is valuable for both translation of terms and types as they are ´animals´ of the same kind.

Formal Description of Programming Concepts - III
M. Wirsing (Editor)
Elsevier Science Publishers B.V. (North-Holland)

© IFIP, 1987

PX: a system extracting programs from proofs

Susumu HAYASHI

Research Institute for Mathematical Sciences,
Kyoto University, Sakyo, Kyoto, Japan

This paper is a report on a system **PX** which realizes the paradigm of "proofs as programs" or "formulas as types". The aim of **PX** is to verify programs and to extract programs froms proofs. We will give a brief description of the system and present some techniques extracting programs from proofs.

0. Introduction

Recently, many computer scientists and logicians are taking interests in the paradigm of "formulas as types" (see [8] for an extensive bibliography on the subject). Among many approaches to the paradigm, Martin-Löf's type theory is most popular in computing society. His system is beautiful and satisfactory from theoretical point of view. But there are problems from practical points of view and some alternatives to his system have been designed [6,9,18]. One of the problems is unnecessary use of the principle of formulas as types. For example, the expression on propositional equality is computationally meaningless. Another problem is too heavy constraint of the totalness. Both of these problems come from the same source that "computing" and "reasoning" are fused too tightly in Martin-Löf's system. Consequently, alternative systems seem to tend to separate logical parts and computational parts.

On the other hand, we introduced a formal theory **LM** in [14] , in which logical parts and computational parts are clearly separated. We can write any kind of general recursions as programs of pure Lisp in **LM** and can infer properties of programs directly by logical rules without awareness of the principle of "formulas as types". The principle of "formulas as types" is realized by the aid of q-realizability interpretation, which enabled us to extract programs from constructive proofs.

In this paper, we introduce a new system **PX** (Program eXtractor) which is an improvement of **LM** and has been implemented on an actual machine. **PX** is also based on the formal systems of Feferman[10] as **LM** was. The most important improvement of **PX** is the introduction of the principle of CIG (Conditional Inductive Generation), by which we can define various data types and can represent a wide class of recursions, called CIG-recursion, by induction principles. In a sense, **PX** is *extensionally complete*, since CIG-recursions subsume all "iterations". Actually we can represent *all* partial recursive functions by constructive proofs of **PX**. The representation of a CIG-recursion by an induction principle leads us to a natural definition of a domain on which the recursion terminates. Since the termination of the recursion is assured only on the domain, the incompleteness results of formal logic do not conflict with the completeness of **PX**. We will show this provides a methodology by which we can separate the problems of termination and partial correctness even in the framework of "proofs as programs".

Another improvement is the presentation of axiom system. The formal system of **LM** was based on traditional intuitionistic logic. **LM** has a predicate which represents a graph of an interpreter of pure Lisp without function closure mechanisms. Form it we developed a logic of partial terms and defined an interpreter of pure Lisp with a function closure mechanism. On the contrary, **PX** is directly based on pure Lisp with a function closure mechanism and a logic of partial expressions. This change made the formalism of **PX** much more understandable than that of **LM**.

Yet another improvement is an introduction of new logical constructs $\Diamond$, ∇ and $\rightarrow$. $\Diamond$ is a modal operator corresponding to double negations by which we can avoid unnecessary use of the principle of "formulas as types". $\rightarrow$ is a logical connective resembles $if-then-else$ construct in programming languages. This enables us to represent $if-then-else$ expressions by proofs naturally. Similarly, ∇ is a quantifier corresponding *let* construct in programming languages.

In this paper we focus on the aspect of **PX** as a system extracting programs from proofs. But **PX** also provides mathematical foundations of some type disciplines and semantics of computations as logical framework of Matrin-Lõf[18] does.We leave these aspects of **PX** to [15], which includes also mathematical semantics of **PX** and proofs of theorems of this paper.

1. Formal theory

1.1. Expressions

In this section, we will define expressions (terms) and functions of **PX**. The objects (values) which expressions describe are *S-expressions*, i.e. the objects are generated from atoms by successive applications of dotted pair operations.

Expressions and functions of **PX** are defined by the following:

$$\begin{aligned} e ::= & x|c|fn(e_1,\ldots,e_n)|cond(e_1,d_1;\ldots;e_n,d_n) \\ & |\Lambda(x_1=e_1,\ldots,x_n=e_n)(fn)|let\ p_1=e_1,\ldots,p_n=e_n\ in\ e \\ fn ::= & f|\lambda(x_1,\ldots,x_n)(e) \end{aligned}$$

Here $e, e_1, d_1, \ldots$ and fn range over expressions and a function, respectively, and x ranges over variables, c ranges over constants, and f ranges over function identifiers. Besides these official expressions we use *case expression* defined by

$$case(e,e_1,\ldots,e_n) \equiv_{\text{def}} cond(equal(e,1),e_1;\ldots;equal(e,n),e_n).$$

These are mathematically refined M-expressions of a class of well-formed Lisp programs. So **PX** may be thought a system based on Lisp. The semantics of the expressions are given by a Lisp interpreter. To the end we translate the above M-expressions to S-expressions as usual. Applications, conditional forms, let forms, and λ-notations are translated as usual. The patterns $p_1,\ldots,p_n$ of the let form are patterns in the sense of Franz Lisp[11]. But they may include constants, e.g. $(1\ .\ x)$, which is not a pattern of Franz Lisp[11]. The Λ-notation $\Lambda(x_1=e_1,\ldots,x_n=e_n)(fn)$ is translated into an expression whose value is the function closure of fn with the local environment $\{x_1=[\![e_1]\!],\ldots,x_n=[\![e_n]\!]\}$, where $[\![e]\!]$ stands for the value of e. The point is that *all of the free variables of the function fn, $FV(fn)$ in symbol, must be included in $x_1,\ldots,x_n$.* Otherwise it is an illegal expression. Besides, two Λ-expressions are α-convertible only when their functions are *literally* equal. The translation of Λ-notation is arbitrary as far as translated Λ-notations satisfies axioms given in 1.3.1. One possibility is to translate e.g. $\Lambda(x=e)(\lambda(y)(pair(x,y)))$ to an expression whose value is the expression

```
(lambda (y) (let ((x ⟦e⟧)) (pair x y))).
```

Since e is evaluated when the translated Λ-form is evaluated, the Λ-notation has a value only when e has a value. Λ-notation corresponds to S_n^m function or Λ-notation of Kleene[16].

We may introduce functions by recursive definitions as in usual Lisp. The scoping is lexical so that a function cannot be declared unless its arguments do not include all of free variables of its body of definition.

We assume at least the following functions are included in the basic (built-in) functions of **PX**:

$$app,\ app*,\ list,\ atom,\ fst,\ snd,\ pair,\ equal,\ suc,\ prd.$$

These ten function identifiers are intended to be the following Lisp functions, respectively:

$$apply,\ funcall,\ list,\ atom,\ car,\ cdr,\ cons,\ equal,\ add1,\ sub1.$$

In our theory, neither a variable nor a constant need have values. This is unusual but quite convenient to describe a programming language. The constants (variables) are divided into two groups. One is called total constants (variables), which are supposed to have values. The other is called partial constants (variables), which need not have values. Total variables are further divided into two groups. One is individual variables, which range over all of the objects (S-exps.) and the other is class variables, which range over classes. Total constants are also divided in the same manner.

Constants and partial variables may be thought as names of global special variables of Lisp in the sense of Steele[21] which are not assigned to nor bound in executions of programs. But the global environments may be arbitrary, i.e. constants and partial variables may be valueless or may have arbitrary global values except total constants are supposed to have fixed global values. The role of partial variables are virtually identical to the role of *constants* in our intended semantics of **PX** as a programming language. But their roles in the logic of **PX** are different from those of constants. We may substitute any expressions for partial variables in the derivations of **PX**, on the contrary, we must not substitute for constants. On the other hand, total individual variables play rather distinguished role in the programming language of **PX**. They are exclusively used for names of lexical variables in the sense of Steele[21]. Our intended evaluator can bind only lexical variables, so the variable x of $\lambda(x)(e)$, $let\ x = e_1\ in\ e_2$, or $\Lambda(x = e)(fn)$ *must* be a total individual variable.

1.2. Formulas

Formulas of **PX** are defined by the following grammer:

$$\begin{aligned} F ::= & E(e)|Class(e)|[e_1,\ldots,e_n]:e|e_1 = e_2|\top|\bot \\ & |F_1 \wedge \ldots \wedge F_n|F_1 \vee \ldots \vee F_n|F_1 \supset F_2|e_1 \to F_1;\ldots;e_n \to F_n|\neg F|\Diamond F \\ & |\forall \vec{x}_1 : e_1,\ldots,\vec{x}_n : e_n.F|\exists \vec{x}_1 : e_1,\ldots,\vec{x}_n : e_n.F|\nabla p_1 = e_1,\ldots,x_n = e_n.F. \end{aligned}$$

where $F, F_1,\ldots$ are formulas and $e, e_1,\ldots$ are expressions. We will explain the meaning of formulas informally. $E(e)$ means e has a value or the execution of e under the current environment terminates. $Class(e)$ means that e has a value which is a description of a class. Classes are particular sets of objects. Since classes are considered as data types, **PX** is a system of the discipline of "types are first class objects". The equality $e_1 = e_2$ is Kleene's equality, i.e. if e_1 has a value then e_2 has the same value and vice versa. $[e_1,\ldots,e_n] : e$ means $e_1,\ldots,e_n,e$ have values, say $v_1,\ldots,v_n,v$, respectively, and v is a description of a class to which the tuple $[v_1,\ldots,v_n]$ belongs. (The meaning of the tuple notation $[\alpha_1,\ldots,\alpha_n]$ is as follows: if $n = 1$, then $[\alpha_1]$ means α_1 and if $n \neq 1$, then $[\alpha_1,\ldots,\alpha_n]$ means $list(\alpha_1 \ldots \alpha_n)$.) $\top$ and $\bot$ mean true and false respectively.

The logical connectives except $\to$, $\Diamond$ are as usual. The modal operator $\Diamond$ is just double negations. $e_1 \to A_1;\ldots,e_n \to A_n$ means there is m such that $e_1 = \ldots = e_{m-1} = nil$ and

e_m has a non nil value and A_m holds. Note that if all of $e_1, \ldots, e_n$ have the value *nil* then the formula is false. Since this semantics resembles MacCarthy's conditional form, we call this formula a *conditional formula*. As in the case of conditional form we can define "serial or" and "case formula".

$$
\begin{aligned}
Sor(e_1, \ldots, e_n) &\equiv e_1 \to \top; \ldots; e_n \to \top, \\
Case(a, A_1, \ldots, A_n) &\equiv equal(a, 1) \to A_1; \ldots; equal(a, n) \to A_n.
\end{aligned}
$$

The universal quantifier and existential quantifier are as usual except that we may use *tuple variables* (tuples of variables) as bound variables. For example $\forall[x, y] : C.R(x, y)$ means that $R(x, y)$ holds for all x, y such that $[x, y] : C$. We will denote tuple variables by vector notations like $\forall \vec{x} : e.A$. (Exactly it should be $\forall[\vec{x}] : e.A$. But we abbreviate square brackets for simplicity.) Since we identify a tuple variable $[x]$ with x, we write $\forall x : e.A$ instead of $\forall[x] : e.A$. We abbreviate $\forall \ldots, x : V, \ldots$ as $\forall \ldots, x, \ldots$, where V is the class of all objects. Bound variables must be total variables.

The ∇-quantifier resembles *let* of Lisp. $\nabla p = e.A$ means e has a value which matches to the pattern p and under the matching A holds. We use tuple notations as patterns, e.g. $\nabla[x, y] = a.A$ is $\nabla(x\ y) = a.A$ and $\nabla[x] = a.A$ is $\nabla x = a.A$. Bound variables of ∇-quantifier also must be total variables.

Note that we can define ∇ by universal quantifier and also by existential quantifier. For example $\nabla x = e.A$ is defined by $E(e) \wedge \forall x.(x = e \supset A)$ and also by $\exists x.(x = e \wedge A)$. But our realizability interpretation of $\nabla x = e.A$ is different from the realizability interpretations of these two formulas. This is one of the reasons why ∇ is a primitive logical sign. The reason why $\to$ is a primitive logical connective is the same.

For each formula A, we associate a non-negative integer, called the type of A. We will write it $type(A)$. Types of formulas will be used for defining **q**-realizability interpretation.

Definition 1 (type of formula).

1. The type of atomic formulas and formulas of the forms $\neg A$ or $\Diamond A$ is zero.
2. A is $A_1 \wedge \ldots \wedge A_n$. If all of $A_1, \ldots, A_n$ are of type 0, then so is A. Otherwise, set

$$type(A) = \#\{i | type(A_i) > 0\},$$

   where $\#$ means the cardinality.
3. A is $A_1 \vee \ldots \vee A_n$. If all of $A_1, \ldots, A_n$ are of type 0, then $type(A)$ is 1. Otherwise, $type(A)$ is 2.
4. A is $B \supset C$. If C is of type 0 then so is A. Otherwise, $type(A)$ is 1.
5. A is $\forall \vec{v}_1 : e_1, \ldots, \vec{v}_n : e_n.B$. If B is of type 0 then so is A. Otherwise, $type(A)$ is 1.
6. A is $\exists \vec{v}_1 : e_1, \ldots, \vec{v}_n : e_n.B$. Then $type(A)$ is $m + type(B)$, where m is the number of variables in $\vec{v}_1, \ldots, \vec{v}_n$.
7. A is $e_1 \to A_1; \ldots; e_n \to A_n$. If all of $A_1, \ldots, A_n$ are of type 0, then so is $type(A)$. Otherwise, $type(A)$ is 1.
8. A is $\nabla p_1 = e_1, \ldots, p_n = e_n.B$. Then $type(A)$ is $type(B)$.

1.3. Axiom system

We will give a virtually full presentation of the axiom system of **PX** below. Only the axioms on basic functions and some other miscellaneous axioms are not included. The axiom system has two parts. One is the logic of partial terms (expressions). The other is the axioms on classes.

1.3.1. A logic of partial terms

The logic of partial terms presented in this section is a refinement of the logic of **LMI** of Hayashi[14]. It resembles the logics of Beeson[4,5], Plotkin[19] and Sato[20].

Axioms for primitives

$$E(e) \quad (e \text{ is a total constant or a total variable}),$$
$$Class(e) \quad (e \text{ is a class constant or a class variable}),$$
$$[e_1,\ldots,e_n] : e \supset Class(e), \quad Class(e) \supset E(e), \quad [e_1,\ldots,e_n] : e \supset E(e_i),$$
$$E(fn(e_1,\ldots,e_n)) \supset E(e_i), \quad E(\Lambda(v_1 = a_1,\ldots,v_n = a_n)(fn)),$$
$$e = e, \quad e_1 = e_2 \supset e_2 = e_1, \quad (E(e_1) \vee E(e_2) \supset e_1 = e_2) \supset e_1 = e_2,$$
$$a = b \vee \neg a = b, \quad \frac{\Gamma \Rightarrow P(e_1) \qquad \Pi \Rightarrow e_1 = e_2}{\Gamma \cup \Pi \Rightarrow P(e_2)},$$
$$app(\Lambda(v_1 = a_1,\ldots,v_n = a_n)(fn), list(e_1,\ldots,e_n)) = (fn\sigma)(e_1,\ldots,e_n),$$
$$app{*}(\Lambda(v_1 = a_1,\ldots,v_n = a_n)(fn), e_1,\ldots,e_n) = (fn\sigma)(e_1,\ldots,e_n),$$
$$(\lambda(v_1,\ldots,v_n)(e))(a_1,\ldots,a_n) = e[a_1/v_1,\ldots,a_n/v_n],$$
$$cond(e_1,d_1;\ldots;e_n,d_n) = a \ \supset\subset \ e_1 \rightarrow a = d_1;\ldots;e_n \rightarrow a = d_n; t \rightarrow a = nil,$$
$$(let\ p_1 = e_1,\ldots,p_n = e_n\ in\ e) = a \ \supset\subset \ \nabla p_1 = e_1,\ldots,p_n = e_n(e = a),$$

where $a, b, a_1,\ldots,a_n$ are total variables and σ is $[a_1/v_1,\ldots,a_n/v_n]$.

Structural rules

$$(assume) \ \{A\} \Rightarrow A, \quad (\top) \ \Gamma \Rightarrow \top, \quad (\bot) \ \frac{\Gamma \Rightarrow \bot}{\Gamma \Rightarrow A},$$
$$(thin) \ \frac{\Gamma \Rightarrow A}{\Gamma \cup \Pi \Rightarrow A}, \quad (cut) \ \frac{\Gamma \Rightarrow A \quad \Pi \Rightarrow B}{\Gamma \cup (\Pi - \{A\}) \Rightarrow B},$$
$$(inst) \ \frac{\Gamma \Rightarrow A \quad \Pi \Rightarrow SC(\sigma)}{\Gamma\sigma \cup \Pi \Rightarrow A\sigma}, \quad (alpha) \ \frac{\Gamma \Rightarrow A}{\Pi \Rightarrow B},$$
$$(replace) \ \frac{\Gamma \Rightarrow A[B]_+ \quad \Pi \Rightarrow Env_{A[*]}[B \supset C]}{\Gamma \cup \Pi \Rightarrow A[C]_+}, \quad \frac{\Gamma \Rightarrow A[C]_- \quad \Pi \Rightarrow Env_{A[*]}[B \supset C]}{\Gamma \cup \Pi \Rightarrow A[B]_-},$$

where $SC(\sigma)$ of $(inst)$ is the *substitution condition* of σ, e.g. if σ is $[e/a]$ and a is a total variable then it is $E(e)$. The upper and lower sequents of $(alpha)$ must be α-convertible. $A[*]$ of $(replace)$ is a *context* which is a formula with *just one* "hole" $*$. Subscripts $+, -$ indicate if the hole appears positively or negatively. B, C of $(replace)$ must be type 0 formulas. $Env_A[*]$ is a context represents the local environment of the hole, e.g. if A is $\forall x : e_1.\exists y : e_2.\nabla p = e_3.(* \wedge F)$, then Env_A is $\forall x : e_1.\forall y : e_2.\nabla p = e_3.(* \wedge F)$. Namely $Env_A[*]$ is obtained from $A[*]$ replacing every existential quantifier by universal quantifier as far as the hole $*$ is in its scope.

Rules for ordinary logical constructs

The logical rules for ordinary logical constructs are more or less standard except some substitution conditions are required when an expression is substituted for a total variable.

$$(\wedge I) \ \frac{\Gamma_1 \Rightarrow A_1,\ldots,\Gamma_n \Rightarrow A_n}{\Gamma_1 \cup \ldots \cup \Gamma_n \Rightarrow A_1 \wedge \ldots \wedge A_n}, \quad (\wedge E) \ \frac{\Gamma \Rightarrow A_1 \wedge \ldots \wedge A_n}{\Gamma \Rightarrow A_{i_1} \wedge \ldots \wedge A_{i_m}},$$
$$(\vee I) \ \frac{\Gamma \Rightarrow A_i}{\Gamma \Rightarrow A_1 \vee \ldots \vee A_i \vee \ldots \vee A_n}$$

$$(\vee E)\quad \frac{\Gamma_1 \Rightarrow A_1 \vee \ldots \vee A_n \quad \Pi_1 \Rightarrow C, \ldots, \Pi_n \Rightarrow C}{\Gamma \cup \Pi_1 - \{A_1\} \cup \ldots \cup \Pi_n - \{A_n\} \Rightarrow C},$$

$$(\supset I)\quad \frac{\Gamma \Rightarrow B}{\Gamma - \{A\} \Rightarrow A \supset B}, \quad (\supset E)\quad \frac{\Gamma \Rightarrow A \supset B \quad \Pi \Rightarrow A}{\Gamma \cup \Pi \Rightarrow B},$$

$$(\neg I)\quad \frac{\Gamma \Rightarrow \bot}{\Gamma - \{A\} \Rightarrow \neg A}, \quad (\neg E)\quad \frac{\Gamma \Rightarrow \neg A \quad \Pi \Rightarrow A}{\Gamma \cup \Pi \Rightarrow \bot},$$

$$(\forall I)\quad \frac{\Gamma \Rightarrow A}{\Gamma - S \Rightarrow \forall \vec{v}_1 : e_1, \ldots, \vec{v}_n : e_n.A},$$

$$(\forall E)\quad \frac{\Gamma \Rightarrow \forall \vec{v}_1 : e_1, \ldots, \vec{v}_n : e_n.A \quad \Pi \Rightarrow SC(\sigma)}{\Gamma \cup \Pi \Rightarrow A\sigma},$$

$$(\exists I)\quad \frac{\Gamma \Rightarrow A\sigma \quad \Pi \Rightarrow SC(\sigma)}{\Gamma \cup \Pi \Rightarrow \exists \vec{v}_1 : e_1, \ldots, \vec{v}_n : e_n.A},$$

$$(\exists E)\quad \frac{\Gamma \Rightarrow \exists \vec{v}_1 : e_1, \ldots, \vec{v}_n : e_n.A \quad \Pi \Rightarrow C}{\Gamma \cup \Pi - \{A, \vec{v}_1 : e_1, \ldots, \vec{v}_n : e_n\} \Rightarrow C},$$

S of $(\forall I)$ is $\{\vec{v}_1 : e_1, \ldots, \vec{v}_n : e_n\}$. $SC(\sigma)$ of $(\exists I)$ and $(\forall E)$ is the substitution condition. The subscripts $\{i_1, \ldots, i_m\}$ of $(\wedge E)$ is a subset of $\{1, \ldots, n\}$.

Rules for ∇ and $\rightarrow$

The logical meanings of $e_1 \rightarrow A_1; \ldots; e_n \rightarrow A_n$ and $\nabla p_1 = e_1, \ldots, p_n = e_n.A$ are

$$(e_1 : T \wedge A_1) \vee (e_2 : T \wedge e_1 = nil \wedge A_2) \vee \ldots \vee (e_n : T \wedge e_{n-1} = nil \wedge \ldots \wedge e_1 = nil \wedge A_n),$$
$$\exists \vec{x}.(exp(p_1) = e_1 \wedge \ldots \wedge exp(p_n) = e_n \wedge A).$$

$exp(p)$ is the *expansion* of a pattern p, which is defined as $exp(v) = v$ and $exp((p_1 \,.\, p_2)) = pair(exp(p_1), exp(p_2))$ etc.. T is the class of non-nil objects. These validates the following rules. Each rule for ∇ $(\rightarrow)$ has a counter rule for $\forall$ and $\exists$ ($\wedge$ and $\vee$) as indicated by the names of rules.

$$(\rightarrow \vee I)\quad \frac{\Gamma \Rightarrow A_i \quad \Pi \Rightarrow \bigwedge S_i}{\Gamma \cup \Pi \Rightarrow e_1 \rightarrow A_1; \ldots; e_n \rightarrow A_n}$$

$$(\rightarrow \vee E)\quad \frac{\Gamma \Rightarrow e_1 \rightarrow A_1; \ldots; e_n \rightarrow A_n \quad \Pi_1 \Rightarrow C, \ldots, \Pi_n \Rightarrow C}{\Gamma \cup \bigcup_{i=1}^{n}(\Pi_i - \{A_i\} - S_i) \Rightarrow C},$$

$$(\rightarrow \wedge I)\quad \frac{\Gamma_1 \Rightarrow A_1, \ldots, \Gamma_n \Rightarrow A_n \quad \Pi \Rightarrow Sor(e_1, \ldots, e_n)}{\Pi \cup \bigcup_{i=1}^{n} \Gamma_i - S_i \Rightarrow e_1 \rightarrow A_1; \ldots; e_n \rightarrow A_n},$$

$$(\rightarrow \wedge E)\quad \frac{\Gamma \Rightarrow e_1 \rightarrow A_1; \ldots; e_n \rightarrow A_n \quad \Pi \Rightarrow \bigwedge S_i}{\Gamma \cup \Pi \Rightarrow A_i},$$

$$(\nabla \exists I)\quad \frac{\Gamma \Rightarrow A\sigma \quad \Pi \Rightarrow \bigwedge R}{\Gamma \cup \Pi \Rightarrow \nabla p_1{=}e_1, \ldots, p_n{=}e_n.A}, \quad (\nabla \exists E)\quad \frac{\Gamma \Rightarrow \nabla p_1{=}e_1, \ldots, p_n{=}e_n.A \quad \Pi \Rightarrow C}{\Gamma \cup (\Pi - \{A\} - Q_1) \Rightarrow C},$$

$$(\nabla \forall I)\quad \frac{\Gamma \Rightarrow A \quad \Pi \Rightarrow \bigwedge R}{(\Gamma - Q_1) \cup \Pi \Rightarrow \nabla p_1{=}e_1, \ldots, p_n{=}e_n.A}, \quad (\nabla \forall E)\quad \frac{\Gamma \Rightarrow \nabla p_1{=}e_1, \ldots, p_n{=}e_n.A}{\Gamma \cup Q_2 \Rightarrow A},$$

where

$$S_i = \{e_1 = nil, \ldots, e_{i-1} = nil, e_i : T\},$$
$$R = \{exp(p_1)\sigma = e_1, E(e_1), \ldots, exp(p_n)\sigma = e_n, E(e_n)\},$$
$$Q_1 = \{exp(p_1) = e_1, E(e_1), \ldots, exp(p_n) = e_n, E(e_n)\},$$
$$Q_2 = \{exp(p_1) = e_1, \ldots, exp(p_n) = e_n\}.$$

Rules and axioms for $\Diamond$

The modal symbol $\Diamond$ is just double negations. We may think that the formula $\Diamond A$ stands for "A holds classically", i.e. the logic in the scope of $\Diamond$ is the ordinary classical logic. The axiom ($\Diamond$2) is the principle of "double negation shift" of constructive logic.

$$(\Diamond 1)\ \neg\neg A \supset\subset \Diamond A,$$
$$(\Diamond 2)\quad \forall \vec{x}_1 : e_1, \ldots, \vec{x}_n : e_n.\Diamond F \supset \Diamond\forall \vec{x}_1 : e_1, \ldots, \vec{x}_n : e_n.F,$$
$$(\Diamond 3)\ A \supset\subset \Diamond A \quad (A \text{ is a type 0 formula}).$$

By virtue of these axioms we can prove the following proposition which shows type 0 formulas obey classical logic.

Proposition 1. *A type 0 formula is provable in* **PX** *iff it is provable in* **PX**+*(classical logic).*

1.3.2. Classes: data types as objects

A class is a *name* of a set of objects. Classes and axioms on them play very important roles in **PX** in two ways. For one thing we can define various kinds of data types including dependent types of Martin-Löf. Since a class is a mere a code of a set, we can program various operations on types in the way of the usual programming. So data types are first class objects and the type discipline of **PX** is close to those of the typed languages Russell and Pebble, although it does not have the type of all types. For another the induction principle is quite useful for representations of recursions called CIG-recursions and their domains of terminations are also representable by classes.

The axioms on classes are divided into two groups. One is the axioms of conditional inductive generations (CIG), which maintains the existence of a particular kind of inductively defined sets. It is an extension of the principle of inductive generation of Feferman[10]. The other is the axioms of dependent types, which maintains the dependent types in the sense of Martin-Löf exist. We will present the latter in Appendix B, since we need not them in this paper. See [5,10,14,15] for the mathematical semantics of classes.

In the following, variables $\vec{X} = X_0, \ldots, X_n$ are always class variables. Formulas called *CIG-templates with respect to* $\vec{X}$ and n_0, $CIG_{n_0}(\vec{X})$ for short, are generated by the following grammer:

$$\begin{aligned} H ::= & E(e) | [e_1, \ldots, e_{n_0}] : X_0 | [e_1, \ldots, e_n] : X_{i+1} | e_1 = e_2 | \top | \bot \\ & | H_1 \wedge \ldots \wedge H_n | e_1 \to H_1; \ldots; e_n \to H_n | \Diamond P | K \supset H | \neg K \\ & | \forall \vec{x}_1 : e_1, \ldots, \vec{x}_n : e_n.H | \nabla p_1 = e_1, \ldots, p_n = e_n.H, \end{aligned}$$

$$\begin{aligned} P ::= & H | P_1 \wedge \ldots \wedge P_n | e_1 \to P_1; \ldots; e_n \to P_n | K \supset P | P_1 \vee \ldots \vee P_n \\ & | \forall \vec{x}_1 : e_1, \ldots, \vec{x}_n : e_n.P | \exists \vec{x}_1 : e_1, \ldots, \vec{x}_n : e_n.P | \nabla p_1 = e_1, \ldots, p_n = e_n.P, \end{aligned}$$

$$\begin{aligned} K ::= & E(e) | [e_1, \ldots, e_n] : X_{i+1} | e_1 = e_2 | \top | \bot \\ & | K_1 \wedge \ldots \wedge K_n | K_1 \vee \ldots \vee K_n | e_1 \to K_1; \ldots; e_n \to K_n | \Diamond K | P \supset K | \neg P \\ & | \forall \vec{x}_1 : e_1, \ldots, \vec{x}_n : e_n.K | \exists \vec{x}_1 : e_1, \ldots, \vec{x}_n' : e_n.K | \nabla p_1 = e_1, \ldots, p_n = e_n.K, \end{aligned}$$

where $H, H_1, \ldots$ range over $CIG_{n_0}(\vec{X})$, $e, e_1, ..$ range over expressions which contain neither elements of $\vec{X}$ nor any free partial variables, and all of the variables of $\vec{x}_1, \ldots, \vec{x}_n$ are individual variables. $P, P_1, \ldots$ $(K, K_1, \ldots)$ are formulas in which X_0 appears positively (negatively). Note that the length of the argument tuple of X_0 *must* be n_0. For each $A \in CIG_n(\vec{X})$ and variables $\vec{a} = a_1, \ldots, a_n$, there is an expression $\mu X_0\{\vec{a}|A\}$, whose free variables is just $FV(A) - \{X_0, a_1, \ldots, a_n\}$. It is the smallest fixed point of the monotone map "$X_0 \mapsto \{\vec{a}|A\}$" so that the followings are axioms:

$$(CIG\ def)\quad Class(\mu X_0\{\vec{a}|A\}),\quad \nabla[a_1,\ldots,a_n] = x.A[\mu X_0\{\vec{a}|A\}/X_0] \supset\subset x : \mu X_0\{\vec{a}|A\}.$$

If X_0 does not appear in A, we write $\{\vec{a}|A\}$, then it is the usual set notation. The induction rule for $\mu X_0\{\vec{a}|A\}$, called CIG-induction, is as follows:

$$(CIG\ ind)\qquad \frac{\Gamma \Rightarrow F(\vec{a})}{\{[\vec{a}] : \mu X_0\{\vec{a}|A\}\} \cup \Gamma - \{A[F(\vec{a})/X_0], A[\mu X_0\{\vec{a}|A\}/X_0]\} \Rightarrow F(\vec{a}).}$$

We substituted a *formula* $F(\vec{a})$ for a class variable X_0. This means to replace all of the subformula of the form $[e_0, \ldots, e_n] : X_0$ by $F[e_0/a_1, \ldots, e_n/a_n]$.

The actual CIG is more flexible than the version of CIG presented here with the following respects.

(0) Simultaneous definitions of classes are possible.
(1) If e is an expression whose class variables belong to $X_1, \ldots, X_n$ (X_0 not allowed) and confirmed to be a class by a specific algorithm, then not only $[e_1, \ldots, e_n] : X_{i+1}$ but also $[e_1, \ldots, e_n] : e$ is allowed as H and K in the grammer of CIG-templates.
(2) For a class whose body of definition is a conditional formula, a more convenient form of CIG-induction is available.
(3) A class may be specified as a superset of the class to be defined.

To illustrate (1)-(3) we define the class of non-empty lists. In the actual system it is declared as follows (syntax is different, see Appendix A):

$$a : Dp = \{a|\nabla(x\ .\ y) = a.\top\}$$
$$\textbf{deCIG}\ a : List_1(X) \equiv_{Dp} snd(a) \rightarrow fst(a) : X, snd(a) : List_1(X),$$
$$t \rightarrow fst(a) : X.$$

The arrow sign $\rightarrow$ in the definition is not the logical sign so that the right hand side of the definition is not a formula. The class defined by this is

$$\text{(A)}\qquad \mu X_0\{a|a : Dp \wedge (snd(a) \rightarrow fst(a) : X \wedge snd(a) : X_0; t \rightarrow fst(a) : X)\}.$$

Dp is the class of dotted pairs and it is to be a superset of $List_1(X)$ so that all lists of the class are non-nil. After defining these, $[e_1, \ldots, e_n] : List_1(X)$ is allowed as a CIG-template for it is a class whenever X is a class. So the class of lists of lists are defined by

$$\textbf{deCIG}\ a : List_2(X) \equiv a : List_1(List_1(X)).$$

The induction principle ($CIG\ ind$) associated to $List_1(X)$

$$\text{(B)}\qquad \frac{\Gamma \Rightarrow A(a) \qquad \Pi \Rightarrow A(a)}{\begin{array}{l}\{\ a : List_1(X)\ \} \\ \quad \cup \left(\Gamma - \left\{\begin{array}{l} a : Dp,\ snd(a) : T,\ fst(a) : X, \\ snd(a) : List_1(X),\ A(snd(a)) \end{array}\right\}\right) \\ \quad \cup (\Pi - \{\ a : Dp,\ snd(a) = nil,\ fst(a) : X\ \})\end{array} \Rightarrow A(a)}$$

By virtue of this form of CIG-induction we may avoid cumbersome applications of the rules $(\to \vee E)$,$(\wedge E)$ and (cut), which are necessary to derive (B) from $(CIG\ ind)$ for (A). The following is called the *generalized CIG-template with superclass Dp* of $List_1(X)$:

(C) $$(snd(a); fst(a) : X, snd(a) : X_0), (t; fst(a) : X).$$

The class variable X_0 is used for the variable representing the class that is defined by this template. $(CIG\ def)$ associated to $List_1$ is just the $(CIG\ def)$ of (A).

2. Giving computational meanings to logic

There are many ways giving computational meanings to constructive proofs. We use q-realizability interpretation to give computational meanings to proofs of **PX** as Beeson[4] and Hayashi[14]. The advantage of q-realizability interpretation is that if a theorem is q-realized, then it is also valid in the sense of classical logic. So we need not change our intended semantics to interpret a theorem as a specification of extracted algorithms. The q-realizability interpretation below is due to Robin Grayson. It is essentially the sheaf semantics of the topos obtained by gluing Hyland's realizability topos and the topos of sets. It is *not* equivalent to the traditional q-realizability interpretation. The relation between Grayson's q-realizability interpretation and the traditional one is that a is a realizer of A in Grayson's sense, if and only if a is a realizer of A in the traditional sense and A holds. Since we think only valid sequents, these two interpretations are virtually the same. Our realizability is more complicated than Grayson's original one for "optimizing" realizers.

2.1. q-realizability

For each formula A, we assign a formula aqA, A^q for short, whose type is 0, and we call it the q-realizability interpretation or q-realization of A. When aqA holds, we say "a is a realizer of A". An important point is that a is a total individual variable not occurring in A. So a realizer must be a value (object). The variable a will be called a *realizing variable* of A. We assume that if two formulas are α-convertible then their realizing variables are the same. We denote the set $\{A^q | A \in \Gamma\}$ by Γ^q.

Grayson's q-realizability interpretation reads as follows in our setting:

1. A is an atomic formula. Then $a\,\mathrm{q}\,A$ is $A \wedge a = nil$.
2. $a\,\mathrm{q}\,A_1 \wedge \ldots \wedge A_n$ is $\nabla(a_1 \ldots a_n) = a.((a_1\,\mathrm{q}\,A_1) \wedge \ldots \wedge (a_n\,\mathrm{q}\,A_n))$.
3. $a\,\mathrm{q}\,A \supset B$ is $E(a) \wedge A \supset B \wedge \forall b.((b\,\mathrm{q}\,A) \supset \nabla c = app{*}(a,b).c\,\mathrm{q}\,B)$.
4. $a\,\mathrm{q}\,A_1 \vee \ldots \vee A_n$ is $\nabla(b\ .\ c) = a.Case(b, c\,\mathrm{q}\,A_1, \ldots, c\,\mathrm{q}\,A_n)$.
5. $a\,\mathrm{q}\,\forall \vec{x}_1 : e_1, \ldots, \vec{x}_n : e_n.A$ is
$$E(a) \wedge \forall \vec{x}_1 : e_1, \ldots, \vec{x}_n : e_n.\nabla y = app{*}(a, a_1, \ldots, a_m).y\,\mathrm{q}\,A.$$
6. $a\,\mathrm{q}\,\exists \vec{x}_1 : e_1, \ldots, \vec{x}_n : e_n.A$ is
$$\nabla(a_1 \ldots a_m\ b) = a.(\vec{x}_1 : e_1 \wedge \ldots \wedge \vec{x}_n : e_n \wedge (b\,\mathrm{q}\,A)).$$
7. $a\,\mathrm{q}\,\nabla p_1 = e_1, \ldots, p_n = e_n.A$ is $\nabla p_1 = e_1, \ldots p_n = e_n.a\,\mathrm{q}\,A$.
8. $a\,\mathrm{q}\,e_1 \to A_1; \ldots; e_n \to A_n$ is $e_1 \to a\,\mathrm{q}\,A_1; \ldots; e_n \to a\,\mathrm{q}\,A_n$.

In 5 and 6 $a_1, \ldots, a_m$ is the concatenation of $FV(\vec{x}_1), \ldots, FV(\vec{x}_n)$. ($FV(\vec{x})$ is the variables appearing in the tuple of variables $\vec{x}$, e.g. $FV([x,y])$ is x, y.) From the definition we see if $a\,\mathrm{q}\,A$ holds then A holds.

This q-realizability interpretation is satisfactory for mathematical use but for computational use it has some redundancies. So we adapt it to computational use as follows:

Definition 2 (q-realizability interpretation).

1. Suppose A is of type 0. Then $a\,\mathbf{q}\,A$ is $A \wedge a = nil$.
2. Suppose $A = A_1 \wedge \ldots \wedge A_n$. Let A_i^* be the formula A_i in the case of $type(A) = 0$ and $a_i\,\mathbf{q}\,A_i$ in the other case. Let $i_1 < \cdots < i_m$ be the list of the indices i such that $type(A_i) \neq 0$. Then $a\,\mathbf{q}\,A$ is

$$\nabla[a_{i_1}, \ldots, a_{i_m}] = a.(A_1^* \wedge \ldots \wedge A_n^*).$$

3. $a\,\mathbf{q}\,A \supset B$ is

$$E(a) \wedge A \supset B \wedge \forall b.(b\,\mathbf{q}\,A \supset \nabla c = fn(a, b).c\,\mathbf{q}\,B),$$

where fn is $app*$ if $type(A_1) = 1$, and app otherwise.
4. Suppose A is $A_1 \vee \ldots \vee A_n$. If $type(A_1) = \cdots = type(A_n) = 0$, then

$$a\,\mathbf{q}\,A \equiv Case(a, A_1, \ldots, A_n),$$

else

$$a\,\mathbf{q}\,A \equiv \nabla(b\ c) = a.Case(b, c\,\mathbf{q}\,A_1, \ldots, c\,\mathbf{q}\,A_n).$$

5. $a\,\mathbf{q}\,\forall \vec{x}_1 : e_1, \ldots, \vec{x}_n : e_n.A$ is

$$E(a) \wedge \forall \vec{x}_1 : e_1, \ldots, \vec{x}_n : e_n.\nabla y = app*(a, a_1, \ldots, a_m).y\,\mathbf{q}\,A,$$

where $a_1, \ldots, a_m$ is the concatenation of $FV(\vec{x}_1), \ldots, FV(\vec{x}_n)$.
6. Suppose A is $\exists \vec{x}_1 : e_1, \ldots, \vec{x}_n : e_n.A_0$. Let $a_1, \ldots, a_m$ be the concatenation of the variables $FV(\vec{x}_1), \ldots, FV(\vec{x}_n)$. If $type(A_0) = 0$ then

$$a\,\mathbf{q}\,A \equiv \nabla[a_1, \ldots, a_m] = a.(\vec{x}_1 : e_1 \wedge \ldots \wedge \vec{x}_n : e_n \wedge A_0),$$

else

$$a\,\mathbf{q}\,A \equiv \nabla p = a.(\vec{x}_1 : e_1 \wedge \ldots \wedge \vec{x}_n : e_n \wedge b\,\mathbf{q}\,A_0),$$

where p is $(a_1 \ldots a_m\ b)$ if $type(A_0) = 1$, and $(a_1 \ldots a_m\ .\ b)$ otherwise. The last dot of the latter pattern is an actual dot.
7. $a\,\mathbf{q}\,\nabla p_1 = e_1, \ldots, p_n = e_n.A$ is $\nabla p_1 = e_1, \ldots p_n = e_n.a\,\mathbf{q}\,A$.
8. $a\,\mathbf{q}\,e_1 \to A_1; \ldots; e_n \to A_n$ is $e_1 \to a\,\mathbf{q}\,A_1; \ldots; e_n \to a\,\mathbf{q}\,A_n$.

Theorem 1 (soundness of q-realizability). *If $\Gamma \Rightarrow A$ is a provable sequent of* **PX** *without free partial variables, then we can find an expression e from its proof effectively so that $\Gamma^q \Rightarrow e\,\mathbf{q}\,A$ is also provable in* **PX**. *Furthermore, we may assume $FV(e)$ is a subset of $FV(\Gamma^q \cup \{A\})$.*

The condition on the variables is necessary to validate the q-realizability interpretations of $(\forall I)$ and $(\supset I)$ etc.. Any sequent without partial variables, if it is provable, can be proved without partial variables, besides partial constants may occur. So it is not a serious restriction. From the definition of q-realizability interpretation, we can easily conclude the following corollary.

Corollary. *If $\forall[x_1, \ldots, x_n] : e.\exists y.F(x_1, \ldots, x_n, y)$ is a provable sentence in* **PX**, *then we can find a closed function fn such that the following is provable:*

$$\forall[x_1, \ldots, x_n] : e.\nabla y = fn(x_1, \ldots, x_n).F(x_1, \ldots, x_n, y).$$

PX uses this corollary as a way introducing new functions. In the terminology of constructive logic, it reads as a derived rule of choice:

$$(choice) \qquad \frac{\Gamma \Rightarrow \exists x_1, ..., x_n.A}{\Gamma \Rightarrow \nabla(x_1...x_n) = f(a_1, ..., a_m).A,}$$

where f is a *new* function with arity n and Γ is a set of type 0 formulas. This means whenever you can *prove* the upper sequent you may introduce a new function f which satisfies the lower sequent. Note that we do not think this as an official inference rule of **PX**, since this contradicts to classical logic when we read it as "if the upper sequent is *valid* then there is a computable function f such that the lower sequent is valid".

2.2. The extraction algorithm

We present a detailed description of the algorithm by which **PX** extracts a realizer from a proof. We will refer this as the extraction algorithm or the extractor, *extr* in symbol.

We have to introduce some auxiliary functions to describe the extractor. If A is a formula, then $rvars(A)$ is a sequence of mutually distinct variables of length $type(A)$. It is considered as a tuple variable that realizes A. We call it the realizing variables of A. We assume $rvars(A)$ and $rvars(B)$ are identical, if and only if A and B are α-convertible. $rpattern(A)$ is the pattern $[a_1, \ldots, a_n]$, where $a_1, \ldots, a_n = rvars(A)$. $rpatterns(A_1, \ldots, A_n)$ is the sequence $rpattern(A_1), \ldots, rpattern(A_n)$. $newfunc()$ is a new function name. $new(n)$ is a sequence of n new variables. $dummy(n)$ is a list of n atoms. $upseqs(P)$ is the upper sequents of a proof P. $rule(P)$ is the last rule of the proof P. $con(P)$ is the conclusion of the proof P. $asp(P)$ is the assumptions of the proof P. When $rule(P)$ is $(\vee E)$, $disch_{\vee E}(P)$ is the sequence of the discharged formulas. $disch_{\supset I}(P)$ is the discharged formula of $(\supset I)$. When $rule(P)$ is $(inst)$, $subst(P)$ is the substitution σ of the rule of $(inst)$. $delete0(P_1, \ldots, P_n)$ is the subsequence of $P_1, \ldots, P_n$ obtained by deleting proofs whose conclusions are of types 0. $tuple[e_1, \ldots, e_n]$ is another notation for the tuple $[e_1, \ldots, e_n]$. If $rule(P)$ is $(\wedge E)$, then $indecies_{\wedge E}(P)$ is the indecies $i_1, \ldots, i_m$ of $(\wedge E)$. If $rule(P)$ is $(\vee I)$, then $index_{\vee I}(P)$ is the index i in the rule of $(\vee I)$. $eigenvars_{\forall I}$ etc. denote the sequence of eigenvariables of each rule. Let $rule(P)$ be $(\forall E)$ and $[e_1/a_1, \ldots, e_m/a_m]$ be the substitution σ of $(\forall E)$. Then $instances_{\forall E}(P)$ are the expressions $e_1, \ldots, e_m$. $instances_{\exists I}$ is defined similarly. $body_{\exists}(A)$ is the immediate subformula of an existential formula A. $body_{\forall}(A)$ and $bodys_{\rightarrow}(A)$ are similarly defined. $conditions(A)$ is the sequence of conditions of a conditional formula. Let ϕ be $\lceil \nabla p_1 = e_1, \ldots, p_n = e_n.A \rceil$. Then $patterns(\phi)$ is $p_1, \ldots, p_n$ and $bindings(\phi)$ is $e_1, \ldots, e_n$. $disch_{CIG}(P_i)$ is the sequence of discharged formulas of the subproof P_i.

We associate a term $pred(A; f; \vec{b})$, $pred(A)$ for short, for each CIG-template A, and a function name f, and a finite sequence of variables b. We call $pred(A)$ the *CIG-predecessor* of A.

Definition 3 (CIG-predecessors).

1. A is of type 0 formula not containing X_0. Then $pred(A)$ is nil,
2. $pred([e_1, \ldots, e_n] : X_0; f; \vec{b})$ is $f(e_1, \ldots, e_n, \vec{b})$,
3. $pred(A \supset B)$ is $\Lambda(\lambda().pred(B))$,
4. $pred(A_1 \wedge \ldots \wedge A_n)$ is $[pred(A_{i_1}), \ldots, pred(A_{i_m})]$, where $A_{i_1}, \ldots, A_{i_m}$ is the subsequase of the non type 0 formulas of $A_1, \ldots A_n$. So m is $type(A)$.
5. $pred(\forall \vec{v}_1 : e_1, \ldots, \vec{v}_n : e_n.A)$ is $\Lambda(\lambda(\vec{x}).pred(A))$, where $\vec{x}$ is the concatenation of the varibles of $\vec{v}_1, \ldots, \vec{v}_n$.
6. $pred(e_1 \rightarrow A_1; \ldots; e_n \rightarrow A_n)$ is $cond(e_1, pred(A_1); \ldots; e_n, pred(A_n))$,
7. $pred(\nabla p_1 = e_1, \ldots, p_n = e_n.A)$ is $let\ p_1 = e_1, \ldots, p_n = e_n\ in\ pred(A)$.

If $(e_1; A_1, \ldots, A_n)$ is a clause of a generalized CIG template, then $pred(A_1, \ldots, A_n)$ is $pred(A_1), \ldots, pred(A_n)$.

Besides these functions, we use functions for optimizations $Optimize_{case}$, $Optimize_{\beta}$, $Optimize_{\eta}$, and **subst** constructs which does some substitution and/or builts a let form in an optimized way. $Optimize_{\beta}$, $Optimize_{\eta}$ are Lisp versions of β- and η-reductions. $Optimize_{case}$ does an optimization such as

$$case(cond(e, 1; t, 2), e_1, e_2) \quad \longmapsto \quad case(e, e_1, e_2).$$

What **subst** does is rather complicated, but essentially it is a *let* form. The value of the expression **subst** $p \leftarrow e$ **in** e_1 is always equivalent to the value of $let\ p = e\ in\ e_1$ as far as the both have values. However, if the pattern p (exactly $exp(p)$) occurs only once in e_1, then **subst** does a partial evaluation by replacing p by e, e.g. **subst** $(a\ .\ b) \leftarrow e$ **in** $pair(a, b)$ is just the expression e. Furthermore, if p is the empty pattern () (or nil), **subst** neglects the substitution for p, e.g. **subst** $() = e_1$ **in** e_2 is just e_2. In this paper it suffices to assume **subst** does only these optimizations. See [14] for a full description.

In the following description of the extraction algorithm, the above auxiliary functions, which are *meta-level* functions in the sense that they deal with syntactic entities of **PX**, will be typed in `this type writer like font`. Metavariables for such entities are also typed in the font. On the other hand, the program constructs of **PX** are typed in the font of mathematical formulas. Some meta-level program construct, like **def, let, case**, are in bold face letters.

The extraction algorithm

```
def extr(P)=
 let type=type(con(P)), P1,...,Pn=upseqs(P) in
  if type=0 then nil else
   case rule(P) of
    (= 5):  cond(equal(a,b),1;t,2)  ; (= 5) is the axiom a = b ∨ ¬a = b
    (assume):  rvars(con(P))
    (⊥):  dummy(type(con(P)))
    (inst):  let A1,...,An=asp(P1), σ=subst(P) in
            extr(P1)σ[rvars(A1σ)/rvars(A1),...,rvars(Anσ)/rvars(An)]
    (cut):  subst rpattern(con(P1))←extr(P1) in extr(P2)
    (∧I):  let Q1,...,Qm=delete0(P1,...,Pn) in
                tuple[extr(Q1),...,extr(Qm)]
    (∧E):  let a1,...,an=new(n), i1,...,im=indecies∧E(P) in
                subst [a1,...,an]←extr(P1) in tuple[ai1,...,aim]
    (∨I):  if type(con(P))=1 then index∨I(P)
                              else pair(index∨I(P),extr(P1))
    (∨E):  if type(con(P1))=1 then
                Optimizecase(case(extr(P1),extr(P2),...,extr(Pn)))
           else
              let c,r=new(2), p1,...,pn-1=rpatterns(disch∨E(P)) in
      Optimizecase(subst (c . r)←extr(P1) in
        case(c,subst p1←r in extr(P2),...,subst pn-1←r in extr(Pn)))
    (⊃ I):  let a1,...,am=rvars(disch⊃I(P)) in
                Optimizeη(Λ(λ(a1,...,am).extr(P1)))
    (⊃ E):  let f = if type(con(P2))=1 then app* else app in
                Optimizeβ(f(extr(P1),extr(P2)))
```

```
(∀I):  let a_1,...,a_m=eigenvars_∀I(P)in
          Optimize_η(Λ(λ(a_1,...,a_m).extr(P_1)))
(∀E):  let e_1,...,e_m=instances_∀E(P) in
          Optimize_β(app*(extr(P_1),e_1,...,e_m))
(∃I):  let e_1,...,e_m=instances_∃I(P),u=type(body_∃(con(P_1))) in
       if u=0 then list(e_1,...,e_m)
          else if u=1 then list(e_1,...,e_m,extr(P_1))
               else  pair(e_1,pair(e_2,···,pair(e_m,extr(P_1))···))
(∃E):  let a_1,...,a_m=eigenvars_∃E(P),
          b_1,...,b_u=rvars(body(con(P_1))) in
       if u=0 then subst [a_1,...,a_n]←extr(P_1) in extr(P_2)
          else if u=1 then subst (a_1...a_n b_1)←extr(P_1) in extr(P_2)
               else let b=new(1) in
    subst (a_1...a_n . b)←extr(P_1) in subst (b_1...b_u)←b in extr(P_2)
(→∨E):  let c_1,...,c_n=conditions(con(P_1))
          p_1,...,p_{n-1}=rpatterns(bodys_→(con(P_1)))
          e=extr(P_1),e_1=extr(P_2),...,e_{n-1}=extr(P_n), in
        cond(c_1,subst p_1←e in e_1;...;c_n,subst p_n←e in e_n)
(→∧I):  let c_1,...,c_n=conditions(con(P)) in
          cond(c_1,extr(P_1);...;c_n,extr(P_n))
(∇∀I):  let p_1,...,p_m=patterns(con(P_1)),
          e_1,...,e_m=bindings(con(P_1)) in
        let p_1=e_1,...,p_m=e_m in extr(P_1)
(∇∃E):  let p=rpattern(body_∇(con(P_1))),
          p_1,...,p_m=patterns(con(P_1)),
          e_1,...,e_m=bindings(con(P_1)) in
        subst p_1=e_1,...,p_n=e_m,p←extr(P_1) in extr(P_2)
(CIG ind):  let a⃗=eigenvars_CIG(P),
              b⃗=FV(con(P))∪FV(asp(P))−eigenvars_CIG(P),
              f=newfunc(),
              (e_1;A⃗_1),...,(e_n;A⃗_n)=template(P),
              pred⃗_1=pred(A⃗_1;f;b⃗),
                 ...
              pred⃗_n=pred(A⃗_n;f;b⃗),
              r⃗_1=rpatterns(disch_CIG(P_1)),
                 ...
              r⃗_n=rpatterns(disch_CIG(P_n)) in
        begin
           def f(a⃗,b⃗)=cond(e_1,subst r⃗_1←pred⃗_1 in extr(P_1);
                                  ...
                            e_n,subst r⃗_n←pred⃗_n in extr(P_n))
        end
        f(a⃗,b⃗)
  default:  extr(P_1)
end.
```

Let us look at how the extraction algorithm associates a recursion to a CIG-induction (B) of 1.3.2. The CIG-predecessors of the clauses of (C) are as follows:

$$pred(fst(a) : X, snd(a) : X_0; f) \quad \text{is} \quad nil, fst(snd(a)),$$
$$pred(fst(a) : X; f) \quad \text{is} \quad nil.$$

Let the realizers of the upper sequents of (B) be e_1, e_2. Let us assume the type of A is 1 so that $rpatterns(A(snd(a)))$ is a single variable, say r. Assume r appears only once in e_1. Then the extraction algorithm declares a function f such that

$$\textbf{def } f(a) = cond(snd(a), e_1[f(snd(a))/r]; t, e_2),$$

and returns the realizer $f(a)$. If r appeared more than once in e_1, then $e_1[f(snd(a))/r]$ would be replaced by $let\ r = f(snd(a))\ in\ e_1$.

3. Writing programs via proofs

It is well-known that the principle of mathematical induction represents primitive recursion. Further correspondence between some structural induction principles, like list induction, and recursions on data structures, like list recursion, are known. However, the known variety of the recursions represented by induction principles has not been presented in a systematic way, and seemed too peculiar to use as control structure of an actual programming language. Furthermore, it has not been clearly demonstrated how *all* computable functions are programmable by constructive formal proofs. (Goad[12] describes a way associates a proof schema for every recursion schema. But his proof schema is only partially correct. Namely it is a valid proof, only when its normalization process terminates.) We solve these problems by the aid of the general scheme of CIG induction, and a technique representing a domain of partial functions by classes. By virtue of CIG every computable (partail) function can be programmed by a proof of **PX**. To show we can actually write enough efficient programs by our programming methodology, we will prove a theorem which shows how a tail-recursive representation of any regular imperative program is programmed in **PX**. Constable & Mendler[7] have presented essentially the same idea in the context of the type theory of nuPRL. Hagiya & Sakurai [13] also have presented a related idea in the context of verification of logic programming.

3.1. CIG-recursion

A recursion generated by the extraction algorithm from $(CIG\ ind)$ is called a *CIG-recursion*, which has the following form:

$$(*) \qquad f(\vec{a},\vec{b}) = cond(e_1, let\ \vec{r}_1 = \overrightarrow{\mathbf{pred}_1}(\vec{A}_1)\ in\ e'_1; \ldots; e_n, let\ \vec{r}_n = \overrightarrow{\mathbf{pred}_n}(\vec{A}_n)\ in\ e'_n).$$

CIG-recursion is not a full form of recursion, but it is complete in a sense. The aim of this section is to explore it.

CIG-predecessors are defined by the following grammer without help of CIG-templates. So CIG-recursion is a logic-free concept except that $e'_1, \ldots, e'_n$ of (*) must be derived from proofs.

$$\begin{aligned} \alpha ::= & f(e_1, \ldots, e_n) \mid list(e_1, \ldots, e_n) \\ & \mid cond(e_1, \alpha_1; \ldots; e_n, \alpha_n) \mid \Lambda(\lambda(x_1, \ldots, x_n)\alpha) \\ & \mid let\ p_1 = e_1, \ldots, p_n = e_n\ in\ \alpha, \end{aligned}$$

where $e_1, \ldots, e_n$ are arbitrary expressions in which f does not appear. The point is that $f(\alpha_1, \ldots, \alpha_n)$ is not a CIG-templates although $f(e_1, \ldots, e_n)$ is. Consequently CIG-recursions tends not to be nested. But by the aid of higher order programming some nested recursions can be programmed by CIG-recursions. Actually we will later show Ackerman function is programmable in **PX**.

To illustrate CIG-recursions we give some examples below. The first example is the quotient-remainder-algorithm:

$$\text{(I)} \qquad \{a : N,\ b : N^+\} \Rightarrow \exists q : N, r : N.(a = b * q + r \wedge r < b).$$

N^+ is the class of positive integers. For readability, we use infix operators like + and some functions like < will be used as functions and predicates both. Assume $e(a,b)$ realize (I). Then it returns a list $(q\ r)$ in which q and r are the quotient and the remainder of the division of a by b as far as $a : N, b : N^+$. Set

$$\textbf{deCIG}\ a : D(b) \equiv_N a < b \to \top, t \to a - b : D(b).$$

A natural number a belongs to $D(b)$ iff a eventually becomes smaller than b by successive applications of subtraction by b. Namely $D(b)$ is the domain on which Euclidian division algorithm by divisor b terminates. (Note that $D(0)$ is the empty set.) We abbreviate $a = b * q + r \wedge r < b$ by $\phi(a,b,q,r)$. We assume the following type 0 sequents (sequents with type 0 conclusions) have been known:

$$\text{(A1)} \qquad \{a : N, b : N, a < b\} \Rightarrow \phi(a,b,0,a),$$
$$\text{(A2)} \qquad \{a : N, b : N, q : N, r : N, \phi(a-b,b,q,r), \neg a < b\} \Rightarrow \phi(a,b,q+1,r).$$

By applying $(\exists I)$ to (A1) and by applying $(\exists I)$ and $(\exists E)$ to $(A2)$ we prove

$$\text{(A3)} \qquad \{a : N, b : N, a < b\} \Rightarrow \exists q : N, r : N.\phi(a,b,q,r),$$
$$\text{(A4)} \quad \{a : N, b : N, \neg a < b, \exists q : N, r : N.\phi(a-b,b,q,r)\} \Rightarrow \exists q : N, r : N.\phi(a,b,q,r).$$

Let a_1, a_2 be the realizing variables of the formula $\exists q : N, r : N.\phi(a-b,b,q,r)$. Then $list(a_1+1, a_2)$ is extracted from $(A4)$ thanks to the optimization done by **subst**. Applying CIG-induction to $a : D(b)$ with $\exists q : N, r : N.\phi(a,b,q,r)$ we prove the following sequent from $(A3)$ and $(A4)$:

$$\text{(A5)} \qquad \{a : D(b), b : N\} \Rightarrow \exists q : N, r : N.\phi(a,b,q,r).$$

From the proof $f(a,b)$ is extracted where f is a function defined by

$$f(a,b) = cond(a < b, list(0,a); t, let\ (a_1\ a_2) = f(a-b,b)\ in\ list(a_1+1, a_2)).$$

This recursion has the form of iteration in the sense of Backus[3]. So far, we have established only *partial* correctness of f, since $\{(a\ b) | a : D(b) \wedge b : N\}$ is a domain on which f terminates. To see $f(a,b)$ realizes (I) it is sufficient to prove

$$\text{(A6)} \qquad \{a : N, b : N^+\} \Rightarrow b : N, \qquad \{a : N, b : N^+\} \Rightarrow a : D(b).$$

These sequent, which maintain the termination of f on the domain $\{a, b | a : N \wedge b : N^+\}$, are of type 0 and are easily proved. By applications of (*cut*) we finally prove the total correctness statement (I) from the partial correctness statement (A5) and the termination statement (A6). Since the sequents of (A6) are of type 0, the applications of (*cut*) do not change the realizer, i.e. $f(a,b)$ is again extracted from the proof of (I).

This example shows how to separate "termination" and "partial correctness" in the framework of "proofs as programs". No formal systems are complete for the termination problem. Since "proofs as programs" discipline involves total correctness it looks like there is no way to program all computable functions by proofs of a single formal system. But the above example shows we can overcome this difficulty by "cutting out termination problems" by the aid of CIG-induction. In fact we can prove the following theorem:

Theorem 2. (extensional completeness of PX). *For each partial recursive function $\phi(x_1, \ldots, x_n)$, in the sense of Kleene[16], there are classes D_ϕ, G_ϕ which represent the domain and graph of ϕ, respectively. Furthermore, there is a proof Π_ϕ of*

$$\forall [x_1, \ldots, x_n] : D_\phi \exists y.[x_1, \ldots, x_n, y] : G_\phi$$

such that $extr(\Pi_\phi)(x_1,\ldots,x_n)$ *equals to* $\phi(x_1,\ldots,x_n)$ *provided* $[x_1,\ldots,x_n] : D_\phi$.

We do not give a proof of this theorem, but we will give a detailed proof of a more refined result Theorem 3 in the next section. In fact their proofs are essentially the same.

Let us explain how to use this theorem for verification problem. If one wants to verify that a function ϕ, which is extracted from the proof Π_ϕ, has a property, say

$$(**) \qquad \forall x_1,\ldots,x_n.(Input(x_1,\ldots,x_n) \supset Output(x_1,\ldots,x_n,\phi(x_1,\ldots,x_n))).$$

Then it is sufficient to verify the following two conditions

$$Input(x_1,\ldots,x_n) \supset [x_1,\ldots,x_n] : D_\phi,$$
$$Input(x_1,\ldots,x_n) \wedge [x_1,\ldots,x_n,y] : G_\phi \supset Output(x_1,\ldots,x_n,y)$$

The first condition says, as far as the input $x_1,\ldots,x_n$ satisfies the input condition, ϕ terminates on the input. The second condition says if ϕ terminates on the input with an output y, then it satisfies the output condition. Hence these are just the conditions of terminations and partial correctness of the statement of (**). Note that the input and output conditions may be thought of type 0, since it is merely a statement on data, i.e. does not embody any computational (or constructive) meaning. Hence the above two conditions are of type 0. So you may prove them by virtue of classical logic. Even you may verify them by a semantic consideration. This resembles the fact that in Hoare logic formulas which is valid in the intended interpretation of a assertion language are used as axioms in the consequence rule. Note that the point is that we can write down those verification conditions naturally by the language of **PX**. Later we will see a closer relationship of **PX** to Hoare logic.

We derive Ackerman function as an example of this programming methodology. It is also an example of nested CIG-recursion. First we define a graph of Ackerman function.

$$\mathbf{deCIG}\ [x,y,z] : Ack \equiv_{N\times N\times N}$$
$$equal(x,0) \rightarrow suc(y) = z,$$
$$equal(y,0) \rightarrow [prd(x),1,z] : Ack,$$
$$t \rightarrow \Diamond(\exists z_1 : N.([x,prd(y),z_1] : Ack \wedge [prd(x),z_1,z] : Ack)).$$

Next we define a class whose CIG-induction is just the double induction.

$$\mathbf{deCIG}\ [x,y] : Db \equiv_{N\times N} equal(x,0) \rightarrow \top,$$
$$equal(y,0) \rightarrow [prd(x),1] : Db,$$
$$t \rightarrow [x,prd(y)] : Db, \forall y : N.[prd(x),y] : Db.$$

By CIG-induction for Db with $(\exists I)$,$(\exists E)$, and $(\forall E)$, we can prove

$$\{[x,y] : Db\} \Rightarrow \exists z : N.[x,y,z] : Ack.$$

Its realizer is $f(x,y)$ where f is defined by

$$f(x,y) = cond(equal(x,0),suc(y);equal(y,0),f(prd(x),1);t,f(prd(x),f(x,prd(y))).$$

Without the optimization by $Optimize_\beta$, the third clause of the above function definition would be

$$app*(\Lambda()(\lambda(y).f(prd(x),y)),f(x,prd(y))).$$

We prove the termination statement $\{x : N, y : N\} \Rightarrow [x, y] : Db$ by nested applications of mathematical induction and by (cut) we finally prove

$$\text{(II)} \qquad \{x : N, y : N\} \Rightarrow \exists z : N.[x, y, z] : Ack$$

and the realizer is the same as the above. The clauses of the definition of the class Ack may be thought a Prolog program of Ackerman function. What we did is to compile it to a deterministic functional program and verify total correctness of the compiled code.

Next we give an example from list processing. The theorem we prove is

$$\text{(III)} \qquad \{a : List_1(N)\} \Rightarrow \exists m : N.(m \in a \wedge \forall x : N.(x \in a \supset x \leq m)).$$

The formula $m \in a$ means m is an element of the list a and we suppose it is expressed in a type 0 formula. We define a class

$$\begin{aligned}\textbf{deCIG } [n, a] : M \equiv_{N \times List(N)} \\ & equal(a, nil) \rightarrow \top, \\ & n < fst(a) \rightarrow [fst(a), snd(a)] : M, \\ & t \rightarrow [n, snd(a)] : M.\end{aligned}$$

where $List(N)$ is the class of lists of natural numbers possibly empty. Set

$$\phi(m, a) = m \in a \wedge \forall x : N.(x \in a \supset x \leq m),$$
$$\psi(m, n, a) = \Diamond(m = n \vee m \in a) \wedge \forall x : N.((x = n \vee x \in a) \supset x \leq m).$$

Suppose the following three valid type 0 sequents:

$$\text{(B1)} \qquad \{equal(a, nil) : T, [n, a] : N \times List(N)\} \Rightarrow \psi(n, n, a),$$
$$\text{(B2)} \qquad \Gamma \cup \{\psi(m, fst(a), snd(a)), n < fst(a)\} \Rightarrow \psi(m, n, a),$$
$$\text{(B3)} \qquad \Gamma \cup \{\psi(m, n, snd(a)), n \geq fst(a)\} \Rightarrow \psi(m, n, a),$$

where Γ is $\{equal(a, nil) = nil, [n, a] : N \times List(N)\}$. Applying $(\exists I)$,$(\exists E)$, and CIG-induction to these sequents we can prove

$$\text{(B4)} \qquad \{[n, a] : M\} \Rightarrow \exists m : N.\psi(m, n, a).$$

Its realizer is $f(n, a)$ where f is defined by

$$f(n, a) = cond(equal(a, nil), n; n < fst(a), f(fst(a), snd(a)); t, f(n, snd(a))).$$

This recursive definition is tail recursive and $f(n, a)$ computes the maximum element of the list $pair(n, a)$. By CIG induction for $List_1(N)$ we can prove

$$\text{(B5)} \qquad \{a : List_1(N)\} \Rightarrow [fst(a), snd(a)] : M$$
$$\text{(B6)} \qquad \{a : List_1(N)\} \Rightarrow \forall m : N(\psi(m, fst(a), snd(a)) \supset \phi(m, a))$$

Substitute $fst(a)$ and $snd(a)$ for n and a of (B4) and apply (cut) with (B5). Then the result is

$$\{a : List_1(N)\} \Rightarrow \exists m : N.\psi(m, fst(a), snd(a)).$$

By $(replace)$ with (B6) we can finally prove (III). Its realizer is $f(fst(a), snd(a))$. This example suggests a possibility to program all "iterative programs" as tail recursions in **PX**, which is the subject of the next section.

3.2. Simulating Hoare logic

In this section we present a method by which we can "simulate" Hoare logic in **PX**. In light of the technique of developing programs with proofs of correctness, e.g. of Alagić & Arbib[1], a derivation in Hoare logic may be thought not only a verification of a program but also a "trace" or "history" of a program development. In Hoare logic of Pascal-like regular programming language, each program construct has exactly one logical inference rule by which the construct is newly introduced. Morally, a verified program is determined by the structure of its correctness proof. Hence we can extract or reconstruct a program from a derivation of Hoare logic whose programs are eliminated. This observation is a key to relate the notion of "propositions as types" and Hoare logic. A system based on this idea has been implemented by Takasu & Nakahara[22]. Their system constructs a Pascal program through an interactive development of a proof of an existence theorem. They used logical inference rules tailored to their specific purpose. In essence, their inference rules are rules of Hoare logic hiding programs. We will show the inference rules of **PX** can be used for the same purpose, although they were designed for other general purposes. We formulate our technique of the simulation as the following mathematical theorem.

Theorem 3. *Let* **HL** *be the Hoare logic given below with an assertion language L. If* $\{Q\}B\{R\}$ *is provable in* **HL** *with all of true statements of the assertion language as axioms, then there is a proof, say* Π, *of* **PX** *with all of true type 0 sequents as axioms satisfies the following conditions:*

(a) $extr(\Pi)$ *is an iterative program which is equivalent to* B *under* Q.
(b) The assumption of Π *is* Q *under the interpretation of* L *in* **PX**.
(c) The conclusion of Π *is* $\exists\vec{x}.R$ *under the interpretation of* L *in* **PX**, *where* $\vec{x}$ *is the sequence of variables which* B *assigns values to.*

PX does not have imperative programming features, so we have to represent them by state transition functions. A functional program is called an iterative program if its recursions involve only tail-recursion so that a compiler or an optimizer can *directly* transform them to actual Pascal-like imperative programs. In the notations of Backus' FP, the set of iterative programs, say S, is defined by

(1) Let $e_1, \ldots, e_n$ be expressions such that $FV(e_i) \subseteq \{x_1, \ldots, x_n\}$. Then the function

$$\langle x_1, \ldots, x_n \rangle \longmapsto \langle e_1, \ldots, e_n \rangle.$$

belongs to S.
(2) If $f_1, f_2 \in S$, then $f_1 \circ f_2 \in S$.
(3) If e is an expression and $f_1, f_2 \in S$, then $e \to f_1; f_2 \in S$.
(4) If e is an expression and $f_1 \in S$, then the function f defined by the tail-recursion

$$f = e \to id; f \circ f_1.$$

(This definition is not quite complete. In reality, sometimes length of tuples must be adapted.) These (1)-(4) are counterparts of the statements of assignment, composition, conditional, and while, respectively.

A program e of **PX** is said to be equivalent to an imperative program P under Q iff $FV(e)$ is a subset of $Var(P)$, the set of *all* variables appearing in P, and under the function declaration

$$\textbf{function } foo(x_1, \ldots, x_n, y_1, \ldots, y_m) \textbf{ begin } P;\ foo := [x_1, \ldots, x_n] \textbf{ end}$$

e equals to $foo(x_1,\ldots,x_n,y_1,\ldots,y_m)$ under the condition Q, where $x_1,\ldots,x_n$ is the variables to which the program P assigns values and $y_1,\ldots,y_n$ are the rest of the variables appearing in P. We call $x_1,\ldots,x_n$ the *program variables* of P and write it $PV(P)$.

We assume there is an interpretation of L in **PX**. The interpretation of expressions of L in **PX** must have values. Especially, $true$ and $false$ must be interpreted as t and nil, respectively. We assume that L does not have logical symbols $\exists, \vee$. Since the logic of L is classical, this is not a restriction. Furthermore, we assume that $\{\vec{x}|P\}$ is a class in **PX** for any formula P of L. This mild assumption is not actually necessary but simplifies the proof. The rules and axiom of **HL** is as follows:

Assignment Axiom :

$$\{P(\vec{t})\}\ \vec{x} := \vec{t}\ \{P(\vec{x})\},$$

Composition Rule :

$$\frac{\{P\}A\{Q\} \quad \{Q\}B\{R\}}{\{P\}A;B\{R\}},$$

Conditional Rule :

$$\frac{\{P \wedge e = true\}B_1\{Q\} \quad \{P \wedge e = false\}B_2\{Q\}}{\{P\}\ \mathbf{if}\ e\ \mathbf{then}\ B_1\ \mathbf{else}\ B_2\ \{Q\}},$$

while Rule :

$$\frac{\{P \wedge e = true \wedge \vec{x} = \overrightarrow{snap}\}B\{P \wedge \overrightarrow{snap} \succ \vec{x}\}}{\{P\}\mathbf{while}\ e\ \mathbf{do}\ B\ \mathbf{od}\{P \wedge e = false\}},$$

where $\overrightarrow{snap}$ is a sequence of "snapshot variables" appearing neither in the program B nor in the formula P and $\vec{x}$ is $PV(B)$, e is a boolean expression, and the binary relation $\succ$ is well-founded.

Consequence Rule :

$$\frac{P' \supset P \quad \{P\}A\{Q\} \quad Q \supset Q'}{\{P'\}A\{Q'\}}.$$

We prove Theorem 3 by the induction on the structure of proofs of Hoare logic. For simplicity we assume the domain of the assertion language is the domain of **PX**.

For the assignment axiom we associate

$$\Pi = \frac{\{P(t_1,\ldots,t_n)\} \Rightarrow P(t_1,\ldots,t_n)}{\{P(t_1,\ldots,t_n)\} \Rightarrow \exists x_1,\ldots,x_n.P(x_1,\ldots,x_n)}(\exists I).$$

Then $extr(\Pi)$ is $[t_1,\ldots,t_n]$ and it may be regarded as an assignment statement of $\mathcal{S}$, i.e. $\langle t_1,\ldots,t_n\rangle$, satisfying the conditions of the theorem.

Assume

$$\Pi_1 \vdash \{P\} \Rightarrow \exists \vec{x}'.Q, \quad \Pi_2 \vdash \{Q\} \Rightarrow \exists \vec{x}.R.$$

are associated to the premisses of the composition rule. Then Π is

$$\frac{\Pi_1 \quad \Pi_2}{\{P\} \Rightarrow \exists \vec{x}.R}(\exists E)$$

and

$$extr(\Pi) = \mathbf{subst}\ \vec{x}' \leftarrow extr(\Pi_1)\ \mathbf{in}\ extr(\Pi_2).$$

This may be regarded as a composition statement of iterative programs $\mathcal{S}$.

Let Π_1 and Π_2 be assigned to the premisses of the conditional rule. Since P is a type 0 formula, by the aid of $(\wedge I)$ and (cut) there are Π_1' and Π_2' such that

$$\Pi_1' \vdash \{e : T, P\} \Rightarrow \exists \vec{x}'.Q, \quad extr(\Pi_1') \equiv extr(\Pi_1),$$
$$\Pi_2' \vdash \{e = nil, P\} \Rightarrow \exists \vec{x}''.Q, \quad extr(\Pi_2') \equiv extr(\Pi_2).$$

Then Π is

$$\frac{\dfrac{\Pi_0}{Sor(e,t)} \quad \begin{array}{c}\Sigma_1\\ \{P, e : T\} \Rightarrow \exists \vec{x}.Q\end{array} \quad \begin{array}{c}\Sigma_2\\ \{P, e = nil\} \Rightarrow \exists \vec{x}.Q\end{array}}{\{P\} \Rightarrow \exists \vec{x}.Q} (\rightarrow \vee E)$$

where $\vec{x}$ is the union of $\vec{x}'$ and $\vec{x}''$, and

$$\Sigma_1 = \frac{\begin{array}{c}\Pi_1'\\ \{e : T, P\} \Rightarrow \exists \vec{x}'.Q\end{array} \quad \dfrac{\{Q\} \Rightarrow Q}{\{Q\} \Rightarrow \exists \vec{x}.Q}}{\{P, e : T\} \Rightarrow \exists \vec{x}.Q} (\exists E),$$

$$\Sigma_2 = \frac{\begin{array}{c}\Pi_2'\\ \{e : T, P\} \Rightarrow \exists \vec{x}''.Q\end{array} \quad \dfrac{\{Q\} \Rightarrow Q}{\{Q\} \Rightarrow \exists \vec{x}.Q}}{\{P, e = nil\} \Rightarrow \exists \vec{x}.Q} (\exists E).$$

Then its realizer is

$$if\ e\ then\ \mathbf{subst}\ \vec{x}' \leftarrow extr(\Pi_1)\ in\ \vec{x}\ else\ \mathbf{subst}\ \vec{x}'' \leftarrow extr(\Pi_2)\ in\ \vec{x}.$$

Except the adaptation of length of the tuple variables $\vec{x}', \vec{x}''$, this may be thought as a conditional statement of iterative programs $\mathcal{S}$.

Suppose

$$\Sigma \vdash \{P \wedge e = true \wedge \vec{x} = \overrightarrow{snap}\} \Rightarrow \exists \vec{x}.(P \wedge \overrightarrow{snap} \succ \vec{x})$$

is associated to the premiss of **while** rule. Let $\vec{x}$ be $x_1, \ldots, x_n$ and let $extr(\Sigma)$ be b. Set

$$b_i = nth(i, b), \quad \vec{b} = b_1, \ldots, b_n,$$

where $nth(i, b)$ is the function fetches the i-th element of the list b. By $(choice)$ we may regard $\vec{b}$ as a sequence of expressions defined in **PX**. So we can declare a class $W(\vec{s})$, where $\vec{s} = (FV(\vec{b}) \cup FV(e)) - \{\vec{x}\}$, such that

$$\mathbf{deCIG}\ \vec{x} : W(\vec{s}) \equiv e \rightarrow \vec{b} : W(\vec{s}), t \rightarrow \top.$$

Set

$$F(\vec{x}) = \exists \vec{x}'.\vec{x} : R(\vec{x}', \vec{s})$$
$$\mathbf{deCIG}\ \vec{x} : R(\vec{x}', \vec{s}) \equiv_{\{\vec{x}|P\}} e \rightarrow \vec{b} : R(\vec{x}', \vec{s}), t \rightarrow \vec{x} = \vec{x}'.$$

Apparently $\{P, e = nil\} \Rightarrow \vec{x} : R(\vec{x}, \vec{s})$ is provable. Let Σ_1' be its proof. Set

(1) $$\Sigma_1 = \frac{\begin{array}{c}\Sigma_1'\\ \{P, e = nil\} \Rightarrow \vec{x} : R(\vec{x})\end{array}}{\{P, e = nil\} \Rightarrow F(\vec{x})} (\exists I).$$

Then $extr(\Sigma_1)$ is $\vec{x}$. By $(CIG\ def)$

(2) $$\{e : T, P\} \Rightarrow \forall \vec{x}'.(\vec{b} : R(\vec{x}', \vec{s}) \supset \vec{x} : R(\vec{x}', \vec{s}))$$

is provable. Set

$$\Sigma_0 = \frac{\{F(\vec{b})\} \Rightarrow F(\vec{b}) \quad (2)}{\{e : T, P, F(\vec{b})\} \Rightarrow F(\vec{x})}(replace)$$

Then $extr(\Sigma_0)$ is just the realizing variables of $F(\vec{b})$. By (*CIG ind*) we derive a proof Σ such that

$$\Sigma = \frac{\begin{matrix}\Sigma_0 & \Sigma_1 \\ \{e : T, P, F(\vec{b})\} \Rightarrow F(\vec{x}) & \{e = nil, P\} \Rightarrow F(\vec{x})\end{matrix}}{\{\vec{x} : W(\vec{s}), P\} \Rightarrow F(\vec{x})}.$$

Then its realizer is $f(\vec{x}, \vec{s})$ and f is defined by

$$f(\vec{x}, \vec{s}) = cond(e, f(\vec{b}, \vec{s}); t, [\vec{x}]).$$

This is the **while** statement of iterative programs $\mathcal{S}$. But this is not the end of the proof. We have to adapt Σ so as to satisfy the conditions (a),(b) of the theorem. By the definition of W we see from the validity of the premiss of **while** rule

(3) $$\{P\} \Rightarrow \vec{x} : W(\vec{s})$$

is a true type 0 sequent so that we may use it as an axiom. (This is the assumption that we may have to assume without a formal proof of **PX**.) On the other hand, there is a proof Σ_3 such that

$$\Sigma_3 \vdash \{\ \} \Rightarrow \forall \vec{x}'.(\vec{x} : R(\vec{x}', \vec{s}) \supset (P \wedge e = nil)[\vec{x}'/\vec{x}])$$

Set

$$\Pi = \frac{\dfrac{(3) \quad \Sigma}{\{P\} \Rightarrow F(\vec{x})}(cut) \quad \Sigma_3}{\{P\} \Rightarrow \exists \vec{x}.(P \wedge e = nil)}(replace)\&(alpha)$$

Then $extr(\Pi) = extr(\Sigma)$ and Π satisfies the conditions of the theorem.

The counterpart of the consequence rule is just (*replace*). It does not change the program (realizer). This ends the proof of Theorem 3.

What we have proved can be summerized up by the following diagram:

$$\begin{array}{ccc} \Sigma \vdash_{\mathbf{HL}} \{P\}A\{Q\} & \longrightarrow & \Pi \vdash_{\mathbf{PX}} \{P\} \Rightarrow \exists \vec{x}.Q \\ \downarrow & & \downarrow \\ A & \cong & extr(\Pi) \end{array}$$

The important point is that $extr(\Pi)$ is not only extansinoally equivalent to A but also *essentially intensionally equivalent* to A, i.e. the imperative program A is directly reconstructible from the functional program $extr(\Pi)$. The correspondence between **HL** and **PX** used in the above proof are summerized up by the following table:

HL	**PX**
Assertion formula	Type 0 formula
$\vdash \{P\}A\{Q\}$	$\Pi \vdash \{P\} \Rightarrow \exists \vec{x}.Q$
Assignment	$(\exists I)$
Composition	$(\exists E)$
Conditional	$(\rightarrow \vee E)$
While	(*CIG ind*)
Consequence	(*replace*)

As an example of the above method we derive another program of the quotient-remainder theorem (I) of 3.1. Set

$$D(a,b) = \{q,r|q : N \wedge r : N \wedge a = b * q + r\}$$

and

$$\textbf{deCIG } [x,y] : W(a,b) \equiv_{D(a,b)} y \geq b \rightarrow [x+1, y-b] : W(a,b), t \rightarrow \top.$$

$$\textbf{deCIG } [x,y] : R(q,r,a,b) \equiv_{D(a,b)} y \geq b \rightarrow [x+1, y-b] : R(q,r,a,b),$$
$$t \rightarrow x = q, y = r.$$

In the symbols of the proof of Theorem 3, $\vec{x}$ is q, r, $\vec{x}'$ is q_1, r_1, and $\vec{s}$ is a, b. As in the proof we can derive a program Σ such that

$$(4) \qquad \Sigma \vdash \{a : N, b : N^+, [x,y] : W(a,b)\} \Rightarrow \exists q : N, r : N.[x,y] : R(q,r,a,b)$$

and $extr(\Sigma)$ is $f(x,y,a,b)$ whose f is defined by

$$f(x,y,a,b) = cond(y \geq b, f(x+1, y-b, a, b); t, list(x,y)).$$

Substitute $0, a$ for x, y in (4). Since $[0,a] : W(a,b)$ holds provided $a : N, b : N^+$, we can eliminate this from the assumption of (4). Since R is inductively defined, if $R(q,r,a,b)$ is non empty, then there is a value $[x_0, y_0]$ of $[x,y]$ satisfying the conditions of the base case:

$$[x_0, y_0] : D(a,b), \ y_0 < b, x_0 = q, \ y_0 = r.$$

So $a = b * q + r \wedge r < b$ holds. Formalizing this consideration we can derive

$$(5) \qquad \forall q : N, r : N.([0,a] : R(q,r,a,b) \supset a = b * q + r \wedge r < b).$$

So the sequent (I) of 3.1 is derived by $(replace)$ and its realizer is $f(0,a,a,b)$. This is just a tail-recursive version of the usual Euclidian division algorithm.

4. Conclusion

PX is a system which realizes the principle of "proofs as programs", which is based on Lisp and Feferman's theory of functions and classes[10]. It is a type free system but have the concept of classes which may be thought as carriers of data types as first class objects. We introduced the principle of CIG which is a generalization of the inductive generation of Feferman[10]. By virtue of CIG and a logic which is consistent with all classically valid statements, **PX** may be thought as a "complete" computational logic in the same sense that Hoare logic is complete. In fact we "simulated" a complete system of Hoare logic of total correctness. We have established a methodology to separate "partial correctness" and "total correctness" in the frame work of "proofs as programs".

The relation to the other works are as follows. The aim of **PX** is virtually the same to those of nuPRL of Constable & Bates[6], the system of Dijyr[9], and the logical framework of Martin-Lőf[17]. But the approaches of nuPRL and **PX** to achieve the goal are opposite. nuPRL starts with some basic types then gradually "builts up" complex data types over them. On the contrary, **PX** starts with the universal sapce of S-expressions and "carves out" all data types as its subtypes. nuPRL started with Martin-Lőf's type theory, all functions of which are total, and imported partial function spaces and subtypes. On the contrary, **PX** is basically a monotype theory of partial functions. Constable & Mendler[7] introduced the concept of the domain of algorithms into nuPRL, by which they could reason about the properties of the algorithms. So in nuPRL functions are defined first and verification comes later. On the other hand we built up a proof first and extract a program from it. But, since we may extract the program without proving totalness, the actual program developments in nuPRL and **PX** are quite similar.

PX was originally implemented on VAX/UNIX at the Computer Centre of University of Tokyo. Now it is running on SUN3 at Kyoto University. It consists of about 7,000 lines of Franz Lisp. Its specification and core system has been completed and is under use of experiments. All of the examples of this paper have been experimented on the machine among others. A tautology checker has been extracted from a proof of the completeness theorem of propositional logic. It returns a proof of a given formula, if it is a tautology, and returns a function closure which is a valuation refuting the formula, if it is refutable. The system is still experimental and in the stage of development. The next step of the development will be improvement of human interface, which enables us to conduct with large scale experiments.

Acknowledgements

I would like to express my hearty thanks to Prof. S. Takasu for encouraging me to write this paper and helpful criticisms on the system **LM**. I would like to thank Prof. M.J. Beeson, M. Hagiya, Prof. P. Martin-Löf, H. Nakano, Dr. G.R. Renardel de Lavalette, and Prof. M. Sato for valuable discussions and comments. I would like to thank Prof. S. Feferman and Prof. D. Scott for their interests. I am grateful to Nakano and Tatsuta for proof reading.

Appendix A

In this appendix we present an actual session of deriving a proof of (A5) of 3.1. In the following proof, LEMMA1, LEMMA2, LEMMA3 are proofs of (A1), (A2), and $\{q : N\} \Rightarrow q+1 : N$, respectively. They are assumed to have been proved, for their proofs do not change the extracted codes.

```
(deCIG {a :(DD b)} (in N)
   ((lessp a b) {TRUE}) (t {(diff a b):(DD b)}))

(dp BASIS
  (exI '{(EX q r :  N)
             (a = (plus (times b q) r) & (lessp r b)  :  T)}
      LEMMA1 (assume '{a  :  N})))

(dp STEP
  (exE (assume
  '{(EX q r :  N)
       ((diff a b) = (plus (times b q) r) & (lessp r b)  :  T)} )
      (exI '{(EX q r :  N)
             (a = (plus (times b q) r) & (lessp r b)  :  T)}
      LEMMA2 LEMMA3 (assume '{r :  N}))))

(dp THM (cigIND '{a :  (DD b)}  BASIS STEP))
```

`(DD b)` is the class $D(b)$ and `EX` is existential quantifier and `&` is conjunction. Note that in the actual system all formulas are surrounded by braces. `(dp name prf)` is the same as `(setq name prf)`. Reading these expressions with those lemmas, **PX** binds proofs of

(A3), (A4), and (A5) to BASIS, STEP, THM, respectively. **PX** extracts (<rec0> a b) from the proof THM, declaring a function <rec0>.

```
(defrec <rec0> (a) (b)
       (cond ((lessp a b) (list 0 a))
             (t
              (let (((@1:1 @1:2) (<rec0> (diff a b) b)))
                   (list (add1 @1:1) @1:2)))))
```

Since b is not an eigen variable of the CIG induction, it does not change its value through the computation of (<rec0> a b). The function defined by defrec does not push the value of b on a value stack when <rec0> is called.

Appendix B.

In this appendix we present the axioms of joint and product. **PX** has a basic function Σ whose arity is two, and the following is an axiom, provided A is a class variable:

(*Join*)

$$\forall a : A.Class(app*(f,a)) \supset Class(\Sigma(A,f)) \\ \wedge \forall x.(x : \Sigma(A,f) \supset\subset \nabla(a \;.\; b) = x.(a : A \wedge b : app*(f,a)))).$$

This corresponds to Martin-Lõf's dependent sum. By the aid of this axiom and CIG, we can derive the existence of dependent products. But, for symmetry, **PX** has the axiom of the dependent products.

(*Product*)

$$\forall a : A.Class(app*(f,a)) \supset Class(\Pi(A,f)) \\ \wedge \forall x.(x : \Pi(A,f) \supset\subset \forall a : A.app*(x,a) : app*(f,a)).$$

By these two dependent types and the types introduced by CIG, we can interpret a version of Martin-Lõf's type theory $\mathbf{ML_0}$.

References

[1] Alagić, S. & Arbib, M.A., *The Design of Well-Structured and Correct Programs*, Springer-Verlag, New York, 1978.

[2] Apt, K.R., Ten Years of Hoare's Logic: A Survey-Part I, ACM TOPLAS 3 (1981), 431-483.

[3] Backus, J., Can programming be liberated from the von Neumann Style?, CACM 21 (1978), 613-641.

[4] Beeson, M.J., Programming proofs and proving programs, In *Logic, Methodology, and Philosophy of Science VII*, North-Holland, 1985.

[5] Beeson, M.J., *The Foundations of Constructive Mathematics*, Springer-Verlag, 1986.

[6] Constable, R.L. & Bates, J.L., The Nearly Ultimate PEARL Technical Report TR 83-551, Department of Computer Science, Cornell University, 1984.

[7] Constable, R.L. & Mendler, N.P., Recursive Definitions in Type Theory, In *Logic of Programs*, Lecture Notes in Computer Science, 193, Springer-Verlag, New York, 1985, 61-78.

[8] Coquand, T. & Huet G., A Selected Bibliography on Constructive Mathematics, Intuitionistic Type Theory and Higher Order Deduction, J. Symbolic Computation 1 (1985), 323-328.

[9] Dijyr, P., Program Verification in a Logical Theory of Constructions, In *Functional Programming Languages and Computer Architecture*, Lecture Notes in Computer Science, 201, Springer-Verlag, New York, 1985, 334-349.

[10] Feferman, S., Constructive theories of functions and classes, In *Logic Colloquium '78*, North-Holland, Amsterdam, 1979, 159-224.

[11] Franz Lisp, *The Franz Lisp Manual*, Franz Inc., 1984.

[12] Goad, C., Computational uses of the manipulation of formal proofs, Ph.D. Thesis, Stanford University, 1980.

[13] Hagiya, M. & Sakurai, T., Foundation of Logic Programming Based on Inductive Definition, New Generation Computing 2 (1984), 59-77.

[14] Hayashi, S., Extracting Lisp Programs from Constructive Proofs: A Formal Theory of Constructive Mathematics Based on Lisp, Publ. of the Research Institute for Math. Sci. 19 (1983), 169-191.

[15] Hayashi, S., **PX**: a computational logic, in preparation.

[16] Kleene, S.C., *Introduction to Metamathematics*, D. Van Nostrand, Princeton, N.J. 1952.

[17] Martin-Löf, P., Constructive mathematics and computer programming, In *Logic, Methodology, and Philosophy of Science VI*, North-Holland, 1982, 153-179.

[18] Martin-Löf, P., On the meanings of the logical constants and the justifications of the logical laws, Lectures given at Siena, April 1983, included in Proc. of the Third Japanese-Swedish Workshop, Institute of New Generation Computing Technology, 1985.

[19] Plotkin, G., Lectures given at ASL Stanford meeting, July 1985.

[20] Sato, M., Typed Logical Calculus, Technical Report 85-13, Department of Information Science, Faculty of Science, University of Tokyo, 1985.

[21] Steele, G.L., *Common Lisp, The Language*, Digital Press, 1984.

[22] Takasu, S. & Nakahara, T., Programming with mathematical thinking, In *IFIP 83*, North-Holland, 1983, 419-424.

QUESTIONS AND ANSWERS

Tennent: You say that your system PX is complete in the sense of Stephen Cook, but relative to what?

Hayashi: Relative to all type-zero formulas. Type-zero formulas are the PX counterpart of the assertion language of Hoare's logic.

Felleisen: It seems to me that your proofs actually not only correspond to programming but they really are 'programming'. Namely the structure of your CIG induction is so close to a tail recursion that I almost can't see the difference and I would suspect that if you specify a maximum function, that has some real exception conditions, you would have just to list the exception conditions and you will get the same conditions on the proofs. So I don't really see what big advantage you get by programming in a proof system. And then getting the program extracted?

Hayashi: I think this is a big debate. There are a lot of theorems in logic which are constructive. I´m very interested in proof-checking of theorems. Actually we have a project at ICOT to build a proof checker of mathematics. I believe if we can extract programs from that kind of verified mathematical theorems, that´s fine. I do not maintain that a programmer should program his proofs. I think this is hopeless. But it is very interesting to extract programs from proofs, to see how actual algorithms are embodied in mathematical proofs. So this is a kind of experimental logic.

Blikle: I would like to know your opinion about the possible range of applications of this. The idea of extracting programs from proofs has been investigated for about 15 years maybe (tracing it back to Igarashi´s papers) and so far I think it has not been applied to the development of large programs. It seems more suitable for the development of small tricky programs or maybe of smart algorithms, but I haven´t heard about any concrete applications. Can you comment on this?

Hayashi: Well, I don´t know what a large program is. I have constructed a program which checks whether a propositional formula is a tautology. This program consists of about one and a half page. It contains four or five functions which call each other. Probably it is a toy program for actual Computer Science. For that kind of area related to logic the method of extracting programs from proofs is very promising.

Felleisen: Is it correct that you claim at one point, if I am understanding you correctly, that all problems extracted from your proofs are tail recursive?

Hayashi: No.

Felleisen: OK, that´s what I have expected. It could not really be the case; otherwise you could not have specified the ´maximum´ function in different ways.

Formal Description of Programming Concepts - III
M. Wirsing (Editor)
Elsevier Science Publishers B.V. (North-Holland)
IFIP, 1987

Polymorphic Types, Fixed-point Combinators and Continuous Lambda-Models (+)

M. Dezani-Ciancaglini (++)
I. Margaria

Dipartimento di Informatica - Universita' di Torino - Via Valperga Caluso 37, 10125 TORINO (Italy).

1. Introduction.

Over the last several years there has been an increasing interest in studying polymorphic type disciplines for the untyped λ-calculus. In fact, it is well known that many problems concerning programming languages can be stated in a "pure" form for the λ-calculus, which can be considered as the kernel of functional languages.

The idea of assigning types to terms was introduced by Curry [Curry and Feys 58] in the context of his foundational program. Many extensions of Curry's systems have been proposed in the literature.

The quantification discipline [Mac Queen and Sethi 82, Leivant 83, Mac Queen et al. 84, Mitchell 84] is based on the F-system of Girard [Girard 71] (called second-order lambda-calculus in [Reynolds 74]). The main difference with Curry's system is the introduction of the universal quantifier "∀" as type constructor. The soundness and completeness of this discipline are proved in [Mitchell 85].

In the intersection discipline the set of types is extended by adding the constant type "ω" (which plays the role of universal type) and the intersection operator "∧" of type formation [Coppo and Dezani 80, Coppo et al. 81, Barendregt et al. 83]. This discipline is proved to be sound and complete in [Hindley 82, Barendregt et al. 83, Dezani and Margaria 84].

A drawback of Curry's system and of the previously mentioned extensions is that many interesting terms do not have meaningful types. In particular the well known fixed-point combinator $\mathbf{Y}=\lambda f.(\lambda x.f(xx))(\lambda x.f(xx))$ has no type in the quantification discipline, since in this discipline we can assign types only to terms which are strongly normalizable [Girard 71]. In the intersection discipline we cannot deduce

---

(+) Research partially supported by M.P.I. 40% Comitato per l'Ingegneria
(++) Centro Linceo Interdisciplinare di Scienze Matematiche e loro applicazioni (for the Academic years 84-85, 85-86 and 86-87).

the expected type $(\sigma\rightarrow\sigma)\rightarrow\sigma$ for **Y** (where σ is arbitrary), even if **Y** has infinitely many types.

In the literature there are essentially two ways of extending a type assignment system in such a way that also fixed point combinators are correctly typed. One proposal is to allow recursively defined types [Morris 68, Mac Queen et al. 84, Coppo 85] as it has been done in the language ML [Gordon et al. 79]. Otherwise, following [Coppo 84] we can add two new rules (called (Ω) and (C)) to the type assignment system. The terms which are typed using recursively defined types depend on the assumed type equations, while all terms are typed by means of rules (Ω) and (C). In both cases we are naturally led to consider continuous λ-models only [Barendregt 84, 19.3] (where **Y** is interpreted as the least fixed point operator) and to interpret types as ideals [Coppo 84, Mac Queen et al. 84, Coppo 85].

In the present paper we consider two type assignments obtained by adding rules (Ω) and (C) respectively to the natural deduction systems of the quantification and intersection disciplines. We prove that these type assignments are sound and complete with respect to the inference and simple semantics of types (as defined respectively in [Mitchell 85] and in [Böhm 75, open problem II.4]). The completeness of these systems with respect to the **F**-semantics remains an open problem. We prove instead the **F**-completeness of a restricted system of type assignment.The models used in these proofs are P_ω [Scott 76] and **B** (the model of Böhm-like trees) [Barendregt 84, 18.3].

We assume the reader to be familiar with the basic concepts of λ-calculus and λ-models [Barendregt 84, Part I].

2. The $\forall$**Y** *discipline.*

2.1. Type assignment.

In this section we consider the type expressions of the F-system [Girard 71].

2.1. *Definition.* Let V be a set of variables. The set T of *quantification types* is the minimal set such that

1. $V\subseteq T$
2. $\sigma,\tau\in T \Rightarrow \sigma\rightarrow\tau\in T$
3. $\varphi\in V\ \sigma\in T \Rightarrow \forall\varphi.\sigma\in T$.

Let $\forall\vec{\varphi}.\tau$ where $\vec{\varphi} = \varphi_1,\ldots,\varphi_n$ be short for $\forall\varphi_1\ldots\varphi_n.\tau$. Possibly n =0 and, in this case, $\forall\vec{\varphi}.\tau = \tau$.

We need the standard definitions of λ-Ω-terms and Ω reduction (called $\lambda\bot$-terms and $\bot$-reduction in [Barendregt 84, 14.3]). The notion of β-Ω-conversion $=_{\beta\Omega}$ is introduced in the usual way [Wadsworth 76].

A λ-Ω-term A is a *β-Ω-normal form* (β-Ω-n.f.) iff A cannot be reduced using β and Ω-reduction rules. Let M be a λ-Ω-term and A a β-Ω-n.f., A is *a direct approximant* of M ($A\sqsubseteq M$) iff A matches M except at occurences of Ω in A. A is an *approximant* of M ($A\sqsubseteq M$) iff $\exists M'$ such that $M \twoheadrightarrow_\beta M'$ and $A\sqsubseteq M'$. Lastly define $\mathcal{A}(M)=\{A \mid A\sqsubseteq M\}$.

Types are assigned to terms by means of a natural deduction system which is obtained by adding rules (Ω) and (C) of [Coppo 84] to the system given in [Mitchell 85].

2.2. *Definition.* (i) A *quantification statement* is of the form σM with $\sigma\in T$, $M\in \mathbf{\Lambda\Omega}$ (set of λ-Ω-terms). M is the *subject* and σ is the *predicate* of σM.
A *basis* B is a set of quantification statements with only variables as subjects and such that no two statements in B have the same subject.
(ii) The *∀∀ type assignment* is defined by the following natural deduction system:

$$(\to I)\ \frac{\begin{matrix}[\sigma x]\\ \vdots \\ \tau M\end{matrix}}{\sigma\to\tau\ \lambda x.M}\ (+) \qquad\qquad (\to E)\ \frac{\sigma\to\tau M \quad \sigma N}{\tau MN}$$

$$(\forall I)\ \frac{\sigma M}{\forall\varphi.\sigma M}\ (++) \qquad\qquad (\forall E)\ \frac{\forall\varphi.\sigma M}{\sigma[\tau/\varphi]M}$$

$$(\Omega)\ \frac{}{\sigma\Omega} \qquad\qquad (C)\ \frac{\sigma A \text{ for all } A\in\mathcal{A}(M)}{\sigma M}$$

(+) if x not free in assumptions on which τM depends other than σx.
(++) if φ is not free in assumptions on which σM depends.

(iii) If σM is derivable from a basis B in the ∀∀ type assignment, we write $B \vdash \sigma M$.
If $\mathcal{D}$ is a derivation showing this, we write $\mathcal{D}$: $B \vdash \sigma M$.

For example we have $\vdash \forall\varphi.(\varphi\to\varphi)\to\varphi\mathbf{Y}$ since for all $n\in\omega$ $\vdash \forall\varphi.(\varphi\to\varphi)\to\varphi\ \lambda f.f^n\Omega$.
Let $FV(B)=\{x \mid \sigma x\in B\}$ and $B/x=\{\sigma y \mid \sigma y\in B \text{ and } y\not\equiv x\}$.
For our proof of completeness it is useful to show that the following is a derived rule of the ∀∀ type assignment:

$$(\sqsubseteq)\ \frac{\sigma M \quad A\sqsubseteq M}{\sigma A}$$

To this aim let us associate with each statement of a deduction $\mathcal{D}$ an ordinal number $\mathcal{O}(\mathcal{D})$ in the following way. 0 is associated with each assumption and with each statement obtained by (Ω). The ordinal associated with the conclusion of an inference rule is greater than all ordinals associated with its premises. The ordinal $\mathcal{O}(\mathcal{D})$ is the ordinal associated with the end-statement of $\mathcal{D}$.

2.3. *Lemma*. (i) $B \vdash \sigma M \Rightarrow B[\tau/\varphi] \vdash \sigma[\tau/\varphi]M$.
(ii) $B \vdash \forall\vec{\varphi}.\sigma\rightarrow\tau\ \lambda x.M \Rightarrow B/x\cup\{\sigma x\} \vdash \tau M$.
Proof. (i).The proof is by transfinite induction on $\mathcal{O}(\mathcal{D})$ where $\mathcal{D}: B \vdash \sigma M$. The only interesting case is when the last applied rule is $(\forall I)$:

$$\frac{\rho M}{\forall\psi.\rho M}\ (\forall I).$$

If $\varphi \equiv \psi$ then $(\forall\psi.\rho)[\tau/\varphi] \equiv \forall\psi.\rho$ and $B[\tau/\varphi] \equiv B$ since ψ cannot occur free in the premises.
If $\varphi \not\equiv \psi$ we have
$B \vdash \rho M \Rightarrow B[\tau/\varphi] \vdash \rho[\tau/\varphi]M$ by the induction hypothesis
$\Rightarrow B[\tau/\varphi] \vdash (\forall\psi.\rho)[\tau/\varphi]M$ by $(\forall I)$ (possibly after a renaming of ψ).
(ii).By transfinite induction on the ordinals associated with deductions. If the last applied rule is $(\forall E)$:

$$\frac{\forall\psi\vec{\varphi}.\sigma\rightarrow\tau\ \lambda x.M}{(\forall\vec{\varphi}.\sigma\rightarrow\tau)[\rho/\psi]\ \lambda x.M}\ (\forall E).$$

$B \vdash \forall\psi\vec{\varphi}.\sigma\rightarrow\tau\ \lambda x.M \Rightarrow B/x\cup\{\sigma x\} \vdash \tau M$ by the induction hypothesis
$\Rightarrow B/x\cup\{\sigma[\rho/\psi]x\} \vdash \tau[\rho/\psi]M$ by (i) since ψ cannot occur free in B.
If the last applied rule is (C) notice that $\mathcal{A}(\lambda x.M) = \{\lambda x.A \mid A\in\mathcal{A}(M) \text{ and } A\not\equiv\Omega\}\cup\{\Omega\}$.□

2.4. *Theorem.* (i) $B \vdash \sigma M,\ M\rightarrow\!\!\!\!\rightarrow_\beta M' \Rightarrow B \vdash \sigma M'$.
(ii) $B \vdash \sigma M,\ A\sqsubseteq M \Rightarrow B \vdash \sigma A$.
Proof. (i). Clearly it is sufficient to prove $B \vdash \sigma(\lambda x.M)N \Rightarrow B \vdash \sigma M[N/x]$.
We prove this claim by transfinite induction on the ordinals associated with deductions. The most interesting case is when the last applied rule is $(\rightarrow E)$:

$$\frac{\tau\rightarrow\sigma\ \lambda x.M \quad \tau N}{\sigma(\lambda x.M)N}\ (\rightarrow E).$$

$B \vdash \tau\rightarrow\sigma\ \lambda x.M$ implies $B/x\cup\{\tau x\} \vdash \sigma M$ by Lemma 2.3(ii). Therefore we obtain a deduction of $B \vdash \sigma M[N/x]$ by replacing each premise τx by a deduction of τN and x by N in $\mathcal{D}: B/x\cup\{\tau x\} \vdash \sigma M$.
For rule (C) notice that $\mathcal{A}((\lambda x.M)N) = \mathcal{A}(M[N/x])$.
(ii).$A\sqsubseteq M$ iff there is M' such that $M\rightarrow\!\!\!\!\rightarrow_\beta M'$ and $A \sqsubseteq M'$. By (i) there is $\mathcal{D}: B \vdash \sigma M'$. The proof of $B \vdash \sigma A$ by transfinite induction on $\mathcal{O}(\mathcal{D})$ is rather standard.
The only interesting case is when $A\not\equiv\Omega$ and the last applied rule is $(\rightarrow E)$:

$$\frac{\tau\to\sigma P \qquad \tau Q}{\sigma PQ}\ (\to E).$$

In this case we must have $P\equiv x\vec{P}$ for some $x,\vec{P}$ and $A\equiv x\vec{A}A'$, where $x\vec{A} \sqsubseteq P$ and $A' \sqsubseteq Q$. Then the induction hypothesis applies. □

As an immediate consequence of 2.4(ii) and rule (C) we have that the following rule:

$$(Eq_{\beta\Omega})\ \frac{\sigma M \qquad M =_{\beta\Omega} N}{\sigma N}$$

is a derived rule of the $\forall\mathbf{Y}$ type assignment.

2.2. *Type semantics.*

Let $\mathcal{M}$=<D,·,ε> be a λ-model and $[\![\ ]\!]^{\mathcal{M}}$ be the interpretation of λ-Ω-terms in it. Following [Barendregt 1984, 19.3] we say that $\mathcal{M}$ is a continuous λ-model iff there is a partial relation ⊑ on D such that

(1) <D,⊑> is a c.p.o.

(2) "·" is continuous (with respect to the Scott topology induced by ⊑, see [Barendregt 1984, 1.2])

(3) for all terms M and environments ξ, the set $\{[\![A]\!]^{\mathcal{M}}_{\xi} \mid A\in\mathcal{A}(M)\}$ is directed and $[\![M]\!]^{\mathcal{M}}_{\xi}=\sqcup\{[\![A]\!]^{\mathcal{M}}_{\xi} \mid A\in\mathcal{A}(M)\}$ (where ⊔ is the supremum operator in D and Ω is interpreted as the least element of D).

Most interesting λ-models are continuous λ-models, for example P_{ω}, D_{∞} and $\mathbf{B}$ (the model of Böhm-like trees) [Barendregt 84, 19.3.2]. In continuous λ-models all fixed point combinators are equated and represent the least fixed point operator on D [Barendregt 1984, 19.3.4].

We want to interpret types in continuous λ-models as sets of values. As remarked in [Milner 78, Mac Queen and Sethi 82, Mac Queen at al. 84, Coppo 84, Mitchell 85] we must require that these sets are *ideals*, i.e. non-empty left-closed sets closed under lubs of increasing sequences.

2.5. *Definition.* Let $\mathcal{M}$ = <D,·,ε> be a continuous λ-model. A mapping $\mathcal{V}:T\to\mathbf{P}(D) = \{X \mid X\subseteq D\}$ is a *type interpretation* iff:

(1) $\mathcal{V}(\sigma)$ is an ideal

(2) $d\in\mathcal{V}(\sigma\to\tau) \Rightarrow$ for all $e\in\mathcal{V}(\sigma)$ $d\cdot e\in\mathcal{V}(\tau)$

(3) for all $e\in\mathcal{V}(\sigma)$ $d\cdot e\in\mathcal{V}(\tau) \Rightarrow \varepsilon\cdot d\in\mathcal{V}(\sigma\to\tau)$

(4) $\mathcal{V}(\forall\varphi.\sigma) = \bigcap_{\tau\in T}\mathcal{V}(\sigma[\tau/\varphi])$

for all $\sigma,\tau\in T$ and $\varphi\in V$.

Other notions of type interpretations are given in the literature.

Following [Hindley 83-a] we say that a type interpretation $\mathcal{V}$ is *simple* iff

$$\mathcal{V}(\sigma\to\tau) = \{d\in D \mid \forall e\in\mathcal{V}(\sigma)\ d\cdot e\in\mathcal{V}(\tau)\} \text{ for all } \sigma,\tau\in T.$$

Instead, an *$\mathcal{F}$ type interpretation* $\mathcal{V}$ is a type interpretation satisfying

$$\mathcal{V}(\sigma\to\tau) = \{d\in\mathbf{F} \mid \forall e\in\mathcal{V}(\sigma)\ d\cdot e\in\mathcal{V}(\tau)\} \text{ for all } \sigma,\tau\in T$$

where $\mathbf{F}$ is the range of ϵ.

These notions of type interpretations lead naturally to the following definitions of semantic satisfability (called respectively inference, simple and $\mathbf{F}$-semantics).

2.6. *Definition.* Let $\mathcal{M}=\langle D,\cdot,\epsilon\rangle$ be a continuous λ-model, ξ an environment and $\mathcal{V}$ a type interpretation.

(i) $\mathcal{M},\xi,\mathcal{V} \models \sigma M$ iff $[\![M]\!]^{\mathcal{M}}_{\xi}\in\mathcal{V}(\sigma)$

$\mathcal{M},\xi,\mathcal{V} \models B$ iff $\mathcal{M},\xi,\mathcal{V} \models \sigma x$ for all $\sigma x\in B$

$\mathcal{M},B,\mathcal{V} \models \sigma M$ iff for all ξ: $[\mathcal{M},\xi,\mathcal{V} \models B \Rightarrow \mathcal{M},\xi,\mathcal{V} \models \sigma M]$.

(ii) $\mathcal{M},B \models \sigma M$ iff for all $\mathcal{V}$: $\mathcal{M},B,\mathcal{V} \models \sigma M$

$\mathcal{M},B \models_s \sigma M$ iff for all simple type interpretations $\mathcal{V}$: $\mathcal{M},B,\mathcal{V} \models \sigma M$

$\mathcal{M},B \models_{\mathcal{F}} \sigma M$ iff for all $\mathbf{F}$ type interpretations $\mathcal{V}$: $\mathcal{M},B,\mathcal{V} \models \sigma M$.

(iii) $B \models \sigma M$ iff for all $\mathcal{M}$: $\mathcal{M},B \models \sigma M$

$B \models_s \sigma M$ iff for all $\mathcal{M}$: $\mathcal{M},B \models_s \sigma M$

$B \models_{\mathcal{F}} \sigma M$ iff for all $\mathcal{M}$: $\mathcal{M},B \models_{\mathcal{F}} \sigma M$.

2.3. *Inference Semantics.*

The soundness of the $\forall\mathbf{V}$ type assignment can be easily proved. Since (C) is an infinitary rule, we must use transfinite induction on the ordinal $\mathcal{O}(\mathcal{D})$ associated with $\mathcal{D} : B \vdash \sigma M$.

2.7. *Theorem* (Soundness). $B \vdash \sigma M \Rightarrow B \models \sigma M$.

Obviously $B \models \sigma M$ implies $B \models_s \sigma M$, $B \models_{\mathcal{F}} \sigma M$. But we will see that other rules are sound for the simple and $\mathbf{F}$ type interpretations.

We use the model $\mathbf{B}$ to prove completeness. Let us recall that the *Böhm-tree* of a λ-Ω-term M (BT(M)) can be informally defined by:

BT(M) = $\bullet$ if M is unsolvable

BT(M) = 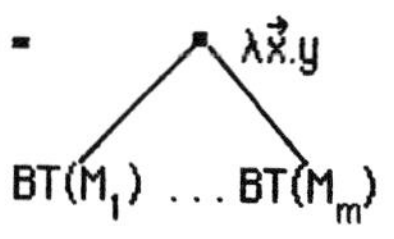 if $M =_{\beta\Omega} \lambda\vec{x}.yM_1 \ldots M_m$

Roughly a *Böhm-like tree* is a (possibly infinite) tree whose internal nodes are labelled by $\lambda\vec{x}.y$ and whose terminal nodes are either unlabelled or labelled by $\lambda\vec{x}.y$ for some variables $\vec{x},y$. Obviously, there are infinite Böhm-like trees which are not Böhm-trees of any λ-Ω-term.

Formal definitions are given in [Barendregt 84, 10.3].
If $\mathcal{A}$ is a Böhm-like tree, $\mathcal{A}^k$ is the finite Böhm-tree resulting from $\mathcal{A}$ by cutting off all subtrees at depth k.
If $\mathcal{A}$ is a finite Böhm-tree, we can define (by induction on the depth of $\mathcal{A}$) a β-Ω-n.f. $A_{\mathcal{A}}$ such that $BT(A_{\mathcal{A}}) = \mathcal{A}$:

(i) if $\mathcal{A}$ = • then $A_{\mathcal{A}} \equiv \Omega$

(ii) if $\mathcal{A}$ =

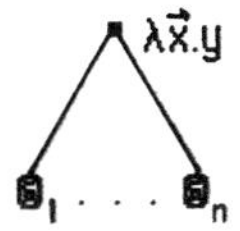

then $A_{\mathcal{A}} \equiv \lambda\vec{x}.yA_{\mathcal{A}_1} \ldots A_{\mathcal{A}_n}$ $(n \geq 0)$.

The set $\mathbb{B}$ of Böhm-like trees is a (coherent algebraic) cpo with respect to the order relation $\subseteq$ defined by:
$\mathcal{A} \subseteq \mathcal{B} \Leftrightarrow \mathcal{A}$ results from $\mathcal{B}$ by cutting off some subtrees (where $\mathcal{A},\mathcal{B} \in \mathbb{B}$).
Following [Barendregt 1984, 19.3] let $\mathfrak{B} = \langle \mathbb{B}, \cdot, \mathcal{I} \rangle$ where $\mathcal{I} = BT(\lambda xy.xy)$ and "$\cdot$" is defined by:
$\mathcal{A} \cdot \mathcal{B} = \bigcup_{k \in \omega} BT\,(A_{\mathcal{A}^k}\, A_{\mathcal{B}^k})$ for $\mathcal{A},\mathcal{B} \in \mathbb{B}$.

As proposed in [Hindley 83-a], given a λ-Ω-term M we can extend any basis B to a basis B^+ which contains infinitely many statements $\sigma x_{\sigma,i}$ for all $\sigma \in T$ and $i \in \omega$, where the variables $x_{\sigma,i}$ are all distinct and do not occur in B and M. Notice that $B \vdash \sigma M$ iff $B^+ \vdash \sigma M$.
Let Var denote the set of term variables.

2.8. *Definition*. (i) For all $\sigma \in T$ define $\mathcal{V}_0(\sigma) = \{\mathcal{A} \in \mathbb{B} \mid \forall k\ B^+ \vdash \sigma A_{\mathcal{A}^k}\}$.
(ii) ξ_0: Var$\to\mathbb{B}$ is the environment defined by $\xi_0(x) = BT(x)$.

It is easy to verify that $[\![M]\!]^{\mathfrak{B}}_{\xi_0} = BT(M)$.
We must show that Definition 2.8 (i) is correct, i.e. that $\mathcal{V}_0$ satisfies the conditions given in 2.5.

2.9. *Lemma*. (i) $\mathcal{V}_0$ is a type interpretation.
(ii) $BT(A) \in \mathcal{V}_0(\sigma) \Leftrightarrow B^+ \vdash \sigma A$.
(iii) $\mathfrak{B}, \xi_0, \mathcal{V}_0 \models B$.
Proof. (i). First we show that $\mathcal{V}_0(\sigma)$ is an ideal.
$\mathcal{A} \subseteq \mathcal{B} \Rightarrow \forall k\ A_{\mathcal{A}^k} \sqsubseteq A_{\mathcal{B}^k}$ by 14.3.11 of [Barendregt 84] .

$\mathbf{b}\in\mathcal{V}_0(\sigma) \Rightarrow \forall k\ B^+ \vdash \sigma A_{\mathbf{b}^k}$.

$\forall k\ A_{\mathbf{a}^k} \sqsubseteq A_{\mathbf{b}^k}$ and $B^+ \vdash \sigma A_{\mathbf{b}^k} \Rightarrow \forall k\ B^+ \vdash \sigma A_{\mathbf{a}^k}$ by 2.4(ii)

$\Rightarrow \mathbf{a}\in\mathcal{V}_0(\sigma)$ by 2.8(i).

Let $\mathbf{a}=\bigcup_{i\in\omega}\mathbf{b}_i$ be a direct union and $\mathbf{b}_i\in\mathcal{V}_0(\sigma)$ for all i.

$\mathbf{a}=\bigcup_{i\in\omega}\mathbf{b}_i \Rightarrow \forall k\ \mathbf{a}^k \subseteq \bigcup_{i\in\omega}\mathbf{b}^k_i$

$\Rightarrow \forall k\ \exists j\ \mathbf{a}^k \subseteq \mathbf{b}^k_j$ since $\mathbf{a}^k$ is a compact element of $\mathbf{a}$ [Barendregt 84, p.488]

$\Rightarrow \mathbf{a}\in\mathcal{V}_0(\sigma)$ as before since $\mathbf{b}_j\in\mathcal{V}_0(\sigma)$.

So we can conclude that $\mathcal{V}_0(\sigma)$ is an ideal.

$\mathbf{a}\in\mathcal{V}_0(\sigma\to\tau)$ and $\mathbf{b}\in\mathcal{V}_0(\sigma) \Rightarrow \forall k\ B^+ \vdash \sigma\to\tau A_{\mathbf{a}^k}$ and $B^+ \vdash \sigma A_{\mathbf{b}^k}$

$\Rightarrow \forall k\ B^+ \vdash \tau A_{\mathbf{a}^k} A_{\mathbf{b}^k}$ by rule $(\to E)$.

Barendregt in [Barendregt 84, proof of 18.3.4] shows that $\forall k\ \exists j\ A_{(\mathbf{a}\cdot\mathbf{b})^k} \sqsubseteq A_{\mathbf{a}^j} A_{\mathbf{b}^j}$.

So we may conclude by 2.4(ii) $\forall k\ B^+ \vdash \tau A_{(\mathbf{a}\cdot\mathbf{b})^k}$ which implies $\mathbf{a}\cdot\mathbf{b}\in\mathcal{V}_0(\tau)$.

For all $\mathbf{b}\in\mathcal{V}_0(\sigma)$ $\mathbf{a}\cdot\mathbf{b}\in\mathcal{V}_0(\tau) \Rightarrow \mathbf{c}\equiv\mathbf{a}\cdot BT(z)\in\mathcal{V}_0(\tau)$ where $\sigma z\in B^+$ and $z\notin FV(B)$

$\Rightarrow \forall k\ B^+ \vdash \tau A_{\mathbf{c}^k}$

$\Rightarrow \forall k\ B^+ \vdash \sigma\to\tau\ \lambda z.A_{\mathbf{c}^k}$ by rule $(\to I)$.

$\mathbf{a}\cdot\mathbf{c} = \bigcup_{k\in\omega} BT(A_{\mathbf{a}^k}A_{\mathbf{c}^k}) = \bigcup_{k\in\omega} BT(\lambda z.A_{\mathbf{c}^k}z)$ since $A_{\mathbf{c}^k} \equiv \lambda yz.yz$ for k>1.

Therefore $A_{(\mathbf{a}\cdot\mathbf{c})^k} =_{\beta\Omega} \lambda z.A_{\mathbf{c}^k}$ and we conclude $\mathbf{a}\cdot\mathbf{c}\in\mathcal{V}_0(\sigma\to\tau)$.

$\mathbf{a}\in\mathcal{V}_0(\forall\varphi.\sigma) \Leftrightarrow \forall k\ B^+ \vdash \forall\varphi.\sigma A_{\mathbf{a}^k}$

$\Leftrightarrow \forall k\ \forall\tau\ B^+ \vdash \sigma[\tau/\varphi] A_{\mathbf{a}^k}$ by rules $(\forall E)$ and $(\forall I)$

$\Leftrightarrow \mathbf{a}\in \bigcap_{\tau\in T}\mathcal{V}_0(\sigma[\tau/\varphi])$.

(ii)and (iii). Easy.□

The desired completeness result can easily be stated now.

2.10. *Theorem.* (Completeness). (i) $\mathbf{B}, B \models \sigma M \Rightarrow B \vdash \sigma M$.
(ii) $B \models \sigma M \Rightarrow B \vdash \sigma M$.

Proof. (i) $\mathbf{B}, B \models \sigma M \Rightarrow [\![M]\!]^{\mathbf{B}}_{\xi_0}\in\mathcal{V}(\sigma)$ by 2.9(iii)

$\Rightarrow BT(M)\in\mathcal{V}(\sigma)$

$\Rightarrow \forall A\in\mathcal{A}(M)\ BT(A)\in\mathcal{V}(\sigma)$ since $BT(A)\subseteq BT(M)$

$\Rightarrow \forall A\in\mathcal{A}(M)\ B^+ \vdash \sigma A$ by 2.9(ii)

$\Rightarrow B^+ \vdash \sigma M$ by rule (C)

$\Rightarrow B \vdash \sigma M$.

(ii) Immediate from (i). □

2.4. *Simple Semantic.*

As suggested in [Mitchell 85] the typing rule

$$\text{(simple)} \qquad \frac{\sigma\to\tau\ \lambda x.Mx}{\sigma\to\tau M} \qquad \text{where } x\notin FV(M)$$

is sound for simple type interpretations since $(\lambda x.Mx)y =_\beta My$ whenever $x\notin FV(M)$. (simple) is not a derived rule of the $\forall\forall$ type assignment, since for example $\{\sigma\to\tau x\} \vdash (\forall\varphi.\varphi)\to\tau\ \lambda y.xy$ but $\{\sigma\to\tau x\} \nvdash (\forall\varphi.\varphi)\to\tau\ x$.
We write $B \vdash_S \sigma M$ if σM is derivable from B using the rules of 2.2(ii) together with rule (simple). $\mathcal{D}$: $B \vdash_S \sigma M$ is as in 2.2 (iii).
It is useful to show that $(\sqsubseteq)$ is a derived rule of the $\vdash_S$ type assignment.

2.11. *Theorem.* (i) $B \vdash_S \sigma M,\ \ M \to\!\!>_\beta M' \Rightarrow B \vdash_S \sigma M'$.
(ii) $B \vdash_S \sigma M,\ \ A \sqsubseteq M \Rightarrow\ B \vdash_S \sigma A$.

The (rather technical) proof of this Theorem involves the introduction of another system of type assigment and it is given in the Appendix.
2.11(ii) and rule (C) imply that also $(Eq_{\beta\Omega})$ is a derived rule of the $\vdash_S$ type assigment.

2.12. *Theorem.* (Soundness) $B \vdash_S \sigma M \Rightarrow B \models_S \sigma M$.
Proof. Easy by induction on $\mathcal{O}_S(\mathcal{D})$ where $\mathcal{D}$: $B \vdash_S \sigma M$ and $\mathcal{O}_S$ is defined similarly to $\mathcal{O}$. □

The proof of the completeness of $\vdash_S$ with respect to the simple semantics is similar to the previous one.

2.13. *Definition.* For all $\sigma\in T$ define $\mathcal{V}_S(\sigma)=\{\mathbf{a}\in\mathbf{B} \mid \forall k\ B^+ \vdash_S \sigma A_{\mathbf{a}}{}^k\}$.

2.14. *Lemma.* (i) $\mathcal{V}_S$ is a simple type interpretation.
(ii) $BT(A) \in \mathcal{V}_S(\sigma) \Leftrightarrow B^+ \vdash_S \sigma A$.
(iii) $\mathbf{B},\xi_0,\mathcal{V}_S \models B$.
Proof. (i) We can prove that $\mathcal{V}_S$ is a type interpretation just mimicing the proof of 2.9(i) using 2.11(ii) instead of 2.4(ii).
To show that $\mathcal{V}_S$ is simple notice that, if $\mathbf{a},\mathbf{e},z$ are as in the proof of 2.9(i):

$$\begin{aligned}\forall k\ B^+ \vdash_S \sigma\to\tau\ \lambda z.A_{\mathbf{e}}{}^k &\Rightarrow \forall k\ B^+ \vdash_S \sigma\to\tau\ \lambda z.A_{\mathbf{a}}{}^k z \text{ by } (Eq_{\beta\Omega})\\ &\Rightarrow \forall k\ B^+ \vdash \sigma\to\tau\ \ A_{\mathbf{a}}{}^k \text{ by (simple)}\\ &\Rightarrow \mathbf{a}\in\mathcal{V}_S(\sigma\to\tau).\end{aligned}$$

(ii) and (iii). Easy. □

2.15. *Theorem* (Completeness). (i) $\mathbf{B}, B \models_S \sigma M \Rightarrow B \vdash_S \sigma M$.

(ii) $B \models_S \sigma M \Rightarrow B \vdash_S \sigma M$.

Proof. (i) Similar to the proof of 2.10(i).

(ii). Immediate from (i). □

2.5. *$\mathcal{F}$-semantics.*

It is easy to verify that the rule

$$\frac{\forall\varphi.\varphi M}{\forall\varphi.\varphi\ \lambda z.Mz} \quad \text{where } z \notin FV(M)$$

is sound for the $\mathbf{F}$ type interpretations since $[\![M]\!]^{\mathcal{M}}_{\xi} \in \bigcap_{\sigma \in T} \mathcal{V}(\sigma)$ implies $[\![M]\!]^{\mathcal{M}}_{\xi} \in \mathbf{F}$.

This argument can be generalized. Let us define *fin*: $T \rightarrow \{$*true*, *false*$\}$ by induction on types:

fin(φ) = *fin*$(\forall\psi.\psi)$ = *true*

fin$(\forall\varphi.\varphi)$ = *fin*$(\sigma \rightarrow \tau)$ = *fin*$(\forall\varphi.\sigma \rightarrow \tau)$ = *false*

fin$(\forall\varphi.\forall\psi.\sigma)$ = *fin*$(\forall\varphi.\sigma)$ *and* *fin*$(\forall\psi.\sigma)$

where $\varphi, \psi \in V$ with $\varphi \not\equiv \psi$ and $\sigma, \tau \in T$.

Informally *fin*(σ) = *false* means that $\sigma \equiv \forall\vec{\varphi}.\tau$ and there are $\vec{\rho}, \mu, \nu$ such that $\tau[\vec{\rho}/\vec{\varphi}] \equiv \mu \rightarrow \nu$. Then also the rule

$$(\mathbf{F}) \quad \frac{\sigma M \quad fin(\sigma) = false}{\sigma\ \lambda z.Mz} \quad \text{where } z \notin FV(M)$$

is sound for $\mathbf{F}$ type interpretations.

It is easy to verify that the type assignment obtained by adding rule ($\mathbf{F}$) to the rules of 2.2(ii) is not complete since it does not preserve types under $\sqsubseteq$ between terms. For example from $\{\forall\varphi.\varphi x\}$ we can deduce $\forall\varphi.\varphi\ \lambda z.xz$ but we cannot deduce $\forall\varphi.\varphi\ \lambda z.x\Omega$. Therefore we consider the type assignment whose rules are the rules of 2.2(ii) together with rules ($\mathbf{F}$) and ($\sqsubseteq$). We write $B \vdash_{\mathcal{F}} \sigma M$ if σM is derivable from B in this type assigment. It is clear that $(Eq_{\beta\Omega})$ is a derived rule of $\vdash_{\mathcal{F}}$.

2.16. *Theorem.* (Soundness) $B \vdash_{\mathcal{F}} \sigma M \Rightarrow B \models_{\mathcal{F}} \sigma M$.

We do not know whether $\vdash_{\mathcal{F}}$ is complete with respect to the $\mathbf{F}$-semantics.

3. *The $\wedge\forall$ discipline.*

3.1. *Type assignment.*

3.1. *Definition* . (i) The set T^* of *intersection types* is the minimal set such that:

1. $V \subseteq T^*$
2. $\sigma,\tau \in T^* \Rightarrow \sigma\rightarrow\tau,\ \sigma\wedge\tau \in T^*$.

(ii) The preorder relation $\leq$ on T^* is the smallest relation satisfying:

1. $\sigma \leq \sigma\wedge\sigma$
2. $\sigma\wedge\tau \leq \sigma,\ \sigma\wedge\tau \leq \tau$
3. $(\sigma\rightarrow\tau)\wedge(\sigma\rightarrow\tau') \leq \sigma\rightarrow(\tau\wedge\tau')$
4. $\sigma \leq \sigma',\ \tau \leq \tau' \Rightarrow \sigma\wedge\tau \leq \sigma'\wedge\tau'$
5. $\sigma \leq \sigma',\ \tau' \leq \tau \Rightarrow \sigma'\rightarrow\tau' \leq \sigma\rightarrow\tau$

plus reflexivity and transitivity.

(iii) $\sigma\sim\tau$ iff $\sigma \leq \tau \leq \sigma$.

We write equality "=" between types with the conventions that $\sigma\wedge\tau=\tau\wedge\sigma$ and $(\sigma\rightarrow\tau)\wedge(\sigma\rightarrow\tau') = \sigma\rightarrow(\tau\wedge\tau')$. I, J, H, ... denote finite sets and $\wedge_I\, \sigma_i$ is short for $\wedge_{i\in I}\sigma_i$.
The definitions of intersection statement and basis are standard.

3.2. *Definition.* (i) The *∧∀ type assignment* is obtained from the ∀∀ type assignment of 2.2(ii) by replacing rules (∀I) and (∀E) by the following rules:

$$(\wedge I)\ \frac{\sigma M \quad \tau M}{\sigma\wedge\tau M} \qquad (\wedge E)\ \frac{\sigma\wedge\tau M}{\sigma M} \quad \frac{\sigma\wedge\tau M}{\tau M}$$

$$(\leq)\ \frac{\sigma M \quad \sigma\leq\tau}{\tau M}.$$

(ii) If σM is derivable from a basis B in the ∧∀ type assignment, then we write $B \vdash^* \sigma M$. *D*: $B \vdash^* \sigma M$ is defined as usual.

Rule (∧E) is superfluous since it is directly derivable from rule ($\leq$).

3.2. *Type semantics.*

As in previous section, we need a continuous λ-model in which types are interpreted as ideals. The definition of type interpretation can be easily obtained from Definition 2.5 by replacing T by T^* and condition (4) by:

$$(4^*)\ \mathcal{V}(\sigma\wedge\tau) = \mathcal{V}(\sigma)\cap\mathcal{V}(\tau).$$

The conditions for a type interpretation to be simple or $\mathcal{F}$ remain unchanged.

The notions of semantic satisfability induced by these type interpretations are as in Definition 2.6 and will be denoted by $\models^*$, $\models^*_S$, $\models^*_{\mathcal{F}}$.

3.3. *Inference and simple semantics.*

The soundness of $\vdash^*$ can be easily proved.

3.3. *Theorem.* (Soundness).(i) $\sigma\leq\tau \Rightarrow \forall\mathcal{M}$ and $\mathcal{V}$ $\mathcal{V}(\sigma)\subseteq\mathcal{V}(\tau)$.

(ii). $B \vdash^* \sigma M \Rightarrow B \models^* \sigma M$.

Proof. (i). By induction on $\leq$.

(ii). By transfinite induction on the ordinals associated with deductions (in the obvious way). For rule ($\leq$) use (i).□

The continuous λ-model we use to prove completeness is P_ω [Scott 76, Barendregt 1984, 18.1] . We recall here the basic concepts concerning P_ω. $P_\omega = \{x \mid x \subseteq \omega\}$ is the power set of ω, partially ordered by set inclusion $\subseteq$. (m,n) represents the coding of the pair of integer m,n whereas e_n denotes the finite set of ω coded by n (we assume the standard coding of [Barendregt 1984, 18.1]). The abstraction and application in P_ω are defined as follows:

$$\lambda z.t = \{(n,m) \mid m \in t[e_n/z]\}$$

$$x \cdot y = \{m \mid \exists e_n \subseteq y\ (n,m) \in x\}.$$

An element x of P_ω is *saturated* iff $(n,m) \in x$ and $e_n \subseteq e_k$ imply $(k,m) \in x$. Notice that each element x of P_ω such that $x = \lambda z.t$ is saturated.

Following [Coppo 1984] we define, for each type $\sigma \in T^*$, an element $t_\sigma \in P_\omega$ which induces the principal ideal interpreting σ.

3.4. *Definition.* If $\sigma \in T^*$, $t_\sigma \in P_\omega$ is inductively defined by:

1. $t_{\varphi i} = \{(0,n) \mid n \in \omega\} \cup \{(2n,0) \mid n \neq i\} \quad (i > 0)$
2. $t_{\sigma \to \tau}$ is the representative of the continuous function f such that

$$f(x) = \begin{cases} t_\tau \text{ if } x \subseteq t_\sigma \\ \omega \text{ otherwise} \end{cases}$$

3. $t_{\sigma \wedge \tau} = t_\sigma \cap t_\tau$.

It is easy to verify by induction on σ that $t_\sigma \neq \omega$, $t_\sigma \neq \{0\}$ and $0 \in t_\sigma$ for all σ. From $0 = (0,0) \in t_{\sigma \to \tau}$ we have $\forall n\ (n,0) \in t_{\sigma \to \tau}$ since $t_{\sigma \to \tau}$ is saturated for all σ, τ.

3.5. *Lemma.* (i) All the subsets of $t_{\varphi i}$ are not saturated.

(ii) $\forall x \quad t_{\varphi i} \cdot x = \omega$.

(iii) $\forall \sigma \quad t_\sigma \cdot x \neq \omega \Rightarrow \exists\, \tau$ such that $t_\sigma \cdot x = t_\tau$.

(iv) $\forall \sigma, \tau\ t_\sigma \subseteq t_\tau \Leftrightarrow \sigma \leq \tau$.

Proof. (i). Notice that $e_{2n} \cup \{0\}$ is coded by 2n + 1.

(ii). Immediate from 3.4 (1).

(iii). Let $\sigma = (\wedge_I\ \varphi_i) \wedge (\wedge_J\ \mu_j \to \nu_j)$. It is easy to verify that:

$$t_\sigma \cdot x = \begin{cases} \cap_H\, t_{\nu h} = t_{\wedge_H \nu h} \text{ if } \exists H \subseteq J,\ H \neq \Phi \text{ such that } x \subseteq \cap_H\, t_{\mu h} \\ \omega \text{ otherwise.} \end{cases}$$

(iv). (⇐). Easy by induction on the definition of $\leq$.

(⇒). Let $\sigma = (\wedge_I \varphi_i) \wedge (\wedge_J \mu_j \to \nu_j)$. The proof is by induction on σ and τ.

Case 1. $\tau \equiv \varphi_h$. If $h \in I$ then $\sigma \leq \tau$. $h \notin I$ is impossible since, in this case, we would have $(2h,0) \in t_\sigma$ and $(2h,0) \notin t_{\varphi h}$.

Case 2. $\tau \equiv \mu \to \nu$.

$t_\sigma \subseteq t_\tau \Rightarrow \forall x\ t_\sigma \cdot x \subseteq t_\tau \cdot x$

$\Rightarrow t_\sigma \cdot t_\mu \subseteq t_\nu$

$\Rightarrow \exists H \subseteq J, H \neq \Phi$ such that $\cap_H t_{\mu h} \supseteq t_\mu$ and $\cap_H t_{\nu h} \subseteq t_\nu$

$\Rightarrow \exists H \subseteq J, H \neq \Phi$ such that $\wedge_H \mu_h \geq \mu$ and $\wedge_H \nu_h \leq \nu$ by the induction hypothesis

$\Rightarrow \sigma \leq \tau$.

Case 3. $\tau \equiv \mu \wedge \nu$. Easy by induction. □

3.6. *Definition.* (i) For all $\sigma \in T^*$ define $\mathcal{V}_*(\sigma) = \{x \in P_\omega \mid x \subseteq t_\sigma\}$.

(ii) Given a basis B define

$$\xi_B(x) = \begin{cases} t_\sigma & \text{if } \sigma x \in B \\ \omega & \text{otherwise.} \end{cases}$$

We must prove that our definition of $\mathcal{V}_*$ is correct, i.e. that $\mathcal{V}_*$ is a type interpretation. Really, $\mathcal{V}_*$ turns out to be a simple type interpretation.

3.7. *Lemma.* (i) $\mathcal{V}_*$ is a simple type interpretation.

(ii) $[\![A]\!]^{P\omega}_{\xi_B} \in \mathcal{V}_*(\sigma) \Leftrightarrow B \vdash^* \sigma A$.

(iii) $P_\omega, \xi_B, \mathcal{V}_* \models^* B$.

Proof. (i) $\mathcal{V}_*(\sigma)$ is obviously the principal ideal generated by t_σ.

$x \in \mathcal{V}_*(\sigma \to \tau) \Rightarrow x \subseteq t_{\sigma \to \tau}$

$\Rightarrow \forall y \in P_\omega\ x \cdot y \subseteq t_{\sigma \to \tau} \cdot y$ by monotonicity

$\Rightarrow \forall y \subseteq t_\sigma\ x \cdot y \subseteq t_\tau$ by 3.4 (2)

$\Rightarrow \forall y \in \mathcal{V}_*(\sigma)\ x \cdot y \in \mathcal{V}_*(\tau)$.

$\forall y \in \mathcal{V}_*(\sigma)\ x \cdot y \in \mathcal{V}_*(\tau) \Rightarrow \forall y \subseteq t_\sigma\ x \cdot y \subseteq t_\tau$

$\Rightarrow \forall y \in P_\omega\ x \cdot y \subseteq t_{\sigma \to \tau} \cdot y$ by 3.4 (2)

$\Rightarrow \epsilon \cdot x \subseteq \epsilon \cdot t_{\sigma \to \tau}$ by definition of λ-model

$\Rightarrow x \subseteq t_{\sigma \to \tau}$ since $x \subseteq \epsilon \cdot x$ and $t_{\sigma \to \tau} = \epsilon \cdot t_{\sigma \to \tau}$ (cf. [Barendregt 84,18.1.9,18.1.10])

$\Rightarrow x \in \mathcal{V}_*(\sigma \to \tau)$.

$\mathcal{V}_*(\sigma\wedge\tau) = \{x \mid x\subseteq t_{\sigma\wedge\tau}\} = \{x \mid x\subseteq t_\sigma \text{ and } x\subseteq t_\tau\} = \mathcal{V}_*(\sigma)\cap\mathcal{V}_*(\tau)$.

(ii). ($\Rightarrow$). By induction on A.

$A\equiv\Omega$. Trivial.

$A\equiv x$. $[\![x]\!]^{P\omega}_{\xi B}\in \mathcal{V}_*(\sigma) \Rightarrow [\![x]\!]^{P\omega}_{\xi B}\subseteq t_\sigma$

$\Rightarrow \exists\tau x\in B$: $t_\tau\subseteq t_\sigma$

$\Rightarrow \exists\tau x\in B$ $\tau\leq\sigma$ by 3.5 (iv)

$\Rightarrow B \vdash^* \sigma x$ by rule ($\leq$).

$A\equiv\lambda x.A'$. By induction on σ.

$\sigma\equiv\varphi_i$. Impossible by 3.5 (i).

$\sigma\equiv\rho\rightarrow\tau$.

$[\![\lambda x.A']\!]^{P\omega}_{\xi B}\in\mathcal{V}_*(\rho\rightarrow\tau) \Rightarrow [\![A']\!]^{P\omega}_{\xi B[t\rho/x]}\in\mathcal{V}_*(\tau)$

$\Rightarrow B/x \cup\{\rho x\} \vdash^* \tau A'$ by the induction hypothesis

$\Rightarrow B \vdash^* \rho\rightarrow\tau\ \lambda x.A'$ by rule ($\rightarrow$).

$\sigma\equiv\rho\wedge\tau$. Easy by induction.

$A\equiv xA_1...A_n (n>0)$:

$[\![A]\!]^{P\omega}_{\xi B}\in\mathcal{V}_*(\sigma) \Rightarrow \exists\tau x \in B : t_\tau\cdot[\![A_1]\!]^{P\omega}_{\xi B}\cdot...\cdot[\![A_n]\!]^{P\omega}_{\xi B}\in\mathcal{V}_*(\sigma)$.

Let $\tau = (\wedge_I\varphi_i)\wedge(\wedge_J\mu_j\rightarrow\nu_j)$.

$t_\tau\cdot[\![A_1]\!]^{P\omega}_{\xi B}\cdot...\cdot[\![A_n]\!]^{P\omega}_{\xi B}\subseteq\mathcal{V}_*(\sigma) \Rightarrow \exists H\subseteq J$, $H\neq\Phi$ such that $[\![A_1]\!]^{P\omega}_{\xi B}\subseteq\cap_H t_{\mu h}$ and

$(\cap_H t_{\nu h})\cdot[\![A_2]\!]^{P\omega}_{\xi B}\cdot...\cdot[\![A_n]\!]^{P\omega}_{\xi B}\in\mathcal{V}_*(\sigma)$.

Let $\nu \equiv \wedge_H\nu_h$.

$[\![A_1]\!]^{P\omega}_{\xi B}\subseteq t_{\mu h} \Rightarrow [\![A_1]\!]^{P\omega}_{\xi B}\in\mathcal{V}_*(\mu_h)$

$\Rightarrow B \vdash^* \mu_h A_1$ by the induction hypothesis

$\Rightarrow B \vdash^* \nu x A_1$ by rules ($\leq$), ($\rightarrow$E) and ($\wedge$I).

$(\cap_H t_{\nu h})\cdot[\![A_2]\!]^{P\omega}_{\xi B}\cdot...\cdot[\![A_n]\!]^{P\omega}_{\xi B}\in\mathcal{V}_*(\sigma) \Rightarrow [\![yA_2...A_n]\!]^{P\omega}_{\xi B[t\nu/y]}\in\mathcal{V}_*(\sigma)$

$\Rightarrow B/y\cup\{\nu y\} \vdash^* \sigma yA_2...A_n$ by the induction hypothesis.

Then we can obtain a deduction of $B \vdash^* \sigma A$ by replacing the premise νy by a deduction of $B \vdash^* \nu xA_1$ and y by xA_1 in $\mathcal{D}$: $B/y\cup\{\nu y\} \vdash^* \sigma yA_2...A_n$.

($\Rightarrow$). Immediate from 3.3 (ii).

(iii). Easy. □

Now we can state the completeness result.

3.8. *Theorem*.(Completeness). (i) P_ω, $B \models^*_s \sigma M \Rightarrow B \vdash^* \sigma M$.

(ii) $B \models^*_s \sigma M \Rightarrow B \vdash^* \sigma M$.

Proof. (i) P_ω, $B \models^*_s \sigma M \Rightarrow [\![M]\!]^{P\omega}_{\xi B}\in\mathcal{V}_*(\sigma)$ by 3.7(iii)

$\Rightarrow \forall A\in\mathcal{A}(M)\ [\![A]\!]^{P\omega}_{\xi B}\in\mathcal{V}_*(\sigma)$ since $[\![A]\!]^{P\omega}_{\xi B}\subseteq[\![M]\!]^{P\omega}_{\xi B}$

$\Rightarrow \forall A \in \mathcal{A}(M)\ B \vdash^* \sigma A$ by 3.7 (ii)

$\Rightarrow B \vdash^* \sigma M$ by rule (C).

(ii) Immediate from (i). □

As a consequence of 3.3 and 3.8 we have that rules ($\leq$), ($Eq_{\beta\Omega}$) and (simple) are derived rules of the $\wedge\forall$ type assignment.

3.4. *$\mathcal{F}$-semantics.*

It is easy to see that the rule:

$$(\mathcal{F}^*)\ \frac{\varphi \wedge \sigma \to \tau M}{\varphi \lambda z.Mz} \qquad \text{where } z \notin FV(M)$$

is sound for the $\mathcal{F}$ type interpretations since $\forall \mathcal{V}\ \mathcal{V}(\sigma \to \tau) \subseteq \mathcal{F}$.

The type assignment obtained by adding rule ($\mathcal{F}^*$) to the rules of 3.2 (i) is not complete, since ($\leq$) is not a derived rule. For example from $\{\varphi \wedge \sigma \to \tau x\}$ we can deduce $\varphi\ \lambda z.xz$ but we cannot deduce $\varphi\ \lambda z.x\Omega$. Moreover, types are not invariant under β-expansion of λ-Ω-terms. For example from $\varphi \wedge \sigma \to \tau x$ we deduce $\varphi\ \lambda z.xz$, but we cannot deduce $\varphi\ \lambda z.(\lambda u.xz)v$. Therefore it is natural to consider the rules of 3.2(i) together with ($\mathcal{F}^*$) and ($\leq$).

We write $B \vdash^*_{\mathcal{F}} \sigma M$ if σM is derivable from B is this type assignment. It is immediate to prove that ($Eq_{\beta\Omega}$) is a derived rule of this type assignment.

3.9. *Theorem.* (Soundness). $B \vdash^*_{\mathcal{F}} \sigma M \Rightarrow B \models^*_{\mathcal{F}} \sigma M$.

We do not know whether $\vdash^*_{\mathcal{F}}$ is complete with respect to the $\mathcal{F}$-semantics.

Instead, in the rest of the paper we prove the completeness with respect to the $\mathcal{F}$-semantics of a type assignment where we allow "restricted types" only. Types are restricted since the intersection can be applied only to types which have the same number of arrows. Note that in the so obtained formal system rule ($\mathcal{F}^*$) does not have any meaning since $\varphi \wedge \sigma \to \tau$ is not a restricted type.

3.10. *Definition.* (i) $|\ |: T^* \to \omega$ is defined by:

$|\varphi| = 0$

$|\sigma \to \tau| = 1 + |\tau|$

$|\sigma \wedge \tau| = \max(|\sigma|, |\tau|)$.

(ii) The set $RT \subseteq T^*$ of restricted types is the minimal set such that

1. $V \subseteq RT$
2. $\sigma, \tau \in RT \Rightarrow \sigma \to \tau \in RT$
3. $\sigma, \tau \in RT$ and $|\sigma| = |\tau| \Rightarrow \sigma \wedge \tau \in RT$.

(iii) $\sigma \leq_R \tau$ iff $\sigma, \tau \in RT$ and $\sigma \leq \tau$. $\sigma \sim_R \tau$ iff $\sigma \leq_R \tau \leq_R \tau$.

(iv) A *restricted basis* B is a basis such that all predicates are restricted types.

(v) $B \vdash^R \tau M$ iff τM is derivable from the restricted basis B in type assignment obtained from the $\wedge\forall$ type assignment of 3.2.(i) by replacing $\leq$ by $\leq_R$ and by restricting rule ($\wedge$I) as follows:

$$(\wedge I')\ \frac{\sigma M \quad \tau M \quad |\sigma|=|\tau|}{\sigma\wedge\tau M}\ .$$

We prove that when B is restricted and $\tau\in RT$, $\vdash^*$ and $\vdash^R$ have the same expressive power. This result looks relevant and rather unexpected.

3.11. *Lemma.* (i) $(\wedge_I\mu_i\to\nu_i)\wedge(\wedge_H\varphi_h)\leq\sigma\to\tau\wedge\rho \Rightarrow \exists J\subseteq I$ such that $\sigma\leq\wedge_J\mu_j$ and $\wedge_J\nu_j\leq\tau$.
(ii) $\rho\leq\sigma_1\to\sigma_2\to\ldots\to\sigma_m\to\tau \Rightarrow \rho=(\wedge_J\mu_1^{(j)}\to\ldots\to\mu_m^{(j)}\to\nu^{(j)})\wedge\rho'$, $\sigma_i\leq\wedge_J\mu_i^{(j)}$ $(1\leq i\leq m)$ and $\wedge_J\nu^{(j)}\leq\tau$ for some $\mu_i^{(j)}$, $\nu^{(j)}$ and ρ' $(1\leq i\leq m)$ $(j\in J)$.
(iii) $B\vdash^* \tau x\vec{A} \Rightarrow \exists\sigma_1,\ldots,\sigma_n$ $B\vdash^*\sigma_i A_i$ $(1\leq i\leq n)$ and $B\vdash^*\sigma_1\to\ldots\to\sigma_n\to\tau x$.
(iv) $B\vdash^* \sigma\to\tau\wedge\rho\ \lambda x.A \Rightarrow B/x\cup\{\sigma x\}\vdash^*\tau A$.
Proof. (i). By induction on $\leq$.
(ii). By induction on m. Let $\tau\equiv\sigma_{m+1}\to\tau'$. By the induction hypothesis $\rho=(\wedge_K\mu_1^{(k)}\to\ldots\to\mu_m^{(k)}\to\nu^{(k)})\wedge\rho'$ and $\sigma_i\leq\wedge_K\mu_i^{(k)}$ $(1\leq i\leq m)$, $\wedge_K\nu^{(k)}\leq\tau$. Without loss of generality we can assume $\wedge_K\nu^{(k)}=(\wedge_P\alpha_p\to\beta_p)\wedge(\wedge_H\varphi_h)$. By (i) this implies $\exists Q\subseteq P$ such that $\sigma_{m+1}\leq\wedge_Q\alpha_q$ and $\wedge_Q\beta_q\leq\tau'$. Therefore we can conclude:
$\rho=(\wedge_Q\mu_1^{(\chi(q))}\to\ldots\to\mu_m^{(\chi(q))}\to\alpha_q\to\beta_q)\wedge\rho'$ where $\chi(q)=k$ implies $\nu^{(k)}=(\alpha_q\to\beta_q)\wedge\overline{\nu}^{(k)}$ for some $\overline{\nu}^{(k)}$.
(iii) and (iv). Easy using 3.7(ii). □

3.12. *Theorem.* (i) Let B be a restricted basis and $\tau\in RT$. Then $B\vdash^*\tau M \Leftrightarrow B\vdash^R\tau M$.
(ii) $B\vdash^R\tau M$ and $A\sqsubseteq M \Rightarrow B\vdash^R\tau A$.
Proof. ($\Leftarrow$). Obvious.
($\Rightarrow$). Notice that $B\vdash^*\tau M$ and $A\sqsubseteq M$ imply $B\vdash^*\tau A$ by 3.3 and 3.8. We prove by induction on A that $B\vdash^R\tau A$ and we conclude $B\vdash^R\tau M$ using rule (C).
$A\equiv xA_1\ldots A_m (m\geq0)$.
$B\vdash^*\tau xA_1\ldots A_m \Rightarrow \exists\sigma_1,\ldots,\sigma_m$ such that $B\vdash^*\sigma_i A_i$ $(1\leq i\leq m)$ and $B\vdash^*\sigma_1\to\sigma_2\to\ldots\to\sigma_m\to\tau x$ by Lemma 3.11(iii).
$B\vdash^*\sigma_1\to\ldots\to\sigma_m\to\tau x \Rightarrow \exists\rho x\in B$ such that $\rho\leq\sigma_1\to\ldots\to\sigma_m\to\tau$
$\Rightarrow\rho=(\wedge_J\mu_1^{(j)}\to\ldots\to\mu_m^{(j)}\to\nu^{(j)})\wedge\rho'$, $\sigma_i\leq\mu_i^{(j)}$ $(1\leq i\leq m)$ $(j\in J)$ and $\wedge_J\nu^{(j)}\leq\tau$ by Lemma 3.11(ii).
$B\vdash^*\sigma_i A_i \Rightarrow B\vdash^*\mu_i^{(j)}A_i$ $(j\in J)$ by $(\leq)$
$\Rightarrow B\vdash^R\mu_i^{(j)}A_i$ $(j\in J)$ by the induction hypothesis since $\mu_i^{(j)}\in RT$.
Therefore we obtain a deduction of $B\vdash^R\tau A$ as follows:

$$\rho x$$
$$\overline{\qquad\qquad\qquad} (\leq_R)$$
$$\mu_1^{(j)}\to\ldots\to\mu_m^{(j)}\to\nu^{(j)}x \qquad\qquad \vdots \qquad\qquad \mu_1^{(j)}A_1$$
$$\overline{\qquad\qquad\qquad\qquad\qquad\qquad\qquad\qquad} (\to E)$$
$$\mu_2^{(j)}\to\ldots\to\mu_m^{(j)}\to\nu^{(j)}\,xA_1$$
$$\vdots \qquad\qquad\qquad\qquad \vdots$$
$$\mu_m^{(j)}\to\nu^{(j)}xA_1\ldots A_{m-1} \qquad\qquad \mu_m^{(j)}A_m$$
$$\overline{\qquad\qquad\qquad\qquad\qquad\qquad\qquad\qquad} (\to E)$$
$$\nu^{(j)}xA_1\ldots A_m$$
$$\overline{\qquad\qquad\qquad} (\wedge I')\ \forall j\in J$$
$$\wedge_J\nu^{(j)}xA_1\ldots A_m$$
$$\overline{\qquad\qquad\qquad} (\leq_R).$$
$$\tau xA_1\ldots A_m$$

Notice that ρ, $\wedge_J\nu^{(j)}\in RT$ since B is a restricted basis.

$A\equiv\lambda x.A'$.

$B\vdash^{*}\sigma\to\tau\wedge\rho\ \lambda x.A' \Rightarrow B/x\cup\{\sigma x\}\vdash^{*}\tau A'$ by Lemma 3.11 (iv)

$\Rightarrow B/x\cup\{\sigma x\}\vdash^{R}\tau A'$ by the induction hypothesis since $B/x\cup\{\sigma x\}$ is a restricted basis and $\tau\in RT$

$\Rightarrow B\vdash^{R}\sigma\to\tau\ \lambda x.A'$ by $(\to I)$.

(ii). $B\vdash^{*}\tau M$ and $A\sqsubseteq M\Rightarrow B\vdash^{*}\tau A$ since $(\sqsubseteq)$ is a derived rule of $\vdash^{*}$; so the statement follows by (i).□

3.13 *Theorem.* (Soundness). (i) $\sigma\leq_R\tau\Rightarrow\forall\mathcal{M}$ and $\mathcal{F}$ type interpretation $\mathcal{V}$ $\mathcal{V}(\sigma)\subseteq\mathcal{V}(\tau)$.

(ii) $B\vdash^{R}\tau M\Rightarrow B\models_{\mathcal{F}}\tau M$.

Proof. (i) By induction on $\leq_R$.

(ii) By transfinite induction on the ordinals associated with derivations. For rule $(\leq_R)$ use (i). □

We prove the completeness of $\vdash^{R}$ with respect to the $\mathcal{F}$-semantics of types using the model $\mathbf{B}$.

3.14. *Lemma.* (i) $\sigma\leq_R\tau\Rightarrow|\tau|=|\sigma|$.

(ii) $B\vdash^{R}\sigma x\underbrace{\Omega\ldots\Omega}_{m}\Rightarrow\exists\rho x\in B\ \ |\sigma|+m=|\rho|$.

Proof. (i). Easy by induction on the definition of $\leq_R$.

(ii). By transfinite induction on the ordinal associated with $\mathcal{D}$: $B\vdash^{R}\sigma x\underbrace{\Omega\ldots\Omega}_{m}$.

If the last applied rule is $(\to E)$:

$$\frac{\tau\to\sigma x\underbrace{\Omega\ldots\Omega}_{m-1} \qquad \tau\Omega}{\sigma x\underbrace{\Omega\ldots\Omega}_{m}}\ (\to E)$$

$\exists\varrho x\in B$ such that $|\tau\to\sigma|+m-1=|\sigma|+m=|\varrho|$ by the induction hypothesis.
If the last applied rule is $(\leq_R)$:

$$\frac{\tau x\underbrace{\Omega\ldots\Omega}_{m} \qquad \tau\leq_R\sigma}{\sigma x\underbrace{\Omega\ldots\Omega}_{m}}\ (\leq_R)$$

$\exists\varrho x\in B$ such that $|\tau|+m=|\varrho|$ by the induction hypothesis and $|\tau|=|\sigma|$ by (ii).
The other cases are trivial.□

Given a restricted basis B we define

$$m(x)=\begin{cases}\lambda z_1\ldots z_n.xz_1\ldots z_n & \text{if } \sigma x\in B \text{ and } |\sigma|=n\\ x & \text{otherwise.}\end{cases}$$

3.15. *Lemma.* $B\vdash^R\sigma M \Rightarrow B\vdash^R\sigma M[m(x)/x]$.
Proof. By transfinite induction on the ordinal associated with $\mathcal{D}$: $B\vdash^R\sigma M$. If $\sigma x\in B$ and $|\sigma|=n$ then $m(x)=\lambda z_1\ldots z_n.xz_1\ldots z_n$. Let $\sigma=\wedge_I\alpha_1^{(i)}\to\ \ldots\to\alpha_n^{(i)}\to\varphi^{(i)}$. We can deduce $\sigma m(x)$ as follows:

$$\frac{\dfrac{\dfrac{\sigma x}{\alpha_1^{(i)}\to\ldots\to\alpha_n^{(i)}\to\varphi^{(i)}x}\ (\leq_R) \qquad \alpha_1^{(i)}z_1}{\alpha_2^{(i)}\to\ldots\to\alpha_n^{(i)}\to\varphi^{(i)}xz_1}\ (\to E)}{\vdots}$$

$$\frac{\dfrac{\alpha_n^{(i)}\to\varphi^{(i)}xz_1\ldots z_{n-1} \qquad \alpha_n^{(i)}z_n}{\varphi^{(i)}xz_1\ldots z_n}\ (\to E)}{\alpha_n^{(i)}\to\varphi^{(i)}\lambda z_n.xz_1\ldots z_n}\ (\to I)$$

$$\frac{\qquad}{\alpha_1^{(i)}\to\ldots\to\alpha_n^{(i)}\to\varphi^{(i)}\ \lambda z_1\ldots z_n.xz_1\ldots z_n}\ (\to I)$$

$$\frac{\qquad}{\wedge_I\ \alpha_1^{(i)}\to\ldots\to\alpha_n^{(i)}\to\varphi^{(i)}\lambda z_1\ldots z_n.xz_1\ldots z_n}\ (\wedge I')\ \forall i\in I.$$

If the last applied rule is (C)

$$\frac{\sigma A \qquad \forall A\in\mathcal{A}(M)}{\sigma M}\ (C)$$

we have by definition $\mathcal{A}(M[m(x)/x]) = \{A' \mid A' \sqsubseteq A[m(x)/x] \text{ and } A\in\mathcal{A}(M)\}$.
By the induction hypothesis for all $A\in\mathcal{A}(M)$ σA implies $\sigma A[m(x)/x]$. Therefore by 3.12(ii) we have $\sigma A'$ for all $A'\in\mathcal{A}(M[m(x)/x])$.
The other cases are trivial. □

If B is a restricted basis, for any finite $\mathfrak{b}\in\mathfrak{B}$ define $\mathfrak{b}^*$ as the tree obtained by replacing each subtree of the shape

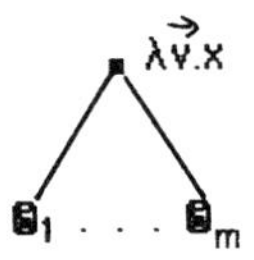

where $x\in FV(A_{\mathfrak{b}})$ and $\sigma x\in B$ with $|\sigma|=n>m$ by

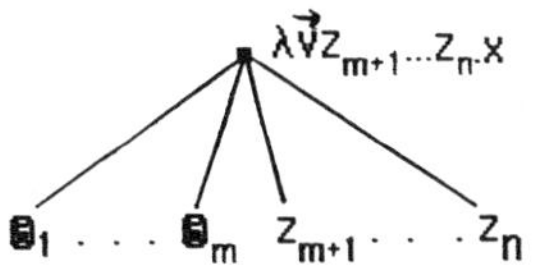

$(z_{m+1},\ldots,z_n\notin FV(A_{\mathfrak{b}}))$.

It is easy to verify that for all restricted B and all A:
$(BT(A))^* = BT(A[m(x)/x \mid \forall x\in FV(A)])$.
Given a restricted basis B and a λ-Ω-term M, $B^{\oplus}$ is the basis obtained by adding to B infinitely many statements $\sigma x_{\sigma,i}$ for all $\sigma\in RT$ and $i\in\omega$, where the variables $x_{\sigma,i}$ are all distinct and do not occur in B and M. Obviously $B \vdash^R \sigma M$ iff $B^{\oplus} \vdash^R \sigma M$.

3.16. *Definition.* (i) For all $\sigma\in RT$ define $\nu^*_{\mathfrak{F}}(\sigma)=\{\mathfrak{b}^*\in\mathfrak{B} \mid \forall k\ B^{\oplus} \vdash^R \sigma A_{\mathfrak{b}^k}\}$.
(ii) Given a restricted basis B define : $\xi^{\mathfrak{F}}_B(x) = BT(m(x))$.

It is easy to verify that $[\![A]\!]^{\mathfrak{B}}_{\xi^{\mathfrak{F}}_B} = (BT(A))^*$.

3.17. *Lemma.* Let $\sigma\in RT$ and B be a restricted basis.

(i) $\mathbb{a}\in\mathcal{V}^*_{\mathcal{F}}(\sigma) \Rightarrow \forall k\ B^{\oplus} \vdash^{R} \sigma A_{\mathbb{a}^k}$.

(ii) $\mathcal{V}^*_{\mathcal{F}}$ is an $\mathbf{F}$ type interpretation.

(iii) $[\![A]\!]^{\mathfrak{B}}_{\xi_{\mathcal{F}_B}} \in \mathcal{V}^*_{\mathcal{F}}(\sigma) \Leftrightarrow B^{\oplus} \vdash^{R} \sigma A$.

(iv) $\mathfrak{B},\xi_{\mathcal{F}},\mathcal{V}^*_{\mathcal{F}} \models B$.

Proof. (i). $\mathbb{a}\in \mathcal{V}^*_{\mathcal{F}}(\sigma) \Rightarrow \exists\mathbb{b}\in\mathbb{B}$ such that $\mathbb{a}=\mathbb{b}^*$ and $\forall k\ B^{\oplus} \vdash^{R} \sigma A_{\mathbb{b}^k}$.

$B^{\oplus} \vdash^{R} \sigma A_{\mathbb{b}^k} \Rightarrow B^{\oplus} \vdash^{R} \sigma A_{\mathbb{b}^k}[m(x)/x \mid \forall x\in FV(A_{\mathbb{b}^k})]$ by Lemma 3.15

$\Rightarrow B^{\oplus} \vdash^{R} \sigma A_{\mathbb{a}^k}$ by 3.12(ii) since $A_{\mathbb{a}^k} \sqsubseteq A_{\mathbb{b}^k}[m(x)/x \mid \forall x\in FV(A_{\mathbb{b}^k})]$.

(ii). It is easy to verify that:

$\mathbb{a}\subseteq\mathbb{b}^* \quad \Rightarrow \mathbb{a}\equiv\mathbb{a}^*$

$\mathbb{a}=\bigcup_{i\in\omega} \mathbb{b}_i^* \Rightarrow \mathbb{a}\equiv\mathbb{a}^*$.

Using these facts and (i) we can mimic the proof of 2.9 (i) (using 3.12(ii) instead of 2.4(ii)) to show that $\mathcal{V}^*_{\mathcal{F}}$ is a type interpretation.

To check that $\mathcal{V}^*_{\mathcal{F}}$ is an $\mathbf{F}$ type interpretation, let us consider $\mathbb{a}^*\in \mathcal{V}^*_{\mathcal{F}}(\sigma\to\tau)$. If $A_{\mathbb{a}^1}\equiv\lambda x.A'$ then $\mathbb{a}^*\in\mathbf{F}$.

Otherwise, if $A_{\mathbb{a}^1}\equiv x\underbrace{\Omega\ldots\Omega}_{m}$ we have $B^{\oplus} \vdash^{R} \sigma\to\tau A_{\mathbb{a}^1}$ by definition.

$B^{\oplus} \vdash^{R} \sigma\to\tau A_{\mathbb{a}^1} \Rightarrow B \vdash^{R} \sigma\to\tau A_{\mathbb{a}^1}$

$\Rightarrow \exists\rho x\in B$ with $n=|\rho|=|\sigma\to\tau|+m$ by 3.14(ii)

$\Rightarrow A_{\mathbb{a}^1}{}^* \equiv\lambda z_{m+1}\ldots z_n.x\underbrace{\Omega\ldots\Omega}_{m}z_{m+1}\ldots z_n$

$\Rightarrow \mathbb{a}^*\in\mathbf{F}$.

(iii) and (iv). Easy. □

3.18. *Theorem.* (Completeness). Let $\sigma\in RT$ and B be a restricted basis.

(i) $\mathfrak{B},B \models_{\mathcal{F}} \sigma M \Rightarrow B \vdash^{R} \sigma M$.

(ii) $B \models_{\mathcal{F}} \sigma M \Rightarrow B \vdash^{R} \sigma M$.

Proof. (i). $\mathfrak{B},B \models_{\mathcal{F}} \sigma M \Rightarrow [\![M]\!]^{\mathfrak{B}}_{\xi_{\mathcal{F}_B}}\in\mathcal{V}^*_{\mathcal{F}}(\sigma)$ by 3.17(iv)

$\Rightarrow \forall A\in\mathcal{A}(M)\ [\![A]\!]^{\mathfrak{B}}_{\xi_{\mathcal{F}_B}} \in\mathcal{V}^*_{\mathcal{F}}(\sigma)$ since $[\![A]\!]^{\mathfrak{B}}_{\xi_{\mathcal{F}_B}} \subseteq [\![M]\!]^{\mathfrak{B}}_{\xi_{\mathcal{F}_B}}$

$\Rightarrow \forall A\in\mathcal{A}(M)\ B^{\oplus} \vdash^{R} \sigma A$ by 3.17(iii)

$\Rightarrow B^{\oplus} \vdash^{R} \sigma M$ by rule (C)

$\Rightarrow B \vdash^{R} \sigma M$.

(ii) Immediate from (i). □

References

[Barendregt 84] Barendregt, H.P., The Lambda Calculus: Its Syntax and Semantics, (North Holland, Amsterdam, 1984).

[Barendregt, et al. 83] Barendregt H., Coppo M., Dezani-Ciancaglini M., A Filter Lambda Model and the Completeness of Type Assignment, J. Symbolic Logic 48, (1983), 931-940.

[Böhm 75] Böhm C., ed., Open Problems II.4, in: λ-Calculus and Computer Science Theory, LNCS 37, (Springer-Verlag, Berlin ,1975), 368.

[Coppo 84] Coppo M., Completeness of Type Assignment in Continuous Lambda Models, Theor. Computer Science 29, (1984), 309-324.

[Coppo 85] Coppo M., A Completeness Theorem for Recursively Defined Types, in: Brauer W., ed., ICALP 85, LNCS 194, (Springer-Verlag, Berlin, 1985), 120-129.

[Coppo and Dezani 80] Coppo M., Dezani-Ciancaglini M., An Extension of the Basic Functionality Theory for the λ-Calculus, Notre Dame J. of Formal Logic 21-4, (1980), 685-693.

[Coppo et al. 81] Coppo M., Dezani-Ciancaglini M., Venneri B., Functional Characters of Solvable Terms, Z. Math. Logik. Grundlag. Math. 27, (1981), 45-58.

[Curry and Feys 58] Curry H. B., Feys R., Combinatory Logic I, (North Holland, Amsterdam, 1958).

[Dezani and Margaria 84] Dezani-Ciancaglini M., Margaria I., F-Semantics for Intersection Type Discipline, in: Kahn G. et al., eds , Semantics of Data Types, LNCS 173, (Springer-Verlag, Berlin, 1984), 279-300.

[Girard 71] Girard J. Y., Une extension de l'interpretation de Gödel à l'analyse, et son application à l'élimination des coupures dans l'analyse et la théorie des types, in: Fenstad J. E. ed, 2 Scandinavian Logic Symp., (North Holland, Amsterdam, 1971), 63-92.

[Gordon, et al. 79] Gordon M. J., Milner R. and Wadsworth C. P., Edinburgh LCF, LNCS 78,(Springer-Verlag, Berlin, 1979).

[Hindley 81] Hindley R., The Simple Semantics for Coppo-Dezani-Salle' Type Assignment, in: M. Dezani-Ciancaglini, U. Montanari, eds, International Symposium on Programming, LNCS 137, (Springer-Verlag, Berlin, 1981), 212-226.

[Hindley 83-a] Hindley R., The Completeness Theorem for Typing λ-terms, Theor. Computer Science, 22 (1), (1983), 1-17.

[Hindley 83-b] Hindley R., Curry's Type-Rules are Complete with respect to F-semantics too, Theor. Computer Science, 22 (1), (1983), 127-133.

[Leivant 83] Leivant D., Polymorphic Type Inference, Proceedings 10-th ACM Symposium Principles of Programming Languages, Austin Texas, (1983), 88-98.

[Mac Queen and Sethi 82] Mac Queen D., Sethi R., A Semantic Model of Types for Applicative Languages, ACM Symposium on LISP and Functional Programming, (1982), 243-252.

[Mac Queen et al .84] Mac Queen D.,Plotkin G., Sethi R., An Ideal Model for Recursive

Polymorphic Types, Proc. 11-th ACM Symp. on Principles of Prog. Lang., (1984), 165-174.
[Milner 78] Milner R., A Theory of Type Polymorphism in Programming, ICSS, 17, (1978) , 348-375.
[Mitchell 84] Mitchell J. C., Type Inference and Type Containment, in: Kahn G. et al., eds, Semantics of Data Types, LNCS 173, (Springer-Verlag, Berlin, 1984), 257-278.
[Mitchell 85] Mitchell J. C., Polymorphic Type Inference and Containment, (1985), to appear in Information and Control.
[Morris 68] Morris J. H., Lambda Calculus Model of Programming Languages, Dissertation, MIT, (1968).
[Reynolds 74] Reynolds J. C., Towards a Theory of Type Structure, in: B. Robinet, ed., Programming Symposium, LNCS 19, (Springer-Verlag, Berlin, 1974), 408-425.
[Scott 76] Scott D.S., Data Types as Lattices, SIAM J. Comp. 5 , (1976), 522-587.
[Wadsworth 76] Wadsworth C., The Relation between Computational and Denotational Properties for D_∞-models of the Lambda-Calculus, SIAM J. Comp. 5, (1976), 488-521.

Appendix.

We prove Theorem 2.11 by introducing a new type inference system based on a preorder relation $\leq_+$ between types, defined following [Mitchell 85].

A.1. *Definition.* The relation $\leq_+$ on T is inductively defined by:

1. $\forall\vec{\varphi}.\sigma \leq_+ \forall\vec{\psi}.\sigma[\vec{\tau}/\vec{\varphi}]$ where $\vec{\psi}$ are not free in $\forall\vec{\varphi}.\sigma$
2. $\forall\vec{\varphi}.\sigma\to\tau \leq_+ (\forall\vec{\varphi}.\sigma)\to\forall\vec{\varphi}.\tau$
3. $\sigma' \leq_+ \sigma, \tau \leq_+ \tau' \Rightarrow \sigma\to\tau \leq_+ \sigma'\to\tau'$
4. $\sigma \leq_+ \tau \Rightarrow \forall\varphi.\sigma \leq_+ \forall\varphi.\tau$
5. $\rho \leq_+ \sigma, \sigma \leq_+ \tau \Rightarrow \rho \leq_+ \tau$.

Consider the system $\vdash_S$ and replace rule (simple) by:

$$(\leq_+)\ \frac{\sigma M \qquad \sigma \leq_+ \tau}{\tau M}.$$

$B \vdash^+ \sigma M$ denotes derivability in the resulting system.

A.2. *Lemma.* (i) $B \vdash^+ \sigma M \Rightarrow B[\tau/\varphi] \vdash^+ \sigma[\tau/\varphi]M$.

(ii) $\forall\vec{\varphi}.\sigma\to\tau \leq_+ \rho \Rightarrow \rho \equiv \forall\vec{\psi}.\mu\to\nu$ for some $\vec{\psi},\mu,\nu$.

(iii) $B/x \cup \{\sigma x\} \vdash^+ \tau M,\ \forall\vec{\varphi}.\sigma\to\tau \leq_+ \forall\vec{\psi}.\mu\to\nu \Rightarrow B/x \cup \{\mu x\} \vdash^+ \nu M$.

(iv) $B \vdash^+ \sigma\ \lambda x.M \Rightarrow \sigma \equiv \forall\vec{\varphi}.\mu\to\nu$ for some $\vec{\varphi}, \mu, \nu$.

(v) $B \vdash^{+} \forall\vec{\varphi}.\sigma\to\tau\ \lambda x.M \Rightarrow B/x\cup\{\sigma x\} \vdash^{+} \tau M$.

Proof. (i). Transfinite induction on the ordinals associated with deductions (cf. the proof of 2.3(i)). If the last applied rule is ($\leq_{+}$) notice that $\rho\leq_{+}\sigma$ implies $\rho[\tau/\varphi]\leq_{+}\sigma[\tau/\varphi]$.

(ii). Induction on $\leq_{+}$.

(iii). The proof follows by induction on $\leq_{+}$ using (i) and (ii).

(iv). Transfinite induction on the ordinals associated with deductions. If the last applied rule is ($\leq_{+}$) use (ii).

(v). By transfinite induction on the ordinal associated with the deduction

$\mathcal{D}: B \vdash^{+} \forall\vec{\varphi}.\sigma\to\tau\ \lambda x.M$.

If the last applied rule is ($\forall$E) use (i).

If the last applied rule is ($\leq_{+}$) use (iii) and (iv).

If the last applied rule is (C) notice that $\mathcal{A}(\lambda x.M)=\{\lambda x.A \mid A\in\mathcal{A}(M) \text{ and } A\not\equiv\Omega\}\cup\{\Omega\}$.□

A.3. *Theorem.* (i) $B \vdash^{+} \sigma M,\ M\to\!\!>_{\beta} M' \Rightarrow B \vdash^{+} \sigma M'$.

(ii) $B \vdash^{+} \sigma M,\ A\sqsubseteq M \Rightarrow B \vdash^{+} \sigma A$.

Proof. Mimic the proof of 2.4 using A.2(v) instead of 2.3(ii).□

As an immediate consequence of A.3(ii) and rule (C), ($Eq_{\beta\Omega}$) is a derived rule of the $\vdash^{+}$ type assignment.

We prove Theorem 2.11 by showing that the systems $\vdash_{S}$ and $\vdash^{+}$ are equivalent, i.e. $B \vdash_{S} \sigma M \Leftrightarrow B \vdash^{+} \sigma M$.

A.4. *Lemma.* (i) If φ does not occur in σ then $\forall\varphi.\sigma\to\rho\leq_{+}\sigma\to\forall\varphi.\rho$.

(ii) $B/x\cup\{\sigma x\} \vdash^{+} \tau\vec{y}Mx$ and $x \notin FV(\vec{y}M) \Rightarrow B \vdash^{+} \sigma\to\tau\vec{y}M$.

Proof. (i). $\forall\varphi.\sigma\to\rho\leq_{+}(\forall\varphi.\sigma)\to\forall\varphi.\rho\sim_{+}\sigma\to\forall\varphi.\rho$ since if φ does not occur in σ then $\sigma\sim_{+}\forall\varphi.\sigma$ by 1 of Definition A.1.

(ii).The proof is by transfinite induction on the ordinals associated with deductions.
If the last applied rule is ($\forall$I):

$$\frac{\begin{array}{c}\sigma x\\ \vdots\\ \rho\vec{y}Mx\end{array}}{\forall\varphi.\rho\vec{y}Mx}\ (\forall I)$$

by the induction hypothesis we have $B \vdash^{+} \sigma\to\rho\vec{y}M$ which implies $B \vdash^{+} \forall\varphi.\sigma\to\rho\vec{y}M$ by rule ($\forall$I) (notice that φ cannot occur in B and σ) and lastly $B \vdash^{+} \varphi\to\forall\varphi.\rho\vec{y}M$ by (i).

If the last applied rule is ($\forall$E):

$$\frac{\begin{array}{c}\sigma x\\ \vdots\\ \forall\varphi.\tau y\vec{M}x\end{array}}{\tau y\vec{M}x}\ (\forall E)$$

by the induction hypothesis we have $B \vdash^+ \sigma\to\forall\varphi.\tau y\vec{M}$ which implies $B \vdash^+_S \sigma\to\tau y\vec{M}$ by rule $(\leq_+)$.

The other cases are trivial.□

A.5. *Theorem.* $B \vdash^+ \sigma M \Leftrightarrow B \vdash_S \sigma M$.

Proof. It is sufficient to show that $(\leq_+)$ is a derived rule of the $\vdash_S$ system, whereas (simple) is a derived rule of the $\vdash^+$ system.

The proof that $(\leq_+)$ is a derived rule of $\vdash_S$ is by induction on the $\leq_+$ definition. The most interesting cases are 2 and 3 of Definition A.1.

$B \vdash_S \forall\vec{\varphi}.\sigma\to\tau M \Rightarrow B \vdash_S \sigma\to\tau M$ by $(\forall E)$

$\Rightarrow B\cup\{\forall\vec{\varphi}.\sigma y\} \vdash_S \tau My$ by $(\to E)$ since $B\cup\{\forall\vec{\varphi}.\sigma y\} \vdash_S \sigma y$ by $(\forall E)$ $(y\notin FV(M)\cup FV(B))$

$\Rightarrow B\cup\{\forall\vec{\varphi}.\sigma y\} \vdash_S \forall\vec{\varphi}.\tau My$ by $(\forall I)$

$\Rightarrow B \vdash_S \forall\vec{\varphi}.\sigma\to\forall\vec{\varphi}.\tau\ \lambda y.My$ by $(\to I)$

$\Rightarrow B \vdash_S \forall\vec{\varphi}.\sigma\to\forall\vec{\varphi}.\tau M$ by (simple).

$B \vdash_S \sigma\to\tau M \Rightarrow B\cup\{\sigma'y\} \vdash_S \tau My$ by $(\to E)$ since $\sigma'y \vdash_S \sigma y$ by the induction hypothesis $(y\notin FV(M)\cup FV(B))$

$\Rightarrow B\cup\{\sigma'y\} \vdash_S \tau'My$ by the induction hypothesis

$\Rightarrow B \vdash_S \sigma'\to\tau'\ \lambda y.My$ by $(\to I)$

$\Rightarrow B \vdash_S \sigma'\to\tau'M$ by (simple).

We prove that (simple) is a derived rule of $\vdash^+$, i.e. $B \vdash^+ \sigma\to\tau\ \lambda x.Mx$ with $x \notin FV(M)$ implies $B \vdash^+ \sigma\to\tau M$, by cases on M.

If M is unsolvable $B \vdash^+ \sigma\to\tau M$ by rules (C) and (Ω).

$M=_\beta\lambda y.M'$. In this case $M=_\beta\lambda x.Mx$.

$M=_\beta y\vec{M}'$.

$B \vdash^+ \sigma\to\tau\ \lambda x.Mx$ and $x \notin FV(M) \Rightarrow B/x\cup\{\sigma x\} \vdash^+ \tau Mx$ by A.2(v)

$\Rightarrow B/x\cup\{\sigma x\} \vdash^+ \tau y\vec{M}'x$ by $(Eq_{\beta\Omega})$

$\Rightarrow B \vdash^+ \sigma\to\tau y\vec{M}'$ by A.4(ii)

$\Rightarrow B \vdash^+ \sigma\to\tau M$ by $(Eq_{\beta\Omega})$. □

QUESTIONS AND ANSWERS

Tennent: Is the C-rule a finitary rule?

Dezani: No, it is an infinitary rule.

Jouannaud: I would like to ask some questions about the type system where you have intersection. When you have intersection in some way you have a partial order on types because you have a notion of subtype. We have this notion for example in the OBJ language [cf. e.g. K. Futatsugi, J. Goguen, J.-P. Jouannaud, J. Meseguer: Principles of OBJ2. In: Proc. 12th Symposium on Principles of Programming Languages, ACM, 1985, 52-66] and it happens that if we don´t assume that there is a universe or a finite number of distinct universes, then the models don´t work at all for the OBJ language. So I am a little bit surprised, that you have said, that here you don´t have any assumption about a universe. And I wonder how it can work without any universe.

Dezani: I do not know OBJ. Here we have a universe in some sense since all types are interpreted as a subset of the domain of a λ-model.

Tennent: You have described two approaches to types, explicit types and type inference on a basicly type-free language, but would it not be concievable to have compromises between these in which the language designer allows for types to be omitted in certain contexts? The compiler could infer the types in restricted contexts rather than in the whole language.

Dezani: I think that such a kind of compromise is the best thing that you can practically do. There are a lot of proposals and to find the good compromise is not easy.

Tennent: Well, but actually I´m surprised that you say there are a lot of proposals. I´m really aware of only one which is McCracken´s at the semantics of data types conference [N. McCracken: The typechecking of programs with implicit type structure. In: G. Kahn, D.B. MacQueen, G. Plotkin (eds.): Semantics of Data Types. Lecture Notes in Computer Science 173, Berlin: Springer, 301-316]. Are there also other approaches?

Dezani: McCracken´s algorithm presented in Antibes does not succeed in all cases; but it is a good compromise.

Longo: Just a comment to your question. You are dealing with the most complicated form of classical polymorphism, the ML framework. There you need the type-free model. In the background, you need the universe. McCracken considers explicit polymorphism as you find for example in Burstall and Lampson´s language PEBBLE [R. Burstall, B. Lampson: A kernel language for abstract data types and modules. In: G. Kahn, D.B. MacQueen, G. Plotkin (eds.): Semantics of Data Types. Lecture Notes in Computer Science 173, Berlin: Springer, 1-50]. There you do not have a universe in the background.

List of Participants

Pierre AMERICA	Eindhoven, The Netherlands
Krzysztof APT	Paris, France
Egidio ASTESIANO	Genova, Italy
Ralph-Johann BACK	Aabo, Finland
Jos BAETEN	Amsterdam, The Netherlands
Jaco DE BAKKER	Amsterdam, The Netherlands
Marek A. BEDNARCZYK	Brighton, England
Gerard BERRY	le Chesnay, France
Eike BEST	St. Augustin, Germany
Carsten BJERNAA	Lyngby, Denmark
Dines BJØRNER	Lyngby, Denmark
Andrzej BLIKLE	Warsaw, Poland
Ed K. BLUM	Los Angeles, California, USA
Frank S. DE BOER	Amsterdam, The Netherlands
Luc BOUGÉ	Orleans, France
L. CHADILI	Palo Alto, California, USA
Palle CHRISTENSEN	Lyngby, Denmark
M. COPPO	Torino, Italy
Philippe DARONDEAU	Rennes, France
Daniel DAVIS	Monterey, California, USA
Ulla Barbara GAMVELL DAWIDS	Gentofte, Denmark
Pierpaolo DEGANO	Pisa, Italy
M. DEZANI-CIANCAGLINI	Torino, Italy
Mansour FARAH	Damaskus, Syria
Matthias FELLEISEN	Bloomington, Indiana, USA
Nissim FRANCEZ	Haifa, Israel
Daniel P. FRIEDMAN	Bloomington, Indiana, USA
Harald GANZINGER	Dortmund, Germany
Rob GERTH	Eindhoven, The Netherlands
Graham D. GOUGH	Manchester, England
Michael Reichhardt HANSEN	Lyngby, Denmark
Susumu HAYASHI	Kyoto, Japan
Eric C.R. HEHNER	Toronto, Canada
Takayasu ITO	Sendai, Japan
Suresh JAGANNATHAN	Westbury, New York, USA
Neil JONES	Copenhagen, Denmark

J.-P. JOUANNAUD	Orsay, France
Ulrik JØRRING	Lyngby, Denmark
Fred KRÖGER	München, Germany
Leslie LAMPORT	Palo Alto, California, USA
Jean-Louis LASSEZ	Yorktown Heights, New York, USA
Peter E. LAUER	Ontario, Canada
Hans Henrik LØVENGREEN	Lyngby, Denmark
Giuseppe LONGO	Pisa, Italy
Peter LUCAS	San Jose, California, USA
Michael J. MAHER	Yorktown Heights, New York, USA
Brian MAYOH	Århus, Denmark
J.-J. Ch. MEYER	Amsterdam, The Netherlands
G. MIRKOWSKA	Warsaw, Poland
Bernhard MÖLLER	München, Germany
Peter MOSSES	Århus, Denmark
Erich J. NEUHOLD	Wien, Austria
Rocco DE NICOLA	Pisa, Italy
Mogens NIELSEN	Lyngby, Denmark
Maurice NIVAT	Paris, France
Ernst Rüdiger OLDEROG	Kiel, Germany
Fernando OREJAS	Barcelona, Spain
Manfred PAUL	München, Germany
Amir PNUELI	Rehovot, Israel
Willem P. DE ROEVER	Eindhoven, The Netherlands
Scott A. SMOLKA	Stony Brook, New York, USA
J. STEENSGAARD-MADSEN	Lyngby, Denmark
Robert E. STROM	Yorktown Heights, New York, USA
Reino KURKI-SUONIO	Tampere, Finland
Satoru TAKASU	Kyoto, Japan
Andrzej TARLECKI	Warsaw, Poland
Robert D. TENNENT	Edinburgh, Scotland
David A. WATT	Glasgow, Scotland
Martin WIRSING	Passau, Germany

-- with no guarantee for correctness --

Author Index